Successful
Pistol
Shooting

Other Books By Bob Hickey

Mental Training
(A book for shooters)

Laundry Room Poems
In The Room Of Poems
Little Rooms Of Poems

SUCCESSFUL PISTOL SHOOTING

By
Bob Hickey
and
Art Sievers

STP Books

Library of Congress Cataloging in Publication Data

Hickey, Bob & Sievers, Art
Successful Pistol Shooting
Includes bibliographical references
Indexed
Orig. Ed.
STP 11/1996
ISBN: 0-939-414-03-1
Library of Congress Catalog Card Number: 96-93004
Status: Active Entry
Illustrated
PBIP SUBJECT HEADINGS:
   Shooting (00428619)
   Health and Physical Education-Sports (00001302)

STP $Books$

3350 West Desert Turtle Way
Tucson, AZ 85742-9019
Phone: 520-744-8805
Fax: 520-744-8810

Dedication

To our respective wives:

June Jewell Sievers
20 May 95

50 years Partners
25 years Active Navy
25 years Retired

Mary Jane Hickey

This book would not have been possible in this form without Mary Jane. Mary Jane's constant proofing, criticisms and perspective insights cannot be underrated. Her ability to spot technical errors was uncanny and most welcome. Her comments regarding the manuscript were top flight and astute.

Forward

"So, Mr. Wright, is that the rifle
you used to shoot All American at
the Naval Academy?"
"Yes, Sir."
"So tell me, Mr. Wright, what size
is the front aperture?"
"Oh, I don't know, Sir. Whatever
was in it when I got the rifle."
"That's what I thought, Mr.
Wright."

So began the summer of 1964, an experience that I would not trade for a million dollars. Also, one that I would not go through again for two million. As explained to me, many years later, I became a *"training aid"* for the most knowledgeable, most demanding teacher of shooting of this era. I grew to hate every time I, the boy Ensign on the United States Navy Service Rifle Team, made a mistake. The line was halted and the error discussed so the lesson was fresh for the entire team. It hurt, but I learned so much, so quickly. Even though a Collegiate All American Rifle Shooter, I didn't understand the true rudiments of marksmanship.

It was a summer in which I began to learn a system which would eventually take me shooting in 15 countries representing the United States. The path included five Distinguished Awards, several World and National Records and teaching directly or supervising the smallarms training of more than 90,000 people in the military, police and civilian communities.

It was also the beginning of a lifetime association with the most personally influential, yet most nationally underrated shooting *"guru"* in my forty plus years of firearms activity.

Art Sievers was the oldest Lt.(Junior Grade) in the United States Navy when he asked me those first questions. A former Chief Aviation Enlisted Pilot and Marine Corps First Sergeant, he had the reputation of being one of the toughest coaches in the US Military forces. The time was in the *"Golden Years"* of shooting when marksmanship programs received military and government support unknown before or after the years 1957 to 1970. There were a lot of famous coaches generated through Army and Marine Corps marksmanship training systems. These programs selected from standard troop training and then placed selected individuals in units which did, essentially, shooting as a full time profession. Army and Marine Corps coaches then *"molded and honed"* to produce champions. We used to joke about *"monkeys and typewriters"* as we watched the Army enter 250 shooters and the Marine Corps enter another 147 at Camp Perry for High Power Rifle. We then looked at our Navy Rifle and Pistol Teams that numbered between 16 and 23 and who were mostly released from commands for only three months in the summer.

Interestingly, we always gave the giants a run for the money, winning proportionally more with both guns, including national individual and team championship. It was obvious that our three month summer training program was superior to the others' permanent duty station concept. The question then became, were the other service coaches famous because of their teachings or, rather, because their shooters won as a result of the *"monkey and typewriter"* system.

In those days, Art Sievers was, by his own description, *"bigger, badder and meaner"* than the total of strong willed shooters on his teams. His experience told him that was the way to run military marksmanship units.

He is one of the very few individuals who was able to analyze large numbers of champion shooters and glean the true fundamentals of marksmanship, separating them from techniques and legend. He devised competitive and mass training systems that were, and remain, classics in condensed learning. His conviction that *"all shooting is the same,"* is the major truth and the base of his teachings.

Especially in international rifle shooting, US competitors were the most winning in the world prior to 1980. These World Champions were essentially self taught, coming from diverse backgrounds. In the 1970s it became vogue to emulate these individuals in the hopes of continued national success. Eventually the Champions created long lists of *"fundamentals"* (Army Marksmanship Manuals and National Rifle Association training publications) necessary to make a good shot. These *"fundamentals"* changed in number while the actual training normally consisted of attempting to memorize what were actually the techniques (*"fundamentals"*) of those winning shooters. Then, if a shooter was having problems, he was given more things to memorize to try to *"work the way"* out of the problem. That system has now become nearly *"set in concrete"* in today's training environment. National Rifle Association coaches and instructors are chastised if they vary, even minutely, from the lesson plan. The result is that many young people can attain reasonably good results rather quickly. Since, however, they don't really know how they arrived at that point, they can't go any further. The expression *"hit a plateau"* applies.

The goal of Sievers' method, which has also been successful in international coaching, is to make the shooter think for himself and realize *"how a point was reached."* The shooter can then continue using his brain to analyze and increase performance. In most cases, analyzing consists of reducing the thought process again, to the true fundamentals. A group of us, disciples if you will, follow this logic as presented by the master, Art Sievers.

The tragedy is, that because Art was never in the highly advertised training programs, there are only a few of us who use the *"thinking man's"* system. The good news is, the number of disciples grows as thinking coaches and shooters become disgruntled with the current *"monkey see, monkey do"* systems.

Hopefully this book will bring Art to the level of recognition he deserves.

I am pleased to announce that Art Sievers is a *"pussycat"* compared to the old days. Now he generally *"pitches"* to younger, civilian groups who listen more easily.

Art claims that shooting is so simple that it can be reduced to one page. When I asked him how he, then, planned to write a 500 page book, he replied, *"We're just going to write the same thing 500 times, back to back so you won't forget."*

I doubted that his writing partner, Bob Hickey, would allow that.

I have known Bob since the early 1970's when I was the rifle coach at the US Naval Academy. He has always been interested in helping young people, especially in the shooting arena. The mental aspects of the sport, especially, have intrigued Bob. His written works on the subject were some of the first and remain among the best produced.

The association of these two should create a classic in the literature of shooting.

By the way, Art and I talk on the phone every couple of weeks. If this shooting stuff is so simple, how come I learn something new in every conversation?

Webster M. Wright, Jr. LCDR USN (RET)
Distinguished International Shooter Badge
Distinguished Marksman (Service Rifle)
Distinguished Pistol Shot
NRA Distinguished Smallbore Rifle Prone Award
NRA Distinguished Smallbore Position Award
Military Rifle Champion of the World 1978, Gotland, Sweden
World Champion (Team), World Championships 1978, Korea
National Champion and Record Holder, Several Disciplines.
International Rifle Coach
NRA Training Counselor and Coach Instructor
Founder and OIC, US Navy International Shooting Team
Founding and eight year member, NCAA Rifle Committee

Preface

The purpose of this book is to present an alternative to currently accepted methods of teaching pistol shooting. This alternative is based principally upon the discoveries about pistol shooting training by Art Sievers.

The chapters in this book are designed to be complete in and of themselves. We do not direct you to other chapters when the information should be available in the chapter you are reading. Each of the chapters is designed with the person who may have a personal interest in a particular area of pistol shooting. This leads to duplication, but we believe it is better for the reader.

For example, if you are interested in occasional recreational shooting, then Chapter 1, Head Start is the place for you. The focus of the training in the Head Start Chapter is designed to allow the shooter to obtain consistent *"hits"* in the tin can arena.

For a historical background on the new *Philosophy of Shooting* advocated in this book, see Chapter 2, *Pistol Shooting, It's Simple, Keep It Simple*. This is where we start the training in the new method of shooting. **The whole of this book can be summed up in the idea that the training must be kept simple, if anything is added to the simplicity of the two fundamentals, you have wasted your time.**

Chapter 3 highlights the myths of shooting past. We show what shooting *"facts"* are myths and why. This is probably something you have never seen in print before.

In Chapter 4, we lower the age at which youngsters can start to shoot pistol competitively. It is also where we look at a very valuable and completely honest contribution to marksmanship training. It is the book we call the Coast Guard book. The other chapter titles are self-explanatory.

The information in this book is a summary of the authors' hundred plus years involvement in competitive and other forms of shooting. No outside input has been solicited, nor included in this book with respect to the development of this new philosophy of shooting. Many shooters and researchers have been cited when their writings touch upon some aspect of this new philosophy. We are rare birds in the shooting world. We are professional shooting coaches for the single discipline, shooting. We are not professional shooters moonlighting as coaches.

If you have science and skill, good shooting! If not, lots of luck, but it won't help.

We want it clearly understood, that this information is not a rehash of the *"put your little foot here"* philosophy, which is, and has been the accepted philosophy pre-eminent in the public domain.

If you are looking for a reinforcement of the old pistol training methods you may be used to and feel comfortable with, you will not find it in this book. We do not claim the old tried and true methods are wrong, just that they have proven to be ineffective at what shooters and instructors have claimed they would do. The pistol training methods described in this book are based on science and in accordance with the immutable laws of gravity and motion here on earth.

Contents

Contents

Head Start

Head Start

How To Successfully Shoot A Pistol...
It's Easier Than You Ever Thought!

If you have not said it yourself, you have most likely heard someone say, "*I can shoot a rifle (or shotgun) okay, but I can't shoot a pistol worth a darn!*" If you're like a lot of people, you've figured you just don't have the stuff to shoot a pistol. This is especially true if you have ever paid for pistol shooting instruction from your local Pistol Instructor. Sometimes this instruction is thrown in as *Free*, when you purchase a gun from a gun store or a local dealer. *To find out if you will be getting your money's worth for the instruction you are about to purchase, ask the question:*

Just what is shooting?

If the instructor comes back with something like "*have to,*" or "*try to hit the target,*" you may not be getting what you want with respect to learning how to shoot the pistol. You see, to the average person, shooting is getting the bullet out the barrel and making a noise.

We are a hitting oriented society. We "hit" a baseball with a bat, we "*hit*" a golf ball with a club, we "*hit*" a tennis ball with a racket. Therefore, it is not odd that we fall into the trap of thinking that we have to "*hit*" a target with a bullet. When we have a focus on "*hitting,*" then our attention is naturally drawn to the target.

We neglect to remember the cause and effect relationship which put the hole in the target. In all of the other examples of "*hitting*" we have named, the cause is something coming into contact with, in these cases, a ball. The effect of the "*hitting*" is the ball being directed into a particular path.

In shooting the cause of what happens is the trigger being moved by the finger. The effect is the strike of the bullet appearing on the target. In the "*hitting*" examples we have used, the focus of the eye is on the ball until it has been "*hit.*" In shooting if the focus of the eye is on the target, what is being neglected or overlooked?

The sights! In our shooting game, we point a tube somewhere. We line that tube up with our eye. Then we point that eye-tube system at the target area and move the trigger finger smoothly. We want the strike of the bullet to be indicated by a hole appearing on that target. In this book, what are we talking about when we use the word **shooting**?

Shooting is lining up the barrel with the eye, pointing it at the area we want the bullet hole to appear, and moving the trigger finger smoothly to cause the bullet hole to appear.

Good marksmanship is not mysterious, not magical and not something to be restricted to a few highly trained athletes. The basics of shooting are so simple they are easily understood by elementary school students, as demonstrated so vividly here in Tucson.

One of our nine year old girls, before she attended her first day of school in the 4th grade, in other words, a 3rd grader, achieved a place in the history of US Pistol Shooting by being a member of a team which broke the NRA National Women's Team Record over the International 3-Person Rapid Fire Event by 206 points.

This is an event where each person fires 20 shots in 5 shot strings in 8 seconds, 20 shots in 5 shot strings in 6 seconds and 20 shots in 5 shot strings, each fired in 4 seconds at 25 yards. Her name, for the record, is Michal Newhouse.

Unfortunately, lack of awareness of the basics of shooting has led to misconceptions in the training priorities of shooting. A brief review of these simple basics will aid us in arranging our training priorities in a logical order.

If we can visualize a bullet issuing from the muzzle of a loaded pistol, it is simple to perceive that the only place the bullet could possibly strike *is wherever the barrel happened to be pointed when the bullet emerged.*

If this is true, and it is, then it becomes obvious that if we find the bullet hole it tells us precisely where the pistol was pointed on discharge. A brief reflection on this point will quickly

15

lead us to the conclusion that it is immaterial whether or not anyone is holding the pistol, this still holds true. For example, it could be set up in a vise and fired by an electric impulse.

The next elementary step in this basic awareness exercise will lead us to the inescapable conclusion that if we wish the bullet hole to appear in a particular place, only one thing has to happen, the barrel must be pointed there when discharged. How this is done is of no consequence. To summarize:

> ⇒ The bullet *"hits"* wherever the barrel is pointed when the pistol is discharged
> ⇒ it is immaterial how this is done
> ⇒ the bullet hole is merely a visual indicator telling us where the barrel was pointed on discharge.

Let us now put on our thinking caps and turn our thinking to consider the process of getting "hits." If the shooter can point the pistol anywhere he wants, and he can, and the pistol "hits" wherever it is pointed on discharge, and it does, why don't people simply point the pistol where they want the bullet to strike?

The reasons and rationalizations for *"why not"* are infinite in number, but only one is valid. The shooter doesn't *"know how"* to have the pistol *"pointed"* where he wants to hit. Getting a hit is normally considered the problem in shooting. Not so! In learning to shoot this can actually be a distraction!

The problem is learning the *how* of having the pistol *"pointed"* wherever the shooter wants to hit, when it discharges. This is the **cause** of the "hit." The "hit" is after the fact, it merely tells the shooter the quality of his pointing in regards to precision and consistency, and is the **result** of the **cause**. We're certain all of you are aware of the concept of cause and effect.

Just to check the instructor out a bit more, ask the instructor one more question:

What kinds of things will I have to learn to be able to shoot good?

If correct position, correct grip, correct breath control, sight alignment, trigger squeeze and follow-through are part of the instructor's list of what he will teach you, then you can probably figure you won't get what you are paying for. This type of response will indicate that you are talking to an instructor who is still living in the time of the dinosaurs.

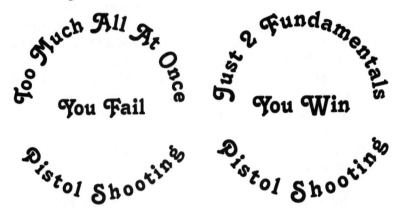

The instructor has no idea that the information he is using to teach people how to shoot the pistol does not even meet modern teaching theory about how to teach any physical skill. Bear in mind that the instructor is not, on purpose, destroying your effort to learn how to shoot. The record and research clearly demonstrate that this instructional method is ineffective in doing what the instructors claim it will do, teach people to shoot to a very high level.

Oscar [Fingal O'Flahertie Wills] Wilde 1854-1900, once wrote in *Personal Impressions of America (Leadville)* [1883]:

Over the piano was printed a notice:

> *Please do not shoot the pianist.*
> *He is doing his best.*

We, too, believe that the Pistol Instructor is doing his best.

There's an old adage which is appropriate here:

> *"It ain't what ya don't know what hurts ya,*
> *It's what ya know what ain't so!"*

17

Wilde, in **The Critic as Artist** [1891], pt. II, said, *There is no sin except stupidity.* In the case of the Pistol Instructor, we can forgive ignorance, but stupidity is forever.

When an instructor spends a lifetime of using methods which have the effect of making it nearly impossible for a person to learn how to shoot a pistol effectively, and continues to use the same information to produce that type of product time after time, it is beyond what is commonly thought of as stupidity.

What manufacturing company could continue to profit from a product which could not produce the results advertised. If the company marketed a frying skillet which could only burn eggs at whatever setting the stove burner was set to, how long would that company be able to continue producing such a product? Word about that product would surely get out to the buying public.

In the case of pistol training, because of the magic often thought to be associated with someone able to shoot the short gun very well, both the instructor and the students of that training, placed the blame squarely on the student, as just not being able to hack it.

There are even times when this teaching service is provided free from your local shooting club. In nearly every case, the person receiving this currently available pistol shooting instruction is not really satisfied that he got his money's worth. Oh, the instructor may wax proud about the student's ability to **hit** the target. The target being probably placed at 5 or 7 yards from the shooter and probably 36 inches square. And for the methods currently available in the public domain, this is probably fairly good.

Using the method described in this book, you can start teaching yourself how to shoot hand size groups at 50 feet with a pistol, or at 10 meters with an air pistol.

You will no longer be the subject of snickers behind the firing line at your local shooting range because you have to have the target brought to about 10 feet in front of you before you can start to get some shots on it.

No longer will people laugh when they see the difficulty you have in putting some holes in that man-sized piece of paper. Instead, you'll much more likely be the subject of glances

18

admiring your small groups appearing in the center of your target.

This is now your chance to teach yourself to shoot a pistol and be as successful as you want. If you are one of the guys who kept at it, this book is a must read! If your friends get their hands on this book, and you don't, get ready to be surprised the next time you guys or girls go out to a range for some pistol shooting.

Here in America, people often go out to a vacant area and set up some empty food cans or soda pop cans or plastic bottles, **Plastic Only! No glass targets!,** for a bit of informal target practice. This book is the *Head Start* you need to be the best tin can shooter in your group.

On the other hand, if you decide to work to win a shooting medal in a future Olympics, this book will give you the training method and the theoretical background to help you make that medal a reality.

But, now onto your **Head Start!**

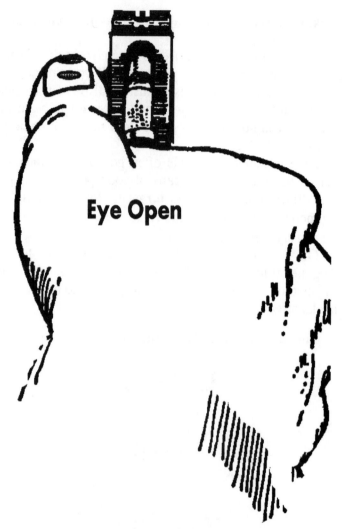

Eye Open

Me and mah gun!

Think about it! Without you, your gun is an inanimate object. But, once you join your handgun to your hand, it is now *"Me and mah gun!"* You can point that handgun anywhere you want. You can also move your trigger finger when and how you want. That's this thing we do which we call *shooting.* If you like the way you are shooting, look in the mirror. That's your buddy. If you do not like the way you are shooting, look in the mirror and grit your teeth. That's the nincompoop that did it to you!

Head Start

We come now to the heart of the affair. In this book we will show you something different from what you are used to with respect to handgun shooting training. We have done the unthinkable. We have questioned the validity of the handgun training information available in the public domain of the United States. There have been occasions when others have questioned the handgun shooting training information available to them in their times. One notable person was Ed McGivern, in his *Fast and Fancy Revolver Shooting.*

> *I recall that it most certainly looked, at that time, as though the voluntary and always very willing critics were going to have the best of the argument; some similar views and prophesies later appeared in print, in some cases with very well-meaning and, no doubt, honest conviction on the part of the writers. At other times such advice was coupled with much sarcasm, and a generally "know it all" attitude. Time, however, with the very funny way that time so often has of doing such things, showed that these wise ones were-well-"just slightly in error."* (Reprinted from FAST & FANCY REVOLVER SHOOTING copyright 1984 by New Win Publishing.)

The authors of this book, like McGivern before them, have found many people with whom they have had contact are sincerely concerned that this program does not give a new shooter enough information. Often they will judge the information in this program against what they know, from their lifetime of shooting experience, and find it lacking. So, the first thing many of these sincerely concerned people say is,

> *"Oh yeah, we have those two fundamentals of (1) looking hard at the sights and (2) moving the trigger finger smoothly. We just use different terms. We use the terms, sight alignment and trigger control. But, then we do have some other sub-fundamentals. You*

> *gotta admit that you gotta have stability, so*
> *you gotta get a stable platform to shoot from*
> *and you gotta control your breathing so you*
> *can keep the gun from moving around. We*
> *know you gotta do these things to get good*
> *shots on the target."*

We describe these concerned people as being the **gotta people**. Does it matter to them that the people they teach seem to often fall short of their expectations? Very often their pistol shooting students fall woefully short when it comes to demonstrating what is being taught them by this gotta have coach.

Notice, they **have the two fundamentals** we have found necessary to produce excellent results with the pistol, but then they cannot keep from adding something to **"make it better."** They shake their heads in bewilderment, over the failure of their shooting students to do what they are telling them to do. The blame is promptly placed squarely on the heads of their students. They have given them all the best of the *gotta do* stuff. But, the students "just won't do what we tell them they *gotta do*!"

Our research clearly **points definitively to the information** which is **currently being given to the new shooter** as being the problem.

It is not the student. The student who comes to learn to shoot the pistol has a desire to learn and a wholehearted willingness to try to do all of the *gotta do's* listed for him by the instructor or coach.

So, what happens when the pistol instructor lists the 61 elements from the 1981 US Army Pistol Marksmanship Manual, on page 42, which are required as being necessary for the firing of one accurate shot? We'll tell you what! The student's system goes into overload.

There are, of course, some instructors and coaches who insist that the student keep only six or seven things in mind when they begin to learn to shoot a handgun. Generally, educators acknowledge that, when learning a basic skill, the student can only focus on one item of the skill being learned. When the focus has to be on two things, the boundary of skill acquisition is being pushed to the edge.

In the past, what has hindered the students in pistol courses from achieving results commensurate with their efforts and the efforts of their instructors? Take a look at what was being taught in 1959 and the decade of the 1960's.

Imagine the student having to try to do 14 things in order to fire one shot!

The problem is that the instructors mistook an academic observance of what had to happen in order to produce an accurate shot with what the student had to have his attention directed toward in order to fire that shot which the academicians observed and recorded.

The instructor misunderstood his role in the teaching process. He attempted to teach the pistol student all that he knew had to be learned for the student to end up with his knowledge of pistol shooting.

It is like the nuclear physicist teaching a high school freshman all he knows during the first 10 hours of class meetings. Many in the pistol instruction community do not realize the harm they are doing with their *"they gotta have it all, if they're going to learn to shoot right!"* Over the years, it has never dawned on them that it is their zeal to include everything which has spawned their ineffectiveness as teachers.

NRA 1959 Pistol Instructors Guide
"A Mental Checklist To Follow In Order To Fire One Shot"

1 Foot Position	2 Body Erect	3 Arm Straight	4 "Other" Arm	5 Elbow
6 Grip High	7 Grip Firm	8 Thumb High	9 Trigger Finger Position	10 Trigger Finger Clear
11 Sight Alignment	12 Sight Picture	13 Breath Control	14 Squeeze	

Successful Pistol Shooting
A Mental Checklist To Follow In Order To Fire One Shot
Our Method Is Successful By Eliminating Distractions

1	2
Visually Align the barrel with the eye, using the top of the front sight as a reference, point the aligned system at the area where you want the indicator (bullet hole) to appear..	Instantaneous Smooth Trigger Finger Movement

It gets back to *"Me and mah gun!"* When you point it, look hard at the sights. Notice, we did not say to look at the target!

We do say that if you want to put a bullet hole in a piece of paper, then you must point the handgun at the paper, using the front sight as a reference point for doing the pointing. Look at the sights! Look *Hard* at the sights!

Some people look through the sights to the target. This has the effect of altering the attention from the sights to the target. Looking *through* the sights to the target produces a condition that can produce "ball park" "hits," such as on a tin can, but will not yield the precision performance obtained by looking at the sights.

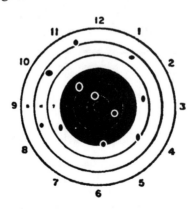

When someone picks up a handgun, it is assumed that he intends to do some precision pointing with it. How can you point any gun? You can point it anyway you want. Wouldn't it be nice to be able to point the handgun in such a way as to obtain consistent results each time you perform an action to cause a bullet to come out the muzzle.

One of the terms which has become a part of our shooting vocabulary is the term, **sight alignment**. When questioned, some old time shooters and coaches will admonish the new shooter to line up the sights with the target.

Once the shooter lines up the sights with the target, he then leans his head over so as to look through the sights at the target. This action guarantees random strikes on the target. In this situation, it is almost impossible to have the head returned to the exact same position from one shot to the next.

Consider the tool. The sights are affixed onto the top of the barrel.

They are in a straight line with each other. You may turn the gun any way you wish. However, you will not be able to get the sights out of line with each other.

You can point the gun at a piece of paper or any other place. But, to get consistent results, you must line up the barrel with the eye. This means lining up the sights with your pointing eye. It is then very easy to determine when the sights are lined up with your eye. In other words, you can see it.

Extensive research by the authors has demonstrated conclusively that in all shooting instruction, attention is directed at the effect, which is the hit or strike of the bullet. In our instruction, by deliberate contrast, the attention is directed at the cause, which is the pointing of the pistol.

All the hit does is to evaluate the pointing. When the instructional process, deliberately or unintentionally, directs the attention of the shooter to the effect, it is not like putting the cart before the horse, it is getting in the cart and forgetting all about having a need for the horse.

When you direct the attention to the effect, the hit, or the hole, in the target, you find that you still obtain results which are satisfactory to many of the shooters. It is entirely possible to obtain satisfactory alignment of the barrel with the eye. You can shoot dinner plate size groups all day long.

It is only for those people who wish to compete at a very high level of precision pointing, that it becomes necessary to focus the eye very hard at the sights instead of looking through the sights to the target.

Looking really hard at the sights causes the shots to be sucked into a tight group, provided your trigger finger movement is very smooth.

Safety

Before you start to shoot, let us direct your attention to safety with a handgun. What we need is a safety rule which will never fail. We have just such a safety rule.

It is completely obvious, that the only place a bullet can strike, is where ever the barrel happens to be pointed when the bullet exits the barrel. In other words, the only reason a bullet hole is anywhere is because that happens to be where the barrel was pointed when the bullet left the barrel.

Whoever is handling the shooting tool is completely responsible for the pointing. So, the person handling the shooting tool has to be held completely responsible for any bullet hole which is caused by his handling of the shooting tool.

When the *unintentional discharge* occurs, this is proof positive that every safety rule has failed. The only solution to this problem is for the handgunner to be aware, at all times, of where he or she is pointing the shooting tool.

With pointing as the sole safety focus, whatever happens, when we have an *unintentional discharge*, the bullet will exit the barrel in a safe direction. So, pointing is safety's salvation. There can be no secondary safety consideration. You have to place 100% of your safety awareness on where your shooting tool is pointed.

Always Keep The Gun Pointed In A Safe Direction

You must always be conscious of where you are pointing your handgun. Should any little gremlins load your handgun, you will always be safe if you keep the gun pointed in a safe direction.

There are many other safety rules espoused by many shooting organizations and magazines. Many include the rule we advocate above. But, then they also add such rules as *keep the gun unloaded until ready to use.* But, sometimes, the little gremlins slip a cartridge into the chamber. Or, there will be a gremlin loaded magazine in the gun.

The authors feel certain that many of the *I didn't know the gun was loaded* accidents could, with certainty, be attributed to the mischievous actions of the little gremlins. That would certainly have to be the case. Otherwise the gun owners *who didn't know the gun was loaded* would not have been so uninformed as to the loaded status of their handgun.

We know from newspaper accounts that the authorities cleared some of these *didn't know the gun was loaded* gun owners of blame in what they termed *gun accidents.* The authors of this book believe that these incidents should not be termed accidents.

The gun functioned exactly the way it was intended. When the trigger was pulled or the hammer dropped, the bullet came out the barrel and indicated where the barrel was pointed.

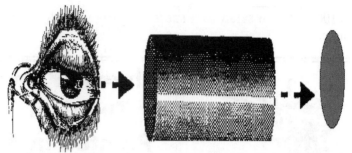

In any personal gun injury incident, it is completely obvious where the barrel was pointed when discharged. All you have to do is to find where the bullet hole appeared. Ricochet strikes are out of control and not included in this context.

The focus of much pistol coaching has been directed at, the bullet hole, and it's location. By and large, the cause has been ignored, the pointing.

Cause and Effect

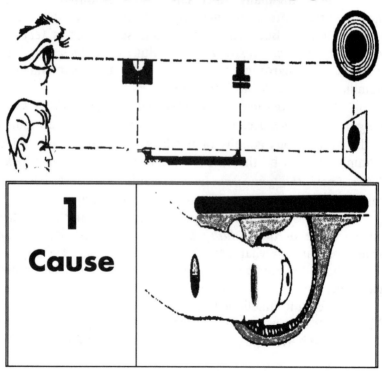

1

Cause

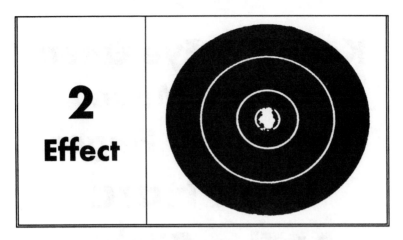

Once You Have Decided Where You Want To Point The Gun

Shift The Focus From The Target Look Hard At The Sights

Keep The Eye Open As You Move The Trigger Finger

Look Hard At The Sights

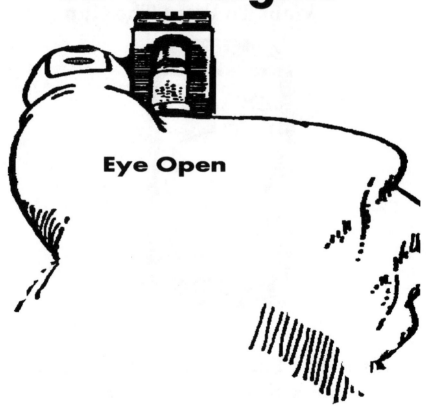

Eye Open

Move The Trigger Finger Smoothly

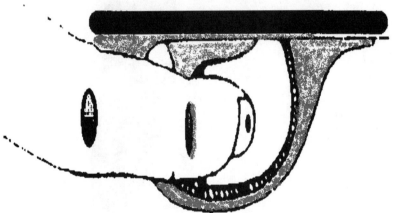

Makes for Successful Pistol Shooting

A Standing Plinking Platform

Establishing the Plinking Shooting Platform

- For a target, use a blank 8½" x 11" sheet of paper. Or, you can use the blank or back side of a target.
- Point the pistol at the target area, similar to the previous illustration.
- Look at the sights and use the top of the front sight as the pointing reference to point at the desired area.
- With the eye open, move the trigger finger smoothly, so the barrel is not pushed out of alignment with the eye when the bullet leaves the barrel.

The Orientation for the plinking shooting platform is based on the target location. The only time we base the platform on the target location is in recreational shooting, hunting, police or military applications.

For playing competitive precision shooting games, we base the platform on precise internal alignment between the barrel and the eye within the shooting unit. The normal shooting activities in the areas we have mentioned are satisfactorily performed with ballpark pointing.

By this, we mean that the target is comparatively large. For example, in shooting at a tin can, any strike on the tin can would be a satisfactory result. A bullet hole in the center of the tin can would not enhance the performance. In plinking, the question asked is *how many times did you hit the tin can*, never **where** did you hit the tin can.

In competitive shooting, the question asked is, *"Where did you hit the target?"* Never *"**How many times** did you hit the target?"*

Step-By-Step Hints In Setting Up The Platform:

- Stand erect and relaxed. Avoid any *Hollywood Type* stance.
- Head Erect
- Get a normal two handed grip on the pistol
- Thrust the pistol out at a 45° angle
- Grip firm, wrist firm and elbow firm
- Then raise the pistol to shoulder height, eye level

33

- Align the barrel with the eye, rather than the eye with the barrel.
- Avoid ducking the head to align the eye with the barrel, which is the normal action.
- Keep the head erect.
- Look at the sights.

With this stance, we can use either eye to look at the sights.

- Observe where the pistol is pointed.
- If the pistol is pointed left or right of the target, maintain the position and rotate the entire platform by moving the feet and rotate the aligned system onto the target area.
- Use the top of the front sight as a reference for pointing the internally aligned system at the desired area, the center of the blank target.
- Move the finger smoothly causing the pistol to discharge.
- Immediately recover and point the pistol at the desired area and setup the alignment as though to fire another shot before lowering the pistol.
- This automatically establishes a desirable technique known as follow-through without any conscious thought on the part of the operator

If you do these two simple things, you will get consistent *"hits"* wherever you point the pistol, no matter what else you do.

1. Align the barrel with the eye by observing sight alignment and
2. moving the finger smoothly.

If you do not do these two simple things, it will not make any difference what else you do, you will not get consistent *"hits"* where you want.

If the results are unsatisfactory, you are probably:
- not attentive to the sight alignment
- not moving the finger in a reasonably smooth manner,
- *or you have added something to improve the performance.*

This information constitutes the Sievers Simplified Shooting Method and has a built in self-destruct, if you add anything, it will not work.

What happens is, you overload the students physical capability of handling a maximum of two elements when teaching themselves a basic skill. Suppose someone tells you that you must breathe a certain way or stand a certain way. If you put your attention on these things, you will find your attention focused on something other than

(1) looking hard at the sights
and
(2) moving your finger smoothly.

It is this shifting of the focus of your attention which contributes to your self-destruct in pistol shooting. When you are first starting to teach yourself how to shoot, things other than these two fundamentals distract your concentration or attention. Just work on perfecting these two fundamentals and you will enjoy successful pistol shooting.

Look
Hard
At The
Sights

Move
The
Trigger Finger
Smoothly

Makes for Successful Pistol
Shooting
Point Good!
Move The Finger Smooth!
Eye Open!
"Let's Shoot!"

Chapter 2

The Sievers Simplified Shooting Method has been in continual use by associates of the authors since its inception in 1960. No new shooting philosophy has been deliberately subjected to such scrutiny in the history of marksmanship. The authors feel the 36 years proving has produced results which provide them with the data to say, unequivocally, that this training method is the most effective pistol shooting training program available in the world today.

Shooting:
It's Simple,
Keep It Simple!

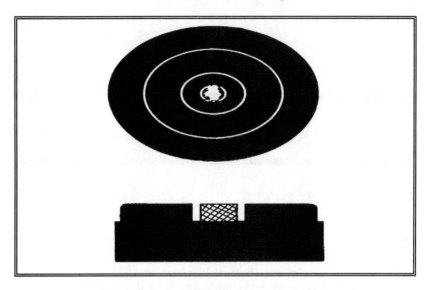

This is a do it yourself
book for the only
person
for whom it is possible
to teach you how to
shoot:

Yourself!

Rules
Of Safe Gun Handling

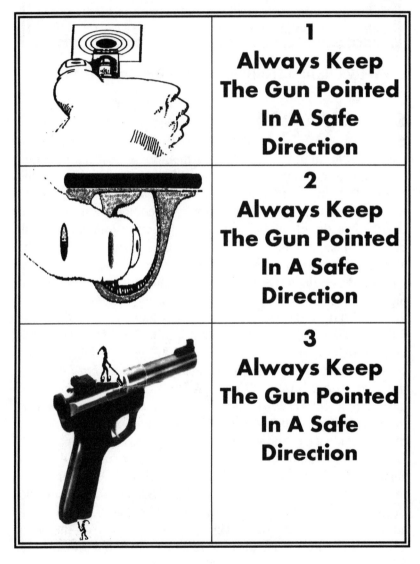

	1 **Always Keep** **The Gun Pointed** **In A Safe** **Direction**
	2 **Always Keep** **The Gun Pointed** **In A Safe** **Direction**
	3 **Always Keep** **The Gun Pointed** **In A Safe** **Direction**

> While references to previous shooting literature have been made in this work, we have neither solicited nor used outside information in establishing the *Philosophy of Shooting* defined in this book. The philosophy defined in this book is *Precision Pointing*. This philosophy is the sole inspiration of Art Sievers. It is rooted in the adversity he suffered as a result of a 40 year immersion in the outdated, inefficient shooting philosophy of, *"Hit the target!"*

Why change from what we have been doing?

What would you say if we told you that the accepted methods of pistol shooting training have been demonstrably a recognizable failure? These failed methods have been repeated so often, for so long, by so many, that they have taken on the status of **Divine Truth** and are embedded in concrete! Manure by any other name does not change it's composition. This, of course, has the effect of insuring that their continued use will produce results which are completely unacceptable to the authors, even at the recreational level. For many years the authors were included among the adherents of these failed methods.

What is the obvious evidence which demonstrates the failure of the training being provided for the pistol shooters of the United States? It is the most obvious evidence of all. It is the common statement, *I can shoot a rifle pretty good, but I can't hit anything with a pistol!* When queried as to why, the standard answer is *I can't hold it still!* The solution for this problem is thoroughly discussed and solved in this book. A more objective piece of evidence of the scope of this problem, is the listing of the Gold Medals won by the Elite US pistol shooters in the Olympics since 1896. In one hundred years, the US pistol shooters have won a total of 8 Olympic Gold Medals. Between the Silver and Bronze medals, the US Pistol Shooters have captured 8 additional Olympic Medals. The US Rifle Shooters, on the other hand, during this same time period, won 15 Gold Medals, 15 Silver Medals and 8 Bronze Olympic Medals.

40

Since 1948, in the recent era of the Olympic Games, the US Pistol Shooters have won two Gold Medals. The US Rifle Shooters have won 10 Gold Medals.

Olympics	Gold Medals Won	Shooting Game
1896	Sumner Paine	Free Pistol
1896	John Paine	Military Revolver
1900	None	
1904	At St. Louis there were no sport shooting events in rifle or pistol.	
1908	None	
1912	Alfred Lane	Free Pistol
1912	Alfred Lane	Rapid-Fire Pistol
1920	Karl Frederick	Free Pistol
1924	Henry Bailey	Rapid Fire Pistol
1928	None	
1932	None	
1936	None	
1948	None	
1952	Joe Benner	Free Pistol
1956	None	
1960	Bill McMillan	Rapid Fire Pistol
1964	None	
1968	None	
1972	None	
1976	None	
1980	The United States Did Not Participate in the 1980 Olympics	
1984	None	
1988	None	
1992	None	
1996	None	

Suppose you own your own business. Down the street is another person in the same line of business you are. You decide to change the way you have been advertising. Up to this point you and your competition have been on a pretty level field of

41

commercial competition. So you then hire an ad agency to produce an ad which will give you prestigious name recognition and get people to purchase your product instead of that of your competitor down the street.

After couple of weeks you notice people on the street seem to have developed disrespect for your business name. You have noticed that people seem even a bit contemptuous of the product you are selling. At the same time, you see an objective survey which shows conclusively that your competition is doing even a better job of moving their product than before you started your present ad campaign.

How long would you stay with running that particular ad? Some business people we have mentioned this to, have invariably responded that they would be on a phone to another ad agency before they finished reading the results of that objective survey.

Our fellow competitor down the street is the rifle shooter. The rifle shooters of America have won nine Gold Medals during the 40 years stretching from 1956 to 1996. During the same time, the US Pistol Shooters took home one Olympic Gold Medal.

The pistol training fraternity of the United States has continued to produce mediocre entries when measured each four years in the Olympics of their Quadrennial against the competitors from the rest of the world. We do not believe that the blame can be placed on the bureaucrats at the National Rifle Association. They only reflect training trends which are current during their time on the job. There is no blame to be attached to the National Rifle Association. As a matter of indisputable fact, there is no blame to be ascribed to anyone, not the American pistol shooters, and most certainly not the coaches and instructors of the American pistol shooters. You see, most were not aware of any different information available. No one in the pistol shooting fellowship was aware of anything which offered even the most remote hope, that doing something different would produce more positive results. They attributed their *"hitting the wall"* to a defect in themselves. So they looked inward and eagerly looked to mental training or mental management to get them over the wall. Or they ascribed their inability to continue positive performance improvement to a lack of time or a lack of

Shooting: It's Simple, Keep It Simple

finances to be able to afford either the equipment or the ammunition. Often they felt that if only they could afford the best guns and the best ammunition, in sufficient quantities to get more practice training than they were doing, they could really move the wall down the road.

For example, take the photograph of Jasna Seharic, of Yugoslavia, in the January 1996 issue of the *UIT Journal*, with her *golden-plated* air pistol. Her score of 393 points at Munich's International Competition would be attributed by many American pistol shooters to her being able to afford a gold plated air gun. You see, we Americans, because of our culture as developed since the end of World War II, believe that the more something costs, the better it *just has to be.* Being able to add 103.4 points in the finals is the mark of a champion, not her equipment. It is a testament of her training. Whatever else she was doing, she had to have been looking very hard at the sights and moving her trigger finger very smoothly. This is what all shooters have to do in order to move forward of any levels beyond what they are producing year after year.

This book offers such an opportunity for improvement. The track record where **methods anchored on this philosophy** have been employed, demonstrates conclusively the validity of this brand of information. For example, here is a listing of results obtained in cases where this philosophy has been used:

★ 1960   Art Sievers: Marksmanship Instructor for the 14th Naval District *Simplified Pistol Training* first initiated.

★ 1965   Art Sievers: US Naval Academy. Coaching Midshipman Intercollegiate Pistol Team with a 40 man Midshipman Squad From 1965 to 1970. 533 personnel, other than midshipmen, stationed at Naval Station Annapolis and the U.S. Naval Academy, ranging in grade from Seaman to Captain have graduated from LCDR Sievers' pistol courses with a 64.4% Navy Expert pistol shot qualifications record.

★ 1967   Tom Treinan: 1976 US Olympic Rapid Fire Team. Trained under the *Navy Simplified Method of Pistol Instruction* by Art Sievers after being kicked off the pistol range by the elite Navy pistol team as being "too dangerous."

43

★ 1968   Art Sievers: US Naval Academy **Results:** 45% **Expert** qualification of participants in the Midshipmen Summer Marksmanship Training Program for the Class of 1972.

★ 1969   Art Sievers: US Naval Academy **Results:** 62% **Expert** qualification of participants in the Midshipmen Summer Marksmanship Training Program for the Class of 1973.

★ 1970   Art Sievers: US Naval Academy. **Results:** 71% **Expert** qualification of the 1500 participants in the Midshipmen Summer Marksmanship Training Program for the Class of 1974.

★ 1970   Art Sievers: Received citation from Chief of Naval Operations for **Developing** outstanding training course for the .45 caliber service pistol.

★ 1971   Nevada Highway Patrol. The *Sievers Simplified Method of Pistol Instruction* adopted as the Nevada Highway Patrol Basic Pistol Training Program by Lt. Neil R. Lunt, Training Officer.

★ 1971   Deleware Highway Patrol. The *Sievers Simplified Method of Pistol Instruction* adopted as the Delaware Highway Patrol Basic Pistol Training Program by Cpl Val Fox.

★ 1978   Bob Mason: Shelton, Washington. Bob Mason, a science teacher at the Shelton Middle School begins to employ the *Sievers Simplified Method of Pistol Instruction* as he sets up a junior pistol club at his school.

★ 1978   John Watkins: Shelton, Washington. John Watkins, a real estate broker, took over coaching the Shelton High School Rifle Team. He begins to employ the *Sievers Simplified Method of Pistol Instruction* as he starts his efforts with the rifle team. Imagine! Using air pistols to train rifle shooters! Prior to his coming on board as their coach, the Shelton High School Rifle Team was a perennial occupant of last place in their high school rifle league. Since then, Watkins' coached rifle teams, using the *Sievers*

Simplified Method of Pistol Instruction and Daisy Model 717 air pistols, have won the high school league a good number of years. The sorriest position they placed under his tutelage was 2nd. As an integral part of his coaching program, Watkins has the team members warm up with the air pistol for about 35 to 40 minutes each practice session before they get on to the .22 caliber rifles.

★ 1979   National NRA Junior Olympic Training Program. The *Sievers Simplified Method of Pistol Instruction* used by Art Sievers. One of the participants was an 17 year old boy, Steve Collins.

★ 1979   National NRA Coach's Clinics. The *Sievers Simplified Method of Pistol Instruction* used by Art Sievers as a part of the NRA Coach's Class C Clinics at the Olympic Training Center in Colorado Springs. Participants were certified as NRA Class C Pistol Coaches.

★ 1980   Steve Collins ranks 1st in US Olympic Rapid Fire Team Selection. Use of this method proves successful in International Rapid Fire Olympic Shooting Game. US did not participate in the 1980 Olympics. Collins shoots a score in the mid 590's in Rapid Fire Match in China.

★ 1980   National NRA Coach's Clinics. The *Sievers Simplified Method of Pistol Instruction* was used by Art Sievers as a part of the NRA Coach's Clinics at the Olympic Training Center in Colorado Springs. Participants were certified as NRA Class C Pistol Coaches. This Coach's Clinic was video taped and the tape is in our files. One of the participants of this Coach's Clinic, on October 1, 1980, wrote a letter to NRA President Harlon B. Carter. In it he wrote, "I attended Art Siever's pistol session. Sievers taught me more about teaching techniques than I have learned in the past 35 years of professional experience." Signed: Benjamin D. Fremming, D.V.M., Director, Professor of Pharmacology, Schools of Medicine and Pharmacy, University of Missouri-Kansas City, Laboratory Animal Center.

⭐1980   Bob Mason: Shelton, Washington. The Shelton Middle School won the 2nd Place NRA Sub-Junior Air Pistol Team.

⭐1981   Minnesota 4-H Shooting Sports. The *Sievers Simplified Method of Pistol Instruction* introduced to the 4-H Shooting Sports Program at Brainard, Minnesota. This seminar was video taped and the tape is in our files.

⭐1981   Bob Mason: Shelton, Washington. The Shelton Middle School won the NRA Sub-Junior Air Pistol Team Championship.

⭐1981-87   Crosman Airguns.   The *Sievers Simplified Method of Pistol Instruction,* used in conjunction with the services of Frank Briggs as Director of Crosman Airgun Department of Shooting Services, for their Pistol Shooting Instruction.

⭐1987   Minnesota 4-H Shooting Sports. The *Sievers Simplified Method of Pistol Instruction* adopted as the National 4-H Shooting Sports Program for Pistol Shooting Training at the 4-H Meeting in Reno, Nevada.

⭐1992   Bob Mason: Shelton, Washington. The former Shelton Middle School student, Kelly Morris, won the 1992 Men's Air Pistol Junior Olympic National Championship at Colorado Springs, CO.

⭐1993   Bob Hickey: The Tucson Pistol Shooting Training Project. The *Sievers Simplified Method of Pistol Instruction* employed as the instructional method for the Flowing Wells Junior High School Pistol Shooting Project of the Saguaro 4-H Shooting Sports Club. **Results:** May 6, 1993, the Flowing Wells **Junior High School Pistol** team beat the Flowing Wells **High School ROTC Rifle Team**, with a score of 1333 for the Pistol Team to 1195 for the Rifle Team. Without context, these scores have little meaning. So, consider, the match required the pistol shooters to fire on the 10 meter pistol target and the rifle shooters to fire on the 10 meters air rifle target, both from the standing position. All shooters fired 40 shots with their respective shooting tools.

The pistol shooters had been learning to shoot the pistol using the *Sievers Simplified Method of Pistol Instruction* since March of 1993. Many of the rifle shooters had been on their ROTC Rifle Team for three or more years. So, they were juniors and seniors, firing against junior high kids. For an evaluation of the results the *Sievers Simplified Method of Pistol Instruction* can produce in a relatively brief time, look at the top four scores of the winning junior high school pistol team: Jeremy Hudgens, 360; Josh Gardner, 325; Nicole Cervantes, 319; Todd Albrecht, 329.

★ 1993 Kelly Morris, Shelton, Washington. Still using the *Sievers Simplified Method of Pistol Instruction* while in Shelton High School, Kelly Morris, won the 1993 Men's Air Pistol Junior Olympic National Championship at Colorado Springs, CO.

★ 1994 Bob Hickey: The Tucson Pistol Shooting Training Project. The *Sievers Simplified Method of Pistol Instruction* continues to be used with exciting results. On July 15, 1994 The Flowing Wells Junior High School Pistol Team set two new National Junior Pistol Team Records. One over the NRA National Match Course 4-Man Team course of fire and the other over the NRA Short Course 4-Man Team course of fire. These were fired outdoors at the 25 yards and 50 yards distances.

★ 1994 Kelly Morris, Shelton, Washington. Still utilizing the *Sievers Simplified Method of Pistol Instruction,* Kelly Morris, for the third consecutive year, won the 1994 Men's Air Pistol Junior Olympic National Championship at Colorado Springs, CO. In doing so, he sets the National Junior Air Pistol Record at 577 points. In addition, he scored 102.8 points in the Finals for a total of 679.8. These are still the National Junior Records as of the publication of this book.

★ 1995 Bob Hickey: The Tucson Pistol Shooting Training Project. The *Sievers Simplified Method of Pistol Instruction* continues to be used with exciting results. On April 23, 1995, The Saguaro 4-H Shooting Sports Club

Pistol Team set three new NRA National Junior Pistol Team Records. The boys set one record. Theirs was over the 3-Person Junior Men's Team course of fire. The girls set two new NRA National Women's Pistol Team Records. Their records were over the NRA Free Pistol 3-Person Team course of fire. The other was over the NRA International Rapid Fire 3-Person Team course of fire. These were fired outdoors at the 50 meters and 25 meters distances. **June 24, 1995** The Saguaro 4-H Shooting Sports Club Pistol Team set another new NRA National Junior Pistol Team Record. The boys set the record this time. It was over the NRA 3-Person Junior Men's Sport Person Team course of fire.

☆ **July 30, 31 & August 1, 1996.** The Saguaro 4-H Shooting Sports Club Pistol Team set 2 individual junior records, 3 Junior Team records and 3 Women's Team NRA National Records. That's a total of eight National Pistol Records over a three-day period, outdoors in temperatures ranging from 103 degrees to 107 degrees, with wild afternoon thunderstorms, making it difficult to keep the target papers on the frames.

The four members of the NRA National Match Course Junior Team Record.

Cade Wilson, age 14, 263-6X points.

L to R: "Bugsy" Barstow, age 11, 244-2X points, Jason Neill, age 13, 242-5X points and Grant Morgan, age 12, 229-2X.

Many of the elite pistol shooters whose opinions are solicited by the shooting management, often we suspect, have ignored the results of the Olympics in their games of Pistol Shooting. They ascribe the loss of face, of their friends in the matches of the Olympiad, to the fanciful notion that the other nations of the world have more people shooting pistol than do we here in America. What a cop out! Take a look at the size of some of the countries beating us in the Olympics. When it comes down to a comparison, take a look at the rifle shooters of Great Britain versus the United States. In England, there are more smallbore rifle shooters who shoot in their National Championships at Bisley, than there are Americans who shoot in our National Smallbore Rifle Championships at Camp Perry, Ohio. According to the rationale of the pistol shooters, American rifle shooters should never be able to beat the British since they have more shooters than we do firing in their National Championships as compared to the number we have shooting in ours. This, historically, has not been the case.

For example, in 1970, Hickey took a group of junior rifle shooters from his training program in Alaska to England. They participated in the Smallbore Rifle Championships of Great Britain. Now, everyone knows that Alaska is far from the continental United States. All of the youngsters learned their shooting techniques in the Alaska training program. Could a team of five of the Alaskan girls, ages 14 to 16, ever expect to defeat the women's national teams representing England, Scotland and Wales? They did, not by much, but the fact that they did invalidates the idea rationalized by many pistol shooters, that the quantity of shooters makes the difference. With a population base of less than 100,000 to draw upon, how can such a local Alaska shooting club be expected to even be competitive with national teams drawing on populations of millions?

In the normal course of events, visitors do not expect to win. Especially on the opponents home ground, using the courses of fire the opponents were used to firing on their home ranges, on targets foreign to the Alaskans. No one gave the Alaskans much of a chance. Much of the Alaskan youngsters' practice had to be conducted indoors due to the severity and length of their winter. And, like the junior rifle teams in the *South 48* of the United States, the Alaskans devoted much of their practice time to 3-position shooting. In England, they fired their international team matches in the prone position. But, look at what they did!

49

Ladies Friendly Match

Bisley, England	50 Meters		24th June 1970

ALASKA

Glacier Cadet Squadron

1,929

Betsy Fleishauer	196	197	393
Genelle Scott	195	192	387
Valorie Walker	193	194	387
Marie Steadman	195	188	383
Nancy Jensen	186	193	379

ENGLAND: CROSS of ST GEORGE

ENGLAND

1,927

Mrs. J. Jordan	197	193	390
Miss M. A. Watson	196	191	387
Mrs. S. Carveth	193	191	384
Mrs. A. Travis	195	188	383
Miss C. A. Lowe	191	192	383

SCOTLAND: CROSS of St. ANDREW

SCOTLAND

1,907

Mrs. S. Robertson	198	194	392
Miss J. Adamson	193	191	384
Mrs. J. Miles	193	188	381
Mrs. E. McNairn	189	186	375
Miss A. M. Simpson	185	190	375

WALES

WALES

1,896

Mrs. J. Dornin	195	194	389
Olga K. Moses	188	190	378
Janet Reed	192	186	378
Mrs. C. Mortimer-White	189	187	376
Mrs. V. C. Martin	185	190	375

British Juniors *versus* Glacier Cadet Squadron

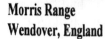

UNITED KINGDOM

ALASKA

Morris Range	60 Shots - Prone	28 June 1970
Wendover, England	50 Meters	
	Metallic Sights	

British Juniors	5,502	Glacier Cadet Squadron	5,804
K. Tilbury	583	S. Brooks	588
C. Every	572	L. Moran	584
R. McEwen	563	B. Fleishauer	582
S. Albon	552	D. Ash	582
Toogood	549	M. Hopkins	580
S. Talbot	545	B. Mellish	580
V. Caudrey	537	M. Steadman	580
F. Dunnett	535	V. Walker	579
K. Dutton	535	D. Landacre	578
P. Hammond	531	G. Scott	571
	5,502		5,804

Shooters Firing - Scores Not Counted For Team Scores

S. Rockell	531	N. Jensen	568
J. Booth	528	D. Shofner	562
R. Arnott	444	D. Sill	559
G. Rutter	Did Not Fire	R. Blanton	557
		K. Rudolph	541

How could such depth in a local club, far from the mainstream of their natural competition, be developed? The authors speculate that it was because of the nature of the shooting training each of these groups of juniors received. The British, it is speculated, trained shooting 10 shots or so, before attempting to change sights. They rationalized that the shots out of the location they expected were due to something they did. So, they kept shooting until the location of the shot group told them they should move their sights.

On the other hand, the Alaskan juniors had been trained to trust their shot calls, and to then move their sights if the shot hole was in a location different than that where they knew the barrel had been pointed when the shot left the muzzle. So, the Alaskan juniors were continuously keeping up with wind conditions and light changes.

The training methods under which the Alaskan juniors had been developed probably played a part in the international matches in which they participated. It was not the quantity of shooters each team had available for the international competition which made the difference in this case. It was the quality and nature of the training.

It is the contention of the authors of this book, that the evidence plainly demonstrates that the American methods of teaching pistol shooting, have failed to produce shooters who have won Olympics in recent years

It is a fact, that in American pistol shooting, the level of acceptance of shooting performance during basic instruction is extremely low. Take for example, the technique which appeared in the May/June, 1983 issue of *InSights (NRA News For Young Shooters)*. The article was written by the then *Pistol Team Coach for the National Development & National Training Teams.*

> *Put up a blank sheet of white paper that is approximately 30" by 30" for a target.*

The elite level coaches **expect and know from their personal experience**, that students learning to shoot their very first shots, under their tutelage, will not be able to fire shots in an area less than that 30-inch square piece of paper. The shooters

52

who learn to shoot in our program start off their training at an 8 ½" by 11" piece of blank paper. And routinely keep all of their shots in groups of less than a 6-inch circle. Just as the elite pistol coach referenced above knows what his information can produce in his students, so too we know what our information produces. Our program starts our shooters off at 10 meters, as does the program that the then national pistol coach advocates. But take a look at what shooters in his program are expected to do:

> *Practice shooting in this position and at this distance until you can place the shots in a 12-inch circle.*

Shooters in both programs are doing their initial training by firing from a benchrest. That pistol coach has his beginning students start the initial phase of their training and

> *"kneel or sit down behind the table."*

Shooters starting in our program start off in the standing position, using an extended benchrest, or sitting down at a table using a sandbag rest. So, both programs start off in the benchrest position.

Is what that pistol coach advocates *wrong*? No way! If he can live with the results he is getting, how could it be wrong? Is it efficient? No way! The authors cannot live with the results of this kind of instruction. Our program can produce, **right from the start**, shooters who are able to fire groups within a circle with a diameter of 6 inches from a distance of 10 meters. This normally is done during the same training session and after ten shots. So, during the firing of the third five-shot group, our shooters usually can produce a group within a circle of **3 inches**. On the other hand, consider the one which produces, **right from the start**, shooters who are able to fire groups within a circle of 30-inches. In that pistol coach's training, a 12-inch circle is the **goal** of the training. Progress occurs when the student can finally manage to obtain groups, with all of the shots in a 12-inch circle. The article cited does not state how many shots are expended in finally producing this 12-inch shot circle. However, the impression is that it may require quite a few since it is not expected that the student will be able to produce such a result until after "probably the second or third visit to the range." This probably includes the expenditure of several boxes of ammunition. Our program is ammunition cost effective. Our program can produce better results with the expenditure of 10 rounds of ammunition. With a program based around the same information provided by a program such as that pistol coach describes, after the student can produce a 12-inch group, he is then allowed to put up a regulation target. Most pistol shooters know that pistol coach's expectations are right in line with what their experience has demonstrated in their initial training and in training they have put on for someone else.

Why have the American pistol shooters not looked at this problem and tried something different? Nothing different has been available! Because the information available in the public domain has been enshrined as holy grails. No one doubts a holy grail. They constitute the **facts of shooting**. Everyone knows facts do not change. Or do they? Several hundred years ago, it was a *fact* that the earth is **flat**. Today, it is round or oblong. In pistol shooting, how can so many have been so led astray for so long?

Why did no one look at the inadequacy of the training methods to produce the results the coaches and instructors claimed would occur? Because the inadequacy was blamed squarely on the student! It never occurred to anyone to look at the information being provided to the student. The student, under this method, was given a task which was physically impossible to accomplish. The maximum number of things which the student can physically perform simultaneously, hits the wall at two! The minimum number of things we have found in our investigation of current shooting teaching programs is five, running to 60 in a US Army Pistol Shooting Marksmanship Training Manual in order to fire one accurate shot. Distractions which had nothing to do with the shooting process were introduced and elevated to the status of fundamentals. For example, one of these is commonly known as breathing. Here a natural body function which adjusts to any physical activity was touted as a pistol shooting fundamental and had to be relearned. If you want to breath in a particular manner, it requires 100% of

54

your attention continuously. At the microsecond your attention wanders from this attempt to control the process of breathing, it goes back into full automatic. So, unless you are in a breathing contest, forget it! Let sleeping dogs lie. Accept the natural function of our breathing! It normally operates without distracting our attention from whatever we are doing. Why did no one look at the information which served as the backbone of the modern pistol training methods to see if it met the standards of educationally sound teaching theory? Well, one man did, Art Sievers. And, in February of 1970, an article was printed in *The American Rifleman* describing his new philosophical approach to the teaching of shooting.

The article points out that the product of this training was the qualifying of 62% of the plebes at the US Naval Academy as <u>Experts</u>. Notice they qualified as <u>Experts</u>, not merely qualified as marksmen! Over 99% of the group achieved some qualifying score. And this was with the service issue .45 caliber pistol. That reflected the qualification scores fired in 1969. In 1970, the number qualifying as <u>Experts</u>, out of a pool of 1,500, went up to in excess of 71%.

In the same time frame, the US Coast Guard, in 1971, was achieving a 46% of 7,868 people obtaining at least a minimum pistol marksman qualification rating. This was also over the Navy F qualification course. In 1972, the Coast Guard achieved only 38.5% minimum marksman qualification rating out of 9,269.persons sent through the pistol qualification course. This brings up the question of *"in how many other Coast Guard training classes do they expect that their instruction will produce a 60% failure rate?"*

Why should pistol shooters change from teaching pistol shooting as they always have in the past? Because it has not been doing the job at the level they claim they are striving to achieve.

It is a scientific fact that the earth is round. However, or in spite of this, there are people who believe that the earth is flat. They are numbered among the members of the *Flat Earth Society*. If you continue to support a pistol training system that is a proven failure by its track record, feel free to apply for membership in the *Flat Earth Society*.

Pistol shooters urgently need to consider changing to a new philosophy of shooting. Why a philosophy? What does that mean? It is a new way of thinking about pistol shooting training. Under this new philosophy, in shooting, hitting the target is worshipping a false god. This is easily understood once you understand how a shooting tool really works. The new philosophy has been in continued use since 1960. In every pistol training situation where it has been used, it has been an exemplary success.

This program has been in continual testing by associates of the authors since its inception in 1960. No new shooting philosophy has been deliberately subjected to such scrutiny in the history of marksmanship. The authors feel the 36-year testing has produced results, which provide them with the data to say unequivocally that this training method is the most efficient program that is available in the world today. Should another method, upon being subjected to the duration and critical analysis which has been shown on this program, and which can produce better training results, then the authors of this book stand ready to employ it. We would then know two methods!

This philosophy is thoroughly analyzed and presented in this book.

Just what is this new philosophy?

In essence, *it is Precision Pointing with a precision pointing tool!* We focus all of our training around the establishment of just two fundamentals, **with never ceasing repetition.** We are going to call the **combination** of the shooter and the shooting tool, the *shooting unit, "Me and Ma Gun."*

1	2
Visually Align the barrel with the eye, using the top of the front sight as a reference, point the aligned system at the area where you want the indicator (bullet hole) to appear..	## Instantaneous Smooth Trigger Finger Movement

When we exceed two fundamentals of instruction during the learning of a physical skill, then, we are beyond the student's physical and mental capacity to easily master that skill. This is not to say that such a skill cannot be eventually learned. However, it will neither be easy, nor immediately rewarding.

When we mention this simple idea to old *hard-holding pistol shooters,* the response we invariably get is something like,

> *Oh, yes, we teach both those two fundamentals, but we give them the other fundamentals or sub-fundamentals also.*

And, you see therein lies the difference between our philosophy of focusing our entire program around only these two fundamentals and the old *hard-holding pistol shooters* and their **multitude of fundamentals**.

Take for example, *hard-holding pistol shooters* and their espousal of a multitude of fundamentals. This is best illustrated by the outline of more than 60 fundamental things, needed to be done, to fire one accurate shot. We first found this list in the 1964 edition of *The United States Army Marksmanship Unit Pistol Marksmanship Guide.* It was added to and refined in various reincarnations.

1964 Page 93 *The Advanced Pistol Marksmanship Manual*
1969 Page 43 *Pistol Marksmanship Manual*
1972 Page 42 *Pistol Marksmanship Guide*
1975 Page 34 *Basic Pistol Marksmanship Guide*
1981 Page 42 *Pistol Marksmanship Guide*

Of particular interest is the 1975 *Basic Pistol Marksmanship Guide*, cited above. It has only 37 total pages.

57

The experts who wrote the pistol guide must have felt that it was very important to retain this *Outline Of The Complete Sequence Of Firing One Accurate Shot.* The 1964 manual, at 396 pages, contains the most pages of any of the pistol manuals and guides, which we have researched.

The 1981 publication, on page 1, documents what the *hard-**holding** pistol shooters* believe the fundamentals of pistol marksmanship comprise,

> *The fundamentals of pistol marksmanship embrace all of those physical factors essential to the firing of an accurate shot.*

You can evaluate our new philosophy of shooting with what has been taught for a long time in American pistol training. Consider, how many things can you think about and really concentrate on at one time? Most of you will probably say, ONE. We agree with you! When you get TWO things to have to keep in mind when you are first learning to do something, then you are stretching the limit of what most humans are capable of accomplishing with some degree of success. If you have to remember 30 or 60 things that you must learn to do, the wonder is that so many people selected *Sight Alignment and Trigger Control* from among all of the options they were told they had to keep in mind in order to fire one accurate shot.

Does it matter how you think when you assume the task of training others to shoot?

Yes, it most certainly does! For example, in our training, we know that we obtain our *Sight Alignment* from our stance. This goes to the root of the differences in the kinds of training a person receives under our philosophy of shooting and what was taught as the purpose of the stance under the old failed training method. Our training focuses on the establishment and refinement of the conditional reflex between the eye, the brain and the trigger finger. Therefore, we get our *Sight Alignment* through our stance. We want our shot to be fired while on full automatic. If the stance is not set up so that when the sights reach eye level, the brain initiates the conditional reflex of moving the trigger finger, then we are interrupting that conditional reflex by trying to muscle the sights into alignment. So, under our philosophy of shooting, what is the grip of the pistol used for? We use the grip of the pistol to get finger placement in order to provide for a consistent **Moving The Finger To Actuate The Trigger**. The grip of the pistol is used to place the finger in exactly the same place on the trigger so that the conditional reflex can occur automatically as it is designed to do. If the brain senses that the finger is not in the same position that it is expecting, then the conditional reflex is again thrown off by a slight amount. This will then cause random indicators to appear on the target.

On the other hand, consider what page 1 of *The United States Army Marksmanship Unit Pistol Marksmanship Guide* has to say about how they obtain *correct sight alignment*:

> *To obtain correct sight alignment, **it is necessary for the shooter to grip the pistol in a manner which guarantees that he is holding the pistol firmly** and that trigger pressure is applied straight to the rear....However, since the shooter cannot achieve complete immobility when assuming the stance and position, **the trigger has to be pressed** during some movement of the pistol. In order to deliver an accurate shot within his ability to hold, the shooter must not only **press the trigger evenly**, but he must do so with correct sight alignment. The size of the shot group will, therefore, not exceed the dimensions of the arc of movement, provided the shot breaks as a surprise **and no reflex action of muscles disturbs the delivery of the shot**.*
> (Selections bolded by authors)

Under this still current method of teaching pistol shooting, the student is taught to get sight alignment through the grip. Remember, this method has been unable to develop Olympic level shooters. But, it sounds reasonable. Under that method, shooters were told to *press the trigger evenly*. This idea of *press the trigger evenly* has the effect of distracting the shooter from the developing of the conditional reflex we are showing shooters in our program how to acquire. In fact, the old method described in the **Pistol Marksmanship Guide** actually holds up the development of a reflex action of the muscles as being wrong, so *no reflex action of muscles disturbs the delivery of the shot.*

Now, a philosophy is a way of thinking. You may be starting to see the difference in how we think about our shooting, compared to the shooters of the old school. In the century of the 2000's, we need shooters with a new way of looking at their pistol shooting. For example, we stress that the pistol shooter must develop his act of shooting as a conditional reflex. This means that when the sight alignment gets to eye level and is pointed at the desired area, the eyeball transmits this information to the brain instantaneously. This, in turn, generates an instantaneous reflexive reaction by the trigger finger. This trigger finger movement is what we call instantaneous smooth. Consider, on the other hand, how the **Pistol Marksmanship Guide** handles the teaching of the act of shooting:

> *In order to apply coordinated pressure on the trigger,* **the shooter must wait** *for those very definite times* **when all control factors are optimum and firing conditions become favorable.** *The* **rule that must be observed** *as the first step in attaining control of the shooting is:* **"You must never attempt to fire until you have completely settled into a minimum arc of movement."** (Selections bolded by authors)

By focusing the training of the shooter on **waiting**, the pistol coach or instructor is creating a hesitant shooter. Research shows that one of the traits of a champion is an attitude of aggression toward his shooting. So, here is a coach, probably unwittingly to be sure, actually training a shooter right from the start to be a loser. By focusing attention on the *rule that must be observed,* the coach is circumventing the early development of the conditional reflex.

60

So, you see, our research clearly demonstrates that the old established methods are inefficient at what they set out to do, create Olympic Pistol Champions.

If after reading this information and what you read on the following pages, you prefer the old method, then by all means get your kid into one of the old programs. If you do, we will wish you luck and good shooting. If you choose to keep your kid with us, we will imbue him or her with our new shooting philosophy. We have found it to be a much more efficient philosophy in the teaching of shooting than the old method. If another more efficient method comes along, we will embrace it.

What is shooting?
(Technical Definition)
Just so that we are communicating, just what is this thing we are learning to do called *Precision Shooting*?

Precision Shooting is being able to align the barrel of a shooting tool with the eye, precisely and consistently, and being able to point as desired and move the finger instantaneously smooth, without introducing angular misalignment between the barrel and the eye.

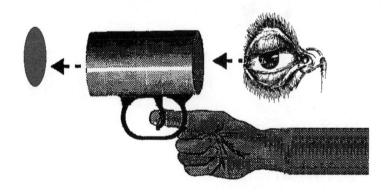

What is shooting?

(A Kid's Definition)

Just so that we are communicating, just what is this thing we are learning to do called *Precision Shooting*?

Precision Shooting is being able to put the barrel of a shooting tool in line with the eye, the same way each time, and being able to point as desired and move the finger instantaneously smooth, without causing the barrel and the eye to not be lined up with each other.

Conditional Reflex Development Phase
Forming the Shooting Template

The formation of the Shooting Template is really a visual motor reflex loop. This loop becomes more refined or perfect each time you do it. The template formed by this shooting action gets to be more precise each time it is practiced. The formula for this template can be conceptualized as:

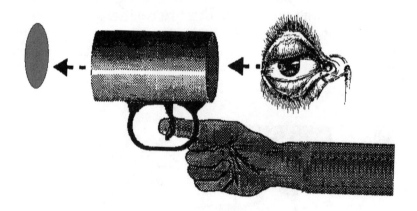

Visual Perception of the sight system
+
A Kinesthetic Reaction
=
The Output: motor response
(the finger is moved)

A kinesthetic reaction, is described by *The American Heritage Dictionary*, (Houghton Mifflin, 1987) as *"the sensation of bodily position, presence, or movement resulting chiefly from stimulation of sensory nerve endings in muscles, tendons, and joints."* In the case of shooting, our attention is focused on the movement of the finger. To make the movement of the finger smoothly moving the trigger a reflex action, we practice smoothly moving it to the rear, over and over and over.

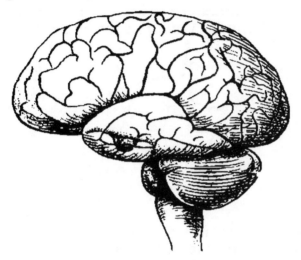

Visual Motor Reflex Loop Process:

❶ **Visual Perception of the sight system**
The shooter decides to perform the action of moving the trigger finger with the arm extended out from the body while pointing at a place where he wants the impact of the pellet or bullet to strike.

❷ **A Kinesthetic reaction occurs**
The brain acts on the shooter's intention by sending commands to the arm to rise to the shooting

63

position with the proper hand
grip.

❸   The Output
A motor response sub-program is
initiated by the brain and the
result is the trigger is moved.

Method of Training Your Trigger Finger Control:

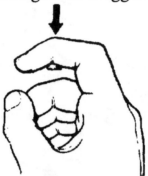

1. Put your arm out in front of you.
2. Make your wrist firm and your elbow firm.
3. Make a fist in the normal pistol gripping position, that is, with the thumb facing forward and the lower three fingers closed in the palm of the hand.
4. Insert the fingers of your non-shooting hand into the pocket formed by the fingers of your shooting hand.
5. Bend your trigger finger to the position it occupies on the trigger.
6. Now, smoothly move your trigger finger straight back.
7. Focus on the effort to eliminate the sympathetic reaction of the fingers of the trigger hand to move when the trigger finger moves.
8. Repeat steps 1 through 7 for a minimum of ten minutes at a time.
9. Repeat step 8 for a series of 5 times.

Shooting: It's Simple, Keep It Simple

As we begin to teach ourselves to shoot, our attention is focused on the movement of the trigger finger. But, that is only in the beginning. Our attention is focused on the trigger finger movement only in the very beginning, until we have established it as a conditional reflex. The reason we put our attention on the movement of the trigger finger is so that we can train this movement to the way we want it to perform when we shoot. We do this so that when we actuate the trigger finger, we do not introduce angular misalignment between the barrel and the eye.

The effort of the beginning competitive shooter is directed toward creating a conditional reflex between the eye, the brain and the finger. We want the trigger finger movement to be instantaneously smooth. This reflex action is initiated as soon as the brain is satisfied with what the eye sees as flawless internal alignment of the system, pointed at the desired area.

Precision Shooting is being able to put the barrel of a shooting tool in line with the eye, the same way each time, being able to point as desired and move the finger instantaneously smooth, without introducing angular misalignment between the barrel and the eye.

LOOK

HARD

AT

THE

SIGHTS

+

MOVE

THE

TRIGGER FINGER

SMOOTHLY

MAKES FOR SUCCESSFUL PISTOL SHOOTING

Chapter 3

Please understand it is not the intention of the authors to single out any person or organization for any derogatory comment. We are using their published works to illustrate common pistol shooting concepts. We do not say that the comments selected for illustration in this book are either good or bad. In some cases, they differ from that which we advocate. However, we want the reader to understand that we do not make a judgment as to their being right or wrong. We have selected them solely for the purpose of showing how our philosophy and methods differ from prevailing concepts.

Pistol

Shooting

Concepts

Traditional concepts of pistol

shooting training have not changed for most of the last century. One premise of traditional pistol shooting instructional design strategies calls for linking marksmanship theories and teaching methods so as to provide the most efficient means for the greatest number of students to acquire the greatest amount of knowledge. Wells, in his book about the history of marksmanship instruction in the US Coast Guard, mentioned that the pistol instructors were told they could use any method they wanted provided they did not change the traditional theories of marksmanship. William R. Wells, II book, *Shots That Hit, A Study of U.S. Coast Guard Marksmanship 1790 - 1985,* is unique in the annals government publications. The authors expected a self-serving puff job for the Coast Guard marksmanship program. Instead, it is a book both well researched and very comprehensively documented.

Much of pistol shooting training has been built upon the traditional theories of marksmanship. In essence, these theories constitute a philosophy of control that requires a pistol instructor centered classroom. These marksmanship theories assume that properly managed instruction enables most pistol students to acquire the skills and knowledge needed to continue to learn. Practice and repetition, with frequent participation in pistol matches, characterize this approach. This approach is the only one that many pistol shooters, coaches and instructors have ever known, Their level of comfort with this model will make it very difficult to supplant. Many of today's pistol instructors entered the field of pistol shooting during this last half century and still believe in focusing on out-dated content.

Many pistol coaches might admit that perhaps someday we will know how to teach beginning shooters more effectively, but for the present we must *"make do"* with what we have and are sure of, as *"tried and true"*. Most of the pistol coach trainers seem to assume that the information required for this more complete and effective kind of pistol training doesn't exist, and that is why we are not seeing it applied. Well, we couldn't agree less! Over the past several decades, in a wide variety of pistol training situations, a new technique and method has been quietly devised, applied, and tested -- techniques that at the very least promise to give the pistol shooters at large, significantly increased access to their own potentials and capacities. The puzzle remains: Why are we not applying this technique more extensively, and how does it happen that mainstream pistol trainers have largely ignored even the most conservative pieces of information regarding these matters? The method in this book was first publicly described in a 1970 article in *The American Rifleman.*

Despite the publishing of the investigative report of this new and unique training method, *The American Rifleman* did not receive even one inquiry pertaining to it's availability and applicability. Not one! There was a response received from an Australian civilian who stated that he was pleased with the article and in full agreement with the concept.

Just think, here was a prime opportunity for the Coast Guard pistol instructors to have picked up on this method and evaluated it's training effectiveness. After all, *The American Rifleman* article mentioned that the training method involved the use of the service .45 caliber pistol. It further noted that the Siever's pistol training method produced 65% Expert ratings in 1969. This was achieved out of a group of over 1,500 midshipmen, and was fired over the Navy F Course. These Navy midshipmen recorded a unheard of 99% over-all qualification achievement. This means that almost all of the 1,500 made at least the minimum qualifying marksman score. That was the very same qualification course the Coast Guard was using at that time. While the Navy was producing a 99% qualification rating, the Coast Guard was producing less than 50%. Why did they miss this opportunity.

Why indeed? We ignore things not only because they seem valueless; we also ignore things because we see them as a threat to the comfort zone we have created in our pistol shooting.

We fear our highest possibilities, as well as our lowest ones. We are generally afraid to become that which we can glimpse in our most perfect moments, under conditions of greatest courage. Winning an Olympic Pistol Shooting Gold medal, we enjoy and even thrill to the godlike possibilities we see in ourselves in such peak moments. And yet we simultaneously shiver with weakness, awe, and fear before these very same possibilities.

Courage is the power to let go of the familiar, and we are not over-endowed with courage. Pistol shooters are no less prone than others to cling tenaciously to the safe, the established, the accepted. After all, *"if I innovate, I draw attention to my actions and will be held responsible for them. But if I stick to the tried and true, it is not I who bears responsibility"* -- responsibility falls upon the established method, so no one is responsible. How comforting! How easy! How irresponsible!

Pistol shooters, for years, like scavengers, intent upon finding the secret ingredient responsible for the successes of great pistol champions, poke around in the didactic effluvium until they find a likely morsel. They then subject it to statistical analysis, then triumphantly announce a high correlation between the "secret" characteristic and successful shooting. Their disciples, swooping in for the kill, hastily confuse statistical correlation with causation and declare that use of the secret ingredient will cure all pistol shooting ills. If circumstances contrive to produce a wave of enthusiasm for the *new* pistol training "method," then good results ensue -- for a while. But, note that as enthusiasm wanes, positive results wane! Even so, after a few years the training secret is enshrined in shooting mythology. If it doesn't work for a shooter, then *"Aw, he just doesn't have it."* The blame is placed squarely on the shooter, not the information he was working under.

Is it not time that we learned something from this pattern? Perhaps we are looking in the wrong place for the key to pistol shooting success.

Looking where the light happens to be best, may be an approach worthy of a drunken man, but sober pistol coaches and instructors ought to have learned from half a century of an inability to produce successful pistol shooters from their instruction. The presupposition that technique can solve all of our problems involves an attitude most unbecoming to anyone posing as a pistol coach.

Perhaps the most enduring and pervasive principle in pistol shooting training, is that students learn by emulation. Socrates induced a fundamental alteration in his students by serving as a model of inquiry unfettered by the popular prejudices of his time. Youngsters are often confronted with pistol coaches and instructors who know all of the answers. It becomes apparent to thinking pistol shooters that these pistol coaches and instructors are not themselves learners. It is obvious that those pistol coaches who insist that there is only one correct way, who are unimaginative, whose sole criterion of worth is performance, can learn to be creative, open, self-reliant and responsible pistol coaches only by default, that is, by not being "good" students in their own coach trainer's eyes. But encouraging pistol coaches to defy their coach trainer would be throwing out the baby with the bath water. If the bath water needs changing, then change it while exercising care to preserve the baby. It is the pistol coach's consciousness which needs "cleansing" so that students come forth from the pistol shooting educational bath with that fresh set of principles, insights, skills, and knowledge necessary for the kind of pistol shooting competitive world which the students will inhabit.

The pistol shooting concepts we have identified in the following pages are those which we hold up for your inspection. We look at them and identify their merits or defects from the perspective of the new shooting training method we have set forth in this book. We judge these concepts as neither right nor wrong. We look at each of them to identify their efficiency at being able to produce positive results under our method of pistol shooting training.

◎ **Source of Pistol Concept:** Just think, what is the biggest problem in the world? Some of you might claim hunger is the biggest problem, others might claim people are the biggest problem and you are close. But if something is the biggest problem in the world, it has to be present where you are now, where you go tomorrow and where you went yesterday. Consider this, do you recall hearing anyone comment something to the effect,

I can't talk to my old man,
he doesn't know what I'm talking about.

Or, I'm sure you have heard somewhere along the line,

That darn youngster of mine,
I can't talk to him,
in one ear and out the other.

☞**comment:** Could you go along with *communication* as being the biggest problem in the world? Sure. You, the reader, can find value in this book if you first understand just what we, as authors of this book, mean when we use the term *shooting.* In other words, you and I have got to *communicate* on just what is this thing we all call, *shooting.*

To get down to brass tacks, our definition may not quite jibe with your definition of shooting. Do you have to agree with our definition? Absolutely not! However, you must **understand** our definition of *shooting.* If you find yourself **applying your definition of shooting** to what we are talking about when we use the term *shooting,* within the pages of this book, you may find that you become confused about what we mean.

How do we get to our definition of *shooting?* First, let's eliminate some of the things which do not enter into our definition of *shooting.* From there you can see how we proceed to define *shooting.*

Shooting

Shooting is a word which can stand alone. If you go out to the shooting range and see someone on the firing line and ask him what he is doing, you are likely to get the reply, *shooting.*

72

Here we have added another word to the term *shooting*. What is the rifle with respect to *shooting*? I think you can agree that it refers to the tool we are using in doing our *shooting*.

Now we have added a new term. What is the relationship of **prone** to rifle. It describes the position being used to do the shooting. Instead of using the word position, we will use the term platform to describe how the shooting is being done. In other words,

- we shoot the rifle prone
  - we shoot the rifle standing
    - we shoot the rifle kneeling
      - we shoot the rifle sitting
        - we shoot the rifle benchrest.

The only difference lies in the stability that each of the various platforms contributes to the shooting tool for the shooting being done.

Here we have added another word to the term *shooting*. What is the pistol with respect to *shooting*? I think you can agree that it refers to the tool we are using in doing our *shooting*.

Now we have added a new term. What is the relationship of **benchrest** to pistol? It describes the position being used to do the shooting. Instead of using the word position, we will use the term platform to describe how the shooting is being done. In other words,

- we shoot the pistol benchrest
    - we shoot the pistol standing
        - we shoot the pistol kneeling
            - we shoot the pistol sitting
                - we shoot the pistol prone.

The only difference lies in the stability that each of the various platforms contributes to the shooting being done.

Here we have added another word to the term *shooting*. What is the shotgun with respect to *shooting*? I think you can agree that it refers to the tool we are using in doing our *shooting*.

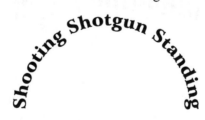

Now we have added a new term. What is the relationship of **standing** to shotgun. It describes the position being used to do the shooting. Instead of using the word position, we will use the term platform to describe how the shooting is being done. In other words,
- we shoot the shotgun standing
  - we shoot the shotgun prone
    - we shoot the shotgun kneeling
      - we shoot the shotgun sitting
        - we shoot the shotgun benchrest.

The only difference therefore lies in the stability and flexibility that each of the various platforms contributes to the shooting being done. But, all shooting is the same.

Only the tool used for the shooting is different.

	Tool	**Platform**
shooting	**rifle**	**prone**
		benchrest
		standing
shooting	**pistol**	**benchrest**
		standing
		sitting
shooting	**shotgun**	**standing**
		sitting
		benchrest

Not Talking About Platforms

When we are talking *tools* we are not talking *shooting*. When we are talking *platforms*, we are not talking *shooting*. If we are not talking about *platforms*, we shall eliminate them from our discussion of *shooting*. They have nothing to do with *shooting*. They are only the *platforms* we use to do our *shooting*.

	Tool	Platform
shooting	rifle	~~prone~~
		~~bench rest~~
		~~standing~~
shooting	pistol	~~bench rest~~
		~~standing~~
		~~sitting~~
shooting	shotgun	~~standing~~
		~~sitting~~
		~~benchrest~~

Not Talking About Tools

If we are not talking *tools*, we will eliminate them from our discussion of *shooting*.

	Tool	Platform
shooting	~~rifle~~	
shooting	~~pistol~~	
shooting	~~shotgun~~	

All Shooting Is The Same.

That being done, we are left with the obvious, *all shooting is the same*. Only the tools used and the platforms used to create stability are different. Until you read this book, you probably fell into the trap of thinking shooting with different tools was different somehow. You probably felt that shooting shotgun was different from shooting rifle. You did not know that you were talking about the tools and the platforms used to achieve that level of performance you set for yourself. In the future, if you are comparing platforms and tools, say so. Understand that *shooting* has nothing to do with such extraneous things. When you are talking *shooting*, these things constitute distractions.

Hit The Target

When you shoot, do you try to hit the target? Sure, I think that most of you can honestly say that is what you try to do when you shoot. But, shooting does not work that way. We'll take this up further on in this chapter. For now, try to figure out why we say shooting does not work that way.

No one can teach anyone how to shoot. I've never heard of anyone who has taught anyone how to shoot. So who has taught you how to shoot? You are the one who has taught yourself how to shoot. Someone may have given you some information about shooting. But, you had to select from that information just what you would use in teaching yourself to shoot.

Who can decide what you will teach yourself about shooting? Only you can decide what you are going to teach yourself about shooting. You may have a coach, but only you can decide what you will teach yourself. Most people who shoot think of themselves as experts. And, they are willing to share their expert knowledge with anyone who will listen. So, you are faced with a massive amount of information that you can use to teach yourself about shooting. You have to make a decision about what you want to teach yourself so that your shooting performance will be at the level of satisfaction you want from the shooting you do. You must reduce this information to two elements to remain within your physical envelope.

Assume the gun is loaded and we cause it to be discharged, perhaps by remote control. What is the major thing that happens? The bullet comes out the barrel. That is what it is supposed to do. And, what is the bullet's purpose, when you are teaching yourself to shoot? It will verify absolutely where the barrel is pointed when the bullet is discharged out the muzzle.

What does the bullet hole tell us? It tells us where the

barrel was pointed when the bullet exited the barrel. The figure above is based on one which appeared in the 1960 US Army translation of Yev'yev's book, *Sportivnaya Strel'ba Iz Vintovki.*

The illustration above supposes *that no forces act on the bullet after it leaves the bore. In this case, as indicated above, the bullet would move by inertia infinitely, uniformly and rectilinearly, in the direction of the axis of the bore. During each second it would travel the same distance at a constant velocity equal to the muzzle velocity. In this case, if the barrel of the weapon were pointed directly at the target, the bullet, travelling in the direction of the axis of the bore, would strike the target. (Yev'yev, A.A., Sportivnaya Strel'ba Iz Vintovki,* Competitive Marksmanship With Rifle and Carbine, Moscow, 1957, Translation Department Of The Army, Office Of The Assistant Chief Of Staff, Intelligence, 1960, pp 48) That's it! Now, there are naysayers who will object, using terms such as trajectory, elevation, windage, and etc.

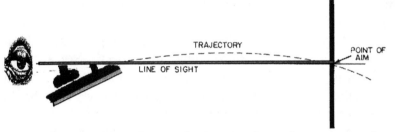

But, at this point we don't care about these terms. Just for the record, the trajectory is the same for a particular load every time. So, for our purposes, we can call it a straight line. It won't make a bit of difference. When playing a game of precision pointing, the sights on the pistol are adjusted to account for the trajectory. Since the bullet is acted upon by gravitational forces once it is propelled out the barrel, the pistol has to be angled upwards to compensate for the dropping of the bullet. The sights are adjusted so that the point of aim and the point of impact on the target are identical. Thus, when we say the bullet *"hits"* when the pistol was pointed, we can leave the concept of trajectory out of the discussion.

Once we find the bullet hole, we know exactly where the barrel was pointed when the gun went off. What does the bullet hole tell us? It tells us where the barrel was pointed when the bullet was discharged. What information did we get from that bullet hole? It gave us *Instantaneous Feedback* about where the barrel was pointed when the bullet was discharged. What word are we trying to call to your attention? Pointing!

    If we want to have a bullet hole appear at a particular spot, what is the only thing which has to happen? The barrel has to be pointed at that spot when the bullet leaves the barrel. Would it make any difference at all how that was done? Absolutely none at all. All that has to happen is that the barrel has to be pointed at that particular place when the bullet leaves the barrel.

    Have we said anything in the previous paragraph about *"hitting"* anything? No! Hitting is an effect. Not a cause. When you shoot, if you are trying to *"hit"* the target, that is a distraction. The gun does not even work that way. You should be learning how to have it pointed where you want the bullet to indicate when you shoot. Where does a gorilla sleep? *Anywhere he wants.* Where can you point one of these tubes used for shooting? *Anywhere you want.*

◎ **Source of Pistol Concept:** Art Sievers, 1968.

    Back in the late 1960's Art Sievers introduced the concept of the shooting unit. What he did was to call the combination of the shooter and the shooting tool, the *shooting unit, "Me and Ma Gun."* Sievers used a concept, which he referred to as the *"Shooting Diagram,"* to divide the shooting unit into three systems.

☛**Comment:** An analysis of the three systems enables us to derive our definition of shooting..

The Shooting Diagram

Composed

of

Three Systems

The Internal Alignment System

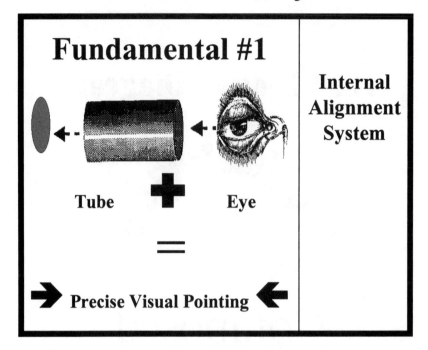

Fundamental #1

Internal Alignment System

Tube **✚** Eye

=

➡ **Precise Visual Pointing** ⬅

Visually aligning the axis of a tube on an external point. The accepted term for this action is called "aiming."

System I consists of the eye, the barrel and the sights, all within the shooting unit, hence internal.

Note the position between the barrel and the eye. If there is the slightest random misalignment between the barrel and the eye, it is obvious that a random point is the most that can be expected at the external area.

For the ultimate in pointing precision, it is again obvious that the maximum acceptable error in internal alignment, between the barrel and the eye, is "zero."

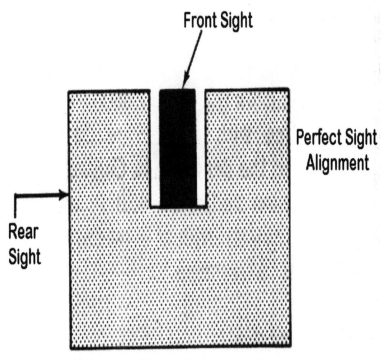

This perfect sight alignment produces perfect barrel alignment with the eye.

The Indicating System

Fundamental #2

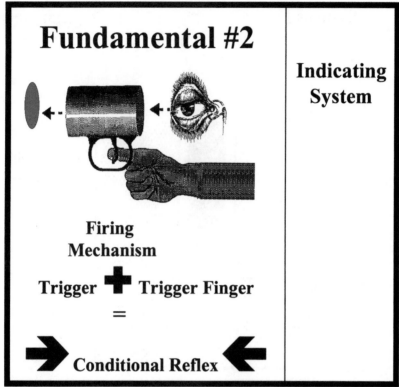

Indicating System

Firing
Mechanism

Trigger ✚ Trigger Finger

=

➡ Conditional Reflex ⬅

This system consists of the firing mechanism and the actuating finger. With the firing mechanism in an operating mode, physically moving the finger on the trigger will cause a missle, commonly referred to as a bullet, to be expelled from the barrel. Because of the guiding nature of the barrel, the only place the bullet can strike is where ever the barrel happened to be pointed on the bullet's exit.

The strike of the bullet, commonly referred to as a bullet hole, positively indicates, as feedback, precisely where the barrel was pointed on the exit of the bullet. This action generates the name "Indicating System."

Systems I and II of the Shooting Diagram are the heart and soul of precision pointing and are the basis of our definition of shooting.

"To be able to align the barrel with the eye precisely and consistently and be able to indicate as desired, without introducing angular misalignment between the barrel and the eye."

To be valid, the definition must apply to any shooting tool by any able bodied users.

Aligning the barrel with the eye is completely within the physical capability of the average person. To *"Indicate as desired"* means moving the finger to get the bullet out the barrel. The shooter can point the internally aligned system anywhere he wants, any way he wants, any time he wants and move the finger whenever. Avoiding the introduction of angular misalignment is self explanatory.

From this, it is completely obvious that if you use the "definition of shooting," to apply systems I & II of the "Shooting Diagram," you will get consistent indicators where ever the barrel is pointed, no matter what else you do. If you do not do this, it doesn't make any difference what else you do, you will have random points!

III
The Support System

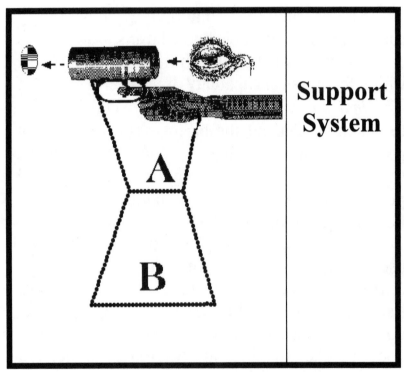

Support System

System III consists of everything not included in systems I and II.

The support system provides two distinct services to the shooting unit. The primary service "A" in accordance with System I, must establish and maintain internal alignment. The secondary service "B" provides maximum support and stability for the entire shooting unit.

1. Internal Alignment System

Aligning the barrel with the eye.

We will visually align the axis of the tube with an external point. The eye is the place where we start building any platform. We cannot see through the barrel because it is plugged up. So, we have a couple of references on the outside of the barrel which we call *sights.* If we align these two sights <u>with the eye</u> each time, then we are *aligning the barrel with the eye* each time. The number one purpose for which we use the sights is not to aim at the target at all. <u>We use the sights to get this precise and consistent alignment between the barrel and the eye</u>. That is the number one purpose for which we are going to use the sights. The secondary purpose for which we are going to use the sights is to use the front sight, when placed between the blades of the rear sight, as a reference to point the system around the desired area.

If we have any random misalignment between the tube and the eye, the best we can get is a random indicator in the external area. For precision shooting, we have to have absolute precise alignment between the barrel and the eye. Any misalignment, however slight, between the barrel and the eye, and the best we can get, at the aiming area, is a random point. For the ultimate in precision pointing, the maximum acceptable alignment error is zero!

◎ **Source of Pistol Concept:** Dr. Heinz Lösel of Germany, points out the shooting philosophy that most people have with respect to the pistol and it's relationship to the bullseye. They try

"to bring the gun in exact alignment with the bullseye."

☛**comment:** In theory, this statement is indisputable. In practice, it is physically impossible. It sounds completely reasonable, but it is not possible to execute in the practice of the precision pointing we need to have done at the level of consistency we require. You see, the pistol is moving at all times. That is the pure physical fact we are dealing with here. This is the core point at which the shooting philosophy which is advocated in this book, the Sievers Simplified Shooting Program, differs in a very revolutionary manner from the one described in the above quote by Dr. Heinz Lösel. In our program, shooters are taught, right from the start that they must line up the barrel with the eye, using the reference elements known as *sights*. If there is any misalignment between the barrel and the eye, the most the shooter can expect is to produce random strikes on the target.

◎ **Source of Pistol Concept:** We have noticed, throughout the years, the proliferation of the number of Advanced Shooting Classes and Camps.

☛**Comment:** Yet, here in America, the evidence seems to point out that the more such camps a shooter attends, the less able he or she is to produce world class scores in the Olympics. What seems to have come about is the closing of any cracks in the process whereby champions like a Gary Anderson, a Jack Writer, a Lones Wigger or a Margaret Murdock can make it onto a US National Shooting Team. Shooters are being coached out of techniques they have developed naturally, because those techniques do not meet the preconceptions of those shooting leaders who have designed the national programs. These shooting leaders do not comprehend that their policy of *monkey see, monkey do*, is not the way champions are developed. Some coaches even have pictures of past champions and when coaching, pull out these photos and try to match body conformations with those they are coaching. To try to fit someone into the mold of a champion is the ultimate *monkey see, monkey do*. Has it worked? The evidence is plain, no way has it even come close for American pistol shooters.

Many people involved in shooting have noticed that since the inauguration of the national coaching program, as an established part of the shooting training of America's shooters, our shooters have won fewer gold Olympic medals. It is plain to see that since the coaching has been formalized, shooter performances have stabilized below world performance levels. Now, in America, coaching results are measured by the statistics reported, rather than the results of the shooters being coached.

The most obvious purpose of an advanced coaching school is to provide the shooters with the really **have-to-have** information which someone left out of their beginning training. Wouldn't it have been nice if their starting coach or instructor could have had the skill to give them that information right at the start of their training?

Remember, someone who goes to an Advanced Shooting Camp, will expect to learn the **good stuff**, the stuff his coach left out. So, the shooter going to one of these Advanced Shooting Camps, has to know that he is setting himself up for a period of retraining. Retraining is the hardest type of training known to us. It is our wholehearted wish that this book provide the reader with information which allows him to develop his skill to whatever level he desires, starting with the first shot. McGivern points out that

> *any "average person" ...who is willing to study, practice, and persist in the effort, can master every subject treated. There are no "magic mixtures" which will take the place of ability developed by practice and study, and, contrary to popular belief, there is no need of any supernatural or out of the ordinary ability, or supernatural development required. There is no need of possessing any of the qualifications of a "wizard" in order to achieve success.* (Reprinted from FAST & FANCY REVOLVER SHOOTING copyright 1984 by New Win Publishing.)

It gets back to *"Me and mah gun!"* When you point it, look hard at the sights. Notice, we did not say to look at the target!

We do say that if you want to deliberately put a bullet hole in a piece of paper, then you must point the handgun at the

89

paper, using the front sight as a reference for pointing the aligned system. Look at the sights! Look **Hard** at the sights! Some people look through the sights to the target. This has the effect of altering the attention from the sights to the target. Once the attention is diverted from the sights, the result is a random strike on the paper. This means the position of the bullet hole on the paper could land in any of the scoring rings with no predictable consistency. Looking **through** the sights to the target produces a condition that does not yield the same outcome or consequences every time it occurs.

When someone picks up a handgun, it is assumed that he intends to do some precision pointing with it. How can you point any gun? You can point it anyway you want. Wouldn't it be nice to be able to point the handgun in such a way as to attain consistent results each time you perform an action to cause a bullet to come out the muzzle.

◎ **Source of Pistol Concept:** One of the terms which has become a part of our shooting lexicon is the term, **sight alignment.** When queried, some old time shooters and coaches will admonish the new shooter to line up the sights with the target. Once the shooter lines up the sights with the target, he then leans his head over so as to look through the sights at the target. This action guarantees random strikes on the target. In this situation, it is almost impossible to have the head returned to the exact same position from one shot to the next.

☛**Comment:** Consider the tool. The sights are affixed onto the top of the barrel.

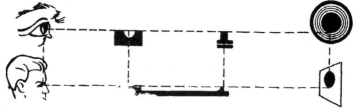

They are in a straight line with each other. You may turn the gun any way you wish. However, you will not be able to get the sights out of line with each other. You can point the gun at a piece of paper or any other place. But, to get consistent results, you must line up the barrel with the eye. This means lining up the sights with your pointing eye. It is then very easy to determine when the sights are lined up with your eye. In other words, you can see it.

◎ **Source of Pistol Concept:** Extensive research by the authors has demonstrated conclusively, that in all shooting instruction, attention is directed at the effect, which is the hit or strike of the bullet. In our instruction, by deliberate contrast, the attention is directed at the cause, which is the pointing of the pistol. All the hit does is to evaluate the pointing. When you direct the attention to the effect, the hit, or the hole in the target, you will find that you are misdirecting the shooter's attention from the internal alignment to the target.

☛**comment:** This method has the shooter looking through the sights and concentrating on the target. This is the method touted by Col. Charles Askins, *The Pistol Shooter's Handbook*, Collier Books, Ed. 1962, Page 122. The use of this method physically prevented pistol shooters from breaking the NRA 2600 barrier. In 1947 and 1948, Huelet Benner and Harry Reeves broke the 2600 barrier with the tactic of looking at the sights. This action spread quickly through the competitive American pistol shooting community. Askins' concept of looking through the sights at the target had already been relegated to the scrap heap of pistol shooting forever in the world for those involved in precision shooting. Askins apparently never did get the word about this, since his looking through the sights had been shown to be inefficient since Benner and Reeves found a better way some sixteen years before.

When the instructional process intentionally or inadvertently directs the attention of the shooter to the effect, it is not like putting the cart before the horse, it is getting in the cart and forgetting all about having a need for the horse. When you direct the attention to the effect, the hit, or the hole, in the target, you find that you still obtain results which are satisfactory to many shooters. It is entirely possible to obtain satisfactory alignment of the barrel with the eye for *"ballpark"* shooting. You can shoot dinner plate size groups all day long. It is only for those people who wish to compete at a very high level of precision pointing, that it becomes necessary to focus the eye very hard at the sights instead of looking through the sights to the target. Looking really hard at the sights causes the shots to be sucked into a tight group, provided your trigger finger movement is very smooth.

Misaligning the Sights

Some shooters think that the sights are used for aiming at the target.

They are NOT.

Champions use the sights:

1.   To align the barrel with the eye precisely and consistently.

2.   They use a single point in the system, normally the front sight, as a reference, to point the aligned system at the desired area.

So, sights are used to align the barrel with the eye,
in precision shooting,
not to aim at the target.

3.   Remember pointing the aligned system at the desired area means just that:

pointing the aligned system.

4.   Pointing the aligned system means keeping the top of the centered front sight on a level with the top of the wings of the rear sight with equal light, or space, on each side of the front sight.

5.   Some of you may have noticed that you are positioning the front sight in a different area of the rear sight each time you shoot. This will give you a random dispersion of your little bullet holes. Is this what you want? If not, what must you do to avoid this random misalignment of your system? Of course, the answer is obvious. Just align the sights the way you desire.

6.   As shown in figure 3-1, the little bullet holes will deviate in the direction in which the front sight is positioned in the notch. This is caused by Angular Misalignment of the aligned system

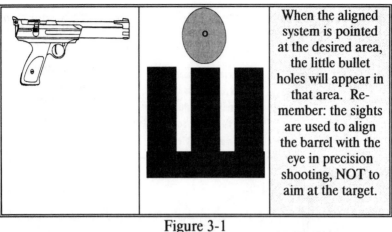

When the aligned system is pointed at the desired area, the little bullet holes will appear in that area. Remember: the sights are used to align the barrel with the eye in precision shooting, NOT to aim at the target.

Figure 3-1

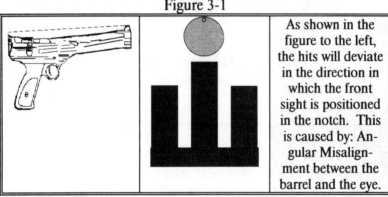

As shown in the figure to the left, the hits will deviate in the direction in which the front sight is positioned in the notch. This is caused by: Angular Misalignment between the barrel and the eye.

Figure 3-2

2. Indicating System
The firing mechanism and the trigger.

When we see that the sights are aligned the way we want them, and the aligned system is pointed at the desired area, the finger should move all by itself. This trigger movement is called a conditional reflex. Many of you have probably been shooting long enough that you have developed a habit whereby you make a conscious effort to maintain your sight alignment in an Arc of Movement. Then when you see the Arc of Movement becoming small enough for your acceptance criteria, you move your finger. This type of control prevents a conditional reflex from being formed.

93

◎ **Source of Pistol Concept:** 1981 *U.S. Army Marksmanship Unit's Pistol Guide.*

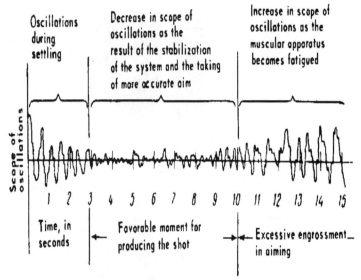

Attaining A Minimum Arc Of Movement

"It is necessary during firing to press the trigger under varying conditions of pistol movement in conjunction with correct sight alignment. In order to apply coordinated pressure on the trigger, the shooter must wait for those very definite times when all control factors are optimum and firing conditions become favorable. The rule that must be observed as the first step in attaining control of your shooting is: "You must never attempt to fire until you have completely settled into a minimum arc of movement. "

In order to learn how to fire a shot at the proper time, the shooter must make analysis of the time needed to settle and the duration of the minimum arc of movement.

The entire system, consisting of the shooter's body and the pistol, always undergoes a degree of movement. This is sometimes a pulsating, swaying or erratic arc of movement during aiming and firing a shot, The cause of this movement aside from conditions such as weather, is the action of the muscles maintaining the shooter's body in a definite position. Other action such as blood

94

pulsation, causes movement of individual parts of the shooter's body and the pistol. The nature and extent of the arc of movement changes within the time being devoted to delivering a shot. For example, when the shooter is first getting his sight alignment and has not yet had time to settle his body and pistol, the extent of the movement is relatively great. As the body becomes balanced and the aiming is more precise, the arc of movement minimizes. After a certain length of time, the minimum arc of movement begins to increase, because the muscles begin to fatigue, and the shooter does not have enough air in his lungs to continue holding his breath. If we record the arc of movement, we will see a wavelike line with varying amplitude of oscillations

It is obvious that under such circumstances the shooter must begin his smooth pressure on the trigger while not devoting too much attention to the arc of movement as long as it remains at the minimum. Continue to apply pressure on the trigger and intensely concentrate on keeping the sights in alignment. The resulting five to seven second period is the most favorable time for firing an accurate shot."

☛**Comment:** The Arc of Movement concept, by it's track record, will not provide the precision pointing efficiency we require in our pointing. There is constant erratic movement within the arc. The arc is ever increasing, because of the inherent instability of the platform, which is the erect human body.

On the other hand, precision pointing, according to the concept of the Shooting Diagram, requires two physical actions, both of which can be physically self-taught. Bill Blankenship, of the US Army AMU, was dissatisfied with his "trigger control." In 1959, he made a three month in depth study of this area and came up with some revolutionary conclusions. He found three physical requirements for the finger movement itself, i.e. Fast, Smooth, and Continuous. There was another major problem. The finger movement had to be activated at a particular time in order for the bullet hole to appear in a particular place.

This problem had a visual solution, *"What you sees is what you gets."* Blankenship's visual solution has two visual elements. Number one, which he thoroughly stresses, is *to align the barrel with the eye by establishing and maintaining zero error sight alignment.* In the authors' vernacular, this is referred to as **internal alignment**. Element number two, *is to use the top of the front sight as a reference to point the* internally aligned system at the desired area. In Blankenship's world, this is the "ten ring" of a standard American pistol target. When the eye directs this information to the brain, the finger movement is instantaneously and automatically activiated. In Blankenship's comfort zone, he refers to this action as "habit." So be it. Blankenship wrote a beautiful description of how he established his finger movement in *The Pistol Shooter's Treasury* edited by Gil Hebard. In our comfort zone, we interpret this a classic example of how to deliberately establish and activate a desirable conditional reflex.

The continued use of the Arc of Movement concept in pistol training, which has proven itself a failure will prevent our pistol shooters from moving into the top elite of the pistol shooters of the world. Stability is their god under the Arc of Movement concept. This stability is based on an inherently unstable platform, the erect human body. R.J. Shephard, in a study reported in *Endurance In Sport,* a part of the *The Encyclopaedia of Sports Medicine, an IOC Medical Commission Publication*, reported something of interest to pistol shooters:

> *Like most machines designed by humans, the body is an imperfect device for converting stored energy into external work.*

This has a direct impact on pistol shooters expending the amount of energy required for each shot during the pistol holding process called the Arc of Movement. Shephard points out that the normal relationship of energy expended to output of useful athletic work is around 25%. On the other hand, the figure can be as low as 1% in a novice swimmer. For pistol shooters, this is significant. Shephard notes the in *"in highly skilled activities ... the difference in mechanical efficiency (and thus the energy cost of a given performance) between a novice and an international competitor is at least fourfold, and very substantial gains of performance can result from an upgrading of technique."*

In the face of both the results achieved by American pistol shooters, and substantial research about the efficiency of techniques applicable to pistol shooting training, why haven't the American pistol shooters upgraded their techniques?

◎ **Source of Pistol Concept:** Our studies indicate that, in American competitive pistol shooting circles, the Arc of Movement concept has been elevated to the status of super-stition. One thing about superstition, "everyone knows it." Since "everyone knows it," it is no longer subject to scrutiny. It is accepted as the way things are and, in the case of the Arc of Movement concept, as superstition it is not even ques-tioned. It is much like the superstition surrounding the num-ber 13. Everyone knows it has a connotation of "bad luck" in Christian culture. Lost in history, is the information that it reached the status of superstition based on the number of persons attending the *Last Supper* of Jesus Christ.

☛**Comment:** The Shooting Diagram concept, on the other hand, has it's basis in the establishment of a conditional re-flex between the eye recognizing that the perfectly aligned sights have reached the pre-selected area of the target. At this moment, the self taught conditional reflex causes the trigger finger to instantaneously smoothly move the trigger so the shot is fired. Now, this means the pistol shooter is working with his body. The amount of time from the moment the gun reaches eye level until it is fired, under the Shooting Diagram method is less than three seconds. That is what we mean by the statement that the pistol shooter is working with his body under the Shooting Diagram conditional reflex concept. Re-member "work" is the product of force and distance. Pistol shooting is an act of physical work. In other words, the body must perform physical work whenever pistol shooting activity is undertaken. So, when pistol shooting, by definition, stores of potential energy are modified. Pistol shooting is viscous work performed against internal or external resistance, and the kinetic energy of the body and associated equipment, the pistol, is altered. We know body stores of chemical energy are used to effect these changes in the body. These reserves are replenished later through the consumption of food.

◎ **Source of Pistol Concept:** For pistol shooters, an example of external *viscous work* is encountered when the pistol rises

97

from a 45 degree ready position. The viscous work performed by a pistol competitor may be calculated as the distanced travelled times the resisting force, which is the product of gravitational acceleration, the mass of the shooter's arm, plus the pistol.

☛**Comment:** Current in much of American pistol shooting training is the idea that the limb and it's associated equipment, the pistol, must be raised quickly at first and then slowed down during the remaining one third of the way to eye level, for the International Rapid Fire game. What they fail to take into account is that work is performed not only in accelerating the body or its parts, but also in deceleration. Is it wrong to do it the way they have been teaching and doing? No way. Is it the most efficient use of the body? We do not think so. Will the old, inefficient method of pistol shooting work? Sure it will. But, instead of focusing his whole attention on moving the trigger finger smoothly and quickly, the shooter has, instead, had to focus his attention on defying several physical laws of life here on earth. Unfortunately, that is not something for which prizes are awarded in our shooting games. These shooters are employing what they lovingly call the Arc of Movement. They are to be heard in many back-of-the-firing-line discussions explaining how to shoot using this Arc of Movement. Sounding like gurus of shooting training, they seem to have a feeling of evangelism about their efforts to explicate this information to naive junior pistol shooters. It is much like a member of the *Flat Earth Society* being invited to give a lecture to a graduate collegiate program in Astronomy proving the theory of the earth being flat, and debunking the idea that the earth is a globe.

Those pistol shooters using the Arc of Movement concept, by their attempts to defy the laws of movement, take about
eight to sixteen seconds once the gun reaches eye level before the
shot is fired. It is our evaluation that the Shooting Diagram, with
it's basis in an instantaneous movement of the trigger finger at
the instant the gun reaches eye level through the self taught establishment of a conditional reflex is a much more efficient pistol
shooting method.

Why? For an important and often overlooked physiological fact. A distinction has to be drawn between the external
power output and the internal energy consumption. The internal
energy consumption is usually four times as great as the external
power expenditure. This reflects not only the energy consumed
by the muscles engaged in the raising of the pistol to eye-level,
but also the resting energy consumption and unavoidable ancillary costs of the Act of Shooting. The ancillary costs of the pistol
shooting activity includes increases of energy expenditure in the
heart and the respiratory muscles. So, we say that any pistol
shooting method which increases internal energy consumption of
the muscles has the effect of increasing shooter fatigue. Some
pistol shooters make a big effort to build up the strength of their
upper bodies. They know they have to have good upper body
strength to work to achieve a longer hold time waiting as they
attempt to stabilize their Arc of Movement. The authors speculate that by doing this, the pistol shooters are attempting to prove
Newton's Laws of Motion and Gravity in error on each and every

shot, or perhaps they have come to believe that such laws do not apply to them.

In our Tucson Junior Pistol Training Program, the youngsters have made a game out of seeing who can be the first to spot the pistol shooter in a match who spends the longest holding time in his Arc of Movement. The giggling which results from this information is a bit embarrassing. Fortunately none of the other pistol shooters have any idea of what the youngsters are doing. What happens is, they call each other over to watch these shooters working at their extended Arc of Movement. We have deliberately encouraged this game amongst our young pistol shooters. By allowing this Arc of Movement method to be held up to ridicule by the young boys and girls, we are helping to ensure that they are not affected by pistol shooters coming up to them and harming their training by suggesting that they should slow down and take their time. Since they have made a private game out of the hold long crowd, they get tickled when they come back to their coaches and friends to report the latest "hold longer" advise.

But, of course this technique of timing the number of seconds it takes for a shooter fire a shot from the moment it reaches eye level, gives the coach a tool to observe whether the shooter is performing a an acceptable level when using the conditional reflex method.

◎ **Source of Pistol Concept:** We have many conditional reflexes. If you have ever fed an infant or seen one being fed, you know that we use a spoon as we start the strained food feeding. Once the infant can grasp the spoon, you can observe the development of the conditional reflex. You can also see why the infant is started with a spoon. When the arm comes up, the food gets all over the infant. A fork would be a painful disaster for the infant. But, pretty soon the infant begins to hit the mouth. That's a conditional reflex. Every time the hand comes up, the mouth opens. It becomes full automatic.

☛ **Comment:** When we start *shooting* the finger will not move all by itself. We have to train it. This is the critical part. We have to start training it from the first shot. Habits

100

start quickly and habits are hard to break. We want to form the habit of having the sight system formed perfectly and moving around the point where we want the indicator to appear and for the finger to move all by itself, really smooth. We want it to be just like what happens when that infant's mouth opens when the arm is brought up.

Generally, most people form a conditional reflex wherein they pull the trigger in an instantaneous convulsion each time they align the sights. Why do they do that? Because they taught themselves to do that. Did they mean to teach themselves to do that? Does it make any difference whether they meant to teach themselves to do that? It does not make a bit of difference. So, you see, we have to know exactly what it is we want to teach ourselves to get the job done at the quality level we want.

3. Support System

A. *To establish and maintain the internal alignment between the barrel and the eye with any shooting tool.*

B. *To provide support and maximum stability for the entire shooting unit.*

If we have any misalignment between the barrel and the eye, however slight, the more stability we have in our support system, the more positive we are of getting random indicators on our aiming area. We have some of our top flight international competitors who are in this very situation. In their most stable position, they are getting random indicators on their targets. This is happening because they do not understand *shooting*. They are getting angular misalignment in their sighting system and they do not recognize the alignment error, everything looks the same to them. They cannot understand why these random indicators are appearing when they fire their shots. They just do not understand *shooting*. Consider the parts of our *Shooting Diagram* :

101

1. Internal Alignment System

> *Aligning the barrel*
> *with*
> *the eye.*

and

2. Indicating System

> *The firing mechanism*
> *and*
> *the trigger.*

Because of the interrelationship between alignment of the barrel with the eye and movement of the trigger finger, it is necessary that we teach them to ourselves simultaneously. It is obvious that teaching ourselves two elements simultaneously puts a maximum load on our physical and mental envelope. It should also be obvious, that if anything is added, it will exceed the capabilities of our physical and mental envelopes, and it won't work at the quality level we demand. In the case of pistol training, from good intentions will come low quality output. If you can feel a sense of satisfaction with substandard performance by your students, then of course you will keep on giving them **ALL** the **good stuff**. Will it work? Yes, if you are satisfied, unless your students read this book, they will probably never notice the difference.

3. Support System

A. *To establish and maintain the internal alignment between the barrel and the eye with any shooting tool.*

B. *To provide maximum support and stability for the entire shooting unit.*

Now, lets look at what we have talked about so far.

☛When *Shooting* we want to do precision *pointing.* That little bullet hole gives us instantaneous feedback as to the quality of our *pointing,* how precise, how consistent.

☛There are no "**shooting**" problems outside the shooting unit.

☞What is the interaction between a bullet and a piece of paper? *Answer.* A hole is punched in a piece of paper.

☞Wind doping has absolutely nothing to do with shooting. That is when we are talking about atmospheric conditions on a body that is moving freely in space.

☞*Mental conditioning* is knowing your business, knowing you know your business and being able to demonstrate that you know your business.

☞Remember, ignorance is no problem, but stupidity is forever.

☞We are looking for **pointing** efficiency.

☞This book is not designed to teach what is *right* or *correct.* We do not know what is *right* or *correct* for any particular person. But the shot groups will tell what sight picture that person can repeat most consistently and precisely.

☞We are looking for the most efficient way to get the pistol pointed at a pre-determined area, within the framework of the rules regulating whatever shooting game we are playing.

Pistol Marksmanship

In this book, the myths of shooting past are relegated to history, where they properly belong, as curious to the readers of this book as the readers of the once revolutionary theory that the earth is of a rounded nature, not flat as everyone knew that it was in the 1200's. Various shooting myths are likewise exposed for

103

what they are, the musings of old shooters trying to identify the things which helped them become shooting champions. Then, when they could not find the words, they slipped into repeating the myths which had been likewise repeated to them. The Sievers Simplified Shooting Method has been in continual testing by associates of the authors since its inception in 1960. No new shooting philosophy has been deliberately subjected to such scrutiny in the history of marksmanship. The authors feel the 36 years testing has produced results which provide them with the data to say, unequivocally, that this training method is the most efficient pistol shooting teaching program available in the world today.

The lexicon of marksmanship is replete with myths which over time have been elevated to the status of Holy Grails or superstition. This is not unique in human history. Recall that Galileo Galilei around 1600 found, experimentally, that bodies do not fall with velocities proportional to their weights. This conclusion was received by the scientific authorities of that time with ridicule and hostility because it contradicted the accepted teaching of Aristotle. Aristotle's teaching had been accepted as gospel for about hundreds of years. At the time Galileo Galilei lived, Aristotle, an ancient Greek philosopher who lived in the 4th century B.C., said that the Earth was the center of the universe. Everything else, the moon, the Sun, the planets and the stars, moved around the Earth. For hundreds of years, no one questioned this idea, especially when the Roman Catholic Church said that Aristotle was right. Finally, in 1543, someone DID question the Church's teachings. A Polish astronomer named Nicholas Copernicus said that the Sun was the center of the Universe, and that everything, including the Earth, went around the Sun. If Copernicus was right, the Church was wrong. The Church, in response, denounced the Copernican system. Galileo using a telescope he invented proved the Sun was the center of the Universe. The Church prohibited him from teaching the Copernican system. He was tried and found guildty of heresy. Finally, in 1992, three years after Galileo Galilei's namesake had been launched on its way to Jupiter, the Vatican formally and publicly cleared Galileo of any wrongdoing. We are in much a similar situation with the myths of shooting.

104

The world is replete with *facts* being turned into *myths*. Remember the Earth was once *flat*, now it is *round*. We offer our observations in an effort to make the study of shooting more precise. To do this, we have had to address what we perceive as *myths* which have become established *dogma* in shooting training.

Through out the history of marksmanship, many people have investigated the methods current in different periods. As in our book, these investigators looked at what the process was designed to produce as a final product, for example, Timothy Pickering, Jr., in a book titled, *An Easy Plan of Discipline for a Militia*, and published in 1775 in Salem, New-England, took a look at some of the practices current then. As we have in this book, he also found the training methods of his time inefficient for what the instructors claimed they would accomplish.

AN EASY

PLAN

O F

DISCIPLINE

FOR A

MILITIA.

By TIMOTHY PICKERING, jun.

. " Almoſt every *free* State affords an Inſtance of a NATIONAL MILITIA :
" For *Freedom* cannot be maintained without *Power*; and Men who are not
" in a Capacity to *defend* their *Liberties*, will certainly *loſe* them."
Treatiſe on the Militia, in Four Sections, by C. S, London, 1753.

SALEM, NEW-ENGLAND :
PRINTED BY SAMUEL AND EBENEZER HALL, 1775

Ed McGivern, in his *Fast and Fancy Revolver Shooting*, which was published in the 1930's, raised the specter that *a great*

106

part of our shooting information came to become a part of shooting myth based on what sounded good, but which was not how it actually worked in shooting, "or did one writer, basing his opinions on theory, express such views, and other writers repeat them and then keep on repeating what some other one had said, and pass it on in that way from one to another? It now seems highly probable that this was the case, which makes us wonder if at least a great part of our shooting information is not handed out to us in that manner. The results of many of our actual tests carried out to determine the lack of reliability of some such handed down information seem to point that way quite conclusively."

In discussing the use of *Single and Double Action*, with respect to their uses in his work of fast revolver shooting, McGivern noted that, from his *"profitable experience,"* fast shooting could not be done by the hand-cocking single-action method of operating any revolver or by any

"...other method of operating any single-action revolver, so it naturally follows that if done at all it must necessarily be done with double-action revolvers and by the double-action method of operating them. And, right here is where we come "slap bang!" up against a wall of opposition. According to the "sacred" code of the "Rule of the Dead Men," and in accordance with such tradition—"double-action revolver shooting should never be indulged in," although double-action revolvers of very fine quality and very dependable actions have been manufactured and sold for years in large quantities in the United States by Smith & Wesson, Colt Patent Firearms Company, and others. A rather odd situation is it not? Why make such wonderful double-action guns as these firms make if they are not intended to be used that way?

I decided this question for myself many years ago, and have been successful in teaching this double-action system of shoot-

107

ing in the face of an opposition, which, I am at this time pleased to say, was brought to bear on me in relation to this subject in rather liberal quantities. Books, catalogues, articles in periodicals and elsewhere denounced it. Surely these writers really believed they were right, and if these, no doubt, very fine and sincere persons were right, I certainly must have been wrong.

As I progress with this subject these points can easily be decided, on the merits of the case, and in keeping with the evidence submitted. Quoting just a little of such opinions in reference to double-action shooting, without any harmful intent on my part toward any particular person may help to make the situation better understood and furnish only food for thought. I quote from a noted writer—"As such shooting (double-action) will ruin any shooter's holding, and still more so his scores, and other make hitting or grouping of shots quite impossible." (?) From another of today's books, in reference to quick-draw training— "While it may be the possible that there can be a situation wherein double action is necessary." (?) Another reads—"The use of double action in this work (fast drawing, pointing and shooting) is almost sure to throw the aim off." And these are only a few from many that could be quoted.

With this, of course, I did not and do not agree for the very simple reason that it has been demonstrated beyond any reasonable doubt that such arguments against using revolvers "double action" are not supported by facts. The fastest, accurately controlled shooting up to now has been done with double-action revolvers, and all of the fast-shooting results described in this book were secured with double-action revolvers, while using the double-action method and the standard double-action mechanism for operating the guns, all such guns being held in the hands and operated entirely by hand, and entirely free of any other attachments, mechanism, or mechanical device of any sort whatever that could in any way assist in their operation.

The important point at issue is—just what caused such positive, though unfounded, opinions to be formed so very generally? Can it be possible that none of these persons ever discovered that astonishingly fast shooting could be done, and excellent accuracy could be secured, by this method of operating these revolvers, or did one writer, basing his opinions on theory, express such views, and other writers repeat them and then keep on repeating what some other one had said, and pass it on in that way from one to another? It now seems highly probable that this was the case, which makes us wonder if at least a great part of our shooting information is not handed out to us in that manner. The results of many of our actual tests carried out to determine the lack of reliability of some such handed down information seem to point that way quite conclusively. *(Highlighted by the authors)*

In the past it was quite a general custom for men to settle disputes by quoting words spoken by some individual or statements from some books; perhaps in some cases this custom is still in favor. I am, of course, interested in this angle of the situation to the extent of wanting to have the material contained in this writing, which relates to this

109

particular subject, to be reliable enough in every way, so that if someone should decide to quote from it, the quotation will at least be fairly correct and reasonably reliable even though we must allow for the usual variations that generally —though possibly unintentionally—creep into quotations.

If this book serves no other purpose than to clear up this situation and kindred matters relating to this system of shooting, and thereby establish only part of the real possibilities of the double-action revolvers, I will surely feel fairly well-paid for the effort put forth to gather together the data and other valuable material so necessary to produce it.

On this basis I will proceed with the description of methods used and the results that can be expected along this line of endeavor."(Reprinted from *FAST* & FANCY RE-VOLVER SHOOTING copyright 1984 by New Win Publishing. *pp 112-113)*

It is in the spirit of taking up that illuminating torch, which Ed McGivern thrust into the information, current in the public domain of his day, that the authors of this book have continued his probe into the information available to today's shooters.

◎ **Source of Pistol Concept:** A coach from the Soviet Union, Aleksandr A. Yur'yev, *Competitive Shooting*, (first published in 1957), led the way into the modern study of marksmanship. Gary Anderson, former Executive Officer, Operations of the National Rifle Association, in his introduction to the third edition of Yur'yev's book as published by the National Rifle Association in 1985, stated *"It was the foundation of many of the teachings in the manuals on international shooting published by the U.S. Army Marksmanship Unit."* He goes on to say, *"That first translation of Yur'yev's original book may well have resulted in the biggest single advance in shooting knowledge that ever took place in this country."* One source reported that the National Rifle Association of America paid $100,000.00

for the Russian translation of Yur'yev's book. Then, it took a couple of American shooters some three years to work it into the shape where it could be published by the NRA.

The 1965 *U.S. Army Marksmanship Unit's Rifle Instructors and Coaches Guide*, signed off by Colonel Joseph J. Peot, SigC, who was the Commanding Officer at that time, is of note because it depicts the spirit of American Coaches in searching for more efficient methods of teaching marksmanship. This training manual represents the best of that spirit of American marksmanship. Colonel Peot makes the point in his **Foreword**, *"While the manual primarily illustrates the methods and techniques endorsed by USAMTC personal it is subject to improvement by suggestion and new development."* That is also a statement the authors of this book maintain. What we point out in this book, *is subject to improvement by suggestion and new development.* Whenever we find techniques which allow us to shoot more efficiently, we will adopt them.

☛**comment:** All these *U.S. Army Marksmanship Unit Training Manuals* are extremely good with respect to the technical aspects of the shooting positions, but concerning several basic shooting concepts, they have contributed to focusing the attention of the shooter away from the refinement of the two basic fundamentals of shooting and toward placing distractions in the way of that refinement, *and for all of his sports medicine research, Yur'yev HIMSELF REPEATED VARIOUS SHOOTING MYTHS.* Yur'yev bought into the mythology of shooting and did not delve into the basic elements of which shooting is composed. He did much to explain that mythology to his readers, adopting most of the myths which had accumulated in that mythological sacred soil. The Russians were doing very well on the international scene at that time, and our top shooters just knew that the Russians must be onto some secret, that was enabling them to win so consistently. The *"Russian Book,"* must have seemed like manna from heaven when it came onto the scene. What it did was make *Shooting* seem to have *pedagogy* just like the other sports which make up the Olympic *Sports* venues. *Now,* our shooters had a vocabulary with which they could wax well into the night discussing their performances. To this day

111

Yur'yev's work is the bedrock of American marksmanship training.

◎ **Source of Pistol Concept:** For example, Yur'yev states as dogma, *"Shooting a series of accurate shots requires the shooter to follow a specific sequence of actions: assuming the position, aiming, holding the breath and releasing the trigger."*

☛**Comment:** When you get down to *Shooting* basics, *assuming the position,* is a distraction to the delivery of *shooting a series of accurate shots.* Position is related to stability. Another distraction is *holding the breath.* It is harmful to *Shooting* progress to harp on *holding the breath* in the beginning process of the development of a shooter. Many of you have threaded a needle. How would you have reacted if you were told you had to have special instructions in how to hold your breath in order to consistently thread a needle? Reinkemeier does just that, but he even goes further, *"Other ways to achieve correct breathing. Probably the best way to learn the fundamental of breathing is to attend a course such as those offered in evening classes...When was the last time you threaded a needle? To do it, you have to hold your breath and concentrate totally on coordinating your fingers and eyes. If you don't succeed right away, your fingers start to tremble, your chest tightens, and everything becomes blurred. It is not uncommon for people to lose their temper."* We believe breathing is automatic. If you need to hold your breath in order to achieve the stability you need to thread that needle, then it is automatic. You do not have to think about it. Remember, the moment you stop concentrating your attention on your breathing, it goes back to normal. If you concentrate your attention on your breathing, you inhibit the subconscious from reacting to the conditional reflex of moving the finger instantaneously smooth as the eye sees the front sight of the internally aligned system move into the pre-selected area of the target.

◎ **Source of Pistol Concept:** Much of the formal modern thinking about breathing can be traced to a Department of the Army translation of a Russian shooting book. The cover sheet for this US Army Intelligence Document is shown on the following page. It was translated and published in an era when there was no copyright cooperation between the United States and the old Soviet Union. It was published by the US Army on April 26, 1960 as a limited edition of 200 copies. As published in this translation, the book contained 304 pages. This edition was devoted to competitive marksmanship with the rifle and carbine.

☛Comment: Of particular interest, to the authors of this book, is the chapter titled, *Pulling the Trigger,* in Yev'yev's book. We find it especially pertinent to the shooting method espoused in this book. It *"...contains information concerning the rapidity of reaction, the processes of excitation and inhibition in the central nervous system and the reflex activity of the human organism during the process of pulling the trigger and producing the shot." (Yev'yev, A.A., **Sportivnaya Strel'ba Iz Vintovki,*** Competitive Marksmanship With Rifle and Carbine, Moscow, 1957, Translation Department Of The Army, Office Of The Assistant Chief Of Staff, Intelligence, 1960).

Using the conditional reflex technique, look at the results these two young shooters achieved.

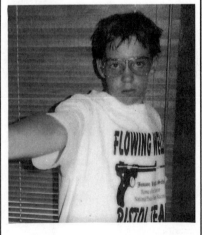

| Jason Neill, 1st of the juniors in the Tucson Junior Pistol Training Program to achieve a score of 569 with the Air Pistol in training. | Cade Wilson, Winner: 1996 Sub-Junior Air Pistol Championship at the Nationals held at Chino, California, with 538 x 600. |

DEPARTMENT OF THE ARMY
OFFICE OF THE ASSISTANT CHIEF OF STAFF, INTELLIGENCE
WASHINGTON 25, D. C.

INTELLIGENCE TRANSLATION NO. H-3205 B

TRANSLATED FROM Russian

SUBJECT: (FOREIGN TITLE)
SPORTIVNAYA STREL'BA IZ VINTOVKI
SUBJECT: (ENGLISH TITLE)
BRIEF HISTORICAL INFORMATION CONCERNING
THE DEVELOPMENT OF
MARKSMANSHIP IN OUR COUNTRY

REFERENCES:

AUTHOR: A. A. Yur'yev
TITLE OF PUBLICATION: *Sportivnaya Strel'ba Iz Vintovki*
(Competitive Marksmanship With Rifle and Carbine)
PARTS TRANSLATED: Entire Publication

PUBLISHER, DATE, AND PLACE OF PUBLICATION:

State Publishing House for Physical Culture and Sport, Moscow, 1957

SUPPLY OFFICER
US Army Advanced Marksmanship Unit
Fort Benning, Georgia

◎ **Source of Pistol Concept:** Consider for example, the breathing example in the US Army Marksmanship Unit Pistol Marksmanship Guide:

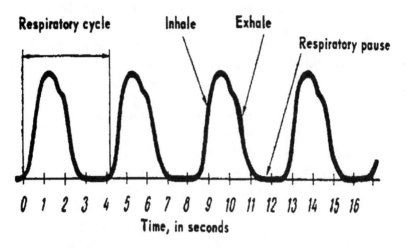

☛**comment:** The information about breathing was lifted verbatim from the Russian book. In the Shooting Manuals and Guides published by the US Army Marksmanship Unit, no attribution for the source of this material was made. The reader was left to assume that this information was coming from the shooting oracles at Fort Benning. More than anything else, what this illustrates is the lack of original research into shooting by the American shooters, their instructors and their coaches at Fort Benning. The breathing technique advocated in the Pistol Guide is:

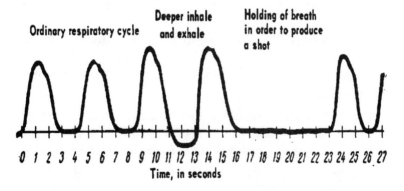

115

◎   This was, again, lifted from the Russian book. In August of 1981, writing in *The American Marksman*, M.O. Wilkerson, D.M. Landers and F.S. Daniels, reported that this breathing method was not being used by any of the 14 sub-elite intercollegiate shooters or any of the 21 world-class elite shooters from college and military teams. This research report should have cleared up the misconceptions surrounding the idea that the US Army Marksmanship Guide shows a correct breathing method. Unfortunately, even as this book is being written, there are still coaches who believe in the validity of the information about breathing in the US Army Marksmanship Unit Manual.

◎ **Source of Pistol Concept:** The basic problem is that the Russian book, and therefore also, the US Army manuals, showed the breathing process wherein the shooter inhales after firing the shot. Whereas, the Wilkerson report demonstrated that all of the shooters, in the research project, exhaled upon firing the shot.

☛**Comment:** In the shooting method described in this book, we do not bother to teach the beginning shooter anything at all about breathing. Page 16 of the 1981 *US Army Marksmanship Unit Pistol Marksmanship Guide* states very clearly, that during actual firing:

The shooter should not be conscious of the need to breathe.

If, during actual firing, the shooter should not be conscious of the need to breathe, why introduce such a concept during the initial stages of his training? Bill Blankenship once wrote in *The Pistol Shooter's Treasury* edited by Gil Hebard, that the average individual does not usually have to think about breathing. He pointed out that the lungs take care of the body without conscious thought.

◎ **Source of Pistol Concept:** *c. During actual firing: The shooter should not be conscious of the need to breathe. If during practice a shooter finds that he cannot hold his breath the twenty seconds necessary to fire a timed fire string, he should make a practice of firing his timed fire strings in less than twenty seconds. However,*

116

if during a timed or rapid fire string, the shooter feels compelled to breathe, he should take a short breath quickly and continue to fire. This causes a lapse of concentration on sight alignment and should not be the normal technique used. (US Army Marksmanship Unit Pistol Marksmanship Guide, 1981, pg 16)

☛**Comment:** If, as the preceding quotation states, transferring the attention to breathing *causes a lapse of concentration on sight alignment*, why ever begin to direct the attention of the pistol shooter to his breathing? In our program, we find breathing to be an automatic process. We do not direct anyone's attention to it.

◎ **Source of Pistol Concept:** Therefore, we are left with *aiming* and *releasing the trigger*. Hundreds of thousands of dollars have been spent on publishing books, manuals and video tapes extoling these five items:

assuming the position
forming the stance
holding the breath
aiming
releasing the trigger

☛**Comment:** These often are touted as the indispensable foundations of *Pistol Shooting*. This has had the effect of sabotaging innumerable beginning pistol shooters who have been exposed to this educational method. At the most, we can expect to put our attention on perhaps two things when we are first learning to shoot. Here, the minimum expectation placed on the beginning shooter is five. Often, it is seven or more.

In this chapter, we have referred to a book by Aleksandr A. Yur'yev, *Competitive Shooting*, (first published in 1957), which led the way into the modern study of marksmanship from the standpoint "of pedagogical science."

Just so that we are communicating, just what is this thing we are learning to do called *Precision Shooting*?

Just What Is Precision Shooting?

Precision Shooting is being able to align the barrel of a shooting tool with the eye precisely and consistently and being able to indicate as desired without introducing angular misalignment between the barrel and the eye.

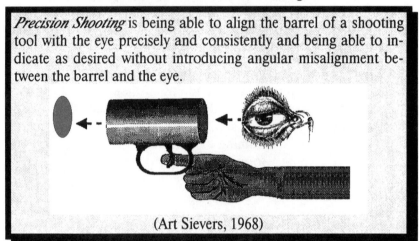

(Art Sievers, 1968)

Yur'yev puts considerable emphasis on breathing. *"Breathing is accompanied by the rhythmical movement of the chest, stomach, and other organs and muscles. During the time required to fire the shot, the shooter must hold his breath."* For a beginning shooter, being admonished to concentrate his attention on breathing acts as a distraction to *Precision Shooting*. For any shooter, being told to focus his attention on his breathing distracts him from concentrating of the basics of *Precision Shooting*.

To tell a recreational shooter that he has to attend a lecture on how to breathe among other things, starts the turning off process from the very beginning of his introduction to *Precision Shooting*. And that is sad. *Precision Shooting* is so simple, that it insults the intelligence.

◎ **Source of Pistol Concept:** The terminology used by Yur'yev's translator in the 1985 edition of *Competitive Shooting* acts to draw attention away from the rudiments of *Precision Shoot-*

118

ing, to fire the shot, the shooter must release the trigger smoothly.

☛**Comment:** *Release,* according to *The American Heritage Dictionary,* (Houghton Mifflin, 1987), has as one of it's key meanings, *"To free, unfasten, or let go of."* Natural speakers of English understand this meaning of release. In *Precision Shooting* what actually happens is that the shooter <u>applies</u> <u>pressure</u> *smoothly, smoothly, smoothly* until there is enough <u>pressure on the trigger</u> to trip the action starting the process which sends the bullet out the barrel. Using the word *release* gives the reader/listener exactly the wrong impression of the way to activate the normal trigger. Of course, there are some specialized guns which do employ a system of the finger engaging the trigger and then actually *releasing* it so as to send the bullet on it's way. But these guns are much the exception.

It is not the **releasing of the trigger** to which the attention has to be placed, it is the effort to make the **trigger finger automatically move smoothly** when the eye determines that the sight alignment is what we want and where we want it. Our effort is to make this a conditional reflex. Just the connotation of the word *release* in and of itself contributes to an erroneous impression of just what the action involved here is all about. Remember, *The American Heritage Dictionary,* (Houghton Mifflin, 1987) defines **release,** as a verb, *To free, unfasten, or let go of. And as a noun, A device or catch for locking or releasing a mechanism.* Most triggers require that something moves them. Generally, the trigger finger does not have to **release** the trigger in order for the mechanism to cause the cartridge to fire. The finger must **move** the trigger. No big deal! That is the usual process in the act of shooting.

$$Act$$
$$Of$$
$$Shooting$$

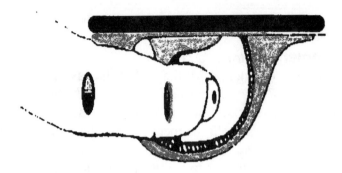

Consider the differences between the NRA 1985 translation and the Department of the Army's 1960 translation of Yev'yev's book. For example, the NRA 1985 translation uses the following language:

Trigger release technique is of major and sometimes decisive importance in producing an accurate shot. First, a proper release does not disturb the aim of the firearm on the target, therefore, the shooter must squeeze the trigger smoothly. Second, the trigger release must be in complete coordination with visual perception of the sight picture so that it occurs at that precise instant when the sights are properly aligned on the bull's-eye.

Compare this with the Department of the Army's 1960 translation:

PULLING THE TRIGGER

The technique of pulling the trigger is of very great, and sometimes even decisive, importance in producing an accurate shot. The pulling of the trigger, first, must not shift the position of the gun which is aimed at the target, that is, it must not spoil the aim; for this purpose the rifleman must be able to squeeze the trigger smoothly. Second, the trigger must be pulled in complete conformity with visual perception, that is, it must be timed to that definite instant when the centered front sight is under the lower edge of the bulls-eye.

The Department of the Army's 1960 translation gives a flavor of objective assurance that the author believes the shooter can carry out this firing of a shot if he just follows the advise laid down in the book. Compare this attitude with the NRA translation. Here's the way the Army's translator perceived what was being said:

Consequently, in order to achieve an accurate shot, the rifleman must carry out actions-smooth squeezing on the trigger and aiming-not separately, in isolation from one another, but in strict coordination with one another.

Now, look at the way the NRA's translator perceived what was being said:

121

> *Accomplishing such a coordinated yet complex action is difficult. The gun oscillates continuously depending on the stability of the position being used. The aligned sights move across the aiming point, stopping at the proper place on the bull's-eye only for short periods of time during which the shooter must complete the smooth release of the trigger and fire the shot.*

So, while the NRA edition hamstrings it's readers by setting a tone of describing the Act of Shooting as being difficult, the Army's translation sets an objective tone. It merely observes what the shooter needs to do to obtain good shots. The NRA's translation promotes the idea that the coordination of sight alignment and trigger pulling is **difficult**. Does this mean that if it is **difficult**, it is not something us mere mortal people can teach ourselves to accomplish with any degree of proficiency? We much prefer the Army's objective view of the process. We suspect that the Army's translation may be closer to the original intention of the author. Through out the Army's translation, there is reflected an optimistic observation of the processes involved in the Act of Shooting. For example, when commenting on the establishment of new conditional reflex links, notice how the Army translation puts it:

...the execution of coordinated actions under such conditions, on the one hand, is in contradiction to habits, instinctive tendencies, and conditional reflexes which are innate in a person or acquired by him during the period preceding his life's work, and, on the other hand, demands the development and formation in the rifleman of new conditional-reflex links increasing the rapidity of reaction and improving the coordination of movements.

Now look at how the NRA's translation puts it:

Executing coordinated actions under such conditions is contrary to inherent human responsive reactions and habits acquired earlier in a shooter's life. This requires the formation of new conditional reflexes directed towards decreasing reaction time and improving the coordination of movement.

The NRA translation directs the attention towards *decreasing reaction time* and the Army's translation directs the attention towards *increasing the rapidity of reaction*. This goes to the heart of the matter between these two translations. By emphasizing such things as decreasing reaction time, the NRA book creates an unconscious sense of hesitation about the shooting. On the other hand, the Army translation, with it's idea of increasing the rapidity of reaction promotes a sense of aggression in the shooter. Shooters seeking to decrease reaction time have to overcome the idea of hesitancy which the word decrease connotes. If you are attempting to decrease your reaction time, there is a built-in connotation that what you are doing is wrong since you have to decrease it.

123

The Army's version, however, states you should look to increase the rapidity of the reaction time. This is what six time American National Pistol Champion, Bill Blankenship meant by his constantly increasing pressure, as he described his trigger finger movement. Remember, if the trigger finger starts from a position of rest, then its movement is conducted with rapidly increasing pressure, which is a very fast trigger finger movement.

Here is a very important point! How you view your shooting is very important. If you approach it with a degree of hesitation, you will most likely lose out to a person approaching his shooting with a sense of aggression. The idea that you should try to increase the rapidity of your reaction fits in very well with the training we suggest, with respect to developing a conditional reflex in this book.

In our Tucson Pistol Training Project, we have been having trouble keeping the youngsters from being influenced by the very helpful adult shooters. In a spirit of helpfulness, they sidle up to the parents of our juniors and suggest that if the youngster will just slow down, he could do a whole lot better. This even includes an elite shooter and coach, who once told Hickey that he did not think youngsters should start shooting until they get to be about sixteen or seventeen years of age.

Of interest is the fact that they never approach either of the authors with this advise. They fail to grasp that such **slow down** advise is the very reason which may have contributed to their not being able to win an Olympic gold medal during the years they have competed.

Blankenship once commented on *"these people who use the system of slowly squeezing the trigger."* He observed that they have a lot of trouble. What they are doing, he says, is they try to squeeze the trigger only when the sights are perfectly aligned. But that is not the big problem, he points out that they then pull the trigger when their perfect sight alignment is sitting **exactly** under the bullseye. The problem Blankenship notes is that as soon as anything moves they stop squeezing or hesitate until everything is perfect again to squeeze a little more. He further notes that these shooters develop serious problems because of jerks, flinches, heeling, etc He says that all of these problems are the result of anticipation. (*The Pistol Shooter's Treasury* edited by Gil Hebard)

124

◎ **Source of Pistol Concept:** Of special importance is what the NRA translation of the book omitted. For example, the following is one of the sequences eliminated from the NRA version. The authors of this book believe that this is a very important element which stresses the importance of smoothly moving the trigger.

☛**Comment:** The authors speculate that the decision to eliminate it harkens back to the assumption that *everybody knows this*. The problem as the authors see it is that this type of information is not stressed during beginning instruction. The coach is usually in a hurry to get on to the good stuff, position, stability, breathing, etc.

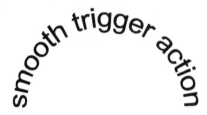

"Factors Providing for the Correct Pulling of the Trigger"

"Independent of the type of trigger action used by the rifleman, it is important for him to observe the principal requirement evolving from the fact that the pulling of the trigger is the completion of all the actions required to produce a shot; therefore, the trigger must be pulled in such a way as not to spoil the aim, that is, smoothly.

The producing of smooth trigger action makes special demands upon the work of the right index finger when squeezing upon the trigger; its correct work determines to a great extent the quality of the shot, since the most careful and most delicate aim will be spoiled by the slightest incorrect movement of the finger.

In order for the index finger to be able to carry out its work without spoiling the aim, it is first of all necessary to have the right hand grasp the small of the stock correctly and thus create the proper support permitting the index finger to overcome the trigger-action tension. The small of the stock must be grasped tightly but without any strain, since muscular tension in the hand can lead to excessive oscillations of the rifle. It is also necessary to find a posi-

125

tion for the hand that will provide for a space between the index finger and the small of the stock, then the movement of the index finger as it squeezes on the trigger will not cause any lateral jerks, which also could shift the position of the rifle, that is, spoil the aim." (Yev'yev, A.A., Sportivnaya Strel'ba Iz Vintovki, Competitive Marksmanship With Rifle and Carbine, Moscow, 1957, Translation Department Of The Army, Office Of The Assistant Chief Of Staff, Intelligence, 1960).

◎ **Source of Pistol Concept:** It is when we get to *aiming* that most of the misunderstandings occur. You know that a person does not understand what *Precision Shooting* is if he talks about aiming at the target.

☛**comment:** *Remember: the sights are used to align the barrel with the eye in precision shooting, NOT to aim at the target.*

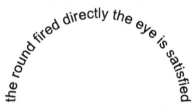

"Once the eye has arrived at the target and the rifle is roughly aligned upon it, the eye must commence consciously to focus the target, foresight and backsight in turn by a process of ac-commo-dation. When finally satisfied that the point aimed at is correct and that the foresight is central in the U, the foresight alone must be focused and the round fired directly the eye is satisfied with the height of the fore-sight...Thus the aim which I have suggested and which I normally use, **though having the appearance of being revolutionary, is really nothing more than the usual aim with the foresight focused instead of the target**." Brigadier J. A. Barlow C.B.E., p.t.s.c. in his book, *The Elements of Rifle Shooting* published in 1932)

◎ **Source of Pistol Concept:** *The sights are used to align the barrel with the eye in precision shooting, NOT to aim at the target.* It is evident that the shooters at the *U.S. Army Marksmanship Unit* in the 1960's time period understood that. They point it out on page 28 of the 1965 *U.S. Army Marksmanship*

Unit's Rifle Instructors and Coaches Guide. Think about what they say, *"This is the most important aspect of aiming, as errors in alignment create angular changes in the position of the axis of the bore."*

☛**Comment:** As we have pointed out, the rifle shooters have done a better job of winning Olympic Gold Medals than have the pistol shooters. Just what have the rifle shooters been doing that the pistol shooters have not been doing? The thrust of our program is internal alignment. Any misalignment between the barrel and the eye and the best you can get is a random point. The internal alignment is simply the alignment between the barrel and the eye. The only place it can happen is within the shooting unit. There are no shooting problems outside of the shooting unit. There may be problems, but they are not shooting problems. There are other types of problems, such as atmospheric effects on the free flying indicator.

The rifle shooters must be doing something different than the pistol shooters. And they are. They start, when they set up their platform, by lining up the barrel with their shooting eye very deliberately. They set up their internally aligned system. Then, if they see that this aligned system is not pointed at the desired area, they adjust the whole internally aligned shooting unit until it is. The rifle shooter adjusts the platform, until the internal alignment coincides with the desired aiming area.

◎ **Source of Pistol Concept:** A pistol shooter will say, *"But, pistol shooters do the same thing!"* No, they do not. They are not even close! The pistol shooters start off by looking at an area outside of the shooting unit. Whereas, the rifle shooters start off by aligning the barrel with the eye, mechanically, and seeing where it is pointed. They then move the whole unit so the aligned system is pointing where they want. The pistol shooters, on the other hand, start off by looking at an area outside of the shooting unit. Then, they point the pistol at it. They next twist their heads around trying to get their eye aligned with the pistol and the target.

☛**Comment:** On the other hand, in our system of establishing internal alignment, we pay no attention to anything out-

127

side of the shooting unit. Out whole interest is setting up our basic stance so that when the pistol is raised to eye level, if we do not have perfect barrel alignment with the eye, then that is not it. We stabilize the eye, get into the position we want and then we move the pistol until we have perfect barrel alignment with the eye, just like the rifle shooters do. Then we adjust the internally aligned system by rotating the shooting unit around until it is pointed at the desired area. This is the same as the rifle shooters use when they establish their internal alignment and then adjust the shooting unit so it points at the desired area.

◎ **Source of Pistol Concept:** The US Army Marksmanship Unit Pistol Marksmanship Guide of 15 April 1964, stated *The proper stance and position will tend to cause the pistol to point naturally at the center of the aiming area.*

☛**Comment:** We agree that this is the way it is. The champions do it. However, they have been notably unsuccessful in instructing others how to teach themselves how to attain the proper stance and position.

Think of it this way. You have a youngster, erect and relaxed, and he has the pistol pointed where he wants it. He fires a shot and recovers the sight alignment, pointing the pistol at the target. He looks at the sights. He should have perfect sight alignment. To obtain this, you need to setup your stance so that you have relaxed alignment and you shift it so that you are on your aiming area. So, when you raise your pistol up to eye level, you should be on your aiming area. That is, when you stick the pistol out in front of your eye, pointed at your predetermined aiming area, you should have perfect sight alignment.

Now, suppose your neck is strained in the alignment of the sights with the eye. And, you fire a shot. Everything collapses. What happens is, the gun, upon recovery of the sights from the recoil, will not return to perfect sight alignment. Or, with the strained neck problem, the gun, upon recovery of the sights, comes up with perfect sight alignment, but is not pointed at the target.

128

What we are looking for is minimum recovery time. So, we want our shooter to setup a comfortable, relaxed stance, which they deliberately setup to give themselves perfect sight alignment, and pointed toward a predetermined area of their choice.

On the other hand, take the case when the neck is strained getting the shooting eye lined up with the barrel. In this situation, the shot is fired. The shot could be a good shot, for one shot, it could be okay. The gun recoils and comes back down. The shooter does not have sight alignment. Or more than likely the shooter does not have the sight alignment for which he is looking. The shooter has to find his sight alignment and re-build it.

In another case, the shooter has a relaxed, comfortable position. But, while he is comfortable, the shooter has not setup his sight alignment through his stance. So, he fires the shot. The sights are recovered from the recoil. But, while the shooter has perfect sight alignment, he does not have his target in front of his sights. He has to find the target at which to point the aligned system.

A rifle shooter, on the other hand, when he has his position the way he wants, fires a shot. He relaxes, checks his eyeball, and he is right back on his target. Pistol shooters, almost every one of them, do not setup like that. They generally have to rebuild their position for every shot. For slow fire, it is no problem. For timed fire, if they are experienced, they can rebuild and fire reasonably well. In rapid fire, they do not have time to rebuild the position and sight alignment in ten seconds. When they get to shooting the International Rapid Fire, where they are required to fire five shots in four seconds, one at each of five different targets, they do not have time for that rebuilding process. They are then dead in the water.

◎ **Source of Pistol Concept:** The US Army Marksmanship Unit Pistol Marksmanship Guide of 15 April 1964, stated *A definite rhythm or cadence is a must, especially in rapid fire, where only 10 seconds is allowed.*

☛ **comment:** Focusing on rhythm in shooting is sheer stupidity. What does it take to have the bullet hole appear where

129

you want it? The gun has to be pointed there when it goes off. The rules specify that the bullet holes should appear in predetermined areas so the shooter can obtain the most points the game rules permit.

What people entranced with the idea of rhythm in shooting want the shooter to do is to have the shots appear in predetermined areas at precise times. Putting shots into the predetermined areas, of a game such as the International Rapid Fire event, is difficult enough, without adding the extra requirement that the bullet holes appear at predetermined, precise times. These people have to be out of their minds to focus such an amount of effort on something which is not required under the rules of the game they are playing. What these people hung up on rhythm have done is to throw something into the game which is physically impossible to cope with. No way can you have your pistol pointed at a particular area, at a precise interval, and get the bullet out the barrel. It cannot be done. You see, champions do not do that. But, they say they do. What the champions do is when they have precise alignment and the pistol pointed at an area they can live with, the gun goes off. So, they fire their shots on the basis of precise internal alignment and acceptable aiming area. It is inconsequential whether it is done in a rhythmical manner. It is completely immaterial when the shots are delivered within the time frame.

With sixty years of shooting experience, Sievers reports that he has seen only one shooter who ever came close to delivering his shots within a specified rhythmic time sequence. That was a shooter on his Navy teams, named Don Hamilton. Another elite shooter would fire "bang", "bang, bang, bang" and then wait and then just before the targets turned, that last shot would go, "bang." Both shooters had that time frame locked in their heads. So, for the elite shooters, it is sight alignment and acceptable aiming area, versus what they say. When a shooter adds rhythm to his repertoire of things needed to be accomplished in order to fire a series of aimed shots, he is taking away the time he can focus on the sight alignment and acceptable aiming area.

Then there is the example of the new shooter who has just fired a real abortion of a series of shots. In no way could the

130

shots be classified as being any semblance of a group. The normal reaction is to try to salvage something out of this embarrassment. So, he'll say to anybody in earshot, *"Well, at least my rhythm was good."*

◎ **Source of Pistol Concept:** The US Army Marksmanship Unit Pistol Marksmanship Guide of 15 April 1964, stated *Follow thru is the continuation of all mental and physical processes brought into play to deliver a surprise breaking, controlled shot.*

☛**Comment:** In our method, the shooter teaches himself to deliver a controlled shot when what the eyeball identifies visually to the brain which acuates the trigger finger to an instantaneously smooth movement. What is the surprise about that? The surprise is, if they do it!

◎ **Source of Pistol Concept:** The US Army Marksmanship Unit Pistol Marksmanship Guide of 15 April 1964, stated *A limited amount of oxygen can be momentarily stored in the respiratory system and the breath can be held comfortably only a short length of time. It stands to reason, that within the first ten or twelve seconds we are in better condition to deliver a good shot on the target. Waiting too long to apply a positive trigger pressure to break the shot may allow the Arc of Movement to increase and the eye focus to blur. The shooter eventually becomes impatient and abruptly speeds up his trigger action. This causes a jerk shot.*

☛**Comment:** Whether or not their reasoning is true, we do not know. But, we agree with their conclusion. They recognize that holding 10 or 12 seconds is a detriment to the firing of a good shot. But, they do not train to shoot before that length of time. They have pointed this out, and then gone into a training system which completely ignores it.

◎ **Source of Pistol Concept:** The US Army Marksmanship Unit Pistol Marksmanship Guide of 15 April 1964, stated *Looking at the Target: The eye can only focus on one object at a time. That object should be the front sight. Valuable time is lost in looking over the sight to the target to adjust the point of hold. During the fleeting instant that you remove your focus*

131

*from the sights, they could become misaligned...It is difficult to
maintain constant point focus on the front sight, but it can be
effectively accomplished through continued emphasis on training in this specific area.*

☛**Comment:** One concept stated above, *Valuable time is lost
in looking over the sight to the target to adjust the point of hold*
has been a source of controversy for many years.   The
authors have speculated that the reason pistol shooters have
been able to move from the high 2500's into the 2600 range is
due primarily to their decision to look at the sights.

◎ **Source of Pistol Concept:** *Colonel Charles Askins, Jr.* in his
book, ***The Pistol Shooter's Book***.   Colonel Charles Askins, Jr.
advocates looking through the sights to the target.

looking at the bullseye

*"Don't look for the sights on the pistol, bring the sights into that
line between your eye and the center of the target. You are looking
at the bullseye, not at the front and rear sights on the weapon. Align
the sights one with the other and with the 10-ring as quickly as you
can. Squeeze with a decisive pressure which has no part of a jerk
about it. When the gun explodes, the strong grip will counteract the
roughness you may have been guilty of at the time the trigger was
mashed. That same powerful hold will dampen the recoil and give
you more time to maneuver the pistol into line with the bull for
squeeze No. 2.*

*You will find after a shot or two that you can see where the bul-
lets are hitting, if you find that the group is piling up at some spot
outside the 10-ring, immediately shift your point of aim slightly to
bring the remaining shots in the string into the center. When you
commence rapid fire you will not be able to do this. To begin with,
the game is difficult and all your time and resources are used up
just firing the 5 rounds in the 10 second interval. After some months
of shooting you will find that you do not seem to be so greatly*

132

rushed and it is then that you will acquire the ability to see holes as they appear in the paper and can slightly shift your aiming point to center following shots."

☞**comment:** Askins is directing the attention of the shooter at the target. In our concept, we direct the shooter's attention to the sight alignment.

◎ **Source of Pistol Concept:** *Colonel Charles Askins, Jr.* in his book, ***The Pistol Shooter's Book.***

"Progress depends very largely on the gun you commence with. None is better than the .22 Olympic High Standard auto pistol. This gun fires the .22 short cartridge which has practically no recoil at all. It is amazing what a big factor recoil assumes in rapid fire shooting. The up-thrust of the muzzle is a sudden and savage thing and it plays disconcerting tricks on the equilibrium. The noise is a harmful element as well. If you will do your first rapid-tempo gunning with the smallest caliber you will never have cause to regret it." (Askins, Pg 118)

☞**comment:** In our program, the shooter is training himself, right from the start to shoot in the rapid fire mode. Sight recovery is taught during training with our electric trigger air pistols. We do this deliberately in order to facilitate the training of the conditional reflex between the eye and the trigger finger. We purposely configure our platform for the establishment of internal alignment. This allows for a natural

133

sight alignment. It is a part of their trained shooting technique. Askins talks about slow fire style. In the slow fire method that he is referring to, the shooter has 60 seconds prorated to fire one shot, ie: ten minutes total time to fire ten shots.

"There IS REALLY only one proper way to shoot a handgun and that is rapidly. All of them are essentially designed for self defense. The very shape of the machine indicates that it is a repeater, and, in the case of the automatics, a very fast sort of a quick-firer gives additional force to the contention. But what probably clinches the argument is that there is more pleasure and satisfaction in shooting a one-hand gun rat-tat-tat.

It is all very well to stand and aim and aim and dawdle over the squeeze and fiddle with the sight picture and finally murder a full 60 seconds to touch off one round-all very well but an exceedingly stuffy business. For a red blooded, double-charged thrill it is a lot better to rip out a magazine in a couple of seconds. Something about the buck of the recoil and the clanging response of quickly-reacting nitrocellulose works an alchemy which is heart tingling." Askins

Michal Newhouse, age 9.
1996 Junior Women's NRA 900 Silver Medalist Grand Canyon State Games

134

In the Grand Canyon Games of 1996, Michal Newhouse, one of our 9 year olds, won the Junior Women's Silver Medal with a score of 385 points over the NRA 900 course of fire. 60 of the shots in the match were fired in time limits of 5 shots in 20 seconds or less. Try taking a 9-year-old out to shoot sometime. Hickey suspects, that if you use the old tried and true methods currently in the public domain that you will not be able to replicate our 9-year-old's performance. The only way this performance can be replicated is, in our opinion, by use of the teaching method we advocate in this book. And, do you know we did not even mention to her, that in order to shoot the timed and rapid strings of her match, she would have to breathe in a special manner. After the match, Hickey spoke with the lady who scored Michal's target. She told him that Michal did very well in the rapid and timed fire events.

Is it even possible for a 9 year old, let alone a 9 year old girl, to score any points at all over the NRA 900 .22 caliber course of fire? That's the course where 30 shots are fired, slow fire at 50 yards. And 30 shots are fired in each of the events at 25 yards. These 25-yard events are comprised of the Timed Fire events, where 5 shots are fired in 20 seconds, for 30 shots. Then there is the Rapid-Fire event, where 5 shots are fired in 10 seconds for 30 shots.

Gil Hebard, former National Pistol Champion and publisher of the well respected *Pistol Shooter's Catalog,* wrote,"*The average beginner often scores between 100 and 200 out of a possible 300 points. You may not even break 100 the first time you try!"* (*The Pistol Shooter's Treasury* edited by Gil Hebard). Hebard is referring to the National Match Course scores. We speculate that he is referring to adult beginners. Interestingly, it has been the experience of the juniors in the Tucson Junior Pistol Training Program that many of them can exceed these expectations.

We completely agree with Askins when he says *"For a red-blooded, double-charged thrill it is a lot better to rip out a magazine in a couple of seconds."* From our experience with youngsters from 9 years of age to collegiate shooters, to mature adults on elite teams representing the United States Navy, they all seem to enjoy the rapid emptying of their pistol magazines out the muzzles of their guns.

135

For those doubters amongst you, who shake your heads at even the mention of a nine year old shooting a pistol, let alone shooting it as a part of the international rapid fire game, I invite you to visit our shooting program in Tucson, Arizona. We have one girl, Michal Newhouse, who shortly after turning 9 joined our pistol-training program at the end of March of 1996. As a part of our conditional reflex training, she participates in the International Rapid-Fire training program. It is a fact of the history of the National Rifle Association of America that she is a member of the 3-person team which, at the writing of this book, holds the current NRA National Women's International Rapid Fire Team Record. This team of which she was a member broke the old women's national record by 206 points. This record was fired in a NRA Registered Tournament at the end of July 1996. This little nine-year-old girl had been in our shooting training program for only four months at the time.

For our conditional reflex training, we train the youngsters only at the 4-second portion of the rapid-fire game. Girls are not allowed to compete in the International Rapid-Fire event of the Olympics or in the international arena. However, they are permitted to compete in the International Rapid-Fire events registered with the National Rifle Association of America.

Askins says *"Unfortunately we all must walk before we run; all must serve a long and somewhat tiresome apprenticeship as slow-fire marksmen before we essay the bang-bang game."* Michal's apprenticeship consisted of training with the air pistol before firing her first shots with the .22 caliber Ruger Model .22/45. We have a couple of club qualification ratings she had to earn before going out to the .22 caliber range. But, after four weeks, she was qualified, under our system, to join the other youngsters on the outdoor range.

Once the youngsters come out to the range, we have them participate in the full training schedule. So, she was introduced to firing 5 shots, in 10 seconds, with the .22, from the benchrest during her first training session. We make no big deal out of the shooting the 5 shots in 10 seconds. It is just normal. Our youngsters do not know any difference.

136

All of our training is geared to training the conditional reflex of the trigger finger moving when the eye sees perfect sight alignment pointed at the area previously selected by the shooter.

If there is one thing which we all know, it is that it is not possible to identify anyone as a **natural** shooter at 9 years of age.

However, our evidence shows clearly that it is possible to show someone how, at 9 years of age, to teach herself the simple methods needed to come out ahead of one of the adult women in the Grand Canyon Games.

One neat thing she taught herself, as a result of her training with us, was to recover the sight alignment during the rapid fire. Each shot she fired was thus an aimed shot. People watching her fire expressed amazement at sight recovery, it was apparent to all that she was firing aimed shots. Very fast aimed shots, but ones which were being deliberately triggered by her eyeball.

This runs counter to the prevailing concept as stated by Colonel Askins,

"I do not believe anyone is ready for rapid fire shooting until he has been shooting very intensively at the slow stages for at least a half-year.

The actions we start generating in our first shot, will be the actions we want in our ultimate goal. And, they should never vary in their direction from reaching this objective. All the other methods, we know about, are trying to teach the beginning shooters a multitude of things. Our students' attention is directed and constantly redirected at internal alignment and developing the finger movement as a conditional reflex, where the finger movement is instantaneously smooth.

Askins again voices another concept we want to comment on, *Rapid fire is nothing in the world except the preliminary stuff greatly speeded up. Everything you have done as a slow fire gunner is followed exactly. The only trouble is that while the trigger is squeezed much more quickly it still must be pressed just as smoothly, just as sweetly. To do this successfully requires a profound grounding in all the fundamentals.* While this concept may fit Askins, it seems obvious to us, that all it requires is the individual teaching herself how, and when, to move the trigger finger.

Another concept, and again we find it expressed in the writings of Askins is that, *"First practices should be commenced at a tempo little faster than your customary slow fire. If it requires a full minute for you to shoot one shot, try firing two shots in the same time interval. Gradually work up until you can get off a full*

138

string." It is our observation that this type of training, by its very nature, creates the idea that shooting rapid fire is somehow *difficult.* We train a shooter to teach himself how to develop his trigger finger movement as a conditional reflex when his eye sees perfect sight alignment pointed at the desired area. Then, we judge the effectiveness of that training by the timing of the action of the conditional reflex after the gun gets to eye level. We are talking about hundredths of a second. No way are we able to live with our shooters taking anywhere near a full minute to fire one accurate shot. It is just not a part of our program. We certainly agree with what Askins says below:

"It has been a longstanding contention of mine that after a man has mastered the fundamentals of pistol marksmanship he should never shoot again in a slow fire style. I mean by that this business of deliberately aiming for a minute or more to fire a single shot. Then, like a lot of gunners, lower the weapon, rest the arm not having fired at all, and finally commence over again. This is tommyrot.

When the weapon is first leveled at the mark the shooter is fresh and strong. His arm is not tired; his eyes are bright and clear; his nerves feel no strain. It is during the first 8-10 seconds of the aim that the shot should be set a-wing. It is simply a matter of courage. If the marksman is strongly determined to squeeze decisively the first time the front sight covers the 10-ring and just as decisive the next time the gun aligns itself, within the space of a very few seconds the piece will explode and the hit will be a good one.

The trouble is, however, we are so hidebound and conventional that this system is looked upon as radical and ruinous. To fire thus quickly will result in a wild hit, and in the case of the targetman result in a low total score. Bosh! It will not do anything of the kind. Regardless of whether the shooter is performing at 10 yards or 50, the bullet should be aimed and fired in not more than

139

*10 seconds. Of course this kind of gunning is not for tyros; it is for the individual who has had a thorough grounding in the basic principles of handgunning. After the pistoleer understands how to aim and squeeze, he should be forever attempting to take advantage of those early stages of his aim when his grip is strong and **unstrained,** his eye is clear, and his nerves unfrayed".* (Askins)

Now, back to a concept described by the folks at Fort Benning. Here, we think they can only be guessing, *"Valuable time is lost in looking over the sight to the target to adjust the point of hold."* No one can know this for sure. It is an unsupported guess. If you deliberately, physically set up the sight alignment with the eye, you will not lose it like that.

We go out of our minds continuously harping on the next concept, *"It is difficult to maintain constant point focus on the front sight, but it can be effectively accomplished through continued emphasis on training in this specific area."* We start our training with this concept of *maintaining constant point focus on the front sight* and we never let up that focus throughout the shooter's association with our program.

◎ **Source of Pistol Concept:** *"The course taught the trainee the principles of effective shooting, under the supposition that an experienced marksman made an effective instructor. This same premise, used in the past at Cape May and elsewhere, was faulty because competent marksmen do not always make competent general service instructors. Neither the Yorktown or Cape May course taught instructional methods or presentation. There may have been some credibility in the theory for the men who had spent most of their careers firing in competition, but most trainees left Yorktown without learning the basic elements of teaching."* **Wells, W.R.,II,** (1993). ***Shots That Hit.*** *A Study of U.S. Coast Guard Marksmanship: 1790-1985.* United States Coast Guard Historian's Office.

☛ **Comment:** The concept that the best pistol shooter makes the best instructor is still in vogue in much of the pistol shooting community today.

◎ **Source of Pistol Concept:** *The US Army Marksmanship Unit Pistol Marksmanship Guide* of 15 April 1964, stated *The instant nature of the reflex action sometimes so closely coincides with recoil that difficulty is often encountered in making an accurate shot call.*

☛**comment:** There is only one thing, only one thing which will interfere with making an accurate shot call. What is that? It is the closing of your eye. Most shooters have never connected an open eyeball with a shot call. A shot call exactly where it is supposed to be, is giving you feedback that you had your eye open and you saw everything going on at the time the shot was fired. Or you made one heck of a lucky guess. When you can call your shots continuously, then that tells you that your eyeball is open. When you cannot see where it went, that tells you that you did not see it, your eyeball was closed.

◎ **Source of Pistol Concept:** *The US Army Marksmanship Unit Pistol Marksmanship Guide* of 15 April 1964, stated *Muscular and/or nervous reflex action takes place and disturbs sight alignment because the reflexes usually react sooner than the actual firing of the shot.*

☛**comment:** When this happens, the reflex action has been misplaced. In our system, what reflex action are we training ourselves to perform? The trigger finger to move when the eye sees that the sights are perfectly aligned in the area we have pre-selected. That is what we want to take place first.

◎ **Source of Pistol Concept:** *The US Army Marksmanship Unit Pistol Marksmanship Guide* of 15 April 1964, stated *A spasmodic, abrupt trigger movement combined with the reflex action of the arm and hand muscles causes a violent disturbance of a sight alignment and results in a bad shot. When this happens, the shooter may be attempting to use point shooting technique but faulty trigger control prevents the application of smooth trigger pressure.*

141

☛**comment:** The only time the shooter sees that the gun is pointed where he wants is in passing. The gun never hesitates at that point for him to think about moving the finger. Thus, the gun continues to move in widening uncontrolled motions as fatigue sets in. Eventually, the NOW syndrome rushes in and the shooter snatches a last hope as the sights go by the target. Invariably this kind of effort is accompanied by eye closure. So, what is the last thing the shooter sees just before the gun fires? It is passing exactly where he wants it to go off. The eye closes and the gun is pointing at some random place as the bullet leaves the barrel. You ask the shooter, *"How did it look?"* The shooter will 9 times out of 10 say, *it looked good.* And the shooter is absolutely correct. It did look good, the last time he had his eye open looking at it. But that was not when the action took place. The Moment of Truth is when the bullet leaves the barrel. And, that was all in the dark. So the only way to find where the barrel was pointed at that time, is to find the indicator, the bullet hole. The shooter will then say something like, *"I don't understand that, that can't be, because I saw it point right there in the middle of the ten!"* But, he is talking about a different time of day, when he saw it there, not when the action took place.

Let's look at the concept of the wobble area. More and more often, if you develop the trigger finger movement control, you will see better and better results. This is noticeable, particularly at long range rifle shooting with a scope, where you accept the wobble area. So then you get the shot off, and instead of trying to get it off on a point, you accept the wobble area. Very often, you will look at it when it goes off and you will say to yourself, *"if I had a choice of where I wanted it to go off, that would be the place."* It starts going off by itself closer and closer to the desired point. This happens because your wobble area gets smaller as you train yourself. Pistol shooting is the same way. More and more often, you will find gun going off on a point. But, if you try to make it go off on a point, forget it. What happens in our program, is development of the trigger finger movement as a conditional reflex to what the eyeball sees. In that context, we use area aiming. The gun has to be pointed in an accepted area when it goes off. We pick up the sight alignment at the foot of the target. The gun goes off when the sight alignment is perfect and the gun is pointed at an acceptable area. In other words, the sight alignment is setup and then we bring that aligned system into the acceptable aiming area. That is what triggers the trigger finger movement. For example, the shooter picks up the sight alignment as the gun is being raised to eye level. Once the sight alignment is picked up, the shooter starts to load the trigger. That way, when the shooter brings the sight alignment up into the acceptable aiming area the shot is gone.

One shooting technique advocates looking at the sights, while the gun is at the 45° ready position for the International Rapid Fire event. In this method, the attention of the shooter is misdirected. The focus should be on the bottom of the target. Once they start to move, the shooter raises his arm into position, catching the sight alignment as the sights reach the bottom of the target and come into his vision. If he does not have perfect sight alignment at that moment, that is not it. He did not set up his sight alignment with his stance. If he has to do any shifting around of the sight alignment, that is not it, he did not set up his stance properly for his sight alignment. So, he picks up the sight alignment at the bottom of the target. It has to be absolutely perfect because he set it up that way. He then continues into the center of the target, having started to load the trigger as his sight alignment came into view and the shot fires as it reaches his predetermined aiming area. As he shifts to the next target, he loads the trigger. The gun fires as he reaches his aiming area. Having set up his sight alignment mechanically, the shooter maintains sight alignment as he shifts from target to target.

◎ **Source of Pistol Concept:** *The US Army Marksmanship Unit Pistol Marksmanship Guide* of 15 April 1964, stated *When the shooter has perfect sight alignment and is able to momentarily freeze the Arc of Movement. This condition is of extremely short duration and the shooter is prone to act quickly and abruptly in applying trigger pressure before the ideal moment passes.*

☛**Comment:** Momentarily impossible. You do not momentarily freeze anything. That is the NOW syndrome. If

143

the shooter had developed the conditional reflex, the shot would have gone off. It has to be instantaneously smooth. How fast should the trigger control be? Instantaneous. That's what all successful trigger control is, instantaneously smooth.

◎ **Source of Pistol Concept:** *"One innovation included allowed instructor latitude while maintaining the traditional theories of marksmanship instruction."* **Wells, W.R.,II,** (1993). Shots That Hit. *A Study of U.S. Coast Guard Marksmanship: 1790-1985.* United States Coast Guard Historian's Office.

☛**Comment:** This says it all! It is the traditional theories of marksmanship instruction which we have found defective. These theories do not constitute an efficient teaching method. This active discouragement of departure from the traditional theories of marksmanship also discourages innovation in marksmanship theory development.

◎ **Source of Pistol Concept:** *The US Army Marksmanship Unit Pistol Marksmanship Guide* of 15 April 1964, stated *Do Not Shoot and Practice Alone: When possible, shoot with someone who is a better shot than you. Observe his methods, the sequence of events he uses and request that he coach you for a few strings. Most good shooters are willing to help another shooter to perfect his performance.*

☛**Comment:** This concept should be labeled **The Kiss of Death!** What most of the so-called experts are putting out, for the most part, is guaranteed to put you on a track which will make the development of your skill much harder and will probably take a much longer time than if you went your own way. Many of these experts have some favorite way of breathing or have a real stable platform which they will most accommodatingly demonstrate for you. The only thing is, much of what these experts have to offer sounds really good, but is really, really bad news for you. Many of them do the things they do because it *sounds good.* Most do not really understand shooting. But, if you tell them this, they will bluster and just walk away. We do things deliberately in our program. Everything we do, with respect to our shooting, we do deliberately and on purpose. Everything we do is judged against whether it will help our sight alignment or help us in forming the conditional reflex of the trigger finger. If it will help one of those two items, we will try it. If it will not help either of those two elements, we will ignore it. If it does not matter, then it becomes a matter of convenience and we have a choice as to whether we want to use it or not.

◎ **Source of Pistol Concept:** *The US Army Marksmanship Unit Pistol Marksmanship Guide* of 15 April 1964, stated *Unresolved Shooting Problems handicapping performance are a continuing burden plaguing a shooter on the firing line. As a shooter knows, persistent shooting faults mean a slump in performance as a result, he is not in the proper mental state when on the firing line and cannot concentrate properly. His anxiety is that these faults will continue to constantly affect his performance and will handicap his scores. A so-called slump need only last until planning for the next shot. The solution of those knotty problems in your shooting can be best resolved by comprehensive shot analysis and application of corrective techniques. A good line coach or one of your teammates can be of great help to you in your dilemma.*

☛**Comment:** There is no such thing as a *slump.* Now, it is possible that some people will think we are saying that these people are wrong to describe some less than expected performances as slumps. That is not what we are saying at all. If some people think we are saying that, then that is their problem. We are in a position where we cannot use that term to describe some result in our program. We have no objections whatsoever to anyone else using this term to characterize some persistent problems they may be having with their shooting performance. But, we find no value in it, other than as a horrible example of how to teach shooting. You see, if you are performing at a particular level and your performance goes down, it means that you have changed something that you are doing. If someone is in a *slump,* meaning that they have changed something that they are doing, they would have to be able to analyze what they have been doing, to see

145

what they have changed and get back on track. For a *slump* to continue, means that they are not able to analyze what they have been doing in order to get back on track. They cannot analyze what they are doing because they did not understand what they were doing in the first place to perform at the level they were performing. A key to remaining out of a *slump* is the mental state of the shooter. For example, we do not care what our shooters do with respect to the Act of Shooting. What we want is for them to understand what they are doing and why. We want everything they do to be done on purpose. So, if they do something they do not like, and the results are shown on the scoreboard, then they can put their finger on it. Once identified, they can change it to something they do like. The basic problem with those who latch on to the idea of a *slump* is that they are proclaiming for all concerned that they do not understand what they are doing.

◎ **Source of Pistol Concept:** *The US Army Marksmanship Unit Pistol Marksmanship Guide* of 15 April 1964, stated *Don't Knock It Until You Have Tried It: Suggested techniques should be fully explored and tested. The old saying that "Rome wasn't built in a day, applies here. When an expert suggests changes in any part of a developing shooter's performance, the shooter should give the new method a thorough trial before discarding it. The master shooter attained his rating by doing many things right.*

☛**Comment:** No, he did not. The master shooter did two things efficiently. We do not even get close to this right or correct stuff. Right, correct and wrong are not in our vocabulary when we look at shooting methods. The only reason those words might appear in our book is to point out that we have eliminated them from our vocabulary and we want to be very specific about it. How many things does the master shooter have to do efficiently in order to be a master shooter? Two. Align the barrel with his eye precisely and consistently and move his trigger finger without introducing angular misalignment between the barrel and his eye. Where can these master shooters point this aligned system? Anywhere they want.

For example, one of our young 13 year old pistol shooters in the 1996 Grand Canyon Games, fired a 74 on one of his timed fire targets. Sievers asked him where could he point his pistol. The youngster replied, *"anywhere I want."* Sievers suggested he point the gun about 6 inches above where he had pointed for that target. The next target showed a 90 score for a 90 group. The youngster, for this stage of his development was pointing reasonably well and he had his trigger movement pretty well in hand. So, he was able to produce the result his holding indicated he should have. We did not monkey around adjusting sights. All the junior did was to point the pistol where he wanted.

◎ **Source of Pistol Concept:** *"All concerned know that the only shots that count are those that hit."* **Wells, W.R.,II,** (1993). *Shots That Hit. A Study of U.S. Coast Guard Marksmanship: 1790-1985.* United States Coast Guard Historian's Office.

☛**comment:** For Shooting Training, *"Hitting"* the target is a distraction. Our interest should be in *"Precision Pointing."*

◎ **Source of Pistol Concept:** *The US Army Marksmanship Unit Pistol Marksmanship Guide* of 15 April 1964, stated *on the back cover:*

> *Prepare For Shot*
> *Plan Shot*
> *Relax Before Shot*
> *Deliver Shot*
> *Analyze Error*
> *Correct Error*

☛**comment:** Is that a good plan? What this says to us, is that the above does not work. If it does work, the last line should say, **Shoot another ten.** What the people who prepared this plan did was to assume that the shooter would always have an error. We wonder why the Army's Advanced

Pistol Marksmanship Unit would assume that what they were teaching would produce errors.

If the shooter has random misalignment, either detectable or undetectable, between the barrel and the eye, the more stable the platform from which the shooter fires, the more assured he is of getting random strikes on his aiming point. We will use as our examples, the rifle prone position and the rifle standing position. Most shooters will generally find that their shooting eye is closer to the rear sight in the prone position. They also usually find that their shooting eye is further away, in comparison to the prone position, when they shoot from the standing position. Prone is a more stable position than the standing position. Let's examine the position of the eye in the prone position.

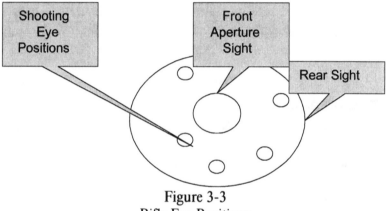

Figure 3-3
Rifle Eye Positions

Notice that the eye positions vary even though the rifle prone position is a very stable shooting platform. Will these eye positions work? That is, will they enable a shooter to attain consistent results? Yes! However, the eye position must be maintained consistently from shot to shot. If the shooter places the whole amount of his attention on the relationship of the target in the front sight, how much attention is he paying to the position of the eye with respect to the rear sight? This is an area where otherwise master shooters cannot figure out why they are getting random hits on their target.

The primary emphasis in sighting is the achievement of mechanical alignment of the sights with the eye. For example,

Art Jackson, one of America's premier elite rifle shooters of the 1950's, uses a shim which he places on the comb of his rifle stock when moving from 300 yards to 600 yards. Mechanical alignment of the barrel with the eye!

Many shooters fall back to placing the blame on the ammunition. They have failed, as Gary Anderson, one of the top gold medal placing Olympians in today's world, put it, to master one of the basic elements of shooting.

Concept of Aiming

Gary Anderson, in his book, *Marksmanship*, published in 1972 by Simon and Schuster, wrote: *"The concept of aiming is the first fundamental of shooting that must be learned.*

"The first thing to master in aiming is sight alignment. If the sights are not properly aligned, then an error is produced which becomes increasingly greater as the bullet nears the target. Particularly for the beginner, concentration should be on aligning the sights until this action becomes almost a habit."

Anyone who has done even a small amount of pistol shooting can recognize that Yur'yev is right on track when he points out, *"It is necessary to keep in mind that this failure to center the front sight in the rear-sight notch leads to an angular misalignment of the firearm and considerable deviation of the shot from the center of the target."* Pistol shooters, especially, know as Yur'yev states, *"This is an especially important point for pistol shooting when we recognize that if the properly aligned sights deviate from the lower edge of the bull's-eye, this will not lower the results of shooting to as great an extent as misalignment of the front sight in the rear sight."* We agree with Yur'yev, *"proper aiming depends upon the shooter's ability to be consistent in the way that he maintains sight alignment and how he aligns the front sight with the bull's-eye (aiming area)."* If the barrel is pointed where the shooter wants it to be, then that is where the bullet will indicate, or in other words, where the bullet will strike.

149

The purpose of sight alignment is to establish a precise and consistent internally aligned system. Once we have the internally aligned system established, any single point in the system can be used as a reference to point the internally aligned system at a predetermined area. The obvious reference point is the top of the front sight where our vision is concentrated to maintain the internal alignment.

When we maintain the internal alignment, we use a single point for aiming. We have parallel error in the movement of the pistol and the effect is that of shooting down a pipe. When angular error is introduced, we have the effect of shooting down a funnel inverted.

We have observed that the rifle shooter is doing precisely what we are talking about. What the pistol shooters are doing is talking about sight alignment and trigger control in passing, and

150

getting hysterical about the platform. Unfortunately the platform is based on a non-existing feature, for the pistol, called the *"Natural Point of Aim"* and stability for an inherently unstable support, the erect human body with arm extended. The deliberate configuration of our platform is vital for the establishment of internal alignment. In the conventional pistol training method, internal alignment has never been mentioned in the configuration of the establishment any pistol shooting platform. In the establishment of conventional competitive pistol shooting platforms, the entire thrust has been on platform stability. In our system, at the beginning stages of training, stability is a secondary consideration according to the Shooting Diagram. The pistol shooters have misplaced the emphasis with respect to the Act of Shooting. That emphasis is what keeps them pecking at the world elite status. We believe that if the pistol shooters shifted their emphasis initially to the internal alignment of the barrel with the eye and the movement of the trigger, they would be very well prepared to later move on to the platform stability. But, that is not the way pistol shooting training is presently conducted in the United States. There is no one outside of our associates around the country who have such an emphasis on that concept.

Unfortunately, the platform is based on a non-existing feature, for the pistol, called the *"Natural Point of Aim"* and stability for an inherently unstable support, the erect human body, with arm extended.

It is interesting to consider the continued initial emphasis on platform and position stability. For example, how could such an emphasis be justified if the pistol coach ever tried to teach a person confined to a wheelchair? The answer is they can't. On the other hand, the technique we use would dovetail nicely with a program for the handicapped, wheelchair confined, shooting athlete. That is because, under our system, it is absolutely immaterial how the pointing is done.

In one of the matches we took our juniors to, the range master and local coach came up and told us, *"none of your shooters has the same position. And, in some of those positions, they cannot be getting very much stability at all!"* Hickey explained that stability is not one of the concepts we are concerned about in this stage of the youngster's development. The coach then dem-

151

onstrated the proper position he uses and showed Hickey how it was a very stable position. Hickey explained that since our shooters are training themselves to employ a conditional reflex, it was not necessary that they devote very much attention to achieving stability in their positions. Hickey informed him that our shooters work to achieve sight alignment in their stance. Therefore, all that was required of their stance was that it enabled their sights to be aligned the same each and every time they brought up the gun to eye level.

He blurted out, *"That's another thing, your youngsters are shooting too fast! They have to be jerking the trigger!"* He was not aware that shooters could teach themselves an instantaneously smooth trigger finger movement. What we have here is a classic example, of where the average pistol shooter's attention is misdirected. This contrasts with the areas to which we direct our shooters' attention. This demonstrates the classic pattern of accepted shooting training where the attention is directed toward *"stability"* and the *"take your time"* myth. We use a more aggressive approach.

Pistol Arm Technique

Directions:

You need a short sleeved shirt or a sleeve rolled above the elbow joint.

1.   Put your hand out in front of you.
2.   Make a fist.
3.   Roll the fist to the right.
4.   Return the fist to pistol holding position.
5.   Raise the fist upwards.
6.   Note what happens to the elbow joint.
7.   The forearm comes straight up.

Now, do the same thing, only turn the fist to the left:

1.   Put your hand out in front of you.
2.   Make a fist.
3.   Roll the fist to the left.
4.   Return the fist to pistol holding position.
5.   Raise the fist upwards.

6.   Note what happens to the elbow joint.
7.   The forearm bends to the left.

PURPOSE:

To deliberately position the elbow joint to control the direction of recoil for the heavy recoilers. We do not have to accept random recoil.

Shooters can be heard commenting, "Sometimes the pistol comes up one way and sometimes it goes the other way." But, we can deliberately position the elbow joint so that the recoil comes straight up or to the left. We do not care which way. That is left up to the individual. But, the shooter needs to be aware that he/she has control over the direction of the recoil.

PROCESS:

We teach shooters, *grip firm, wrist firm, elbow firm* so that we put that elbow joint up on top and our recoil will be normally coming straight up. We are talking efficiency.

With the .22 caliber, it doesn't make much difference. But, with the .38 caliber or the .45, the recoil will go straight up and then the *Recover* will come straight *down,* rather than swinging across the target.

CONCEPT:

We want to make our shooters their own experts, so when we finish the job, they will not need us any more. They will know what they are doing, will be doing it on purpose and they can then evaluate information that comes their way. And if that information will have a *positive effect* on either *internal alignment* or *trigger finger movement* then it is fine. But, if the information will adversely affect either *internal alignment* or *trigger finger movement* then it is bad news. If it will not make any difference anyway, it is a convenience item.

154

Establishing the Shooting Platform

The Position Used By Champions, Tailored To The Individual

Rationale: This page alone is worth the price of this book!!

How the <u>platform</u> is established <u>is based on eye position</u>, not something down range. Then, what the eye wants to see when we have it in that position <u>is absolutely perfect sight alignment</u>. You can then rotate your platform 360° and put it anywhere you want. So then, when the platform is setup, we rotate it so that the aligned system coincides with the desired area. This gives us a basic body angle with the target. So the next time we come to the firing line, we set up in as near that position as possible and then make adjustments to fine tune the position. <u>There is no such thing as a natural place for the arm to point</u>. It is completely flexible. It is set up deliberately, in as relaxed a manner as possible, commensurate with the muscles required to hold it up.

Directions:

Get your normal grip on the pistol. A normal grip establishes the barrel at an angle, NOT to an extension of the forearm.

Stand erect and relaxed.

Basic Head Position

Turn your head to the right until you get strain on your neck.

Turn your head back to the left until you no longer have any strain on your neck.

Raise the pistol to shoulder height.

Swing the pistol <u>from the shoulder</u> off to the right until you see the front sight off to the left of the rear sight.

Swing the pistol from the shoulder off to the left until you see the front sight off to the right of the rear sight.

Somewhere in this arc, the sights cross.

We swing the pistol until we get perfect sight alignment

What Is Our Choice Of A Shooting Tool To Teach The Fundamentals Of Pistol Shooting?

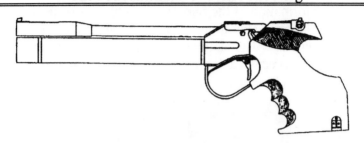

In our simplified shooting program, the Morini Model CM 162E is the air pistol of choice for teaching the fundamentals of shooting.

Why? It has an electric trigger. Sure, you say, but why even let beginning shooters handle a thousand dollar gun, let alone shoot it? Because it can do a better job than a fifty-dollar air pistol. How? First of all, because of the electric trigger, the shooter is taught to fire the shot, then recover the sight alignment and dry-fire a second shot. The shooter who learns in this manner will find that follow through becomes an instinctive process. The trigger is light enough so that the shooter can concentrate on the process of a *smooth* release without being hampered by a rough trigger requiring much focused effort to cause it to be tripped.

Technical Data For The Morini CM 162E

Caliber	4.5 mm (.177)
Weight	Normal: 980 grams
	Junior Model: 960 grams
Total Length	410 mm
Total Height	180 mm
Total Width	50 mm
Length of Sight Line	300 mm to 360 mm
Barrel Length	240 mm
Functioning	Compressed Air
Trigger	Electronic
Weight Of First Trigger Travel	70 grams To 500 grams
Trigger Release Weight	50 grams To 400 grams
Voltage	15 Volts
Battery Life	10,000 firings
Sight Length	4 - 4.5 -5 - 5.5 - 6 mm
Sight Adjustment	Micrometrically Adjustment
Average Pellet Speed	$V^m = 155$ m/s
Number Of Shots Per Cylinder	Normal: 200
	Junior Model: 170

Forming the Shooting Template

The formation of the Shooting Template is really a visual motor reflex loop. This loop becomes more refined or perfect each time you do it. The template formed by this shooting action gets to be more precise each time it is practiced. The formula for this template can be conceptualized as:

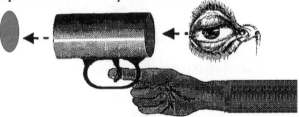

Visual Perception of the sight system
+
A Kinesthetic Reaction
=
The Output: motor response
(the finger is moved)

A kinesthetic reaction, is described by *The American Heritage Dictionary,* (Houghton Mifflin, 1987) as "*the sensation of bodily position, presence, or movement resulting chiefly from stimulation of sensory nerve endings in muscles, tendons, and joints.*" In the case of shooting, our attention is focused on the movement of the finger. To make the movement of the finger instantaneously smooth in launching the contraction of the trigger as a reflex action, we practice smoothly starting the instantaneously movement of the finger to the rear, over and over and over.

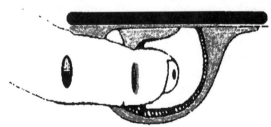

Visual Motor Reflex Loop Process:

❶ Visual Perception of the sight system

The shooter decides to perform the action of moving the trigger finger with the arm extended out from the body while pointing at a place where he wants the impact of the pellet or bullet to strike.

❷ A Kinesthetic reaction occurs

The brain acts on the shooter's intention by sending commands to the arm to rise to the shooting position with the proper hand grip.

❸ The Output:

A motor response sub-program is initiated by the brain and the result is the trigger is moved.

Method:

1. Put your arm out in front of you.
2. Make your wrist firm and your elbow firm.
3. Make a fist in the normal pistol gripping position, that is, with the thumb facing forward and the lower three fingers closed in the palm of the hand.
4. Insert the fingers of your non-shooting hand into the pocket formed by the fingers of your shooting hand.
5. Bend your trigger finger to the position it occupies on the trigger.
6. Now, smoothly move your trigger finger straight back.
7. Focus on the effort to eliminate the sympathetic reaction of the fingers of the trigger hand to move when the trigger finger moves.
8. Repeat steps 1 through 7 for a minimum of ten minutes at a time.
9. Repeat step 8 for a series of 5 times.

As we begin to teach ourselves to shoot, our attention is focused on the movement of the trigger finger. But, that is only in the beginning. Our attention is focused on the trigger finger movement only in the very beginning, until we have established it as a conditional reflex. The reason we put our attention on the movement of the trigger finger is so that we can train this movement to the way we want it to perform when we shoot. We do this so that when we actuate the trigger finger, we do not introduce angular misalignment between the barrel and the eye.

The effort of the beginning shooter is directed toward creating a conditional reflex between the eye, the brain and the finger. We want the trigger finger movement to be initiated as soon as the brain is satisfied with what the eye sees, with respect to the internal alignment of the barrel pointed at the desired area.

Pistol shooters who, through this book, discover that what they know is no longer so, may feel a bit traumatized. The authors suggest that they may want to explore the feasibility of forming peer support groups. Remember, no one understands like someone who's been through it. The authors have had the benefit of having the advantage of being able to be their own support group during the writing of this book. They have *"been there, done that and got the T-Shirt."* In fact, they would still be mired in many of the old concepts without the clarification and support they received from each other as these new concepts were explored and refined.

160

For the past one hundred years alone, untold millions of pistol shooters and instructors have fired untold millions of rounds shooting "misses" or "zeros." The "misses" or "zeros" constituted a loud and clear feedback message that says, "Buddy, that ain't it!"

Their attention has been completely misdirected and focused on an effect, "hitting the target." Methods developed for teaching this are based on ignorance, superstition and throwing stones.

Once the problem is understood, which is "PRECISION POINTING" with a "PRECISION POINTING TOOL," it is a whole new world!

The solution to their dilemma is to realize that they are doing "PRECISION POINTING" with a "PRECISION POINTING TOOL."

The solution for obtaining hits in any desired area is simply a matter of "PRECISION POINTING" with a "PRECISION POINTING TOOL." This applies from a battleship's main 14-inch battery to a hand held pistol. A battleship's main battery has the same requirement as a hand held pistol for aligning the barrel with the eye. With the pistol, we refer to this as internal alignment. For a battleship, the same action is called bore sighting.

Bore Sighting

Chapter 4

Competitive Pistol Shooting, When To Start, What Are The Physical Considerations?

Thinking of competitive pistol shooting?

How precise do you want to point?
Precision pointing takes desire, dedication, time and personal input.

Thinking of competitive pistol shooting? How competitive do you want to be? You have heard the story of the man who went to a dealer to purchase an automobile. He told the dealer, *"I want to drive fast."* The dealer responded with the question, *"How fast do you want to go? All it takes is money."* That is the point of our question, How precise do you want to point? There is the dedication a person has to have who occasionally goes out to shoot at tin cans. There is the dedication a person has to have who goes out to the shooting range once a month or so. Then there is the dedication a person has to have who wants to win an Olympic Shooting Gold Medal. For example, Ralf Schumann, of Germany, the Olympic International Rapid Fire Champion in both 1992 and 1996 says that he fires about six or seven thousand rounds per week. That's .22 caliber shorts in an international rapid fire pistol. Now, that takes desire, dedication, time and personal input. So, consider carefully, **how precise do you want to point?** How much do you desire to become a competitive pistol shooter? Do you just want to shoot in your local club matches? Are your aspirations national? Or, do they also include a desire for international competition? Just What does it take to be above the rest?

Gil Hebard has observed, that it takes a desire which is directed and sustained over a long period of time. *"Desire to improve is a simple thing, but it's surprising how many shooters don't have enough of it to force themselves into directed, sustained action. It is fatal to become satisfied with one's shooting ability, yet many shooters do just that. If some outside force does give them a temporary desire to improve, more often than not that desire is misdirected and the shooter doesn't improve, so he believes he can't*

164

improve and soon reverts to his old bad habits. Some shooters gain 10 years of experience in one year's shooting, others gain one year in 10 years' shooting. The champions belong to the first group, the duffers in the second. You can put yourself in the first group by developing a mental approach that is open minded and scientific in nature. The shooter who has a closed mind, who knows all the answers, will be left standing at the gate. All of our best shooters have this desire to improve, and most of them do. You had better develop it and maintain it, or resign yourself to mediocre shooting the rest of your days." (*The Pistol Shooter's Treasury* edited by Gil Hebard)

Russian Pistol Shooting Starts At Early Age

V.A Kinl', *Shooting With Rifled Weapons*, Moscow, 1989 describes shooting in schools beginning with 9-10 year olds. It was in this book that we realized that the younger the child, the higher the pulse rate: (p. 131)

6-8 year olds average 82-95,
9-10 year olds 72-88,
11 year olds 70-80.

Kinl' also gives a very interesting description of the anatomy, physiology and psychology of school age children. It is surprising how many pistol or rifle coaches do not even consider the anatomical, physiological or psychological factors which have an impact on the pistol training of their young team members.

Women Blamed For The Ineffectiveness Of Their Pistol Instructors

William L. Wells, II, in his book titled, *Shots That Hit*, a "Study of U.S. Coast Guard Marksmanship 1790 - 1985," published by the U.S. Coast Guard Historian's Office, described the problems the women posed with their shooting performance during their pistol training. Wells reports that on December 2, 1976, in a letter from the Reserve Training Center of the United States Coast Guard to OMR-2, C. L. Blaha had some interesting things to say about their female Coast Guard members. The report covered the subject, *"Pistol qualification shooting by USCG women."*

"Small-arms training of the 1970s also included more female Coast Guard members; their training became controversial. The controversy was not over whether women should be trained, but over the weapons they should use. The Reserve Training Center, Yorktown, Virginia, where the majority of female personnel were trained, requested additional .38-caliber revolvers for their training but Headquarters disapproved the request. The Reserve Training Division at Headquarters agreed, stating, "This division would prefer that women not be trained with the .38 revolver, but rather the standard service pistol [.45 caliber M1911 A1]." (*Shots That Hit,* William L. Wells, II)

The firing range personnel at Yorktown were persistent and reported that 210 female shooters were trained between June and August 1976 on the standard U.S. Navy "F" pistol course. The lengthy report explained the reasons that women should not be trained with the .45 caliber M1911 A1 pistol.

The report recommended *"that USCG women be authorized to fire either weapon interchangeably, depending on personal strength and size [physical] demonstration of capability to use either or both weapons."* The report further recommended that once a particular woman was evaluated for weapon type suitability, she would use that weapon only and a certifying statement entered into her service record. The Yorktown Pistol, range personnel outlined their major reasons for supporting this recommendation.

⇒ *"a. The .45-caliber pistol is, in most cases, too heavy for Coast Guard women to fire safely during both timed and rapid fire. Most .45-caliber rounds fired by women during this segment of qualification strike the ground somewhere between the firing point and the target."* (*Shots That Hit,* William L. Wells, II)

166

Wells noted that Surfman Stanley Loyer, of the Coast Guard, made similar remarks about the *"hale and hearty"* surfmen who shot the ground halfway to the target. Loyer made his remarks in the mid-1930's.

⇒ *"b. Most women's hands are not physically large enough to properly grip the weapons and maintain positive control of it between rounds fired.*

⇒ *c. Most women demonstrated a physical strength problem in pulling the .45 slide to the rear. In accomplishing this, the weapon usually was pointed at the shooter next to her or otherwise handled in a manifestly unsafe manner."* (*Shots That Hit*, William L. Wells, II)

The report was neither scientific, nor free of bias. It concluded with a warning that accidents and possible personal injuries could result.

The authors of this book maintain that the problem is not the women trainees in that Coast Guard pistol training program. The problem has to be attributed to the instructors and their instruction information presented to those women. Throughout our research, the student has always been blamed for an ineffectiveness of the instruction information. This is the way it is in every example we have explored in our research.

In training, the proper measurement has to be whether the instructor gets across to the student what he says is his objective. Wells in his book notes, *"One innovation included allowed instructor latitude while maintaining the traditional theories of marksmanship instruction."* This insured that there would be no incentive to explore alternative theories of marksmanship instruction. Even when evaluating the Coast Guard-wide instruction program, the effectiveness of the instruction was noted by Wells in his research. *"There was no improvement in training by the end of 1983. The use of the 1976 practical pistol course came to an end with a meager 61 percent Coast Guard-wide qualification average. This qualification rate mirrored the rate of the Navy "F" pistol course and demonstrated insufficient knowledge of basic marksmanship fundamentals and poor instruction."* So, the authors believe that castigating the female Coast Guard trainees for their inability to learn when exposed to instructors with *insufficient knowledge of basic marksmanship fundamentals and poor instruction* was more a reflection of the inabilities of the instructors than it was of the inability of the women to learn what was being taught. It really represents an inability of the instructors to communicate with their students. In any case, this signalling out the female students for the instructor's inability to communicate, was most certainly not a very gentlemanly thing for the instructors to have done. It seems inconceivable to the authors that these Coast Guard women did not try to do what the instructors told them to do with respect to learning to shoot the pistol. We would pose the question to these Coast Guard Pistol Instructors. *"Do you mean that you told them what you wanted them to do and they refused to do it?"* We are informed by what we consider reliable authority, the **Uniform Code of Military Justice**, that this refusal could have a name. We are told it is called *Mutiny* in the Coast Guard. We believe that if it was within their comprehension, in other words, if these women really understood what the instructors wanted them to do, they would have busted their backs to do it. After all, they were not conscripted into the Coast Guard, they joined willingly and enthusiastically.

We believe that this blaming of the student is not endemic to the Coast Guard. It is a macrocosmic example of what has been prevalent throughout a great part of pistol instruction in the United States. There is no way anyone can even speculate that the pistol instructors have deliberately tried to sabotage their students. What they have done is to destroy their students through commendable good intentions. They have tried to give the students too much of the **good stuff**, much, much too soon. It is not a minor overload of a pistol shooting student, it is a cataclysmic overload of the student's physical capabilities. To stand a chance of success, the information must be reduced to two elements to remain within the student's capability of performance.

What the Coast Guard Historian's Office has done is to give us documentation of an example of this type of justification used by pistol instructors for the failure of their training, We believe that what the Coast Guard experienced was not a shooter or pistol instructor failure, but a management failure. It was a definite management failure for using a training system based on

168

or pistol instructor failure, but a management failure. It was a definite management failure for using a training system based on ignorance and superstition. What other Coast Guard training curricula expect that over 50% of their graduates will be certified as being proficient when they achieve a 49% out of 100% on each of their qualification exams?

If Coast Guard shipboard navigation were based on principles similar to their smallarms pistol training, they would never get a cutter out of a channel. Can you imagine a navigation failure of 50%? Can you imagine turning over cutter navigation to a certified navigator who scored in the 49th percentile of his basic navigation class?

Kids And Competitive Pistol Shooting In The USA

It has been known for years that youngsters as young as 9 years of age have been introduced to pistol shooting in countries other than the United States. How successfully can youngsters this young be introduced to shooting training? Hickey has introduced 8-year olds and one 7-year old girl to pistol training. Hickey cautions that 7 and 8 year olds need the coach's complete attention. In working with youngsters in this age bracket, it is extremely important that the coach keep it simple. No big words like *concentrate*. Through out the work with 7, 8 and 9 year olds, it is important that the coach convey by the tone of his voice on just what the youngster should focus.. For example, put emphasis on the word **hard**, when saying to the youngster, *"Look Hard at the front sight!* At ages 7 and 8, the youngsters have to be led into the discipline of shooting through work off the extended benchrest. We start youngsters this age at 10 meters, firing at blank targets. Kids this young can still keep 5 out of five shots on a blank 8 ½ x 11 inches piece of paper at that distance.

Judging by the results we have obtained in Tucson, Arizona, we can say unequivocally that starting youngsters at these young ages has been a great success. For example, consider the scores fired by the kids in the 1996 Tucson Handgun City Championship. These scores were fired on the Tucson Rod and Gun Club Outdoor Shooting Range in Tucson, Arizona. The National Match Course consisted of 10 shots Slow Fire at 50 yards, 10 shots Timed Fire at 25 yards in 20 seconds and 10 shots Rapid Fire at 25 yards in 10 seconds. The NRA Short Course, with all firing at 25 yards, consisted of 10 shots Slow Fire, 10 shots Timed Fire in 20 seconds and 10 shots Rapid Fire in 10 seconds. Take a good look at both their ages and their scores.

Some Scores Fired In The
1996 Tucson City Junior Handgun Championship

Name	Amount of Time in the Tucson Pistol Training Program	Age	National Match Course	NRA Short Course
Cade Wilson	2 years	14	263	257
Jason Neill	1 year	13	242	244
Bugsy Barstow	1 year	11	244	232
Jeff Planteen	1 year	15	236	217
Danielle Dancho	5 months	16	226	217
Geoff Barstow	1 year	13	229	242
Grant Morgan	1 year	12	229	224

Figure 4-1

Can you set up a similar program in your own club? Yes. We will show how to do this in Chapter 5.

American pistol shooters have traditionally been reluctant to offer pistol shooting training to youngsters below the age of 16 or 17. They have misconstrued the nature of pistol shooting, and followed the universally accepted dogma, that kids need good

170

upper body strength before they should be started on shooting a pistol.

It has been the experience of the instructors and coaches involved in the Tucson Pistol Training Program, that we have had considerable success with youngsters who are aged nine and above. Do these nine year old youngsters have much upper body strength? Are you kidding? They are nine year old kids and they inhabit nine year old bodies! Do they have enough strength to hold up a pistol? No problem! Can they score points at 50 and 25 yards in pistol tournaments? This they have done! It is now a part of the history of our sport here in Arizona. Their scores and their ages are already in the Arizona score books of our pistol shooting sport. One of our nine year olds out-scored the adult Bronze medal winner for the women in this year's 1996 Grand Canyon State Games over the NRA 900 course of fire by 138 points. Was she anywhere near as strong as that lady? No way! What she had though, was three months of training in our Tucson Pistol Training Program. In the normal course of the old pistol training method, no nine year old girl would be expected to score 138 points in that type of course of fire.

So, when can you start competitive pistol training? Given the proper pistol training program, we say age nine will do nicely. However, that is not to say that should an eight year old come along with the proper self-discipline and a good attention span, we would exclude that shooter.

What are the physical considerations? The shooter has to be able to raise the pistol to eye level and move the finger instantaneously smooth. The shooters in our Tucson Pistol Training Program start off by lifting a gallon water bottle filled with about three pounds of water or sand. Once they are able to lift it from a table, and bring it to eye level, we encourage them to see if they can repeat that action. We ask that they set up a schedule at home where they can perform a series of such repetitions. We believe this will give anyone the type of training which will enable them to enter competition and perform acceptably. We also encourage that the beginning shooter do a series of pushups on their fingertips. The objective of our training is to show the shooter how to develop stamina as opposed to upper body strength.

171

We even put a special emphasis on this by including a fingertip pushup contest in each of the USA Shooting or NRA Registered Pistol Tournaments we sponsor. We have even developed special rules to provide structure to this part of our program. See Chapter 5 for an example of the rules we use. In Chapter 5, we also show an example of how we play up the results.

Child Development
And
Pistol Shooting

In the case of youngsters, we must remember that they gain control of the larger muscles, those of the shoulders and limbs, first. It is as a result of knowing that this control is developed first, that we encourage our youngsters to practice the repetition of raising a gallon water jug with three pounds of water or sand in it, to eye level and then back down to 45 degrees. We must not expect youngsters to acquire immediately, movements of the trigger finger sufficiently precise to move the trigger upon recognition that the sight alignment has reached the area of the target where they want an indicator to appear. But since we get all things in life through action, we must remember that motor tracts need as careful training as sensory tracts, and that *there may be undeveloped motor, as well as sensory, cells in the central nervous system.* These spots will remain permanently undeveloped, unless they receive the proper modification while still plastic.

Yev'yev, in his book, *Competitive Shooting*, points out, *"Through the process of training, the plasticity of the cerebral cortex increases, in other words, its capability of forming new, temporary connections faster and of reconstructing old connections increases. Moreover, the capability is developed for a more acute reaction to stimulation corresponding to its magnitude and which is associated with the work of muscles. In this case, the training associated with the primary activities of one*

172

sensory organ can have a progressive influence on the activities of other sensory organs connected with it. To take advantage of this, the shooter must strive in his training to vary his different shooting exercises as much as possible, since this increases his ability to subsequently master new motions faster and to improve on the accomplishment of those already known. In the final analysis, this ensures the improvement of competition results and their consistency under different shooting conditions. Through the training process, stable conditional reflex connections are formed in time into a dynamic stereotype." There are those persons who in vain try in middle life to acquire the necessary correlation of movements for swimming. These movements could have been gained easily and pleasantly while the motor cells were plastic, and in many cases, drowning might thus have been avoided. We also occasionally see persons of both sexes, not over thirty, who, from lack of early motor development, cannot balance themselves sufficiently to learn to ride a skateboard or roller blades.

Roughly speaking, the plasticity of nerve cells is inversely proportional to a person's age. A lumberjack may sharpen his ax as well next week or next year; a man owning mineral land may mine the coal now or wait twenty years, as he chooses, knowing that it will not deteriorate. But the nervous system can be effectively trained only in youth. An adult pistol shooter may be approximately defined as the sum of his youthful nerve reactions, which tend to perpetuate themselves.

Youthful nerve cells are like freshly mixed plaster of Paris, and, like it, they soon lose their plasticity. Many things can be done with the youthful nervous system. But, if the conditional reflex training is deferred, it will soon be too late to accomplish much. Habits are early formed, and after they have once become fixed, they rule us with the grasp of a *Superman.* If you, being a right handed person, have ever tried eating with your left hand, you know what I am talking about. If not, try it today. Hickey started eating with his left hand some 40 years ago. He now has the same full automatic control eating with his left hand as with his right. But, he started training his left hand when he was not yet 17 years of age.

173

Investigations of the growth and increase in weight of the nervous system have served to emphasize the necessity for early training. Vierordt gives the average weight in grams of the male brain at various ages as follows:

New-born child	381 grams
1 year	945 grams
5 years	1263 grams
10 years	1408 grams
15 years	1490 grams
20 years	1445 grams
25 years	1431 grams

Figure 9-2

These figures show that the male brain attains its maximum weight by the age of fifteen. The female brain reaches its maximum slightly earlier, between ten and fourteen.

Youthful nerve cells possess a remarkable power of regeneration and recuperation. A young person recovers quickly from over-fatigue. The old frequently never completely recover from such fatigue, or if they recover at all, progress is very slow. Now, fatigue is a condition of advancement, for this comes as the result of work. The quicker the recuperation, the sooner the work can be again resumed. In this respect, especially, does youth have a vast advantage over age.

We ought not only to begin training the nervous system early, but this training should produce the desired result. We set up the training so that a simple sensation is followed by an invariable motor reaction of the same kind. In this case, it is the eye recognizing the acquisition of the pre-selected target area, with the sights being precisely lined up with the eye. The invariable motor reaction is the instantaneous smooth movement of the trigger finger.

The young person embarking on a pistol training program needs to have the absolute necessity of early training impressed on him. Many shooters drift along feeling that they have plenty of time to develop their skill. Many have the feeling that it will happen by-and-by. We are reminded of something Rueben Post Halleck once wrote, *"here is one motto which a study of the nervous system specially impresses on us"*

"By the streets of By-and-By,
one arrives at the house of Never."

In pistol shooting, it is simply necessary that the foundation for future success must have been laid by a proper youthful development of the central nervous system. Or, as Blankenship has shown us, it will take a very deliberate effort with total dedication and an extremely powerful work ethic to establish the foundation necessary for future improvement in pistol competition.

Halleck notes: *"The modifiability which is characteristic of the nervous organism as a whole during its earliest stages, continues to show itself in each individual organ until its evolution is complete. Thus it is a matter of universal experience that every kind of training for special aptitudes is both far more effective, and leaves a far more permanent impress, when exerted on the growing organism, than when brought to bear on the adult. The effect of such training is shown in the tendency of the organ to 'grow to' the mode in which it is habitually exercised..."*

When Hickey was 16 or 17 years old, he came home from school each day and set up a dry firing range in the driveway of his front yard. Although he did not know it at the time, those hours spent developing his trigger finger movement so as not to disturb the sight alignment, were responsible for any medals and shooting honors he subsequently won. *The effect of such training is shown in the tendency of the organ to 'grow to' the mode in which it is habitually exercised,* which was what my eyeball recognized as perfect sight alignment and smooth trigger finger movement. Hickey laments that this book was not available at the time he started shooting, so that he could have more deliberately trained his eye/trigger finger combination to a conditional reflex.

What research has demonstrated, in recent years, is that the unconscious mind may understand and respond to meaning from emotional responses and guide most actions. Research has shown that much of this response is largely independent of conscious awareness. The studies show that people are guided far more than they know by the unconscious mind. In fact, a lot

175

of perception is automatic and independent of conscious intention or awareness. The pistol shooter needs to understand that the subconscious is there to help. However, the shooter is responsible for guiding the subconscious in what kind of help to provide.

For example, Benjamin Libet, a professor of physiology at the University of California, San Francisco, conducted research measuring brain waves. In his study, the subjects were instructed to flex a hand spontaneously, and with the aid of an electronic device, he was able to register the millisecond at which the subjects became aware of their intent to move. That movement was generally two-tenths of a second before the movement actually occurred.

Libet found that the subjects' brain waves showed that the brain started to initiate the movement about four-tenths of a second before a person is aware of wanting to do it. Libet said, *"This means that you don't initiate voluntary actions consciously, but decide to make them somewhere in the brain outside of awareness. The part of the mind that becomes aware of a decision to act is not the part that decides; a person's decisions come to him already made."* So, the pistol shooter, attempts to overcome the effects of gravity and negate the laws of motion on that piece of metal at the end of his arm. He does this by a conscious attempt to make the arc of the pistol's movement smaller. This interrupts the subconscious process. The pistol shooter, using the current training methods, feels he has to have control and does not allow his subconscious to take over. We see this during every club training session. The beginning pistol shooter pays full attention to the task of bringing the pistol to eye level and triggering the shot when the sights reach the desired area. Then as the shooter masters that task, he pays less and less attention to raising the pistol to eye level and triggering the shot. What happens is that the shot goes instantaneously smoothly, actuated in the subconscious.

When an error in an automatic routine occurs, it enters the consciousness. We know that one of the main functions of the conscious seems to be making repairs in routines where a slip has occurred.

176

Chapter 5

The Junior Pistol Shooting Club/Team

The State of Junior Pistol Shooting In America.

Then and Now!

The future is brighter than we have known in the past. So, we will begin with the now and future of junior pistol shooting training here in America. One event occurred in 1993. Charlie Jackson built a state-of-the-art indoor shooting range, which even includes some electronic scoring targets, in Poway, California. With 50 meters and all of the ranges in between, including air pistol, Jackson limited the facility to pistol shooting. In addition, Jackson set up an entity to provide for the maintenance and upkeep of that facility. It is known as the Black Mountain Shooting Club.

The club is organized to accept both senior and junior members. In the beginning, Jackson provides juniors a basic introduction to pistol marksmanship, then gives the youngsters an opportunity to train on the range, as their time and interest permits. Ammunition and pistols are provided. If the youngster stays interested and practices his pistol training for about a year, he is encouraged to purchase his own pistol. If these youngsters want individual coaching, they are permitted to seek it from other sources. One youngster we interviewed indicated he had his own personal coach.

Jackson also takes those youngsters showing exceptional talent aside, providing them coaching from himself. In addition, the Black Mountain Shooting Club provides support to the youngsters in Jackson's program by providing funding for them when entering matches specified by Jackson. He even took a dozen or so of the youngsters to New Zealand for a match. They had an excellent shoot in New Zealand, winning the Sport Pistol Team Match, beating the Australian Junior National Team in the process. This program offers exceptional promise for providing a significant upgrade of America's international pistol prospects.

The Junior Pistol Shooting Club is, at this time in America, pretty much of an anomaly. When such a group exists, it often revolves around the National Rifle Association and it's affiliated Rifle and Pistol Clubs. Most shooting clubs in the United States share a common range facility accommodating both rifle and pistol interest groups. The NRA Club is often the first contact for all those juniors interested in beginning pistol shooting instruction. Those who aspire to the Olympics or other international competition then gravitate to shooting in competitions conducted under *USA Shooting* auspices. This is because *USA Shooting* is the National Governing Body of the Shooting Sports in the United States. But, there are many paths to the Olympic. One is the 4-H shooting sports club. The Boy

Scouts Explorer Program offers another opportunity to refine marksmanship skills.

The problem is that, while these groups do a good job at introducing an ever expanding core of people to recreational shooting, they are not organized to produce Olympic level shooting athletes. Neither, of course, do they make any claim to do so.

The focus of this chapter is on training juniors for international pistol competition. There are many other forms of recreational pistol shooting and this chapter will touch briefly on them. Shooters are considered juniors until December 31st of the calendar year in which their twentieth birthday occurs.

The first contact a junior typically should have with a junior club is through a basic pistol safety and marksmanship training course. In fact, juniors who decide to practice with the club and earn USA Shooting Junior Olympic Qualification Program certificates and brassards, need first to have successfully passed just such a training course. This requirement is part of the first qualification rating.

Interview With A Typical American Junior Pistol Coach

The guiding impetus behind the production of this book was the determination to first, find out why American pistol shooters have continued to do so poorly in competition with their peers in the Olympics of several decades. Second, to see if American training methods were in line with sports medicine research known facts. In the course of our research, it became completely apparent that American pistol training was pervaded with myths which had been elevated to the status of fundamentals. Many of the pistol techniques run completely counter to recognized research results. Bill Blankenship, six times US National Pistol Champion, provided the first written account of how to acquire the kind of habit which needs to be developed in order to become a champion pistol shooter. It is this technique which is an integral part of this book. This book will show you methods of training which will allow you to train juniors in the Blankenship manner.

We surveyed quite a few of the junior pistol programs around the United States. Many of the replies were made by people like Larry N.C. Forman of Billerica, Massachusetts who wrote, *"I'm pleased to offer whatever help I can, in the interests of promoting Jr. Pistol Shooting."* George E. Alves, of New Castle, Delaware provided a very insightful picture of the development of the shooting sports in his area. Hickey's daughter, Sharon, at age nine, fired the full NRA Prone events at Camp Perry at the same time George's daughter, Ethel Ann was shooting there.

This portion of the chapter which we have called an interview is typical of the way training is conducted in American junior pistol training. It is a compilation of the responses we received from this survey and *is not an actual interview*. It is merely a literary device. There is no consistency in the relationship of the terms, *Coach 1, Coach 2,* or *Coach 3,* to the names of the coaches who participated in this survey.

Question: Do you have a junior pistol program?

> **Coach 1:** *We do not have a junior pistol program or air pistol program. We do have rifle and encourage them to try pistol. We do have good rifle program. We do the International 3 position shooting. We've been doing air rifle for about 10 years. In that time two of our shooters made the national junior development team. We generally start our juniors at about age 12. Once in a while, we start them at 10 or 11 years. We have a very strong junior rifle program and do cross over into air rifle. Some of older kids carry on with the rifle program in high school. Right now it is considered a varsity sport. Our club provides everything for the program*
>
> **Coach 2:** *There is no specific "class start up" date. Monday evenings is our range time. A youngster*

can start on any Monday evening, except holidays, bad weather conditions, etc. The first step is orientation which takes about 1 to 2 hours depending upon the interest and the questions asked by the youngster or parents. Such orientation covers:

⇒ *what is the program about*
⇒ *what are the objective*
⇒ *appreciation & basic use of firearms*
⇒ *participating in another sport (a lifetime sport)*
⇒ *learning mental discipline*
⇒ *sportsmanship*
⇒ *competing against peers*
⇒ *discussion of firearm safety*
⇒ *NRA "Gun Safety Rules"*
⇒ *NRA "A Parents Guide to Gun Safety"*
⇒ *discussion of Range Safety Rules*
⇒ *discussion of the particular firearm*
⇒ *NRA's "A Guide to Firearm Operation"*
⇒ *Checking for dominant eye*
⇒ *and finally registering youngster for the program*

The fees cover such expenses as awards, club memberships (NRA, USA Shooting, and local club fees.)

The youngster starts shooting the first day (THIS IS MOST IMPORTANT!) The youngster is given instruction as needed during subsequent practice sessions.

The length of the practice session is about two hours.

As the youngster progresses in the program, additional reading material is given or lent to the youngster and (USAMU Shooting Guides, books on pistol shooting, books and literature on mental training). The youngsters who attend the National JOSC also receive "professional" training at the clinics.

We encourage match competition as soon as possible (local matches, JOSC's). The program consists of

181

a few "lectures" and much "guided" shooting by trained dedicated instructors.

Comment: This is a very common occurrence in America. Junior pistol training is often a sideline. Charlie Jackson, a coach in Ohio, Don Davis, and Bob Mason, in Shelton, Washington, have the only programs of which we are aware iin which the entire emphasis is on pistol. Most programs have a low age limit of about 12 years for starting their shooters.

Question: At what age do you start youngsters in your junior pistol program?

Coach 1: *I've found that most Juniors under the age of 12 are seldom large enough or strong enough to safely handle and hold steady enough to aim a .22lr or match grade air pistol, however there are exceptions! Generally, I feel by attempting to train them before they are physically capable will only discourage them and "turn them off" because of their inability to compete. In order to help alleviate this problem, I choose Browning Buckmarks for my .22 target pistols. These guns are lightweight, highly reliable and with 2 different grips (the larger one is weighted with thumb rests) sizes available Buckmarks can be fitted across a wide range of hand sizes from childrens hands up to and including most adults.*

Coach 2: *What age to start juniors in shooting?. Around here, we say as soon as they can hold a gun and can follow instructions, i.e. of sufficient maturity. For air pistol, our youngest starting youngster was a boy 7 years, 9 months. The youngest to start shooting one hand, a boy 8 years, 2 months and a girl 8 ½ years. Both of these after starting with bench rest and working towards one hand. We should start youngsters as soon as* *possible or we will lose them to soccer, Little League, and other school activities.*

Coach 3: *I teach in a Middle School, so I get the kids from 6th grade to 8th grade. They're probably between 11 and 12 years of age. I recruit kids from the school. Generally, I have more than half the kids who are in the 8th grade, the 6th and 7th graders make up the remaining half. Usually, I start out with about 20 kids. One year I started with 65. The way I recruit the kids is I go around to teachers classrooms and I put it on the school announcements, that sort of thing. I started this in 1978 and been doing it each year since then. I talk to the teachers ahead of time. Those who let me, I go in and talk to the kids. The teachers who don't want me to visit their classrooms, I leave alone.*

Comment: Under the training program proposed in this book, the youngsters are actively discouraged from attempting to hold the handgun up for extended hold times. Therefore they only must be physically capable of lifting the gun to eye position. This does not require any inordinate amount of strength.

Because of the nature of our training, we have selected Ruger .22 caliber pistols for our club. We have 5 Ruger Mark II's and 7 Ruger .22/45's. Both of these handguns have firing pins which do not protrude beyond the face of the bolt. This means the guns may be dry fired without peening the face of the chamber. In our training, we fire a live shot, then immediately recover the sights and dry fire another shot. So, when we fire our one-handed, standing-on-our-hind-feet 20 shots groups at 25 yards, our guns get a lot of dry firing work.

We especially like the Ruger .22/45's because of their straight grip. We find this type of grip to be very efficient in the nature of the work placed on the various muscles in the Act of Shooting.

We have found that taking them from a little past 9 years of age is about right. At that age, we have found that they have good attention span and are starting the responsibility maturation process. You know traditionally we have assumed that beginning pistol shooters had to have a lot of upper body strength to engage in a systematic pistol training program. I have found that is not exactly an accurate picture of what pistol shooting is. It requires stamina. Of course stamina does not mean to have to bulk up or to build up the muscles. We have found that our little 9 year old girls can shoot tight groups with the air pistol and the 22.caliber pistols. We focus much of our training on firing from the bench rest, both dry firing and with ammunition. One thing which drives our program is what Yev'yev, in his book, **Competitive Shooting**, points out, *"it should be kept in mind that additional external stimuli also create additional foci of stimulation and can disrupt these unreinforced connections. This occurs during the initial period of training when temporary connections in the cortex have not yet been reinforced. In the subsequent course of training, however, conditional reflexes become solidly established, the completion of an exercise becomes automatic, and extraneous stimuli do not have a harmful influence. Consequently, in the initial steps of training, the shooter must have ideal conditions for perfecting the technique of shooting. It is in this phase of training that he must work out the separate elements of shooting techniques so to firmly reinforce them and to make them automatic. Then, after mastering the complex series of actions needed to produce a shot, he start training under less ideal conditions, including different meteorological conditions, competition conditions and intentionally complicated conditions. In this manner, stable conditional reflex connections and firm motor skills which can accommodate themselves to variable shooting conditions will be worked out."*

Question: How and why did you start your junior pistol training program?

    Coach 1: *We do not have a junior pistol program or air pistol. I was disappointed to learn that when* *the JOSC ended, the kids had no program or opportunity to practice their newly acquired skills until the next JOSC. This seemed such a waste of talent and enthusiasm, I decided to offer a on-going Jr. Program, to promote JR. OLYMPIC Pistol Shooting. My club gave me permission to operate a program and supported my efforts with: the club's liability Insurance, expenses for ammo and targets, and team entry fees, and providing us with reserved range time on the indoor range. At first, I offered just .221r pistol and only during the school year. I was pleasantly surprised to find that there.was a demand to operate the program nearly all year long, especially considering that several important tournaments take place during the summer and the kids wanted to participate and naturally be at their best. I've adjusted the Program accordingly and now we operate nearly all year around, with several long breaks of 2-4 weeks spread out through the year.*

Coach 2: *When we started, it was my intention to prepare the kids shooting pistol to then go into the high school rifle program when they got over there. That has worked pretty well, except that once the kids got to shooting pistol, they thought it was a real kick in the pants. So, they didn't really want to have to move a big heavy gun. I think shooting pistol sort of spoiled them.*

Comment: *Coach 1* has an outstanding example of a local club supporting the development of a junior pistol training program. These supporting elements are essential for a junior pistol program:

⇒ the club's liability Insurance
⇒ expenses for ammo and targets
⇒ team entry fees
⇒ providing reserved range time on the indoor range

185

Coach 2 shows a different kind of philosophy. Under the Art Sievers program, the attitude is shape them up on the pistol before you put them on the rifle. Once they have the concept of lining up the barrel with their eye and moving the trigger finger smoothly, put them on the rigid rifle system and you will see outstanding results. And a number of them have gone on to the rifle.

Question: What kind of training program do you have the youngsters on for the pistol?

> **Coach 1:** *I basically try to get them to concentrate on sight picture and hold. Done nothing on physical training yet. Have a senior lady and I've picked up some bits and pieces here and there with weights and things like that and I'm going to get her started on that. Basically we take the skills they've learned in rifle and show how the same skills, breathing and stuff can be related to pistol. No formal program to follow. Hope your new book can help us. I'm new at working with the kids in a formal program for pistol shooting. I've been shooting and self taught because there is nothing available in the area where I live. I started with silhouettes and worked into bullseye shooting. I then sort of worked out of the 2700 game and worked into international style shooting. I've talked to another pistol coach and he more or less gave me a few tips. I take the **NRA Shooting Sports** and my own kids get the **Insights**. So I read them, and I find I get a lot of stuff out of that. I can build up and really get the basics. I find it to be a good source, pretty condensed and in terms written for kids and I've found it to be helpful. I can see your book might give me a whole lot of help.*

The Junior Pistol Shooting Club/Team

Coach 2: *The youngest begin shooting using two hands off a bench rest, and working toward shooting with one hand.*

Coach 3: *I use Art Sievers' program. What I do is have the kids start shooting from off a bench rest. I have them dry firing, using the Daisy Model 717. I was using the Smith & Wesson, but they got to be too expensive. I usually have them dry firing for the first two sessions. Usually, by the end of the second day, we start firing some pellets. Most of the time, the kids lose interest in just coming down and popping air. After that, I start them off each session doing some dry firing, calling their attention to looking at the sights and moving the trigger finger smoothly. When a kid questions me about why we spend so much time on the looking at the sights and moving the finger, I tell him the truth. I tell him that if he is just going to come down and keep looking at the paper, trying to punch holes in it, then he's wasting my time and I'm wasting his time. I tell him, shooting is not a hitting game, it is a pointing game.*

I keep the kids working on the basics from when we start in October until Christmas. And when I say basics, I mean only lining up the barrel with the eye and moving the trigger finger smoothly. But, after Christmas, those kids who are interested in competition, I work with getting them ready. Usually, that involves going up to Seattle to shoot in the Junior Olympics. The school provides a bus. It makes for a long day, but the kids have a lot of fun. One year we won the National Sub-Junior Team Championship, Then, one of my shooters, Kelly Morris, won the Individual Junior Championship for three years in a row.

What I do with the kids is keep them on the bench rest, training them to recognize what they want to see in order to get a good group. What

I'm doing is training their conditional reflex where the trigger finger moves real smooth when the eye sees the sights in the area of the target they want them in. I start training their conditional reflex from the first shot. That's why we work on the bench rest so often. If they've never seen what a ten looks like so they can repeat it off the bench rest, how can they ever see it consistently when they have it held up by one hand. Don't get me wrong, most of our time is spent working with the sights pointed at a blank target. But, you see, you train the conditional reflex off the bench. My kids never see a bullseye target until after Christmas. You see, the bullseye is a distraction if you are actively training the kids' conditional reflex.

Then when they're shooting good groups off the bench, you stand them up and have them work with two hands holding the air pistol. Once they get good groups with the two handed methods, stand them up shooting one hand. But, you have to be certain they get their sight alignment through their stance. Otherwise, the conditional reflex will not work. If the trigger is not moved real fast and real smooth when the eye sees the sights where the kid wants them on the target, then that's not it. They got to put the gun down and re-establish their sight alignment through their position.

I never stop talking to the kids about moving the trigger finger real smooth when the sights are lined up with their eye and pointed where they want them on the target. Even after Kelly won his championships, that is what we would talk about. You know, how his sight looked. We talked about body position as it relates to sight alignment. I'd have him bring the pistol up to eye level, get into a relax position, and then move the whole unit to where he wanted to point on the target.

Comment: This effort to draw the attention of the beginning youngsters to sight picture and hold is the dominant feature of the American pistol shooting training program at all of the club level programs we have

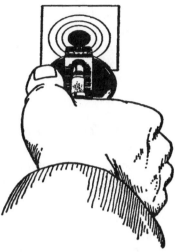

investigated. It is symptomatic of what ails the pistol shooting program for beginning shooters. First, the shooter's attention is drawn to the sight picture. Now, let us understand what sight picture means in the parlance of the pistol shooting trainer. It is the alignment of the sights on the pistol with the target. What we have found to be more efficient at teaching a beginner to shoot a pistol is to draw his or her attention to the alignment of the sights with the eye. Notice, the one big difference between what we do in our initial instruction is to show the beginner how to line up the barrel with the eye. **It is inefficient and by it's very nature, designed to produce random shots if the sights are lined up with the target and then the eye is laid over to the barrel.**

We agree with Yev'yev's reason for using a blank target. He says, *"This requires less concentration on the pattern of the firearm's oscillations and prevents switching from one dominant activity to another. This allows the motor center in the cerebral cortex, which is responsible for the functioning of the finger flexor muscles, to remain dominant.*

Question: What type of character development methods do you employ?

> **Coach 1:** *Oh, for one thing, I will not permit my shooters to bug the tournament officials to find out*

their scores. But, I have no objection to the kids knowing the scores of other shooters before they shoot. I think it builds character to be able to perform up to your skill level even when you have the pressure of knowing the score your opponent shot.

Coach 2: *As a result of the methods I employ, when inviting a Junior to join my year round program, I tend to encourage those Juniors that are used to exercising self-discipline and are high achievers in school. The points I try to emphasize directly in a sit-down conference with each new junior and his parents are:*

⇒ *I will NEVER lie to you! You must promise to NEVER lie to me, including lies by omission!*

⇒ *My program requires a long-term commitment from both the Junior and his parents if we are to be successful in reaching our goals.*

⇒ *Whenever you are with me, I will try to always treat you as if you were a member of my own family.*

⇒ *I refuse to waste my time with undisciplined children, so if you are not willing to learn and practice what I teach, we aren't going to do well together.*

⇒ *I will treat you as an adult and you must act accordingly whenever around guns and/or at a shooting facility. I will arrange "PLAY TIME" occasionally, so you can behave as a NORMAL KID BUT ONLY WHEN I have expressly given permission "TO RELAX AND PLAY"!*

⇒ *Failure to remain a citizen in good standing in your community and in your school will likely result in suspension from my programs.*

⇒ *My goal is to prepare you to earn an invitation to join the Junior Olympic Development Team and then perhaps, someday represent the United States of America in an Olympic Games Pistol event. However, while winning is great stuff, that is NOT what my program emphasizes! I believe honor, ethics, and performing at your personal best is what is important, and if we win something that's swell, but not my main goal!*

By clearly establishing codes of behavior (for both of us) and with mutual promises to back them up, new juniors are more open to my inputs, more trusting and willing to try new things and ultimately they progress faster than otherwise. My best students are usually used to performing under similar conditions at home, and I've found another excellent student to train! On the other hand, I've accepted students that were borderline and nearly flunking out of school, who were afraid I would throw them out of my program and are now beginning to bring home B's and A's! Most of "MY KIDS" continue on to college, and I've even had some limited success with High School dropouts resuming their education. I think if kids feel they can trust you, can count on you to "be there" if needed, are capable of achieving nearly anything asked of them!

Comment: Coach 2 has an excellent program orientation method. We are indebted to Larry N.C. Forman for sharing this with us. If you are going to be involved in coaching junior shooters, then this is something you should seriously think about adopting for use in your program.

Question: What we've done is look at past information. You see no one in the past has looked critically at the information that's available in the public domain to see if it has been doing the job it was presumed to be doing. A lot of information has been built up mythologically through someone's theory who has been a shooter and because it sounded reasonable people just repeated it. What we have done, is scrutinized this. For example, are you familiar with the *Army Marksmanship Pistol Manual?*

> **Coach:** *Yes, that's where I've learned what I've learned.*

Question: We think on about page 42 or something like that, they have a listing of what you have to do to fire an accurate shot. I think they have 61 of those items. When you are teaching a kid how to shoot could he remember our two fundamentals and master them or would he be able to remember the 61 things to fire one accurate shot?

> **Coach:** *Right, I can see your point.*

Question: In other words the basic information these people have provided has actually worked against these kids or these people going to those books. Its actually worked against what might have actually been their ability.

> **Coach:** *What we have been telling the kids is the basics, relax, breathe, aim and squeeze. That's basically what I've been telling them. Do those four things while you are trying to keep that front sight in sharp focus and doing the rest of it. Some kids it works and some kids it doesn't work. We're trying and hopefully someday we'll get more pistol shooters than rifle shooters.*

Comment: This is normal, except that often the junior coaches and instructors have seven to ten fundamentals. Many of these so-called fundamentals are actually

192

distractions to the act of getting well aimed shots out the barrel of the pistol.

Question: Where and how do you do your recruiting for the pistol team/club?.

> **Coach:** *We run the NRA personal protection course, I'm not one of the instructors on it, but the head of the Junior club is, and he has a police officer who was also involved at one time in the Junior program and another gentleman who was involved in the junior program. Between the three of them they do it with adults and it has gone from a gun club thing to an adult education course. They promote it as personal protection/handgun safety. We are explaining the guns and the Eddie Eagle program behind it in the local kindergartens, 1st and 2nd grades and these kids are remembering it from year to year and coming back and hopefully we are going to get a feeder program that way when they get old enough they can get into our junior programs.*

Comment: In Tucson, we conduct Handgun Safety Education Courses for the general public. Often we identify a gun as a firearm, pistol or revolver. Well, we've stopped doing that and we now call it a handgun. A Handgun Safety Education Course as a result at going to this approach, the media here in Tucson grabbed a hold of it and highlighted this Handgun Safety Education Course on 3 prime-time networks here with 137,000 households, So nearly a quarter million people probably watched it as it carried a very uplifting message across the video waves, all in a very positive note. Not a negative thing about it at all and we think a lot of it had to do with using the term handgun.

Question: What influences outside of your club have you identified as helpful to your program?

Coach 1: *As we can afford another Crosman, we do kind of another trade off. We can put another cylinder in and not worry about bulky tanks and the accuracy on them is very good. But we've had no shooters up to Olympic caliber. We've had a couple of shooters on the National Team come up and shoot our matches and promote interest. So, we are starting to get the names and people are starting to recognize them and saying maybe someday I can shoot like him. They are seeing them shooting, and shooting with them, and we tell them you can beside an Olympic shooter and he is just like shooting beside your friend. We saw it happen a couple years ago when we had a pistol match and a couple of shooters who were on the development team were shooting side by side with our kids. It kind of promoted the attitude of "hey we can do this too!" We saw some good results from that. Just the exposure for the kids like you say puffed them up and made them feel good they were shooting in the same matches with these people. So we try to take our kids all over when we can. Last weekend we brought six juniors to shoot up in a local tournament for their spring championships. It was a good experience for them.*

Coach 2: *This past year "MY KIDS" did rather well for themselves (aged 12-15), they swept the Jr Air Pistol medals at the Bay State Games with Gold, Silver, and Bronze medals, and in Sept they set 3 new Jr Team National Records in .22, CF, and .45. I'm very proud of "MY KIDS" and I've just received State level authority to field a Jr PISTOL Team to the Nationals this summer at Camp Perry! This will be the first JR Mass Pistol team ever! A co-ed team, too! I am truly certifiable! Ho! Ho! Wish me luck!*

Coach 3: *Our DSPC Jr. Division air pistol shooters have done well. Each year at least one* *receives an invitation to compete in the National JOSC. One of our members, Carl Elkins, was the National Junior Olympic Air Pistol Champion for three consecutive years. He then graduated high school, went working in the crafts and the next year with little practice, took 2nd place at the National JOSC.*

Comment: One influence on a well developed junior program is the desire of parents and others to try to help the kid to improve his or her shooting performance. With that in mind, some figure that what they need to do is to get the kid a membership in a local gym where he can work out with weights. If you have such a situation, then read what Yev'yev, in his book, **Competitive Shooting**, points out, *"as sports medicine research has shown, the acute muscular-articular sensation developed for shooting disciplines is dulled considerably if the shooter uses auxiliary training exercises which require excessive muscular effort with heavy loads. This means that the shooter, after spending many years developing a fine, distinguishing capability of the motor analyzer, can significantly lower that capability if he practices those forms of sport which are associated with heavy physical overloads such as gymnastics on apparatus and weight lifting."*

We can very well relate to **Coach 2.** On a extremely windy Friday afternoon, four of the youngsters in our Tucson Pistol Training Program, ages 11 to 14, broke this coach's *Woburn Sportsman's Assocication's* National Junior 4-Person Pistol Team Record of 874-10X over the .22 caliber National Match Course. The news release had this to say:

Sample News Release:

The Tucson .22 Caliber Handgun Championships' most exciting match was the effort by the Tucson kids to overturn the National Rifle Association's National Match Course Junior Pistol Team Record. The National Match Course is one of the oldest pistol courses of fire in the history of pistol shooting in the United

195

States. First, each shooter fires 10 shots at a target placed 50 yards from the shooter. Each target has an "X" ring which has a diameter of just over 1 and a half inches. The number of bullet holes in the "X" ring are used to break numerical ties in competition. The "X" ring has the same value as the "10" ring. The shooter then fires 10 shots from a distance of 25 yards. Each of these 10 shots is fired under Timed Fire conditions. Each shooter loads five of the ten rounds into a magazine at a time. Then the shooter must fire those five shots within a time limit of 20 seconds, and then repeats that for the second five shot magazine. The third stage of the National Match Course consists of the shooter firing two more five shot strings, this time each magazine of five rounds must be fired in ten seconds at a target 25 yards distant.

On the 50 yard target, the Tucson kids who kept their shots in the 3 1/3" center ring of the target received ten points. That is quite a feat for kids between 11 and 14 years of age to accomplish.

In real life terms, that is putting holes through the open end of a medium sized drinking glass, at a distance of half a football field, while shooting the handgun with only one hand. In scoring those 15-X's, the Tucson kids would have put holes in a "Liberty" silver dollar fifteen times, if the silver dollar had been placed at the bottom of the drinking glass, with the glass laying on end facing them.

In September of 1995, that NRA pistol team record, of 874 points with 10Xs, was set by a 4-person team of Juniors from the Massachusetts Woburn Sportsmen's Association.

This particular match generated much on range excitement as the shooters were informed of the record prior to shooting. This match generated a very different feeling among the shooters. This time, they were fully aware that they were seeking to overturn this National Record. They knew it to be within their capabilities. After each stage of the match, the shooters huddled together to figure out what they had to shoot on the next stage of the match. So, they knew what they had to do, they were confident they could do it and they went out and did it. Knowing what you have to do, knowing it to be within your skill level and then demonstrating that skill level in front of all of your club members builds a very different type of personal character.

196

> *The current National Junior Pistol Team Record was overturned, by 104 points, with 978 points with 15Xs, by a team of Tucson kids, one of whom, Cade Wilson, is 14 years old, who led the record breaking effort with 263-6X. The other three Tucson team members were Jason Neill, 13 years old, with 242-5X, Grant Morgan, 12 years old, scoring 229-2X and anchored by 11 year old, Bugsy Barstow's 244-2X. All of the handguns used in the tournament are .22 caliber.*

Question: Do you use any mental training techniques with your shooters?

Coach 1: *The only thing we try to tell them is when they come up to a 45 degree ready position, to relax their breath, bring their arm up and as they are bringing the arm up inhale and then go back down and when they are settling in the position with the gun up and relax their breathing and close their eyes, have a mental sight picture where the sights are suppose to be on the target and go from that, relaxing the breathing and the aiming and the squeezing and the follow through. That's basically what we use. After listening to what you are doing, I'm going to look forward to reading the book and trying to apply some of that to what tools we have to work with.*

Coach 2: *I begin introducing "MY KIDS" to mental training techniques immediately after they have successfully completed our mandatory Pistol based Firearms Safety Course. I've found that long lectures on Mental Management techniques puts young Jrs. to sleep! They need only to be enlightened to a technique with a brief example and an even briefer explanation of how and why it works. I introduce my students to key elements they can apply immediately to help solve a shooting performance problem or to attain a higher performance level. They tend to absorb and utilize these "new" techniques like sponges soaking up*

197

*water and generally produce positive results almost
instantly. I'm blessed with some exceptionally high
IQ students and their ability to achieve quick
results using new techniques can be very
impressive, indeed! The best part is their fellow
teammates/competitors are always keenly
interested in learning any "tricks" being used by
anyone else, so when they see a teammate get
instant results they are eager to learn the technique
too!*

Question: Do you encourage the use of a shooting diary by your
shooters? And if so, in what way do you have them use it?

> **Coach 1:** *We do very heavily in the rifle program.
> We instruct them when they get either a shooting
> diary or a spiral bound notebook they can stick in
> their pocket, whatever they want to use, is to write
> down the day, we are shooting indoors and I shot
> prone and kneeling today and my goal is to keep in
> scoring ring and as kids progress we try to
> encourage increasing the goal, not by much, just a
> little, so they can attain that goal and a couple
> more steps and they can attain another goal. We
> don't try to shoot all 8's today when they can't
> even hit the target. We start them off slow with a
> real small goal and they have that goal written in
> the front of their notebook and they write down that
> day I shot x number of shots in this position and in
> that position and my score was and we have them
> keep track of their score from week to week and
> have them put down how they felt when they were
> shooting whether I was concentrating on my
> shooting, was my mind wandering, was I thinking
> about going home and watching television, was I
> thinking about a school test I just had, did I pass it
> or fail It? How did I feel when I came in to shoot.
> How do I feel I shot? Basically that's it. I don't*

know again if that is how you follow anything or not.

Coach 2: *I have some of the high school kids who drop around to shoot with us pick up on using a diary. I worked with Kelly on doing that.*

Question: The system we use is a little different because the process we use is a little different. We are looking at the relief of stress and things like that. Do you have any – you listed those 4 fundamentals you use with your training with the kids. Are there any of the pistol NRA fundamentals that you might think are a waste of time for a shooting coach to stress in pistol training? You know from observing your kids.

Coach: *I really don't know how to answer that one. We have the basic fundamentals that we try to get across to them we don't try to push any kid into doing it because we don't want them to feel stressed about it. We want them to go at their own pace but, as far as the fundamentals themselves gee I don't know how to answer that one.*

Question: What training process do you use in training/teaching sight alignment, pistol especially?

Coach: *OK We have several things that we use. We have a big cardboard cutout of a front & rear sight and a bullseye and we explain to them the 6 o'clock hold or the center of mass hold. We start them at the 6 o'clock hold. And then at the basic fundamentals because the NRA wall charts are all made that way and we have the wall charts for them to follow along. We have a 12 inch rear sight we have cut out of cardboard and with a notch cut out of that with the front sight up in front and we can show them the sight alignment. We can move the front sight from left to right so we can show them how the impact would be when they don't keep the proper light between the front sight and*

199

the rear sight for that sight alignment. Then basically we try to check their dominant eye so they are not crossing over or something like that. To try to straighten them out, if they use their non-dominant eye for aiming, we use scotch tape over the glass if they wear glasses or something like that. Basically, I guess we use your average sight alignment training just from shooting pistols. Most of our stuff is trial and error. We have learned ourselves and we try to catch what they are doing wrong at the time and try to straighten them out. I don't know if that is the answer you are looking for or not.

Question: Do you have any training methods that you employ to produce the process of accommodation from interfering with the shooters consistent acquisition of an efficient sight alignment?

Coach: *No, I would say no on that. We just try to work on them and we try to get them to get everything back to the same every time. We try to watch them when they get into their stance. We have them raise their firing hand without a gun in it. And try to show them how to get lined up on the target. Get their body position right and come up to the firing line, get in position, raise their hand, get sighted up and come back down and stand there. Then we have them do the whole thing again and close their eyes and tell them to "bring your arm up and let your arm relax and then open your eyes and see where your hand is pointing in relation to the target." If it's not right, then we show them how to try to shift their body right or left after they've told us where their hand is in relation to the target. We ask them, "Where's your hand pointing in relation to the center of the target, are you pointing to the left, are you pointing to the right with your hand"*

200

The Junior Pistol Shooting Club/Team

We try to teach them to take the top knuckle, the second knuckle where it goes into the palm of their hand and keep the sight, if they are right handed, keep the knuckle to the left of the bullseye so the black of the bull is just touching their knuckle so it would be more or less where the sight would be when they were lined up.

We found that one of the biggest helps is for the kids to come up to the line and get in their standing position as though they were going to fire the gun, but with no gun in their hand, come up and sight on the target through the web of their hand and get that bullseye right in there and then come back down close their eyes again and come back up and see where everything is. This is to see if they are in the same position they were when their eyes are open and then have them shift and come back down until things were lined up. We found that pretty good way to find a stance.

After we get them doing that and hitting the target we'll watch them and see what they do when they are ready to pick up the gun. We watch them pick the gun up and aim and fire to see if they are settling into position before they raise the gun or waited until they bring the gun up and then trying to settle into position while they are holding the gun up getting ready to squeeze.

What we are trying to teach them when they do that is to come up and they are in position and the target is down range, to settle themselves in just getting the gun in place, getting the head where they want it, getting relaxed, getting their body where they want it and then bringing the gun up. At this point, all they have to do is follow the gun up with their eyes. This way they don't have to follow it up with their head. Once the gun is in place they don't have to think, "now I gotta get my head this way, now I gotta get my body this way and then try to relax to squeeze off the shot." By

201

having them do physical preparation prior to bringing up the gun has made a difference we have found. They seem to be more settled into their position. Then when the gun comes up, all they have to think about it that mental picture of the sight alignment on the bullseye. They know where it is it is going to go into the 10. Bringing that gun up get them relaxed a little bit. They then bring it up the rest of the way. Then when it is up there, we have them relax their breathing a little bit and aim and squeeze. When they are doing that squeezing they are not going to know when that shot is going off. It should go off as a complete surprise to them. Instead of saying OK now I'm up here, Now I've got to make that trigger let go and we want them to have that constant pressure on it and as they get that sight alignment, get it where they want, it will go off by itself when everything is ready. We found that to work pretty good. Basically that is what we are doing on that part of it.

Question: Where are you having the kids get their sight alignment?

Coach: *Where are we having them get their sight alignment meaning?*

Question: In what part of their body are they obtaining sight alignment?

Coach: *In what part of their body are they obtaining sight alignment. You mean when they have raised the gun and they are up onto the target?*

Question: Is it being done through the grip or how is it being done?

Coach: *I'm trying to think how to answer that one. We have them step up to the line and their body and* *their arm lined up to the target without the gun in it. Ok. Then they come back down and they load their gun, put it in their hand and come up about a 45 degree angle and they are watching the bullseye. And then what I tell them to do is I say all right I've got the gun up there, I bring my eyes back down when the gun is on the 45° and the gun is lined up. Then I put my eyes on the rear sight, to change the depth from where they are looking at the target at 10 meters. Now they are coming back down and they are looking at the gun. As I raise the gun up and my eyes are concentrating and they pick up the front sight, because they are looking at the rear sight and bringing the gun up, and when they are bringing the gun up I tell them to change their focus to the front sight and align the front sight up on the target with the rear sight and they get their sight picture that way and to keep their focus on that front sight. Some kids say that their target goes a little fuzzy and we tell them that is the way it should look. We don't want them to look at the target, we want them to look at the front sight and concentrate on that front sight and keep their front sight centered in the rear sight and then squeeze the shot off. So then I would say we are looking at the rear sight to get things started. Kind of a 1,2,3, look at the target, change your focus to the rear sight bring your gun up with your focus now on the front sight and aiming at that black spot you see down range that's kind of on the fuzzy side. So I would say we are going rear sight, front sight.*

Question: OK, I guess I was actually trying to figure out what you believe is the function of the grip?

Coach: *The function of the grip, if I had to explain it to them, would be for you to hold on to without squeezing it to death and basically relying on your middle finger and your thumb wrapping around it*

203

your 4th and 5th finger just to keep the thing from flopping around. That is how I would explain it to them if they asked me what the grip was for.

Question: OK. Do you have any of your shooters involved in the NRA or USA shooting qualification programs?

> **Coach 1:** *I used to spend a lot of training time working on the NRA Qualification program, initially it was fun and the kids loved it. Later as they started to reach more difficult levels, I became disappointed with the resulting reactions from my juniors. They were so eager to achieve the next step and win the material award (certificate and patch) that they were becoming too reward/award oriented. They were becoming programmed to: shoot and win, shoot and win! and nothing else! As a group, they were objecting to any training other than being allowed unlimited time and ammo to shoot the Qualification Program. They didn't want to practice basics or any other part of their training, so I put the program on a long term hold. It took me about 2 months to get them back to shooting for intrinsic awards and they rediscovered the fun in shooting. Since that time, I have not re-introduced the Qualification Program back into my training program. I have a group of highly motivated juniors. They are having fun shooting, and all work hard to establish new "PB's" (personal bests) and are true sharks when it comes to a competition. They set 3 new National records this past year ('95) and numerous other achievements. I'm unlikely to resume the Qualification Program again, until I need outside motivation for a new group of entry level juniors.*

> **Coach 2:** *You asked about programs. That is the problem today. There is not a good junior air pistol qualification program today. The "split" of the NRA a couple of years ago has not as yet*

benefited the juniors. The NRA qualification program is too difficult for very young shooters. It takes too long to obtain awards. The NRA qualification program is satisfactory for youngsters 14 years old or so - if you can find youngster of that age who are not into other sports. We are still using the old NRA Junior Olympic Air Pistol program as we still have certificates and brassards on hand. The old NRA JOSP's were the best for youngsters. These were used in our rifle, pistol and shotgun program, and will be used until the brassards etc., are used.

Question: What types of motivational techniques do you employ in your training program?

Coach: *Goal setting is our biggest motivation that we have. The kids do it to attain the goals they set for themselves and when they attain that goal we more or less talk to them now you've made your goal, what does it feel like? Do you think you can do better and what do you think would be better? Sometimes the younger kids seem to set a goal a little bit out of reach beyond reach rather and we explain to them you know that is kind of a big goal you set and it is going to be a long time before you get there what do you say if we drop back to this? Again, we go to that small step, and we more or less have them come up with an obtainable goal. We feel they can establish an obtainable goal, and as they get into the program you can see them set a little tougher goal for themselves as they get older. We've got a couple boys that are about a year apart in age and it has for the last three years been a see-saw. One comes out on top one time and then next time, it's other's turn to come out ahead. It's vice-versa and it's just been one after the other and they both are trying to get to Colorado and they*

205

have just come short of getting it here for the last three years on the both of them.

Question: Is that right?

Coach: *This year they will both make it.*

Question: How old are they?

Coach: *One is 16 and the other one will be 17 in a couple of weeks. So they are pretty close in age and they've come up together in the program. When the adults go to a match, we'll bring them down and we'll watch their scores come out, because we try to keep them on the same relay, but in different ends of the range*

Question: Why put them in different ends of the range?

Coach: *So they can't watch each other. We watch their scores and we can see them with half of us rooting for one and half rooting for the other because they are from different schools. It kind of goes that way and it's made for good competition between the two boys and the goals they've accepted. Now the one that won the gold last weekend, lost it the year before, and the other boy won the gold. They just reversed places this time. It was interesting to watch. They started out the same. One went ahead of the other and dropped back and then the other went ahead and it was like that through the entire match.*

Question: Wow! Do you encourage them to watch the scores that they put up?

Coach: *No, as a matter of fact, when we go into a traveling match, the first thing we tell them, is* **"don't even look at the scoreboard. You are not here to shoot against them. You are here to shoot the best you can shoot. If you don't win we don't**

care. We just want you to shoot the best you can shoot this particular day." Usually one of us will stand in front of the score board just to make sure the younger kids don't look at it. The older kids have learned not to look at the scoreboard until they are all done shooting and they come out. Sometimes on a two day match, it is hard to do. On a one day match we usually bring them in and have them sitting there. Some places will be slow in posting the scores for that particular reason. We have kind of a gentleman's agreement between us in our matches around here and sometimes we'll be a little slow in posting their scores so the kids won't look at the scoreboard. Well, they're not done yet so, they will just sit there and do their mental thinking about their sight alignment and their breathing before they go into shoot. Get themselves into a match condition before they get in there and lay down and now I'm going to start thinking

Question: AH...

Coach: *We get them early enough to get them there, get them signed up, get their gear ready fill out all the paper work they have to fill out. Once they get ready they know they have to start forgetting about this and forgetting about that and start thinking about - we always tell them to think about shooting a 10. Every time you squeeze that trigger off you are shooting a 10 and get your sights lined up and get your mind cleared up to thinking of nothing else but getting that sight alignment and that trigger squeeze in. It works pretty good with the older kids. The younger kids, their minds tend to wander, but they do pretty good as a whole.*

Question: What's the primary source of funding for your program?

207

Coach 1: *Primary source is my senior matches. I kind of defer the junior cost. I cut the cost in half. Say if I charge $12 for a senior I'll charge $6.00 for a junior. The excuses, "I don't have a gun, I don't have any pellets," is not acceptable. We will provide the gun, we will provide the pellets for you. Mom and Dad can bring you to the match and provide the entry fee. We'll even pick you up and bring you home if we have to. If you can't get there, we'll get you to a match and we'll bring you home. Basically, we try to keep the cost down to minimal and provide all the equipment for the kids. We don't require them to buy their own guns at all. If they want to have their own guns that's up to Mom and Dad. If Mom and Dad come in and ask questions we give them all the answers. It's not mandatory they have their own guns.*

Coach 2: *Until right now after quickly reviewing my sources of funding, I've just realized how heavily I've committed my resources to Jr. shooting. My primary source of funding is me, with my club in distant 2nd place, and then followed by solicited (by me) donations from my former adult students. I personally bought and paid for 12 Buckmarks, 7 Skanakers, and 5 Gold Cups (Yes, I'm slightly crazy, and no I'm not wealthy!), that are primarily used just for Jrs. As a matter of fact, each of my Juniors has one of each gun assigned to him for as long as he is in my programs. I loan (with parental permission and proper licensing of course) Skanakers to be taken home, to promote additional practice when not shooting with me. I also supply just about everything else except hearing and eye protection for which each Jr. is personally responsible. I pay for my own gun maintenance, perform my own repairs and tuning, use my own car for Jr. transportation with occasional help from parents to transport the kids.*

The Junior Pistol Shooting Club/Team

My club pays for: staples, pasters, targets, C02, .22 ammo, and some .45 ammo, liability insurance and team entry fees. The kids pay for their own match grade pellets (I supply practice pellets, thanks to Crosman Co.), and the kids also pay for most of their own .45 match grade ammo. including all individual entry fees and personal expenses, plus a modest $15 annual Jr Club membership fee. Through generous assistance from Browning, Crosman, and Colt I'm able to equip my firing lines with new, quality equipment and offer .221r, air pistol and recently .45, including the usual array of patches and pins for incentives for "MY KIDS". Without Browning, Crosman and Colt assistance, I would not be offering all these disciplines to my Juniors.

Question: So the matches provide the funds to buy these extra guns or are they yours?

Coach: *The junior program when it started had nothing. It bummed and borrowed from the senior shooters. And they went out and raised money selling candy, having paper drives, bottle drives, a shoot-a-thon to raise money and they would buy some equipment. For kneeling rolls we went out and bought rug remnants and rolled them up and made kneeling rolls. Basically we made everything from scratch when we started. We are up to the point now we have guns for the littlest tykes up to the kids that are almost adults. We have six Anschutz Achievers now and different weights of Anschutz rifles for them and basically that is what we are doing now with the air program. We are slowly building up as we go. I've got Crosman CO^2 pistols, One is one of my own I put into the program for the kids to use which makes it kind of hard when I go back to shoot because we have to re-sight the thing every time because we are* *teaching the kids how to sight the guns, using the clicks.*

Question: Oh?

Coach: *We are basically going that route. We started out with nothing Five years ago. Some of the adults bring in their own guns for them to use. Most of it is out of our own pockets to get it going and keep it going.*

Question: In this exchange of pistols between two kids, what method do you use to teach them how to get the sights changed from one to another?

Coach: *OK. The younger kids, we will until they are confident, we will have spotting scopes set up and we will go over and make the correct adjustments. Once they have reached a plateau of being confident of what they are doing, we will spot for them in practice. They will shoot their three sighter shots and we will tell them to come right so many clicks, up or down so many clicks, left or right so many clicks and then they will fire three more sighters and make what adjustments are necessary.*

Of course in a match we can't do that. But, once we have them doing that, then we have them using their own spotting scope and making their own decisions on how many clicks they have to go. We also have charts on the wall, whether it is the European style or the American style as to which way to turn the knobs. We also have little plastic coated file cards they take to the line with them when they are first learning how to do this so they will know which way to turn the knob. We even let them use them in the match. These are the newer ones who haven't built up the confidence to go without the cards. This lets them feel they will

*know which way to turn the sights when they have
to make an adjustment.*

Question: Do you do the same thing with both the rifle and the
pistol?

> **Coach:** *Yes. What's nice, the Daisy rifles and
> pistols, they are marked so they know which way
> they are turning the sight and they know what it is
> going to do when the pellet goes down range. On
> the other hand, on the Anschutz sights, or
> something like that, we more or less require them
> to use the cards. That way the kids learn in their
> minds to have them translated from the European
> markings to the English markings.*

Question: In the initial stages of your training, especially with
the pistol, do you use the bench rest or what method do you use?

> **Coach:** *On the younger kids we have them use two
> hands at first because, like I said, the Daisys are
> the heavier guns. We are starting to use the
> Crosmans because they are a little lighter and little
> easier to handle. They are not quite as heavy.
> They don't have to struggle quite as hard to cock
> the gun. What I've done in the past, I have set them
> down in a chair, because we have a drop down leaf
> on the firing line in the booth so it falls out of the
> way if you're in the kneeling or prone position and
> if standing you can bring it down and you've got
> your bench. I'll set them in a chair and put a prop
> under the fore-end of the gun and have them rest
> the stock on the table and have them shoot at the
> target that way to show them they can hit the
> target. After we've done that for a while we have
> them come up and use the two hands. I had an 8
> year old boy come in with his father and he said
> he's been shooting at home with two hands. And he
> asked me, "Do you mind if he shoots beside me in
> the match? You know just fires a few shots."*

211

We've gotten a couple father and son teams started that way.

Question: How did that work out?

Coach: *One of the other clubs where they go shoot .22 conventional pistol. One of our club members takes his kid to a match up the road. But the guy running the match never had any arrangements for juniors. So the guy shoots and pays the full adult fare for his kid. The next time he shows up without the kid. The guy asked him, "where is your son?" And our club member says "Gee, I can't afford to pay adult fees for him and myself too and bring him to other matches along with me." The fellow running the match says, "What are these other clubs doing?" The man who's our club member says, "Well, they have junior fees which are cut in half." The upshot is they started doing it.*

Question: Oh, that's good.

Coach: *It's catching on. There is a father-son team in pistol like that. We have three teams like that in rifle.*

Question: When you are starting the youngsters off, what distance do you start these kids shooting pistol?

Coach: *We go right with the full 10 meters.*

Question: OK.

Coach: *With the rifle they go with the 50 foot indoors.*

Question: What type of air pistol do you train your juniors with?

Coach 1: *I'm very pleased with the Crosman/Skanaker #88's, together with 4 owned by* *my club (The Woburn Sportsman's Assoc.) which are reserved exclusively for my Junior Program, I own 6 more and control a total of 10 at this moment. The only down side of these guns is that they are highly adjustable and cannot be used as a "CLUB GUN" because they are custom adjusted to each Junior's shooting hand, it would become a nightmare to allow the guns to be used by the general membership. The guns would never survive all the adjusting and the juniors could never have a gun to use that was setup the same as the last time they used it. I compete with a Skanaker, a Challenger III and a Gold cup (if you hadn't already guessed). I never could promote something if I didn't truly believe in it, myself. So, I shoot in competition, side by side with "MY KIDS" using the same basic equipment I provide for the juniors.*

Coach 2: *In the pistol program we use air pistols. I have reliable 717 Daisy and we have had kids go up to Styre. I got hold of a couple of Crosman CO2 pistols and we found those to be quite acceptable to the kids 14 years and older because of the size of the grip. We found the Daisy's to be rather on the heavy side.*

Coach 3: *The shooters start using Daisy 717 or 747 air pistols. For youngsters with small hands, the grips are replaced with taped on thin pieces of plywood. Club pistols are available, but a youngster can use his or her folks' air pistol if it is suitable for target shooting. We find that the Daisy 747 is a good beginner pistol. Later the advance shooter can obtain an FWB, etc. Several parents purchase their own air pistol, Daisy, Crosman, as then air pistol shooting can become a family sport at home.*

Comment: In the Tucson Pistol Training Program, we have gone to using the Morini 162E for use with our beginning shooters. We use that air pistol because of the electric trigger. Being electric, it does not have to be recocked after the firing of each shot. So, the shooter can teach himself, right from the first shot, to recover the sight alignment and dry fire another shot. This way, follow through is be learned as an instinctive process, a habit if you will. Yev'yev once pointed out, *"It is very important not to develop conditional reflexes harmful to shooting, such as using the shot as a signal to rest. To overcome this evil, the shooter must force himself to follow through or hold the gun on target a little bit longer, not lowering it immediately after the shot. Some experienced shooters mobilize their will and consciousness to convince themselves to continue the hold longer than is actually necessary for the bullet to pass through the bore after releasing the trigger. By using such psychological methods, shooters have better success in maintaining muscle tone at the constant level while firing a shot. In this case, the use of an extended follow-through makes the holding of the gun in position independent of the shooter's actions in releasing the trigger."* The Morini Model 162E air pistols were purchased through a grant from the **Friends of NRA** Banquets here in Arizona.

The How-To Of A Junior Pistol Program

Setting Up A Junior Pistol Program!

What does the previous section tell us loud and clear? It is perfectly obvious that your program will be a success if you, very personally, decide what it is you want to do with your junior pistol shooting program. In other words, someone has to have the vision of where the program will go. Consider this. If your vision is confined to local competition, that will usually be a limiting cap on the performance of your shooters. Hickey has found that what unifies a club is a purpose of attaining something outside of their local area. It is fine to set a goal of having some of your shooters make a National Development Team. And, it is really worthwhile to talk to your shooters about someday attaining a berth on a US Olympic Pistol Team. But, if competition is your thing, why not talk to your shooters about winning an Olympic gold medal? If you are into competition, the ultimate is the winning of the Olympic gold in the shooting game you are teaching the youngster to play.

Now, on the business of getting a junior pistol program up and started. Where do you get the youngsters? You recruit them. The proven way Hickey has done it has always been

215

through a basic handgun safety course. If you are associated with a club which has access to a shooting range, all the better. If not, it is relatively easy to set up an air pistol range in your home.

When we say *relatively*, that is exactly what we mean. Hickey set up a range in his kitchen, shooting air pistol into the attached garage. It takes an outstandingly cooperative and understanding spouse to allow an air pistol to be fired past the refrigerator into the garage.

When you conduct a handgun safety class, course or camp, you are providing a very valuable service to your community. In many communities in our present day society, *handguns and kids* are perceived to be the problem. Hickey says the solution is *handguns and kids*.

In setting up a Handgun Safety Camp, you can use the words class, camp and course, interchangeably for your advertising. However, there is one thing to keep in mind, choose your illustrations with some discretion. For example, we ran into a problem with one of the illustrations shown below:

Figure 5-1   Figure 5-2

We took a flyer, Figure 5-3, to the Tucson Unified School District's main office to obtain permission to place the fliers in various schools. The reaction of the bureaucrats was one of being horrified at the picture of the girl with the gun, obviously very young, and out on a range shooting a handgun. If you cannot get your message out, what good does it do you to have a message? So, we redesigned the flyer.(See Figure 5-4)

Summer Handgun Safety Camp
For Kids Ages 9 To 18

Choose to attend either one of two
Handgun Safety Camps
on the Tucson Rod & Gun Club's .22 caliber range

The Saguaro 4-H Shooting Sports Club will conduct two NRA Handgun Safety Camps for boys and girls, ages 9 to 18. You may choose to attend either one of the following camps:

Camp #1: June 3rd to June 24th each MONDAY, **8:00 am to 11:30 am.**
Camp #2: July 8th to July 29th each MONDAY, **8:00 am to 11:30 am.**

The Handgun Safety Camp is designed for an intense immersion in all aspects of handgun safety. This will include constant handgun safety awareness, safety considerations while shooting a handgun and actual hands on practice in cleaning a handgun.

FREE Handgun Safety Camp.

Our program has the use of Ruger Mark II and .22/45 target pistols, courtesy of the Southern Arizona Firearms Educators through a grant from the **Friends of NRA Banquets** state fund. The Arizona Arms Association has donated ammunition for this youth training program. **The youngsters will be required to join the Saguaro 4-H Shooting Sports Club since this is a 4-H project. There is no charge to the boys and girls for this camp or to join the 4-H Club.** All young people who would like to join a formal summer Handgun Safety Camp, please contact Bob Hickey at 744-8805

Figure 5-3

Summer Handgun Safety Camp
For Kids Ages 9 To 18

Choose to attend either one of two
Handgun Safety Camps
on the Tucson Rod & Gun Club's .22 caliber range

The Saguaro 4-H Shooting Sports Club will conduct two NRA Handgun Safety Camps for boys and girls, ages 9 to 18. You may choose to attend either one of the following camps:

Camp #1: June 3rd to June 24th each MONDAY, **8:00 am to 11:30 am.**
Camp #2: July 8th to July 29th each MONDAY, **8:00 am to 11:30 am.**

The Handgun Safety Camp will be held at the Tucson Rod and Gun Club Range on the north end of Sabino Canyon Road. The Handgun Safety Camp is designed for an intense immersion in all aspects of handgun safety. This will include constant handgun safety awareness, safety considerations while shooting a handgun and actual hands on practice in cleaning a handgun.

FREE Handgun Safety Camp.

Our program has the use of Ruger Mark II and .22/45 target pistols, courtesy of the Southern Arizona Firearms Educators through a grant from the **Friends of NRA Banquets** state fund. The Arizona Arms Association has donated ammunition for this youth training program. **The youngsters will be required to join the Saguaro 4-H Shooting Sports Club since this is a 4-H project. There is no charge to the boys and girls for this camp or to join the 4-H Club.** All young people who would like to join a formal summer Handgun Safety Camp, please contact
Bob Hickey at 744-8805
to arrange to participate. Parents, should any youngster not be able to attend the start of the Handgun Safety Camp, please call Bob Hickey and we'll work out a process to get him or her started so your kid can get Handgun Safety Training this summer.

Figure 5-4

All clubs should consider consulting an attorney about setting up procedures to protect the club and the people who assist with the club. As a starting point, we have included the some sample liability items you need to discuss with your attorney.

☛ Consider a power of attorney and authorization to consent to medical treatment. You need this in order to be prepared in the event of an accident. If one of your young shooters trips over a rock and breaks a leg, you need to be prepared to see that the proper treatment is given promptly.

☛ Much of what we do involving, as we do, kids and handguns, is often newsworthy. So, to avoid having to keep coming back to the parents for permissions for each instance of news coverage, see if your attorney thinks you ought to include a blanket permission specifically authorizing the use of photographs and names of youngsters for publication by Television and print media news reports and for club advertising of club projects.

☛ Be aware that there may be occasions, such as in a very nasty divorce, that the parent would prefer that the child not be allowed to be in any photo shoot or news interview.

☛ Do recognize up front, that participation in activities at a shooting range involves exposure to lead which may result in bodily injury, disease and/or death.

☛ See if your attorney thinks it necessary to include your club range rules as a part of any waiver of liability you ask the parents of your youngsters to sign. Here are the range rules we use in the Tucson Pistol Shooting Program.

SAGUARO SHOOTING SPORTS CLUB
RANGE RULES

1.   Obey all safety rules and range rules at all times.

2.   ALWAYS KEEP YOUR MUZZLE POINTED IN A SAFE DIRECTION.

3.   Actions must be kept open unless on the firing line.

4. Always check your air pistol for pellets, or your pistol for bullets, <u>before</u> you take it from the line.

5. Uncased air pistols are allowed in the range only, unless authorized by instructor.

6. NO HORSEPLAY IN RANGE OR PREP AREAS.

7. Eye/Ear protection must be worn on the range at all times.

8. All shooters will arrive on time and complete each practice sessions fully unless excused.

9. Obey all commands of range officer.

10 Inform range officer of any equipment malfunctions immediately.

11. Upon calling a cease fire, immediately open action, remove pellets or bullets and cease further handling of guns. <u>Step back behind the Safety Line</u>. Do not retrieve targets until range officer calls "Bring back your targets!"

12. Keep your firing position uncluttered and neat.

13. All shooters should keep a shooter's scorebook.

14. To minimize lead exposure, keep exhaust fans on at all times, wash hands and change clothes after range use. <u>Do not eat anything until you have washed your hands.</u>

15. All persons under 18 must have an adult present at all times when shooting.

Now that you have the youngsters in your Handgun Safety Camp, wouldn't it be nice to insure that they are safe? Many organizations have their own safety rules. Many are variations of the following three:

☞ Always keep the gun pointed in a safe direction at all times.

☞ Always keep your finger off the trigger until ready to fire.

☞ Always keep the action open until ready to fire.

We also have three rules of gun safety, and the shooter is allowed to pick the one he thinks is the most important to memorize and to follow at all times:

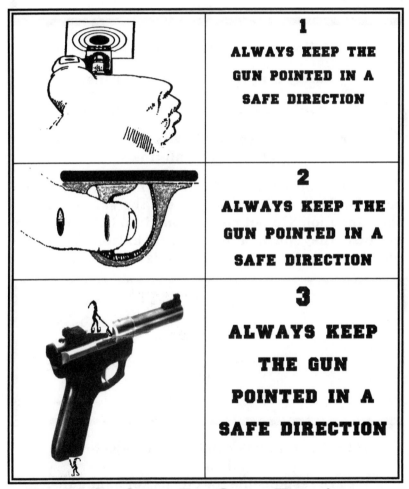

Gun Safety Is Our Business

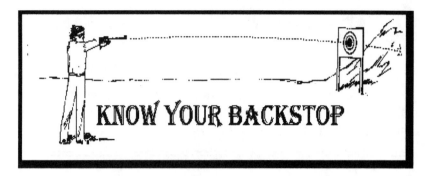

Pointing is safety's salvation.

Safety is always 100% on pointing.

Safety should be the only thing you think about.

Pointing Safely should have everyone's 100%
attention at all times.

In a positive controlled range situation, no
one should permit anyone to set the safety on any
shooting tool. Do not con anyone into believing that
because they push a lever or a button from one
position to another, that the gun is now SAFE.

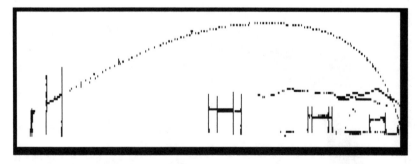

.22 caliber bullets can travel a considerable
distance.
We are responsible for our use of handguns.

222

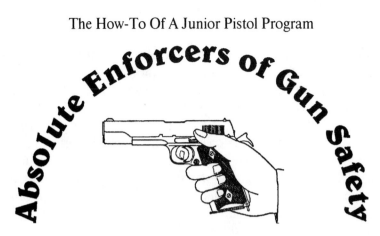

Absolute Enforcers of Gun Safety

In order for us to play our handgun games, we must be the absolute enforcers of gun safety. We must setup all of our training sessions with safety built-in. How do you do this? First of all, we will assume that the firing will be done on a shooting range. As the person responsible for safety, you must make certain that you have an unobstructed view of the area between the safety line and the firing line, probably a distance of around 12 feet. That space must be absolutely clear at all times, except when the line is active and the shooters are in the process of preparing to fire, or are engaged in their shooting training.

Training One Person

As the person responsible for safety, consider how you train your beginning pistol shooters. If you are training just one person at a time, then you can setup sandbags, or an *Extended Benchrest*, on a shooting bench. Be certain to place the handgun firmly in the sandbag or on the support lever of the *Extended Benchrest*. Both you and your beginning shooter should sit down at the benchrest. You, as the coach should coach from the opposite side of the gun from which the shooter is moving the trigger. If the shooter is moving the trigger with a finger on his right hand, the coach should place himself or herself on the left side of the shooter. If the shooter is moving the trigger with a finger on his left hand, the coach should place himself or herself on the right side of the shooter. In any case, the coach has to be constantly alert that the shooter does not forget and point the handgun somewhere other than down range. If there are other shooters on the range, the coach must be especially alert so the gun is not misdirected to the side of the shooter.

Stop

Hands ON

Methods

In our research, we have noticed a wide spread tendency among pistol coaches and instructors, graphically illustrated in one particular pistol shooting training video, to employ a special **hands-on** training technique. This is where the pistol instructor is physically touching and or manipulating the shooter into position. We noticed this technique being especially outrageous in the 4-H video, ***Shooting FUNdamentals,*** produced by the 4-H Youth Development Minnesota Extension Service and Daisy Manufacturing Company. On the other hand, there is an excellent example of the instructors being able to talk the shooter into position in the 4-H video, *Basic Rifle Shooting, **A Better Way,*** produced by the 4-H Youth Development Minnesota Extension

Service and Federal Cartridge Company. This is an excellent film from both a technical viewpoint and from a training viewpoint.

In the educational field, *hands on* training means that the student gets to perform some learning task while the teacher observes. Hands-on learning is learning by doing. It is not having the teacher *"laying on of the hands"* onto parts of the student's body. Vocational education has always understood that if you want someone to learn to repair an automobile, you need an automobile for the person to repair. If you want to teach someone how to cook, you put him in a kitchen and let him help prepare the family meals.

Real *hands on* is what we do before the shooters fire the first shot in our initial training session. We explain the process of clearing a pellet from the barrel. Then, when it occurs, as it often does, the student picks up the cleaning rod in his hand and clears the mis-fed pellet. That is *hands on* in the normally accepted sense of the term. It is the student actually handling things, and doing for himself, various thing connected with the learning experience.

Hands-on learning means many different things to different people. It has become a slogan and is often used to describe any activities in classrooms that use materials. Hands-on learning, however, does not, in any use of the term, except when used by pistol coaches, involve physically manipulating pistol students. It is the student engaging in in-depth investigations with objects, materials, phenomena, and ideas and drawing meaning and understanding from those experiences. Other terms for this are inquiry learning, hands-on, and minds-on learning

Hands on learning is the only way pistol students in our program can directly observe and understand pistol shooting. We guide our pistol students to develop effective techniques for observing and testing everything they see and hear about pistol shooting. They learn the what, how, when, and why, of things with which they interact in their game of pistol shooting. These experiences are necessary if the youngsters of today are to remain "turned-on" to pistol shooting and become the champions of tomorrow. Pistol coaches and instructors, using their perversion of the term *hands-on*, need to re-evaluate what they are doing.

Hands-on quite literally means having **students manipulate** the **things** they are studying, air pistols, pellets, .22 caliber pistols, spotting scopes, ammunition, magazines, sights, cleaning rods, extended benchrests rulers for measuring shot groups and stop watches for measuring the progress of the development of their conditional reflex. In a more general sense, it means learning by experience. And nowhere in that list have we mentioned manipulating people, either by the student or the coach or instructor. That is just not a part of the real meaning of the hands on process.

The Thesaurus of ERIC Descriptors defines manipulative materials as *"instructional materials that are designed to be touched or handled by students and which develop their muscles, perceptual skills, psychomotor skills, etc."* (U.S. Department of Education, 1990, p. 249).

Somewhere along the line, pistol shooting coaches and instructors have bastardized and perverted the meaning of this very respected educational method and turned it into a *touchy-feely* procedure. Often a spectator is left with the impression that the instructor cannot use language alone to get a person into what the instructor feels is the "best" position for that person's particular body conformation.

The spectator is treated to the spectacle of the pistol instructor adjusting arms, kicking feet either wider apart, or nudging them inwards. The pistol instructor will be seen to be wrapping her arms around the young man, and clasping his forearms from a very intimate position, bringing her body in contact with his posterior, then elevating his forearms to his eye level. We see this particular example in the above mentioned 4-H video, *Shooting FUNdamentals.* Watching the video, one wonders just what the instructor is trying to accomplish with her special *hands-on* technique. But, she is not alone. Many pistol coaches seem to feel that unless they are able to physically manipulate their students into a specially *hands-on* molded position, that they have not done their job.

It is the contention of the authors that any such physical *hands-on* methods are counter-productive. First of all, they start, right from the first instance, to destroy the shooter's independence. Quite often, the pistol instructor will ask his student, *"Do you mind if I touch you? I want to move you into a more stable position."* From the vocalizing of that question, it is apparent that the instructor is aware that most people, even kids do not like to be touched. The pistol instructor is probably reacting to an awareness, that in some cases, his or her touching could be interpreted as a form of sexual harassment.

Even to single out a student for such public physical manipulation, is somewhat demeaning for the student's self-image. The pistol coach will usually come back with the justification that the student probably feels thankful to have him/her place him in a more stable position. However, because of the unique authority position the pistol instructor occupies, the student, in permitting the *touchy-feely* manipulation, during the shooting instruction, thereby surrenders some part of his independence to the instructor. This contributes to the weakening of the mental hardiness we believe the pistol coach or instructor ought to be attempting to instill in his/her students.

This *hands-on* procedure seems to have become a deeply ingrained method in pistol shooting methodology. The authors believe this teaching process has been partially at fault for the beginning pistol shooters requiring a long training process to negate the effects of this type of training method.

Next, the authors do not believe this *touchy-feely* process contributes to the effectiveness of the instructor. We believe that competent instructors should be able to find the words with which to *"talk"* the shooter into the proper position. There is no need to push, kick, pull or manipulate pistol students into any type of *"correct"* position or stance.

Kick The Touch-feely Habit

Training A Group Of People

When training a group of people, we have found the *Extended Bench Rest* to be very well suited to mass training. It has a number of features which recommend it as a training aid for pistol training. In addition, it is excellent for the plinker who goes to the range just occasionally. It takes up very little space and is light weight, yet very sturdy. Plus it is inexpensive and can be assembled with a small amount of time and effort.

The Extended Benchrest

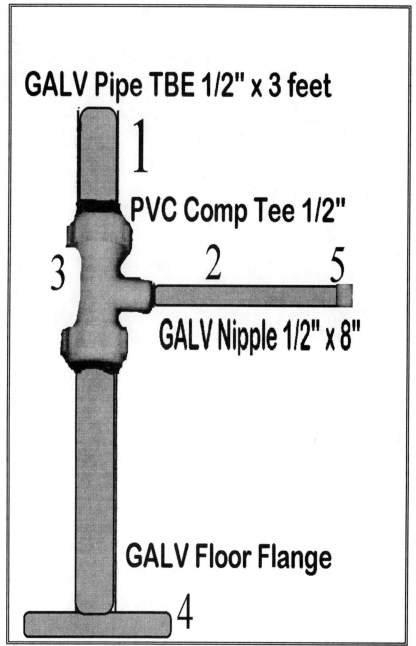

GALV Pipe TBE 1/2" x 3 feet

1

PVC Comp Tee 1/2"

3   2   5

GALV Nipple 1/2" x 8"

GALV Floor Flange

4

The Extended Benchrest

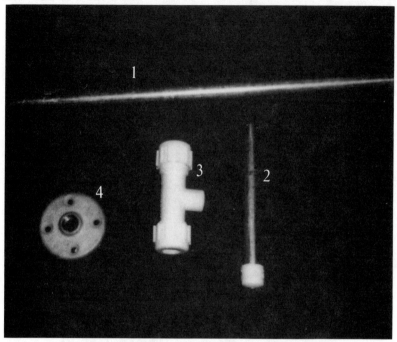

Assembling The Extended Benchrest #1
Easy And The Cost Is Right Around $12.00!

Materials

1) **$ 4.19**   1 each GALV Pipe TBE ½ inch x 3 feet
2) **$ 1.87**   1 each GALV Nipple ½ inch x 8"
3) **$ 2.37**   1 each PVC Comp Tee ½ "
4) **$ 3.45**   1 each GALV Floor Flange ½"
5) **$ 0.50**   2 each PVC Cap Slip ½"
  $12.38   Total without tax
This system does require the use of a C-Clamp.

We start our shooters in the standing position. We do this by having them use our extended benchrest for these reasons:

☞ It modifies the safety factor of the firing line on the range by establishing a safety limit on the travel of the handgun during training.

☞ By having the two hands gripping the handgun, placed on the support lever of an upright pole on the offside from the trigger finger, the coach, when the coach/pupil method is used, only has to look for the handgun being swung in his direction.

☞ The coach/pupil method places two students of equal learning status together. One of the pair acts as a coach and the other takes the gun as the shooter. They then trade positions and each takes a turn in each capacity.

☞ When using the *Extended Bench Rest,* the upright pole physically helps insure that the shooter cannot move the handgun past the upright pole, on the side having the handgun support.

☞ Out of an instinct of self-survival, the coach will notice immediately if the gun starts to swing in his direction. The coach places himself on the shooter's opposite shoulder from the side the shooter's trigger finger is on.

☞ The *Extended Bench Rest* is designed to provide support for shooters when shooting a pistol.

☞ It takes the beginning shooter directly to the standing position.

Art Sievers Assembling The Extended Benchrest #1

⇒ The PVC Tee has two rubber seals.
⇒ Cut a 1/8 inch section out of each seal to permit it to make a sliding adjustment of the tee on the upright galvanized pipe. This allows for quick, easy height adjustment on the vertical pipe. This permits the extended benchrest to be used with a variety of people of varying heights. It also permits the shooter to be seated or standing.
⇒ Place the Tee over the galvanized pipe.
⇒ Place the slit-cut rubber seals around the pipe, one on each side of the Tee.
⇒ Slide the Tee caps into place. Tighten.
⇒ Screw the 8" nipple into the Tee.
⇒ Screw the floor flange onto the 3 foot pipe.
⇒ Put the caps on the open end of the nipple acting as the support and the other one on the top of the pole. These caps will prevent shooters scratching themselves on the threads of the pipe.

Art Sievers, using the Extended Benchrest from a sitting position. Notice the C-Clamp holding the base plate onto the table or bench. The authors have found this little, inexpensive device to be a very stable system. It is both easy to assemble, using no tools, except your hands, and it is very durable. In addition, it is light weight and easy to transport and to store when not in use. It is an excellent training aid which each shooter can construct him or herself and use to dry fire at home with their own guns. This allows for the training of the conditional reflex while the youngster takes a break from homework. Under our method, it is very necessary that the shooter identify precisely where he or she wants the barrel, as referenced by the front sight to be located when the pistol is fired. Dry firing off a bench rest will provide the most efficient training for that purpose that we know of. We have never heard of a case of dry firing burn out.

233

Art Sievers using the Extended Benchrest
in the standing position.

The coach or shooter may prefer not to have to
remember to put a C-Clamp in with the Extended Benchrest each

time it is being taken out for training. For that person we offer an alternative design of the Extended Benchrest.

Assembling The Extended Benchrest #2
Easy And The Cost Is Right Around $22.00!

Materials

1) **$ 4.19** 1 each GALV Pipe TBE ½ inch x 3 feet
2) **$ 1.87** 1 each GALV Nipple ½ inch x 8"
3) **$ 2.37** 1 each PVC Comp Tee ½ "
4) **$ 11.75** 1 each No. 52 Pony Clamp Fixture ½"
5) **$ 0.50** 2 each PVC Cap Slip ½"
   $21.68 Total without tax

This system does **NOT** require the use of a C-Clamp.

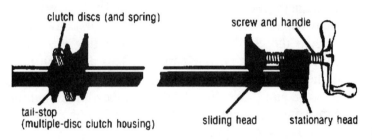

clutch discs (and spring)   screw and handle

tail-stop
(multiple-disc clutch housing)   sliding head   stationary head

This is the No. 52 *Pony* Clamp Fixture ½"

To assemble this clamp fixture:
1. Use the GALV Pipe TBE ½ inch x 3 feet.
2. Make sure the O.D. of the pipe is not "oversize," NOT EXCEEDING .848".
3. Both ends of the pipe should be threaded with regular pipe threads.
4. Screw the head assembly onto the pip threads at one end.
5. Screw the cap over the threads at the other end. It prevents the shooter from

accidentally scraping a hand or arm on
the exposed threads.

6. Follow the instructions for assembling the
remaining parts from the instructions for
assembling the Extended Benchrest #1.

Pistol Shooting Simple & Easy

In this chapter we will demonstrate how to inspire the
juniors in a club to decide to teach themselves what they need in
order to achieve shooting success, at the level to which they
individually aspire. This starts to happen the first day on which
they come to the club. We stress that shooting is really very
simple, it is something anyone can do. This approach has the
effect of helping to defuse some concerns about picking up a
mean looking gun. We first take the superstition that pistol
shooting is somehow magic and replace it with the concept that
pistol shooting is very simple.

Introducing The Idea That Pistol Shooting Is Simple and Easy

☛We have the students point to the instructor or to a
point on a wall with their shooting hand, arm
extended.

☛We additionally ask that they tightly fold their bottom
three fingers into the palm of that pointing hand.

☛We ask that the forefinger, the one next to the thumb
be pointed straight out.

☛The instructor makes a point of noticing that this is
something all of them are able to do.

☛While the arms are still extended, we ask all of the
shooters to smoothly, smoothly, move the forefinger

of their shooting hand back toward the palm of their hands.

☞ We repeat this several times.

☞ We then find out if anyone thought this was a difficult thing to do.

☞ At this time we find out who they think taught them to point and to move their finger the way they did.

☞ Usually the response is that the instructor, or Dad, or another relative, taught them to move their finger.

☞ We then find out how that relative or instructor did this.

☞ We focus on the point that no one can get inside their minds and make them learn anything.

☞ If they were successful at this effort, then it was something they decided to do.

☞ Therefore the person who taught them was none other than themselves.

☞ We get them to enunciate the awareness that, *I taught myself.*

☞ This phrase, *I taught myself,* is the foundation of our whole shooting program.

☞ Right from the beginning, we strive to make each shooter independent of the coach or instructor.

Developing Mental Hardness

Developing mental hardness begins before the firing of the first shot. We spend time showing the shooters how to remove a pellet from the barrel if they happen to put the wrong end in the chamber. We have some cleaning rods made out of the horizontal portion of a vinyl covered clothes hanger. These are placed on the shooting benches. The shooter who experiences such a problem merely picks up the rod and drops it down the air pistol barrel, always keeping the barrel pointed in a safe direction - down range. The pellet generally falls right out. But if it is jammed tightly, a bit more pressure is exerted. What does this do for the mind-set of the shooter? Simply, it gets him ready to recover from jams when he graduates up to firearms prone to jams. It helps make him an independent arbitrator as to whether or not he needs the assistance of the range officer.

Now contrast that to the shooter, who when this happens has to call the coach over and have the coach un-jam the pellet. A coach who does this is making his shooter a mental cripple.

Then there is the situation where the coach sits behind his or her shooters watching the shots fired and then going up and moving the shooter's sights to more precisely center the shot group. This has the effect of creating a sense of dependency on the coach by the shooter.

The focus of our training program is to develop a strong, confident shooter. This requires that the coach let the shooter make his own decision about moving the sights.

We want to help our shooters become alert, thinking competitors, not wimps needing the security of the coach's presence to accomplish what they want with their shooting.

The USA Shooting Junior Olympic Qualification Program is a way to spark interest during junior club or team practices. USA Shooting has developed this program as a part of

238

it's responsibilities as the National Governing Body of the Olympic Shooting Sports in the United States. The forms we use in our junior pistol club are designed to help us keep track of shooter progress and to promote shooter knowledge of the shooting game. Additionally, we use the forms shown on the following pages to advance our agenda of showing the shooter how to focus on the size of the shot group as of more importance than the score on the target. We do this by requiring the shooters on our team to compute the group size of each target submitted for awards in the Junior Olympic Qualification Program. Please note, this is not a requirement of the USA Shooting Junior Olympic Program, nor the National Rifle Association's Pistol Qualification Program. It is something we have added for the shooters training under our tutelage. It has been developed to focus the attention of the shooters in our training program on the size of the group, as opposed to being score oriented.

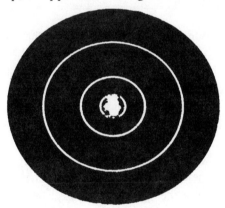

How does this work in an outdoor setting? The first training session starts as a warm up of the conditional reflex. The shooter starts initially at 10 meters. The shooter fires 20 shots, using the method whereby he fires a shot, recovers the front sight of the aligned system, then dry-fires a shot. He recovers again, pauses, looks at the sights and brings the pistol down for reloading of another shot. This process is repeated at 25 meters. The shots are all fired at blank targets. Here is a sample form we use to show the youngsters how to go about the process of measuring the size of their shot groups.

239

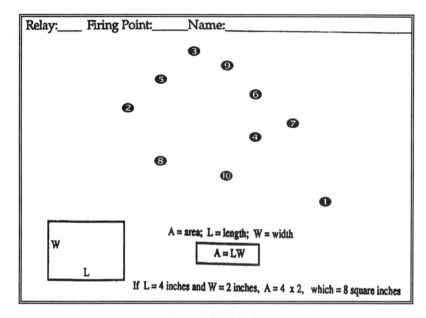

To compute the size of the group, the shooter draws a horizontal line through the center of the top shot of the group. Then he does the same with the bottom shot of the group. He then draws a vertical line through the shot furthest to the left. He does the same for the shot farthest to the right. This gives the shooter a rectangle. We then ask that the area of the group be computed. This, of course calls on the youngsters to go to the formula of Area equals length times width. In this shot group exercise, we ask them to compute the area of the first five shots and then to compute the group size for all ten shots. The more astute of the youngsters discover quickly that they are both the same.

Notice the subtlety of this method. The shooter is led into focusing on the size of the group, compared to any effort to focus on bullseye scores. With this system, the shooter is drawn into comparing the size of his group with others. This has the effect of emphasizing the smallness of the group. Since this opens each practice, while the coach is emphasizing that the purpose is to warm up the conditional reflex, the shooters are really bearing down on making each shot the same so the group is as small as possible. How does this work in practice? Take a look at the example on the next page.

240

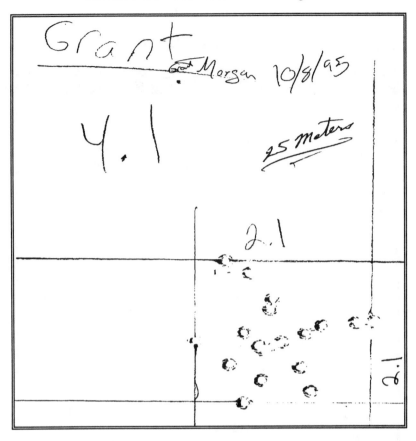

The boy in the example above, was 11 years old at the time and in the sixth grade of Flowing Wells Junior High School.

Lesson Plans

Pistol Shooting Training Program	
	Purpose of this Exercise 1. *Shooter to teach himself or herself the shooting platform which is most __efficient__ for himself or herself.*

241

Lesson Plans

Pistol Shooting Training Program

Purpose of this Exercise

1. *Shooter to teach himself or herself the shooting platform which is most __efficient__ for himself or herself.*

Establishing the Shooting Platform

☛ Have the students pair up and follow the directions on page 243, showing how to do this.

☛ Working in pairs, follow the directions, use coach/pupil method.

☛ Coach of coach/pupil pair to read the *Purpose of this Exercise* and then the *Directions.*

☛ Pairs then switch and repeat the __whole process.__

Directions:

Get your normal grip on the pistol. A normal grip establishes the barrel at an angle, NOT to an extension of the forearm.

Stand erect and relaxed.

Basic Head Position

Turn your head to the right until you get strain on your neck.

Turn your head back to the left until you no longer have any strain on your neck.

Raise the pistol to shoulder height.

Swing the pistol <u>from the shoulder</u> off to the right until you see the front sight off to the left of the rear sight.

Swing the pistol from the shoulder off to the left until you see the front sight off to the right of the rear sight.

Somewhere in this arc, the sights cross.

We swing the pistol until we get perfect sight alignment.

Pistol Arm Technique

Directions:

You need a short sleeved shirt or a sleeve rolled above the elbow joint.

1. Put your hand out in front of you.
2. Make a fist.
3. Roll the fist to the right.
4. Return the fist to pistol holding position.
5. Raise the fist upwards.
6. Note what happens to the elbow joint.
7. The forearm comes straight up.

Now, do the same thing, only turn the fist to the left:

1. Put your hand out in front of you.
2. Make a fist.
3. Roll the fist to the left.
4. Return the fist to pistol holding position.
5. Raise the fist upwards.

244

6.   Note what happens to the elbow joint.

7.   The forearm bends to the left.

PURPOSE:

To deliberately position the elbow joint to control the direction of recoil for the heavy recoilers. We do not have to accept random recoil.

Shooters can be heard commenting, "Sometimes the pistol comes up one way and sometimes it goes the other way." But, we can deliberately position the elbow joint so that the recoil comes straight up or to the left. We do not care which way. That is left up to the individual. But, the shooter needs to be aware that he/she has control over the direction of the recoil.

PROCESS:

We teach shooters, *grip firm, wrist firm, elbow firm* so that we put that elbow joint up on top and our recoil will be normally coming straight up. We are talking efficiency.

With the .22 caliber, it doesn't make much difference. But, with the .38 caliber or the .45, the recoil will go straight up and then the *Recover* will come straight *down,* rather than swinging across the target.

CONCEPT:

We want to make our shooters their own experts, so when we finish the job, they will not need us any more. They will know what they are doing, will be doing it on purpose and they can then evaluate information that comes their way. And if that information will have a *positive effect* on either *internal alignment* or *trigger finger movement* then it is fine. But, if the information will adversely affect either *internal alignment* or *trigger finger movement* then it is bad news. If it will not make any difference anyway, it is a convenience item.

Establishing the Shooting Platform

The Position Used By Champions, Tailored To The Individual

Rationale: This page alone is worth the price of this book!!

How the platform is established is based on eye position, not something down range. Then, what the eye wants to see when we have it in that position is absolutely perfect sight alignment. You can then rotate your platform 360° and put it anywhere you want. So then, when the platform is setup, we rotate it so that the aligned system coincides with the desired area. This gives us a basic body angle with the target. So the next time we come to the firing line, we set up in as near that position as possible and then make adjustments to fine tune the position. There is no such thing as a natural place for the arm to point. It is completely flexible. It is set up deliberately, in as relaxed a manner as possible, commensurate with the muscles required to hold it up.

Pistol Shooting Training Program

Purpose of this Exercise

*Shooter to teach himself or herself to identify the relationship of the **front sight** to the rear sight at the moment when the trigger is moved very smoothly and the gun fires.*

.22 caliber training
Use A Blank Target For This Exercise

☞ Live firing with dry firing exercise.

☞ Shooters to load ONE round in the magazine.

☞ DROP the magazine.

☞ FIRE a shot.

☞ RECOVER the sight alignment.

☞ Keep the ARM UP and,

☞ Fire the DRY FIRE shot.

☞ RECOVER the sight alignment.

☞ Focus on **PERFECT FRONT SIGHT ALIGNMENT - LOOK REAL HARD TO OBSERVE THAT THERE IS AN EQUAL AMOUNT OF LIGHT ON EACH SIDE OF THE FRONT SIGHT.**

☞ Repeat this 20 times for a total of 20 shots and 20 dry fires. That's 40 training rounds in this exercise.

This is a way to get twice the training for half the amount of rounds.

Pistol Shooting Training Program

I. <u>Shot Group Match</u> of 10 shots w/.22 on blank target.

Setup targets at 10 meters

II. <u>Precision Shot Training</u>:

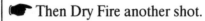 30 shots at 25 meters slow fire using the single shot loading technique without the magazine.

☞ Recover the sight alignment after the shot recoil.

☞ Then Dry Fire another shot.

III. <u>Video Analysis Training</u>

☞ During Phases I & II of today's training, Mr. Hickey will be using the camcorder to record individual training.

☞ Shooters **must** have about <u>5 feet</u> between frames down range and the shooters on either side of their firing points.

☞ After the range is cleaned, we will retire to the trailer for analysis of shooter training.

☞ The pistols will be cleaned after the video analysis.

☞ Targets to be scored at end of day.

How Do You Spot Naturals?

If your purpose in conducting a Handgun Safety Course is purely that of providing a service for your community, then you may miss out on some recruiting opportunities. As a coach, if you are going to join in the effort to help train youngsters for the Olympics of the 21st Century, then you have to identify for yourself that your primary purpose is to recruit youngsters for our game of pistol shooting. When you do this you will start being able to identify those who may excel in our sport.

It is when you set your mind to something that you start noticing things which may otherwise pass unnoticed in the background of things around you. For example, if you buy a particular brand of computer, suddenly you start noticing mentions of that computer in advertisements. You notice it if you see it in an office setting or in a friend's home. In other words, your mind is open to a new dimension of awareness. This awareness is focused on what you have identified in your mind as being important to you.

We call this shooter identification process, *spotting naturals* because that is what other competing coaches think we do. At the US Naval Academy, Sievers would select shooters for his teams on the basis of the size of their shot groups. These were midshipmen who answered the poster he put up informing the students of the tryouts for the pistol team. That sign read:

249

Pistol Team Tryouts
Previous Experience not only not required, but undesirable. 1300 on the range

Sievers discovered that shooters with previous shooting experience with the pistol were already destroyed. Destroyed? Yes, it does not take long to establish a conditional reflex. Under previous pistol shooting instruction, these shooters had taught themselves to shoot using an Arc of Movement or within a wobble area and spot shooting. These shooters have generally taught themselves to be trigger snatchers. To have changed them over to a more efficient method of shooting would have required a substantial effort of retraining. Sievers deliberately took one of these previously experienced shooters on one occasion. The shooter did make the 2nd Team College All-American during his senior year, but, he never did pull his weight on the team.

Sievers built motivation into the initial contact. He deliberately did not supply any directions to the range on his recruiting poster. This meant the prospective shooter had to exert some effort to discover the location of the range.

Every good junior pistol coach, worth his salt, learns what to look for in recruiting young shooters for our pistol shooting game. To aid in this purpose, Hickey uses a form which he designed many years ago and used with the rifle teams he put together during the 30 years he was in Alaska. For the pistol

250

program in Tucson, he merely substituted a picture of a pistol for a rifle.

Shooting Sports Club Test #1

Grade:	Name:
3 4 5 6 (7) 8 9 10 11 12 Circle Grade	*(signature)* B Franklin

Reason for joining the Shooting Sports Club: *My friend asked me to go with her.*

1: _____
2: _____
3: _____
4: _____
5: _____
6: trigger
7: _____
8: _____
9: _____
10: _____
11: _____
12: _____
13: _____
14: _____

Name the parts of the gun at the left.

My Best Liked School Subject:	My most Average Subject:	I have grade problems in this Subject:	The Time I get up each Morning is:	The Time I go to bed each evening is:	Amount of Daily AT HOME Study Time:
Social Studies	Math	none	6:00 on school days 8:00 weekends	9:00	1 hour

| When your parent asks you, "How'd it go today?" Do you

A) describe, in detail, the day's occurrences
B) give out with your usual, *Nothing.*
C) highlight the interesting bits

Circle Your answer:
A   B   (C) | About school, I think:

A) school's a drag!
B) school's okay
C) I have to go don't I?
D) I like it a lot

My Answer: __b__ | Amount of Daily TV Watching Time:

2 hours | My teachers
A) like me
B) hate me
C) don't know I exist
D) Other, explain

Circle Your answer:
(A) B C D |

| Do you sometimes daydream happenings in your imagination?

A) Never   B) Sometimes   C) A lot

Circle Your answer:
A   (B)   C | When I get home, I
A) watch my favorite soap opera
B) talk a lot on the phone with friends
C) usually do not have anything to do
D) my parents always have things for me to do
E) go mall-crawling
F) do my homework
G) other, explain | Circle Your answer:

(A) B C D E F G |

How Do You Spot Naturals?

Test #1 is the primary tool used to identify potential *naturals*. Each coach needs something to help him or her to identify which shooters will get a portion of his limited attention. Some coaches talk about seeing something in a shooter's eyes. Others find themselves giving more of their attention to those who pester them with questions and make demands on their consideration. And others place a great deal of importance on the academic achievement of their shooters. Even USA Shooting has fallen into the trap of believing that academic talent should be the deciding factor in a junior being selected to National Teams. The authors believe that this focus on the academic elite deprives the United States of some otherwise outstanding available pistol shooting talent. If only one character trait is to be used as a criteria for selection to a national junior team, we believe selection based on being a high achiever would be more pertinent. Still others always find themselves focusing on the shooter who shows the greatest initial promise as demonstrated by his or her tight first group. Many coaches who rely on these things to identify *naturals* may find themselves left behind when encountering a team coached by someone using evaluation tools which provide more in depth analysis.

How can *Test #1* be used to help identify *naturals*? The situation in nearly every American Gun Club probably is in the position of taking everyone who shows up and working with them. Often they are the sons and daughters of club members. It is the intent of the authors that this book will change that. This part of the book assumes that you have taken to heart the suggestion elsewhere in this book that you start a junior handgun safety training program. You see, obviously you need young people whom you will test to see if they show some personality traits which you think you can develop. The authors feel it is in the personality area that you can develop shooters with the proper attitude needed for the competitive sport of pistol shooting.

It is with this in mind that the *Test #1* was developed and has been used over the years by Hickey with such outstanding success, both in Alaska with rifle teams and in Tucson with pistol teams. So, let's look at how the coach uses *Test #1*.

Grade: 3 4 5 6 ⑦ 8 9 10 11 12 **Circle Grade**	A-1 This item is a no counter. It is a diversion. Of course, it does give you the grade the youngster is in.
 1:_____ 2:_____ 3:_____ 4:_____ 5:_____ 6:_____ 7:_____ 8:_____ 9:_____ 10:_____ 11:_____ 12:_____ 13:_____ 14:_____ Name the parts of the gun at the left	A-2 This item is of value in two ways. 1st It gives an idea of how familiar the student is with guns. 2nd It is used as a part of the shooter's handwriting analysis evaluation.

My Best Liked School Subject: Social Studies	B-1 This item starts your inventory into the personality of the shooter. A person who likes English or Social Studies is apt to have begun developing the mind. These studies place a premium on recall of information and written expression. Someone who likes gym is probably still into instinctive reactions to stimulus, such as catching a ball.
My most Average Subject: Math	B-2 This item identifies a possible weakness in the student's academic talents. However, a choice of an average subject such as math may indicate that the student is not yet able to work responsibly on his own. Math often requires a student to stick-to-it to complete a long series of the same type problems.
I have grade problems in this Subject: none	B-3 This item further helps to identify those students who are not academically talented. It also indicates a student who often cannot keep up with assigned school work. On the other hand, we are always looking for those students who do not have grade problems in any subject.
About school **A) school's a drag** **B) school's okay** **C) I have to go do** **D) I like it a lot** **My Answer:** B	B-4 This item starts to give you a picture into the mind of the shooter. Someone who thinks school is a drag will most likely not be a good candidate for a pistol team. If a person cannot find an interest in school, then they may not have the mental mind set to be able to meet the regular practice requirements of being on the pistol team.

The Time I get up each Morning is: 6:00 on school days. 8:00-weekends	C-1 This item gives an insight into the inner workings of the family. Research has clearly demonstrated that familial support is crucial to the success of a youngster in sports. Notice that this shooter has identified a difference in get-up-time between school days and weekends. The weekends show an 8:00am get-up-time. For teenagers, this is most likely a parental requirement indicating an established family structure. A child taught to respect structure is a good candidate for success on the pistol team.
The Time I go to bed each evening is: 9:00	C-2 This go-to-bed time indicates whether the shooter lives in a family which is adult driven or child driven. A 9:00pm bedtime for a 7th grader indicates that this is a family with structure. On the other hand, a late go-to-bed time would be indicative of a family which is child driven. Students who do not learn structure at home are less than tractable candidates for the pistol team.

Amount of Daily AT HOME Study Time: 1 hour	C-3 This item starts to identify the student's ability to do work away from school. But, it is tempered by whether it is child driven or adult driven. But, it does give a clue to the student's work ethic.

Amount of Daily TV Watching Time: 2 hours	C-4 The responses to this item have continued to surprise me over the years. Most of the respondents to this item do not seem to watch as much TV per day as most of their peers are reported to do in many studies published in the popular media. However, as in this case, the TV watching time is usually double that used for at home study. This gives the coach an idea of what he or she is up against in trying to work with the shooter in planning for any at home mental training time or bottle lifting time or dry firing time.

When I get home, I

A) watch my favorite soap opera

B) talk a lot on the phone with friends

C) usually do not have anything to do

D) my parents always have things for me to do

E) go mall-crawling

F) do my homework

G) other, explain

Circle Your answer:

(A)   B   C   D   E   F   G

C-5 This again is a reflection of the structure of the family. Are there things for the youngsters to do? Or is this shooter a mall crawling type? A shooter who is into socialization as evidenced by talking on the phone or doing the mall thing, is not a very promising candidate for the pistol team.

My teachers

A) like me

B) hate me

C) don't know I exist

D) Other, explain

Circle Your answer:

(A)   B   C   D

D-1 This goes to the basic feeling of the self-worth of the individual. As a coach, if the other personality indicators are positive, then this will give the coach an idea of what type of reinforcement the shooter needs. In recent years, a great deal of interest has focused on the relationship between self-confidence and performance. This item goes to the shooter's acquisition of the cognitive mechanism called *self-efficacy* which acts as a major determinant of individual behavior. Self-efficacy is the conviction that one can successfully execute the behavior required to produce certain outcomes. Actually, self-efficacy develops from four sources:
⇒ previous performance successes
⇒ the vicarious experience of observing others achieve success
⇒ verbal persuasion
⇒ reduced physiological arousal.

In addition, there is a considerable body of research which has shown that self-efficacy has a substantial impact on performance. It was shown that following failure, high self-efficacy subjects persisted significantly longer on a muscular endurance task than low self-efficacy subjects. In one research project, on the first trial, the high self-efficacy subjects maintained their contraction significantly longer than the low self-efficacy subjects. Following a report of failure, the high self-efficacy subjects exhibited an increase in persistence on the next trial whereas the low self-efficacy subjects showed a decrease. For pistol shooters, this is a very significant finding. It is for this reason that this item deserves the coach's attention. This is one of the items which allows the coach to have an insight into the prediction of a *"natural."*

The research we have studied, with respect to self-efficacy, has demonstrated a high reliability in the contexts of youth, interscholastic, intercollegiate, and adult recreational sport. The pistol coach should be aware that these results suggest that a proneness for being task- and/or ego-involved in sport has been reliably measured among participants who are of a wide variety of ages. The research has looked at those 10 years of age through adulthood. It has looked at these subjects who are involved in different levels of sport competition. It is important that the coach be aware that the experience of ego involvement is not truly realized until a child is approximately 10 years of age. At this stage of development, children begin to understand and use a differentiated conception of ability, which lays the basis for ego involvement. This personal goal state is meaningful and operational among children of this age group.

The pistol coach has to be alert to when a child reaches a level of cognitive maturity to understand that ability is a capacity separate from exerted effort. When this occurs, the coach should know that one's proneness for a task or ego involved goal is dependent on many factors. Pistol team socialization will have an impact on a person's degree of ego and task orientation. It is at this time that the pistol coach can make a difference by providing the shooters of the club or team differential experiences with social environments which reinforce the demonstration of superior ability or learning and personal mastery. In other words, the coach needs to find ways of making public acknowledgments of the shooter's performances. Sometimes, it will be just a private word of praise, other times it will be in a small group meeting where the performance is recognized publicly. This will have a positive impact on a person's degree of ego and task orientation.

We know that shooting athletes, taken as a group, who participate at a higher level of competitive shooting, where winning becomes more notable, are bound to be more ego-oriented than sport participants involved in a less competitive shooting atmosphere. Pistol coaches should, however, value personal mastery and skill improvement, or task orientation, regardless of competitive level. Bear in mind that, at any level of shooting, there is always room for improvement.

The research has shown that, shooters who are involved in the highest competitive level, International and Olympic pistol shooting are significantly higher in ego orientation than their adult counterparts who participated in recreational activities or athletes at a lower level of sport involvement, such as junior pistol shooters.

There is an abundance of literature which indicates that gender also influences the socialization process in terms of the development of achievement goal orientations. Males tend to be more concerned with winning and demonstrating their ability in competitive contexts than females. One thing pistol coaches might want to be aware of is that research indicates that a main effect for gender has emerged. Male athletes were significantly higher in ego orientation than females regardless of competitive level. This result is consistent with previous studies of gender differences in goal orientation in sport.

But the news in research is not all one sided. Males who participated in interscholastic or recreational sport were less task-oriented than high school or recreational female sport participants. These males also were lower in task orientation when contrasted with males who were just beginning their involvement in competitive sport. This would include junior pistol shooters. This pattern was similar when compared to those involved at the elite level, which in this case compared intercollegiate athletes. What is interesting too, is why males of these age/competitive groups are down playing the conspicuity of learning and personal improvement in sport. From the standpoint of contemporary social cognitive theories of achievement motivation, they are at risk to encounter motivational difficulties when faced with threats to their perceived competence and repeated occurrences of failure. This has major implications for the pistol coach. He must stand ready to bolster the male ego development.

Often, the pistol coach will use this information to predict performance variability and the cognitions relevant to such variation. However, we suggest that a more compelling model of achievement motivation would allow us to better understand the meaning of achievement activities to individuals. The pistol coach needs to develop a greater insight into why people decide to participate, or not participate, in competitive pistol shooting.

Coaches should be observant and take special note of any new pistol shooters who emphasize mastery-based achievement goals. The coach should be alert to those shooters who tend to judge their level of competence in terms of self-referenced criteria. This will tell the coach that they participated in pistol shooting so that they could develop their pistol skills. In other words, new pistol shooters who are high in task orientation will perceive the opportunities for learning, practice and regular training as important dimensions of the pistol sport experience. These reasons for involvement are fundamentally more intrinsic to the process of moving and performing pistol skills and they are typically individually-referenced.

To a lesser degree, pistol coaches need to be aware that task orientation is linked to the Affiliation, Team Membership, and Competition participation motives. In regard to the Competition participation motives, it has been suggested in previous research, that task-oriented individuals can indeed be attracted to the competitive features of sport. Although a pistol shooting participant can show that he or she is good at the sport by enjoying competition, one can also desire to compete so that personal improvement might result, accomplishing a task-involved goal.

Just so the pistol coach does not attempt to put a single goal onto each shooter, he must understand the *meaning* of competition will vary as a function of an individual's goal orientation.

Persons considering becoming college or junior pistol team coaches need to be aware that modern research has demonstrated over and over again, the finding that task orientation positively related to the importance of Team Membership and Affiliation as reasons for sport participation. This research has consistently found an interdependence between an emphasis on task-involved goals and the importance of cooperation and the social dimensions of the sport experience.

However, the pistol coach must not neglect those shooters with a strong ego orientation related to the importance of competition. These shooters have a need for the potential for recognition and social status in their shooting. Remember shooters high in ego orientation are engaged in the sport of pistol shooting so that they can compete with others and be socially rewarded for their accomplishments in that setting. Keep in mind that strongly ego-oriented pistol shooters appear to become involved in pistol shooting so that they can demonstrate superior ability in a socially acceptable manner.

When your parent asks you,
"How'd it go today? **Do you**

A) describe, in detail, the day's
occurrences
B) give out with your usual, *Nothing.*
C) highlight the interesting bits

Circle Your answer:

A   B   Ⓒ

E-1 This is one of the indicators as to the readiness of the shooter for mental training. What this does is give the coach a perspective into how the shooter utilizes memory. The functioning of memory mechanisms has been employed to explain how mental training enhances learning. Memory for anything requires rehearsal to achieve ultimately long-term storage. Decribing the day's happening at school is one indicator of readiness for mental rehearsal in pistol shooting. This rehearsal can take the form of overt movements or, apparently, of covert rehearsal. In other words, mental training may have some of the same characteristics of activating and maintaining short-term memory processes as overt practice, and in so functioning will bring about a more robust long-term memory. Mental practice can be viewed, then, as a process of recalling the happenings to maintain the material in short term memory. The effect of this enhances the consolidation of the material into long-term memory. The research evidence is substantial that differences in proficiency on various tasks is due in large part to differences in rehearsal strategies, and that rehearsal is an effective method to move information between short-term memory and long-term memory.

**Do you sometimes daydream
happenings in your imagination?**

A) Never   B) Sometimes   C)A lot

Circle Your answer:

A   (B)   C

E-2 This item serves as a guide for the coach as to the readiness of the shooter to engage in mental training. It is known that people use either imagery or words when they are engaged in thinking.

The pistol coach has to be aware of the shooter's mental preference for either verbal rehearsal or image rehearsal. To force the shooter into a mode of rehearsal which is foreign to him or her will often be ineffective. For a person who uses imagery naturally, the effectiveness of imagery training for the improvement of motor performance will come naturally through imagery vividness.

For example, one of our nine year old girls answered this item indicating that she engaged in daydreaming sometimes. So, the coach then made an effort to see just how developed this mental ability was. He asked her to see if she could visualize something in her mind. She screwed up her forehead, then said, *"Okay, I got a picture."* The coach asked her what it was. She replied that it was a picture of a yard. The coach wanted to know if she daydreamed in color or black and white. Since we live in Arizona and the yards here are typically a sandy brown most the time. The coach asked, what color is it. She looked up puzzled and said, *"brown."* The coach then asked her if she could put something in the yard. She screwed up her forehead again again and said, *"Okay, I got it."* The coach asked, what is it? She replied, *"A chicken."* The coach's next question, what color is it? *"Red."*

Bear in mind that coaches who work with shooters and employ visualization as a training method, need to understand that they must be aware that people are classified by the variable of Preferred Cognitive Style. This classifies people according to their preference for imagic versus verbal thinking. It is known that imagic subjects benefit more from imagery training than Verbal subjects because mental imagery constitutes a mode of thinking that Imagic subjects prefer and use more often.

Name:

F-1 As a pistol coach, your shooters' handwriting is a tool you can use together with your observations and other personality inventory tools. It is NOT to be depended upon all by itself. However, a look at your shooters' handwriting will give you a quick idea of the type of person with whom you will be working. Take the sample above, every movement and line is carefully made. The signature proceeds in a straight line. The signature ends with a final flourish. This large, slightly adorned signature shows pride and egotism, but this is overshadowed by the good flow, pressure and general arrangement. The leftward movements and umbrella-like structures show a need for structure and protection. We term this type of handwriting, where the writer's lowercase *m's* and *n's* are rounded or curved over, arcades. Arcades have a need for psychological protection. They get it by wearing a shell of privacy. However, they also have a desire to be leaders and to set rules for others to follow. They tend to be meticulous, methodical problem solvers. Often they are not quick learners. However, they do persist and they are thorough.

Arcaders tend to stay away from fanatics and fanatical thinking and theories. They accept what they see and are not fans of the *"just trust me"* crowd. For pistol coaches, this type of person will excel at doing detail things. Pistol shooting practice for this person will be something that he or she can obtain satisfaction from performing.

Reason for joining the Shooting Sports Club: *My friend*

asked me to go with her.

F-2 The angle of the lines can tell the pistol coach something about the shooter. The line of writing in this sample waves up and down. This indicates an emotional person. It also shows that the writer is slightly unstable.

The use of a devise such as *Test #1* allows the modern coach more insight into his shooters. Remember, the youngsters who come to a civilian club for shooting instruction are there because they want to be there. In the military, there will be some who are there in order to get out of regular duty. But, in a civilian junior club, the more tools you have to work intelligently with your youngsters, the more you will be able to retain. On the other hand, these tools may support your intuition about a youngster whom you do not feel comfortable having around handguns. Hickey has found handwriting to be invaluable. This is a method which will help the coach to determine which shooters have personality traits such as:

☞Self-confidence

☞Self-esteem

☞Intellectual imagination

☞Emotion

☞Sensitivity to criticism

☞Pursue goals relentlessly

☞Perfectionist - a stickler for details

☞Procrastinator

☞Optimism

☞Jealousy

☞Pride

☞Self-indulgence

☞Self-confidence

☞Sincerity

☞Vanity

☞Honesty

☞Greed

☞Inconsiderate

☞Inferiority complex

☞Hypocrisy

☞Intellectual balance

☞Accuracy

☞Egoism

☞Conscientiousness

☞Ambition

☞Cowardice   ☞Bully

☞Cunning   ☞Distrust

☞Deceit   ☞Emotional nature

☞Caution   ☞Enthusiasm

Remember, a coach has only so much time available to spend with shooters. He or she uses this to maximize the coaching time. If several indicators, including the coach's personal evaluation, indicate that the shooter lacks certain qualities which the coach feels are significant in being able to develop into a top flight pistol shooter, then it allows the coach to provide more help to someone with a better prospect. Of course, as a coach, you must be able to put up with the accusation that you pre-select those youngsters who will be the future champions.

Does a coach have to make use of the tools being made available to him or her in this book? Of course not! But, these tools will help you to know how to work with your juniors in order to bring them along to the goal they select.

The authors of this book do not pretend to be experts in the analysis of handwriting. There are many books about this subject in your local library. These books are also available in local book stores.

The Pistol Shooter's Scorebook

One thing which we believe promotes awareness of one's shooting is to record information about the shooting as close to the happening as possible. We have the youngsters in our Tucson Pistol Training Program maintain a shooting scorebook. Used in conjunction with other observations, character trait analysis tests, analysis of handwriting, and interviews, a coach can get a very good idea of the type of youngster with whom he is dealing. By periodically going over the shooter's scorebook or diary, with the youngster, the coach is able to keep on top of the shooter's progress.

The How-To Of A Junior Pistol Program

Name:_____

Starting Date: _____

Ending Date: _____

Diary Book #:_____

Date:

_____

     Sun Mon Tue Wed Thu Fri Sat

Time:

_____

Food Intake:

_____

_____

Personal Notes: _____

_____

_____

_____

Individual Shot Goal: _____

_____

_____

_____

Shooting Goal Statement:_____

_____

_____

Total Score:_____

Shots Meeting Shot Goal:_____

Number of Hits of value below:

10: _____ 9: _____ 8: _____ 7: _____ 6: _____

5: _____ 4: _____ 3: _____ 2: _____ 1: _____

0: _____

Examples of Goal Statements:

I have an excellent sight alignment recovery after the shot is fired.

I use a fast deliberate movement to bring the gun to eye level.

I focus hard on my front sight for each shot.

I fire each shot under 1 second of bringing the sights in line with my eye, with my front sight where I want it on the target.

I have an instantaneous smooth let-off.

I move my trigger finger quickly and smoothly.

I recover the sight alignment of each shot after it fires.

I have a smooth and instantaneouse trigger let-off.

I have a good solid focus on the front sight.

Shot Estimates

SS ☐ ☐ ☐ ☐ ☐

SS ☐ ☐ ☐ ☐ ☐

1-5 ☐ ☐ ☐ ☐ ☐

6-10 ☐ ☐ ☐ ☐ ☐

11-15 ☐ ☐ ☐ ☐ ☐

16-20 ☐ ☐ ☐ ☐ ☐

21-25 ☐ ☐ ☐ ☐ ☐

26-30 ☐ ☐ ☐ ☐ ☐

31-35 ☐ ☐ ☐ ☐ ☐

36-40 ☐ ☐ ☐ ☐ ☐

Thoughts About
Shooting Performance

_____

_____

_____

_____

_____

_____

_____

_____

_____

_____

_____

_____

Illustrations

To move the sights down, turn screw clockwise.

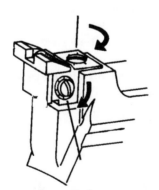

To move the sights left, turn the side screw clockwise.

The How-To Of A Junior Pistol Program

Timed Exposure Technique

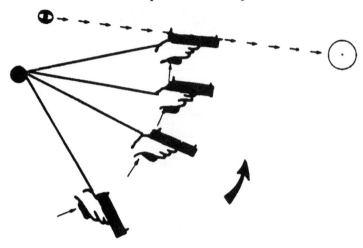

Directions:

> From the first shot, we teach the *rapid fire* techniques.
> Use the .22 caliber pistol for this.
> Magazines out and on the bench
> Load the pistols single shots
>> We do this so that when the shot fires, the pistol
>> cycles and leaves us with a cocked pistol
> We go through the routine
>> ⇒ **wrist firm**
>> ⇒ **elbow firm**
>> ⇒ **grip firm**
>> ⇒ **pistols to eye level.**
> Shooter required to stay on that target, <u>and dryfire</u>
>> <u>the second shot</u>

PURPOSE:

The shooters are learning right from the first shot, to
fire successive aimed shots. Thus, they do not know any other
technique. Within very short order, the shooters are shooting
groups, on the blank target, within the size of the 8 ring. So, as
soon as they do that, have them fire blank targets with a three

as soon as they do that, have them fire blank targets with a three seconds exposure. The idea is to get the dry fire shot off within the three seconds exposure. When they are shooting 8 ring sized groups on that, *then we go to the magazine.*

We use the Ruger .22/45 for the training tool of choice. We like this Ruger for two reasons:

1. In our opinion, the grip angle establishes a "natural" horizontal alignment between the barrel and the eye with a minimum of physical effort.

2. It has a rebated bolt face. This permits unlimited dry firing without peening of the breech face.

The How-To Of A Junior Pistol Program

The American Method

Use with the magazine:

Use three exposures for five shots

Exposure 1: 2 shots in three seconds

Exposure 2: 2 shots in three seconds

Exposure 3: 1 shot in three seconds

This is with the American Method, where they are allowed to have the pistols aimed when the targets are exposed.

The International Method

Use with the magazine:
Use three exposures for five shots

Exposure 1: 2 shots in four seconds
Exposure 2: 2 shots in four seconds
Exposure 3: 1 shot in four seconds

This is with the International Method, where they must come up from the *Ready* position when the targets are exposed.

When the shooters are shooting the 8 ring sized groups, on the blank target, with two shots, then we can go to five shots in ten seconds. There is no need to learn three separate methods for firing different shot strings under different time sequences We just need one method and it works for all.

Use whistle signals when firing fixed targets without a turning mechanism.

Training A Successful Intercollegiate Pistol Team

Introduction

Sievers was intimately associated with the training and management of many United States Navy rifle and pistol teams from 1955 through 1970. The six year period from 1965 to retirement in November 1970, was served in the billet of Small Arms Marksmanship Instructor, U.S. Naval Station Annapolis, Maryland. Included in the assigned duties was that of coach of the Midshipman Pistol Team, U.S. Naval Academy.

Sievers had slowly been developing a simplified method of pistol instruction dating from 1960 and the Naval Academy assignment presented an opportunity to thoroughly test the concepts. That the simplified methods are extremely effective is born out by the record of Intercollegiate Pistol Championships won, both team and individual, and the number of Midshipmen selected for first and second team All Americans pistol honors by the National Rifle Association.

During this association with intercollegiate pistol shooting a number of things were noted in relation to the program:

1. There was very limited participation nationwide, with the majority of teams participating exhibiting a low level of proficiency. Failure to improve proficiency results in rapid loss of interest of the participants in competitive pistol shooting, leading to the early demise of teams which had probably been launched with great enthusiasm.

2. There is no junior pistol program available which would correspond to the junior rifle programs offered throughout the country, many with local and state championships as well as

273

National Championships. This puts every college and University in the country, from Podunk U to the Service Academies on the same basis in pistol competition. There is no pool from which to recruit pre-trained talent. All schools have the same basic untrained students and any pistol team success can be directly equated with the knowledge and teaching techniques of the coach.

3. Although innumerable books and articles have been written by many authors on the subject of pistol shooting, this writer is not aware of any directed primarily at the training of the Intercollegiate Pistol Team.

This information is written with the hope that it may be of assistance to some Intercollegiate Pistol Coaches in improving team performance. No abstract ideas are entertained herein nor is range safety considered. The text deals primarily with the why and the how and the exercises used to develop the how to the point where the aspiring student reaches the level of proficiency necessary to be competitive in the front rank of intercollegiate shooters.

No claim is made or implied that any information presented is *"Right"* or *"Correct."* What is claimed is that the use of the methods delineated here has consistently produced high quality performance from the majority of the students exposed to its application.

If you have science and skill, good shooting. If not, lots of luck but it won't help.

This evaluation was true in circa 1965. Thirty one years down the road, circa 1996, the identical evaluation holds true.

Fundamentals

A logical starting point is a definition of what we mean by fundamental as applied to pistol shooting. This point of view will be that a fundamental is an element that is indispensable in order to get consistent *"hits"* with the pistol. An analysis of the shot process will enable us to isolate the elements considered as fundamentals.

If the pistol barrel can be lined up in exactly the same way, repeatedly, not with any target, simply with the eye, and the pistol can be caused to fire without introducing any angular misalignment to the barrel during discharge process, consistent "hits" will be produced wherever the pistol is pointed no matter what else is done. If the barrel cannot be lined up in a consistent manner with the eye or if angular misalignment is introduced between the barrel and the eye during the discharge process, it is immaterial what else is done; consistent "hits" cannot be produced where desired.

This analysis isolates two elements, consistent barrel alignment with the eye and discharge of the pistol without introducing angular movement between the barrel and the eye as indispensable ingredients required for getting consistent "hits" with the pistol. Ergo, there are two and only two "Fundamentals" of pistol shooting. What happened to stance, grip, breathing, rhythm and various other things that have been advanced and espoused as fundamental by the majority of pistol coaches and shooters? The answer is that these items are not now, and never have been fundamentals of pistol shooting, but merely techniques for the application of the two fundamentals delineated above. It is felt that lack of understanding, by instructors, on this particular point, is a major cause for the student's failure to show progress in the initial phases of instruction. The student's attention is misdirected toward mastering the techniques for a simple physical skill neither the student nor the instructor really understands. The simple physical skill is simply pointing a tube at a piece of paper. The instructor must not permit techniques to be equated with or take precedence over fundamentals during pistol instruction. To do so is to place an unnecessary obstacle in the path of progress. Techniques have their place in the general scheme and should be kept in their place.

The Meaning of Sight Alignment

Consistent barrel alignment with the eye has been determined to be one of two pistol shooting fundamental. The primary purpose for which the sights are used is as reference to obtain this precise barrel alignment. There is only one requirement for correct sight alignment; it must be the same for every shot. Consistent!

It should be thoroughly understood by the student that the term "Sight Alignment" is a translation of the term "Barrel Alignment" and that when the term "consistent sight alignment" is used, what is implied is "consistent barrel alignment with the eye."

The Meaning of Trigger Finger Movement

Discharge of the pistol without introducing any angular misalignment between the barrel and the eye has been determined as the second of two pistol shooting fundamentals. The discharge is normally initiated by manually moving the trigger, disengaging the sear. Therefore this vital element can be translated to the term *"Trigger Finger Movement"* meaning of course, simply being able to discharge the pistol without introducing angular misalignment between the barrel and the eye. Learning the technique of moving a finger to perform this seemingly simple task in an effective manner is unquestionably the most difficult hurdle to clear on the way to pistol mastery.

Techniques

In considering what techniques to teach the student, the two fundamentals, barrel alignment and trigger finger control, must be constantly kept in mind. Anything that is done to distract the student's attention from these vital elements will decrease training effectiveness. Any method of instruction that instills some understanding of the two fundamentals will show some measure of positive results. Pistol shooters seldom reach the performance potential of which they are physically capable, but peak out at some lower performance level dependent on their understanding and the application of the two fundamentals. To realize the maximum results from instruction, everything the student does should have a positive effect on sight alignment and trigger finger movement. This may be too much to expect, but more realistically the coach should not permit any techniques that would adversely effect either of the fundamentals.

Whatever techniques are taught, they must be within the physical capabilities of the student. If the student is required to perform a task that sounds completely reasonable but is physically impossible to accomplish, he can become thoroughly frustrated in short order.

Barrel Alignment With The Eye

It is an almost universal belief that the primary purpose for which the sights are used is to aim the pistol at the target. Practice of this belief is a sure road to inadequate pistol performance. The primary purpose for which the sights are used is to implement the fundamental, barrel alignment with the eye. The secondary purpose for which the front sight is used, is as a reference to point the aligned system at the desired area.

With the excellent and widely used Partridge Type sights, a particular alignment, the top of the front sight aligned with the top of the rear sight and equal lines of light on each side of the front sight, has long been acclaimed as the "correct" sight alignment. This method of instruction also calls this alignment the "correct" alignment with understanding that "correct" is an arbitrary designation. This honor is accorded this particular alignment for the sole reason that it is felt that this particular relationship of the front and rear sights is the easiest one to align consistently and to detect the slightest misalignment.

Eye Usage

Only minimum eye usage is stressed; at least one eye open, looking at the sights when the pistol is discharged. Either eye may be used with the preferred eye being on the same side as the pistol.

In all previous activities, such as throwing a ball, throwing a stone, or shooting a slingshot, the concentration has been on the target. The pistol shooter must be made aware of and learn to change a lifetime habit pattern of target fixation.

277

Therefore, the shooter must be actively taught how to look at the sights with specific exercises designed for this purpose.

A ready reference enabling the student to tell if the eye is open when the pistol is discharged is to see the fired cartridge case pass through the line of vision.

To summarize and stress: one eye must be open looking at the sights when the pistol is discharged.

Grip

There are several features that we would like to encompass in the grip but first we must establish the primary purpose of the grip. Relating to the fundamentals we have a choice between barrel alignment and trigger finger movement. A little thought here will readily lead us to the conclusion that our only contact with the pistol is in the grip. Therefore, if we do not get trigger finger movement in our grip, we will never get it. Unless we establish trigger control as the primary purpose of the grip, anything else we do, in relation to the grip, is wasted effort.

The student must learn to avoid holding the pistol in such a manner that the barrel forms an extension of the arm. This grip automatically requires the line of sight to pass through the shoulder joint.

Grasp the pistol with the hand high on the butt and the barrel at a slight angle to the forearm. Place the tip of the finger on the trigger and apply pressure. Observe the barrel for angular displacement to the left as pressure is applied to the trigger. This movement is a mechanical problem and no amount of practice will overcome the error. Now place the finger as far as possible through the trigger guard and repeat the test. The barrel misalignment now is normally slightly to the right. Somewhere between these two extremes, we can find a finger placement that will eliminate the mechanically induced misalignment. This is our starting point for finger placement on the trigger.

Grip firmness is essential to maintain control of the pistol in firing successive aimed shots. How firm is firm? Firmness is tailor to each individual. The pistol grip is squeezed until a tremor is induced then relaxed until the tremor stops. That's firm! Just below the trembling threshold. The firm grip is maintained and only the finger is moved to discharge the pistol.

In the matter of moving the finger the student can only be given guidance! He must perfect the action himself. I have long believed that the top performers in competitive pistol shooting have developed their trigger finger movement to a conditional reflex. When they have their very precise sight alignment pointed in an acceptable aiming area, the pistol discharges without conscious effort. Students don't start this way and must make a conscious effort to move the finger, applying continuous pressure and waiting for the pistol to discharge. If the pistol is discharged knowingly by a slightly convulsive movement of the finger, angular misalignment will be unavoidably introduced to the barrel. Simultaneous with this action the central nervous system will cause the eye to blink preventing observance of the telltale sight misalignment. This abrupt movement of the trigger is referred to as "trigger snatching" or "jerking" and is the major cause of unsatisfactory shooting performance. Physical habits, whether desirable or not, can be formed very quickly. Consequently, effective trigger finger movement habits must be started with the first shot the student fires.

Wrist

Keep the wrist firm, in the normal position it assumes when the clenched fist is thrust out. Under no circumstances flex the wrist to get sight alignment. This is a fatal error for top level performance because it cannot be done consistently. We get our sight alignment elsewhere.

Elbow

We want all of the student's physical actions to be purposeful. In the simple matter of straightening the arm, random positioning of the arm bones in the elbow joint can occur. To observe the results of positive positioning, hold the right arm out with the elbow joint exposed. Clench and rotate the fist as far as possible to the right then back to an upright position.

279

Flex the elbow and note that the forearm rises vertically. Repeat, rotating the clenched fist as far as possible to the left. Again flex the elbow and note that the forearm rises at an angle to the left. The point here is that the student can deliberately and consistently position the bones in the elbow joint as desired which in turn has an effect on the direction of recoil of the pistol. Position the bones in the joint in the same relative position each time prior to raising the pistol and maintain the elbow straight and as firm as possible when holding the pistol in a firing position.

Stance

In common with sight alignment, there is almost universal misunderstanding of the pistol shooting stance. Many writings concerning this element are replete with misinformation.

The competitive rules require the shooter to be standing with the pistol held in one hand only, thus setting up requirements which must be included in the development of the stance. As with the grip, there are several features we would like to encompass in the stance, but first we must establish the primary purpose of the stance. Relating again to the two fundamentals, we are left with barrel alignment with the eye, having assigned trigger finger movement as the primary function of the grip. Therefore the primary purpose of the stance is effortless and precise barrel alignment with the eye. Once understood, this readily explains the variation in the stances that have been successfully used.

We will start building the stance from the ground up and establish a stable eye position.

⇒ The feet are spread comfortably but no wider apart than the shoulders.

⇒ The body is erect and relaxed.

⇒ Head erect and turned to the right until the neck muscles are slightly strained then turned back until the strain is relieved. This usually leaves the head turned at about forty-five degrees to the right. We now have the basic stance established with the features desired and are prepared for the crucial step of establishing barrel alignment with the eye.

⇒ The pistol is grasped with the grip that gives trigger control and thrust out in the "International Ready Position," wrist firm and elbow firm.

⇒ The pistol is raised to eye level

⇒ Do not move the head!

⇒ Do not move the body!

⇒ Move the arm swinging the pistol in a horizontal arc following the movement with the eye only! As the pistol is moved to the right the relationship of the sights will change with the front sight moving to the left of the rear sight. As the pistol is moved back to the left, at some point on the arc the sights will align and continued movement to the left will cause the front sight to appear to the right of the rear sight. Again swing the pistol back to the right until the sights align. This is the position we are looking for!

We have put it all together! Grip, foot position, body position, head position, and arm position and have come up with effortless barrel alignment, the position used by champions tailored to any individual.

It is a simple matter to shuffle the feet and rotate this entire system full circle. Once the system is set up the entire system is rotated until the focus, sight alignment, is centered on the aiming area. In short order a body angle relationship can be established with the target and only minor changes, if any, are required to rotate the system onto the aiming area. Check the position for sight alignment each time the pistol is replaced in the hand because minor changes in the grip will change the relationship of the sight alignment and the aiming area for any given stance. If there is no variation in the grip, there will be no variation in the sight alignment established for any given stance.

Free Arm

Immobilize it as desired. Let it hang. Place the hand in a pocket, front or rear. Hook a thumb in the belt. Forget it!

Aiming

Aiming is the act of pointing the aligned system at the desired area. Notice that aiming is treated as a separate action from sight alignment although they appear to be a single action. This is a critical area where some instructional techniques can actively teach trigger *"jerking."* No instructor would knowingly do this thus we encounter the situation of requiring the student to do something that sounds completely reasonable but is physically impossible to accomplish. Any technique requiring the sights to be aligned on a particular point on discharge will invariably produce "trigger snatchers" and the consequent unsatisfactory performance.

To illustrate a disastrous aiming technique, in particular, is the one where-in the student is told to apply pressure when aligned on the aiming point and to hold pressure when off the point and that the pistol will then discharge at some time on the aiming point. Sounds great, but it is physically impossible for the student to control the trigger finger in such a sequence. The only time the shooter sees the required point alignment is "on the fly" so to speak, as the aligned system passes the point with insufficient time for any trigger pressure to be applied.

Muscle and mental tension will increase rapidly and the shooter will discharge the pistol with a convulsive finger movement, which this writer refers to as the "NOW" syndrome. The convulsive finger movement is normally accompanied by automatic eye closure preventing the shooter from observing the resulting misalignment as the pistol discharges. The student has extreme difficulty correcting erroneous performance if the error cannot be observed as it occurs.

The most successful aiming method used and the one specifically recommended is the widely known *"Area Aiming."* This method accepts and utilizes the fact of movement that it is impossible to hold the pistol still. The area of movement observed when the pistol is held in the firing position is called the *"wobble area."* When a specific aiming point is used as the center of the wobble area, the whole is called the *"Aiming Area."*

282

With the aligned system pointed at the aiming area, constant pressure is applied to the trigger until the weapon discharges. The aligned system traces a random pattern in the aiming area and frequently passes the center. If the system alignment is maintained and no misalignment introduced on discharge, we will have parallel aiming error in relation to a longitudinal line passing through the center on the aiming area. The parallel error will give the effect of shooting down a pipe and every shot will strike in the aiming area.

The average student is physically capable of performing the functions required for successfully delivering a deliberate aimed shot using the area aiming technique. The student can maintain system alignment. The student can point the aligned system at the aiming area. The student can discharge the pistol, without introducing misalignment or eye closure, by applying continuous pressure to the trigger and waiting for the pistol to discharge. The inevitable result of this performance is a *"hit"* on the aiming area.

Considering the situation from the skill standpoint, there are only three reasons for the shot to strike outside the desired aiming area:

☞1. The aligned system is not pointed at the desired aiming area.

☞2. Sight misalignment (Barrel misalignment with the eye).

☞3. Faulty trigger finger movement causing pistol misalignment.

Reason one seldom appears as a problem. Reason two and three are the focal points of pistol shooting performance. Any thing that adversely effects either of these fundamental, at any time, will adversely effect the performance.

Breathing

Breath control has not been found to be a problem area. Its instruction is considered an extraneous added distraction for the beginning pistol shooter.

Rhythm

Rhythm in pistol shooting is a gross canard, an inconsequential which has been repeated so often for so long by so many that it has taken on the status of divine truth.

Champions deliver successive shots on the basis of precise sight alignment and acceptable aiming area. Whether or not this is done in a rhythmical manner has absolutely no bearing on the results.

Rhythm is merely another distraction to take the student's attention away from the fundamentals of sight alignment and trigger finger movement.

Basic Exercises

In order to teach the fundamental and the techniques for their application, with the minimum expenditure of time and ammunition, four basic exercises were developed as instructional tools. Each exercise is named to indicate its function and is used with both blank and bullseye targets.

Slow Fire Exercise

The student is required to count out the required number of rounds for the exercise. Example: *"Shooters count out ten rounds of ammunition."* With the magazine out, single rounds are loaded on appropriate command, by placing a single round in the chamber and closing the slide. The shooters are then directed to the international ready position by the command *"Extend Pistols."* The standard commands, *"Ready on the right," Ready on the left,"* and *Ready on the firing line,"* are used to have shooters raise their pistols to eye level and fire one round followed by an immediate recovery, picking up sight alignment, area aiming and firing one round dry fire, then clearing the pistol without further command.

The key word *is "line"* in the command, *"Ready on the firing line."* The shooter is directed to adjust his movements to arrive at the firing position on the word *"line."* This is also the command to commence firing one round.

First Shot Exercise

The same as the slow fire exercise using a three-second target exposure with turning targets, or whistle signal with fixed targets and standard NRA commands. Dry fire portion of the exercise is completed even though the targets edge or the whistle sounds.

Two Shot Exercise

Five rounds loaded in the magazine. Three consecutive exposures as in the first shot exercise with the single round fired at the shooters option. After the second round the student will recover and pick-up the sight alignment in preparation for a third shot before lowering the pistol.

Five Shot Exercise

A standard string of rapid fire of five rounds with ten second exposure.

Application

This section will present a broad picture of the training to avoid foundering in minutia.

Team Selection

Any able-bodied student who has the desire and the opportunity can be developed into a competent intercollegiate pistol shooter. Any student who has the foregoing plus above average coordination can be developed into an intercollegiate champion.

If you have more candidates than you can support, make the selections on the basis of interest, willingness to follow instructions, and coordination. If the squad has been organized for a year or more, select only from the freshman class. To have a continuous going operation, you must have a continuous freshman input.

Equipment

Do not worry about what you lack. Do the best you can do with what you have and you will be amazed at how well you can do. Austerity is generally the rule in any shooting program.

The minimum equipment required would include a suitable pistol, safety glasses, ear protectors, and NRA rule book per shooter, plus an adequate supply of .22 caliber long rifle standard velocity standard grade ammunition, cleaning equipment, and NRA B-2 and B-3 targets. Any additional equipment such as scopes and shooting boxes is certainly nice to have.

Suitable pistol mean a semi-automatic with adjustable sights, two magazines, and a minimum five inch barrel. Avoid the use of a muzzle brake attachment as it can be unnecessary source of trouble. The S&W Mod 41 with the 5 1/2 inch barrel or the High Standard "Victor" would be considered first class equipment. Bear in mind NRA International rules limit barrel length to 6 inches.

Initial Training: First Phase

This area is the nucleus of a successful training program. The foundation can be laid so that the student will make continuous progress or, unfortunately and all too often, so that the student will be prevented from progressing.

If possible, schedule team practice for ninety minutes per day, five days per week. Plan thirty minutes for lecture time and sixty minutes for shooting. Compute ammunition expenditure at one hundred rounds per shooter per session.

Utilize the first session to lecture and discuss fundamentals and techniques as presented herein and introduce the NRA rule book with intent on page one and rules 2.8 and 3.5.

Second and future sessions, review fundamentals and techniques and introduce one new item. If shooters are divided into two sections, have one section shoot then lecture all before the second section shoots.

Introduce shooting with the Slow Fire Exercise. Fire ten shot exercise on the blank target. Any scratch paper approximately target size is satisfactory. Designate the center of the blank target as the center of the aiming area.

Maintain positive control over the students and direct their actions with explicit instructions between commands.

The following illustration has the instructions in quotation marks.

Establish Position

"Grasp the pistol with the grip that will give you trigger control." "Grip firm, wrist firm, elbow firm." "Raise the pistol to eye level." "Swing the arm and pickup sight alignment." "Shuffle the feet and rotate the system onto the aiming area." "Pistols down." The above instructions will establish the position giving sight alignment with the system pointed at the aiming are and are used continuously to impress the student with the inseparable relationship between grip, trigger control, sight alignment, and stance.

Dry Fire

Dry fire five or more cycles using the following sequence. Simulate one round load. Magazine out, close slide on an empty chamber. Extend pistol. International ready position. Ready on the right, Ready on the left, Ready on the firing line. Pistols at eye level on the word *"line." "Look at the sights." "Move the finger." "Eye open." "Move the finger smoothly."* Keep the

287

student's attention centered on the elimination of sight misalignment as the hammer falls.

Slow Fire Exercise

Fire five two shot slow fire exercise with the procedure described under Basic Exercises described earlier. Use whatever time is needed. Probably two sessions. Again stress the elimination of sight misalignment on both the live round and the dry fire. Using a clear plastic overlay of the B-3 target, the objective is to fire a nine-ring size group anywhere on the paper. Do not adjust sights. This comes later. Evaluate and critique targets after each ten round exercise. Trigger control problems are immediately apparent and corrective action can be taken before undesirable habits develop.

First Shot Exercise

Fire five First Shot Exercises using the procedure described earlier. By the completion of the fifth exercise the dry fire shot should be completed within the exposure time and the group size should equal slow fire.

Two Shot Exercise

Fire fifty rounds of Two Shot Exercises. By the completion of the last exercise, firing should be completed within exposure time and group size should equal slow fire.

Initial Training: Second Phase

Repeat the Basic Exercise in sequence, fifty rounds each. Introduce sight adjustment on the first Slow Fire Exercise. Continue adjusting sight so that groups are centered on the blank target by the completion of the sequence.

Again repeat the sequence, as above, alternating between blank and bullseye target each ten rounds. Readjust the sights on the bullseye target using the six o'clock point as the center of the aiming area.

On the completion of the last sequence you are ready for the first gallery course. Eliminate timed fire and shoot two rapid fire stages. Scores generally range from the 240's to the 270's, with the average in the low 260's.

Routine Training

This you must play by ear. Some suggestions follow.

Do not permit individual practice until the student has completed the initial training.

Start each session with a sight alignment exercise by firing on a blank target.

Fire at least one gallery course per session, with selected exercise, using both blank and bullseye targets.

Do not waste ammunition on timed fire. Substitute rapid fire except for matches.

Fire a 900 aggregate where all scores are posted as fired at least once per week. Observe NRA rules and no alibis to teach the importance of pistol maintenance. For other gallery courses use alibis to teach malfunction procedure when allowed.

Summary

If the shooter is having problems, something is adversely effecting the sight alignment or the trigger control or both.

The following 1971 news article is a vivid demonstration of the effectiveness, on the collegiate level, of the Sievers Simplified Shooting Method.

Naval Academy Wins Second Straight Intercollegiate National Team Championship, ANNAPOLIS, MD.

NATIONAL INTERCOLLEGIATE PISTOL TEAM CHAMPIONS – CONVENTIONAL

Seated: (From left) R.C. Mayes (Team Captain), G.D. Appenfelder, J.M. Jacobs, J.R. Harris

Standing: (From left) LCDR G.R. Nakagawa, USN (Officer Rep), J.G. Kimball (Manager), MAJ L.D. Brugh, USA (Coach)

For the second consecutive year, Navy marksmen have captured the Intercollegiate National Championship in conventional pistol. Announcement of the Midshipmen's achievements was made recently by the National Rifle Association after a tabulation of sectional results front throughout the country.

In addition to the number one team, the Midshipmen also boast the number one and number two individual shooters on conventional targets. Senior Gary Appenfelder of Melbourne, FL, topped the college marksmen with an 862 in the individual match, two points better than senior teammate Jody Harris of Big Springs, Tex., who finished as the National runner-up with an 860.

Appenfelder and Harris also contributed to Navy's title-winning 1131 team total. Appenfelder was high man with a 286, Harris and fellow seniors Bob Mayes had 282's, and sophomore Mike Jacobs rounded out tile scoring with a 281. Appenfelder

290

and Mayes were members of the team. that fired a 1136 to win the pistol crown in 1970.

The Midshipmen narrowly missed another individual. championship in the International section of the NRA tournament. Freshman Rodolfo Firpo, who shot a 262, placed second nationally. Firpo's score was also a National Junior record for the International course.

Eight Midshipmen, headed by captain Bob Mayes who was selected for the third straight year, were listed on the first two All America teams. Mayes, Individual International Champion as a sophomore, headed a quartet of midshipmen on the first team.

Seniors Appenfelder and Harris and sophomore Tom Martin of Wilkes-Barre, PA, were the other Navy gunners among the nation's top ten. Second team selections included seniors Jim Gokey of McLean, VA, Mike Scherr of Alexandria VA, sophomore Hugo Blackwood of Raleigh NC, and freshman Tom Roberts of Morgantown, VA. Additionally, Mike Jacobs was listed as an Honorable Mention.

The NRA has also certified that the Navy Freshmen, topped by Roberts with a 285, established a new National Junior team record on conventional targets with a 1094, breaking the old record by five points. In addition to Roberts, the Freshman team was composed of Firpo , Don Villnow , and Dwight Pitman.

The selection of the nine shooters as All-Americans brought to eleven the number of All-Americans presently on the Academy pistol team. Senior Ron DeLoof and junior Steve Konopa, second team choices in 1970, are also member s of the talent laden squad.

VARSITY PISTOL TEAM 1970-1971

Seated: (From left) R.C. Mayes (Team Captain), T.O. Martin, J.W. Gokey, M.R. Scherr, G.D.Appenfelder, J.M.Jacobs, J.G.Kimball, J.R. Harris

Standing: (From left) LCDR G.R. Nakagawa, USN (Officer Representative), R.B. Kennedy, B.L. Bullough, W.L. Groves, D.J. Crane, D.B. Marshall, R.J Borro, C.S Tomlinson (Assistant Manager), MAJ L.D. Brugh, USA (Coach)

Not shown: M. E. Lee, H.G. Blackwood, S.J. Konopa, R.M. DeLoof

Coach for the team was Major Larry D. Brugh, US Army, an instructor in the Mechanical Engineering Department at the Academy. Major Brugh was the assistant coach to Art Sievers, well known in Navy shooting circles, for two years and then assumed the coaching role upon Sievers' retirement from the Navy.

All of the Navy shooters used High Standard Model 106 Military pistols. Appenfelder, Mayes, and Jacobs used Oxford Illuminated gun sights and Harris used a 1.5x Tasco Pistolscope in the team and individual conventional competition. The illuminated gun sights were first tried by the team two years ago primarily as a training device for developing trigger control. A very graphic picture of the results of poor trigger control is obtained by watching the dot of light in the sight. However, most of the shooters found they could shoot better scores in competition with the sights so they have been used quite successfully the last two years. The sights were also used by the firing members of the 1970 championship team.

Service Pistol Qualification

The information on military and police training will be combined because of their similarity. The ultimate use of this skill must be considered in the method of presentation.

Targets

Targets can be classified in many ways. We will classify them in two broad categories, passive and active. A passive target is one which poses no threat to the shooter. An active target could pose a lethal threat to the shooter or his environment. For the military and police user, the pistol is not an assault weapon but a survival tool in an adversarial situation. Visual contact must be maintained with the target at all times.

These students are trained with the precision techniques to help them understand the potential accuracy of the pistol. In the field, targets are ballpark size and looking through the sights will produce the required pointing accuracy.

We have based this section on a definitive study of the Coast Guard small arms training, "SHOTS THAT HIT". A study of U.S. Coast Guard marksmanship by William R. Wells, II. This report is outstanding for it's authenticity of information based on official Coast Guard records. We feel that all services and the great majority of police agencies have suffered the same deficiencies in their handgun training. These deficiencies continue to the present day. Our remarks in regard to Coast Guard handgun training are not meant or implied to be disparaging. This may be misconstrued because some statements will be very blunt.

The study by Wells contains 158 pages in seven chapters plus a bibliography. We will pick up our first reference from chapter three, titled "Eternally on a War Footing".

Shots That Hit

A Study of
U.S. Coast Guard
Marksmanship
1790 - 1985

by
William R. Wells, II

United States Coast Guard
Historian's Office
1993

In 1932 Surfman Stanley L. Loyer visited many stations each summer. His evaluation: "the 45 (pistol) training was a disaster... Recruits and many old surfmen shot into the ground half way to the target...very few surfman qualified."

"More changes were in store when Franklin D. Roosevelt took office in January 1933. Nearly a year later Henry Morgenthau became Treasury Secretary replacing William

Woodin. Upon taking office, Secretary Morgenthau, following presidential desires to professionalize the eight regularly armed agencies under him, ordered an inspection of all bureaus' small-arms training and maintenance. Except for the Coast Guard, the inspectors found all the bureaus deficient in knowledge of use and maintenance in their weapons".

"In the following months more inspections revealed many weapons in such poor maintenance that it was doubtful they would fire. Morgenthau ordered the Coast Guard to begin training all Treasury civilian employees who carried weapons. Rear Admiral Harry G. Hamlet, Commandant since 1932, obliged the secretary by assigning trained instructors where they were needed."

"Coast Guard small-arms instructors traveled to all parts of the nation and territories, training agents from Customs, Border Patrol, Secret Service, Internal Revenue, mail carriers, and other agencies."

Coast Guard's Lethal

Virus

It is obvious from the above that the Coast Guard's disastrous training methods spread like a lethal virus throughout the Treasury Department Bureaus.

We move up to the 1942 era and this was still the opinion of the Coast Guard headquarters. "After years of experience and competition with the .45 caliber pistol, Headquarters still considered it a difficult weapon to teach and shoot. This may have been because of personal preferences within Coast Guard Headquarters and the close association with training of the Treasury Department civilians, whose primary arm was the .38-caliber revolver. The revolver preference remained strong in spirit and the influence of the Treasury bureaus continued for many years."

We will now move up to the period of the late 60s and early 70s. "In 1970, in the midst of a deteriorating small-arms program, the Coast Guard instituted its own two-week small-arms instructor (SAI) course at the Reserve Training Center, Yorktown, Virginia. The intent was to prevent further decline in quality. The 1971 course graduated 24 instructors with plans to train 24 more later in the year."

"The course taught the trainee the principles of effective shooting, under the supposition that an experienced marksman made an effective instructor. This same premise, used in the past at Cape May and elsewhere, was faulty because competent marksmen do not always make competent general service instructors. Neither the Yorktown or Cape May course taught instructional methods or presentation. There may have been some credibility in the theory for the men who had spent most of their careers firing in competition, but most trainees left Yorktown without learning the basic elements of teaching."

From the distant past it has been accepted as a divine precept, particularly among elite pistol shooters, that the most skilled shooter was, ergo, the best coach. Our present instructional method evolved from this background. The difficulty of learning to shoot the pistol is well established. Horror tales are freely exchanged among instructors attesting to the stupidity of their students. In all of Sievers years in shooting he has never seen the onus for pistol shooting failure placed anywhere but on the student. *"They can't hack it."* Is it possible in all this time that Sievers has never encountered an incompetent instructor? Not likely. Instructors come in all shades of proficiency. The only thing that has never changed is the basic method of instruction and the course content. The track record for this type of instruction is plain to see for anyone who would care to look. The elite shooters emerging from this system are so few that they are looked upon with awe and adulation. The failures, of which Sievers is one, are legion, the reason being ascribed as a lack of some indefinable attribute which is a divine gift to the anointed few. Sievers genuflected to this interpretation as a way of life for more years than he cares to remember. Sheer chance bounced him out of this rut and started him on an evaluation process of what was really required to get consistent "hits" with the pistol versus what was assumed to be required.

Complete and Utter Failure

The results for a military pistol course are foreordained before the first shot is fired. Complete and utter failure. Failure is completely expected and accepted as normal. In thirty-six years in the military Sievers never saw it any other way until his thirty-third year of service when, while stationed at the US Naval Station, Annapolis, MD. He had the opportunity and sufficient rank to turn this situation around in the US Navy. For this, on 22 October, 1970, Sievers was awarded the Meritorious Service Medal in the name of the President of the United States. His commendation reads in part; *"Displaying exceptional leadership and technical and professional competence, Commander Sievers developed a training method for the service pistol which resulted in outstanding advances in the proficiency attained by the midshipman at the United States Naval Academy. His innovative techniques in the small-arms training of all personnel have contributed directly and measurably to naval readiness and national defense, and reflected great credit upon himself and the United States Naval Service."*

The Naval Academy management wanted the best in small-arms training for the midshipmen. As a consequence, the Plebe summer marksmanship training was conducted by the United States Marine Corp. The training was presented in four identical one week periods to accommodate twelve to fourteen hundred Plebe Midshipmen. This had been in vogue long enough to become a tradition. Infrequently, because of unstable international conditions, the Marines were unable to staff the

297

program and make do instruction was instituted. This happened in the summer of 1968 when the Marines were unable to staff the pistol training. LCDR Conn, the director of the Navy shooting program in NAVPERS, volunteered the Navy shooting teams to take up the slack. In Midshipmen pistol training, the previous high mark reached in quality was a 28% Expert qualification established by Marine instruction in 1967. In 1970 with the only change being the employment of Sievers concepts of pistol shooting instruction, his Navy instructors under his direct supervision raised the quality standard to an unbelievable 71% Expert qualification and 99% total qualification for fourteen hundred Midshipmen. This result was not within any instructors experience and for the majority of them it was beyond their comprehension. It was EASY! The hard part was getting the chance to do it.

Let us revert to 1968 and explain how the chance came about.

At this time the head of the Weapons Department was the Academy Officer responsible for the small-arms training program. He normally appointed Marine officers from his department as his representatives. Because of Navy participation he appointed LCDR Gordon Nakagawa as his officer representative for pistol. His assistant was Major Larry Brugh, U.S.A., an exchange instructor in the engineering department. The third officer was Lt. Sievers, Marksmanship Instructor, US Naval Station, Annapolis. In our Academy association these three officers were involved with the Midshipmen pistol team. LCDR Nakagawa was the officer representative, Lt. Sievers was the head coach and Major Brugh was the assistant coach. They had considerable experience working together as a team and had similar goals and outlooks. They assimilated into their team a fourth member, Chief Petty Officer Willy "The Bull" Martin. CPO Martin was double Distinguished and the first of the elite shooters who understood Sievers concepts. His service for putting this program on track and keeping it on track in the face of massive opposition was invaluable. The major obstacle in the implementation of this pistol course was the overt resistance displayed by the Navy elite pistol shooters. Every known Navy elite pistol shooter was physically present and a member of the

Navy pistol team. No elite pistol shooter was consulted for input into this training program nor was any input considered. A national pistol champion was among the elite shooters.

For the physical setup, 50 firing points with electric turning targets were available. Assistant instructors were assigned on the basis of two students per instructor. The instructors were thoroughly briefed that the only information they would pass on to the student would pertain to "looking at the sights, to align the barrel with the eye and move the finger smoothly." Nothing else was to be brought to the student's attention. On the initiation of the first period of the first session the pistol coaches, in spite of their specific instructions to the contrary, started giving the students all the *"good stuff."* They knew they had been provided with insufficient information to teach anyone how to shoot and it was their duty to save this inefficient management from its' folly. Chief Martin recognized the situation instantly and halted proceedings. He physically relieved the elite pistol shooters on the line with rifle shooters. He required the pistol shooters to stand silently behind the ready line and observe operations. The rifle shooters did not have the pistol shooters knowledge of all the *"good stuff."* They had no problem following instructions and putting out only the minimum information they were given. With the pistol shooters out of the action, Chief Martin immediately had the program on track. Chief Martin made the pistol shooters observe the training until the third day when he replaced them on the firing line with the admonition to keep their mouths shut about all of the *"good stuff."*

The first week qualification resulted in 98% qualification with 37% Expert. A quality level never before produced. The elite pistol shooters contribution to this is referred to as active resistance.

The second week record firing produced 42% Expert qualification. The elite pistol shooters contribution to this is referred to as passive resistance.

The third week record firing produced 47% Expert. The elite pistol shooters contribution to this is referred to as pouting.

The fourth week the Expert average was 54% with the elite pistol shooters completely neutral.

The overall qualification average produced 45% Expert qualification for the Midshipmen class of 1972. This quality qualification with the service pistol had never been produced anywhere by any organization civilian or military.

The Academy management specifically requested NAVPERS to staff the pistol instruction for 1969.

In 1969 with the elite pistol shooters now on track the identical program produced 62% Expert and 99% overall qualification with the service pistol. An article published in the American Rifleman, February 1970 issue, publicized this program. On the completion of the 1969 program the Academy management requested NAVPERS to staff the pistol training program and also the rifle training program.

In 1970 the Navy elite pistol shooters with two years of this training system under their belts were completely motivated. Because of their previous success and motivation they completed the training by producing in excess of 71% Expert qualification and 99% overall. NAVPERS said it was unconscionable to award 71% of the participants medals and the standards were obviously too low. LCDR Nadagawa asked the question, "What percent of Experts they could live with?" NAVPERS came back and said, *"They could tolerate 50%,"* and also gave him figures for Sharpshooter, Marksman, and Unqualified. LCDR Nakagawa and Major Brugh ran the 1970 results through the computer. The first revelation was that the 15 yard stage of the "F" course was nondiscriminatory. NAVPERS said, *"eliminate it."* They evaluated the 1970 figures and came up with qualification scores for a new 300 point course that would meet NAVPERS qualification specifications.

The following year, 1971, with LCDR Nakagawa and Major Brugh running the pistol training program with the Navy pistol team as assistant instructors, the predicted averages came out on the nose, 50% Expert. To the best of our knowledge this is the only pistol training course we have heard of where it was possible to produce predicted results on demand. In other words, we knew exactly what our training was worth and how to produce and reproduce it.

How was this training job accomplished?

What it really was was a communication job. What we did was reach more people at one time, with a simple message in this area, than had ever been reached before.

Shooting instruction is based on a complete distraction which is "hitting the target" and compounded in its' presentation based on ignorance, superstition and throwing stones.

A time honored axiom, probably based on the stone ax, is that *"a good workman knows his tools."* The authors believe this is a valid axiom to review the operation of a pistol.

It is completely obvious to any person, man, woman or child, that when a pistol is discharged the one big thing that happens is that a bullet comes out the barrel. We have yet to find anyone who can remember when they didn't know this. So obviously, this information is and has been common knowledge in the public domain. Our next question is will the *"bullet"* come in contact with something? The immediate retort is, *"Certainly."* The next question posed is where will that be that the contact is made? In short order the answer is apparent that the only place this could be is where the barrel happened to be pointed when the bullet exited the muzzle. We then ask the question if anyone can remember when they didn't know this once it has been brought to their attention. We have found no one who denied knowing this information after it had been brought to their attention.

The next question we ask is how can we tell exactly where the barrel was pointed when the bullet exited the barrel? The more experience an individual has in the shooting the more difficulty they have coming up with a reasonable answer to this question whereas a 10 or 12 year old who has never experienced the shooting myths will immediately reply, *"Find the bullet hole."* In other words, if we can find the bullet hole it gives us instantaneous feedback on where the barrel was pointed on discharge. The bullet hole is an effect not a cause. Obviously, if we wish to have the bullet hole appear in a particular place only one thing has to happen, the barrel must be pointed at that place on discharge. It's completely obvious that how the pointing is done is completely immaterial as long as the barrel is pointed at the area where we wish the bullet hole to appear. In this analysis it's completely obvious that the pointing is the problem for having a bullet hole appear in a predetermined area.

The pistol is a precision pointing tool. If we accept pointing, with a precision pointing tool as the problem, we are in a whole new world. Hitting and pointing have nothing in common. If the bullet hole is visible all it does is give us instantaneous feedback on the quality and consistency of our pointing. How precise, how consistent. Where can anyone point a pistol? The answer is so simple it insults the intelligence. Anywhere they want to. When can they point the pistol? Again, anytime they want to. How can they point the pistol? Again, the obvious, anyway they want to. In competitive shooting games rules define how the pointing must be done to equalize the competition. In military and police applications the name of the game is survival. How the pointing is done is completely immaterial. A Civil War General summed up his philosophy with a simple phrase, *"Get there fustest with the mostest."*

Whatever is required must be within the physical capabilities of the student. When learning a physical skill the average person can only handle one element. When they get past one they are starting to get into trouble. When they are past two they are in trouble. Obviously, in learning a simple physical skill such as pointing a tube at a piece of paper, we are limited to a maximum of two elements. If we exceed two elements we are outside the shooters envelope. It becomes obvious that the physical requirements must be reduced to two elements for any reasonable expectation of successful pointing. The shooting diagram clearly establishes the two elements as precise and consistent barrel alignment with the eye and the instantaneous smooth movement of the finger to get the bullet out the barrel.

302

This internally aligned system can be pointed where ever, whenever, however and moving the finger instantaneously smooth will produce indicators i.e. bullet holes as desired.

The methods and exercises for producing positive results are exceedingly simple. It is normal in most situations that to improve a course something is added. In shooting training to improve the course it is necessary to delete. We have never seen a shooting course that did not include, in some manner, the two elements that we have just proposed. Unfortunately these two elements are camouflaged by so much ignorance and superstition passed off as expertise that their importance is completely unrecognized.

If you wish to upgrade your current course, simply eliminate anything that does not refer to the two elements which we have pinpointed. If you wish to further improve your course, we suggest you try the simple basic exercises we will delineate.

Chapter 6 of the Coast Guard study makes a strong statement of the inability of female shooters to cope with the .45 caliber service pistol. If there is any study to show that the service pistol is aware of gender, we would like to be privy to this information.

Also Chapter 6 states, *"Headquarters modified the navy "F" course for Coast Guard use that was in essence the U.S. Navy Qualification course. The change deleted the entire ten-round string, 15-yard string. Fired in its entirety from the 25-yard range it now consisted of 30 rounds for a 300 possible."*. As stated earlier this change was made by NAVPERS in 1971 based on the Nakagawa - Brugh study at the US Naval Academy.

The Coast Guard study is focused on the title *"Shots That Hit."* *Hitting* the target is a valid measure of a person's skill in throwing stones. It has no connection with precision pointing using a precision pointing tool. In shooting, hitting the target is an effect not a cause. In the summary by Wells at the end of Chapter 7 he states, *"All concerned know that the only shots that count are those that hit."* It is obvious that his complete focus on a distraction, hitting the target, will never permit the self evident solution which is precision pointing. All the bullet hole does, at best, is provide instantaneous feedback on the pointing. How precise. How consistent.

It is completely obvious that the Coast Guard experts have never understood or taught precision pointing with a precision pointing tool and the management bought their expertise. We can say, fortunately, they used the information we have cited for the use of their shipboard batteries.

What are we really trying to teach the embryo pistol shooter to hit? The bullseye? Again, unfortunately, yes. Are the results encouraging? Definitely not, because the bullseye is part of the problem. It is nothing but a snare and a delusion in the instruction of basic pistol marksmanship. What are we trying to teach the embryo pistol shooter? three SIMPLE ACTIONS: to LOOK AT THE SIGHTS IN ORDER TO MAINTAIN SIGHT ALIGNMENT, POINT THE PISTOL AT THE *TARGET AREA*; AND DISCHARGE THE GUN WITHOUT DISTURBING THE SIGHT ALIGNMENT, aiming eye open.

From this we can establish the fundamental of accurate pistol marksmanship. But first, what is a fundamental? By fundamental we are mean a foundation, an essential something we cannot do without. As applied to pistol shooting there are only two fundamentals. Sight alignment and the ability to discharge the gun without disturbing the sight alignment which will be referred to as trigger control. If we can do these two things we will get consistent *"hits."* when the gun is pointed at the target area, no matter what else we do. If we cannot apply, these two fundamentals it is immaterial what else we do, we will not get consistent "hits" in the target area.

If these fundamentals are accepted we can then develop the hypothesis that in order to attain maximum accuracy performance with the pistol, every thing we do in delivering a shot must contribute something positive to sight alignment and trigger control. This is probably physically impossible so to get into the realm of the possible we must analyze our actions in relation to their affect on sight alignment and trigger control and discard or cease any actions which have the slightest adverse effect on either of the fundamentals. We are not trying to make polished competitive marksmen in our qualification instruction. We merely wish to develop a skill level suitable for military purposes. If we can teach a student to look at the sights, point the pistol at the target area, and discharge the pistol without disturbing the sight alignment excessively we will achieve this skill level. This can be readily accomplished in a ten hour course if we know what to teach and how to present our instruction.

It is commonly accepted that the most difficult pistol exercise to master is the one referred to as sustained or rapid fire which consists of firing a prescribed number of rounds within a limited time frame. In the "F" pistol course this is five rounds in 15 sec. With the generally accepted methods of pistol instruction the student is first schooled in the "fundamentals" with sight alignment and trigger control included with various others such as grip, stance, breathing etc. varying with the background and experiences of the instructor. Shooting exercises are started slow fire at a bullseye target. The student is usually told that the rapid fire exercises is very difficult to master and proficiency must first be gained at the slow fire and then the timed fire before any attempt is made to practice the rapid fire. It is also common practice to tell the student to shoot the timed fire just like the slow fire only a little faster and the rapid fire like the timed fire and once again a little faster.

As an instructor what have we done to ourselves and the student by using these techniques? One of the basic principles of instruction is to remove any distractions in the teaching area that could possibly draw the students attention away from the objective of the instruction. If you are *trying to teach the student to look at the sights* and then place a bullseye down range for the student to hit, you have placed a formidable barrier between you and your objective before a shot has been fired. Mere words telling the student to look at the sights will never overcome a lifetime habit of looking at the target. The student must be taught how to change this habit and the bullseye has got to go! In addition you are trying to teach the student three methods of trigger control, one for slow fire, one for timed fire, and one for rapid fire.

And the last cruel blow, unknowingly and unintentional you have built a mental block in the student's head to the effect that rapid fire is *"tough."* If it were possible a much more efficient method of instruction would be one whereby only the rapid fire technique was learned. Once mastered, a single round slow fire or a single round timed fire could be fired with exactly the same technique as a single round rapid fire. The application of the fundamentals required to fire one accurate shot slow fire are exactly the same as the application of the fundamentals to fire one accurate shot rapid fire. It is not only possible to start the new shooter with rapid fire techniques, it is extremely simple. The course presented to accomplish this has been in use for three years with a yield of 70% "Experts". Enough to convince this writer that the average military student is completely capable of qualifying as "Expert" if he is reached by the instruction.

The course, as currently presented requires 10 one hour periods. The first Instructional Tips:

Stay loose - be flexible in presentation - Observe progress by checking shot group spread and match shooting exercise to skill level.

Four basic exercises
1. Slow fire:
   load single round
   magazine out
   Fire: live round
   recover
         pick-up sight alignment
   area aim
   dry fire 1 round.
2. 1st shot exercise:
   Same as slow fire using 3 sec target exposure
   Dry fire portion of exercise is completed even though target edges.
3. 2 shot exercise
   5 rounds loaded in magazine.
   Three 5 second exposures.
   Single round fired at shooters option.
4. 5 shot exercise
   5 rounds loaded in magazine
   15 sec exposure.
   The only reason any bullet hole is any where is because that is where the barrel was "POINTED" on discharge!

306

The Summer Pistol Camp Experience

The United States is now a nation of summer camps. There are summer camps for music, football, baseball, basketball, forestry and shooting. In running a summer outdoor shooting camp in Tucson, we had some considerations that other camp sponsors would not have had. The temperature in the June, July and early August time frame was HOT. The temperature in the 1996 camp was always between 103° and 107°. Our summer day camp was conducted from 8:00 AM to 12:30 PM each week day.

We would advise anyone thinking of conducting a summer camp program to conduct the camp as a part of the NRA Shooting Sports Camp Program. This opens an opportunity for your camp to receive funding by the state Friends of NRA committees.

In addition, the NRA provides a number of camp theme materials, promotional posters, hats, shirts, attendance and appreciation certificates. The NRA also provides grants to help get the camp started.

It is the opinion of the authors that this NRA summer camp program, especially with the grant funding provided, is one of the most exciting shooting development programs the NRA has ever established.

How does our program fit into the NRA Summer Camp Program? Persons wishing to conduct a summer camp according to the new pistol training method described in this book should think about conducting it as an NRA Special Interest Camp. The title of our summer camp in 1996 was the *Training of the Conditional Reflex in Pistol Shooting Camp*.

This type of camp dispenses with lectures about the history of the sport, discussions about gear and accouterments, how the sport is played and all the other types of lectures associated with the programs of competition camps. People not familiar with our program are prone to protest, *"But, how can the kids learn about the sport if you don't include these lectures?*

307

You'll wear the kids out if all they do is shoot. You have to break up the shooting with talks about the sport so they can rest up. You can't have little kids spend several hours out in 105° degree temperatures just shooting!"

It is attitudes such as are reflected in the above comment that have led to the dumbing down of America in many different fields. This is the type of attitude which has led to the sissifying of American pistol shooters. Our good intentioned people have figured they know what is best for seeing that youngsters are not harmed by coaches who overextend the capabilities of the youngsters in sport. It is just people like this, who are part of the liberal touchy-feely good crowd, who want all people to be equal and who definitely do not want to have anyone work harder at something than everyone else. Since they never learned how to work hard to become shooting champions in their own right, they often cannot bear to see others being taught to do something they missed out on.

Or, they come from a recreational mind-set where everyone just shoots to hear the loud bang. If the person is able to have a hole appear in a target, he is given a round of applause. It is the coddling of our youngsters which destroys their competitive spirit. The competitive spirit has taken on a bad meaning in America due to the liberal attitude of *"Let's all just be friends together and not try to beat one another in things."* It is this attitude that coaches should try to desensitize the competitiveness and promote other aspects such as fun and team spirit which has been so destructive of the American competitive spirit in pistol shooting.

One of the 4-H Extension Agents even conducted a meeting, of the youngsters and their parents in our Saguaro 4-H Shooting Sports Club, in which he informed us that the 4-H philosophy did not include having youngsters performing at as high a level as ours were. He said the 4-H idea was that there would be informal competition not going beyond the County Fair Level. At the County Fair, the competition of the shooting aspect of the program is de-emphasized by giving equal points for the preparation of a poster depicting the shooting sports. In other words, the shooter fires 10 shots with an air pistol. His score is a combined point total of what he shoots plus the score he is given for his poster. To be objective about the coaches running the shooting sports section of the 4-H participation in the county fair, their purpose is to do things which will promote the shooting sports. They came up with the idea of having the youngsters in their shooting sports clubs make posters illustrating activities in the shooting sports. That is a worthwhile and noble purpose. However, for a coach with a group of youngsters interested in competition, it is not the way to go.

In a summer camp program where the focus is on the acquisition of the Conditional Reflex in pistol shooting, it is important that the camp stay within that area. One thing the camp director of this type of program has to be continually alert for is the *good adult shooter* who feels you are not offering the youngsters enough information so they can be good shooters. In other words, this *good adult shooter*, in listening to what you are telling the youngsters knows that you are not giving them enough information. So, he tries to save you from yourself, he tries to add what you left out. One thing this *good adult shooter* has is credibility. At the current state of the youngsters development, that *good adult shooter* is visibly better than they are. In the majority of pistol shooting training in the past, not even America's elite shooters have been able to produce groups of successful pistol shooting youngsters. We postulate that the basic difficulty lies in the kinds and amount of the information to which they subjected the beginning student. The initial experience usually determines the path each student will follow long term. Again, youngsters will shy away from areas that do not create immediate success. Our program is designed to create instant pistol shooting success from the very first shot. But, if the *good adult shooter* is allowed to present information you left out, beware, he has started to destroy the youngsters from that very first mouthful of the *good stuff*. He is probably a really good person who is trying to save you from yourself. He knows you have to teach people to breathe if they are to learn to shoot correctly. What he does not understand is that breathing is an automatic process and if left alone, it will adjust automatically to whatever the pistol shooter is doing. Impress, on those who you permit to assist you, that the only things they may say to a shooter is:

309

"Look at the sights!"
or
"Move the finger smoothly!.

Only in the event of a potential safety violation may **ANYTHING** else be said to the shooter.

Now, on to the camp program. We agree with the professional golf instructor who said, *"We like to tell the kids that we'll stay on the tee until they drop, which is usually two hours...The agenda is simple: we begin and end by hitting a lot of golf balls. There is no group lecture...Always remember, you can modify this program regularly, but have a long-term goal in mind."*

Our agenda is also simple, we begin and end by shooting a lot of bullets. There is no group lecture. Lectures often entertain and sometimes bore. In any event, they create a sense of dependance on the lecturer by the shooter. A lecture has the tendency to bankrupt the shooter of his independence.

We begin and never stop working to have the youngsters self-develop a conditional reflex between what the eye sees and the movement of the trigger finger. Remember that throughout the summer camp. Is it possible to have the youngsters do too much shooting? Only if your intention is to develop a bunch of wimps.

1996 Summer Conditional Reflex Training Camp

NRA Special Interest Camp

Training The Conditional Reflex For Pistol Shooting

7:30 AM

Shooters arrive.

Range setup begins. Target frames set up at 10 meters.

8:15 AM

(Keep this brief and to the point.)

1. Introduction and explanation of purpose of camp.

To provide an opportunity for the campers to firmly establish the Conditional Reflex in their pistol shooting.

2. Discuss the Conditional Reflex and how and why it is effective.

The Conditional Reflex is effective because it creates an automatic instantaneous smooth movement of the trigger finger when the eye sees that the front sight of the internally aligned system has reached the desired area of the target.

It is effective because it is subconscious. When something is subconscious, it is more efficient than when it is done consciously. When something is done consciously, the timing of the act is less efficient due to the extra time that elapses from the time the decision is made to perform the action than if it is under subconscious control. The less time spent with the pistol at eye level, the less time for energy expenditure attempting to maintain the relationship of the pistol in it's relationship with the target.

3. Short discussion of Pavlov and his dog. Use this to explain how a conditional reflex is established. Keep it brief.

4. Mention how our method works with Newton's law of motion and gravity's effect on the act of shooting.

5. Today's training will start off with a warm-up of the Conditional Reflex. We will start the warm-up by firing 20 shots from the benchrest at 10 meters on the blank target. Your effort in this exercise to is to move the trigger finger instantaneously smooth when your eye sees the front sight of the aligned system is in the area of the target you want. The way this will be done is that you will:

☛ load one round into your magazine.

☛ Insert the magazine into the pistol.

☛Drop the slide.

☛Release the magazine and take it out of the pistol.

☛Focus on perfect alignment of the sight system with the front sight as the reference while firing the shot.

☛Recover the sight system.

☛Focus on moving the trigger finger without allowing any movement of the pistol while you dryfire a shot.

☛Repeat this process until finished with the 20 shots and 20 dryfires.

Let's Set Up To Shoot!
8:45 AM

9:00 AM	
Allow 20 minutes	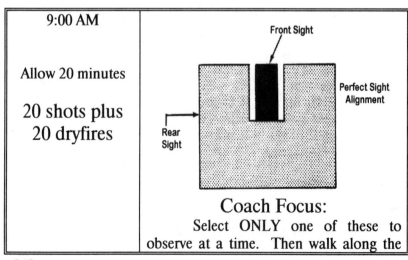
20 shots plus 20 dryfires	

Coach Focus:
Select ONLY one of these to observe at a time. Then walk along the

line to another shooter and observe another of these items. Use a stopwatch. Use with the

Coach's Firing Line Observation Form

shown below.

1) Smooth trigger finger movement.
2) Time from eye acquiring the sights until the shot is fired.
3) Time from eye recovering the sights until the shot is dryfired.
4) If there is a perceivable time difference check with the shooter to see if the shooter understands and can tell why there is a difference.

Coach's Firing Line Observation Form

Firing Point	Name	Trigger Finger Movement	Time of Shot From Eye Level	Time of Dryfire From Sight Recovery	Time + or −
1	Cade	smooth	2.14	0.87	-1.27

Comments

Point 1: Shooter's shot time and dryfire times are too far apart. This type of difference may indicate either a hurried dryfire or an excessive amount of time being taken to fire the live shot.

It is the author's intention that our program develop solid people with a well developed trait of hardiness. Can hardiness be developed by coddling the youngsters? Absolutely not! It is our plan to develop youngsters who will be world beaters. Is this accomplished by having a youngster fire one shot and then have the whole camp stand around analyzing that shot? No way! In our summer camp program, the focus is development of the conditional reflex in pistol shooting. All of the youngsters in our 1996 summer camp program had been training between three months and two years with our program.

We regarded this camp as an intermediate or advanced camp for the further development of their conditional reflex. Unlike most advanced pistol camps around the country, our camp does not pretend to give the youngsters the secrets the coach left out during their initial instruction. No!

A summer camp conducted under the program explained in this book, thinks of advanced training in an entirely different context. We believe an advanced camp focuses on development of the conditional reflex through the spirit and the intensity in which it is practiced, rather than the techniques used. The goal is still to continually develop and to win. The attributes of a top-grade pistol shooter are a combination of physical and psychological factors. It is often said that between high level pistol shooting athletes there is only a minute difference in the level of their skills. However, on a psychological level, the evaluation of their level can be quite different. It is the same in all individual sports.

For example, in 1961, the world of Judo was turned upside down when it was realized that Japan could be beaten at it's own game. Anton Geesink of Holland, in a historic match, defeated Koji Sone of Japan to capture the World Judo Championship title. At that time none of the world's Judo experts could even visualize a non-Japanese Judo Champion. Anton Geesink did, and he made a reality of his dream of being the best. Of course, he also worked very hard.

How was this done? Champions have to have both the ability plus the necessary psychological drive. Regardless of the motivation that keeps them training it is essential they have a dream or higher goal. Many American pistol shooters have had the dream. Many have trained very hard. Many also have had the necessary psychological drive. But, suppose your training flies against certain immutable laws of nature. Suppose your training is designed to defy the laws of gravity and motion? To train in this manner is to train to fail.

Everyone has heard those classic sayings, *"Quitters never win and winners never quit,"* or *"When the going gets tough, the tough get going."* They are hung in many locker rooms to remind individuals that it takes hard work, guts and determination to succeed. On your way to becoming the best you can be, you will

314

run into many plateaus, and in striving to improve, at times it may feel as if you are actually getting worse. Many advanced pistol shooters complain of being in a slump or feeling that they cannot improve beyond a certain level.

Can you imagine a top of the line machinist being in a slump? How long do you think his employer would keep a person who has slumps lasting weeks or months? He would not allow himself even one cut which was off specs. That's because he knows his business. When a pistol shooter tells someone he is in a slump, he is telling that person that he does not know what he is doing in shooting the pistol. Like the machinist, if he knew what he was doing, he would have stopped, taken a look and then made the change to get back on track.

In the summer camp, the shooters are trained to know their business of pistol shooting. If something is not right, they are trained to look at trigger control and the conditional reflex functioning. We follow Bill Blankenship's advice, *"Before I start shooting for a season I work very hard on getting my trigger finger to start moving when I see a still weapon with perfect sight alignment. In other words I'm trying to make it automatic. I have had good results using this system of trigger control and at times it is completely automatic and I never have to think about it. If I do have trouble, it is necessary for me to dry fire until it again becomes automatic."* (*The Pistol Shooter's Treasury* edited by Gil Hebard).

In the camp setting, the coach should always direct the attention of the shooter to only trigger finger movement and the functioning of the eye. Is the eye open at the time the shot fires?

The 2nd Relay

9:20 AM

      At the end of the 20 minutes of benchrest shooting, go through this process:

1) Cease fire.
2) Clear and bench guns
3) Coaches check guns
4) Shooters go forward and move the frame of the shooter on your right to 25 yards.
5) Give your Rapid Fire target to the person on your right to put up for you.
6) Shooters you will have 15 minutes to move the frames and hang targets.

9:35 AM

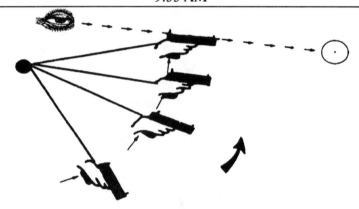

Conditional Reflex Training

Training Procedure:

☞ Using NRA Rules for the Rapid Fire event, there will be 12 five shot rapid fire strings fired on the Rapid Fire target at 25 yards. That is a total of 60 shots. To be fired immediately, one string right after the other.

☞ No breaks between strings.

☞ The firing of the 60 shots will generally take 15 minutes.

☞ Encourage the use of multiple loaded magazines for this exercise.

☞ Alibis will be run after the 12th string. 3 alibis maximum.

☞ Do not allow any talking between strings. Keep the process very professional.

☞ Remind between strings, the purpose is to make the conditional reflex automatic.

☞ When finished, repeat the changing target process of taking down and putting up the shooter's target on the right.

☞ No scoring of targets between relays.

☞ Stress quick changing of targets.

☞ REPEAT THIS FOR FOUR (4) RELAYS.

☞ This will be a total of 240 shots.

☞ As the campers become more efficient at changing targets, another relay can be added by about the 3rd week of the camp.

☞ Targets will be scored after the range has been cleaned.

☞ Guns will be cleaned after the targets are scored.

☞ Targets are scored by the person to the right of the shooter.

Coach Focus During Rapid Fire:
Select ONLY one shooter to observe during a 10 seconds relay. Then walk along the line to another shooter and observe the firing of another 10 seconds relay. Use a stopwatch.
Use with the

Coach's Firing Line Observation Form

shown on page 313.
1) Smooth trigger finger movement.
2) Time from eye acquiring the sights until the shot is fired.
3) Time from eye recovering the sights until the next shot is fired.
4) If there is a perceivable time difference between the two shots check with the shooter to see if the shooter understands and can tell why there is a difference.

317

> 5) If the shooter reports not being able to reacquire the sights after the first shot. More than likely he has not setup his stance with the internal alignment of his sights.

Many potential great pistol shooters quit as they run into training obstacles; yet there are others who meet and overcome even the greatest of obstacles. Continuous and rigorous training requires a special perseverance. This Conditional Reflex Summer Camp is set up to teach that special perseverance. We do this through a rigorous training program. It is designed to promote the development of a hardiness of spirit in the shooters. It is not done by treating them as wimps. The camp is conducted on a matter of fact assumption that the shooters will shoot. To paraphrase the golf pro, we will shoot until the shooters drop. Again about two hours. But, boy, what a two hours! We will fire between 200 and three hundred rounds per shooter. Each coach will remind the shooters that their purpose is to develop the conditional reflex.

The shooters must get the alignment of their sights through their stance. If they do not, they will find that they have to search for their desired area of the target when the pistol reaches eye level.

Coaches must make absolutely certain that they do NOT bring ANYTHING beyond the two fundamentals of:

1	2
Visually Align the barrel with the eye, using the top of the front sight as a reference, point the aligned system at the area where you want the indicator (bullet hole) to appear..	**Instantaneous Smooth Trigger Finger Movement**

In any instance, determination plays an important role in the psychological development of the pistol shooting athlete. The shooter has to be persistent in training. This camp will teach persistence. Coaches must allow the shooters and **expect the shooters to participate in each relay.** Again, it comes down to consistent training.

318

This procedure continues throughout the duration of the camp. Some camp sponsors believe that they must vary the camp schedule to entertain the youngsters. The authors disagree with that supposition. We found during the Conditional Reflex Camp that the youngsters were kept too busy doing the actual training. The idea of a formal entertainment schedule did not enter into the thoughts either of the campers or the coaches.

The authors realize that this camp varies from that which is most common in today's pistol training world. For one thing, the shooters in our camp do not fire over whole courses of fire. In other words, there is not any firing of a National Match Course during training.

We do vary the schedule on two days of the week. During those two days, we divide the campers into two groups. One group of three fire the International Rapid Fire target at 25 meters. What we do is to set up three bays of rapid fire target, five target frames set one next to the other. These are not turning targets. The International Rapid Fire shooters of the future will be firing at non-turning targets. They will shooting according to a series of red and green lights. That is what we are training our shooters on.

The training is done with relays of 4 seconds per relay. Each shooter fires five shots on each 4 seconds relay for twenty relays. That is a total of 100 shots. The targets are changed and scored after the completion of the 100 shots. The purpose of this training is further development of the conditional reflex.

While the one group is training at 25 meters over the 4 seconds conditional reflex program, the other remaining campers are engaged in a 2nd Amendment day exercise of sighting in their pistols. One of the hallmarks of the conditional reflex is the selection of the area of the target where the shooter decides to point the aligned sights using the front sight as a reference point. But how do you know where to decide to point the aligned sights? This is done during sighting exercises conducted from off a benchrest. Using the benchrest, the shooter is able to determine which area will give him or her the most consistent results. If a shooter has never fired a score of 100 out of 100 points from off the benchrest, how can that person expect to do it from the one handed shooting position? So, the benchrest is an integral part of the training we do of the conditional reflex.

We combine this with developing an awareness in the youngsters of how the 2nd Amendment to the Constitution of the United States is a part of their shooting heritage. We therefore designate a day or two in the camp as 2nd Amendment day. We do this sighting in at 25 yards from off the benchrest. To explain the meaning of the significance of the 2nd Amendment, we even employ poetry. Not being able to find anything which adequately explained the concept behind the term *"well regulated militia,"* Hickey wrote a poem which explains the meaning within the context of the times during which the 2nd Amendment was written.

The 2nd Amendment
Constitution of the United States
by Bob Hickey

On the farms
Men picked up rifles
long since well-regulated
by gunsmiths expert
in hammer and
sight shaping rasps

Men hammer lengths of steel
into swords tasty for freedom
Women, water ladled in preparation
for part in sword
hardening process
anxiously helping
husband and sons
get ready, liberty to defend

The Summer Pistol Camp Experience

At Valley Forge
never ending full body disheartening chill
all unbearable by day's boredom
dreading night's colder yet
thoughts of freedom from King George
turning now to freedom from rebellion
thoughts encompassing desertion
as more weak hearted patriots flee
liberty's price

Only the few and the proud endured
blood soaked scant rags
encasing feet blood clotted
Hands, fingers and noses
frost bit many times over
endured the price liberty extracted.
As across the overcast morning sky
the eagle spread it's wings
going after it's prey
And through battles lost,
the war was won
By the few joined in the bondage
of freedom
Joining hands frost bit with
hands farm labor scared
and hands of citified artisan
Creating a Constitution
world envied.
Guaranteed by patriots not yet born
Guaranteed by the people's
Right to bear arms!

Upon getting their handguns sighted in, the campers were each given a certificate.

2nd Amendment Day

July 9, 1996
The Bill of Rights
AMENDMENT II
Right to keep and bear arms.

A **well-regulated** militia, being necessary to the security of a free State, the right of the people to keep and bear arms, shall not be infringed.

Be It Known That:

Michal Newhouse

Age 9,
Has Sighted In Her Pistol, On This Date, For The Year 1996, at 25 Yards, as admonished by the 2nd Amendment of the U.S. Constitution, and is a Well-Regulated Member of the Saguaro Shooting Sports Club.

reg·u·late (rég'y -lät') ——tr. v.-lat·ed., -lat·ing., -lates.

3.   To   adjust   (a mechanism) for accurate and proper functioning.

[*Lat. regulare, regulat- < Lat. regula, a rule.*]

The American Heritage Dictionary, Copyright © 1986, 1987 by Houghton Mifflin Company.

A sight is a mechanism.

The Summer Pistol Camp Experience

Consider what we are doing during our summer camps. First of all, notice, that the camp is a day camp. It is not the length of the camp day which is important, it is the type of training which is practiced. In our camp program, the shooter actually shoots for only about two hours. Yet, notice what we have done, we have made that two hours a very efficient two hours for what we want to accomplish. Our purpose is the furthering of the development of the shooters conditional reflex. Many training programs we have researched have the shooters firing over particular established courses of fire. Often neither the shooter nor the coach or instructor has any real idea of what the shooter should be learning from such practice. Notice we have not referred to it as training.

Under our program the pistol shooting athletes must focus all their attention or the task at hand. Nothing should enter the mind but the task at hand. This ability to think of only one thing is the virtue of single-minded concentration and devotion to exactly what the shooter is doing at the time. It is this single-minded concentration that the camp program is designed to train. By setting up a training program such as we have outlined here in this chapter, you will find that you have established a professional attitude about the training in your camp. By keeping the youngsters busy and focused on the conditional reflex development, you do not give them much opportunity to think of what others are doing around them, what they have to do after training or what they did before training, etc. This methods helps the shooter to concentrate on the act he or she is doing right now, right here. In Western philosophy we try to fill our minds in order to know something, in Eastern philosophy, the idea is to empty the mind in order to know something. The goal of these two seemingly opposite philosophies is the same, for by either standard, concentration means to lose yourself in the activity, not to be conscious of time or space but totally committed. In other words, we want to train the youngsters to lose themselves in the activity of pistol shooting. We do not focus on the score, but on the process of making the act of shooting a subconscious action.

This is how we are training the youngsters to specific character traits. For example, we want to instill a sense of competition into all activities the youngsters engage in. As a part of this effort, we formalize the process of developing strength in the forearms and shoulders by having the youngsters be tested on the number of pushups they can do on their fingertips. We conduct a fingertip pushup as a part of every registered tournament we run. As a part of this process, we pit the boys against the girls. Take a look at just how this is done:

Fingertip

Pushups

by Vince Blair for the Saguaro Shooting Sports Club.

The push-up event measures the strength and endurance of the chest and shoulder muscles, triceps, wrists, hands and fingers.

It is not a measure of form.

On the command:

Get set

assume the front-leaning rest position by placing the fingertips of your hands where they are comfortable for you. Your feet may be together or up to twelve inches apart. When viewed from the side, your body should form a generally straight line from your shoulders to your ankles. *The palms of your hands may not touch the ground.*

On the command:

Go

begin the pushup by bending your elbows and lowering your entire body as a unit until your upper arms are parallel to the ground. Then return to the starting position by raising your entire body until your arms are fully extended. **Your body must remain in a generally straight line and move as a unit for the entire repetition.**

At the end of each repetition, the scorer will state the number of repetitions you have completed correctly. If you fail to keep your body generally straight, to lower your entire body until your upper arms are parallel to the ground, or to extend your arms completely, that repetition will not count; the scorer will repeat the number of the last correct repetition. If you fail to perform the first few fingertip pushups correctly, the scorer will tell you to go to your knees and will explain what your mistakes are. You will then be sent to the end of the line to be re-tested. However, after the first ten fingertip pushups, no restarts are allowed. The test will continue, and the incorrect fingertip pushups will not be counted. An altered front-leaning rest position is the only authorized rest position. That is, you may sag in the middle or flex your back, but you must return to the correct starting position before continuing. If you rest on the ground, or raise either hand or foot from the ground to 'shake it out', the event will be terminated. You may reposition your hands or feet during the event, but you may not allow the palms of your hands to touch the ground. Correct performance, not speed, is important. You will have ten minutes in which to do as many correct fingertip pushups as you can.

Your score will be the number of correct fingertip pushups performed in a ten minute period.

Alternate position for females, fingertip pushups

Choice #1

The event for the females will be the same as the above except with the following exceptions:

Females may choose a starting position where the arms are fully extended and vertical; palms must not touch the ground, and body must be generally straight from the shoulders to the hips. Knees must be resting on the ground and ankles must be crossed. Toes may not touch the ground. Females are to use their knees as a fulcrum and not pivot their hips while using the alternate position. In addition to this, the toes or the palms of the hands may not touch the ground during the entire repetition.

Choice #2

Females may use the primary fingertip pushup position in which case, the number of repetitions will be multiplied by 1.7 to compare their score to the males'.

Basis for above alternatives for females:

Physiological Differences Between Sexes

SIZE:

The average 18 year old male is 70.2 inches tall and weighs 144.8 pounds. The average female of the same age is 64.4 inches tall and weighs 126.6 pounds.

MUSCLES:

The percentage of muscle mass compared to total body weight is 50 percent greater in males. A female who is the same size as her male counterpart is only 80 percent as strong as the male. Therefore, males usually have the advantage in both speed and power over females.

FAT:

Females carry about 10 percent more fat than males of the same age. The location of this fat is important to know. Men accumulate fat primarily in the back, chest and abdomen. Women accumulate fat in the buttocks, arms, and thighs. Because the center of gravity is lower in females than in males, females must overcome more resistance in activities that require movement of the lower body.

HEART SIZE & RATE:

The female's heart is 25 percent smaller than the male's. Thus, the male's heart can move more blood with each heartbeat.

327

The larger heart makes the male's heartbeat slower (five to eight beats per minute). The slower heartbeat causes males to become fatigued less rapidly than females.

LUNGS:

Males' lung capacity is 25 to 30 percent greater than that of females. This gives males still another advantage in processing oxygen.

Awards will be given for Male Champion, Female Champion, and Overall Champion.

Excerpted by Vince Blair, from *Department of the Army manual FM 21-20 "Physical Fitness Training,"* August, 1985.

In conclusion, to train youngsters to be better than the rest is really determined by their state of mind, not what courses of fire they are practicing, but how they are training. Words like spirit, intensity, drive, motivation, hard work, guts, determination, perseverance, determination, focus, concentration, devotion and commitment are the real key to their development of the physical skill of moving the trigger finger automatically when activated by what the eye sees. By allowing the youngsters to train with the proper attitude they can do nothing but improve. If they constantly improve they will find themselves being the best they can be and rising above the rest. Remember, it is the individual and what he or she does, not the established system or method that is important.

Take a look, on the next two pages, at the pushup results being produced in this training. These results show that upper body strength is not necessary to produce champions.

Tucson's Most Powerful!!!

| | 1st(tie) | 1st(tie) | 2nd |

	Competitor	M/F	# Pushups	Rank
	Heather Mitchell	F	47	#1
	Meghan Mitchell	F	47	#1
	Michal Newhouse	F	30	#2
	Competitor	M/F	# Pushups	Rank
	John Jackson	M	27	#3

	Competitor	M/F	# Pushups	Rank
	Wayne Vernon	**M**	**27**	**#3**
	Rose Planteen	**F**	**26**	**#4**
	Danielle Dancho	**F**	**25**	**#5**
	Vince Blair Coach	**M**	**20**	**#6**
	Brent Barstow	**M**	**16**	**#7**
	Geoffrey Barstow	**M**	**12**	**#8**
	Sarah Neuman	**F**	**12**	**#8**
	Matt Planteen	**M**	**10**	**#9**
	Kelly Lara	**M**	**8**	**#10**
	Cade Wilson	**M**	**6**	**#11**
	Mike Lara	**M**	**4**	**#12**
	Ryan Lara	**M**	**4**	**#12**
	Justin Neuman	**M**	**3**	**#13**
	Jeff Planteen	**M**	**2**	**#14**
	Grant Morgan	**M**	**1**	**#15**
	Chance Neuman	**M**	**1**	**#15**

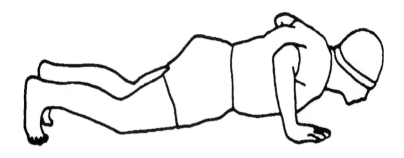

Not all of the campers chose to enter this competition. As a coach, you must recognize that there is a time to let go and not push shooters into events with which they are not comfortable. Remember, the benefits of the training you offer your shooters will go only to those who fully accept the challenges you offer them.

On the other hand, as a coach it must be borne in mind that youngsters, whether or not they are shooters, have a more finely tuned sense of pride than most adults realize. For youngsters fear of being humiliated far outranks many concerns that adults assume they are most troubled by. This is most likely the reason that some of our shooters did not enter the pushup contest. It does not do the shooter any good to insist that he put himself in a situation where the outcome will cause humiliation in the face of his or her peers. The coach has to be aware of just how easily a youngster is embarrassed. Remember, the youngsters' perception of accomplishment and personal worth is shaped predominantly by their school and peer life. Much research underscores how an embarrassment or humiliation can be an especially stinging blow to the youngster's emerging sense of worth. Bear in mind that injuries to the shooter's self-esteem, in the shooter's mind, can come to define their whole identity.

Coach's, in whatever competitions you devise for your pistol shooters, be aware of any clues you may pick up that it may be a bit overwhelming for the youngster at that point. Avoid harassing the shooter to participate in something, such as fingertip pushups, he has concerns about.

331

This is not to say that the coach not encourage some risk-taking by the young shooters. Risk-taking is part of the natural exploration and assertion of independence that every healthy teenager goes through to one extent or another. Remember, the pursuit or new activities and taking of initiative are crucial for the psychological growth that youngsters go through during adolescence. The coach can tap this natural tendency of risk-taking to encourage activities beneficial to the shooter's development in his sport, such as fingertip pushups.

A Note To Shooting Training Administrators:

Rosemary E. Herr, is the person in charge of the National Rifle Association's Shooting Sports Camp Program. Shooting Training Administrators should take their lead from Rosemary Herr. She has setup a summer camp program which allows for an extensive amount of creativity on the part of the sponsors of the NRA's Summer Camp Program. This encouragement of creativity is what permitted the conduct of the Tucson Summer Camp titled Training the Conditional Reflex for Pistol Shooting.

On the other hand, there are some shooting administrators who require that everything be done by the book. There would be no place in their scheme of training for a training camp devoted to training the conditional reflex in pistol shooting. Administrators in this mold stifle innovation. Shooting needs more administrators like Rosemary Herr.

It is interesting to the authors that the best shooting administrators in the United States at this time are women. Another outstanding innovator is NRA's Margaret J. Schoap. Margaret is in charge of the Intercollegiate Shooting Program.

These two women share a common trait, they look at the overall objective of their programs and allow innovation in reaching a goal. For example, the 1997 Guide for *Special Interest Camps* points out, *"Potential is limited only by your own imagination."* Unlike many shooting administrators, they are not adherents of the *monkey see, monkey do* philosophy. Instead of stifling advancement in shooting training methodology, they permit it to leap forward.

Chapter 6

The Coaching 2000 Program

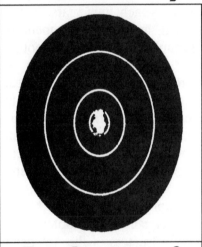

| Development of the conditional reflex between the eye, the brain and the trigger finger. | Identification, development and/or modification of personality traits associated with Olympic and World Champion Gold Medalists in the shooting sports. |

Our training is based on a special new shooting philosophy. It has an entirely different focus than probably anything in the shooting world that you have ever experienced. It is based on the deliberate formation of a conditional reflex between the eye and the trigger finger.

Read on to find out first of all, just why we decided it was necessary to develop a new philosophy of shooting and how it is different from the way others learned to shoot.

Why Change
From What We Have Been Doing?

The pistol-training establishment has continued to produce mediocre entries, when measured each four years, in the Olympics of the current Quadrennial, against the competitors from the rest of the world. For example, in the Men's Shooting 10 Meters Air Pistol Game of the 1996 Olympics, out of 50 shooters, the top representative from the United States, Neal Caloia, placed in a tie for 41st place, with a shooter representing Chinese Taipei. The other American representative, Ben Amonette, tied for 44th place with a man from Slovakia and one from Iraq. Where the Olympic medal winners of the Air Pistol were shooting between 584 and 587, Caloia fired a 571 and Amonette a 569.

Now, as a matter of indisputable fact, there is no blame to be ascribed to anyone, not the American pistol shooters, and most certainly not the coaches and instructors of the American pistol shooters. You see, there was no information available to anyone in the pistol shooting fellowship, which offered even the most remote hope, that doing something different would produce more positive results, or at any levels beyond what was then being produced year after year.

This book offers such improvement. The track record where **methods anchored on this philosophy** have been employed, demonstrates conclusively the validity of this brand new information.

Many of the pistol shooters who obtained the ears of the bureaucrats often, I suspect, ignored the results of the Olympics

334

in their game of Pistol Shooting. They attributed the loss of face of their friends, in the matches of the Olympiad, to the fanciful notion that the other nations of the world have more people shooting pistol than do we here in America. What a cop out! Take a look at size of some of the countries beating us in the Olympics. I would think that proportionally, we would have as many pistol shooters as many of the countries involved in the Olympics. For example, Friedhelm Sack, of Namibia, scored 583 points to capture 8th place in the Air Pistol. Arthur Gevorgian, of Ghana, scored 580 to tie for 9th place in the same event. Jakkrit Panichpatikum, of Thailand, scored 574 to place in a tie for 29th place. Is it really the case that these countries have more shooters in pistol training than does America?

Okay, so the Air Pistol was fired indoors. How did the real men do when it came to the Men's Shooting at 50 Meters, outdoors, with the Free Pistol? Sorry to say, it was more of the same. America's hopes went down as our top representatives finished dismally in the lower half of the 43 entries in the event. While the winners of the Olympic Free Pistol medals scored between 570 to 565, Amonette was America's top shooter, garnering a tie for 25th place with a score of 555. Caloia, the other American representative finished in 39th place with a score of 544. On the other hand, Sergio Sanchez, of Guatemala, scored 563 to place 8th overall. Is it possible that Guatemala has more pistol shooters than does the United States?

When it comes down to a comparison, take a look at the smallbore rifle shooters of Great Britain versus the United States. In England, there are more smallbore rifle shooters who shoot in their National Championships at Bisley, than there are Americans who shoot in our National Smallbore Rifle Championships at Camp Perry, Ohio. According to the rationale of some pistol shooters, American rifle shooters should never be able to beat the British since they have more shooters than we do firing in their National Championships than we have shooting in ours. This, historically, has not been the case.

It is the contention of the authors of this book, that the evidence plainly demonstrates that it is the American methods, of teaching pistol shooting, which have failed to produce shooters who have won Olympics in recent years. Why have the American pistol shooters not looked at this problem and tried something different? Probably because the information available in the public domain has been enshrined as holy grails. No one doubts a Holy Grail. They constitute the facts of shooting. Everyone knows facts do not change. Or do they? Several hundred years ago, it was a *fact* that the earth is flat. Today, it is round or oblong. In pistol shooting, how can so many have been so led astray for so long?

Why did no one look at the inadequacy of the training methods to produce the results the coaches and instructors claimed would occur? Well, one man did, Art Sievers. In February of 1970, an article in ***The American Rifleman*** described his new philosophical approach to the teaching of shooting. The article pointed out that the product of this training was the qualifying of 62% of the plebes at the US Naval Academy as Experts. Notice they qualified as Experts, not merely qualified as marksmen! Over 99% of the group achieved some qualifying score. And this was with the service issue .45 caliber pistol. That reflected the qualification scores fired in 1969. In 1970, the number qualifying as Experts went up to in excess of 71%.

Why should pistol shooters change from teaching pistol shooting as they always have in the past? Because it has not been doing the job at the level they claim they are striving to achieve.

It is a scientific fact that the earth is round. However, or in spite of this, there are people who believe that the earth is flat. To prove it they will walk you to the nearest window, pull back the curtains, and say, *"See, go ahead and look!, As far as the eye can see..., it's flat. How can you doubt the evidence of your own eyes?"* These folks are numbered among the members of the *Flat Earth Society.* If you continue to support a pistol training system which is a proven failure by its track record, feel free to apply for membership in the *Flat Earth Society.*

A Change Of Philosophy In Pistol Shooting Training!

Pistol shooters need to change to a new philosophy of shooting. Why a philosophy? What does that mean? It is a new way of thinking about pistol shooting training. Under this new philosophy, in shooting, hitting the target is worshipping a false god. This is easily understood once you understand how a shooting tool really works. The new philosophy has been in continued use since 1968. In every pistol training situation where it has been used, it has been an exemplary success.

Just What Is This New Philosophy?

In one word, *simplicity.* That's it! We focus all of our training around the establishment of just two fundamentals:

1 Visually Align the barrel with the eye, using the top of the front sight as a reference, point the aligned system at the area where you want the indicator (bullet hole) to appear..	2 Instantaneous Smooth Trigger Finger Movement

When we mention this simple idea to old *hard-holding pistol shooters,* the response we invariably get is something like, *"Oh, yes, we teach them, but we give them the other fundamentals or sub-fundamentals also."* Therein lies the difference between our philosophy of focusing our entire program around only these two fundamentals and the old *hard-holding pistol shooters* and their multitude of fundamentals.

For example, *hard-holding pistol shooters* and their espousal of a multitude of fundamentals is best illustrated by the 60+ fundamentals needed to fire one accurate shot, on page 42, of the 1980 edition, of *The United States Army Marksmanship Unit Pistol Marksmanship Guide.* The same publication, on page 1, documents what the *hard-holding pistol shooters* believe the fundamentals of pistol marksmanship comprise, *"The fundamentals of pistol marksmanship embrace all of those physical factors essential to the firing of an accurate shot."*

You can evaluate our new philosophy of shooting with what has been taught to beginning shooters for a long time in American pistol training. When you are learning a new physical skill, how many things can you think about and really concentrate on at one time. Most of you will probably say, ONE. We agree with you! When you get TWO things to have to keep in mind when you are first learning to do something, then you are stretching the limit of what most humans are capable of accomplishing with some degree of success. If you have to remember 30 or 60 things that you must learn to do, the wonder is that so many people selected *Sight Alignment and Trigger Control* from among all of the options they were told they had to keep in mind in order to fire one accurate shot.

Does it matter how you think when you assume the task of training others to shoot?

Yes, it most certainly does! For example, in our training, we know that we obtain our *Sight Alignment* from our stance. This goes to the root of the differences in the kinds of training a person receives under our philosophy of shooting and what was taught as the purpose of the stance under the old failed training method.

In the *Coaching 2000 Program*, our training focuses on the establishment and refinement of the conditional reflex between the eye, the brain and the trigger finger. Therefore, we get our *Sight Alignment* through our stance. We want our shot to be fired while on full automatic. If the stance is not set up so that when the sights reach eye level, the brain initiates the conditional reflex of moving the trigger finger, then we are interrupting that conditional reflex by trying to muscle the sights into alignment.

So, under our philosophy of shooting, what is the grip of the pistol used for? We use the grip of the pistol to get *Trigger Control*. The grip of the pistol is used to place the finger in exactly the same place on the trigger so that the conditional reflex can occur automatically as it is designed to do. If the brain senses that the finger is not in the same position that it is expect-

338

ing, then the conditional reflex is again thrown off by a slight amount. This will then cause random indicators to appear on the target.

On the other hand, consider what page 1 of *The United States Army Marksmanship Unit Pistol Marksmanship Guide* has to say about how they obtain *correct sight alignment.*

> *To obtain correct sight alignment, **it is necessary for the shooter to grip the pistol in a manner which guarantees that he is holding the pistol firmly** and that trigger pressure is applied straight to the rear....However, since the shooter cannot achieve complete immobility when assuming the stance and position, **the trigger has to be pressed** during some movement of the pistol. In order to deliver an accurate shot within his ability to hold, the shooter must not only **press the trigger evenly,** but he must do so with correct sight alignment. The size of the shot group will, therefore, not exceed the dimensions of the arc of movement, provided the shot breaks as a surprise **and no reflex action of muscles disturbs the delivery of the shot.***
> (Selections bolded by authors)

Under this still current method of teaching pistol shooting, the student is taught to get sight alignment through the grip. Remember, this method has been unable to develop Olympic gold medal winning shooters. But, it sounds reasonable. Under that method, shooters were told to *press the trigger evenly.* This idea of *press the trigger evenly* has the effect of distracting the shooter from the developing of the conditional reflex we are training shooters in our *Coaching 2000 Program* to acquire. In fact, the old method described in the *Pistol Marksmanship Guide* actually holds up the development of a reflex action of the muscles as being wrong, so *"no reflex action of muscles disturbs the delivery of the shot."*

Now, a philosophy is a way of thinking. You may be starting to see the difference in how we think about our shooting, compared to the shooters of the old school. In the century of the 2000's, we need shooters with a new way of looking at their pistol shooting.

For example, we stress that the pistol shooter must develop his act of shooting as a conditional reflex. This means that when the sight alignment gets to eye level and the reference point of the front sight reaches the desired area of the target, the brain activates the trigger finger. Consider, on the other hand, how the *Pistol Marksmanship Guide* handles the teaching of the act of shooting:

> *"In order to apply coordinated pressure on the trigger, **the shooter must wait** for those very definite times **when all control factors are optimum and firing conditions become favorable.** The **rule that must be observed** as the first step in attaining control of the shooting is: "**You must never attempt to fire until you have completely settled into a minimum arc of movement.**"* (Selections bolded by authors)

By focusing the training of the shooter on *waiting*, the pistol coach, or instructor, is creating a hesitant shooter. Research shows that one of the traits of a champion is an attitude of aggression toward his or her shooting.

For example, we focus the attention of our nine year old girls on the idea that they approach their trigger finger movement with the same attitude they have as they swat a particularly annoying mosquito. What this does is to make the idea of that type of aggression acceptable thus providing the nine year old girls with the idea needed for the development of a sense of aggression toward their shooting.

In this way, the coach starts showing the beginning shooters how to acquire a sense of *closure* with respect to their

340

trigger finger movement. We use the term closure because we live in a politically correct era. Previous times knew this as the development of the *killer instinct* in people.

In the old pistol shooting training methods, you have a coach, probably unwittingly to be sure, actually training a shooter right from the start to be a loser. By focusing attention on a *rule that must be observed* the coach is circumventing the early development of the conditional reflex. This is especially true when that rule says, *"You must never attempt to fire until you have completely settled into a minimum arc of movement."* This type of training breeds hesitation. Hesitation trains failure. The *Coaching 2000 Program* is designed for developing competitive shooters. It is not designed for the development of recreational shooters.

As a coach, be aware that the development of the closure instinct is vital to the development of a champion attitude. The authors suggest that coaches give consideration to requiting youth members of the Safari Club International or children of such members who already have experience hunting and killing game. They will already have acquired the necessary closure trait. The coach can then help to further refine this trait.

Our research clearly demonstrates that the old established methods of pistol shooting training are inefficient at what they set out to do, create champion shooters. Remember, *Precision Shooting* is being able to put the barrel of a shooting tool in line with the eye, the same way each time, and being able to point as desired, without introducing angular misalignment between the barrel and the eye. See **Candace Abrams below, at age 11.**

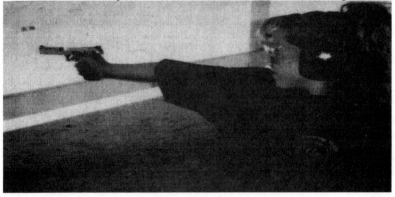

The Coaching 2000 Program

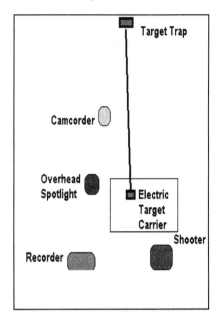

The year, 2000, is not only the start of a new century, but the beginning of a new millennium. As a shooting coach, you might want to adopt as your new millennium motto, *out with the old, in with the new.* Change for the sake of change you say? Not so! But, how about change for the better? For years, we instructors and coaches have mouthed the words*, individualized instruction*, and then gone ahead with our *one way suits everyone.* In your 21st Century, you can change that! Notice, we did not say we would change it! Take a good look at the **Coaching 2000 Program.** It will provide you with the methods and the philosophy needed to upgrade your coaching skills.

Did we say philosophy? Sure did! So, why do you need a philosophy to coach shooting? Don't you just show the kids how to shoot and correct them when they do it wrong? Isn't that the way everyone does it?

Well, not exactly. It is a little bit like sex. Everyone does it, and most people do it exactly the same. But, if you are just one of the crowd doing it just like everyone else, don't you wonder sometimes at what is being left out of your sex life? Many people go through their whole life and never have a sexual experience the least bit out of the ordinary. They are happy in their ignorance.

So it is with a lot of coaches. They do the same thing year after year and never seem to notice that the methods they have used to teach shooting to their youngsters just never seem to produce champions even once in a while, let alone consistently, from one group of youngsters to another, year after year.

As a coach, haven't you ever wondered at how some junior coaches just seem to attract natural shooters, or to somehow just seem to trip over them as they step outside to get the morning paper? If you attribute these *natural shots* to a coach's good luck, then you better take another look at what you are seeing. In the **Coaching 2000 Program** we train ourselves to spot these *natural shots* deliberately. See page 249 for more information about this.

For example, at a Preliminary Pistol Tryout for the 1996 Olympics, a shooter from northern Arizona, told Hickey, *"I happened to notice what a good follow through one of your juniors had, then I looked further down the line and all of your kids had the same sort of superb follow through! I didn't think that kind of thing could be taught to such young kids! What are they, 13 or 14?"* When Hickey pointed out that he had only one 14 year old and the rest were between 10 and 13, the fellow just shook his head in amazement.

Teaching follow through is just like sex education. The words mean little without the touch. The old teaching school of coaching advocated saying the words, *Follow Through* to the student. Of course, in order for the student to actually follow through, he/she had to put a whole lot of conscious effort into the attempt to *Follow Through.* Now because we cannot readily concentrate on more than one thing, or at the most, two things at a time, at least one of the two fundaments of shooting, trigger control or sight alignment, will fade into the mists of forgetfulness. How does a coach teach a shooter to *Follow Through* when shooting a pistol?

Well, it is the same problem teachers have when teaching a class on sex education. They dare not *really* teach in a way which would truly allow their students to experience the joys of sex. So, they teach **about** sex. So, too, the shooting coach of the old school, teaches about *Follow Through.* The shooting coach often thinks that if he just reminds the shooter enough times to

Follow Through, the shooter will eventually get it. Well, of course he/she will eventually **get it**. But, in the meantime, the coach will be destroying the shooter. How? By continuing to draw the shooter's attention to *Follow Through,* the coach distracts the shooter's attention away from at least one of the two fundamentals of shooting,

1	2
Visually Align the barrel with the eye, using the top of the front sight as a reference, point the aligned system at the area where you want the indicator (bullet hole) to appear..	Instantaneous Smooth Trigger Finger Movement

Thus, the shooter is prevented from allowing these two fundamentals to develop into a conditional reflex.

On the other hand, the coach in the **Coaching 2000 Program** provides for a way for the shooter to develop a superior *Follow Through* without ever saying the words. When something is determined to be important for the efficient firing of a shot, the coach devises a way to allow it to happen without distracting the shooter from trigger control and sight alignment.

For example, in practicing with the air pistol, the coach has the shooter simulate the firing of a dry fired shot after the pellet is fired. The more ambitious coach will find a way to acquire an air pistol with an electronic trigger, such as the Morini Model 162E. With the electric trigger, it is easy to have the shooter fire a shot, then recover the sight alignment and fire a dry fire shot without taking the gun out of eye level.

 This process is continued when training with the .22 caliber pistol. We have Ruger Mark II's and Ruger .22/45's. These pistols have rebated bolt faces. This allows dryfiring without damage to the firing pins.

We use the following sequence:

Objective:
> To train <u>Sight Alignment & Trigger Control</u>

Method:
- ☞ Load magazine with one round
- ☞ Insert magazine into gun
- ☞ Drop the slide
- ☞ Take out the magazine
- ☞ Bring pistol to eye level
- ☞ Fire the shot
    > then dry fire a shot while the gun is still in the extended position.
- ☞ Recover the sight alignment
- ☞ Repeat process for 20 rounds.

TOTAL: 20 shots

See how a coach can do twice the amount of training with 20 rounds, using this program compared to the old method where the coach is just yelling out every so often *Follow Through!* Shooters taught under the old method never realize what they are missing as they hit a wall where self-improvement seems to sort of just stop. It is, figuratively speaking, like the man who comes home from work one day and his wife knocks him to the floor, saying, *"That's for being a lousy lover!"* The husband picks himself up off the floor. He then slugs his wife and tells her, *"That's for knowing the difference!"* After reading this book, you will know the difference between the old style of coaching and the **Coaching 2000 Program**.

The philosophy of the **Coaching 2000 Program** is much like the methodology used in some of the more forward looking American manufacturing companies. The basis of this philosophy is the teaching of self-reliance in the shooter. We do this by helping the shooter become his or her own coach. One of the coaches in our program noted that while he was familiar with this philosophy in the American work place, and more particularly in his, he had not seen it in connection with the teaching of shoot-

345

ing. And when he noticed the connection, he wondered aloud why it was that this philosophy of coaching had not been applied to pistol coaching prior to now.

The basis of the program philosophy lies in two directions,

1) The focus on ONLY the two fundamentals:

1 Visually Align the barrel with the eye, using the top of the front sight as a reference, point the aligned system at the area where you want the indicator (bullet hole) to appear..	2 Instantaneous Smooth Trigger Finger Movement

2) The entire training program is designed to teach the shooter to become his/her own coach.

Packaged Options
The Coaching 2000 Program

Price Estimate	No.	Description
$1,050.00	1	Morini Model CM 162E This air pistol has an electric trigger and is used primarily to train beginning shooters from the first shot to follow through as an instinctive process. IF YOU RESTRICT THIS AIR PISTOL TO ONLY YOUR TOP SHOOTERS, YOU WILL FAIL IN DEVELOPING A PIPELINE OF NEW SHOOTERS WELL GROUNDED IN THE SHOOTING PROCESS.

$259,00	1	13" Color TV/VCR combo This is used in the **Coaching 2000 Program** to play back the videos of the shooters. This is part of the process of showing the youngsters how to become their own coaches and to then be able to evaluate problems, which occur in their shooting. This permits the shooters to see problems, not in the abstract, but down right personal to them.
$599.99	1	8mm or VHS Camcorder This is a key element in the **Coaching 2000 Program**. As the diagram shows: 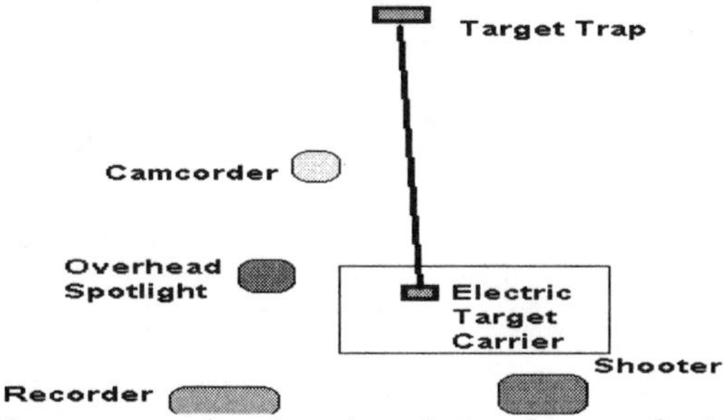 The camcorder is placed in front of the shooter. The distance is about 4 feet from the shooter. The camcorder frames the muzzle of the air pistol and the shooter's shooting eye. This is a very tight frame. We want to be able to see the relationship of the eye to the sound of the air pistol at the time of discharge. The recorder records the time from the moment the gun reaches eye level until the shot is fired. This information is given to the shooter as the video tape is viewed after 10 shots have been fired.
$39.99	1	10 Pack 8mm or VHS Videotapes
$21.00	1	Tripod Needed for the camcorder so that no person has to be in front of the muzzle of the air gun.
$108.00	1 cs	Air Gun Pellets

347

$15.00	2	Stopwatch This is used by the 1ˢᵗ recorder to record the timing of the shot after the gun reaches eye level. The other one is used by the 2ⁿᵈ recorder to record the time it takes the gun to reach eye level after leaving the bench.
$20.00	1	Russian 10 Meter Spotting Scope
$140.00	1	*"Competitor"* Electric Target Carrier **We obtained 11 of these from the Detroit Armor Company.**
$14.00	3	Hearing Protectors
$11.00	3	Eye Protection
$20.00	2	Portable snack tables
$32.50	1 cs	Air Gun Pistol Training Targets
$8.00	2	Clipboards These are used by the recorders to place the **Conditional Reflex Evaluation Form** on clipboards during the training session.

In the table above, you see the options which help make the **Coaching 2000 Program** the success it has become in Tucson, Arizona. The prices are only estimates and will vary from locality to locality. This package may be available in a grant from your local state *Friends of the NRA State Committee.* This *Friends of the NRA Committee* fund raising dinner has proved to be a resounding success at providing seed money to get junior shooting programs the money they need to put on a viable program. Hickey has served on the Tucson *Old Pueblo Friends of the NRA Committee* each year since it began. The authors wholeheartedly endorse this fund raising concept of the National Rifle Association. In addition, they recommend that all readers of this book make contact with your local Friends of NRA Committee and volunteer to become an active member of the committee. You will have fun and you will have a whale of a lot of satisfaction in knowing that you are a part of the rejuvenation of the shooting sports of America.

The role of coach leadership in the **Coaching 2000 Program** has several factors important to effective team performance.

- mutual respect among team members
- effective communication
- feelings of importance
- common goals
- fair treatment

In the **Coaching 2000 Program** mutual respect is generated by having the team members act as recorders for each other. That is one reason for the use of the **Conditional Reflex Evaluation Form**. This particular form teaches the team members to be objective about their teammates. Objectivity comes about through observation of the shooter's performance. You, as a coach stress the help the recorder is to the shooter by giving the shooter objective feedback of his or her shooting performance.

Effective communication is achieved through the coach's never ending emphasis on the two fundamentals of:

1 Visually Align the barrel with the eye, using the top of the front sight as a reference, point the aligned system at the area where you want the indicator (bullet hole) to appear..	2 Instantaneous Smooth Trigger Finger Movement

Many coaches using the old methods of teaching shooting often made themselves into ineffective communicators because their students became confused about which of the 7 to 14 **fundamentals** they were supposed to keep in mind when they were learning to shoot. And, when the shooter seemed to fail to perform one of the seven **fundamentals**, the coach was right there to call the attention of the shooter to the **fundamental** he or she forgot. Thus the conditional reflex between the eye, the brain and the trigger finger was a long time in taking place, if it ever happened before the shooter became discouraged and quit.

Participation in the **Coaching 2000 Program** gives the shooter a feeling of importance. One of the first things a coach does in this program is to set out the results this program is designed to produce.

It has been specially created for the express purpose of providing America with the talent needed to win the Pistol Events of the Olympics of the year 2000. By design, the **Coaching 2000 Program** is structured so that the shooters participating in it will think about setting a goal of participating in a future Olympics. This feeling of importance, at being a part of something bigger than they are, is fostered throughout every aspect of the team training. This is the same type of feeling which was deliberated fostered by the American government as it enlisted the whole population during World War II in the effort to defeat the enemy. It is a feeling that has to be fostered in every gun club in America. National purpose brings success.

This is accomplished in many respects through the ritualization discussed in another part of this book. It is also done by having respected adults, shooters and coaches, provide clinics for the team members. For example, Hickey had Colonel Bill Pullum, USA, Ret., whose rifle shooters won more individual and team international medals than any other coach in the history of United States shooting, give the team members of his pistol team a clinic. His topic was *Winning Characteristics.*

Then, Hickey met International US Shooting Coach, Lieutenant Commander Art Sievers, USN, Ret., for the first time when he visited Tucson looking at and evaluating this **Coaching 2000 Program.** Until that time, Hickey and Sievers spent hours at a time on the phone developing the Tucson Pistol Training Program. After a week investigating the Tucson junior program, he then called our **Coaching 2000 Program,** *"the best shooting training program in the whole country, bar none!"* Sievers, after whom the NRA recently named a new Intercollegiate Air Pistol Team Trophy, and one of the few living American Shooting Coaches to lead a US Palma Team to victory on foreign soil, described the Tucson **Coaching 2000 Program,** *"a national treasure"* for the development of future American Olympic Pistol Champions.

One of the National Pistol Team Members and former Resident Shooting Athlete at the US Olympic Training Center, spent 12 days doing intensive coaching with our Tucson kids in the **Coaching 2000 Program**. After observing it, she pointedly commented, *"Only the Russians or Bulgarians would do something like this!"*

And, she is right. Our international pistol shooters have been like kids playing in a little sandbox while the other kids are up on the swings and the merry-go-round. The purpose of the **Coaching 2000 Program** is to bring our new young international pistol shooters up out of the sandbox and onto the high swings.

We would not dream of trying to change any of the *old established shooters*. Obviously they are satisfied with the level of their shooting performance. If not, we feel sure they would have changed something of what they do. Then again, how could they? They have not been exposed to this new way of thinking about their shooting. Even if they become aware of this new shooting philosophy, retraining is an extremely difficult task to undertake. The ***Coaching 2000 Program*** is designed to provide for the future of America's pistol shooters. The pathways of the central nervous system of the young are plastic enough to easily learn the Conditional Reflex this program teaches. It is through these youths that the future of pistol shooting competition will be forever changed.

Maggie Conlin, Junior Director of the Arizona Rifle & Pistol Association, congratulates Grant Morgan for his medal winning performance in the 1996 Grand Canyon Games.

9 year old Michal Newhouse, cleaning the barrel of her Ruger 22/45 pistol

351

Character Trait Development Phases

Training Phase	Description
1. This is the introductory phase of the **coaching 2000 program**. This provides an overview of the program.	1
2. In this phase, the shooters are identified primarily on the basis of their shot groups fired from an Extended Bench Rest.	
3. Shooters are further identified by Individual On-The-Spot Interviews and the use of Test #1.	
4. Parental attitudes are also identified in this phase during observations and casual conversation.	
5. Most shooters never advance out of this phase.	
6. **Strength Training** is interjected into the shooter's training at this point. Fingertip pushups are the primary strength training items demonstrated to the shooters of this phase.	
7. **Stamina** is developed through use of the gallon milk/water bottle filled to about one fifth of capacity. Shooters are encouraged to hold this water bottle at arm's length during their TV watching and work up to being able to hold it out during the body of the show and to lower it during the commercials.	

Training Phase	Description
1. Shooters in this phase are tested for attitudes and Personality Traits.	2
2. Strength training and stamina training are more rigorous.	
3. Mental Training 2-hour blocks are made a part of the shooter's training in this phase.	
4. Parent involvement *as a motivating force* is reduced through conferences with the parents.	
5. Parents are encouraged not to provide alibis for non performance at this juncture.	
6. **Self motivation** becomes a part of the training. For example, the shooter is encouraged to become the first person awake in the morning. Then, to use that time for strength training and/or mental visualization. At this point, we often refer to visualization as daydreaming.	

Training Phase	Description
	3

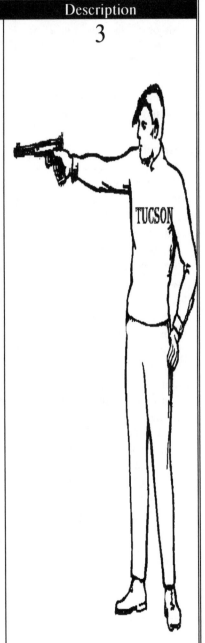

1. All shooters in this phase are encouraged to maintain Shooting Diaries on their computers. Creativity in designing diary entries which illustrate what the shooter wants to easily recall is systematically encouraged through interview feedback.

2. Strength and stamina training is monitored through competitive tests and diary entries.

3. Introduction of the *Sense of Responsibility* through learning to handle the *Fear of Failure*, with penalty, in 10 shot matches based around the Shooter's Individual Shot Goal.

4. Work on tempering or enhancing identified shooter character traits which several world champions have as a part of their mental make up.

5. *Introduction to training in a completely Dark Room, usually a closet or a bathroom with the light leaks covered over.*

6. Video Training designed to help the shooter become his/her own coach.

Training Phase	Description
1. Development of the **_Closure Instinct_** in the shooter through increasingly challenging One Shot Matches, with penalty. **2.** Development of Self Competency through use of the Conditional Reflex Forms. **3.** Development of time and score awareness through use of the timing portion of the Conditional Reflex Evaluation Forms.	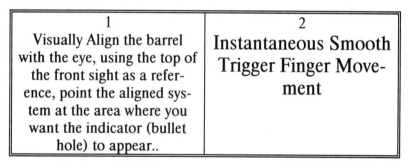

Concept:

We want to make our shooters their own experts, so when we finish the job, they will not need us any more. They will know what they are doing, will be doing it on purpose and they can then evaluate information that comes their way. And if that information will have a *positive effect* on either:

1 Visually Align the barrel with the eye, using the top of the front sight as a reference, point the aligned system at the area where you want the indicator (bullet hole) to appear..	2 **Instantaneous Smooth Trigger Finger Movement**

then it is fine. But, if the information will adversely affect either what the eye sees as *perfect internal alignment of the system* or *the trigger finger movement being made instantaneously smooth,* then it is bad news. If it will not make any difference, it is a convenience item.

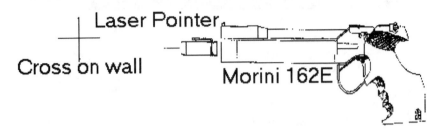

Laser Training

A cornerstone of the ***Coaching 2000 Program*** is training with a laser devise. In this training, a cross is drawn on the back of an 8 ½" x 11" sheet of paper. It is placed on a wall about 5 meters from the shooter. The laser pointer is fastened to a wooden dowel with a sturdy rubber band. The wooden dowel is about 4 inches long. The shooter is then directed to point the pistol at the center of the cross and to dryfire when the sights reach the area of the center of the cross. The shooter's effort is directed at moving the finger quickly and smoothly before the laser's red dot moves from the area of the center of the cross.

This is an extremely important training device for those coaches using the ***Coaching 2000 Program*** method.

1. The shooter can instantly see the deterioration of the hold when the pistol is held over a couple of seconds
2. The coach can continuously direct the shooter's attention to
   a) looking hard at the sights
   b) moving the finger smoothly and quickly

This is used with one shooter using the pistol with the laser pointer attached and an observer recording the results of the shooter's effort to fire the dryfire when the red dot arrives at the center of the cross.

Scoring of observation:

RU= shot fired in upper right quadrant of cross
RD= shot fired in Lower right quadrant of cross
LU= shot fired in upper left quadrant of cross
LD= shot fired in lower left quadrant of cross

356

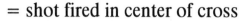 = shot fired in center of cross

It is delightful to observe the beginning shooters as they strive for a smiley face on their laser observation form. The form is very simple. Have the shooters place their names and the date of the observation on a black sheet of paper. Then have them number the paper from 1 to 10, leaving a lot of space between the numbers. Point out to them that they must leave a lot of space for a smiley face.

We use a laser pointer obtained from:

Heartland America
6978 Shady Oak Road
Eden Prairie, MN 55344
1-800-229-2901

Product Number: 7267
Product Description: Infiniter Mini Laser Pointer
Price: $39.99
Shipping: $4.95

Model: Super QPON-650-300

Specifications: 5.9 cm (2.3 in.
Weight: 60 grams. (Including batteries)
Output power: Less than 4mW, Class III A laser product.
Battery: 3 LR44 Alkaline watch battery/90 minutes continuous on.
Battery: 3 SR44 Silver Oxide watch battery/3hr. continuous on.
Warranty: 1 year.

The laser pointer may be obtained from many sources. We like this one, principally due to it's size. Most laser pointers we have seen are between 4" and 5" in length. We believe the shorter laser pointer we obtained provides less displacement of the pistol than would a longer one.

Fill to here

→

Home Training Project #1

Objective:

To train the quick and efficient movement of the arm to eye level.

1. Put about 3 pounds of water or sand into a gallon jug.
2. Make your wrist firm and your elbow firm.
3. Make a fist in the normal pistol gripping position, that is, with the thumb facing forward and the lower three fingers closed around the handle of the gallon jug.
4. Insert the thumb of your non-shooting hand into your belt on the opposite side of your body, over past your belly button.
5. With your wrist firm and your elbow firm, quickly raise the gallon jug to eye level at a spot on the wall.
6. When raised, focus on trying to keep the water from jiggling around.
7. Keep the top of the gallon jug pointing at a spot on the wall.
8. Then lower the gallon jug to a 45° position from your body. Maintain a firm hold on the handle. Do not just let it come to rest after each repetition.
9. Repeat steps 1 through 8 for a minimum of ten minutes at a time.

358

Chapter 7

Coaching The Mind For Pistol Shooting

We are in a decade which is zipping into and through the year 2000. Yet the American Pistol coaching profession is often fast rooted in the past. It seems old models never fade away — they have to be pushed aside by more vigorous counter-models. Most American pistol coaches tend to be position technicians. You see them on the range and in front of shooting classes huffing and  puffing as they demonstrate the correct breathing a shooter has to master. In rifle training, the coach's solution to a shooter's problem very often is, *"Tighten your sling."*

You MUST breathe like this!!!!

Yet these methods have failed to create shooters capable of winning Olympic Gold Pistol Medals in the recent modern Olympics. It is time to look at a coaching method which is radically different. Trying to mold pistol shooters into the **right** position seems to have created a large number of failures. By this we mean failures with respect to being able to win gold medals in the Olympics. The US Olympic Committee

359

says that it judges the effectiveness of a governing body of a sport by it's ability to produce medals in the Olympics.

Isn't it about time that those of us in the pistol shooting games woke up and evaluated why our *"old tried and true"* coaching methods are producing such inept results? Instead, much of the effort being made in the American pistol shooting sports, is to <u>fix it</u> by getting more and more coaches to buy into the failed coaching model which has been spectacularly unsuccessful.

A good pistol coach uses up-to-date research to modify his programs to take advantage of information showing him how

Convergence Zones and Pistol Shooting Training

to instill traits important to marksmanship in his young shooters. For example, using an MRI scanner, Hanna Damasio has examined the living brains of hundreds of patients. She identified regions of the brain which serve as convergence zones in the left hemisphere.

An area in the temporal lobe pulls together information about the names of objects, animals and people. She identified another area in the frontal cortex which appears to act as the

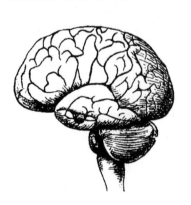

nexus, or point of origin, for verbs. Yet a third area oversees the task of assembling nouns and verbs into sentences.

These convergence zones, thousands of them, spread through the cortex, do more than just process language. They also coordinate every other sort of information the brain needs, perception, memory, and emotion, to be fully functional.

The convergence zones merge miscellaneous pieces of information into a semblance of a whole.

For a pistol shooting coach, this has important implications. We know that it takes many repetitions for these convergence zones to quickly construct it's form of the whole.

360

Take, for example, emotion. The coach decides it would be a desirable trait for the shooter to develop the emotion of pleasure at shooting a ten. Now, we all know that for each ten a beginning pistol shooter fires, he will fire a great number of shots which are not tens. So, introducing the idea of shooting tens is counterproductive.

The pistol coach, at this point, should introduce the concept of an individual shot goal. In this case, we are not talking about the purpose toward which an endeavor is directed. This is a goal or objective which the shooter can feel assured of attaining 80% to 90% of the shots he fires.

Upon firing a shot which meets or exceeds the shooter's individual shot goal, the coach should immediately give the shooter a warm feeling of satisfaction, *"Great shot, Mike!"* We all like to repeat things which are pleasant to us. Therefore, the coach needs to help the shooter nurture a warm, uplifting feeling for each shot which meets or is better than the individual shot goal. When he does this, the coach is giving the shooter a chance to develop a sense of well-being and self-esteem. This will translate into a very desirable character trait for the shooter. The coach introduces the concept of the Individual Shot Goal only after the shooter is grounded in the idea of the Conditional Reflex as used in Pistol Shooting Training.

If the coach is unaware of what modern research is uncovering through special machines such as MRI scanners or highly sensitive devices such as a magnetoencephalograph, then his work with his young shooters is indeed nothing more than baby-sitting.

Marie Alkire, of Tempe, Arizona, former member of the NRA Board of Directors who was also a member of the International Shooting Union Ladies Committee, has reported the results of her research into the woman shooting athlete. She noted that *"In general, the results have shown us that the major factors in a successful shooting performance are high self-esteem and mental preparedness."* As does any excellent coach, Alkire looked at the body characteristics of the female shooter.

Structurally, she pointed out, the most important characteristic of the female body, as far as shooting is concerned, is it's lower center of gravity in comparison with the male body.

For the coach, what is the significance of this? This allows girls to concentrate almost immediately on the refinement of ligament control rather than struggling with larger muscle groups as boys often must do. Boys are, naturally, in a more top heavy, less balanced position. The coach knows the girls' lower center of gravity results from the wider pelvic structure in the female. Thus, the lower the center of gravity, the more stable the structure. Obviously, this is a natural advantage in shooting where one tries to be as steady and motionless as possible.

Self-Directed

Research data from the Sports Research Laboratory at Pennsylvania State University shows that in the force platform experiments, females are more stable than males.

Alkire's other research shows that the girls who rise to the top of the shooting world are *"self-directed."* She reports that their coaches had programs which led them to be confident of their ability. Interviews with their coaches show that these girls also scored highly on tests of achievement motivation. Alkire points out, *"Certainly this is no surprise to women athletes themselves, but may be a revelation to society in general."*

Alkire also reported on a study directly related to females in shooting. The study rearranged the psychological attributes that make up sex differentiation and allows for people to fit into any one of four categories:

⇒masculine
⇒feminine
⇒androgynous
⇒undifferentiated.

The authors of the study, Janet T. Spence and Robert Helmreich, found that both males and females who scored high on the masculinity scale were high in self-esteem. High scores in femininity were correlated with lower self-esteem in males as well as females. But the highest self-esteem scores of all were found in those males and females who rated themselves high in both femininity and masculinity, the androgynous group.

In other words, Alkire says, the study suggested that the male who could be assertive sometimes and dependent other times felt better about himself than the man who was always independent. And the female who was passive sometimes, but could be independent at other times thought more highly of herself than the woman who was always passive. For shooters, this seems to be the a good trait to develop.

Coaching The Psyche For Pistol Shooting Success

Once the pistol coach embarks on the path of being an enlightened practitioner of coaching his or her shooters as individuals, the shooters are limited only by their desire to succeed. If, on the other hand, the pistol coach always seeks to take credit for what his shooters have accomplished, as a direct result of their own hard work, then the coach will find that he has destroyed a portion of those shooters' self-esteem. This is exactly the opposite effect which most pistol coaches think they are accomplishing. It has the effect of harming the spirit or psyche of the shooter.

Remember, as a pistol coach you have to understand that the shooter acquires information which requires routing through the convergence zones of the brain and that it is routed through the left hemisphere. There the emotions are processed into building blocks of the personality, or psyche. Perceptions and memory are also processed in one of these convergence zones. And remember these convergence zones are bombarded by clumps of information about pistol shooting. Outdoors, the shooter may not be consciously aware of the wind or the sun or the gnats flying around. Then again, the shooter may be very aware of the wind and the sun and the gnats flying around and slipping in under the shooting glasses.

Indoors, in the beginning of the pistol shooting training, everything is new and different. It is the coach's job to devise means of helping his pistol shooters to quickly feel at home on the range, this is an important part of shaping the psyche or spirit of the shooter. This will allow the information bombarding these

363

convergence zones to moderate at a good pace. At the same time coaches need to set up a range safety program which leads to safety happening automatically.

Hickey recounts the first time he took a junior pistol team to Phoenix. The other shooters stopped what they were doing as the names of our juniors were read over a loud speaker and gave the youngsters, who were between 10 and 11 years of age, a standing ovation. This type of thing, more than many other things, aids the coach in building the psyche of the young shooters.

The youngsters had shown an attitude toward their shooting and range discipline normally associated only with adults. These people knew only from their own children how youngsters behave on a range. When they see the youngsters from our team, it is generally so out of the realm of their experience to see youngsters knowing what they are doing that it just befuddles them.

While the scores of our beginning shooters do not yet match their range and attitude skills, this will come in time. But, the coach, by giving these youngsters this professional attitude about their shooting, is promoting in them a sense of self-esteem. Your shooters need never know that it is for this reason that you run your ranges in a professional and consistent manner, according to the rule book of the competition for which you are preparing the shooters. This is part of the process of training the shooter to be self confident and to feel independent of the coach when shooting in a match.

Reduce the information deemed important

It is important that the coach reduce, and we do mean reduce, the amount of information he or she designates as being important to a beginning shooter. There are some coaches who break down the firing of a shot into 40 or 50 separate items and the US Army Marksmanship Pistol Manual lists 61 items necessary to the firing of one accurate shot. This bombards the shooter's convergence zones with too much information to process meaningfully all at once. All shooting can be broken down into two fundamentals:

1 Visually Align the barrel with the eye, using the top of the front sight as a reference, point the aligned system at the area where you want the indicator (bullet hole) to appear..	2 Instantaneous Smooth Trigger Finger Movement

Two things! You have given the shooter's mind something it can handle. Notice we have not included breathing as a fundamental you stress to beginning shooters. We believe breathing to be an automatic process. Try to remember the last time you actually thought about your breathing. In humans, breathing is the mechanical operation for getting air to and from the lungs. It is an automatic process. To insist to a person just learning to shoot the pistol, that he must control his breath in a particular manner, distracts him from focusing on the two things necessary to obtain consistent results from his act of shooting.

The selection of the two fundamentals is of critical importance to shooters. For example, at Quantico, the instructors of one of the schools designed to train Non-Commissioned Officers for advancement to Officer status, also had selected two fundamentals. Their two main fundamentals were breathing and stance. One of the men attending the school could not believe his ears. He had been trained in our method as a junior. But, he did not try to fight the program. During the final qualification shoot, which included the instructors firing along side their trainees, he came out on top of everyone, including the instructors. Interestingly, he made it a point to talk with some members of the Marine Corps pistol team stationed there. He mentioned that they seemed to know what they were about. Why this did not filter down to the instructors of the training classes, where it was sorely needed, is anyone's guess.

It is the opinion of the authors, that if anyone needs the proper methods of smallarms training, it is the men and women of our armed forces who may need this to defend our lives and their own. If a military force finds a 40% proficiency rate acceptable, there should be someone called to account.

365

Breath Control for Pistol Shooters Look at this process which pistol shooters are consciously attempting to control. **With so much work being put forth to control their breathing process, how much thought is being directed toward the effort of looking at the sights and task of moving the trigger finger?**	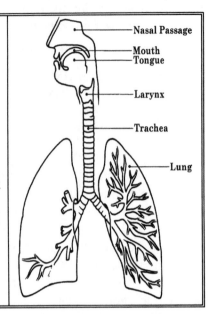

Since you start the shooter from the benchrest position as he starts to learn to shoot, the shooter will automatically adjust his breathing as he shoots, without the distraction of a wandering aiming point. And inasmuch as the gun is stabilized by the benchrest, the shooter will automatically adjust his breathing if he is concentrating on aligning the barrel with his eye, using the sights as references for this job.

Breathing is an automatic process. It occurs because muscular effort enlarges the two lungs in the chest basin. Beneath the lungs is a muscular wall which is called the diaphragm. When we breath, muscular effort enlarges the chest basin. This causes the diaphragm to move down. At the same time, the basin skeleton moves forward and outward. This creates a vacuum in the basin, causing air to pour into the lungs under atmospheric pressure. The lungs enlarge, as a result, and fill out the basin. Bill Blankenship, one of America's premire pistol shooters pointed out, *"It is not often that the average individual would have to think about breathing. The body functions are such that the lungs take care of the body without conscious thought."* (*The Pistol Shooter's Treasury* edited by Gil Hebard).

Breathing out also occurs through muscular effort. The chest basin contracts, which forces the air out of the lungs.

During the stress of a competition, certain things happen to our body. For one thing, the body retains extra sodium. This encourages fluid retention. It also raises the heart rate and the blood pressure. The heart becomes overworked and beats irregularly or too quickly. Now, if you throw in the concentrated effort to manipulate the breathing process by some artificial effort, you have the making of a bit of a minor disaster with respect to your programmed reflex. If you have not trained for controlling your sense of responsibility, stress will be difficult to avoid.

As pistol shooters, you have to be aware that the stress response to the arousal provoked by the competition does some things to your body. Often this will result in unexplained or random strikes of your bullet on the target. For example, the initial stage of arousal remains the same whether you are faced with a major or minor challenge. This can be anything from the front sight dropping off your pistol to spilling your carefully selected match ammo all over your shooting bench.

However, under extreme, prolonged or persistent pressure, the body proceeds to manufacture extra quantities of stress chemicals. This triggers further processes to maintain your energy at a pre-stress level. If the arousal continues, the adrenal glands manufacture anti-inflammatory chemicals that simultaneously speed tissue repair while depressing the body's immune defense system. If all of these changes continue, the body goes on trying to adapt under increasing strain and pressure. Eventually it breaks down. The pistol shooter then experiences feelings of exhaustion. Just imagine what this does to the shooter's spirit or psyche.

Research shows that we may place our body under stress awareness unconsciously. This happens because of our psychological and emotional attitudes to stress.

If, for example, the pistol shooter, during the Act of Shooting, concentrates his effort on adjusting this breathing process to some artificial arrangement, it can be done, but will need nearly 100% of the shooter's mental exertion. This amount of work to contravene an automatic function of the body will

367

seriously impede the Conditional Reflex from being able work properly. Thus the shooter has initiated a quite unnatural amount of stress into his or her body.

It is your job as a coach to arrange for the beginning shooter to assimilate the new information so the convergence zones find it manageable. Through repeated practice some processes associated with shooting become automatic to the experienced shooter. The more automatic the shooter makes his Act of Shooting, the less stress he will place himself under.

What sets the experienced shooter and the new shooter apart is how each shooter takes in large clumps of information. The experienced shooter, on the one hand, discards those clumps which are consistent with past occurrences and which can be discarded or set aside as information which is within tolerable limits. This leaves the shooter with a small amount of information on which to concentrate his efforts. It cannot be stressed enough that the coach has to decrease the amount of information a beginning shooter has his attention directed toward in the beginning stages of his pistol shooting. The importance of continuing the process of focusing the beginning shooter's attention on the two fundamentals of the *Shooting Diagram* cannot waver nor be minimized.

This is the basic reason the coach must make every effort to get the shooters to go to tournaments at every opportunity. Shooting in tournaments is such an important process in helping a shooter to develop his potential that the results can be seen in every club of which we have some knowledge. In Hickey's present pistol club, he has offered the opportunity to all of the shooters to go to many tournaments. When matching the shooting averages against tournaments shot in, it is evident that even though the shooters all started out at the same time, the shooter, with the most tournaments fired, often leads the pack in improved shooting average.

Typically the pistol shooter experiences stress in tournament competition. It is only in competition, when faced with a stressful situation that we can experience the problems associated with the fight or flight choice. The coach should make every effort to give the shooter an opportunity to experience this type of condition. It is then that the coach and shooter can find common ground in learning how to turn off the stress response. This is done by using a conscious relaxation technique. Only then can the body relax again. With relaxation, the heart rate, blood pressure, oxygen consumption, and muscle tension all drop to their normal levels. This allows new blood flows to the muscles, the inner organs and the skin. When this occurs, the organs of the body can regenerate and function normally once more. So, pistol shooters, take heart, it is possible to consciously switch from arousal to relaxation.

Stress And Personality

Personality has the greatest bearing on how we respond to all situations.

Dealing with this is one of the biggest problems a coach has to contend with in trying to formulate a program which will lead a pistol shooter in accomplishing his goals. For example, some parents do not understand the process of letting go of their youngsters and letting them develop their own characters. Some parents have a need to hang on to their youngsters as if they were still small children and not maturing young adults with different needs and goals.

Brent "Bugsy" Barstow, age 10.

369

Then there are parents like some in Hickey's pistol club who let their youngsters work out problems on their own and are there to guide and felicitate the youngster's personality development.

We have one parent of a ten year old boy who let the boy go, by himself, on a hunting trip to Africa. While there, the boy, Brent "Bugsy" Barstow, shot a 5500 pound bull hippo with one shot through the ear canal at 40 yards using a customized .30-06 rifle. This particular hippo had been thoroughly terrorizing a village after leaving the Kruger National Game Preserve and the authorities of the area called in the boy's host, who was a professional hunter, to kill the animal. It was a danger to the villagers who found that throwing rocks had no effect on it while it destroyed their gardens and homes.

"Bugsy" was hailed a hero as the natives celebrated with meat which they seldom had a chance to have in their meals. If the parents of this boy had not allowed this boy this opportunity, it would have been a chance lost for the big step forward in the development of his self-esteem. As a coach, you can only offer youngsters and their parents an opportunity for the youngsters to enter Character Trait Development Sessions and to attend tournaments. In the end, the coach has to live with the parent's decision, even as it sometimes has the effect of destroying the youngster as a true competitor in the game of pistol shooting.

The shooting coach needs to understand the theory of self-consciousness. This is the theory which draws a distinction between the **private self**, that which can be observed only by the experiencing person, and the **public self**, that which is clear and observable. It is evident that **private self-consciousness**, which can be a state or a trait, leads to improved knowledge of the domain of one's **private self** and to the intensification of any associated emotions.

Public self-consciousness, also a state or a trait, results from other people's reactions to one's appearance, style, manners, and general social expression or presentation. Implications of this theory and the pistol shooter's social anxiety need to be considered by the coach. Social anxiety, if observed by the coach in his shooters, is developed in people mostly during puberty. It manifests itself in embarrassment, shame, stage fright, and shyness. When observed by the coach, the social anxiety trait must be attacked systematically and as soon after the coach's observation as is feasible.

However, if the coach is to be able to help his shooter change or eliminate one of these character traits from his personality, the shooter has to be the one to make the decision to change this aspect of his character. Remember, your job as a coach is to provide the kind of shooting training which will help your shooters become their own coaches. That means giving them the freedom to make mistakes.

We know from our experience, that the coach can get so bound up in his shooters, that he has a difficult time letting them make what he feels is a blunder in judgment. The pistol shooting coach knows that social anxiety traits, such as embarrassment, shame, stage fright, and shyness, if allowed to develop unchecked will go a long way to destroying the internal self-worth of a shooter. The shooter will never know why he seems to never get a handle on his shooting. He will hit a wall where nothing he does seems to lead to improvement of his scores.

If the coach persists in attempting to override the shooter's decision not to attempt a modification of one of the social anxiety character traits, he will quickly lose the confidence of the shooter in what he is trying to help the shooter accomplish. Clearly, the coach's own goal has to always remain: *helping the shooter to become his own coach.* If this means walking away from the shooter when his decision is made, which the coach knows to be counter-productive to the shooter's best long term interests, so be it. Remember coaches! You can only help those shooters who are amenable to the kind of help you have to offer.

And, another thing, coaches! Only offer the kind of help with which you personally feel comfortable. As Bill Pullum, former US Olympic Shooting Coach, has said, *"if you do not have rapport with the shooter, you're just wasting your time and the shooter's time in trying to work with that shooter."* While he was in charge of the shooting team at the US Army Marksmanship Unit, Pullum said that if he could not have the kind of rapport he wanted with the shooter, *"that shooter was out of there.*" We think it advisable for any of you aspiring to become top flight coaches to follow Pullum's advise.

Hickey had one shooter on his junior high school pistol team who had a serious problem when he experienced a severe loss of self-esteem. It came about when he fired a qualifying score as a sub-junior in the Arizona Junior Olympic State Air Pistol Championship. This netted him an opportunity for an invitation to the National Junior Olympic Air Pistol Championship being held at the US Olympic Training Center in Colorado Springs, Colorado. You say, he should have experienced a gain in his self-esteem!

However, his parents refused to allow him to go to the Olympic Training Center for the National Junior Olympic Air Pistol Championships. He felt like, *"What's the use of practicing if I can't go anywhere?"* This so did him in, that he became erratic in showing up for practice. When he did, instead of trying to make each shot a good solid, aimed shot, he would stick a target up and just keep shooting shot after shot in one target, without making any real effort to concentrate on each shot. Hickey knew what was happening to him. He knew the boy felt like he had no self worth. His parents had just taken that youngster's self-worth and sent it down the drain. Hickey tried to get him to refocus his attention to his shooting and even offered him the use of one of the club's two 10 meter Russian spotting scopes. He had hoped that through this devise, he could help him start thinking of the importance of each shot he fired. However, the boy declined the offer and said he was just shooting.

As a coach, Hickey knew the boy was making a mistake which would stay with him the rest of his life. We all know that when self-worth is destroyed during puberty, it is hard to establish later in life. But, Hickey also knew that if he tried to hang onto him and help him work through this problem that he would not appreciate it and would probably resent an outside influence involving itself in a matter to which it had not been invited. Hickey knew his decision was misplaced. He knew that by just throwing shots down range, without concern for obtaining a sight alignment with his eye, the boy was developing a conditional reflex which would be counter productive for him.

372

Hickey did what he always does when a shooter of his *decides not to let him help him work through a problem which Hickey knew would eventually hurt his shooting.* He dropped him out of his mind. Hickey no longer went out of his way to offer advice to him. Coaches have to be prepared to drop shooters from their list, of those whom they have singled out in their mind, to receive advanced training, upon receiving that first rejection. Once a shooter has started to reject a coach's offer or suggestions of help, a floodgate of rejections will follow. The coach should not bat his head against a stone wall. Just walk away from that shooter like Hickey did.

What happened next is something which has happened before. After school closed, Hickey received a telephone call from this shooter. He asked Hickey if he would allow him to come back and shoot with the club. Hickey felt that what the boy was really looking for was some way to reestablish his self-confidence. The boy's mother called shortly afterwards and told Hickey she did not know what had happened between us, but she hoped it wasn't anything which could not be repaired. Hickey did not mention to her what the problem was. He told her that her son had just called and he had invited him back into the fold. She mentioned that her son had sold his musical instrument and told her he was going to concentrate just on his shooting. Hickey told her he had no problem with giving him a second chance.

This shooter was really looking for help and he took the first step by reversing his decision to drop out of pistol totally. If Hickey, as his coach, had insisted in trying to *"help"* him at a time when he did not want it or feel good about getting the help, then Hickey would not have left him an opportunity to reconsider his decision. He is now fully and completely involved in the Character Trait Development Sessions and is making excellent progress in working to eliminate the negative self-worth image that had taken root in his mind. Still on the upper edges of puberty, Hickey thinks the boy reconsidered his decision and came back to his program just in time.

As a coach, we think you owe your shooters one mistake, and that for those who reconsider, you need to give them another chance. However, do not allow this to go beyond a second chance. You are not doing your shooters any service by allowing your program to become a Ping-Pong paddle for their ball. As a coach, you must not allow them to leave and rejoin your program at will. If you do, you will loose all track of just where the shooter is in his mental development.

Remember, research shows that the coach who chooses to work with shooters in the 9 to 16 year age bracket, must also prepare himself to deal with *all* of the problems associated with the shooter who goes through puberty during this time. It is during this time that the shooter's **private self** needs the greatest help in developing character traits which, in his shooting persona, will be helpful to have as a part of his or her personality as an adult. One way we do this is through the medium of the one shot match.

The One-Shot Match

As the Michael Wilkinson study of elite pistol shooters tells us, *"in an applied sense, the post hoc analyses yielded findings which could have implications for future sport training techniques...used on an individual basis to simulate competition, individually specific problems of the cognitive, physiological, or behavioral components of the shooting cycle which are the result of competitive stress could be identified. The identification process is currently hampered by the inability to monitor athletes while they are actually engaged in intense competitions. Once the identification process has taken place, individually specific treatment programs could be initiated to alleviate the specified problems. The current use of global or group treatment plans seem unwarranted base on the findings of this study."*

Hickey redesigned his one shot match method to establish the conditions Wilkinson suggested in his study. It is used as Wilkinson suggested, on an individual basis, to simulate competition. The one shot match helps the coach to bridge the gap between the **private self**, which can be observed only by the experiencing person, and the **public self**, that which is overt and observable. The **private self** reveals itself in it's **public self**'s reaction to losing a one shot match. Without the use of this tool, the coach is left with little insight into how to help a shooter to develop the type of character traits which are common in shooting champions.

Internal Self Honesty

The core character trait of internal self honesty is so essentially a key trait possessed by nearly all of the world and Olympic champions we are familiar with, that it is doubtful that anyone can attain this level of shooting success without also learning to make it a part of his or her character.

The Manipulative Person

Take, for example, the manipulative person. He will find himself filled with anxiety when he competes on a level where other shooters and coaches will be watching his every move. For instance, in one of the international final rifle tryouts for the US shooting team some years back, one of the shooters observed one of the best national level shooters firing shots into the dirt of the bank to the side of his target box. It was reported to a range officer who then came and observed the shooter still doing this illegal act. You see, under International Shooting Rules, a shooter is limited to the number of sighting shots and when they may be taken. A shooter having a manipulative character trait who attempts to gain an advantage over his competitors by shooting to the side of his target in order to see what the wind does to the dust kicked up by his bullets is doing something

375

illegal. That shooter will be then disqualified. Wouldn't it have been better for that shooter to have learned early on in his shooting training to substitute that manipulative character trait for one of internal self honesty?

We believe coaches who do not test for this manipulative character trait, and give the shooter the option of training to substitute it with one of internal self honesty, are doing their shooters a disservice. Should a shooter decline to try to change, the coach will have to keep his eyes peeled for manipulative efforts by the shooter. These efforts may lead to:

- efforts to falsify scores so as to make the shooter look good to his peers.

- It may lead to the shooter attempting to manipulate his way onto teams assured of winning a medal for the shooter.

- It may lead to the shooter attempting to manipulate the coach into accepting targets fired out of sequence for the qualification ratings.

One way to attack this manipulative character trait is to provide an opportunity for the shooter to shoot a great number of one shot matches.

However, the coach must be aware, that for this strategy to succeed, the shooter must pay the penalty when the one shot match is lost. The coach needs to discern whether the shooter is serious about developing the hard mental attitude necessary to conquer the problem of having his or her attention distracted from the two fundamentals of moving the trigger finger smoothly, after moving the barrel into alignment with the shooting eye by using the front sight as a reference point. What we, as coaches have to do is provide the shooter an opportunity to develop strength of character through an honest expectation that the price will be paid if the one shot match is lost.

If the shooter attempts to bargain his way out of paying the price or attempts to manipulate the coach into allowing *"another chance"* so as to try to improve the score of the one shot match, the coach must be quick to recognize that this attitude of

376

manipulation is the character trait the shooter is interested in developing.

If this occurs, the shooter is obviously not interested in developing the stronger character trait of internal self-honesty. Such a shooter will always be looking for the easy way out. Such a shooter will find himself not having the time for any home practice. Alibis and excuses will forever be that shooter's way of life. Before casting the shooter off from his sphere of influence, the coach owes the shooter an obligation to explain the character trait of internal self-honesty. You coaches may want to have your shooters read this chapter so they truly understand the importance of developing this internal self-honesty.

The one shot match is really a test of what type of character the shooter possesses. If, after explaining how the one shot matches are used to develop or change a character trait, the shooter attempts manipulation of the results, the coach should allow the manipulation since the shooter has obviously decided not to attempt to modify his character trait.

In the January and February issues of the 1990 volume of *The American Rifleman*, Hickey had two articles published about shooting one shot matches as a means of preparing to shoot finals of tournaments. He pointed out that the American shooters in the Seoul Olympics showed that tough preparation and the expectation of high scores are not enough to ensure the kind of mental case-hardening necessary to come through for the gold, silver or even the bronze medal. There is a different type of mental preparation that must be undertaken in expectation of being entered in a shoot-off.

Back in 1972, Jack Writer won the gold medal for smallbore 3-Position rifle at the Munich Olympics. Writer gave a lecture during the 1978 US International Championships. It was reported in *Schiessportschule Dialogues I*. Here is what Writer said on that occasion:

"I was up in Alaska a few years ago giving clinics to Bob Hickey's group, and they had an award presentation which would include me shooting a 10-shot air rifle match with one of the juniors." A little note here, that junior was David Ash, who later won the Junior Air Rifle Championship of Great Britain at Bisley, England, during the 1970 British National Championships.

Writer continued, *"I had more pressure on me in that little 10-shot match than I had in the Olympics or any world championship I had ever shot. I had a day or two to think about shooting the match. I'd never done anything like this before. I could sit down and think, 'Now, I'm one hell of a better shooter than this youngster is, but it didn't help. I still had the pressure. I thought, 'What if he beats me?' This is a good example of not having anticipated the situation."*

"Physically, I know how to go out, hold up the rifle and shoot the match like any air rifle match, but mentally I couldn't anticipate how my thoughts would be running when I actually went up there to shoot. I wasn't able to get my mind straight on it. If I could do this every day for a week or two, I'd learn a little bit more about myself and how I'd react in that situation, and pretty soon I'd have it all squared away upstairs, and I'd beat the youngster real good. I was nervous in Alaska, and I wasn't in Munich. I prepared myself for one a lot better than I did for the other."

"Let me tell you, I spent a lot of time thinking about what I did wrong shooting that little 10-shot air rifle match. I tried to pin down what specifically, not just generally, but what specifically caused me to have pressure. It was a good experience for me in progressing in shooting."

Writer was in Alaska the year prior to the Munich Olympics. He won this little 10-shot Alaska TV air rifle match, 92 to 87. We call it a TV match because we had television cameras on the shooters and also on their targets. Monitors were stationed around the auditorium for the spectators to observe the firing. We used a split screen, one side showing the shooter and the other showing the close-up of the target. The spectators could see each shooter on side by side monitors, along with the shots as they were fired.

We do not claim Writer won the Olympic Gold Medal because we set him up to shoot this match. But, Writer did not have this pressure in the Olympics. We think, because of his having had to contend with the pressure he experienced in this match and the amount of thought and consideration he gave it as he prepared for the Olympics, that it did much to make him *pressure proof* in the Olympics. This very much supports

378

Wilkinson's recommendations. Shooters need to have an opportunity to compete in as many differing match simulating conditions as possible.

Let's consider the pressure Writer was under. For one thing, he had developed himself into one of the best rifle shooters in the world. But, he also had kept in contact with Hickey, his old junior coach, who had taken him to his first National Smallbore Rifle Championships at Camp Perry. During that week in Alaska, he conducted shooting clinics for the youngsters in the rifle program. Talk about pressure, he had just won the Silver Medal for second place at the Mexico City Olympics. And, more than that he did not want to embarrass his psyche. How would that look if he lost to an unknown up and coming junior? He would never live it down in his own mind. His basic problem was a fear of losing. Now we would refer to it as a fear of failure. This was a new thought for Jack.

It is also a new thought for most American pistol shooters as they face the century of the 2000's. In a microcosmic sense, this is what the shooter of future Olympics must prepare to face. You saw how hard it was for Writer to face up to the possibility of losing. If the shooter does not learn to cope with this problem while going through training, he will have an extremely difficult time overcoming it later on.

You saw how an Olympic Champion did not quite get it all together even though he had a couple of days to prepare for the match. His score, according to what he was averaging going into this 10-shot match was a 96. His score of 92 reflects his inability to, as Writer phrased it, *"get it all together."* He told us *"Let me tell you, I spent a lot of time thinking about what I did wrong shooting that little 10-shot air rifle match. I tried to pin down what specifically, not just generally, but what specifically caused me to have pressure. It was a good experience for me in progressing in shooting."* If Hickey had had his one shot match program in place when Writer was with him in that summer practice camp before Camp Perry, you can bet he would have been able to handle that pressure a whole lot better than he did.

What Writer expressed is much what the shoot-off competitor confronts. It is, boiled down to its essence, the possibility of a defeat and a loss of face, or prestige. And, like

Writer, there is the chance that the loss will be to a shooter held in less-than-equal esteem by his opponent.

In all American pistol match preparation, the emphasis is on shooting the highest score in the tournament. Most American courses of fire are long enough that a bad shot in the course of the tournament will probably not penalize the shooter unduly. But, in a shoot-off, where you only have ten shots, a bad shot can undo a great effort. Rob Harbison, an American rifle shooter had to face exactly this situation in the Air Rifle Finals of the 1996 Olympics. Harbison went into the finals in 2nd place, he came out in 7th place.

In most American pistol training, the effort is directed toward shooting good scores. However, when you get in a situation such as described by Writer, the emphasis undergoes a rather subtle change. It is a subtle, but absolutely profound change. As you saw, Writer's focus became that of avoiding a bad performance. That is very important for us to remember, when as coaches, we devise ways of preparing for a finals shoot-off. That little TV match in Alaska was not important in anyone's scheme of things. It did not decide the Olympics, or even a local club championship, yet it placed a world-class shooting athlete under more pressure than he was to feel the following year in the Olympics.

So, coaches, how does one prepare his shooters for shooting in a short final? Do you stop shooting long practice strings? Absolutely not! If you ordinarily shoot 300 shots with your pistol at every training session, by all means continue to do so. In shooting these 300 shots, do you give up trying to make each shot a good shot? No! Hickey still remembers his coach telling him when he was a junior, *"Concentrate on each shot, make each one the best you can!"* It is still a good goal. Now, however, we understand that the emphasis on the phrase *concentrate on each shot* provides an incorrect bit of information to a pistol shooter. *Concentrate on each shot, make each one the best you can* supplies the shooter with misinformation. In pistol shooting, the effort has to be on the establishment of a Conditional Reflex. This means that the emphasis in pistol shooting has to be in allowing the automatic process to operate unimpeded by concentrating on the rather nebulous idea of

380

concentrate on each shot, make each one the best you can! The mental effort has to be to look hard at the sights and allow the trigger finger to move automatically when the eye sees that the sights are aligned with the eye. The idea of *concentrate on each shot, make each one the best you can* introduces a sense of deliberateness. This means that, instead of allowing the subconscious to fire the shot, the shooter is drawn into the concept of conscious control of the shot. So, this well intentioned idea of *concentrate on each shot, make each one the best you can* actually prevents the conditional reflex from operating. With so much of the shooter's attention drawn to making each shot the best he can, fatigue starts to play a more prominent part in the shooter's central nervous system. And, with this idea of *concentrate on each shot, make each one the best you can*, we are into sloganizing. The slogan may sell a soft drink product, but it is an interrupting influence on the pistol shooter's conditional reflex. Under the system advocated in this book, such sloganeers who caution shooters with this admonition are bad news for the pistol shooter. It misdirects the pistol shooter's attention away from allowing the subconscious to function automatically.

In preparing your pistol shooters to fire in a finals shoot-off, you need to provide a way for them to develop a special mental skill.

The nature of our competitive structure here in America really does not provide the experience backdrop we need when we make the finals and our every shot is being scrutinized closely by spectators. If these spectators are antagonistic toward us and favorable to our competitors, and more especially if we feel hostility around us, then our sense of responsibility impacts even more upon our subconscious.

It is in the subconscious that the match must be won. But if you have not prepared your shooters' subconscious to deal with the *sense of responsibility*, then you have added to their burden at a time when it least needs an extra millstone to overcome.

Many coaches of junior pistol shooters in the United States go to great length to keep their shooters from finding out what their competitors have fired in a match. Some go so far as

381

to get the tournament sponsors to delay the posting of the scores until all of the juniors have shot the course of fire. The theory is that knowing the scores would place an undue amount of stress on the juniors. So, in the United States juniors are routinely shielded from the type of stress they will encounter in the real world of international competition.

Training to overcome the problems attending the *sense of responsibility* is not new to European pistol coaches. But, generally, it is completely foreign to most of us American pistol coaches who are, for the most part, superficial coaches. That is to say, most of us do not attempt to train the whole pistol shooter. Many pistol coaches have never even thought about what attitudes a shooter needs to be trained to acquire. Certainly even fewer have identified what type of character traits help a shooter to become a champion. But, here in this book, we are going to change forever, how those of you who read this will coach future shooters.

Back in 1963, Makhmoud Umarov of the Soviet Union, wrote about training for this sense of responsibility, in an article titled, *"Must Master Shots Have 'Nerves Like Steel Cables?,'"* from the **UIT Journal** magazine, the official journal of the International Shooting Union. Umarov wrote:

> *"The chief cause of the drop in performance under actual competitive conditions in relation to the scores reached during training lies in negative influence brought on by the excitement of the start...the results of most shooters will, however, fall as soon as the mind becomes aware of the fact that these results will be important, i.e., as soon as the sense of responsibility begins to assert itself... In a competition, the shooter is in a state of increased nervous tension and reacts more readily to extraneous influences. This increased sensitivity is brought about by the awareness of one's responsibility and by the impressions made by the more or less festive atmosphere attendant upon a competition."*

382

Why American pistol coaches have ignored the coaching techniques of the Europeans is probably due to the insular nature of the American pistol shooting program. There seems to be an ingrained American character trait which says that the American way is the best way. This idea is held even in the face of hard evidence in the number of Olympic Gold pistol medals won by Europeans compared to a drought in recent Olympics for American pistol shooters. American pistol coaches seem to be perpetually in the dark ages of coaching. We know this because they have had decades to produce Olympic Gold pistol medals and their pistol coaching techniques have resulted in abysmal failures, as any look at the Olympic Records will show.

Most pistol coaches do what they have had taught them by their own coaches. However, they are merely piling failure upon future failure. Take for example the *US Army Marksmanship Unit Pistol Training Manual*. It mandates that a coach check off three pages of 61 steps a shooter must take in order to fire one accurate shot. Yet, we all know that a shooter can think about, at the most, two things when he is shooting. Give him a focus of three and you have started to destroy that shooter right from the start of his shooting. The shooter needs only to focus on the two fundamentals of shooting:

1	2
Visually Align the barrel with the eye, using the top of the front sight as a reference, point the aligned system at the area where you want the indicator (bullet hole) to appear..	Instantaneous Smooth Trigger Finger Movement

So, coaches, what we are offering you here, is a method which focuses on the shooter as an individual, not a puppet who you train to do your bidding. Instead of focusing on the shooter's breathing process or his stance, we will show you how to identify the attitudes and personality characteristics or traits of the shooter. But, more importantly, we will show you how to help the shooter to make changes in his attitude or to modify some of his personality traits to become a better shooter.

It is in the mind that the champion shooter is developed. If you are the type of coach who just comes to the range, unlocks the door and tells the youngsters to shoot 10 rounds slow fire, 10 rounds timed fire and 10 rounds rapid fire and then locks up the range and goes home, this book will open your eyes to a way of improving your coaching ability.

Just how do you go about training your shooters in this shooter focused training program? First of all, you must objectively identify just what attitudes and personality traits your shooters possess. If you are working with shooters who are past the stage of puberty, then you will have a much harder task. As is well known, personality is basically formed during puberty. The members of that junior rifle team Hickey took to Bisley, England, in 1970, formed their shooting personality traits while they were involved in the Anchorage, Alaska, shooting program in their junior high school years.

That team of ten junior rifle shooters beat the ten best juniors of that area of Great Britain in a shoulder to shoulder match at Wendover, England, by 302 points over the English Match course of fire which consisted of 60 shots, metallic sights, Prone position at 50 meters. The reason, the shooters spent a lot of training time working in the tournament program. That program was designed to develop the character traits which enabled them to travel 7,000 miles away from their mothers and fathers and friends and families and shoot in the most important match of their lives, and come away with a resounding victory. If

the result had been ten points difference, you could say that might have been luck. But, 302 points?

That definitely demonstrates that these youngsters, all from one small city in Alaska, had to have been training on a different planet than these juniors of England. Consider the population base that Hickey had to draw on in Alaska. Anchorage had almost 100,000 people in it at that time. Alaska had only the youngsters who had trained from their first shot in NRA Basic Shooting Courses only in Alaska. Further more, remember the course of fire is one which is the national course of fire for the rifle shooters of Great Britain. American shooters do not even shoot this course of fire in their National Smallbore Rifle Championships at Camp Perry. It is usually shot only in USA Shooting Preliminary Rifle Trials.

Training of the character traits of shooters takes place, for the most part, during the firing of one shot matches. It is the coach's job to direct positive feelings toward the attainment of positive results. Negative results where the individual shot goal is not attained should be reacted to by the coach with only acceptance. The coach's goal in this training should be to enhance the shooter's self esteem. If the coach gives off negative vibes when the shooter does not achieve his goal, he helps the shooter destroy his self esteem.

Remember, positive vibes enhance self esteem, negative vibes go a long way to destroying the shooter's self esteem. The key to one shot matches is to provide a way for the shooter to feel a sense of responsibility of not losing the match. If the loser just has to buy a coke as the penalty or brush his teeth five minutes longer, then the coach is allowing the shooter to enhance his feeling that he can achieve what he wants by manipulating his way around having to pay a meaningful penalty.

One girl had just such a manipulative trait developing the first time she fired a one shot match. She tried to set the penalty that she would have to take out the garbage for a whole week instead of her brother. She did not want to take his proposal that she would have to clean the rabbit cage in his room for him. We then explained to her just how developing her manipulative trait when it came to her shooting would, in the future, cause her a lot of harm. We explained to her the need for one's own personal internal self honesty. We explained that to develop this internal self honesty, she needed to be able to accept a penalty which she did not want to do. And, she most definitely did not want to clean that rabbit cage! If the loser had to buy the winner a coke, no big deal! Losing a coke, in our society, has no real meaning. Having to clean a rabbit cage, when it is repulsive to you, puts a whole new spin on just what is at stake in the one shot match.

If you, as coaches, allow your shooters to manipulate the results of their one shot matches, then you are doing them a great disservice. Often the shooter is a very intelligent person. Most shooters need only to be made aware of this character trait and how it would impact on their shooting and achieving their long term shooting goal. Knowing this the shooters most often will work very hard at developing this shooting trait. Can you as a coach, train someone who is no longer in the stage of puberty to make this trait a part of their personality? We frankly do not know. We do know that of the ones we have worked with, those who had developed a manipulative personality trait seemed to really have to think about what they would do in situations where someone who had established that trait, as already a part of their personality, acted instinctively.

Of the adults with whom we have worked, who have this manipulative trait, we have noticed that it seems to function in all of their dealings with other people, both at work and in recreational and competitive pistol shooting activities. If your shooter has to think about what action to take when a situation arises on the range, instead of acting instinctively, then that shooter starts to have too much impinging upon him during a match, when his mind needs to be very hardy and razor sharp and focused on his shooting performance.

As a coach, you must learn to keep up with the latest findings produced by the research community of the world, not just that of the United States. Research into the function of the mind, psychological research into the effects of the environment on the molding of the mind, social research into the inter-functioning of human beings with themselves and others, and educational research into how people acquire learning in the most efficient manner are some of the areas we keep up on. To be a well-rounded coach, we think you need to do this if you are to help your shooters to become the most efficient shooters they are capable of becoming.

For example, romantics of all ages can recall occasions when lust interfered with reason. Scientists once believed sex hormones had very little effect on the brain. The chemicals' only target was supposed to be a tiny structure called the hypothalamus, buried deep in the brain, which is the seat for sexual drive and other urges, such as appetite and aggression.

Recent research, however, has shown that the entire brain, including the thought-processing cortex, is awash in sex hormones, even before birth. For the pistol shooting coach, this has great implications on how you set up training programs. You need to show the shooter how to use this information to his best advantage. Left to himself, it is likely that the shooter will direct his efforts toward suppressing the feelings produced by these sex hormones. Allow these hormones to function as pleasure producing feelings each time you fire a shot meeting your individual shot goal. Just remember, heredity and biology are important factors for the coach to keep in mind as he designs programs for his individual shooters.

Consider, for example, the citizens of Botswana, a nation in Africa where Hickey's son was once employed. These are people who are known as the *losers* of Africa because they, historically, were pushed out of the interior by more aggressive tribes. They fled in panic as they were attacked. This heritage has resulted in the present day Botswanan lacking the get up an go to even go out of his way to provide change for someone who does not have the exact money for a transaction. Whereas in Morocco, if you go into a store and the owner does not have change, he will send a boy running next door to get the change. In Botswana, the owner will not sell you the item if you do not have the correct change. The post office in the capital city even has a sign saying that the clerk is not authorized to make change.

For a pistol coach, understanding the heredity and cultural background of each of his shooters helps him to design programs to help the shooter use the things inherent in the roots of his culture, to reach his shooting goals. For example, shooters of Hispanic origin have won pistol championships in the matches at Camp Perry. As all of you know, this is quite an accomplishment.

And, you know, accomplishing this is not an accident. It takes a enormous amount of hard work to win any championship in the nationals at Camp Perry. On the other hand, would you as a coach, want to devote much of your time to working with someone with a losing heritage? You might, out of pity, but the odds are that the shooter will not be able to form the kind of mental hardiness needed in a world class shooter.

This is a case where, even with the best and most innovative training techniques applied at the most opportune time in the shooter's stage of development, will probably have a lesser chance of working than someone with a more aggressive cultural background development. So, the pistol coach has to be aware of the possible limitations imposed on his training efforts by factors rooted deep in his shooters' inner self.

Consider the question, *"Why can't a woman think more like a man?"* That's the sort of question one would expect to hear from an unrepentant chauvinist like Shaw's Professor Higgins, in the book *Pygmalion*. Now, however, a growing number of scientists have begun wondering the same thing. Relying in part on advanced brain-scanning techniques, they have amassed tantalizing hints that men and women use their heads in subtly distinctive ways.

In July of 1995, a study showed that in science tests teenage boys who scored in the top 5% outnumbered girls 7 to 1. Girls, on the other hand, outperformed boys in reading comprehension. In general, males as a group, excel at tasks which involve orienting objects in space, like reading a map without having to turn it so it lines with the road. Females, though, seem to be more adept at communication, both verbal and non-verbal. Readings of MRI scanning results show females have stronger connections between the two brain halves (hemispheres).

What's sauce for the goose need not be a problem for the gander, however. The relative lack of cross talk between their hemispheres may actually benefit males by allowing each half of the brain to concentrate on what it does best. Studies have shown that when males are confronted with problems which deal with spatial orientation, a function which can be handled by both the right and left hemispheres, they tend to use the right hemisphere only. Thus there aren't many distracting messages coming in from the left hemisphere, which concentrates on language. This cerebral division of labor could also explain why

388

there are so many more male architects and chess champions. Their brains may simply be better able to concentrate on solving problems involving spatial relations.

What implications does this information have for the pistol shooting coach? Males generally develop this ability to solve problems of spatial relations because they play sports in which eye-hand coordination is crucial. Conversely females get more practice at reading words and understanding emotions. The coach, on the one hand, must design techniques to promote the development of this ability to solve problems of spatial relations in his female shooters.

It is seldom you see a boy, while he is going through puberty, walk around with a novel in his book bag. But, look around, observe! The females at this age are seldom without a romance or mystery book of one kind or another. While the girls are quietly reading, the boys are engaged in activities mostly requiring some sort of eye-hand coordination, even if it is just measuring how far to deliver a punch to a friend's arm.

The shooting coach has to take note of this type of information in designing programs which will take advantage of the traits which each sex has from a natural inbred ability, but to also nurture that shooter into the acquisition or substitution of traits not inherently developed. If heredity and biology are important to this differentiated development, then it's a pretty good bet that the sex hormones are somehow involved. For that reason, researchers have begun delving into the effects of testosterone and estrogen on the brain.

The larger amounts of testosterone produced by males may predispose their brains toward greater specialization of the two hemispheres. Note here that the key word is *predispose.* Females, given the proper encouragement and training techniques can learn this specialization. Consider Judit Polgar, who at age 15 became the world's youngest chess grand master. Her success does not mean she has a male-wired brain. No, it means her chess instructor taught her how to solve spatial problems. Why teach females this brain use methodology? With respect to the relative lack of cross talk between their hemispheres, it may actually benefit males by allowing each half of the brain to concentrate on what it does best.

Studies have shown that when males are confronted with problems that deal with spatial orientation, a function that can be handled by both the left and right hemispheres, they tend to use the right hemisphere only. For those involved in the game of pistol shooting, this has a specific importance because there are not many distracting messages coming in from the left hemisphere, which concentrates on language.

On the other hand, consider Shakespeare, whose intuitions about women were uncanny. He did not have female wiring. Does this mean that to coach female shooters the male coach must become a sensitive poet? No, of course not! But, coaches, if you feel the urge, writing poetry is an excellent way of learning to feel sensitive to the needs of your female shooters. The old fashioned image of a macho male coach set in the mold of an old rugged, loud talking former sergeant major has gone the way of the dinosaurs as we approach the profession of coaching youngsters into the century of the 2000's.

Ritualization of Club Procedure and Training

The chief designer of a pistol shooting program needs to be aware that youngsters need rituals to feel a sense of attachment with the club. Creating rituals with young adults as active participants requires that the coach give attention to individual differences and stages of development.

Meaningful rituals contribute to bonding of the individual with both the community of the club and the brotherhood of the shooting fraternity. Some of these rituals can be so simple as the announcement of the name of a shooter who is **first** in hanging his target. It can be the ritual of encouraging the clapping of hands when a shooter reaches a new rank in a qualification program, or attains the achievement of a National Standard Score.

The shooting coach can encourage the development of the ritual of clapping for a shooter who shoots a ten in the finals of an air pistol match. Benefits include reverence and respect for the interdependence of all, including multicultural concerns and appreciation for the nature of one's involvement in the shooting sports. Likewise, it is important for the pistol shooting coach to be aware that many of the crises of modern societies are partly the result of our society becoming more and more of a non-religious one, where ceremony is no longer a part of modern society.

The research shows that the intimate involvement of the shooter with the coach emerged as a primary factor in the level of *"perceived"* influence among teenagers. Once out of puberty, the die seems to be cast. The longer past this stage of life, the less likely the shooter is to be able to mold his mind to the type of character necessary to reach the level of National Team performance. The age of 16 was found to be the apex of reported influence.

The pistol shooting coach has to be cognizant of the dynamic pressures of conformity, inferiority, vulnerability, emotional highs and lows, anxiety, self-identity, and puberty, which are specific only to adolescence. These pressures sometimes interfere with the development of a pistol shooter's mental attitude. Teenagers go through a tumultuous time at this period in their lives. The persuasiveness of television, which in today's society leads to premature exposure to adult themes, sexual content, violence and aggression, TV stereotypes, TV news, and TV's legitimizing influences are important powerful factors affecting the formation and development of an adolescent's morals, values and sense of self. The shooting coach needs to deal with these factors on an individual basis. Just remember that not one shoe fits everyone. This is especially true when working to help a shooter mold his mind to a goal he chooses.

It is extremely important that the coach have the shooter identify the goal he wants. The coach needs to undertake an investigation to determine the extent of the shooter's determination to achieve the goal he enunciates. If the shooter's goal is merely a vocalization of something the shooter thinks that the coach wants to hear, then the coach should recognize that he has overstepped his bounds and allowed his expectations for the shooter to become paramount in the shooter's mind.

This is not a good thing to have happen in the training of the shooter. For one thing, it substitutes shooter independence for shooter submersion in the coach's ego process. To build up the shooter's ego, the coach has to devise situations which will allow the shooter to explore success in his mind.

For example, encouraging a shooter to star in and produce a training video on how to clean a handgun is one Hickey has used. An example of this training video is one made by Cade Wilson, one of his shooters, who at 12 years of age, was in the seventh grade at the time of producing the video. In 1996, Cade won the Sub-Junior Air Pistol Championship in the Nationals at Chino, California with a score of 538 out of 600.

Cade Wilson, age 12.

Coaches wishing a copy of this video may obtain a copy by sending a check made out to Cade Wilson for $20.00, including postage. Mail your requests and checks to:

Cade Wilson
Cleaning the Ruger Mark II
3735 N. Romero Road
Tucson, AZ 85705

Let us briefly tell you what you will find in this video. First you will be struck by the serious mien of Cade as the video starts. His eyes are definitely following a TelePrompTer. Cade made the TelePrompTer out of notebook paper he taped together.

Then the cameraman unrolled this makeshift TelePrompTer as Cade moved through what he had written. You can definitely tell when he reached the end of the introduction he read. Once he got into the actual cleaning, he was home free. He was open and natural during the actual cleaning the Ruger Mark II.

Coaches, you will be very impressed with actually seeing the process of strengthening a beginning shooter's ego. Here ego is used to mean a sense of one's own dignity or worth. By the way, if any of you coaches are working with Ruger Mark II's as a club gun, or if any of your shooters have Ruger Mark II's, then this video is a very valuable teaching tool. Cade did a very good job on it. The Ruger Mark II can be somewhat tricky to get back together when you are 9 or 10 years old, even some adults admit to a bit of a problem putting one back together.

Cade is a very good role model for your young shooters to emulate. His interest and knowledge of the task come through loud and clear. A video of this nature helps to demystify the cleaning process. One of the things which sets Champions apart from their peers, is a very keen interest in how their guns work. They will often spend time at home cleaning their guns on their own. A counterproductive process occurs when a parent harps on the shooter to clean his pistols.

The well-grounded coach will set up a non-threatening personality trait testing program. This will allow the coach to determine which mental facets of the shooter's personality need support or modification in order for the shooter to be able to realistically attain his goals. We use an Attitude Test, which gives an indication as to whether the shooter has a tendency toward extroversion or introversion. We have also developed a Shooter Personality Test, which helps us identify the way in which a shooter tends to deal with the stresses of his or her life. These tests help us develop programs to support the shooter to put himself in a position to be able to achieve his goals. Take a look at these tests a little further on in this book.

Pistol coaches need to be aware of the gender differences in adolescents' experiences of puberty, sexuality, and subjectivity. We suggest that recent work on gender differences of adolescence by researchers like Carol Gilligan are important to pistol coaches working with young shooters. Coaches are missing a significant component of adolescent lives and selves by not examining experiences of puberty and sexuality. Pistol coaches should be aware that girls in adolescence have a more difficult time than boys and men in constructing a *"desire of their own."*

Through semi-structured, in-depth interviews with working class, middle class and upper class teenagers from Hickey's rifle shooting teams in Alaska and his pistol shooting teams in Arizona, we find that puberty and first experiences of sex take a greater toll on adolescent girls' selves than on adolescent boys'. Coaches working with youngsters need to observe and note how pubertal events (menarche, breast development, shaving, voice change, weight gain) evoke cultural meanings about gender and gendered bodies that adolescents then use to construct personal meaning.

Pistol coaches be alert for the gender differentiated expectations, decisions, experiences, and consequences of puberty and how these affect adolescent boys' and girls' selves and desires. Throughout, the coach should also examine socio-class differences in the processes which lead to the development of the formation of a strong mental awareness. To do this effectively, there must be a very large degree of openness and trust on the part of both the shooter and the coach. As Olympic Coach Bill Pullum has said, you do need to have rapport with your shooters. Rapport comes about through sincere interest in your shooters. Looking at them as mannequins who show up once a week to learn how to shoot pistols leaves a void in your training program.

The window of opportunity, for the shooter to develop a solid mental state, capable of handling the demands of championship pistol shooting, is not limited to puberty. However, shooters who contact the coach for training after the end of this stage of their life will find it much harder to develop this particular hardiness of mind.

394

It is even more difficult for shooters to do this effectively after they reach adulthood. By then they will more than likely have developed mind sets and myths of what people can and cannot do with guns. Moreover, the pathways of their central nervous system will be less plastic. Thus it will take more effort to make the conditional reflex a subconscious act between what the eye sees and the movement of the trigger finger.

Many older shooters know it to be a matter of fact that no one can pick up a strange gun and do well with it. They assume that the purpose of shooting is to *"hit the target."* Hickey's juniors know that shooting is a pointing game. They know that if they point the barrel using the front sight of the aligned sight system as a reference point, at a piece of paper and move the trigger finger smoothly, so as not to disturb the alignment of the barrel with the eye, they will be able to keep the shots in a good group. We'll give you an example.

On the shooting range recently, one of the line coaches suggested to another of our line coaches, that he let one of our young juniors shoot his Free Pistol. The junior would let the adult, who is also a top flight Free Pistol and Air Pistol competitor, use his Ruger Mark II. They would each fire 10 shots at a blank target at 25 yards. The winner would be determined by the size of the group of the shots. This line coach is a very good competitive Free Pistol shooter. The object was to prove to the whole club that using a thousand dollar Free Pistol would not of and by itself, allow the junior to shoot a good group.

It was not in the experience of either of these coaches to suppose that anyone, much less a junior be able to just pick up an unfamiliar gun and do very well with it. There was a lot of winking going on amongst the adults on the range as they waited expectantly to be able to point out to the club members what they just knew the experiment would prove. Their point was going to be that a shooter did not need a thousand dollar pistol to shoot a super group. The competitive Free Pistol shooter used one of the club Ruger Mark II's. Our young 13 year old junior used the thousand dollar free pistol with a trigger so sensitive that a breath of wind might set it off.

But, what they were not aware of was that our junior was involved in the Special Training Program we conduct wherein we go one on one with the junior and help him deal with developing his mental awareness.

Our junior's competitive mind-set has started it's development. He has started to decide things for himself. For example, at home his father calls him a fanatic because of his devotion to his training of his arm and eye coordination by lifting a partially filled water bottle to eye level for several hours at a time. So this junior had developed a tactic of getting around letting his dad know what he is doing. This junior places a towel over the lamp in his room so the light will not show under his door, and then practices his repetitions with the water bottle in a way that it will not alert his dad of what he is doing. This junior gave me permission to use this anecdote because he says his dad will probably never read it. We intend to keep his confidence and refrain from mentioning this to his parents.

The upshot of this *match* between the coach and the shooter resulted in the junior pistol shooter beating the coach, who is a competitive Free Pistol shooter. Our junior had a considerably smaller group.

The coaches didn't mention a word about what the match was supposed to prove or anything else like it. We were proud of the way the junior took on this challenge.

For those of you who would be coaches, take this to heart. If you show the shooter how to make his own personal mind sharp and clear, then anything is possible. But, success will generally come, and here is the key point, only to those shooters who take a personal and active role in determining their problem. Often this is done in close consultation with the coach. They then act on their own to help solve the problem. Those shooters will be the most successful.

For example, once we learned that this junior was going to such lengths to avoid having his father catch him, we showed him how to practice in a completely dark room. In training in a dark room, such as a bathroom which does not have a window or in a clothes closet, the shooter's training effort is to identify the elements which make up his position. We demonstrated to him how this type of training would be more beneficial than working out in a lighted room.

By focusing his internal visualization on the front sight, the shooter develops the feeling of the gun in hand while visualizing lining up the barrel with the eye in the mind. Using this training method, the shooter is able to identify whether the position he has developed is susceptible to swaying and can then shift things around to correct the position so it is more efficient. This is now something many of the members of Hickey's junior pistol team have adopted.

Pistol shooting coaches must be aware of the up-welling of energy at puberty and the need of the youngsters to break some of the bonds and constraints of parental rules. This energy needs to be channeled if it is to allow the young pistol shooter to live up to the tremendous potential which he has within himself at this time of his life. It is the job of the coach to help uphold the parents in their rules. Where the coach has a program which, if continued, will modify a child's personality trait, he must make certain to discuss this with the parents so they can make an informed decision as to whether they wish to have their youngster continue in that particular program. If the shooters are immersed in a positive mental atmosphere, and can focus their energy on appropriate goals, they will rapidly mature both mentally and emotionally.

If You Are Starting A Junior Pistol Team There Are Some Concepts of Adolescence Of Which A Good Coach Should Be Aware

Nan Deborah Stein, in 1981, authored a study titled, *"Interplay: A Psycho-Social Study Of Sex Role Beliefs And Attitudes And The Physical Activities Of Working Class Adolescent Girls."* It contains some implications for the pistol shooting coach. As a pistol coach, you need to know that gender, class status, and sex role beliefs and attitudes influence participation in sports. Stein's thesis explores the interplay between working class adolescent girls' participation in physical activities and their sex role beliefs and attitudes about physical activities.

She points out that working class adolescent girls are portrayed in the literature as more sex role conventional than middle class girls. Furthermore, she notes, *"the phenomena of "bisexual socialization" (Bardwick, 1971) for prepubertal girls has different meanings and consequences for middle class and working class girls after puberty, as sex role definitions narrow, and class differences preclude certain options."*

So, what she did was to construct a configuration of psycho-social variables derived from the literature. She hypothesized that this configuration has influenced sex role beliefs and attitudes of working class girls toward their physical activities. She spent four months doing observations at a large urban working class high school of two physical education classes comprised of thirty-five older high school-aged girls engaged in a wide range of physical activities previously tested for their sex role appropriateness. What she found was:

☞(1) the phenomena of first time enthusiasm

This has been evident in the

Tucson Pistol Training Program.

☞(2) differential impact of the time of day upon girls' participation levels for different sports.

In the air pistol training we have done at the Flowing Wells Junior High School, many girls joined the program as an after school activity. But, the number continuing on with the program outside of school was way down. For the most part, the students in this junior high school come from working class families where both parents work. It is convenient for the girls to be involved in an after school activity which keeps them at school until close to the time the parents get home from work. It is equally

398

inconvenient for the parents of the girls to have to make the time to bring them to an evening pistol training session. Many of the parents of the children in the attendance area of this junior high school have physically exhausting jobs. In contrast, the work of many middle class families consists of more clerical or office oriented jobs. Pistol coaches, to attain year after year success in your training endeavors have to consider these points.

◎ Working class families often find it difficult to provide extra money for the expenses associated with pistol shooting:

⇒ ammunition costs
⇒ tournament entry fees
⇒ upgrade of pistols from using club guns to keep up with the youngsters from the more affluent families

☞(3) presence of boys creates ambivalent feelings for the girls as their participation levels and their articulated sex role beliefs and attitudes come into conflict.

◎ To create an atmosphere where the girls feel both comfortable and aggressive with respect to their pistol shooting, the coach should promote feelings of both pleasure and competition through such devices as:

⇒ fingertip pushups

When using the fingertip pushups as a method of firming up the minds of the girls of the pistol club/team, encourage the competition aspect of boys against girls.

A special note here. If you find that a girl who has been in a gymnastics program comes to your club, then by all means start the fingertip pushup option in your club. In gymnastics training, the little girls develop upper body strength, including their forearms. You will find that this will give the little girl an advantage over the boys who will not be expecting it. This allows the coach to capitalize on creating a spirit of competition between the sexes, while at the same time reinforcing the confidence of the girls. This confidence will even work vicariously for the girls who are not involved in the competition

399

of the fingertip pushups. This will have the effect of destroying, in the girls mind, the physical invincibility of the boys. The coach uses this to alter the mind-set of the girls.

☛(4) outfits, uniforms, and equipment needed for different sports have a differential impact upon participation depending on one's body type.

Interviews with twenty-eight girls confirmed the first three hypotheses, and challenged number 4.

Stein found that additional very important themes emerged from the interview data: So, if you are going to coach a junior pistol team, keep these findings in mind.

☛(1) the intervention of a job with sport participation

What kinds of jobs are available for the pistol shooting club?

Club officers

Tournament trip coordinator

Telephone tree coordinator

What kinds of jobs are available for the pistol shooting team?

Girls team captain

Range officer

Statistical officer

☛(2) fathers as positive sport influences

This factor has been well proven in our Tucson Pistol Training Program

☛(3) fear of injury limits sport participation

The connotation of pistol shooting is one of danger. This is so even though the shooting sports carries one of the best sports injury free records of any sport. The first thing the pistol coach or instructor has to do is to help the shooter to feel comfortable with the handgun. This is also the point at which the new shooter is most apt to be turned off by the experience. This happens when the coach starts the "naming of the parts." What does knowledge of the names of the parts of a pistol have to do with shooting? If you do not know what we mean when we speak

400

of shooting, please refer back to Chapter 2. In our training program, we specifically direct the beginners' attention to only two things:

1	2
Visually Align the barrel with the eye, using the top of the front sight as a reference, point the aligned system at the area where you want the indicator (bullet hole) to appear..	Instantaneous Smooth Trigger Finger Movement

☛(4) attitudes about different sports as "more" or "less" of a sport.

Stein noted that there are some psycho-social variables and salient themes which were incorporated into an analytical framework of "stimulators" and "limiters" of sex role beliefs and attitudes, and participation in physical activities. The limiters included

☛(a) generalized fear of injury

☛(b) sex role labels and the presence of boys

☛(c) the acquisition of a job

☛(d) scheduling of physical education activities.

The stimulators for overcoming conventional sex role beliefs and attitudes about physical activities and sport participation patterns were fewer in number and included:

☛(a) the interventions and influences of positive role models

☛(b) the girls' abilities to conceptualize, imagine, and plan for a learning environment in which they would experiment, take risks, and demonstrate their courage, desire, and motivation to learn new sports. These limiters and stimulators are not static, and their simultaneous coexistence creates tensions and ambivalent feelings which at times enhance or inhibit changes in sex role beliefs and attitudes about

401

physical activities and participation in physical activities.

Anton Wilhelm Odendal, in a dissertation titled, *Pubescents In Modern Society: A Psychotherapeutic Approach To Early Adolescence.* The physiological changes which occur during puberty have a major effect on the child's experience of his body. Together with this, there is a significant change in the pubescent's thinking style, and this drastically alters his personality, and moral development. The pubescent's interpersonal style also undergoes radical changes. The early adolescent wants to develop his own identity, wants to develop intimacy in his relationships with others, and wants to gain independence from his parents. All these factors influence the way in which the pubescent reacts to pistol shooting training.

Intellectual development is characterized by the expansion of capacities in pubescents to permit the moves to formal operations from concrete operations and to reality from egocentricity. It is also characterized, unfortunately, by the loss of creativity. It is important for pistol coaches to be aware that their intellectual needs include freedom to explore and experiment. They need stimuli to provide environments conducive to exploration and **experimentation without overloads**, feelings of safety and security, freedom to fail, development and improvement of vertical and lateral thinking skills, encouragement to retain and enhance creative capacities, and the feeling of competence. Pistol coaches who overload their pistol students will find that the youngsters are destroyed and drop pistol shooting. They are experimenting to see if they like pistol shooting. Giving the youngster too many things to think about causes a disastrous overload.

Emotional development is characterized by the move from egocentricity to reality, further development of detachment and autonomy from the family, the development of a new identity and commitments to self, friends, and a *"cause,"* and vulnerability to stress. Emotional needs are great. They include skills for coherence or structure, privacy, feelings of acceptance, affiliation and competence, skills for the development of identity, alternatives from which to choose commitments, activities which provide fun and laughter, and skills for managing stress.

402

Social development is characterized by a move away from family into formal, same-sex peer groups. Needs include freedom of association, freedom not to conform to adult mores, recognition, sense of community, skills for cooperation, authoritative guidance, effective communications skills.

When working with youngsters, a pistol coach has to be aware of these kinds of things. With this information, the coach can plan activities which will appeal to youngsters at this time of their lives.

In dealing with adult pistol shooters, the coach should know that extremely superior athletes show mild tendencies towards introversion. Introversion helps the individual to *"keep his own counsel"* and withstand the pressures of competition. Mrs. J.A. Coleman of Great Britain reported that the introverted pistol shooters showed consistently superior shooting results in both Free Pistol and Rapid Fire Events.

This bears out other studies and observations, that in most sports, the very best athletes are often introverts.

With this in mind, pistol coaches can help shooters become more self-reliant through developing the inner self in a positive manner. Help shooters to eliminate negative thoughts caused by being overly concerned about what others may think of them. This is not something which can be done overnight, but requires a long term commitment on the part of the shooter.

Adjustment To Stress By Shooters

Shooters are affected by any circumstances raising their anxiety level.

Coleman's study investigated the extent to which the stress experienced by a shooter in areas of his life not connected with the shooting sport. She found that the study showed that

403

this had a profound and definite affect on the shooter's competitive shooting performance.

The coach must be concerned not only with the on-the-range shooting performance of the shooter, but has to get to know the shooter and understand what is going on at the present time in his life. Without this awareness, the coach is apt to prescribe training methods which may prove counter productive to the rapid development of the shooter.

Coleman observed that the main discrepancies between "A" and "B" National Pistol Squad Members were in areas of Primary Family (Mother, Father and siblings), Secondary Family (Wife and/or children), Shooting Coach, and Personal Life.

The relationship of the shooter to his wife and family can obviously be an area productive of stress which can affect the shooter in competition here and now. What is more surprising, perhaps, is the way in which primary relationships back in the shooter's distant past can affect his potential for future development in his shooting sport. In addition, most of the shooters who made it to the "A" squad and represented their country on an international level, early on in their shooting, developed a close and personal relationship with their shooting coach. This closeness seems to have been an essential spark to their present level of achievement.

The coach has to identify, as early as possible, all conflicts and potential conflicts within the Primary Family. These must be dealt with by helping the shooter to develop strategies for resolving these kinds of conflicts in a positive manner which will help the shooter to go through these situations with a harmonious result. In other words, the shooter has to be taught how to manipulate his environment to his advantage and leave the family members unaware of the manipulation. This manipulation must be shooter initiated. The coach can only offer suggestions. If the shooter is not open in his feedback to the coach, then the coach should consider dropping the shooter from his training team.

Competitive Rifle Shooter's Questionnaire

Results Implications For Pistol Shooters

In 1980-81, Hickey conducted *"A longitudinal study of personality as a contributing factor in the development of skill amongst America's shooting athletes. This study follows the shooting athlete from high school, through college to the date of the questionnaire."*

The authors make no claim for the reliability of this questionnaire. Hickey has used the results of the test as a part of his screening process, along with personal observation, in his work with the juniors of his pistol program in Tucson. He has, in addition based his pistol training methods on what he considers desirable personality traits for pistol shooters to develop. It is during puberty that many character traits may be consciously developed and formed. Once out of this period, the character traits formed are generally theirs forever.

We have included sample copies of portions of the responses to some of the items on the questionnaire. In keeping with the confidentiality of this study, none of the selections in this chapter have been identified. However, many of them are Olympic or World Champions, either as individuals or on teams. Some have been intercollegiate champions, national or state champions. Many of the samples have been selected on the basis of what their handwriting samples show. Hickey designed the questionnaire with the idea that the respondents would have to give samples of their writing. A bonus also occurred in this study. Many of these champions responded with statements clarifying their responses to the questionnaire items. This permitted a more

405

in depth study than has hereto been made of shooting champions and their personality trait as revealed by their handwriting. This handwriting information was matched against Hickey's personal observations of the responders and their answers to the questionnaire items.

In addition, many intermediate and advanced juniors responded to this study, only two of whom later went on to become champions in their own right.

William R. Rigby, in 1978, conducted a study of *"Personality Characteristics of U.S. International Marksmen."* His study *"strongly supports the fact that personality characteristics which distinguish shooters are very stable over a relatively long period of time."* He found that three character traits demonstrated a discernible difference between these elite shooters and the normal population. These were:

- sociability
- tough-mindedness
- self-sufficiency

As Rigby discovered, *"The overall picture of the personality traits of international marksman is that they tend to be somewhat lacking in warmth, tend to be lower in sociability, and more self-reliant. They are self-assured, secure, and are guided more by intellect than by emotions. They differ from other sport groups by being more self-controlled, secure and intelligent, as well as less sociable and tense."*

Competitive

Rifle Shooter's

Questionnaire

Question #1: **During [High School], I wanted to:**
be top shooter in my club
make my school team
make College All-American

win the state championship
win at Camp Perry
represent the US on an International Team
win a gold medal in the Olympics
other, please specify:

The responses to this question did not discriminate between the champions and the intermediate juniors in an NRA Junior Olympic Rifle Summer Camp in Connecticut, nor in an NRA Junior Rifle Training Session in Colorado Springs at the Olympic Training Center. Fifteen years later, the question did not differentiate between the original sample of rifle champions and the juniors entered in the 1996 Junior Olympic Air Pistol Championships at the Olympic Training Center. The authors suspect that the question itself generates the response to the item which, until that time may not have been an actual consideration.

Ammunition use categories, in either practice or matches, did not discriminate at any level of expertise.

When it comes to the sociability trait, consider the results of the champions who answered this item:

High School

> ## When dealing with the opposite sex in High School, I
>
> ## Get along famously = 20%
> ## Don't feel comfortable = 60%
> ## never think about it one way or another = 20%

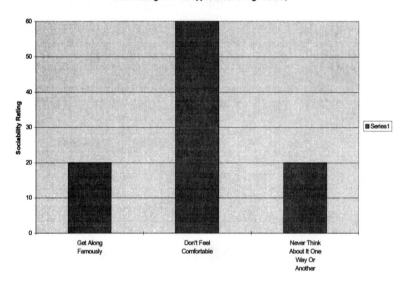

When Dealing With The Opposite Sex In High School, I

As the champions progress through adulthood, notice the changes that maturity and self-confidence produce. While the champions still maintain a relatively high *"Don't feel comfortable with the opposite sex,"* syndrome, there is in general, although not in specific individuals, to either a *get along famously* or a *it doesn't matter either way.* Some champions got along better in high school than others with the sociability rating. One champion explained what he did after school involved,

a particular lady-friend

When dealing with the opposite sex in College, I

Get along famously = 20%
Don't feel comfortable = 33%
never think about it one way or another = 47%

When Dealing With The Opposite Sex In College, I

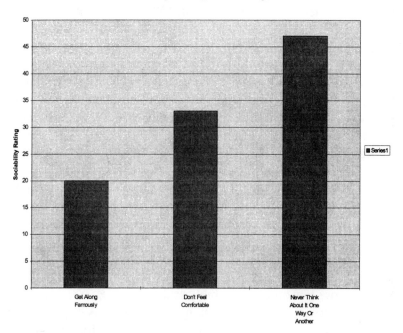

Often persons with lower sociability traits experience social discomfort. So the shooters are not the only part of the population with this trait. Many people fear negative evaluation and thus score low on sociability trait evaluations. Shooters with this sociability trait are easily hurt by criticism or disapproval. Many times such a person will have no close friends or confidants, or maybe only one. This does not include close relatives. The shooters with this trait are hesitant about getting involved with people unless sure of being liked and accepted. They are also diffident in social situations because they fear saying something inappropriate or foolish, or, heaven forbid, being unable to answer a question. Sievers recounts an instance

409

wherein he braced a champion with the question, *"When a firearm is discharged, one big thing happens that we are interested in. What is it?"* It took that Olympic champion seven speculations about what happens until the answer finally came out. *"The bullet comes out the barrel."*

Shooters low on the sociability scale, when they cannot avoid others, stand aloof, looking down or away rather than making contact. If you have ever attended a final social get together at the end of an event at the Olympic Training Center, it is noticeable that, unless the shooters have previously known one another, they a loath to approach others whom they know by sight, but have not talked with before. Many times these shooters are lonely loners. Of course, the selection of a hobby to pursue such as one of the shooting games is the tailor made choice for persons who are low on the sociability scale. To become a champion at any level of the shooting game requires the person to practice his sport, usually by him or her self. These shooters report doing a lot of dryfiring at home. Often this training will go on for several hours at a time. While engaged in this training, they do not have to face others who may cause them some anxiety. Thus they do not have to experience the terrible anticipation of rejection. As a result, other people often perceive them as being cold and not wanting to be included in social affairs. This, of course, contributes to the reinforcement of the trait in those low on the sociability scale.

Shooters with this trait have highly sensitive *"danger-alert systems."* They are always on the lookout for criticism or disapproval. Of course the problem is that even the smallest hint, maybe a cynical word or a odd look, will sound the alarm. Shooters with this trait are generally so over reactive to negative and even neutral evaluation that anything less than total, open acceptance, feels like rejection.

This sometimes carries over into their personal lives, the non shooting related part. Generally, they think that acceptance means unconditional love. In the world of their mind, people who care for each other never become angry with each other. They never hurt each other. They do not point out character flaws. They always accept each other without reservation.

But, then on the other side of the coin, they believe that to be accepted and loved, a person cannot have imperfections. When a shooter with low sociability traits walks into a gathering of other shooters, whom they may not know, they are hyperaware of their inabilities to compete and succeed socially. Often times they will be the *watchers* in a gathering.

WANTED TO SHOOT ON THE COLLEGE TEAM

h. IT IS REWARDING AND I ENJOY THE PEOPLE

Shooters who are aware that they have this trait may be comforted to know that the vast majority of the population experience at least some social anxiety. And a great number of these people find it very upsetting. One estimate is that 15 to 20 percent of all adults experience distressing social anxiety. Often shooters low on the sociability scale believe that they are different from others.

In dealing with shooters with this personality trait, coaches need to be aware that these people are comfortable with routine. They have no problem with following a training schedule. However, remember, they have a need not to be overly involved with their team members. They may also feel uncomfortable when faced with responding to questions from the news media. They can generally shoot and train along side their teammates, but they may remain aloof and to their teammates they may seem standoffish or shy. Some go out of their way to avoid entanglements with teammates even going to the point of not joining any club at all:

all practice is done after school on my own time (I never join a club to shoot in their sessions)

Nearly all of the champions tended to have been self-taught, in significant numbers, after an initial parental involvement. American coaching methods have virtually closed the door to this type of shooter ever being able to move through the cracks like the champions of the 1960's and 1970's.

411

Oftentimes shooters low on the sociability scale are able to find a sense of security by turning inward and allowing creative imagination to take them far away from their anxieties. This is usually the kind of individual who will respond in a positive way to the coach's suggestions about mental training. They will be able to perform this at any time and feel that they are doing a proper and socially acceptable thing. Mental training, like dryfiring is something the shooter does, generally away from the shooting range.

All shooters, at some time in their matches, experience anxiety. This is usually associated with butterflies in the stomach, the wide-open eyes, the pounding heart and the sweaty palms. But people low on the sociability scale are unusually sensitive to that state of physical arousal. A couple of Hickey's junior pistol shooters experienced this type of arousal in the 1996 Junior Air Pistol Championships at the Olympic Training Center. One young 13 year old had fired a very fine score in the Arizona Junior Olympic State Championship. This qualified him to shoot on the top floor range with others having similar scores. When the shooting began, he experienced this problem. He stayed on the line and tried to work through it. Later he told Hickey that he experienced this arousal throughout the duration of the match. He felt that the next time he would not have this problem. The key to the problem was that he had not expected to be shooting against kids in college and juniors and seniors in high school. He did not know any of these shooters from never having fired against them in tournaments. This was something the other boy, an 11 year old also experienced. So not only shooters low on the sociability scale experience this type of arousal in a match, but so do, at some time or other, most all other shooters.

When dealing with the opposite sex Now, I

Get along famously = 26.5%
Don't feel comfortable = 26.5%
never think about it one way or another = 47%

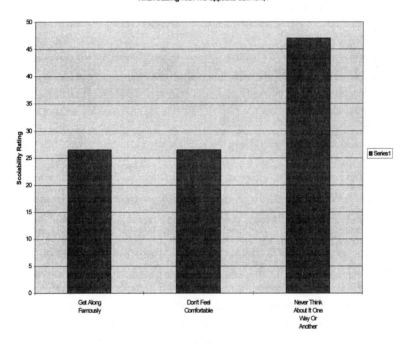

When Dealing With The Opposite Sex Now, I

38. Where ⑩ is most willing, put a vertical line showing your willingness to sacrifice academic progress to attain your ultimate shooting goal:

❶ _____ ⑩

The champions as a group, were more willing to sacrifice academic progress. This seems to be a distinguishing factor which separates the elite of the elite from the sub-champions and the intermediate and recreational shooters.

A number of other factors also showed up in this study. There is a definite difference between young shooters of the upper, more affluent classes and those of the middle class spectrum. For example, the upper class youngsters indicated that they believed that they were able to pull the wool over their parents eyes. Or that their parents did not have a real interest in them or their shooting activities. The middle class youngsters, represented by two 4-H shooting groups from diverse parts of the country, indicated a closer relationship with their parents. This was evident from the responses to specific items designed to elicit this type of information. The 4-H groups showed more trust and understanding between the shooters and their parents. This represents less of a generation gap between parents and their offspring.

With respect to the 4-H shooters, the results were markedly similar over two generations. The first survey of 4-H shooters was conducted 15 years prior to the second survey. Many persons today think that the youth of today in our country do not possess the strength of character of youngsters several years ago. However the results of our survey indicate a consistency between generations, of 4-H shooters. For example, consider the willingness to sacrifice academic progress in these two 4-H sample groups. In each group, the 4-H shooters were less willing to sacrifice their academic progress than were the champions.

We have noticed one thing with respect to the non 4-H shooting sample. What is interesting, the juniors in the 1996 sampling, even though this sampling was taken at the 1996 Junior Olympic Air Pistol Championships at Colorado Springs, showed a significant decline in a willingness to sacrifice academic progress for their shooting goal. This stands out when compared to the sampling results of fifteen years ago. This has serious implications for the future of American pistol competition on the international level. These junior pistol shooters appear to have a

414

significant lack of commitment to what is needed to achieve success in the game of pistol shooting. Academic achievement does not translate into Olympic gold medals. Unlike the National Collegiate Athletic Association, the Olympic movement does not give medals to the physically challenged. The NCAA awards these inferior football players titles such as *Academic All-Americans.* It is assumed by all, that this is merely a sop for the media. This allows the NCAA to look concerned for the academic progress of their football players. The best players go on to assuming their roles in life as sports millionaires. The *Academic All-Americans* recede into obscurity as they dredge out an existence in a job for which their schooling prepared them. Then they can sit back on their couches each Sunday and watch their former millionaire teammates play football.

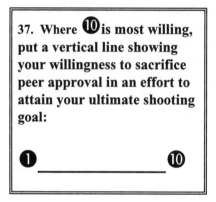

Fifteen years apart, the junior sampling groups indicated that they were willing to sacrifice peer approval to attain their shooting goals. This indicates strong minded individuals, who are not apt to be influenced by a need for peer approval or a need to belong to a group. In today's language, this would indicate that these youths would have the tools with which to withstand the influence of gangs and the attraction of drugs in the school place. At the same time, it demonstrates that these shooters may rate low on the sociability scale. It would appear that persons attracted to shooting may feel comfort in the individuality of the sport. Having this character trait, places them within the character profile of the shooting champions. However, this by itself does not guarantee movement into elite shooter status.

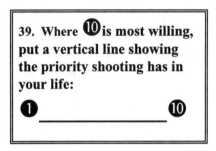

The rifle champions placed shooting as the top priority in their lives. The juniors in the 1981 sampling were attending a Junior rifle camp at Colorado Springs. Those junior shooters of fifteen years ago, by a majority, placed shooting also as their top priority. However, just having this as the top priority did not result in any of them becoming champions in their own right. So, it would seem that just having this priority is not a guarantee of shooting success at the elite level. Interestingly, the juniors in the 1996 sampling, even though this sampling was taken at the 1996 Junior Olympic Air Pistol Championships at Colorado Springs, showed a significant decline in a willingness to have shooting as a priority in their lives, when compared to the sampling results of fifteen years ago. A willingness to have shooting as a priority in the lives of the young shooters was almost doubled in the 1981 sampling. This was a significant decline. It is especially troubling in that these juniors in 1996 were participating in the Junior Olympic Air Pistol Championships. One would think that a junior who spends the time, effort and money to attend the National Air Pistol Championships, would have shooting as a high goal in life. That this was not the case is especially troubling in that USA Shooting has instituted a policy of selecting juniors, not solely on the basis of their pistol shooting performance, but also with academic progress as a vetoing criteria, to the national junior teams which will represent the United States in pistol team competitions with other national junior teams. Like the Russians in 1979, the authors believe that the United States Olympic Body for Shooting should reexamine this potentially disastrous selection policy. It should be the policy of a national governing body to produce the most representative team, not the highest academic talent in the shooting sport. There are no gold medals awarded in the Olympics for the most academically talented shooter. To have a policy which promotes academic talent over shooting performance will continue to lead the United States to more and more failures in the pistol shooting games in the Olympics.

Personality Characteristics Important To Pistol Shooters

The research studies we have looked at, have some rather interesting points for pistol shooters. It was concluded that the adaptiveness of:

- Extraversion
- Sensation-Seeking
- Psychoticism

to sporting activities is likely to be diminished among high performance athletes, at least in non-team sports, because of the long hours of solitary and repetitive training that is required for successful competition. The persons involved in solitary training for individual sporting activities, such as pistol shooting may find the following characteristics helpful.

- Neuroticism
- Toughmindedness
- Psychoticism
- Sensation-Seeking
- Achieving Tendency

Eysenck et al. (1982) make the point that *"Extraversion, and aspects of Sensation Seeking, are likely to be positively associated*

417

with participation and excellence in sport because the inherently low arousal level of the Extraverts makes them more suited to the sensory stimulation obtained from sporting activities." These authors also suggest that traits such as aggressiveness and impersonal attitudes which are characteristic of high Psychoticism should contribute to success in most sports. For pistol shooters, in respect to Neuroticism, however, they point out that moderate levels are probably most adapative for the athlete because too little emotional reactivity makes for poor motivation, and too much, for distraction.

Other studies suggest that Extraversion, Psychoticism, and Thrill-and-Adventure Seeking are related more to interest and recreational participation in sport than to success in sport. Pistol shooters are advised that a moderate degree of stimulation seeking behavior is clearly adaptive to sporting activities. However, it may well be that higher levels diminish the adaptivity of this trait for high performance athletes. On the other hand, Sociability is a central feature of the Extraversion dimension, and yet is a characteristic that is not entirely compatible with the long hours of repetitive, and often solitary, training that is required for success in pistol shooting.

As Rigby found, other studies confirm that elite male athletes are less anxious than their sub-elite counterparts. It was also noted that non-athlete male controls had especially high Neuroticism scores. Some studies have reported that higher emotionality appears to be characteristic of the average female athlete, while normal to low emotionality is more characteristic of the high-performance female athlete

Both elite and sub-elite athlete groups demonstrated a higher degree of Achieving Tendency than the control groups, a findings which is consistent with evidence that persons with a high need for achievement prefer more competitive situations that those with low scores on this variable. This finding suggests that high Achieving Tendency is specifically related to successes in pistol shooting and not simply to interest or recreational participation in pistol shooting.

Chapter 8

Mental Training
For
Pistol Shooters

Pistol shooters, for many years have been stuck in following the lead of the rifle shooters when it comes to mental training techniques. From the observable and reported results, their efforts have had less than the expected success. Why? For the most part they have been dealing with failure.

We believe it is fully apparent to everyone that retraining is the most difficult task going. For those pistol shooters who are looking for something different, you have found it here. However, if you take up this program, you will be *challenged to "not do" what you are already doing.* Sometimes, creating failure is subconscious. For the most part however, simple, conscious changes in motivation, training and education will redirect energy spent failing into activity leading to success.

In other words, by changing a few bad habits, progress toward success gains twice:

☛First, when the failure behavior stops

☛Second, when the energy previously spent failing is redirected to succeeding.

419

If you become involved with this program, we want you to be provoked to do something different! You can do things differently because the challenge before you is to stop doing the things that failures do.

"If you continue to think
in ways you've always thought,
you'll continue to get
what you've always got!"
Gerry Reid

Back in 1994, one of the authors was told by an American Olympic pistol shooter of the 1992 Olympics *"Now I can consider myself one of the veterans. Physically I am no longer struggling as I believe that I have developed the proper stance, grip, etc. for me. But, as you know, the physical attributes comprise but a small portion of the successful shooter's make-up.*

The real competition is with one's own mind. The will and determination to excel must be there as you know. My definition of excelling is not winning, but rather being the best shooter that I can be and boy, does the struggle go on. Some days things go so well and other days I disappoint myself.

You have heard all this too many times, I know! The question now is what am I going to do about it? If I want to change the outcome, then I need to change in input...believe it to be my job to shoot 10's and not muddy the waters with team politics and negative thinking.

While in Milan, ...[I] talked to a former Russian pistol coach at length about their training techniques...[I am] developing a new training plan that in short involves less live shooting, more dry firing and some physical training...[my] goal is to focus less on the outcome (numbers) and more on the components of a good/successful shot. [I am] anxious to start this new program and see how things go. [I am] looking at the 1996 Olympic Games."

The world has seen the result of this training program in the placement of the United States pistol athletes in the 1996 Olympic Games. In the issue of May/June, 1979, of the *UIT Journal,* an article by W. Reschjotilow points out how the Russians reacted to the failure of the leading Soviet shooters in the Montreal 1976 Olympics. Instead of looking for shooting training which *"involves less live shooting, more dry firing and some physical training,"* the Russians deliberately set out to exceed the scores their experts decided it would take *"in order to take a place on the winners rostrum in Moscow"* for the 1980 Olympics. The Russians changed the way shooters were selected to represent their country in the Olympics, *"The first criterion for selection to the team is no longer a place in the medals in the national championships, but regular high performance."* The Russians decided, Reschjotilow pointed out, *"We must do justice to the people responsible for the international selection – they weren't afraid of admitting to their mistakes."* The Russians took a deliberate sight on the winning of individual medals in the Olympic games, *"if one wants to win in shooting, one must have a real fighting spirit."* On the other hand, consider an example of what kind of spirit an American Olympian displayed after the loss of face in the 1992 Olympics, *"My definition of excelling is not winning, but rather being the best shooter that I can be."* This a reflection of how the American pistol shooter thinks of himself.

Instead of a *fighting spirit*, the American pistol shooters want to be *the best shooter that I can be.* With a mental attitude such as this, is it any wonder that when going up against shooters from the rest of the world who *have a real fighting spirit,* they end up just exactly where the mental wimps of the world always end up, second best. Actually our pistol shooters were really more like 18th to 30 something best. And then they wonder why this is so. First of all, they claim that the shooters from the other countries have more pistol shooters to select from. Next, as the pistol shooter referred to above does, they look inward and feel that they must be more mentally prepared.

Yet, when faced with an identical situation in 1976, the Russians initiated training which in resulted developing shooters with a *real fighting spirit,* shooters who came out of a new training process which focused on *"discipline, self control, strict daily routine and definite fulfillment of proposed tasks...even when the trainer isn't nearby."* How different from the American pistol shooter cited above!

How different than the attitude exhibited by 1972 Olympic 3-Position Smallbore Rifle Champion, Jack Writer, after

421

the 1968 Mexico City Olympics where he placed 2nd. Hickey still recalls stopping by the Wheaton (Illinois) Rifle Club with a rifle team from Alaska in 1971. Writer was in the midst of a practice string of 200 shots in the standing position at 50 meters. He was focused on training to eliminate the 8's from his strings. He, like the Russians was into *"discipline, self control, strict daily routine and definite fulfillment of proposed tasks."* In a postcard to Hickey after winning the Gold Medal in Munich in 1972, Writer mentioned that he had eliminated all 8's when firing his standing score. He had worked hard and had the *discipline,* the *self control,* had maintained a *strict daily routine* and through his hard work had achieved a *definite fulfillment* of his own *proposed task* of eliminating the 8's from his standing position at 50 meters. Notice how this differs from the attitude of the American pistol shooter, *"believe it to be my job to shoot 10's."*

With this mental attitude, the American pistol shooters have, to put it very charitably, not fared too well in the Olympics over the past 30 years. Why? Let's look at the mental attitude and the results of the type of mental outlook as evidenced by this American pistol shooter's outlook. With the attitude that *"believe it to be my job to shoot 10's,"* he sets himself up for failure.

Look at the difference in Writer's outlook. Writer expected to shoot 10's, he could accept an occasional 9, but in his mind, an 8 was unacceptable. An 8 was something he worked to eliminate from his strings of 10 shots. He first had to eliminate it during practice.

A shooter cannot normally expect, that under the stress of shooting in an Olympics, he would be able to accomplish what he had never been able to do in practice. Because Writer did not shoot many 8's, he was in the position of having much positive feedback from each shot. If he shot five or six 8's during each 200 shots string, he would have positive feedback on about 194 shots. Look at how that would harden a shooter's mental attitude. This type of training is how winners are developed.

On the other hand, take a look at the American pistol shooter cited above. He *"believe it to be my job to shoot 10's."* Unlike Writer, he is going to do *"less live shooting, more dry firing and some physical training."* So, where Writer chose to do more live firing, the pistol shooter chose to do less. His results

422

placed him lower than his ranking in the Olympics of 1992. But, now let's look at how what he is doing is adversely affecting his mental state. Since he voices the belief that it's *"my job to shoot 10's,"* what does it tell us of what is happening in his subconscious? Unlike Writer, who may be getting 194 positive reinforcements out of 200 shots, the pistol shooter is getting 30 some negative feedbacks out of every 60 shots fired with the air pistol and perhaps 50 or so negative feedbacks out of every 60 shots fired with the Free Pistol at 50 meters. So, at 50 meters Writer gets 6 negative feedbacks, and should the pistol shooter ever fire 200 shots outdoors at 50 meters, he would be getting about 160 negative feedbacks.

What the pistol shooter is doing in this case is designed for failure. First of all, since he is doing less live firing, he is halting the development of a hardened mental attitude. Secondly, he is ensuring a weakened mental state because he is showing his subconscious that he is not able to be as successful as his job of shooting 10's would lead the subconscious to expect. How can you employ your subconscious to aid you when you demonstrate your failure so many times during your shooting? Is it any wonder that our rifle shooters of Writer's time were world beaters? At the same time, our pistol shooters were the laughing stock of the world. Margaret Murdock, in 1974 wrote about the 41st World Shooting Championships - Thun, Switzerland. in a United States Women's International Rifle Organization *Newsletter of October 25, 1974, "The pistol performance was extremely poor – so bad in fact that we heard the Russians were laughing at them behind the line during the rapid fire event."*

Daniel Landers reported on an experiment about attention and performance under high-stress conditions. *"This experiment has one important implication for coaching in skill sports such as archery and shooting. Competitors often report having practice scores far better than those fired in matches. Practice firing is normally done under low or no stress conditions which result in a marksman being ill-prepared to cope with the stress of a competitive match. Increasing the stress to at least a moderate level during practice by such methods as time stress, intrateam competition or "competition" against an individual's best scores would better prepare a competitor for the stress encountered in competition."*

Notice the stress Writer put himself under each of the 200 shots he would fire in a string at 50 meters. In shooting outdoors at 50 meters, he continually had to be alert for wind and light conditions undergoing constant, fluctuating changes. Now, add to that the stress of a goal of eliminating the 8's from that 200 shots string. This is the kind of stress Landers speaks about. Look at the hardiness of spirit Writer was developing on each of those shots. Writer trained himself to shoot very fast, usually on the first hold. He could well fire two or more 200 shot strings in a day of training. Of course, by firing on the first hold, Writer, the authors believe, established a very fine conditional reflex.

On the other hand, consider the pistol shooter. Sure, his job is to shoot 10's. Is it really a job, like in the real world? A machinist who, out of 60 pieces knew he would have 30 that would not meet specs would not have that job very long. However, the pistol shooter expects to retain his position on the National Pistol Team through the 2000 Olympics. So, since there is no penalty attached to not shooting all 10's, both the pistol shooter and his subconscious know it is okay to not shoot 10's. Nothing bad happens when a 10 is not achieved. Oh, the pistol shooter may explode with some under the breath expletives, but that is about all. The Russians, after the 1976 Olympics decided to base their selection of their Olympic squad on the basis of overall performance, not just the performance in their national championships. This placed a premium on sustained overall performance in many different match situations. This helped to ensure that those shooters with a hardened mental state capable of sustained performance would represent the Soviet Union in future Olympics. They would be the ones with a *"real fighting spirit."*

Our pistol shooters verbalize the commercial slogan of *"being the best shooter that I can be."* This very evidently did not get the job done in the 1996 Olympics. Where the Russians methodically looked at the scores expected to win medals in the Olympics, American pistol shooters sloganized. Slogans do not win Olympic medals. Skill and guts do.

Reschjotilow quotes a proverb which says:

424

*"He who sows action will reap habit,
he who sows habit will reap character,
and he who sows character will reap fortune."*

He continues, *"These words can be applied on a large scale to shooters. In shooting, there is no single combat in the real meaning of the word. In shooting, the competitor doesn't even know the other competitor's scores when he is standing in front of the target. He must be able to switch off mentally for some hours in unusual conditions, and only to have the bull's-eye on his mind. One small mistake can ruin everything and so, if one wants to win in shooting, one must have a real fighting spirit."*

Now to the point of all of this. Many pistol shooters vocalize about their mental training. Some will spend 15 minutes to an hour a day, doing their mental training. But, I have heard of only one shooter who spent time refining his trigger finger movement. That shooter was Bill Blankenship. Blankenship has written, *"I spent almost three months, trying to overcome problems in my squeeze. I was trying to develop two things. First, to make my trigger squeeze as much habit as possible and secondly, to be able to squeeze the trigger as fast as I possibly could without disturbing the sight alignment or the lay of the weapon. The harder I worked the better my trigger control became. I had the feeling sometimes that I didn't have to consciously think about the trigger at all. It was becoming habit. Also because I didn't have to think about the trigger, it was much easier for me to concentrate on sight alignment."* (***The Pistol Shooter's Treasury*** edited by Gil Hebard).

The authors believe this type of mental training is much more valuable for pistol shooters than autogenic training, self hypnosis or relaxation exercises. Training your trigger squeeze to a subconscious level is vastly more valuable than mentally rehearsing your shots. You see, first you have to make your trigger squeeze very fast. It has to move without disturbing the way the barrel is pointing. If you do not think this is mental training, try it sometime.

We describe these mental training methods as inducing passivity into the mental state of the shooter. Instead of spinning your mental wheels doing autogenic training, self hypnosis or relaxation exercises, try what Blankenship did, use your time to develop a conditional reflex between when your eye sees the reference mark of the front sight reaching the desired area of the target and the automatic movement of your trigger finger. This is the type of mental training which will be of untold value to pistol shooters.

But, you must also perform activities which will promote a hardiness of spirit, such as the example of Writer above.

The Psychology of Pistol Shooting Training.

Pistol coaches should be aware that efficacy strength exerts a highly significant influence on the performance of competitive pistol shooters. Efficacy is the power or capacity to produce a desired effect. Self-efficacy, refers to the actual amount of belief that a handgun shooter has in his ability to complete a certain task. The task the competitive handgun shooter gives himself is to punch holes in a piece of paper consistently and on purpose and within a predetermined area. This produces a feeling of effectiveness, and is demonstrated in a solid sense of confidence in one's ability to perform within one's expectations. When efficacy is high, performance is enhanced, and when efficacy is low, performance is impaired. Neither skill nor motivation has a significant effect on performance when efficacy is brought into the equation.

We know that although efficacy strength and motivation have a significant positive association, this relationship is not as strong as some have thought. When handgun shooters have a low efficacy, there turns out to be little relationship between efficacy strength and motivation. Interestingly research has discovered there is a highly significant negative correlation between efficacy strength and motivation in the high efficacy competitors. On the other hand, shooters of low skill often exhibit a significant

426

positive relationship between efficacy strength and motivation. But, these two factors are not significantly related in moderate and high skill groups.

The overall implications of research in this area indicates that self-efficacy makes an important contribution to the performance ability of individuals of all skill levels. Efficacy also functions independent of motivation. Therefore, formalized programs designed to enhance efficacy could provide positive outcomes for all levels of sport skill development and performance.

What does this mean to shooting coaches? Merry Miller of the University of Calgary, Canada points out *"Researchers, teachers, coaches, and participants associated with sport are in agreement about the important influence confidence has on athletic performance. It is generally believed that athletes possessing a great amount of confidence are capable of attaining performance excellence while those who lack it experience performance deficits."*

The handgun shooter needs self-efficacy. This is the type of confidence found in the sport environment. Self-efficacy refers to self-belief in personal ability to execute specific courses of action that will produce a particular result. In our case, a bullet hole where we have determined we want to place it. Coaches should know that the handgun shooter's perception of efficacy influences judgment about how effectively a course of action can be planned and then executed in a situation that may possess misleading, unanticipated, or stressful incidents. *"I shot a ten, but the electronic scoring machine reported it as a seven!"*

For efficacy to have a significant influence on performance, there are two qualifying factors which must be present:
⇒ the shooter must be highly skilled
⇒ and a stable motivational base must be provided by ensuring the presence of intrinsic or extrinsic incentives.

Research clearly demonstrates that the *"level of efficacy has a significant influence on skilled performers"*.

But those of you coaches working with young beginning handgun shooters, please know that other research indicates that self-efficacy also exerts a significant influence on the performance of unskilled individuals.

When we try to assess motivation, we need to understand what it is that we are looking at. We will accept the definition of motivation as being *"the direction and vigor of behavior that is present in a situation when an individual knows his performance will be evaluated through comparison to a particular standard of excellence that will subsequently enable success or failure to be determined".*

Recent research examining efficacy's influence on subjects, with various levels of skill, completing the same task, showed that efficacy strength is positively related to performance at all investigated levels of skill. It is now known that a direct relationship between efficacy strength and quality of performance exists. Efficacy strength exerts an enormously significant influence on the performance ability of all subjects. Low efficacy inhibits performance, and high efficacy enhances it. Consequently, these findings challenge the old assumption that efficacy only functions as a major determinant of performance in subjects possessing high skill.

New research results refute the idea that in order for efficacy to exert a critical influence on performance, an adequate level of motivation must be present. Current findings reveal that motivation does not have a significant influence on efficacy or performance. Neither does motivation interact with efficacy to influence performance. Therefore, regardless of an individual's level of motivation, efficacy exerts a significant influence on performance capability.

For the shooting coach, these results indicate that efficacy plays an important role in the practical world of pistol shooting learning and performance. Because self-efficacy exerts a significant influence on the performance of individuals of all skill levels, **regardless of motivation**, it is likely that overall shooting sport performance could be improved through the careful use of efficacy training. Consequently, shooting instructors and coaches should be shown the importance and use of this psychological factor in the sport environment.

Pistol shooting coaches have often assumed that a positive linear relationship exists between motivation and efficacy. Sports training research does not fully support this presumption. Sure, there is definitely a significant correlation between efficacy and motivation. However, research does not reflect the anticipated strength of this supposition. There was however, a significant difference between the motivation scores of the low and high efficacy groups in all skill categories. As expected, the high efficacy group exhibited a high degree of motivation. There appears to be little connection between efficacy and motivation in low efficacy groups. In contrast, in the high efficacy group motivation and efficacy strength had a highly significant **negative** relationship. This unexpected finding indicates a task for which an individual possesses high efficacy to perform, appears to provide little personal challenge. Consequently, motivation is debilitated. This has practical value because it opposes the generally accepted premise that the successful performer exhibiting high efficacy is also fully motivated. Therefore, pistol coaches are encouraged to carefully evaluate the actual motivation level of their highly proficient pistol competitors, rather than merely assuming they are adequately motivated.

So, it appears that the relationship between efficacy and motivation is not as straightforward as pistol shooting coaches of assumed.

While the value of high expectations is not even a disputed concept these days, it is obviously one of the most difficult to operationalize. The undermining of youths' sense of self-efficacy through low expectations communicated by the pistol shooting instructor and coach is the beginning of the insidious process of decreasing motivation and increasing alienation that eventually results in youngsters dropping out of pistol shooting all together. We have to change this.

The authors are calling on pistol instructors and coaches to raise expectations. This has to happen if we are to see improvements in pistol shooting instruction. Of course we are aware that relatively little is known about how to implement both higher and more equitable expectations in pistol shooting training and practice. The pistol coach and instructor needs to be aware of the various aspects of research into *"expectancy communications."* There are *"expressions of belief, both verbal and nonverbal, from one person to another about the kind of performance to be expected."* These *"expressions of belief"* have clearly demonstrated, in our junior pistol training program, the powerful impact of expectancies on shooting performance. Furthermore, research studies consistently have found that expectations of coaches for their students have a large effect on the students' achievement.

In order to plan preventive pistol instruction strategies, we must understand the process by which pistol instructors' expectations are thought to affect pistol student performance. Expectancies affect shooter behavior in two basic ways. First, they directly affect shooting performance by increasing or decreasing the shooter's confidence levels as we approach the task of shooting a pistol and thus affecting the intensity of effort the student is willing to expend. Second, expectations also influence the way we think about or explain our performance outcomes. *"Research in social psychology has demonstrated that the causes to which people attribute their successes and failures have an important impact on subsequent performance"*

We know that when people who are confident of doing well at their pistol shooting and they are confronted with unexpected failure, they tend to attribute the failure to inadequate effort. The likely response to another encounter with the same or a similar shooting problem is to work harder. This is what Jack Writer did. Shooters who come into a shooting game expecting to fail, on the other hand, attribute their failure to lack of ability. Once you admit to yourself, in effect, that *"I don't have what it takes to shoot a pistol,"* you are not likely to approach pistol shooting again with great vigor.

A pistol coach's negative expectancy definitely has a double whammy: It generates failure by its effect on behavior via lack of confidence, and then it entices the person to blame the failure on lack of ability rather than on lack of effort, which is an entirely remediable problem. What we see here is the beginning of a vicious cycle of self-fulfilling prophecy, which for many young shooters is their daily experience with pistol shooting instruction. Eventually, it will lead to an early departure from the sport of pistol shooting.

To create a positive expectancy climate, substantial changes need to be made in the following:

⇒ **Curriculum:** all students should receive simpler, more meaningful pistol shooting instruction.

    1) The air pistol is the most efficient basic training tool for all shooting.

    2) The Sievers Simplified Training Program has only two fundamentals and prohibits the introduction of other items into the basic training process.

    3) Anything the student teaches himself with the air pistol about *"shooting"* is completely transferable to any other shooting tool.

    4) ***Shooting*** *is lining up the barrel with the eye, pointing it at the area we want the bullet hole to appear, and moving the trigger finger smoothly to cause the bullet hole to appear.*

    5) Everywhere we look, we see an air pistol range.

    6) You can get into a basic air pistol for $55.00 retail and feed it for peanuts.

⇒ **Evaluation system:** should reflect the concept of focusing the shooter's attention of the size of the shot group, not on the score of the target.

⇒ **Motivation:** should use competitive pistol teaching strategies and focus on intrinsic motivation based on interest comparison of results with others.

⇒ **Responsibility for learning:** accountability should be placed on the shooter. The shooter has to make an effort at active participation and decision making in their learning to shoot the pistol.

⇒ **Instructor/coach shooter relations:** should develop individual caring relationships with each shooter.

⇒ **Parent-class relations:** should reach out to all parents with explanations of the pistol training program.

In all of the above ways, expectations are communicated to shooters both at the range, in mental training sessions and in tournament trips. And, once again, to change the pistol training environment to convey positive expectations necessitates first and foremost that instructors adopt the attitude that all youngsters can learn to shoot a pistol. With this underlying attitude, the above changes will naturally flow. Of course, we are talking about making a major shift in pistol shooting philosophy, moving from a problem-focused model in which only a few kids are considered intelligent and strong enough to become good shooters to an empowerment model in which all children are recognized as being able to point a tube at a piece of paper, how they want, when they want and to be able to move their trigger finger whenever they want.

L to R: Brent "Bugsy" Barstow, age 10; Grant Morgan, age 12; Danielle Dancho, age 15; Michal Newhouse, age 9; Geoffrey Barstow, age 12.

Chapter 9

It is the aim of the authors to restrict this work to their own proper field of pistol shooting training. In the course of their lives work, the authors have developed methods for the training of the central nervous system for competitive pistol shooters. We, in no way, offer these chapters as a substitute for the thorough study of kinesiology, psychology, physiology, biomechanics or anatomy. We are not and do not pretend to be scientists. This is our interpretation of the material we have studied in the course of designing our pistol training method.

The
Conditional Reflex
In
Pistol Shooting

What Is Meant By The Term "Conditional Reflex"?

A *conditioned reflex is the reaction to an unrelated stimulus by repeated association.* (*Scribner's Bantam English Dictionary*, 1977). Please be aware that we will be using the words *conditioned* and *conditional* interchangably with the word reflex. It appears from our research that the original translator of Pavlov's work may have mistranslated *conditioned* for *conditional*. The authors believe that *conditional* is a more precise term. However, they do acknowledge that *conditioned* is in more general use in the eyes of the public.

Yev'yev, in his book, *Competitive Shooting*, advises, *"It is proper to assign the highest priority to the shooter's coordination of movement and his reaction time to a given stimulus-signal."* (pp 225)

"It should be kept in mind that the functional restructuring of the central nervous system, directed toward perfecting muscle activities, is possible only when training is regular and sufficiently intensive." (pp 311)

The authors show you how to train and measure this stimulus-signal further on in this chapter. Even nine year old girls have achieved success shooting in the one-handed competitive shooting position when trained under the method advocated by the authors of this book. We know of no other method in the country which can have that claim made about it.

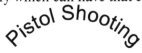

Pistol Shooting

at 9 Years of Age

Success

Figure 9-1
Pavlov's Conditional Reflex Experimental Setup
(Reprinted by permission of the *UIT Journal*)

In 1927, The Oxford University Press of England, published a book by I.P. Pavlov. It was titled **Conditioned Reflexes**, with the subtitle of *An Investigation of The Physiological Activity of the Cerebral Cortex*. It was in this book the world first learned of the training of reflexes from an objective, deliberate and organized experimental viewpoint.

In Lecture I of Pavlov's book, he describes a reflex. *"We are familiar with numerous reflexes which most certainly fuse into chains. Thus, for example, if we stimulate an afferent nerve, e.g. the sciatic nerve, a reflex rise of blood pressure occurs; the high pressure in the left ventricle of the heart, and first part of the aorta, serves as the effective stimulus to a second reflex, this time a depressor reflex which has a moderating influence on the first. Again, we may take one of the chain reflexes recently established by Magnus. A cat, even when deprived of its cerebral hemispheres. will in most cases land on its feet when thrown from a height. How is this managed ? When the position of the otolithic organ in space is altered a definite reflex is evoked which brings about a contraction of the muscles in the neck, restoring the animal's head*

435

to the normal position. This is the first reflex. With the righting of the head a fresh reflex is evoked, and certain muscles of the trunk and limbs are brought into play, restoring the animal to the standing posture. This is the second reflex.

We now know, however, from the recent investigations of Magnus and de Kleijn, that standing, walking and the maintenance of postural balance in general, are all nothing but reflexes. ...We started off with a very simple experiment. The dog was placed in a stand with loose loops round its legs, (See Figure 9-1), but so as to be quite comfortable and free to move a pace or two. Nothing more was done except to present the animal repeatedly with food at intervals of some minutes.

...Let us return now to the simplest reflex from which our investigations started. If food or some rejectable substance finds its way into the mouth, a secretion of saliva is produced. "

The type of pistol shooting training we advocate in *Successful Pistol Shooting* is shooter driven. The purpose of our pistol training is the creation of a dependency between what the eye reports to the brain about the location of the front sight with respect to a pre-selected area on a target. We want to ensure that the contacts between behavior and environment do not vary, and that the behavior to be modified is determined by the pistol shooter rather than by chance.

From a pistol training perspective, there is a certain procedural similarity between experiments on 'superstition' and classical conditioning experiments. In both cases specified stimuli, the Conditional Stimulus and the Unconditioned Stimulus occur independently of behavior. In our case, the behavior we want to influence is the movement of the trigger finger. Just so you know where we are coming from, the Conditional Stimulus, also occurs independently of behavior, though in a consistent relationship to the Unconditioned Stimulus.

Unconditioned Stimulus

Our Unconditioned Stimulus is the visual alignment of the barrel with the eye, using the sights as reference marks.

Unconditional Stimulus

=

visual alignment of the pistol sights with the eye.

Conditional Stimulus

With the visual focus on the front reference mark, the Conditional Stimulus is the visual reference of the front sight located at a pre-selected area on the target.

Conditional Stimulus

=

visual alignment of the pistol sights located
at a pre-selected area on the target.

This suggests that classical conditioning, as pioneered by Pavlov, is essentially the pairing of one stimulus with another, but that operant conditioning, which we use in our pistol training involves the pairing of one stimulus with behavior. An apparent difference between classical and operant conditioning centers on

437

the different types of behavior involved in the two procedures. In the case of classical conditioning, one begins with an unconditional response which is reliably elicited by a stimulus programmed in the experiment.

In operant conditioning, on the other hand, one either has to wait for the 'response' to occur by chance in order to follow it by a reinforcer, or one has to coax an entirely new 'response' from the animal by means of successive approximation techniques, which themselves depend at the outset on some spontaneously occurring pattern of behavior which one can develop. In the case of pistol shooting training, the pattern of behavior which we want to develop is the instantaneously smooth movement of the trigger finger when the front sight of the aligned system reaches an acceptable area of our target.

We believe that the reactions which can be conditioned by means of Pavlov's procedures are the behavior of the autonomic nervous system. This is, in general terms, the part of our physiological system which successfully keeps us alive without our having to pay attention to what we are doing, so to speak. The autonomic nervous system is responsible for regulating our bodily functions, for the distribution of supplies of nutrients throughout the body, for the digestive processes, for the working of the heart, for our glandular reactions, and so on. These reactions of our body occur automatically, and adjust delicately to different internal or external conditions, thereby maintaining our internal environment in a sensitive state of equilibrium.

Operant behavior, on the other hand, is usually behavior which acts on our external environment, for example, 'deliberate' movements of our skeletal system, such as automatic movement of the trigger finger at a particular time. For example, Brian Enos, in the September 1996 issue of the National Rifle Association's **Shooting Sports USA**, noted, *"Taken to the ultimate, as was done and suggested by bullseye pistol legend Bill Blankenship, it is possible to have the gun fire as a reflex to seeing a perfect sight picture. That is a tremendous thing for a bullseye shooter to accomplish."* Enos is into "hitting" the target, which is not the way shooting works. Blankenship is into precision pointing, which Enos apparently does not understand.

It was thought until quite recently, that classical conditioning procedures modify only the activities of the autonomic nervous system and instrumental, or operant, conditioning modifies only the movements of the skeletal system, and that these effects were mutually exclusive. However, this cannot be absolutely sustained in the light of recent work. It implies that the behavior of the autonomic nervous system is unaffected by instrumental conditioning procedures. Thus, for example, if one waits for 'spontaneous' salivation, which does sometimes occur, instead of eliciting it by an obvious stimulus, one should be unable to increase this 'response' merely by associating it with a proven reinforcer. However it is not the case, as shown by the Carmona and N. Miller (1967) experiments.

(Reprinted by permission of the *UIT Journal*)

Natural Stimulus / Unconditioned "Reflex"

Pavlov, in his experiments on conditioning, offered the dog some food. As expected, it was noted that the dog produced a given amount of saliva. This is an **unconditioned** "reflex."

The early apparatus used for recording the salivary secretion in experiments on conditional reflexes is shown at the left. It consisted of a hemispherical bulb which is fixed over the fistula. Then there is a connecting tube leading through the partition separating the animal's room from the experimeter and connecting the bulb, which on the figure to the left is located on the far left. The bulb is connected to the registering apparatus. Then there is the tube connected to the bottle.

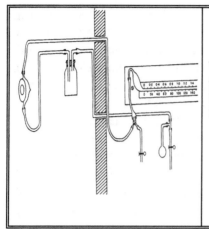

After each observation a vacuum is created in the bottle by depressing the balloon located at the bottom on the lower right of the Figure.

After Pavlov had conditioned the dog to salivate to metronome while being exposed to a bown of meat powder, he discovered that he could use the metronome in place of the unconditioned stimulus. He then discovered that by pairing the metronome and another stimulus, such as an electric light, the dog could be conditioned to slivate to the electric light.

This salivation would occur without bringing the original meat powder in again. Pavlov again paired the electric light to another unconditioned stimulus, for example, the whirling of a fan. The dog began to salivate to the fan, not as much as to the meat powder or the metronome. Thus, Pavlov discovered that the dog could be conditioned to four levels of responding before he stopped salivating. It was this ability for higher-level conditioning that caused Pavlov to conclude it was the basis for higher human learning.

In this illustration, we have a natural stimulus, the dog food. Then we have a neutral stimulus, which is the sound tone. The food generated the expected natural reflex, the saliva. The sound tone produced no result.

Reprinted by permission of the *UIT Journal*)

Natural Stimulus / Neutral Stimulus

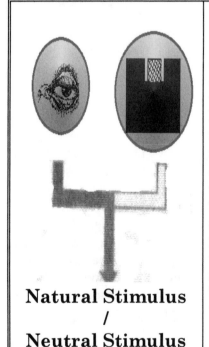

Natural Stimulus / Neutral Stimulus

In this illustration, we have a natural stimulus, the pistol sights in alignment with each other. The eye generated the expected natural reflex, the vision. The vision of the aligned sights produced no reaction. Then we have a neutral stimulus, which is the aligned sights. The eye generated the expected natural reflex, the vision. The aligned sights produced no reaction. In pistol shooting, the eye sees the sights in alignment with each other. This is an unconditioned "reflex."

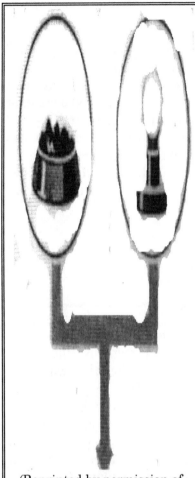 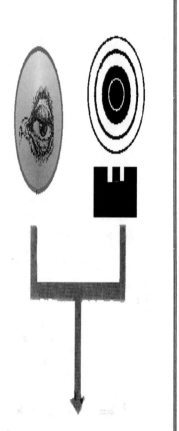

(Reprinted by permission of the *UIT Journal*)

The food is accompanied by the sound of a metronome sounded shortly before the food is introduced. This is continued until the dog becomes accustomed to the sound as a forecasting of the arrival of his food.

The shooter moves his trigger finger instantaneously smooth each time the handgun reaches eye level with the aligned system pointing at a pre-selected area of the target. This training is continued until the trigger finger movement becomes a habit.

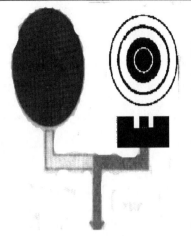

(Reprinted by permission of the *UIT Journal*)

Conditional "Reflex"

No food presented, but the metronome is sounded. The dog salivates to the sound.

Conditional "Reflex"

The shooter moves his trigger finger instantaneously smooth each time the handgun reaches eye level with the aligned sights pointing at a pre-selected area of the target.

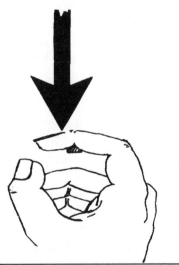

In pistol shooting, we want the trigger finger movement to be instantaneous smooth. This is a reflex action. Bill Blankenship, one of America's elite of the elite, pistol shooters once wrote, *"Trigger control can become a habit. By this I mean when the sights are aligned and the weapon is almost still, the trigger finger reacts automatically to make the weapon fire."* (*The Pistol Shooter's Treasury* edited by Gil Hebard). It is initiated as soon as the brain is satisfied with what the eye sees as perfect internal alignment of the system, **pointed at the desired area.** This movement of the trigger finger is the conditional reflex. The stimulus is what the eye sees as perfect internal alignment of the system, pointed at the desired area. It is the belief of the authors that shooters will achieve more consistent results by placing their primary focus on developing the conditional reflex between what their eye sees and the consequent activation of the movement of the trigger finger when the sights reach the pre-selected area of the target they have chosen. Lanny Bassham, Olympic Gold Medal Winner in Rifle pointed out in his book, ***With Winning In Mind,*** that *"A rifle shooter, who has Sub-Conscious trigger control, will activate the trigger when the sights are aligned. A shooter who Consciously activates the trigger, will most probably move the rifle as he shoots, thereby throwing the shot off."*

How Do You Train Yourself To This Habit?

The authors believe that Bill Blankenship, six times US National Pistol Champion, has produced the best explanation of how to train your trigger finger to this habit, or as we say, conditional reflex, which we have been able to find in our shooting training research. We believe that the best and most descriptive method of explaining how to develop a conditional reflex for pistol shooting, was written by William B. Blankenship, Jr. in *The Pistol Shooter's Treasury* edited by Gil Hebard. Brian Enos, in the September 1996 issue of the National Rifle Association's **Shooting Sports USA**, refered to Blankenships article, *"another way is as Blankenship described where the gun fired the instant he saw perfect sight alignment. He acquired this* *ability through dry-firing at a blank wall with a focus on "connecting" the trigger pull to this image. This method takes a lot of training to acquire, but that is "looking the shot off" and is considered almost universally as the ultimate expression of trigger control-a totally unconscious reflex. That may be what you want."*

What Blankenship discovered with his effort at moving only the trigger in his endeavor to make the movement as smooth as possible and also as fast without causing any movement of the sight alignment or the gun is one of the basic principles of movement performance when temporal accuracy is the major goal. Dr Richard A.. Schmidt, PhD, in his book, *Motor Learning & Performance*, 1991, listed some of the *principles of movement*:

---

* *Increasing speed by decreasing the movement time (with distance constant) decreases, not increases, errors in timing accuracy.*

In this case, the trigger movement distance is constant. So, decreasing the movement time, which means a faster trigger finger movement, ensures that the shooter will be exposed to aiming errors a shorter period of time. Schmidt's research, published in 1991, confirms what Blankenship discovered in 1959, *Increasing speed by decreasing the movement time (with distance constant) decreases, not increases, errors in timing*

445

accuracy. In our pistol shooting training with youngsters here in Tucson, some as young as nine years of age, conclusively demonstrate to our satisfaction that this principle of movement is entirely accurate when measured against our results.

The pistol shooter who developes a *"jerk,"* Yev'yev points out, *"must use the continuous-smooth control method of releasing the trigger. When the smooth pull of the trigger again becomes habitual, and the shooter no longer has to devote special attention to it, he can return to live cartridges fired at a piece of white paper rather than at a target with a bull's-eye."*

Another of Schmidt's *principles of movement* is:

- *The primary determinant of timing accuracy is movement time, with longer movement times generating more timing errors.*

For the pistol shooter, this is a principle which can be applied to the trigger finger movement process. Many pistol shooters are told by *"knowledgable"* peers and coaches that when shooting the Free Pistol at 50 Meters, to take their time. Gil Hebard told Hickey that this may not be how all pistol champions operate. He mentioned watching Hershel Anderson shoot at 50 yards. Anderson would bring up the pistol and "the shot was gone," immediately! However, many develop extended periods of moving the finger, then letting up on the trigger pressure, and continually repeating this process as the sights wander around in their Arc of Movement. Perhaps understanding this movement priciple will show them the "error" of their way. They fail to grasp Brankenship's concept of "continually increasing" trigger finger pressure. Continually increasing does not mean increase it for a while, then let up and do the same again. Continually increasing is a very aggressive concept of trigger finger movement. Yev'yev, in his book, **Competitive Shooting**, points out very clearly, that *"after restoring his cooordination of movement and overcoming the feeling of indecisiveness, the shooter should resume shooting and make every*

446

effort to fire the shot during the first six to nine seconds after beginning the hold. It is during this time period when the shooter can hold the gun with greatest stability and have the best visual acuity."

In a very close approximation of the action of the trigger finger movement on a pistol, Schmidt points out,

> *"These findings about timing errors are not as strange as they seem at first, as you will see if you do the following simple demonstration. Take a stopwatch and, without watching, click it twice to try to generate exactly 2 s. Repeat this 9 more times, noting the amount of error you make on each trial. Now do this same task again, but this time try to generate 4 s. After a little careful practice, you should find that the amount of error you make in estimating 2 s will be just about half the amount of error for 4 s. Why? The system that generates these durations (including both the stopwatch and arm movement tasks) are somewhat noisy, or variable, and the amount of this variability increases, or accumulates, as the duration of the event to be timed increases. The motor programming processes that produce the timing are not affected by the increased forces necessary to alter their movement distance, so altered distance does not affect timing error.*

How about the act of raising the arm from the 45 degrees ready position? Schmidt tells us that when movements are very fast and forceful, reducing the movement time tends to increase, not decrease, accuracy. This, he points out, is because the force variability decreases in this range with decreases in movement time. This runs counter to the prevailing idea that in bringing the pistol arm up, the shooter should start fast, then decrease his speed of raising the arm. Thus, there is a slowing down of the arm down on about the last third of the way to eye level. But, Schmidt's experiments conclusively show that speeding the movement time when it is already quite fast results in a gain in spatial movement accuracy.

From this information, what do we tell the beginning shooter?

⇒ Instructing the shooter to "take your time," in our experience, seriously degrades trigger finger movement performance and should be avoided. I have observed this with two very promising young shooters. In each case, family relatives and respected adult shooters told them to *"slow down, you have plenty of time, this is not a race to see who can finish first."* Did these people intend to sabotage their young shooter? No way! But, what they did was to introduce the attitude of hesitation into the shooter's consciousness. It runs completely counter to Blankenship's concept of continually increasing trigger finger pressure. And we believe he got it right! In a few words, those relatives and well meaning adults destroyed the attitude of aggressiveness we had been training these shooters to develop with respect to the trigger finger movement when triggered by the arrival of their sight alignment at the area of the target they had selected. You have heard the saying, "you can hurt someone by helping them." We agree with the saying which goes something like this:

**It ain't what ya don't know what hurts ya,
It's what ya know what ain't so!**

⇒ When using the gallon water jug to practice your repetitions of bringing the jug to eye level, increasing the weight of the water, but not so much that the maximal upswing slows markedly, can increase spatial accuracy.

⇒ Have the shooter bring up the water jug or pistol almost as quickly as possible, but not so quickly that the movement becomes clumsy and uncoordinated.

⇒ Encourage the shooter to use consistent upswings of the pistol, not only in spatial trajectory but also in initiation time and movement time.

⇒ Allow the shooter to acquire the proper pattern first (relative timing) without undue emphasis on the proper speed or ampliture (parameterization). This, Yev'yev, in his book, *Competitive Shooting*, makes a strong point about, *"One condition for developing a lasting motor skill is to first master it **consciously**. The more consciously a skill is formed, the more strongly it will be consolidated. To form the skill more quickly and solidly, one must picture in his mind every detail of the action being learned, step by step. By relying on this mental image of the action, the athlete can consciously reproduce it in motion. Having a knowledge of the movement being learned **and** a clear concept of how it is preformed are absolutely necessary conditions for mastering it."*

⇒ The learning of relative timing is the hard part, so emphasize it in practice. Learning to parameterize is easy once the proper relative timing is established. This is what Blankenship did when he took three months out of his shooting schedule to work on his trigger finger movement in 1959.

⇒ Altering very well-learned relative timing patterns is difficult, so correct errors in patterning early in your pistol shooting practice. This is one of the reasons which led

449

us to develop the **Conditional Reflex** Evaluation Form, (**Figure** 9-15).

Traditionally, the pistol shooter has placed primary focus on interlimb coordination in control of posture and locomotion. Shooters should be aware of Keiji Nakajima's study, *How Does Interlimb Coordination Occur?* Nakajima, of the Department of Neurosurgery and Casualty Center, Juntendo University School of Medicine, Izunagaoka, Shizoka, Japan, found that when a subject was asked to raise his arm in a standing position, the postural muscles in the trunk and leg were activated before the muscle activity in the arm, and further:

> *"Our loaded arm locomotion study showed that the change of postural activity, as determined by EMG and force plate measurement, preceded the activity in the prime mover of arm swing.*
>
> *Belen'kii' e' al. found that when a subject was asked to raise his arm in a standing position, the postural muscles in the trunk and leg were activated before the muscle activity in the arm. This postural muscle activity would be due to the anticipation of the forthcoming disequilibrium caused by the arm movement and is called anticipatory postural adjustment.*
>
> *In our study, the first EMG finding of the anticipatory postural adjustment was the activation of the ipsilateral TB, which coincided with the ipsilateral directed force exerted by the ipsilateral hand, and later with the deviation of the body to the contralateral side which coincided with the activation of the ipsilateral QD and contralateral TB, the so-called diagonal limb pattern. That is, the initiation of movement is accompanied by an anticipatory postural adjustment which shifts the center of gravity towards the site oppo-*

site to the forthcoming movement to maintain equilibrium.

A movement, especially an alternate and continuous movement like locomotion, causes disequilibrium and compensates for it alternately and continuously. We then asked what mechanism compensates for disequilibrium soon after displacement of the body. To identify whether events at the initiation of arm locomotion are centrally programmed or are a proprioceptive reflex mechanism, we examined the latency of the changes in muscle activity. The beginning of the deviation coincided well with the muscle activity of the ipsilateral TB. Thus, measurement of the muscle activity of the ipsilateral TB, ipsilateral QD and contralateral TB showed the time course at the beginning of deviation to the full development of the diagonal limb postural pattern. The interval between activation of the ipsilateral TB and activation of the ipsilateral QD was about 125 ms, and the interval from the ipsilateral QD activation to contralateral TB activation was about 10 ms. These relatively short intervals indicate that diagonal limb reflex at the bulbospinal level is responsible for the compensation of disequilibrium which is induced by a central command as an anticipatory postural adjustment."

In order to compensate for this automatic limb reflex, pistol shooters have developed elaborate methods of setting up their shooting platforms. The aim has been to provide the ultimate in stability. This means the pistol shooter is forever fighting the automatic reflex to overcome the *"disequilibrium which is induced by a central command as an anticipatory postural adjustment."* Figure 9-3 illustrates the locus of the center of body pressure as recorded by a force plate. Figure 9-2 shows how the

3-D data on each fluctuation of the body was determined by the position of each marker. Because of the on-line computer system with a link between the force plate and the 3-D marker system, all data were collected synchronously.

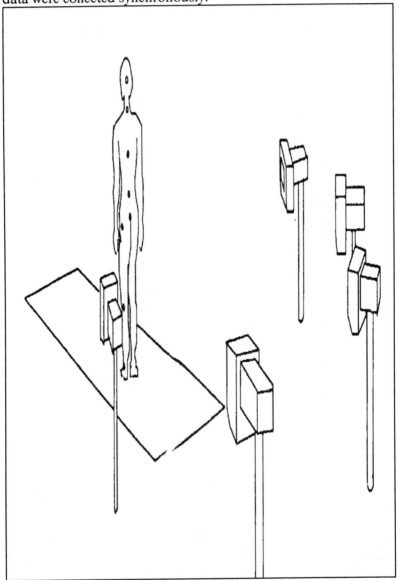

(Reprinted by permission of the *Japan Scientific Societies Press*)
Figure 9-2

The Conditional Reflex In Pistol Shooting

The pistol shooter, *by focusing his attention on this **stability** aspect of his Act of Shooting*, continually interrupts the conditional reflex between his sight alignment and the movement of his trigger finger on the trigger. Look at **Figure 9-3**, the center of pressure is shown in the box between the feet. This box showing the effort to maintain equilibrium is expanded in the box pointed at by the arrow. The pistol shooter is often into *control.* The method current among 2700 bullseye pistol shooters is to **hold hard**. Their effort is to attempt to reduce the movement of the pistol within an *arc of movement*. This requires a concentrated effort at control of the gun during the aiming process. The longer the gun is maintained in an *arc of movement*, the more fatigue is generated. The effort to explain how this works has spawned much shooting literature. Consider for example, the article by Prof. Dr. Andrei Demeter and Prof. Gavrila Barani's article titled *Contributions To A Cybernetic Interpretation Of Performance Shooting.*

They point out that their concept of shooting at fixed targets implies the interaction of three factors: *shooter—weapon—target, each of them having many common, positive and negative characteristics.*

They continue with the observation that from the

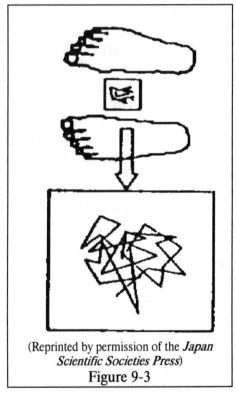

(Reprinted by permission of the *Japan Scientific Societies Press*)

Figure 9-3

functional standpoint this triad should be considered as the dialectic

453

unit of the human organism in its multiple relationship with the weapon and the target, in variable environmental conditions. Just what does the dialectic unit mean? Dialectic is a branch of logic that arrives at truth through deductive reasoning. So, what they are saying is that this triad they have established, 1) shooter, 2) weapon, and 3) target, is what they have determined from deductive reasoning. They point out that *"the major component of this triad—the human organism-functions as a cybernetic system in which the permanent inflow of informations originating in the weapon and the target is picked up by exteroceptors—the peripheral segments of the visual, acoustic, myoarthrokinetic and cutaneous analyzers, and is transformed in nervous impulses that are sent to the cerebral cortex."* (Figure 9-4)

The cerebral cortex is referred by Demeter and Barani as the command center. The cerebral cortex is a mantle, made of a large mass of white and grey neural fiber in the upper cranium, covering the cerebrum. In man, this is the largest portion of the brain. It occupies the entire upper part of the cranium and consists of right and left hemispheres. Sometimes this cerebrum is referred to as forebrain and the midbrain. You may have heard references to cerebral integration. This theory supposes that the cerebrum is the integrating center of man, serving to integrate and unify all parts of the body and all behavior of the organism. This ties in with the idea of cerebral dominance. This principle holds that the cerebrum is the highest control center in the nervous system. It points out that one brain hemisphere is dominant over the other in control of body movement, especially handedness. So, this is why they maintain that *"the cerebral cortex, acts like a central integrating organ, carrying out the de-codification, the analysis and synthesis operations, the fine coordination of the activities of various parts of the organism implicated in the adoption and maintenance of the correct position for shooting, aiming and triggering. The orders elaborated by the cerebral cortex are transmitted to the effector organs the action of which is synergized and results in the motor acts specific for shooting. At the same time the cerebral cortex is informed by feed-back mechanism on the development of the command, allowing thus for corrections to be made when necessary."* The problem with this is that, as the Nakajima's study demonstrates man inhabits a sturcture which is always unstable (see **Figure 9-3**). Focusing primary attention on attempting to establish stability makes little sense. For pistol shooters to attempt to set up stability before anything else is to ignor common sense. Even without the research to prove the instability of the body, a little reflection and personal test will very conclusively prove that stability and the erect human body are at odds with each other. So, since stablity is impossible, why not work more efficiently with this structure called the body with which we are forever stuck? In our program, we have done just that! Since stability is impossible to attain in an erect, unsupported position, does it not stand to reason that the shooter should use a method of pistol shooting which negates, as far as is possible, the amount of time he has to remain in an artificial position, while working to establish stability? In our method, we attempt to decrease the amount of time spent in the erect position during the act of shooting. Our method is something which the shooter can physically accomplish. Since stablity of the pistol shooting platform cannot be attained, no matter how much effort is put into the attempt, we concentrate on something entirely different. We work very hard to decrease the time that the shooters are exposed to the effects Demeter and Barani describe. Our shooters can easily reduce the time they have to spend on target for each shot. What no one can do is to prevent the things Demeter and Barani note as acting upon the shooter in the shooting stance.

Demeter and Barani point out that:

> *"it appears that in high-performance shooting particular attention should be given to*
>> ⇒ *the nervous system (both its central and peripheral sectors),*
>> ⇒ *to analyzers*
>>> ⇒ *visual*
>>> ⇒ *acoustic*
>>> ⇒ *vestibular*
>>> ⇒ *myo-arthro-kinetic*
>>> ⇒ *cutaneous*
>> ⇒ *and to the locomotor apparatus."*

Demeter and Barani highlight what they call, *"some interesting considerations concerning the interrelationships between the triad's factors (shooter—weapon—target)."* They identify seven different types of influences by the handgun. Six of these are on the shooter and one on the target. In **Figure 9-4,** they show *the "target" factor exerts two types of influence, both on the shooter, one of identification by the CNS, and the other concerning the position...identified through the visual analyser and the cerebral cortex."* They use (**Figure 9-4**) to show that *"the "human" (shooter) factor is the most stressed, exerting two types of influences on the weapon (maintaining it in an adequate position for shooting, aiming and triggering), and receiving 8 types of influences from the weapon and target factors, to which one could also add the influences exerted by meteorological factors (wind, rain, changes in light, temperature), and by qualities of the weapons and ammunition."*

Explanation of Abreviations Used in Figure 9-4
SNC: SL - PS = *the central nervous system both its central and peripheral sectors),* **V** = *vestibulal* **A** = *acoustic* **E** = *eye* **M** = *myo-arthro-kinetic* **C** = *cutaneous* **Loc.** Apparatus = *Locomotive Apparatus*

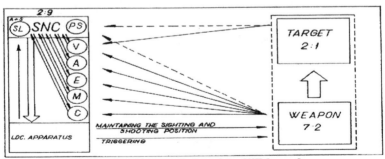

(Reprinted by permission of the *UIT Journal*)

Figure 9-4

456

The Conditional Reflex In Pistol Shooting

On the other hand, we find that the focusing of the attention of the shooter on the stability aspect of his game,(see **Figure 9-6**), gets the shooter involved in a distraction from which he often never recovers. The September 1996 issue of USA Shooting's *QucikShots* reported *"U.S. Army Markmanship Unit **Rob Harbison** (Fallston, Md.) turned in the highest U.S. finish in Olympic shooting competion in men's air rifle. Harbison, 30, went into the final in second place with 594 out of 600 points. During the first eight shots of the final, he fell in the standings but managed to regain the bronze medal position with a near perfect 10.7 (out of a possible 10.9) on his ninth shot. Harbison's last shot, an 8.4, dropped him to seventh place."*

"I know this analogy has been used before, but it you put an I-beam on the floor and walk across it, that's easy; anybody can do it. Take the same beam and put it between two buildings 20 stories high and it's a different story. That's what that last shot was like," said Harbison." Reinkemeier, noted, *"It is typical that the call for psychological help is only heard after a poor performance. Up to that point everyone trusts their common sense."* This may not be Harbison's total fault. The authors speculate that this analogy which he identifies as having heard before may have been relayed to him in some group mental training session. Once a thought is implanted in the mind, it can come back to haunt the shooter at the most inopportune time. If not thought about in advance of the event, the unexpected has a tendency to bite you at a critical time.

Reinkemeier·has pointed out, *"Just after the Olympic Games in Los Angeles it was suggested that the apparent lack of success of German shooters was linked totheir mental preparation. And even at smaller championships at local and regional level many shooters felt that their disappointing performances could only be understood against a background of psychological analysis."* He observed that, *"Behind such statements there are often unrealistic expectations. It is fatal to expect miracles from psychological training methods"*

In 1968, in the Mexico Olympics, Jack Writer faced the unexpected. He found himself far in advance of the rest of the rifle shooters in the three-position event. This was something unexpected, something he had not considered in all of his planning leading up to those Olympic games. This put him off his game so that he finished with the silver medal instead of the gold. He prepared more fully for the 1972 Olympics and won the gold in his three-position game. In any event, the focus on stability and being aware of what the pressure felt like, had to have been a factor in pulling Harbison out of his game.

Coaches have to be aware of this stress and what it does to the mind of the shooter. That is why, in Chapter 7, we talk about coaching the mind for pistol shooting. Coaches who neglect this aspect of training the shooter are, in the eyes of the authors, woefully negligent in their duties to that shooter.

A pistol shooter has to be aware that anything which disrupts the processing of sensory data and the initiation of willful motor processes, such as voluntary muscle flexion, is harmful to their shooting process. For example it is evident that when muscle flexion is voluntary, shooters still using the arc of movement method, will experience problems similar to Harbison's. On the other hand shooters using our method, where the trigger finger movement is automatic or subconscious, avoid that disruption.

Pistol shooters should know there is something called the nervous system in the structure known as the human body, (**Figure 9-5**), which is responsible for:

> ⇒ sending
> ⇒ receiving
> ⇒ and processing nerve impulses.

All of the body's muscles and organs rely upon these nerve impulses to function. There are three systems working together to carry out the lifework of the nervous system:

> ⇒ the central nervous system
> ⇒ the peripheral nervous system
> ⇒ and the autonomic nervous system.

1) The central nervous system, which includes the brain and spinal cord, is responsible for sending nerve impulses and analyzing sensory data.

2) The peripheral nervous system is responsible for carrying nerve impulses to and from the body's many structures, and includes the many craniospinal nerves which branch off of the brain and spinal cord.

3) The autonomic nervous system is responsible for regulating and coordinating the functions of vital structures in the body, for the distribution of supplies of nutrients throughtout the body, for the digestive processes, for the working of the heart, for our glandular reactons, etc.

As pistol shooters, we need to know that the brain is the primary component of the nervous system. It occupies the cranial cavity. Without its outermost protective membrane, the brain weighs an average of three pounds (about 1.4 kilograms), comprising about 97% of the entire central nervous system. The brain is connected to the upper end of the spinal cord and is responsible for:

> ⇒ sending nerve impulses
> ⇒ processing nerve impulse data
> ⇒ and engaging in the higher order thought processes.

The brain is divided into three parts: 1) the large cerebrum, 2) the smaller cerebellum, and 3) the brainstem leading to the spinal cord. The brainstem is divided into the medulla oblongata, the midbrain, and the pons.

The autonomic nervous system is responsible for the self-controlling aspects of the body's nervous network. It is under the control of the cerebral cortex, the hypothalmus, and the medulla oblongata. The autonomic nervous system works in tandem with the central nervous system. It is composed of two subsystems which regulate body functions, such as involuntary smooth muscle movement and heart rate. Harbison likely experienced the involuntary advancement of his heart rate during the firing of his last shot. These two subsystems are called the sympathetic and parasympathetic nervous system. They and their functions operate in opposition to one another, balancing the bodily

459

functions which they control. The sympathetic nervous system causes fight or flight responses in moments of stress or stimulus, such as increased heart rate, saliva flow, and perspiration. The parasympathetic system counterbalances these effects by slowing the heart rate, dilating blood vessels, and relaxing involuntary smooth muscle fibers.

The sympathetic nerves are responsible for contracting involuntary smooth muscle fibers, viscera, and blood vessels, speeding up the heart rate, and dilating the bronchial tubes in moments of stress, such as the stress Harbison was under during the firing of his last shot.

The nerves of the parasympathetic nervous system are responsible for conserving and restoring energy in the body following a sympathetic response to stress.

The cerebellum is the second smaller division of the brain, located below the cerebrum and in the posterior of the brain. It is the responsibility of the cerebellum to coordinate and modify the resultant activity of impulses and orders sent from the cerebrum. It does this by receiving information from nerve endings all over the body, such as the balance and equilibrium centers in the inner ear, and adjusts and fine tunes these actions by passing the regulating signals to the motor neurons of the brain and spinal cord. The cerebellum allows the pistol shooter to maintain precise muscular coordination and fine cooperative actions of the motor processes.

Figure 9-5

The Conditional Reflex In Pistol Shooting

The human body, (**Figure** 9-5), contains more than 650 individual muscles anchored to the skeleton, which provide pulling power so that you can move around. These muscles constitute about 40% of your total body weight. The muscle's points of attachment to bones or other muscles are designated as origin or insertion. The point of origin is the point of attachment to the bone to which the muscle is anchored. The point of insertion is the point of attachment to the bone the muscle moves. Generally, the muscles are attached by tough fibrous structures called tendons. These attachments bridge one or more joints and the result of muscle contraction is movement of these joints. The pistol shooter needs to understand that the body is moved primarily by muscle groups, not by individual muscles. These groups of muscles power all actions ranging from the threading of a needle to the lifting of heavy weights.

In order for the body to stay alive, each of its cells must receive a continuous supply of food and oxygen. At the same time, carbon dioxide and other materials produced by the cells must be picked up for removal from the body. This process is continually maintained by the body's circulatory system. Pistol shooters need to understand that stress will disrupt the normality of the primary circulatory system, which consists of the heart and blood vessels, which together maintain a continuous flow of blood through the body delivering oxygen and nutrients to and removing carbon dioxide and waste products from peripheral tissues. A subsystem of the circulatory system, the lymphatic system, collects interstitial fluid and returns it to the blood. The heart pumps oxygen-rich blood from the lungs to all parts of the body through a network of arteries, and smaller branches called arterioles. Blood returns to the heart via small venules, which lead to the larger veins. Arterioles and venules are linked to even smaller vessels called metarterioles. Capillaries, blood vessels a single cell thick, branch off from the metarterioles and then rejoin them. The network of tiny capillaries is where the exchange of oxygen and carbon dioxide between blood and body cells takes place. The average adult has over 60,000 miles of blood vessels in his body.

The integumentary system is the name given for the skin, hair, nails, and glands covering the body. It also includes the eyes, the ears, the nose, and the mouth, all of which are a part of the body's sensory system. Demeter and Barani point out that the world is perceived by means of coded messages, electrical impulses, sent to the brain by the sensory organs. Our perception is developed by means of the pattern of sound pressure entering the ears and the pattern of light entering the eyes. The senses of touch, taste, and smell, however, are also important to our perception of the world around us.

The eyeballs are located within the two bony sockets of the skull. Of all the senses, eyesight is often considered most important. According to one estimate, four-fifths of everything we know reaches the brain through our eyes. The eyes transmit constant streams of images to the brain by electrical signals. The eyes receive information from light rays. The light rays are either absorbed or reflected. Objects that absorb all of the light rays appear black, whereas those that reflect all the light rays appear white. Colored objects absorb certain parts of the light spectrum and reflect others. When you look at something, the light rays reflected from the object enter the eye. The light is refracted by the cornea and passes through the pupil to the lens. The iris controls the amount of light entering the eye. Then the lens focuses the light onto the retina, forming an image in reverse and upsidedown. Light-sensitive cells in the retina transmit the image to the brain by electrical signals. The brain "sees" the image right side up.

What all of this comes down to is that the pistol shooter has to work within the confines of the body he was born into. It is composed of systems which determine the behavior of the shooter and facilitates his adaptation to the conditions imposed by the contest stresses. But, beware! The pistol shooter is in a situation of GIGO, garbage in, garbage out.

Blankenship seems to be acknowledging this idea of GIGO with his comments in *The Pistol Shooter's Treasury* edited by Gil Hebard, *"frequently, shooters spend too much time waiting for the weapon to become perfectly still and then suddenly apply pressure. This is commonly called the jerk and something to avoid."* You see, by the time the shooter decides to fire, the pistol has moved from that *perfectly still* position and is no longer where it was when the shooter made the decision to shoot.

Garbage in, garbage out. On this point, Blankenship notes, *"Other people have told me they can concentrate on trigger control and get better results. However, it doesn't work as well for me as concentrating on sight alignment. Before I start shooting for a season I work very hard on getting my trigger finger to start moving when I see a still weapon with perfect sight alignment. In other words I'm trying to make it automatic. I have had good results using this system of trigger control and at times it is completely automatic and I never have to think about it. If I do have trouble, it is necessary for me to dry fire until it again becomes automatic.*

I must add here that everyone has a short period of time just after the arm and gun settles, when they will be as still as they will get. It is best to get the shot to break during this period. This explains why it is not desirable to hold too long. What too long is will have to be determined by each individual by how long it takes for the gun to settle and when it becomes as still as it is going to get. After this short period of time that the hold is at optimum stillness, the movements generally increase, making it very difficult to get good results. " (*The Pistol Shooter's Treasury* edited by Gil Hebard).

On the other hand, consider (**Figure** 9-7). We acknowledge the importance of the Locomotive Apparatus. But, we train our system to develop only one primary conditional reflex. When the visually aligned barrel reaches the pre-selected area, we train the trigger finger to move the trigger instantaneously smooth. Are Demeter and Barani wrong? No way! They have identified the process used by the majority of the pistol shooters competing today. Under the current method of pistol training, these factors have a relatively long period of time in which to act on the pistol shooter since he is in the aiming position for such a somewhat long period of time. There is at least one super champion, Bill Blankenship, who apparently decided not to use this method. He recounted the effort he went to during three months of 1959.

"I spent about three months working on specific problems after the shooting season of 1959. The most important of these was trigger control. I knew that the time consumed from the time I made up my mind to apply pressure on the trigger until the hammer fell took a lot more time than was necessary. Therefore, I tried to see how fast I could squeeze the trigger and not disturb the weapon.

When I first started with the fast trigger squeeze, I had sudden movements of the sights to one side or the other. Then I started trying to figure out exactly how to get the trigger to release without any movement. I tried many systems before finding one that worked. I call this "positive pressure."

 ...Then I started dry firing to make the squeeze as fast as possible and to not have any disturbance in either the sight alignment or the stillness of the gun. Without hesitation then, the pressure is a positive pressure straight to the rear in such a way as not to disturb the perfect alignment of the sights or the stillness of the gun." (*The Pistol Shooter's Treasury* edited by Gil Hebard).

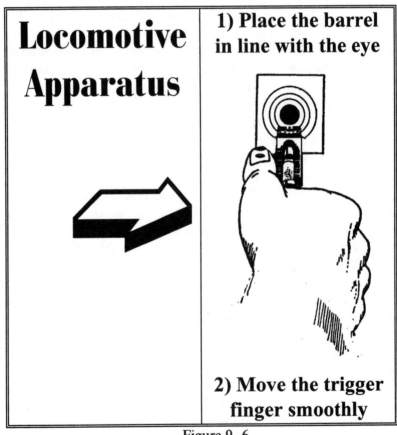

Locomotive Apparatus

1) Place the barrel in line with the eye

2) Move the trigger finger smoothly

Figure 9- 6

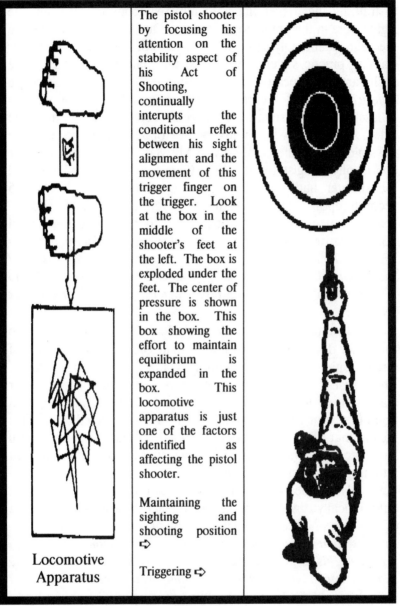

The pistol shooter by focusing his attention on the stability aspect of his Act of Shooting, continually interrupts the conditional reflex between his sight alignment and the movement of this trigger finger on the trigger. Look at the box in the middle of the shooter's feet at the left. The box is exploded under the feet. The center of pressure is shown in the box. This box showing the effort to maintain equilibrium is expanded in the box. This locomotive apparatus is just one of the factors identified as affecting the pistol shooter.

Maintaining the sighting and shooting position ⇨

Triggering ⇨

Locomotive Apparatus

Figure 9-7

It is obvious, when you look at what Yev'yev discussed on page 365 of his book *Competitive Shooting,* that both he and Blankenship were thinking on the same wave length with respect to training the trigger finger to move subconsciously when the sights were in the predetermined area. During the time preceding the 1996 Atlanta Olympics, many studies of the athletes and their training practices were reported in the mainstream press. One such article appeared in the June,1996 issue of *Scientific American* by Jay T. Kearney. A shooting athlete was hooked up to laser tracking system which detects where the shooter aims the rifle. Kearney, who holds a doctorate degree in exercise physiology from the University of Maryland, and who is a senior sports physiologist for the U.S. Olympic Committee, observed the shooter had an exceptionally good hold, for **the first 5 seconds** upon coming into the bullseye. But, then the shooter spent a much longer time attempting to re-acquire that initial hold. Kearney pointed out, *"An analysis of the placement of the beam on the target showed that her aim was nearly flawless. But she continually tried to make adjustments, and so her ability to remain steadily fixed on the target deteriorated after five or six seconds."*

In analyizing a shooter's, performance while hooked up to a laser device, in the National Smallbore Rifle Association of Great Britain's video, the authors made a similar observation. The thrust of our program is designed to help the pistol shooter teach himself to move the trigger finger instantaneously smooth upon first seeing that the sights are in the pre-selected area. This means that all of the factors identified by Demeter and Barani have far less time to act upon the shooter and his effort at attaining perfect sight picture.

How does one train the trigger finger movement to be automatically triggered by the sights reaching a pre-selected area of the target? We refer again to Blankenship, *"I believe very strongly that trigger squeeze can become automatic through practice. This is possible because of the subconscious mind. The subconscious mind controls those things which are automatic that we seldom think about."* (*The Pistol Shooter's Treasury* edited by Gil Hebard).

The following three illustrations are modified from the Russian language book by Lew Weinstein (Vaynshteyn), ***Shooter And Trainer***, Moscow, 1977, (First published 1969).

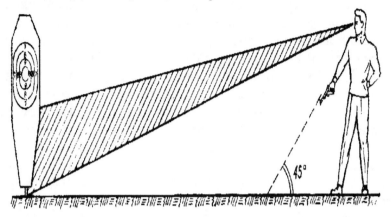

Figure 9- 8

Figure 9-8, shows the starting position of the shooter. Notice his inferior vision field is focused on the bottom of the target. His arm holding the handgun is lined up at 45° to the plane of the ground.

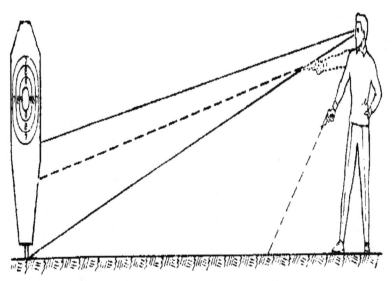

Figure 9-9, shows the shooting unit. The shooter focused on the bottom of the target. The barrel is raised to the bottom of the target. This activates the excitation of the conditional stimulus. Remember, the initial acquisition of the internal alignment must be mechanical. By mechanical, we mean that the sight alignment has to be setup through the stance. This is much like the rifle shooters do with their aligned system. In other words, the rifle shooter, if the sights are not pointed at the area of the target he wants, he moves the entire aligned system. He does not muscle the whole aligned system into alignment. He shifts the whole shooting unit. If pistol shooters have to look for sight alignment, that is not it. That is not what we are looking for. The important point here is that the acquisition of the internal alignment is the exciter for the conditional stimulus of the conditional reflex. The conditional reflex, in this case is the movement of the trigger finger on the trigger.

Yev'yev, in the US Army translation, points out:

> *"All the movements which a person makes are controlled by the nervous system. Under the influence of various stimuli coming in from the immediate environment or from the internal organs, the nervous system enters a state of excitation. The nervous excitation arising at some center of stimulation does not remain there, but extends along the corresponding nerve fibers with great speed, measured in tenths of meters a second."*

It is important to remember when training beginning pistol shooters that as the training proceeds, it is crucial that the shooter perform this raising of the arm to eye level very rapidly. We want the shooter's arm muscles exposed to the effects of gravity for the briefest duration. Now, the coach must not expect more from his shooters than is physically possible for them to achieve. We know, from research, that due to physical limitations of the central nervous system, there is a finite limit on the reaction time of the shooter. Yev'yev points out:

> *"All similar actions by which a person responds to some external stimulus are called reaction. Despite the fact that*

reaction can be very rapid, nevertheless there is a definite interval of time between the beginning of the action of the stimulus signal and the beginning of the response movement. For example, when the rifleman using the method of impulse control of the trigger action begins the rapid movement of the index finger in response to the signal represented by the visual perception of the coincidence of the centered front sight and the lower edge of the bull's-eye, there is a lag of approximately 0.18-0.25 seconds. This reaction time is determined by the fact that it takes a certain amount of time for the image formed on the rifleman's retina by the coincidence of the centered front sight and the lower edge of the bull'seye to be transmitted along the optic nerve to the corresponding cerebral center and to be recognized; there is a certain short interval until the decision to produce the shot, that is, to squeeze on the trigger, is formed, and then it takes time for the corresponding command to be sent by the brain along the centrifugal nerves to the hand muscles and for the finger to squeeze on the trigger."

Many pistol shooters are bound up in doing their training and match competition using the concept of an Arc of Movement or wobble area. They have, in some cases, over many years trained themselves to a conditional reflex wherein they fire the shot within their wobble area. It has been noted that the coordination of the actions of aiming and squeezing on the trigger requires the pistol shooter to be very fast in his reactions. However, in employing an Arc of Movement or wobble area method of shooting, the shooter also, by the nature of the way he interrupts the process of moving the finger while the pistol is not lined up acceptably to him, uses what is known as an interrupted trigger pressure. Just what is the interrupted trigger pressure method?

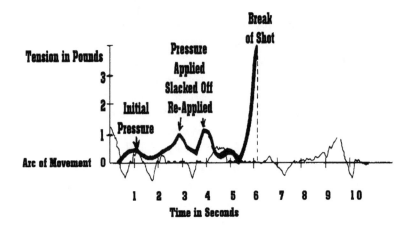

The US Army Pistol Marksmanship Guide of 1981 advises shooters, *"This is a method of trigger control not recommended, although used by some shooters. Some shooters think they can pick the trigger release time even after years of experience.*

The shooter will align the sights and exert initial pressure on the trigger. He will then make every effort to hold the weapon motionless. During extremely brief moments of motionlessness, pressure is applied on the trigger. If the sight alignment changes and is not perfect, or the arc of movement of the weapon increases, the pressure on the trigger is halted and trigger tension maintained. When sight alignment is again perfect and movement diminishes, pressure on the trigger is resumed until the shot breaks, or after the slack in the trigger is taken up, initial pressure is applied and the shot released by a single swift movement of the trigger finger when there is a decrease in the minimum arc of movement. In this case the presence of perfect sight alignment is not considered essential in initiating trigger action. Abrupt action in applying trigger pressure will disturb the existing sight alignment and other fundamental control factors are subordinated to a minimum arc of movement."

Shooters firing within a wobble will have their actions in response to visual perceptions delayed and they will lose their efficiency. The reason is that since the shot will not be fired at the proper time, consequently it will not be accurate. That being the case is the pistol shooter's speed of reaction always fast enough, is the speed of reaction always the same? Yev'yev tells us, *"No, not always, and this is why. The reason is that, in addition*

470

to the process of excitation, which constitutes one of the aspects of the complex nervous activity of the living organism, there is also a process of inhibition in the central nervous system. It has been proven by scientists that inhibition arises in the central nervous system as a process concomitant with stimulation; that means that stimulation and inhibition occur simultaneously in all nervous processes. The state of inhibition must not be considered a state of rest or inactivity; it represents an active state of the nerve cells in which stimulation cannot pass through them. The simultaneous existence of the process of stimulation and inhibition is the only thing that permits the living organism to execute various movements. For example, in order to bend the index finger and thus produce the action of squeezing on the trigger, it is necessary for the stimulating impulses to contract the finger flexors. If only the process of stimulation existed, the coordinated activity of the organism. all kinds of movements executed by it would be impossible."

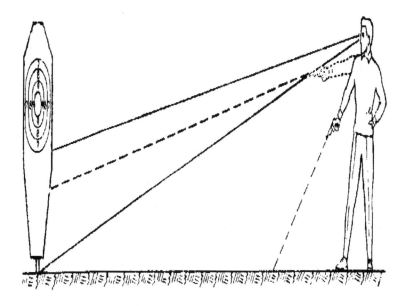

Figure 9-10

Now, **Figure 9-10**, depicts the conditional stimulus, of the eye recognizing the front sight of the aligned system moving into the pre-selected area of the target, which the shooter has trained

471

it to recognize as it comes into the mid-line vision field. Lösel puts it as the *"functioning of the dioptric apparatus and of the optic nerve, which relay the information to the visual analyser in the occipital cortical area, on the border of the calcarine fissure."* What we show in this illustration is the reflex action actuated as soon as the brain is satisfied with what the eye sees as perfect internal alignment of the system, pointed at the desired area This movement of the trigger finger is the conditional reflex.

The identification of the conditional reflex has been with us for about 100 years. It's application for pistol shooters has been pointed out in the UIT Journal on several occasions. For example, Heinz, Dr. Lösel, (Germany), *UIT Journal, (Medicine), Conditioned Reflex and the Psychology of Learning, 1/96, Page 8+,* identified just what are reflexes:

"The most simple reactions to a stimulus are known as reflexes, which take place below the threshold of consciousness (subconsciously) and are hence neither conscious nor controllable." Lösel

What the pistol shooters of America have been unable to do, is to design a training program capable of producing marksmen able to reach the level of expertise to win Olympic gold medals. Until now the Americans have vocalized the idea that youngsters should not be taught to shoot pistols until about 16 years of age.

The youngsers in our Tucson Pistol Training Program may well have put that concept on the scrapt heap of shooting history this July 1996. Shooting over the National Match Course at 50 yards and 25 yards, they shattered the National Match Course Junior Team record by over 100 points. The four boys on the team were between 11 and 14 years of age. The 14 year old scored 263 points and the 11 year old was second high with 244.

Our girls did the same thing to the NRA's International Women's Team Record for the International Rapid Fire event at 25 meters. On this team was one of our nine year old girls. They shattered that WOMEN'S Team Record by 206 points.

Just what does it mean to capture an NRA National Record? It means that in the 125 year history of the National Rifle Association the holder of the National Junior or Women's Record has fired the highest score ever attained over that

472

particular course of fire. To put such a certificate on your wall means the shooters have achieved a level of skill not surpassed by any other team in the sport of pistol shooting.

It was always assumed that youngsters had to have exceptional upper body strength to participate in pistol shooting. In the old method of training, that assumption still holds true. But, developing a conditional reflex does not require any exceptional upper body strength. If anyone thinks the nine year old girl who was a part of this National Women't Team Record is some Amazon, I invite you to look at her picture on the following page. I believe we all know that a third grade school girl does not have the strength of a sixteen year old boy. Nor does she at age nine, have the strength of the grown woman she will grow into. So, it is apparent that it has got to be the method she trained under, not the strength of the shooter which allowed her to produce the results she attained. Is the training method capable of repeatability? We have had more than 70 youngsters between the ages of 9 and 15 prove it over and over again.

Michal Newhouse, Age 9, Winner of the Junior Women's Silver Medal at the 1996 Grand Canyon State Games over the .22 Caliber NRA 900 Course of Fire

Figure 9-11

In **Figure** 9-11, we see the result of a nine year old girl spending 10 hours a week for 8 weeks in the NRA Summer Camp held in Tucson. The camp title was *Training the Conditional Reflex for Pistol Shooters.* When we speak of the conditional reflex we use in **Successful Pistol Shooting**, we are speaking of the trigger finger movement, which we refer to as instantaneous smooth, and is activiated by the brain upon receiving the message from the eye of perfect sight alignment pointed at an acceptable area. We refer to this as *the finger bone connected to the eyebone.* We, therefore, have to get our sight alignment through our stance. We have to eliminate any conscious muscle movement to correct a misalignment of the sights. If we have conscious muscle movement, we no longer have a conditional reflex. It is over-ridden by the conscious exertion.

For years, pistol shooters have acted on the theory that the way to push the envelope of their scores to higher levels of performance consisted solely in modifications of their mental state. One of the American Olympic pistol team members told one of the coaches in our Tucson Pistol Training Program, that his experience in the 1996 Olympics showed him that he had been insufficiently mentally prepared. So, he said he is going to spend the time until the 2000 Olympics preparing a mental program which will carry him to success.

On the other hand, it is pistol shooters like Blankenship, the ones who scientifically investigated what they were doing and questioned the accuracy of the training information current at their time, who have moved our pistol shooting game forward. We believe Blankenship's drive to perfect his performance in the summer of 1959 led him to his six NRA National Pistol Championships and his other awards. He was never, after that, in a **monkey see, monkey do** mode. Many of his peers thought if they just had enough time, money and ammunition, they could be as great a shooter as Blankenship made himself into. Many of the shooters, when they could not achieve Blankenship's results looked inward and tried to harness their mental efforts in place of looking at why the information was not working as it should. This has had the effect of working untold damage. Many believed that the mind never grew old, and that it could be trained as well at one time as at another. From this mistaken notion arose such sayings as, *"It is never too late to be what you might have been."* Unlike Blankenship, what many American pistol shooters failed to grasp is that they are creatures whose mental functions rest upon sensory foundations. In other words, their ability to carry out physical tasks rests upon modifications in nerve cells. So, it is always too late to be the shooter that you might have been. The pistol shooter has to train to be the shooter he or she is to become in the future. This Blankenship did in 1959 when he took three months off to train his trigger finger movement to a habit which would move the trigger when he saw he had perfect sight alignment at the area of the target he desired. Mental training may be nothing more than modifications in the central nervous system, but it is also true that without these modifications no human being can be trained, as Lösel notes:

"The simplest voluntary movements, however, require complicated regulative processes which must first be learned, the movements programmed in the central nervous system are ready for recall.

If the forefinger is at rest, for example, the state of tension between the finger's extending and flexing musculature is almost equal. In order to bend the finger, its flexing musculature must be strained, which triggers an unconscious counteraction of the respective extending musculature." Lösel

This unconscious counteraction is what we build on, in developing a conditional reflex of the trigger finger, actuated when the sights, while aligned with the shooting eye, reach the pre-selected target area. Blankenship pointed out, *"Any muscle movement can become habit through repetitious practice. The movement of the trigger finger can become habit also, but it takes a great deal of practice.*

I spent almost three months, trying to overcome problems in my squeeze. I was trying to develop two things. First, to make my trigger squeeze as much habit as possible and secondly, to be able to squeeze the trigger as fast as I possibly could without disturbing the sight alignment or the lay of the weapon. The harder I worked the better my trigger control became. I had the feeling sometimes that I didn't have to consciously think about the trigger at all. It was becoming habit. Also because I didn't have to think about the trigger, it was much easier for me to concentrate on sight alignment." (*The Pistol Shooter's Treasury* edited by Gil Hebard).

Lösel made the point that, *"Highly coordinated movements require precisely synchronized changes in the tonicity of the active (straining) and counteractive (restraining) musculature. This process is especially difficult when the factor of time is taken into consideration. As early as 1962, Bernstein pointed out that speed and precision dynamically oppose each other."*

Some recent findings indicate that, in some situations, the old saying, *"Haste makes waste,"* does not always hold up. For example, moving the finger on the trigger can be done instantaneously smooth or it can be an instantaneous jerk or snatch. Blankenship points out, *"This does not mean sudden movements on the trigger. This is why the people who use the system of slowly squeezing the trigger have a lot of trouble. In reality they try to squeeze the trigger only when the sights are perfectly aligned and when this perfect sight alignment is sitting **exactly** under the bullseye. When everything is perfect they squeeze, but as soon as anything moves they quit squeezing or hesitate until everything is perfect again to squeeze a little more. These people have a lot of trouble because of jerks, flinches, heeling, etc., all of which are the result of anticipation."* (*The Pistol Shooter's Treasury* edited by Gil Hebard).

When an action becomes a conditional reflex, then you have it for a long time. So, bear in mind that, if you train yourself to an instantaneous jerk or snatch of the trigger finger, that is yours and should you decide to change, you may find it difficult. To switch from one mode to another requires considerable retraining. The unconscious reaction we train, is the smooth movement of the finger on the trigger, when the pre-selected target area is reached while the sights are aligned with the eye. We want our target acquisition to be of such quality that it activates a habit, or conditional reflex, of the trigger finger before random oscillations are generated.

How do we do this training so that the trigger finger moves instantaneously smooth and not in an instantaneous jerk? We use the specially designed pistol shooting training form shown in (**Figure 9-15**). This is used to focus the attention of the

476

shooter and observer where it needs to be, on the internally aligned system reaching the pre-selected area and the finger moving instantaneously smooth. Professor Dr. Andrei Demeter and Prof. Gavrila Barani tell us that *"Obtention of high performances in sports shooting supposes a functional harmony of the perceptual cognitive system of the shooter in the key instant of firing.* In other words, when the internally aligned system has arrived at the pre-selected area of the target, the key instant of firing has to have the trigger finger movement be instantaneously smooth so as not to disturb the harmony of the rest of the internally aligned system.

Demeter and Barani point out further in their 5/6-78 *UIT Jounal* article that *"According to Fitts (1964), the operational definition of an adequate response to the permanently variable stresses of the surrounding environment implies an exact organization, both in time and in space of the receptor-effector processes, as well as of the feedback processes"*. By directing the attention of the shooter to the receptor-effector processes, the implication here is that the shooter needs the feedback in order to make continuous corrections in his pistol holding pattern. It is in ideas such as this, that the concept of the **arc of movement** has come to be such an integral myth in the old fashioned pistol shooting training here in America. Pistol shooters who train to shoot under the **arc of movement** concept, need to be aware that they are continuously testing a couple of the fundamental laws of nature. Often pistol shooters assume that their strength will negate the laws of motion and gravity first identified by Sir Isaac Newton (1642-1727).

Demeter and Barani justifiy the old fashioned pistol training method by pointing out that, *"The model presented by J.T. Gormley (1977) is based on a continuous improvement of the reception and processing of information with the aid of the space and time feed-back mechanisms."* This model assumes that the pistol shooter will continously make adjustments in his aiming based on feedback of the timing of his sight alignment, within his **arc of movement** and as the feedback demonstrates his errors, he then tries to correct the errors. This is just what Blankenship observed, *"This is why the people who use the system of slowly squeezing the trigger have a lot of trouble. In reality they try to*

477

squeeze the trigger only when the sights are perfectly aligned and when this perfect sight alignment is sitting **exactly** *under the bullseye. When everything is perfect they squeeze, but as soon as anything moves they quit squeezing or hesitate until everything is perfect again to squeeze a little more. These people have a lot of trouble because of jerks, flinches, heeling, etc., all of which are the result of anticipation. Using this system they try to know exactly when the gun is going to fire. This is what causes anticipation of one sort or another."* (*The Pistol Shooter's Treasury* edited by Gil Hebard).

"In our concept," Demeter and Barani, point out, *"the shooting at fixed or moving targets implies the interaction of three factors: shooter-weapon-target, each of them having many common, positive and negative characteristics."* It is this type of complexity which has placed an upper limit on pistol shooting training results. Consider what happens when a champion such as Bill Blankenship removes the complexity, *"A person can only concentrate on one subject at a time. To look back at my problem, sight alignment was the only thing about shooting that cannot be controlled by habit, so this is the logical thing to concentrate on while actually shooting. All the other fundamentals of pistol shooting can become habit through lots of hard work on the part of an individual.*

To make trigger control automatic takes a lot of practice, but it can be accomplished. It is definitely worth while putting some effort into an attempt. Just a little bit of thought and any amount of work on a problem will bring some results. The greater the effort, the greater the dividends." (*The Pistol Shooter's Treasury* edited by Gil Hebard).

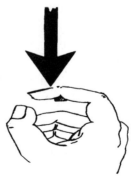

The Conditional Reflex In Pistol Shooting

Under the system explained in *Successful Pistol Shooting*, Blankenship, in the above cited quotation, differs from what we have incorporated in our method when he said, *"sight alignment was the only thing about shooting that cannot be controlled by habit."* In Blankenship's method, this is very true. In our system,

sight alignment is established and controled by the stance or platform. Instead of searching for sight alignment after the pistol arrives at eye level, it has already been established as a part of our stance set-up process. We setup the stance to establish perfect internal alignment. Technically this is known as the exciter for the conditional stimulus of the conditional reflex. Thus, when perfect alignment is pointed at the desired area, the conditional reflex is activated. What has to happen in the method we advocate here in this book, is when the eye sees the perfectly aligned sights reach the pre-selected area of the target, the trigger finger moves automatically. What we are doing is using the perfectly aligned sights reaching the pre-selected area of the target as a conditional stimulus. In other words, we are deliberately using this perfect sight system, perfectly lined up with the eye to stimulate the visual processing center to acutate the trigger finger to produce a response in that finger.

Just how do Demeter and Barani arrive at their concept? They tell us that, *"From the functional standpoint this triad should be considered as the dialectic unit of the human organism in its multiple relationship with the weapon and the target, in variable environmental conditions. The major component of this triad—the human organism—functions as a cybernetic system in which the permanent inflow of informations originating in the weapon and the target is picked up by exteroceptors—the peripheral segments of the visual, acoustic, myoarthrokinetic and cutaneous analyzers, and is transformed in nervous impulses that are sent to the cerebral cortex."* We do not fault Demeter and Barani on their science. We believe that others, involved in the training of pistol shooters have promoted an inefficient use of that science.

Consider the pistol training often seen around this country. The *US Army Marksmanship* Manual, points out that *waiting too long to apply a positive trigger pressure to break the shot may allow the arc of movement to increase and the eye focus to blur. The shooter eventually becomes impatient and abruptly speeds up his trigger action. This causes a jerk shot.* So, this waiting is seen to be apt to cause a problem for pistol shooters. But, there is no effort to scrap the concept of an arc of movement. Indeed, it is still taught to beginning pistol shooters, by coaches using the *US Army Marksmanship* Manual.

How To Train The Conditional Reflex

1) Select the area of the target at which you will point the perfect internal alignment of the system.

2) Move the trigger finger instantaneously smoothly as soon as the eye is satisfied that the internally aligned system, using the front sight as a reference, is pointed at the pre-selected area.

How Do You Evaluate Your Progress Toward Establishing The Conditional Reflex?

This evaluation of the progress of the establishment of the conditional reflex is most efficiently accomplished by working in pairs. One person monitors the time of the interval it takes for the shooter to raise the pistol from the bench, or from the 45 degree ready position, until it reaches eye level. This is done for the first 10 shots. Next the person measures the interval it takes for the shooter to fire the shot from the moment the pistol reaches eye level. Bear in mind what Blankenship says, *"Any muscle movement can become habit through repetitious practice. The movement of the trigger finger can become habit also, but it takes a great deal of practice."* (*The Pistol Shooter's Treasury* edited by Gil Hebard). Do not expect overnight success. We use our stopwatch and the **Conditional Reflex Evaluation Form** in place of the gauge Blankenship used in developing his habit, which we term, a conditional reflex.

480

For an example of a form which assists in tracking the progress explained above, (see **Figure 9-15**).

The progress of the acquistion of the conditional reflex is reflected in the timing of the firing of the shot. The effort is to achieve millisecond timing from the moment the pistol reaches eye leve until the shot fires. The fall of the shot, coupled with the value of the shot will assist in the evaluation process. Fortunately we are pointing at a target with concentric rings. This gives us a precise measurement of the accuracy of our pointing. It also enables us to pick up rather quickly if the shooter is developing an instantaneous jerk rather than an instantaneous smooth movement of the trigger finger. Blankenship has noted, *"Frequently, shooters spend too much time waiting for the weapon to become perfectly still and then suddenly apply pressure. This is commonly called the jerk and something to avoid."*

. In our pistol training, each shooter fires 20 shots at a time. The 20 shots are evaluated in ten shot segments. This is repeated for a total of 60 shots per training session. For the first 10 shots, the **Conditional Reflex Evaluation Form (Figure 9-15)** directs the attention of the observer to the time it takes for the shooter to raise the gun from the bench, or from 45°, until it reaches eye level, (see **Figure 9-12**).

Arm Raises Sights To Eye

Figure 9-12

Purpose of Conditional Reflex Evaluation form: To provide the shooter with objective monitoring, in which the shooter can have his or her visually conditional stimulus evaluated (VCS).

Let's break this purpose down. What is it we want to do? First, we want the shooter to be able to obtain an objective assessment of his or her progress in establishing the conditional reflex as a shooting method. What we are concerned with here is movement behavior. The primary focus is on movement behavior which can be observed directly. The shooters are arranged in pairs. One shoots, the other observes the behavior associated with the practice of the the habit which will lead to the establishment of the desired conditional reflex. What we are doing is building spinal-cord processes that are capable of generating a pattern of skilled activities in the locomotive apparatus.

1ˢᵗ Ten Shots

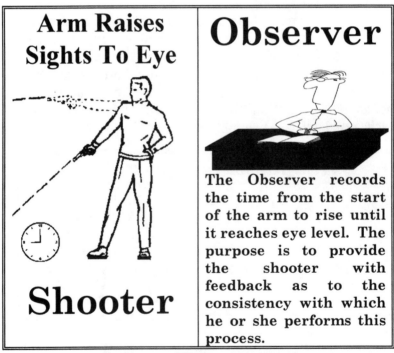

Arm Raises Sights To Eye

Observer

Shooter

The Observer records the time from the start of the arm to rise until it reaches eye level. The purpose is to provide the shooter with feedback as to the consistency with which he or she performs this process.

Figure 9-13

2ⁿᵈ Ten Shots

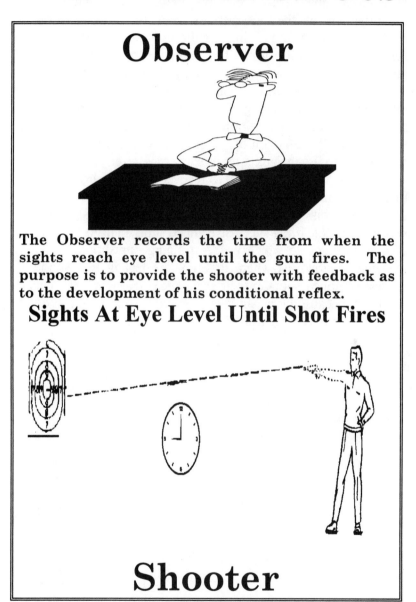

Observer

The Observer records the time from when the sights reach eye level until the gun fires. The purpose is to provide the shooter with feedback as to the development of his conditional reflex.

Sights At Eye Level Until Shot Fires

Shooter

Figure 9-14

483

It is well known in coaching circles of various sports that a person paired as an observer with someone performing the training learns almost as much as the performer. However, the observation must be a directed observation. The coach directs the attention of the observer to what the coach considers important. For example, in a diving experiment, the observers acted as scorers of the dives. This had the effect of directing their attention to those elements of the dives which elicited high scores.

By focusing on the timing, a measure of competition is introduced into the training of the junior at this juncture. For the second 10 shots, the **Conditional Reflex Evaluation** form (**Figure 9-15**) directs the attention of the observer to the time it takes for the shooter to fire the gun after it reaches eye level.

The shooter is directed to recover the sight alignment and dryfire a second shot. This helps to develop follow through as an instinctive habit. It also has the effect of having the shooter feel very comfortable firing successive aimed shots. This is part of the mental attititude to which we are training our shooters. They may never know just where they got the feeling that shooting successive aimed shots is their cup of tea. However, the coach will know because he or she has deliberately trained the shooter in the acquistion of this attitude.

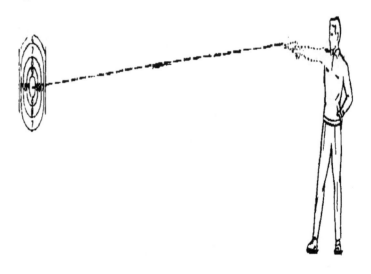

Name: _____ Date: _____

Conditional Reflex Evaluation

Example

Shot #	Seconds	1/100th	Shot Value	Shot Fall
1	2	83	9	

Training Stage #1
Start Time When Pistol Arm Begins To Move Up.

☛Stop TIME When Pistol Reaches Eye Level.

☐ Check when timing

Shot #	Seconds	1/100th	Shot Value	Shot Fall
1				O
2				O
3				O
4				O
5				O
6				O
7				O
8				O
9				O
10				O

Training Stage #2
Start Time When Pistol Reaches Eye Level.

☛Stop TIME When Shot Is Fired.

☐ Check when timing

Shot #	Seconds	1/100th	Shot Value	Shot Fall
1				O
2				O
3				O
4				O
5				O
6				O
7				O
8				O
9				O
10				O

Figure 9-15

Daily Shooting Report
Date: 5/3/96 Friday

Name: Danielle Dancho

	Shot 1	Shot 2	Shot 3	Shot 4	Shot 5	Shot Time Average	Total	
Series 1	1	4	6	6	6		23	
Time 1	3	2	3	3.2	3.5	2.94		
Series 2	8	6	6	7	6		33	56
Time 2	3.1	3.5	4	3.1	5	3.74		
Series 3	5	9	9	8	4		35	
Time 3	3.5	4.6	3	3	3	3.42		
Series 4	6	10	7	8	5		36	71
Time 4	2.5	2.5	2.1	3	3	2.62		
Series 5	6	8	6	4	6		30	
Time 5	2.7	3.5	2	2	2	2.44		
Series 6	6	5	9	10	7		37	67
Time 6	3	4	4	4	2	3.4		
Series 7	7	5	8	6	8		34	79
Time 7	3.5	3	3	3.5	3	3.2		273
Series 8	8	10	8	9	10		45	
Time 8	3	2.8	2.5	2.6	4.6	3.1		
Series 9	10	10	5	9	7		41	
Time 9	3	3.2	2.6	3.1	3.4	3.06		
Series 10	8	7	7	10	4		36	77
Time 10	2	3.3	3	3.5	2.3	2.82		
Series 11	6	6	8	6	6		32	
Time 11	4	3.1	3.2	4	2.2	3.3		
Series 12	6	9	10	8	8		41	73
Time 12	5	2.2	3.1	4	2.6	3.38		

Average Time Per Shot: 2.8 seconds

Total Score For 60 Shots: 423
Shot Average: 7.05

Figure 9-16

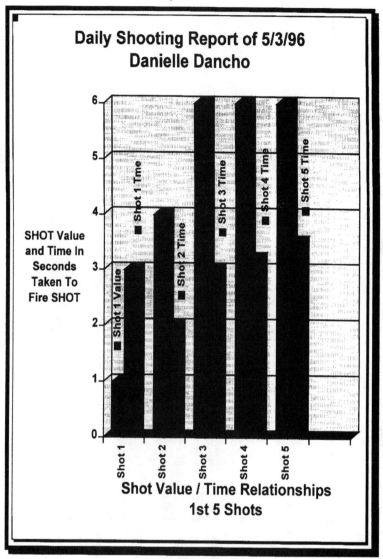

Figure 9-17

Notice the correlation between the value of shot number one and the measurement of the amount of time from when the pistol reached eyelevel until it was fired. Danielle Dancho had been shooting for three months in our training program at that time. A time measurement of three seconds passed before the shot was fired.

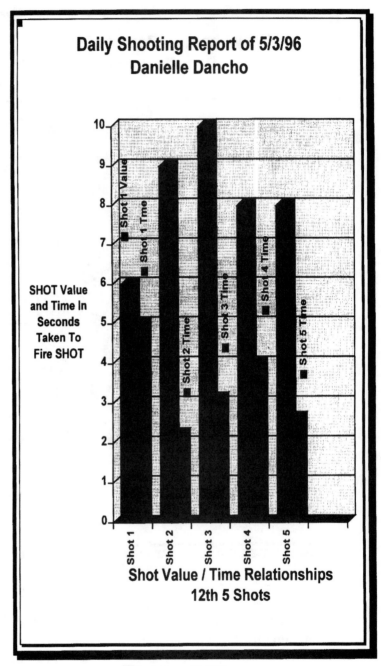

Figure 9-18

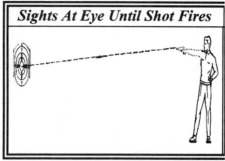

Sights At Eye Until Shot Fires

Figure 9-19

Youngsters 9, 10 or 11 years of age, will not necessarily understand the why of this training, (**Figure** 9-18). And it is not necessary that the coach even try to make them understand at this juncture.

Michael Wilkinson, in May of 1982 reported a study, *"An Examination of Epinephrine and Athletic Performance; Psychophysiological, Cognitive and Behavior Indices of Arousal,"* of eight male pistol shooters and one female pistol shooter attending the United States National Pistol Training and Development Team's camp held during April of 1981 at the Fort Sam Houston Pistol Range in San Antonio, Texas. These pistol shooters, Wilkinson considered highly skilled "by virtue of their past achievements and by their membership on the U.S. National Pistol Team."

What we are concerned with is something which we have not seen recorded other where in our research for this book. Wilkinson recorded the "hold time." This was the time in seconds from the time the shooter started to raise the pistol until the time the shot was fired. He recorded this using a conventional stopwatch having 0.10-second increments. He also recorded the "frequency of aborts." This was recorded on the datagraph paper each time the shooter raised the pistol to fire but decided not to shoot whereupon the gun was put back down on the shooting bench. The authors of this book speculate that the *"frequency of aborts"* represents a failure of the shooter to setup his sight alignment through his stance. In some cases, the shooters recorded a high 90% rate of aborts. That indicates that almost no shot was fired on the first acquistion of the desired

489

target area with the aligned sights. A 10% success rate! How many of you could live with a success rate that low in your business or in any academic class? Imagine! Many of our pistol shooters have lived with that success rate in their competitive games for years. We doubt that they would tolerate one of their children coming home with a grade of 10% in a school class. In our program, a 30% abort rate is cause for an instant re-evaluation of the shooter's technique. It is just not something that a coach in our program is allowed to have happen. We expect between a 98% and 99.5% first hold, first shot success rate. If it is less than that, to us our first task is to evaluate the shooter's stance. We check to see if the shooter has deliberately setup his or her sight alignment with the stance or platform.

After five months of training, Danielle Dancho, at age 15, shooting the air pistol at 10 meters, produced a "hold time" of 2.8 seconds per shot. Many of America's elite pistol shooters have hold times varying from 7 seconds to more than 16 seconds. The information in the Wilkinson report clearly demonstrates a primary difference between the old shooting method and what we advocate. When shooters have hold times in excess over 3 seconds, they are very definitely working with an arc of movement in their shooting. Danielle is definitely seen to be working at establishing a subconscious movement of her trigger finger.

Coaches now have a technique to use to determine the status of the shooter's effort to develop their trigger finger movement as a conditional reflex. This focus on the timing of the shot from bench to eye level is a technique which can be used by all coaches to evaluate the progress of their shooters. For those coaches working in the training program advocated in this book, the well-meaning, often gratuituously given advice of *"slow down, take your time"* is the ultimate destroyer of youngsters training to shoot pistol. Remember, the shooters listed in the Wilkinson study were performing at the top echelon of the pistol games in America at that time. You can easily observe that their shooting technique differs from that advocated in this book. You can easily determine whether a shooter is using this conditional reflex method or the older, more universal method, by timing the shooter from the ready position to eye level. It is normal for beginning shooters to have times of 3 seconds to around 5 seconds. Notice the "hold times" reported in Wilkinson's study.

Shooter	Aborts		Hold Time		Average Shot Value Based on 40 Shots 50 Meters Slow Fire	
	No Epinephrine	Epinephrine	No Epinephrine	Epinephrine	No Epinephrine	Epinephrine
JB	.98	.85	13.92	11.28	9.00 /360	8.50 /340
SC	.53	.48	16.43	15.80	9.55 /382	9.57 /382.8
JD	.13	.15	16.08	11.29	9.05 /362	8.77 /350.8
DH	.30	.38	15.04	12.20	9.15 /366	9.17 /366.8
EX	.08	.05	7.75	10.16	9.70 /388	9.07 /362.8
RK	.75	.40	15.21	15.03	9.05 /362	8.72 /348.8
BO	.20	.18	13.32	12.05	9.60 /384	9.40 /376
RS	.08	.03	16.14	15.21	9.40 /376	8.87 /354.8
JS	.03	.08	14.96	14.17	8.92 /356.8	8.37 /334/8

Figure 9-20

During the 1981 Benito Juarez Championships in Mexico City, D. Cheetham and Dan Landers conducted study of the rapid fire shooting performance of an East German shooter named Weifel. They reported this study in 1981. It was titled, *A cinematographical analysis of rapid fire pistol shooting and running game target shooting.* In this study is a table showing the time reflecting the start of timing for the string of fire to the moment when the arm reached the shooting position(SP). In our program, we term this as being when the gun reaches eye level. Our Conditional Reflex program is designed around the rapid fire events. We find this to be the most conducive to producing the type of Conditional Reflex we are trying to build. With that in mind take a look at the timing reflected in the Cheeetham & Daniels study:

Firing Segment	8-Second Strings	6-Second Strings	4-Second Strings
Ready Position to SP	1.03	.91	.84
SP to Shot 1	.93	.68	.43
Shot 1 to Shot 2	1.21	.92	.63
Shot 2 to Shot 3	1.10	.94	.58
Shot 3 to Shot 4	1.07	.91	.56
Shot 4 to Shot 5	1.12	.91	.60
Total Time to Fire Five Shots	6.46	5.3	3.64
% of Total Time Used	80.8%	88.3%	91.0%
Shot 5 to end of Follow Through	.57	.57	.47

Figure 9-21

These results indicate what the coach and instructor using our **Conditional Reflex Evaluation Form** need to be looking for in the timing of the arm being raised from the bench or ready position to eye level. When you observe American rapid fire shooters doing a slow down of the raising of the gun to eye level during the last third of their arm raise, it is obvious that they have taught themselves something which is not borne out by research results. Compare the hold times in (**Figure 9-20**) to those in (**Figure 9-21.**) Of course, the purists will object to this comparison citing the slow fire course of fire for the hold times reflected in (**Figure 9-20**) to those in (**Figure 9-21**) which are for rapid fire. And they are correct. That is another area where we in this book advocate that all training should be the same. We do not train to shoot one way for slow fire and another way for rapid fire. We are training a Conditional Reflex. We do not try to slow it down when we shoot one course of fire as compared to another course of fire. That is just not an efficient way to train. Of course if the shooter wants to take time out for a rest between shots when the rules permit that, we find it very acceptable. What we do not advocate is changing the time of the shot from either the bench or the ready position to eye level. Nor do we advocate taking more time for one course of fire after the gun reaches eye level until the shot is fired. We want the advantage the Conditional Reflex gives shooters trained under our method.

The purpose of the Wilkinson study was to determine if the injection of epinephrine would be of value to coaches and shooters as a potential competition simulation technique. The results indicated that this was not effective with high level elite pistol shooters. The pistol shooters involved in the study ranged in age from 15 to 45 years. According to Don Hamilton, the 15 year old would have been Steve Collins, DH is Don Hamilton, RS is Ragnar Skanaker and JS is John Smith.

As the Wilkinson study tells us, what is important is that each shooter be rated individually and not against some artificial standard. Individual performance curves plotted over several weeks of practice indicate important long-term trends that can be obscured by short-term plots. One thing we do is to have the shooters plot their own performance charts. We feel this leads to increased involvement with the skills they are trying to teach themselves and sparks an even greater motivation to acquire these skills. We feel this acquistion of the associated skills of:

☛1) Placing The Barrel In Line With The Eye Within The Shooting Unit, Using The Front Sight As A Reference,

☛2) Moving The Finger To Actuate The Trigger

is promoted by the shooters' personal involvement in their training. For example, in our *Coaching 2000 Program*, when we observe that the shooter seems to be having a problem understanding something which is happening between the moving of the trigger finger and eye, we setup the camcorder.

493

Using the camcorder, we focus on the muzzle and the eye. Naturally, with this framing, the trigger finger is also in the frame. By recording a series of shots, the shooter is lulled into the sameness of the procedure and thus fires naturally. After a 10 shot series, the shooter and the coach view the video together. The shooter is allowed to discover things such as the closing of the eye just before let off or the snatching of the trigger. It is this process which demonstrates to the shooter what has to be corrected. It is imperative that these pathways be formed efficiently at the beginning.

When a piece of paper is folded, it can again be folded much more readily in the former crease. Suppose some one asks us to explain why this is the case. Very likely we shall say, here is a piece of paper which does not fold readily in any special place. We now crease it through the middle. You can see for yourselves that it will now fold readily in the middle. Of course, this is no explanation, but our failure to explain facts does not disprove their existence. We may say that there is a new molecular arrangement in the paper, and that it folds more easily because of this. Of course the next question comes promptly: Why is a new molecular arrangement better than an old for this purpose? Because this is the nature of molecules.

The illustration of the paper has been used to show that if we cannot tell why paper folds more readily where it has before been folded, we should not be surprised if we cannot fully understand the changes in the brain corresponding to the formation of habit. We may not be able to explain why practice facilitates actions, but the practice is just as efficient as if we could.

Arm Raises Sights To Eye	Start time when Pistol Arm Starts To Move Up.
	☛Stop TIME When Pistol Reaches Eye Level. ☐ Check when timing

Figure 9-22

The Conditional Reflex In Pistol Shooting

Once trained, the conditional reflex works best when it is warmed up. That is why, in training under the system we advocate, the shooter warms up from a benchrest. In our training, the pistol shooter fires from a benchrest with the objective of producing a score of 100 out of ten shots. If a shooter has never fired a score of 100 from off a benchrest, how can he know how to do it on purpose when firing one-handed? This is true whether the shooter is shooting the air pistol from 10 meters or the sport pistol from 25 meters or the free pistol from 50 meters. The conditional reflex must be developed so that this can be done very frequently from these various distances. During the firing from off the benchrest, the shooter has to continue to develop his conditional reflex. If the shooter attempts to take more time when firing off a benchrest, then he is into developing a bad habit which will interfere with his good conditional reflex. All of his training must be directed toward that one goal, the establishment of his conditional reflex.

A conditional reflex is inherently more precise than a controlled reaction to an external stimulus. Most pistol shooters are into the control business. When you control your shooting process consciously, you prevent a conditional reflex from forming. But, since most pistol shooters train to control an Arc of Movement with respect to the target, they must teach themselves to be in complete control at all points in the Act of Shooting.

Many of the pistol shooters are observed to take up to 13 to 22 seconds once the pistol reaches eye level before they are able to fire the shot. They are seen and understood to be working very hard at their effort. Understand that the authors of this book do not claim that the old pistol training system is "wrong." We do believe that the pistol training method laid out in *Successful Pistol Shooting* is a replacement for that method because our system is more efficient at doing what we want, making our pointing more precise and consistent.

We believe the term *minimum arc of movement* to be a fantasized dream phrase. Uncontrollable oscillations do not tend to settle. They tend to expand their movement. Sir Isaac Newton (1642-1727), in his *Philosophiae Naturalis Principia Mathematica* [1687], with the *First of his Laws of Motion*, noted,

495

"Every body continues in its state of rest, or of uniform motion in a straight line, unless it is compelled to change that state by forces impressed upon it." Thus, it is evident that the normal physical pattern for controlling motion of a handgun is over-control, not under-control.

About three hundred years ago, Robert Hooke looked through a microscope at some plant material. Instead of a single, much enlarged piece of plant material, he saw a group of several small pieces. They looked like miniature prison cells to him, so that is what he called them: cells. Cells are the smallest units of living matter in which basic life processes take place. At the time of Robert Hooke's discovery, he believed cells only existed in plants. It wasn't until 1858 that the cell theory united plants and animals. Rudolph Virchow, a German pathologist, is generally given credit for the theory. He was the first to state that the cell was a fundamental component of all living organisms. Cell's are the body's microscopic building blocks. The human body contains more than 50 billion cells. Cells differ somewhat in structure (shape and size) according to the role they play in the function of a living organism. Four main types of cells compose the human body: epithelial cells, connective cells, muscle cells, and nerve cells. All cells have three main parts: the cell membrane, the cytoplasm, and the nucleus. In addition there are several smaller parts. Many of which were not discovered until the invention of the electron microscope in 1930.

If brain cells are allowed to pass the plastic stage without being subjected to the proper stimuli or training, they will never fully develop. This book calls attention to the importance of early training of the central nervous system while its relatively brief period of plasticity lasts.

Pistol shooters have no more relentless enemy than motor nerve cells which have been inefficiently trained early in their shooting career. Should they desire to effect a change, they will discover, as others before them, that retraining is the most difficult training of all training we human engage in.

It has been known for some time that the higher processes of thought are dependent on modifications in brain cells. In pistol shooting, even the highest intellectual superstructure can be no firmer than the sensory foundation. Even knowing this, pistol shooters have not properly applied this information in training these cells. In pistol shooting, a practical application of research results, lags far behind a theoretical knowledge of them.

The principal object of this book is to describe for our pistol shooters, the training of the complex central nervous system necessary for their development as competitive shooters.

In the pistol shooting world, most of the training management has not yet realized the very important truth, that youthful nerve cells alone are easily modified by training. The old theory that mental training can overcome deficiencies in training methods has proven a disaster. The idea that mental training consists solely in modifications in the mind, has worked untold damage. It was and continues to be an unspoken idea that the mind never grows old, and that it can be trained as well at one time as at another. You still hear this from shooters who take up the pistol shooting competitive game well after they are into their 30's, 40's and even into their 50's. From this mistaken notion came such sayings as: *"It is never too late to be what you might have been."* It would be nearer the truth to say: *"It is always too late to be what you might have been."* With each advancing year, this becomes an absolute truth in the case of the vast majority of us who have passed the age of twenty.

It may be true, as we believe it to be, that pistol shooting training consists in developing the mind as well as mere brain cells. However, the mind, for its nutrients, is completely at the mercy of the nervous system. A well-trained nervous system is the greatest friend that the mind can have. An ill-trained nervous system is a relentless enemy to the mind. It follows its victims, many of whom are pistol shooters, and thwarts their aims until they give up in despair, believing that they do not have what it takes to become a pistol shooting champion. Very often, around pistol shooters, you hear the lament, *"The more I shoot, the worst I get!"* Most place the blame on their inner-self. It is seldom that some time in a conversation with a pistol shooter about shooting, that you do not hear the mantra, *"If I just had more time to practice and more ammunition, I would see a big improvement in my scores."*

Attention

On the physical side, we may define attention as tension in nerve cells.

In pistol shooting, it is useful to distinguish between reflex and voluntary attention. Reflex attention is given, without our seeking or volition, to certain incoming nerve stimuli of great intensity or peculiar quality. For example, the discharge of a pistol, the slamming of a door or a flash of lighting will sufficiently stimulate the auditory, visual or tactile center in the brain to cause attention even against our will. Thus, in reflex attention, there is lack of previous voluntary attention in the appropriate center. The stimulus comes when we are not looking for it.

On the other hand, take voluntary attention. In this type of attention, we are conscious of an effort to make the utmost out of something, whether it is subjective or objective. When we are looking for a special arrangement of the two reference points on the top of a pistol barrel, it is the voluntary attention centered in that direction which serves to make the eye more sensitive to that visual cue in certain brain cells in the proper area of the brain. Voluntary control of attention is fundamental to the free development of the types of consciousness best suited to a rapidly, and often unpredictably, changing situations found during any outdoor pistol match.

"Attention" is much in need of precise definition. Etymologically, *"attention"* derives from Latin "attendere", to stretch toward, which allows considerable latitude of specificity. Scientific research developments in the Western world have made detailed analysis the attentional modes. For most people today *"attention"* is nearly synonymous with *'concentration'*. The hemispheric specialization model of brain functioning, assigns this concentrative type of attention to the left hemisphere and casts the right hemisphere into the role of global awareness.

There are notable differences between the analytic, particulate, causal, linear, quantitative style of attending which we assign to the left hemisphere. The right hemisphere we label as nourishing the synoptic, Gestalt, holistic, simultaneous, qualitative style of attending.

Both ancient wisdom and modern research hold that the wrinkled brow, clenched teeth, tense muscles, high anxiety type of attention, which we identify with *"type A"* personalities, are often seen in our pistol shooting community. This attention is an eliminative, conservative, no-change mode. We often see this type of attention in pistol coaches, especially when they demonstrate the proper breathing technique. This "left hemisphere" type of attention seems essential, under the current process of pistol shooting training. However, it is not an essential element of the authors' shooting training methods. We believe that the wrinkled brow, clenched teeth, tense muscles, high anxiety type of attention is counter productive of the employment of the conditional reflex in pistol shooting.

A knowledge of the fact that attention of any kind is cor-related with expenditure of energy in nerve cells is of the utmost importance in any activity which has a learning component as a part of the process. The majority of shooters and coaches have been singularly neglectful of the physical accompaniments of at-tention. Their importance will be clear when one realizes that without these, there can be no attention of any kind. Even reflex attention will exhaust nerve energy in certain brain tracts if the stimulus is continuous, as on an active firing line. Shooters are sometimes thankful for this, although not for the increasing diffi-culty of hearing, which is the usual accompaniment of such con-tinued over-stimulation of the auditory center.

Voluntary attention makes several more demands upon the brain than reflex attention. Tense voluntary attention will fatigue the strongest brain, which will soon demand rest or a change in the direction of attention. For example, extend your arm as tensely as possible and hold it at right angles to your body. This muscular tension will soon cause weariness. In an analogous way, tension in brain cells soon exhausts their energy for a while. Just as a change of position will enable the arm to do additional work, so a change of subject, involving a different di-rection to the attention, will provide the energy for additional voluntary mental effort. Indeed, this often seems more restful than mere blankness or void of attention.

499

Not only mental effort, but work of any kind, tends to use up the stored energy in nerve cells and to bring on fatigue. Muscular activity and the ensuing fatigue are correlated much more closely with fatigue in the central nerve cells than is popularly thought. Halleck says: *"In the last stages of extreme fatigue, it is the nerve cells, not the muscles, which are exhausted."* When one lifts a weight, he starts by bracing the motor cells which flex the muscles concerned in the work. If the energy in these cells is below the average, the muscular response will also be below the average.

Those who believe in long hours for pistol shooting matches or practice work, ought to remember this observation: *"Fatigue in every shape is fatal to memory."* The impressions received under such conditions are not fixed, and the reproduction of them is very laborious and often impossible. Now, fatigue is regarded as a state wherein, owing to the over-activity of an organ, the nutrition suffers and halts. When the normal conditions are restored, muscle memory comes back again.

Cade Wilson, one of our 14 year old shooters described to me his planning which he did as he prepared to travel to Chino, California for the 1996 USA Shooting International Pistol Championships. What he did was to experiment to determine how soon unacceptable movement was introduced to his pistol while it was in the arm extended position. Using a stopwatch, he determined that the movement became unacceptable to him just before 2 seconds. In practice, he was normally timed at between 3 and 4 seconds for the firing of the shot after the gun reached eye level. Reinkemeier points out, *"When breaks in concentration occur because of excessive stress, the most effective way of dealing with them is by resting, just as with physical tiredness. After you have stopped, breathed deeply and relaxed for a few minutes, you can usually carry on again with renewed energy....The effectiveness of rest periods depends essentially on their length, frequency and how they are organized. We know from occupational psychology that several short breaks are more effective than a few longer ones."*

So, in his dryfiring practice at home, Cade determined to decrease the time for the firing of his shot once it reached eye level. At Chino, he was able to perform at this less than 2 second

500

level for his shots to the extent of winning the 1996 National Sub-Junior Air Pistol Championship with a score of 538 out of 600 points. What he did was to fire ten shots at this timing, then sit out and wait for 5 to 8 minutes before firing the next ten shots. He said it took him almost the full time to fire the whole match, but he felt more confident about his shooting and of course he knew his shots were going well into the center of the target.

A study of the physical aspects of attention is necessary. Notice the type of attention in which Cade engaged. If we notice ourselves carefully, we can often detect a distinct physical strain in attention. Cade made careful observations of the extent of his attention. He noted when his attention focus showed up in more movement of his hold. If we focus our ears to catch the first sound of a coming footstep, if we continuously follow the flight of a bird across the sky, if we pass our fingers over various fabrics to detect a difference, we are conscious of a physical tension, which, if uninterrupted, produces fatigue. When Cade noticed this occurring, he planned for rest time to allow for the attention span to recover.

It follows as a corollary from the physical basis of attention, that it cannot be held at great intensity for a long period. When his physical awareness dictated, Cade rested. There are also two classes of objects to which the strongest will cannot long sustain the attention. The first is an object which does not spark interest, either directly or indirectly. Cade discovered for himself what many persons have never learned, that no amount of compulsion can rivet the attention to such an object over extended periods of time. Many of America's elite and *"want-a-be"* pistol shooters have never learned this. They can be seen on countless firing lines, advocating to all who will listen, *"You gatta take your time, you'll do a whole lot better if you just concentrate on each shot."* They do not understand that the demands of attention over extended periods of time drain their energy, especially in the central nervous system. Reinkemeier makes the point, *"Fatigue always sets in early when parts of the body are not sufficiently accustomed to carrying out a certain action."* This means that all of the efforts of the shooters to establish habits of shooting go down the drain because of their non-awareness of the attention syndrome.

501

The second class of objects which can claim only short-lived attention are those which present one unchanging aspect. It is by no means always necessary that there should be a new object to secure the attention again. A new angle with respect to an old object is equally effective. Any one who can show an old thing in a new light, is always sure of an alert audience. Coal received little attention from men before they learned that it would burn. Then attention was at once directed toward it. So we become interested in the most common insects, flowers, and birds, as soon as a new attribute is discovered. The genius is he who shows us something new in an old thing, so that our attention is again turned toward it.

So far as we know, all energy, whether mental or physical, travels in waves. Attention, or concentration, rises and falls like the waves of the sea, and cannot remain long at the same level. For example, take a windup clock and put it where the ticking is barely heard. You will notice that periods when you can hear the sound, alternate with those when you can not. These periods exhibit wave-like characteristics. If a water faucet at a little distance is turned, the same thing will prove true. The rise and fall of attention corresponds to the periods of the sound waves. Reinkemeier points out, *"If you grip something repeatedly, the muscles gradually get tired and the grip becomes irregular after a time. For the sake of simplicity we shall regard breaks in concentration similarly as a process of fatiguing of the nerve pathways involved, and consider what measures can be used to combat this fatigue."* Cellular vibrations, or some kinds of molecular brain tension, determine this characteristic of attention.

It is matter of everyday observation that youngsters learn with wonderful ease, and that anything, such as foreign languages, which calls only for memory, is readily learned by them. We know, furthermore, that habits, which are one form of memory, are far more easily formed in childhood, in youth, than in maturity. At that period of life, so great is the activity of the nutritive process that new connections are rapidly formed. In the aged, on the contrary, a rapid effacement of new impressions coincides with a considerable decline of this activity.

These physiological and psychological facts all show that there exists between nutrition and retention the relation of cause and effect. There is exact coincidence between their periods of rise and fall. Variations short or long in the one are repeated in the other. If the one be active, or moderate, or feeble, so is the other.

Nutrition of the best kind depends on a state of antecedent fatigue. When nerve cells have been exercised, but not over-fatigued, they are then in the very best condition for receiving fresh nutriment. We sometimes see older persons, who seldom stir out of the house, pick things over at the table without eating scarcely anything, and we tell them that if they would exercise, they would have an appetite and feel more like getting up and about. Analogous advice should be given in the case of the nervous system. Pistol shooters and coaches need to know that nerve cells should be exercised to the point of reasonable fatigue, so as to be put in the proper condition for being made stronger by the nutriment which they will then be in a condition to assimilate.

Sensations exist for the specific purpose of inciting us to action, either immediate or remote. If they fail to initiate the proper action, their failure is absolute. Even in so simple a case as sitting down to dinner, if the sensations due to seeing and smelling the food on our plates do not lead to motor action, we

HOT SURFACE   **503**

would eventually starve. When our barbaric forefathers saw edible wild fruit, they plucked and ate it. A question is asked us, and the sensation of sound acts upon the motor speech region, leading to a reply to the question. We touch a hot surface, and withdraw our hands to escape serious harm. Life in an analogous way exposes good things to our sight. It is not enough for us to see them, we must act in a way best suited to get them. The man of action comes away with the prizes of life. It must not be forgotten that human actions are possible only because nerve cells are capable of undergoing certain modifications. That is the key to our conditional reflex training in pistol shooting. It is that the product of a sensation affects a motor center, and action results in terms of the original capacity and subsequent habituation of that center.

When a sensation first pours into an infant's brain, certain cells are set in action. With this action comes development of connective nerve fibers. Motor connections are thus developed and rendered stable.

In our world, it takes motion to produce anything. Thus, we can see the importance of motor ideas. Unfortunately the world contains a class of people, whose activity in their sensory tracts is not paralleled by action in their motor cells. A sensation may evaporate from the brain without causing the proper action, just as rich land may exist and be further fertilized by showers and yet produce no crops of value. The motor element involves effort and this is not always present.

A glance around us is nearly certain to discover some persons of marked deficiency in the world of action. They may like to learn and to continue absorbing knowledge, but they never make any worthy use of it. A visit to the reading rooms of any library will enable us to find chronic sponge-like absorbers of whatever is written. Their very faces come to have a dreamy relaxed expression. These persons generally fancy that they are *going to do* something soon. But, instead, the motor paralysis becomes more and more complete. Sometimes boys are allowed to bury themselves in book after book, until action becomes extremely irksome to them. They love to absorb ideas and to direct all their motor energy into dreaming or castle-building. In the case of the majority of people, motor action needs to be cultivated, and to be directed to definite ends. It is not enough for one to form an idea of becoming a great pistol shooter; he must do things to make himself great. So, too, in pistol training, the youngsters involved in the program must be given the idea that their training could lead to a possible Olympic medal.

Suggestion has much power in arousing the central nervous system to action. One of the best practical rules that we can formulate for developing the motor tendency in the central nervous system is this, bring suggestion of the proper kind to the attention of the youngsters involved in any pistol training program.

So few people have a really clear idea of what suggestion is, that we must explain just what we mean. When a train of sensations, ideas, or thoughts, in short, when any mental thought, is suddenly interrupted by any object or idea, with strong motor qualities, this new object or idea is specially situated to develop action in its direction. This definition, like all others, requires concrete illustrations to make it plain. An infant's eyes will follow a ball rolling across the floor, although they will speedily lose the ball when at rest. A child playing in a park will chase a butterfly flitting by. In these cases, sense objects in motion broke in upon the child's mental train, and suggested movement of eye or of the entire body in their direction. A part of this movement was of course reflex, but we must remember that reflex movement in nerve cells lies at the basis of every higher act of will. A sensory stimulus pours into a nerve cell, is reflected outward along a motor nerve, and movement results. The Act of Shooting will have deliberation, choice, and inhibition added to these foundation reflexes.

One reaction to stimulus modifies the nerve matter. Repeated reactions, such as bringing the pistol to eye level and moving the trigger finger instantaneously smooth, cultivate new paths in this matter, or change its manner of responding to normal stimuli.

The acquisition of efficient shooting habits is the most important result of motor training. Shooting habit is the process of associating a definite muscular action with a sense impression. In this case, the aligned sights arriving at the pre-selected target area. If a youngster is properly trained, his motor response to the conditional stimulus will be unerring. Such a youngster will not stop with a sensation or with an idea, which amounts to nothing when divorced from action. He will act in the efficient way every time. To show more definitely what we mean by a uniform motor reaction to a sensation in order to form a habit, let us show how the habit of putting things in their places is formed. A child should first be taught that the sensation due to seeing a thing out of its place must be followed by the action necessary to put the article in its place. The sensation must so often be associated with the action, that the one shall flow automatically into the other. There must be at once one definite action resulting from the sensation. This is habit. When a good railroad engineer sees a red light on the track before him, the sensation immediately flows into the motor cells governing his arm, and the throttle valve is closed. There is no hesitation, no thought of an alternative course of action. It is a very fast action. So it is with trigger control, Blankenship describes this process,

> *"Because this pressure is constantly increasing it is very fast. There is no hesitation in this type of trigger control unless the weapon moves suddenly away from the black area of the target such as when a gust of wind moves the arm suddenly. This system takes a great deal of practice to perfect it enough for it to be effective, but it certainly has done wonders for my scores. Do not misunderstand the phrase, "positive pressure." This does not mean sudden movements on the trigger. This is why the people who use the system of slowly squeezing the trigger have a lot of trouble. In reality they try to squeeze the trigger only when the sights are perfectly aligned and when this perfect sight alignment is sitting **exactly** under the bullseye. When everything is perfect they squeeze, but as soon as anything moves they quit squeezing or hesitate until everything is perfect again to squeeze a little more. These people have a lot*

> *of trouble because of jerks, flinches, heeling,*
> *etc., all of which are the result of*
> *anticipation. Using this system they try to*
> *know exactly when the gun is going to fire.*
> *This is what causes anticipation of one sort*
> *or another.*
>
> *The best way to think about trigger*
> *control is that you are going to squeeze the*
> *trigger as soon as the weapon settles and*
> *you have the sights aligned. While you are*
> *applying pressure on the trigger you*
> *concentrate on keeping the sights aligned*
> *until the hammer falls, firing the weapon.*
> *Perfect sight alignment is wasted if you*
> *disturb the firearm just as the hammer falls. "*
>
> (*The Pistol Shooter's Treasury* edited by Gil
> Hebard).

The way to spoil either a child or a young dog, is to allow it to react to a certain sensation one way today and another way tomorrow. Such a child may put a thing where it can be found, occasionally, but no dependence can be placed upon him. A pointer will be worthless as a hunting dog, if he is allowed to point at the game sometimes, and at others to bark or to rush on it. You do the same thing to your trigger finger movement if you do it one way one time and another way the next time. You cannot allow your trigger finger to react to a certain sensation one way today and another way tomorrow. The training you do to get your finger to move automatically when the sights are aligned at the area you want, has to be practiced time and time again. As Blankenship has pointed out, *"when you're practicing squeezing the trigger, concentrate on just the trigger to make the movement as smooth as possible and also as fast as you can without causing any movement of the sight alignment or the gun."* (*The Pistol Shooter's Treasury* edited by Gil Hebard). So, if you move your finger a different way during a match, then your practice training has been wasted. Or perhaps you have a good adult shooter come up to you and say, *"Mortimer, if you will just slow down you'll do a whole lot better."* Instead of slowing down, which is often equated with

507

becoming more hesitant, we believe it to be more efficient for you to take Blankenship's advice, *"I tried to see how fast I could squeeze the trigger and not disturb the weapon."* (*The Pistol Shooter's Treasury* edited by Gil Hebard).

From another point of view we may define habit as motor modifications in nerve matter, which have become stable through the repetition of actions. Blankenship notes, *"Trigger control can become a habit. By this I mean when the sights are aligned and the weapon is almost still, the trigger finger reacts automatically to make the weapon fire."* (*The Pistol Shooter's Treasury* edited by Gil Hebard).   During the time he was in his championship winning form, he had very deliberately made motor modifications in nerve matter. This repetition ensures that the actions will be more easily performed. There is at first friction between sensory and motor nerve cells and this must be decreased. That is why, when we start a youngster in our pistol training program, we suggest that he or she put about three inches of water, or sand, in a gallon milk jug. Then hold it at 45° and lift it so the top of the jug is at eye level. The youngster is then advised to perform a number of repetitions of that lifting process during the day.

From the broadest point of view, memory is habit. In memory the nerve cells are again acting in a way in which they have acted before. So, each repeated action the shooter makes, deepens the tendency to act again in the same way. This is the reason why we remember most easily things or acts which have been most often performed. Thus, we never forget the alphabet or how to walk, so long as our nervous system is not diseased.

Precisely what happens in the central nervous system when habits are formed? Understand that the human nervous system detects changes inside and outside of the body and responds to them. The central nervous system analyzes information and institutes responses. The peripheral nervous system gathers information and sends it to the brain. The brain then issues it's response. Consider what happens when you are gesturing and talking, with one of your hands near a lighted candle. The back of your hand comes to a brief rest directly over the candle. A reflex occurs, as the skin becomes aware of the burning sensation. A sensory receptor sends a message via a sensor fiber to the spinal cord. This triggers a signal which travels via a motor fiber

508

back to a muscle. This causes the muscle to contract drawing the hand away from the hot object. At the same time a message is sent to the brain which initiates, in this case, a vocal reaction. That is why there is an almost simultaneous response of the withdrawal of the hand and the emission of the yowl of pain from the mouth. That is why we are able to train our trigger finger to respond to the stimulus of the sights being lined up the way we want them and then for the trigger finger to move automatically, as Blankenship observed as he was training it.

So, what first has to happen, is that a new path has to be established in nervous matter, so that a motor discharge proceeds more directly and more easily from one cell to another associated one. It sometimes happens that when we wish to go from one place to another, the airplane proceeds only in a roundabout way. At a certain airport hub, we must wait and change planes. Suppose, however, that a new air route is opened up between the two places and that no change of planes is necessary. The trip can now be made much more quickly and easier than before. That is what we are doing when we train our trigger finger to re-act to the conditional stimulus of the eye sending information that the aligned sights have arrived at the pre-selected target area. When we have had little repeated activity of the efficient sort in doing a certain thing, we are like the person who travels two sides of a right-angled triangle, the base and the perpendicular, instead of going by way of the hypotenuse. Habit of the efficient kind discovers that any two sides of a triangle are together greater than the third side, and travels by the shortest path. That is what we are doing in developing the conditional reflex in our shooting training.

Secondly, there may be no new path formed in nerve matter because of repeated actions which lead to habit. For example, consider a new lock which is opened with difficulty. Although no new path is formed in which the lock slides back and forth, it is yet locked and unlocked more easily with use. The rough points in the old path are worn away so that there is less friction. It may be that repeated dynamic associations between cells clear out the path and reduce friction. A current of water in a stream may at last wear its bed smooth, so that the water may flow on more rapidly because there is less friction from projecting

509

particles. For example, we have noticed that in training our youngsters to this conditional reflex movement, that their time at eye level is decreased as their training progresses.

We may gain another view of habit by considering it as organic memory. In strictest truth, all habit is memory. It is acting again in a way in which we have acted before. This organic memory may or may not be accompanied with consciousness. The organic memory of walking remains with us.

When we are talking, we are looked on with pity if we have to center our attention on the pronunciation and grammar, and thereby subtract so much from our thinking power.

All actions, in short, depend on proper motor modifications in the central nervous system. The same is true of expertness in any muscular movements, whether in moving the vocal chords so as to speak a foreign language correctly, or in fingering the piano.

For the formation of habits, there must be repetition of dynamic associations between nerve cells early in life. Remember, the size of the brain and the number of its cells make far less difference than the way they are associated. Good roads and easy means of communication between different parts of our country, contributed in a great measure and were essential to its prosperity. The same analogy holds true of the brain.

Organic memory supposes not only a modification of the nerve elements, but also the *establishment between them of associations adapted to each special action* of certain dynamic associations which by repetition become as stable as the primary anatomical connections. In our opinion the thing that is of importance, as supplying a basis for memory, is not only the modification impressed upon each element, but the way in which various elements are grouped together to form a complex.

A rich and well-stored memory is not a collection of impressions, but an assemblage of dynamic associations, very stable and very readily called forth.

All living substance, especially nerve matter, has the peculiarity in that every irritation produced in a limited region at once spreads to the adjoining parts. It continues spreading as long as it meets with any substance which is capable of being similarly irritated, and which, so to speak, responds to such irritation.

If the virgin substance of the brain is excited and internally agitated by an irritation which has been transmitted through the nerve fibers of the sensory organs, an increased ability to reproduce the same kind of irritation is acquired by a permanent change of its internal structure. When you train the eye to an awareness of the location you want your sights to be on the target when you want your trigger finger to move, that is the irritant you are training. If the sensory nerve again transmits the same irritation, the cerebral substance responds to it more easily. As pistol shooting coaches, we must set up training methods which ensure the early acquisition of the conditional reflex in our shooters.

Habit is a bundle of memories or tendencies to act again in a way in which we have acted before. That is what Blankenship took some three months to train in 1959. Herein lies the tremendous importance of early actions. Their results do not end with the setting sun; they are as imperishable as ourselves. Today a man does something which he determined to do on purpose ten, twenty, thirty, or forty years ago. I recall 40 years ago deciding to begin eating with my left hand. I imagined that this would give me greater control for shooting the rifle in the standing position. It may be that I would gladly have left the deed undone, but the time to have reflected on the undesirability of such an action was not when it was last committed, but at its first occurrence, perhaps forty years before. That is why we say that habits in shooting training are formed at the firing of the first shot. We begin all pistol training firing from a bench rest. In our training, the idea of the importance of the first shot, is such an important concept, that we halt the firing and go down range and point out to the shooter just where the first shot landed on the paper. If it did not make a hole in the paper, we take immediate corrective action. Under our system, there are only two possibilities. For one thing, the shooter's eye may have closed at the moment of truth, the instant the shot is fired. Or, the shooter may have snatched at the trigger. In either of these two possibilities, the desired pointing was destroyed by the action. That one action started the nerve tract to act with greater ease in the same way again. By repeated motor responses in certain ways, the shooter molds his nervous system so that it will continue to react in the same way. At the start he may be the master; at the end he will be the slave. It will be well if he is the slave of an efficient master. If his automatic responses are inefficient, he is also stuck with them and there will be little he can do with them. Retraining is the most difficult training of all.

When training young shooters, coaches should understand that they should not fault themselves for not making the shooters grasp the complexities of the conditional reflex. Those youngsters are specially fortunate who are compelled to acquire certain proper motor reactions before the reasons for them are understood. Such young shooters will find out later that they have a wonderful mechanism properly fashioned to their hand. The sooner the idea is exploded that a young shooter should not be taught to shoot the pistol competitively until he can see the why and wherefore of things, the better it will be for the pistol shooting world. It is only when we stop deluging our beginning shooters with **all the good stuff** that progress occurs. Some very top flight pistol shooters adamantly believe that new shooters ought not to be introduced to the concept of the conditional reflex until they are well along in their shooting. This a myth which probably should have been mentioned in Chapter 3. We have found the very opposite to be true. This is another example of our favorite truism:

> *It ain't what ya don't know what hurts ya,*
> *It's what ya know what ain't so!*

Our research demonstrates the validity of starting the new shooter, right from scratch knowing he or she is developing the trigger finger as a conditional reflex. Or as Yev'yev, in his book, *Competitive Shooting,* points out *"The basic pattern in the development of a motor skill, as we mentioned before, is the formation of new conditioned reflex connection in the central nervous system. In learning the technique for completing a specific action, a person repeatedly performs a series of motions which comprise the entire action. When, by constant repetition, the connections between those motions are reinforced, it becomes possible to complete the entire action in sequence since all parts of the action enter into interconnections with each other, resulting in*

512

the formation of a dynamic stereotype-acomplex balanced system of cortical process." We want the shooter to be absolutely aware of what he or she is doing during their pistol shooting training. They may not need to fully comprehend the theoretical basis for the pistol training, but they must be doing what they are doing very deliberately.

If motor training in its initial stages were to depend on the thinking power of the individual undergoing the training, there would be little progress made until the nervous system had in great part lost its plasticity. Many persons would receive scarcely any training, were it not for the fact that their nervous systems are compelled to undergo motor modifications by intelligent parents. There are hourly illustrations of this. The parent makes the child say *"he sits down"* in place of he sets down, the sun sets in place of *the sun sits*. The child may not understand why he should use *sit* and *set,* both intransitively, but he grows up as correct a speaker as if he could explain the inexplicable. He is not compelled to think which form is correct; he can be thinking about something else, while the motor reactions of speech are habitually right. No person can think about two different things at the same time with equal concentration, and our thinking hours during each day are limited. So, imagine how the beginning shooter feels when he is told he has to think about five or six or sixty-one things at the same time in order to fire one accurate shot.

Shooters can see the importance of becoming a motor automaton in certain directions early in life, so that thought can be occupied with other concerns. When we began to walk, the whole power of conscious would have been necessary to direct the movements. We could not have thought about anything else at the time. When the child first tries to form a letter of the alphabet, his whole power is expended in controlling the muscles. If a writer lived until the age of forty without learning how to write, it would be some time before he could form the letters and think of fitting ideas to be expressed at the same time. When writing comes to be largely the result of an automatic discharge of motor cells, one can center almost his entire attention on the thought while writing at great speed. This is what Blankenship did as he purposely tried to make his trigger finger movement

513

into an automatic, subconscious habit, keyed by seeing his perfect sight alignment arrive at the target area he wanted. He then could focus his full attention on his aligned sights.

Bear in mind that, *"Any movement that has become altogether habitual is made instinctively. An impulse of will is, of course, necessary at the outset; but its effect extends to a whole series of actions, and each particular one takes place without effort and without knowledge: the series once started is continued to its end with the same unconscious certainty. In purposeness is the reflex. The voluntary movements of early childhood are uncertain and awkward; practice has not had time to transform them into instinctive acts. And the same is true of the adult whenever he wishes to perform some as yet unaccustomed action, of however simple a character. Precision and grace of movement, then, depend upon certainty of instinct, not upon firmness of will."* Halleck

It is apparent that the simplest conditions of instinctive action in general are to be found in the cases where it is the result of individual practice. In our pistol shooting training, the instinctive action has been induced by movements often repeated in the past. The performance of the definite complex act of moving a trigger finger and its connection with an adequate sense stimulus have become more and more matters of course, till at last they are rendered completely mechanical. The sense stimulus is the visualization of the sights lined up perfectly with the eye and located in the pre-selected area of the target.

The effect of **practice** and of **habit** can only be due to after effects of excitation, of the kind assumed by us for the explanation of instinctive movements. And, since the expressions of instinct are, customary or habitual actions, their subjection to the control of the general law of practice needs no justification. That law runs as follows:

⇒ the more frequently a voluntary action is repeated
⇒ the easier it is to perform
⇒ and the greater is the tendency of its constituents
⇒ (if it is a complex act)
⇒ to take on the reflex form
⇒ that is, to arrange themselves in a connected series of movements
⇒ which runs on mechanically

514

$\Rightarrow$ **when once initiated by an adequate stimulus.**

The formulation of this law shows us at once that its basis must be physiological. The goal attained by the process of practice is simply the mechanization of movements which were originally dependent upon mental antecedents. That must mean that mechanical, that is, physiological, alterations of the nervous system are at the bottom of the whole matter. There is hardly any movement of the human body, however difficult, which we cannot, by continued practice and repetition, reduce to a mechanical certainty so complete that it will be performed, even without any intention on our part, as the necessary reaction to certain sense-stimuli.

So, it is the conclusion of the authors, that even a most complex series of actions, which essentially depends on guiding perceptions, may be performed by the automatic mechanism, without any other voluntary action than that which starts it when once this mechanism has been developed by the *habitual exercise* originally imposed on the nerve centers by the will. And further, it shows that this mechanism, having been originally so shaped *at* an early period of life, is kept up by nutritive action, even though not called into use; just as the traces of our early mental acquirements are persistently retained in our organism long after we have lost the conscious memory of them.

A study of motor reactions and their resulting habituation's shows us why pistol shooting training should consist largely in doing. The act of doing results in changed physiological disposition. It is of little use for one to be told, or to read, how pistol shooting is done, unless he follows this with the appropriate actions. Telling one how to ride a bicycle, develop a photo negative, tie a knot, perform a chemical experiment, or clean a Ruger .22/45 pistol, is of very little use. But if, for example the shooter, under the proper guidance, is made to perform the necessary actions, he is on the only efficient road leading to the desired result. There was once a boy scout shown how to tie a flat knot and a bowline knot. Instead of making him take the rope and perform the complex movements under guidance, the instructor did all the tying himself. As a result, the person, as an adult, cannot today tie a bowline knot.

515

A rectangle enclosing the shooter's shot group means more to the shooter after he has drawn it, and still more after he has actually measured the area of the shot group within the rectangle. Young shooters will absorb only so much of spoken or written material as they can interpret in terms of their own *active* experience.

Action is the keynote to habit and character. If a shooter wants to built a habit in a given direction, he has to act in that direction. If one wishes a garment or a piece of paper folded in a certain way, he must be sure to see that the first folds are made in the proper way. Anyone can soon demonstrate how well the nervous system is adapted for the formation of habits and how hard it is to overcome the effects of previous action. Give a youngster a pack of cards to sort by suits. Have him put hearts well over to the right side of the table, clubs to the left, the other suits at well separated intervals. Take accurate note of the time it takes to sort the pack. Gather the cards up and shuffle them as before, then have the youngster place clubs to the right, hearts to the left, and the other suits out of their former places. He will now be a much longer time in sorting the pack. The reason for this shows how speedily a tendency toward habit is formed. The sight of hearts had been associated with a muscular movement to the right, and during the second sorting the muscles will tend to move in the direction required for the first sorting. The inhibition of this movement and then turning it in the proper direction takes additional time. Shooters, in so far as possible, ought to do a thing at first as it will be required to be done for all future times. To save such a thing for teaching in an *advanced pistol training clinic, camp or school* is a crime against the shooter. If it is important, it should be taught at the firing of the first shot.

Above all, we must guard against ideas which do not result in action. The idea exists only as a prompter to action, immediate or remote. If the idea is of the efficient kind, the action need not be feared. Pistol shooters spend a lot of effort chasing gadgets. When the USSR went capitalistic, one item which became available in quantity was a small spy-scope. It measures about 2 inches in length. Some pistol shooters attached the scope to the bill of their baseball caps seeking a clearer picture of the sights.

516

Then again, a true pistol shooter wants to find out just what it is that the champions are doing to achieve their results. Many adopt the *monkey see, monkey do* attitude. Often they make superficial judgments as to the effectiveness of what they observe. More often than not, this occurs because they do not have a firm understanding of what shooting is all about. They fall into the trap of talking about platform, thinking they are talking about shooting. They will talk about someone who has outstanding results and sometimes even speculate that they must be using a conditional reflex. Often this speculation ends with the vocal speculation. The problem is, they have not figured out why it would be more efficient to teach themselves to use an effective conditional reflex. Instead many pistol shooters fall back on the idea that *if I just had more time to practice and more money to buy more ammunition with, I could be an Olympic champion.* The great danger from castle building and chronic novel-reading lies in divorcing ideas from action. The dreamer accustoms himself to become incapable of action. In the proper scheme of pistol training every sensation and resulting idea should be made to have a bearing on action. Some valedictorians have amounted to little in the outside world because their ideas did not lead to action.

Hickey often points out a motto he adopted some thirty years ago:

Some men see things
as they are
and say, why?

I dream things
that never were
and say why not?

Robert Kennedy

Quick Summary

The type of pistol shooting training we advocate in *Successful Pistol Shooting* is shooter driven. The purpose of our pistol training is the creation of a dependency between what the eye reports to the brain about the location of the handgun sights with respect to a pre-selected area on a target. We want to merely ensure that the contacts between behavior and environment do not vary, and that the behavior to be modified is determined by the pistol shooter rather than by chance.

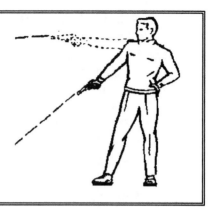

**Sources
of
Successful
Pistol
Shooting**

This chapter is a documentation of those aspects of recent research into areas that buttress our new philosophy of shooting. Please be aware that the authors of this book do not claim their new philosophy of shooting is more correct than the old philosophy. Many of the citations deal with research into personality characteristics, the development of conditioned reflexes and mental training.

The coaching techniques and training methods evolved from this research, work most efficiently when used with the new shooting philosophy developed in this book. Unless the shooting program is based on the Sievers Simplified Pistol Shooting Method, the results obtained can only be random. Remember, any method of operation that encourages the shooter to actively try to control his Act of Shooting process through use of an Arc of Movement, prevents the early development of a conditional reflex in pistol shooting.

In Bob Hickey's earlier book, *Mental Training*, he pointed out that he felt it was instructive to mention where ideas originate. That is one of the purposes of this chapter. The authors of this book have quoted in great detail from those articles not likely to be readily available in local library retrieval systems. We have done this in an effort to accurately illustrate the thoughts of the authors of the articles. On the other hand, for those books and articles readily at hand in the commercial mar-

519

ketplace, or likely to be obtainable in local libraries, we have often merely cited the book or article.

We have listed those works which we could identify as having had an influence on our thoughts and ideas.

We merely claim that our research has demonstrated to us, that this Conditional Reflex methodolgy is a much more efficient philosophy of pistol shooting. This book is not an effort at conversion. It is a delineation of a different way of looking at pistol shooting. The authors maintain that if you are happy with the results you are obtaining with your present philosophy of pistol shooting, then of course stick with it. We make no claim that the philosophy we lay out in this book is more *right* or *correct* than that available in the public domain. We do find it to be more efficient than the old way of thinking about pistol shooting. If another, more efficient, philosophy is discovered by the authors, we have no problem with adopting it.

1996 USA Shooting Media Guide (1996). *Sports Graphics*, Colorado Springs, CO.

Aaro, L.E., Bruland, E., Hauknes, A. & Lochsen, P.M. (1983) *Smoking among Norwegian schoolchildren 1975-1980. III. The effect of antismoking campaign. Scandinavian Journal of Psychology, 24,* 277-283.

⇒ & Wold, B., Kannas, L. Rimpela, M. (1986). *Health behaviour in schoolchildren.* A WHO cross-national survey. *Health Promotion, 1,* 17-33.

Aastryan, D.G., & Fel'dman, A.G. (1965). *Biophysics of complex systems and mathematical models. Functional tuning of nervous systems with control of movement or maintenance of a steady posture.. Mechanographic analysis of the work of the joint on exectuion of a postural task. Biophysics, 10,* 925-935.

Abernethy, B. & Russell, D.G. (1987a). *Expert-novice differences in an applied selective attention task. Journal of Sport Psychology, 9,* 326-345.

⇒ & (1987b). Russell, D.G. *The relationship between expertise and visual search strategy in a racquet sport. Human Movement Science, 6,* 283-319.

⇒ (1987). *Selective attention in fast ball sports II. Expert-novice differences, Australian Journal of Science and Medicine in Sport. 19,* 3-16.

⇒ (1988). *Dual-task methodology and motor skills research: Some applications and methodological constraints. Journal of Human Movement Studies, 14,* 101-132.

⇒ (1988). *Visual search in sport and ergomonics: Its relationship to selective attention and performed expertise. Human Performance, 1,* 205-235.

⇒ (1989). *Expert-novice differences in perception: How expert does the expert have to be? Canadian Journal of Sport Sciences, 14,* 27-30.

Abrami, P. & D'Appollonia (1990). *The dimensionality of ratings and their use in personnel decisions.* In Theall, M. & Franklin, J. (Eds.), ***Student ratings of instruction: Issues for improving practice,*** 97-111. San Francisco, CA: Jossey-Bass Inc.

Abramson, L.Y., Seligman, M.E.P. & Teasdale, J.D. (1978). *Learned helplessness in humans: Critique and reformulation. Journal of Abnormal Psychology, 87,* 49-74.

Adams, J.A. & Bray, S.W. (1970). *A closed-loop theory of paired associate verbal learning. Psychological Review, 77,* 385-405.

⇒ & Creamer, L.R. (1962*). Anticipatory timing of continuous and discrete responses. Journal of Experimental Psychology, 63,* 84-90.

⇒ & Dijkstra, S. (1966). *Short-term memory for motor responses. Journal of Experimental Psychology, 71,* 314-318.

⇒ & Goetz, E.T. (1973). Feedback and practice as variables in error detection and correction. *Journal of Motor Behavior, 5,* 217-224.

⇒ & Hufford, L.E. (1962). *Contributions of a part-task trainer to the learning and relearning of a time-shared flight maneuver. Human Factors, 4,* 159-170.

⇒ & Reynolds, F. (1954). *Effect of shift in distribution of practice conditions following interpolated rest. Journal of Experimental Psychology, 47,* 32-36.

⇒ (1952). *Warm-up decrement in performance on the pursuit rotor. American Journal of Psychology, 65,* 404-414.

⇒ (1955). *A source of decrement in psychomotor performance. Journal of Experimental Psychology, 49,* 390-394.

⇒ (1956). *An evaluation of test items measuring motor abilities.* Research Report AFPTRC-TN-56-55. Lackland Air Force Base.

⇒ (1959). *The second facet of forgetting: A review of warm-up decrement. Psychological Bulletin, 58,* 257-273.

⇒ (1964). *Motor Skills. Annual Review of Psychology, 15,* 181-202.

⇒ (1966). *Some mechanisms of motor responding: An examination of attention.* In Bilodeau, E.A. (Ed.), ***Acquisition of skill.*** New York: Academic Press.

⇒ *(*1967). ***Human Memory.*** New York: McGraw-Hill.

⇒ (1968). *Response feedback and learning. Psychological Bulletin, 70,* 486-504.

⇒ (1969). *Motor Behavior.* Section VII in M.H. Marx (Ed.), ***Learning processes.*** London: MacMillan.

⇒ (1971). *A closed-loop theory of motor learning. Journal of Motor Behavior, 3,* 111-150.

⇒ (1976a). *Learning and Memory: An introduction.* Homewood, IL.: Dorsey.

⇒ (1976b). Issues for a closed-loop theory of motor learning. In G.E. Stelmach (Ed.), *Motor control: Issues and Trends.* New York: Academic Press.

⇒ (1977). *Feedback theory of how joint receptors regulate the timing and positioning of a limb. Psychological Review, 84,* 504-523.

⇒ (1978). *Theoretical issues for knowledge of results.* In G.E. Stelmach (Ed.), *Information processing in motor control and learning.* New York: Academic Press.

⇒ (1987). *Historical review and appraisal of research on the learning, retention and transfer of human motor skills. Psychological Bulletin, 101,* 41-74.

⇒ & Goetz, E.T., & Marshall, P.H. (1972). *Response feedback and motor learning. Journal of Experimental Psychology,* 391-397.

Adams, W. (1990). *Foundations of physical education, exercise, and sport sciences.* Philadelphia: Lea & Febiger.

Adlercreutz, H, Harkonen, M., Kuoppasalmi, K., Naveri, H., Huhtaniemi, I., Tikkanen, H., Remes, K., Dessypris, A. & Karvonen, J. (1986). *Effect of training on plasma anabolic and catabolic steroid hormones and their response during exercise. International Journal of Sports Medicine,* 7 (Suppl.), 27-28.

Aicher, Hans, *UIT Journal* (1/82). *Italian Sport Pistols,* 10-17.

Aiken, L.R. (1964). *Reaction time and the expectancy hypothesis. Perceptual and Motor Skills, 19,* 655-661.

Air Gun Safety Program. North Palm Beach, FL. National Police Athletic League.

Alderman, R.B. (1978). *Strategies for motivating young athletes.* In Straub W.F. (Ed.), *Sport psychology: An analysis of athletic behavior,* 136-148. Ithaca, NY: Mouvement.

⇒ & Wood, N.I. (1976). *An analysis of incentive motivation in young Canadian athletes. Canadian Journal of Applied Sport Science, 1,* 169-176.

Alexander, Leo. (1992). *Conditional reflexes as related to hypnosis and hypnotic technique.* Tufts U Medical School, MA, *Integrative Physiological & Behavioral Science.* Vol 27(4) 371

Alkire, M. (edited by). (1977). *Schiessportschule Dialogues I.* United States Women's International Rifle Organization. Tempe, AZ.: Reliable Reproductions, Inc.

Allard, F. & Burnett, N. (1985). *Skill in sport. Canadian Journal ol Psychology, 39,* 294-312.

⇒ & Starkes, J.L. (1980). *Perception in sport: Volleyball. Journal of Sport Psychology, 2,* 22-33.

⇒ (1980). *Perception and sport skill Coaching Science Update,* 52-55.

⇒ Graham, S. & Paarsalu, M.E. (1980). *Perception in sport: Basketball. Journal of Sport Psychology, 2,* 14-21.

Alloy, L.B., Peterson, C.R., Abramson, L.Y. & Seligman, M.E.P. (1984). *Attributional style and generality of learned helplessness. Journal of Personality and Social Psychology, 46,* 681-687.

Allport, D.A., Antonis, B. & Reynolds, P. (1972). *On the division of attention: A disproof of the single channel hypothesis. Quarterly Journal of Experimental Psychology, 24,* 225-235.

Allred, K.D., & Smith, T.W. (1989). *The hardy personality: Cognitive and physiological responses to evaluate threat. Journal of Personality & Social Psychology, 56. 257-266.*

Alter, J. (8/25/1995). *Cal Ripken and the American work ethic.* Gannett Newspaper: USA Weekend, Tucson Citizen.

Alvermann, D.E. et.el. (9/1996). *Middle- and High-School Students' Perceptions of How They Experience Text-Based Discussions: A Multicase Study. Microsoft Internet Explorer.*

American College of Sport Medicine. (1978). *Position statement: The recommended quality of exercise for developing and maintaining fitness in healthy adults. Medicine and Science in Sport, 10,* 3, 7-10, VII-X.

Ames, C. (1984). *Achievement attributions and self-instruction under competitive and individual goal structures. Journal of Educational Psychology, 76,* 478-487.

⇒ (1984). *Competitive, cooperative, and individualistic goal structures: A cognitive-motivational analysis.* In R. Ames & C. Ames (Eds.), *Research on motivation in education: Vol. 1. Student movitation,* 177-208. New York: Academic Press.

⇒ (1984a). *Conceptions of motivation within competitive and non-competitive goal structure.* In R. Schwarzer (Ed.), *Self-related cognitions in anxiety and motivation,* 229-246 Hillsdale, NJ.

⇒ & Archer, J. (1988). *Achievement goals in the classroom: Student's learning strategies and motivation processes. Journal of Educational Psychology, 80,* 260-267.

⇒ (1992). *Achievement goals, motivational climate, and motivational processes.* In G.C. Roberts (Eds.), *Motivation in sport and exercise,* 161-176. Champaign, IL: Human Kinetics

Ames, L.B., Ph.D., M.D. & Baker, S.M., M.D. (1988). *Your Ten-To Fourteen-Year-Old.* New York: Delacorte Press.

Ammons, R.B. (1951). *Effects of pre-practice activities on rotary pursuit performance. Journal of Experimental Psychology, 41,* 187-191.

Anastasi, A. (1976). *Psychological Testing, Fourth Edition.* New York, N.Y.: MacMillan Publishing Co., Inc.

Anderson, Gary L. (1972). *Marksmanship.* New York, N.Y.: Simon and Schuster.

⇒ *UIT Journal,* (2/96). *XV Benito Juarez - Comments of the New Finals,* 56.

Anderson, J.R. (1982). *Acquisition of cognitive skill. Psychological Review, 89,* 386-406.

⇒ (1985). *Cognitive psychology and its implications.* New York: Freeman.

⇒ (1987). *Skill acquisition: Compilation of weak-method problem so-lutions. Psychological Review 94*, 192-210.

Andreassi, J.L. (1980). ***Psychophysiology, Human Behavior and Physiological Response***. New York: Oxford University Press.

Andreev, A.A. (1924). *Observations upon the functions of the senile central nerv-ous system*. **Collected Papers, Physiol. Labs. I.P. Pavlov**, *vol. i.* No. 1.

Andrew, A.M. (1995). ***The Decade of the Brain - Some comments***. *MCB* Univer-sity Press.

Angel, R.W. & Higgins, J.R. (1969). *Correction of false moves in pursuit tracking. Journal of Experimental Psychology, 82*, 185-187.

⇒ (1977). *Antagonist muscle activity during rapid movements: Central versus proprioceptive influences. Journal of Neurology, Neurosur-gery, and Psychiatry, 40*, 683-686.

Anger, D. (1956). *The dependence of interresponse times upon the relative rein-forcement of different interresponse times. Journal of Experimental Psy-chology, 52*, 145-161. Reprinted in Catania (1968), 101-112.

⇒ (1963). *The role of temporal discriminations in the reinforcement of Sidman avoidance behaviour. Journal of tbe Experimental Analysis of Behavior, 6*, 477-506.

Anrep, G.V. (1917). *A static state of irradiation of excitation. Archive of Biol. Sciences, xx.* No. 4.

⇒ (1917). *Interaction between two different types of internal inhibi-tion. Archive of Biol. Sciences, xx.* No. 4.

⇒ (1917). *Irradiation of conditioned inhibition Russian Jour. Physiol. vol. i.* Nos. 1-2.

⇒ (1923). *Irradiation of conditioned reflexes. Proc. Royal Soc. vol. B.* 93.

Anshel, M.H. & Singer, R.N. (1980). *Effect of learner strategies with modular versus traditional instruction on motor skill learning and retention. Re-search Quarterly for Exercise and Sport, 51*, 451-462.

Appel, J.B. (1963a). *Aversive aspects of a schedule of positive reinforcement. Journal of the Experimental Analysis of Behavior, 6*, 423-428.

Archangelsky, V.M. (1922). *Contributions to the physiology of the motor ana-lyser.* ***Archive of Biol. Sciences***, *vol. xxii.* No. 1.

⇒ (1924). *Comparative intensities of different types of internal inhibi-tion.* **Collected Papers of Physiol. Lab. of I.P. Pavlov**, *vol. i.* No. 1.

Archer, E.J., Kent, G.W. & Mote, F.A. (1956). *Effect of long-term practice and time-on-target information feedback on a complex tracking task. Journal of Experimental Psychology, 51*, 103-112.

Archer, J. (1984). *Gender roles as developmental pathways. British Journal of Social Psychology, 23*, 245-265.

Ardrey, R. (1970). ***The Social Contract***. London: Collins.

Argyle, M. (1967). ***The Psychology of Interpersonal Behaviour***. Harmondsworth: Penguin Books.

Ascoli, K.M. & Schmidt, R.A. (1969). *Proactive interference in short-term motor retention. Journal of Motor Behavior, 1*, 29-35.

524

Askins, C., Jr., (1941). *The Art of Handgun Shooting.* New York: A..S. Barnes & Company.

⇒ (1962). *The Pistol Shooter's Book.* New York, N.Y.: Collier Books.

Astrand, P. & Rodahl, K. (1970). *Textbook of work physiology.* New York: McGraw-Hill.

Atkinson, J.W. (1964). *An introduction to motivation.* Princeton: Van Nostrand.

Atkinson, R.C. & Shiffrin, R.M. (1971). *The control of short-term memory. Scientific American, 225,* 82-90.

Averill, J.R. & Rosenn, M. (1972). *Vigilant and nonvigilant coping strategies and psychophysiological stress reactions during the anticipation of electric shock. Journal of Personality and Social Psychology, 23,* 128-141.

Azrin, N.H. & Holz, W.C. (1966). *Punishment.* In Honig, W.K. (Ed.) *Operant Behavior: Areas of Research and Application,* 380-447. New York: Appleton-Century-Crofts.

⇒ (1956). *Some effects of two intermittent schedules of immediate and nonimmediate punishment. Journal of Psychology, 42,* 3-21. Reprinted in Catania (1968), 227-235.

⇒ (1960). *Effects of punishment intensity during variable interval reinforcement. Journal of the Experimental Analysis of Behavior, 3,* 123-142.

Blair, S.N., Jacobs, D.R. & Powell, K.E. (1985). *Relationships between exercise or physical exercise and other health behaviours. Public Health Reports, 100* (2), 172-180.

Baade, E., Ellertsen, B., Johnsen, T.B. & Ursin, H. (1978*). Physiology, psychology and performance.* In Ursin, H., Baade, R. & Levine, S. (Eds.), *Psychobiology of stress: A study of coping men.* New York: Academic Press.

Bach, G.R. & Wyden, P. (1969). *The Intimate Enemy.* New York: William Morrow.

Bachman, J.C. (1961). *Specificity vs. Generality in learning and performing two large muscle motor tasks. Research Quarterly, 32,* 3-11.

Bachrach, A.J., Erwin, W.J. and Mohr, J.P. (1965). *The control of eating behavior in an anorexic by operant conditioning techniques.* In Ullmann, L.P. & Krasner, L. (Eds.). *Case Studies in Behavior Modification,* 153-163. New York: Holt, Rinehart and Winston, Inc.

Bahrke, M.S. & Morgan, W.P. (1978*). Anxiety reduction following exercise and meditation. Cognitive Therapy and Research, 2,* 323-333.

Bakan, P. (1980) *Imagery Raw and Cooked: A hemispheric recipe.* In J.E. Shorr, G.E. Sobel, P. Robin, & J.A. Connella (Eds.), *Imagery: Its many dimensions and applications,* 35-53. New York: Plenum Press.

Bakker, F.C. & Kayser, C.S. (1994). *Effect of a Self-Help Mental Training Programme.* Department of Psychology, The Netherlands: *International Journal of Psychology, 25,* 158-175.

⇒ Whiting, H.T.A., & Van der Brug, H.H., (1990*). Sport psychology. Concept and applications.* Chichester: John Wiley & Sons.

Balazs, E.K. (1980). *Psycho-social study of outstanding female athletes.* In R.M. Suinn (Ed.), *Psychology in sport.* Minneapolis, Minn.: Burgess Publishing Co.

Bandura, A. & Schunk, D. (1981). *Cultivating competence, self-efficacy, and intrinsic interest through proximal self-motivation. Journal of Personality and Social Psychology 41* (3), 586-598.

⇒ (1977a). *Self-efficacy: Toward a unifying theory of behavioral change, Psychological Review, 84* (2), 191-215.

⇒ (1977b) *Social learning theory.* Englewood Cliffs, NJ: Prentice-Hall.

⇒ (1979). *Reflections on self-efficacy. Advances in Behavioral Research and Therapy, 1,* 237-268.

⇒ (1981). *Self-referent thought: A developmental analysis of self-efficacy.* In Flavell, J. & Ross,L. (Eds.), *Social cognitive development: Frontiers and possible futures,* 200-239. Cambridge, England: Cambridge University Press.

⇒ (1982). *Self-efficacy mechanism in human agency. American Psychologist, 37,* 122-147.

⇒ (1986). *Social foundations of thought and action.* Englewood Cliffs, NJ: Prentice-Hall.

Banquet, J.P. (1973). *Spectral analysis of the EEG in meditation. Electroencephalography and Clinical Neurophysiology, 35,* 143-151.

Baranowski, T. (1988). *Validity and reliability on self report measures of physical activity: An information-processing perspective. Research Quarterly for Exercise and Sport, 59* (4), 314-327.

Bard, C. & Fleury, M. (1976). *Analysis of visual search activity during sport problem situations. Journal of Human Movement Studies, 3,* 214-222.

⇒ & Fleury, M. (1981). *Considering eye movement as a predictor of attainment.* In Cockerill, I.M. & MacGillivary, W.W. (Eds.), *Vision and sport,* 28-41. Cheltenham, England: Stanley Thornes.

⇒ & Fleury, M., Carriere, L. & Halle, M. (1980). *Analysis of gymnastics judges' visual search. Research Quarterly, 51,* 267-273.

⇒ & Fleury, M. & Goulet, C., (1994). *Relationship Between Perceptual Strategies and Response Adequacy in Sport Situations.* Department d'Education Physiqué, Laval, Canada: *International Journal Sport Psychology*, 25, 266-281.

Bar-Eli, M. & Tenenbaum, G. (1988a*). Rule- and norm-related behavior and the individual psychological crisis in competitive situations Theory and research findings. Social Behavior and Personality, 16,* 187-195.

⇒ & Tenenbaum, G. (1988b). *Time phases and the individual psychological crisis in sports competition: Theory and research findings. Journal of Sports Sciences, 6,* 141-149.

⇒ & Tenenbaum, G. (1988c). *The interaction of individual psychological crisis and time phases in basketball. Perceptual and Motor Skills, 66,* 523-530.

⇒ & Tenenbaum, G. (1989a). *A theory of individual psychological crisis in competitive sport. Applied Psychology, 38,* 107-120.

526

⇒ & Tenenbaum, G. (1989b). *Observations of behavioral violations as crisis indicators in competitions. The Sport Psychologist, 3,* 237-244.

⇒ (1985). *Arousal-performance relationship: A transactional view on performance jags. International Journal of Sport Psychology, 16,* 193-209.

⇒ & Taoz, E., Levy-Kolker, N. & Tennenbaum, G., (1992). *Performance Quality and Behavioral Violations as Crisis Indicators in Competition.* Ribstein Center for Research and Sport Medicine Sciences, Wingate Institute, Israel. *International Journal of Psychology, 23,* 325-342.

⇒ & Tenenbaum, G. & Elbaz, G. (1989). *Pre-start susceptibility to psychological crises in competitive sport: Theory and research. International Journal of Sport Psychology, 20,* 13-30.

⇒ & Tenenbaum, G. & Elbaz, G. (1990a). *Psychological performance crisis in high arousal situations: Diagnosticity of rule violations and performance in competitive team handball. Anxiety Research, 2,* 281-292.

⇒ & Tenenbaum, G. & Elbaz, G. (1990b). *Psychological strain in competition: The role of time phases. Sportwissenschaft, 20,* 182-191.

Barling, J. & Abel, M. (1983). *Self-efficacy reliefs and tennis performance. Cognitive Therapy and Research, 7* (3), 265-272.

Barlow, J.A., Brig., C.B.E., p.t.s.c. (1961). *The Elements of Rifle Shooting.* Aldershot, Hampshire: Gale & Polden Limited.

Baron, J. (1996). *Measurement of gender-role attitudes, beliefs, and principles.* University of Pennsylvania: Microsoft Internet Explorer.

Barr, K. & Hall, C. (1992). *The Use of Imagery by Rowers.* Faculty of Kinesiology, University of Western Ontario, Canada. *International Journal Sport Psychology, 23,* 243-261.

Barrani, G., *UIT Journal* (1982). *Scientific Congress of the UIT, Venezuela,* 4/81, 12.

Barrell J.J., Medeiros, D., Barrell J.E. & Price, D. (1985). *The causes and treatment of performance anxiety: An experimental approach. Journal of Humanistic Psychology, 25,* 106-122.

⇒ & Price, D.D. (1977). *Two experimential and orientations toward a stressful situation and their related somatic and visceral responses. Psychophysiology, 14,* 517-521.

Barrett, E.S. (1972). *Anxiety and impulsiveness: Toward a neuropsycholobical model.* In C.D. Spielberger (Eds.), *Anxiety: Current trends in Theory and Research* (Vol.1). New York: Academic Press.

Barron, J.L., Noakes, T.D., Levy, W., Smith, C. & Millar, R.P. (1985). *Hypothalamic dysfunction in overtrained athletes. Journal of Clinical Endocrinology and Metabolism, 60,* 803-806.

Bartlett, F.C. (1947). *The measurement of human skill. Occupational Psychology, 21,* 31-38.

Bartone, P.T. (1989).*Predictors of stress-related illness in city bus drivers. Journal of Occupational Medicine, 31,* 857-863.

Basic Pistol Marksmanship (1959). Washington, D.C.: National Rifle Association.

Basic Pistol Marksmanship Guide (1975). Ft. Benning, GA.: The United States Army Marksmanship Unit.

Basic Smallbore Rifle Guide (1980). United States Army Marksmanship Unit, Washington, D.C.: U.S. Government Printing Office.

⇒ (1981). United States Army Marksmanship Unit, Washington, D.C.: U.S. Government Printing Office.

Basic Rifle Shooting: A Better Way (Video 1988?). *4-H Youth Development.* Minnesota Extension Service and Ferderal Cartridge Co.

Basowitz, H., Korchin, S.J., Oken, D., Goldstein, M.S. & Gussack S. (1956). *Anxiety and performance changes with a minimal dose of spinephrine. Archives of Neurology and Psychiatry, 76,* 98-105.

Bassham, L. (1988). *With Winning in Mind.* San Antonio, TX.: X-Press, Publications.

Bates, J.E. & Bentler, P.M. (1973*). Play activities of normal and effeminate boys. Developmental Psychology, 9,* 20-27.

Beech, H.R. (1969). *Changing Man's Behaviour.* Harmondsworth, Middlesex: Penguin Books, Ltd.

Beek, P.J. (1989) *Timing and phase locking in cascade juggling. Ecological Psychology 1,* 55-96.

Bell, F.K. (1983) *Championship Thinking.* Englewood Cliffs, NJ: Prentice Hall.

Bell, K.F. (1980). *Self instructional methods. Coach,* 29-31.

Bem, S.L. (1974).*The measurement of psychological androgyny. Journal of Consulting and Clinical Psychology, 42,* 155-162.

⇒ (1977). *On the utility of alternative procedures for assessing psychological androgyny. Journal of Consulting and Clinical Psychology, 45,* 196-205.

Benson, H. (1975). *The Relaxation Response.* New York: William Morrow.

Benson, H., Beary, J.F. & Carol, M.P. (1974). *The relaxation response. Psychiatry, 37,* 37-46.

Bereiter, C. (1985). *Toward a solution of the learning paradox. Review of Educational Research, 55,* 201-226.

Berger, A.T. (1967). *Depression: Clinical, experimental, and theoretical aspects.* NY: Harper and Row.

Berger, B.G. & Owen, D.R. (1983) *Mood alteration with swimming - swimmers really do feel better. Psychosomatic Medicine, 45,* 425-433.

⇒ & Owen, D.R. (1988*) Mood alteration with swimming: A re-examination.* In Vander Velden, L., & Humphrey, J.H. (Eds.),*Current selected research in the psychology and sociology of sport: Vol. 1,* 97-113. New York: AMS Press.

⇒ & Owen, D.R. (1988) *Stress reduction and mood enhancement in four exercise modes: Swimming, body conditioning, hatha yoga, and fencing. Research Quarterly for Exercise and Sport, 59.* 56-57.

⇒ & Owen, D.R., (1992). *Preliminary Analysis of a Causal Relation-ship between Swimming and Stress Reduction: Intense Exercise May Negate the Effects*. Department of Physical Education and Department of Psychology, Brooklyn College of the City University of New York. *International Journal Sport Psychology, 23*, 70-85.

⇒ (1984). *Running away from anxiety and depression: A female as well as male race*. In Sachs, M.L. & Buffone, G.W. (Eds.), **Running as therapy: An integrated approach**, 138-171. Lincoln: University of Nebraska Press.

⇒ (1986). *Use of jogging and swimming as stress reduction techniques*. In Humphrey, J.H. (Ed.), **Human stress: Current selected research**, 169-190. New York: AMS Press.

⇒ (1987). *Stress reduction following swimming*. In Morgan, W.P. & Goldston, S.E. (Eds.), **Exercise and mental health**, 139-143. Washington, DC: Hemisphere.

⇒ & Friedmann, E. & Eaton, M. (1988). *Comparison of jogging and other techniques for stress reduction. Journal of Sport Psychology, 10*, 431-447.

Berglas, S. & Jones, E.E. (1978). *Drug choice as a self-handicapping strategy in response to noncontingent success. Journal of Personality and Social Psychology, 36*, 405-417.

Berliner, D.C. (1979). *Tempus educare*. In Peterson, P.L. & Walberg, H.J. (Eds.), **Research on teaching: Concepts, findings and implications** 120-133. Berkeley, CA: McCutcham.

Bernstein, D.A. & Borkovec, T.D. (1973). **Progressive Relaxation Training**. Champaign, IL.: Research Press.

Bernstein, N. (1967). **The co-ordination and regulation of movements**. Oxford: Pergamon Press.

Bijou, S.W. & Baer, D.M. (1961). **Child Development, Vol 1: A Systematic and Empirical Theory**. New York: Appleton-Century-Crofts.

Bikov, K.M. (1925). **Contributions to the question of the symmetrical reproduction of function of the hemispheres**. *Pavlov Jubilee*.

⇒ (1926) *The properties of different components of compound stimuli*. **Collected Papers of Physiol. Laboratories of I.P. Pavlov**, vol. i. Nos. 2-3.

Blackman, D.E. (1967*). Effects of response pacing on conditioned suppression. Quarterly Journal of Experimental Psychology, 19*, 170-174.

⇒ (1974). **Operant Conditioning: An Experimental Analysis of Behaviour**. Cambridge: The University Printing House.

⇒   (1968a). *Conditioned suppression or facilitation as a function of the behavioral baseline. Journal of the Experimental Analysis of Behavior, 11*, 53-61.

⇒ (1968b). *Reponse rate, reinforcement frequency and conditioned suppression. Journal of the Experimental Analysis of Behavior, 11, 503-516.*

⇒ (1968c). *Effects of drugs on conditioned 'anxiety'. Nature, 217*, 769-770.

⇒ (1970a). *Effects of a pre-shock stimulus on temporal control of be-havior, Journal of the Experimental Analysis of Behavior, 14*, 313-319.

⇒ (1970b). *Conditioned suppression of avoidance behaviour in rats. Quarterly Journal of Experimental Psychology, 22*, 547-553.

⇒ (1972). *Conditioned 'anxiety' and operant behavior*. In Gilbert, R.M. and Keehn, J. D. (Eds.). **Schedule Effects Drugs Drinking and Aggression**, 26-49. Toronto: University of Toronto Press.

Blair, S.N., Kohl, H.W., Paffenbarger R.S., Jr., Clark, D.G., Cooper, K.H. & Gibbons, L..W. (1989). *Physical fitness and all-cause mortality. A prospective study of healthy men and women. Journal of American Medical Association, 262* (17), 2395-2401.

Blankship, B. & Fox, R. (Video). **Pistol Shooting Fundamentals**. Washington, D.C.: National Rifle Association of America.

Bloom-Feshbach, J. (1980). *Differentiation: Field dependence, spatial ability and hemispheric specialization. Journal of Personality, 48*, 135-148.

Bloomfield, T.M. (1967). *A peak shift on a line tilt continuum. Journal of the Experimental Analysis of Behavior, 10*, 361-366.

⇒ (1969). *Behavioural contrast and the peak shift*. In Gilbert, R.M. and Sutherland, N.S. (Eds.). **Animal Discrimination Learning**, 215-241. London: Academic Press.

Boe, E.E. & Church, R. M. (1968). **Punishment: Issues and Experiments**. New York: Appleton-Century-Crofts.

Boothroyd, G. (1974). **The Handgun**. New York, N.Y.: Bonanza Books.

Borg, G. (1978). *Subjective aspects of physical and mental load. Ergonomics, 21* (3), 215-220.

Borger, R. & Cioffi, F. (Eds.) (1970). **Explanation in the Behavioural Sciences**. London: *Cambridge* University Press.

Borkovec, T.D. (1976). *Physiological and cognitive processes in the regulation of anxiety*. In Schwartz, G.E. & Shapior, D. (Eds.), **Consciousness and Self-regulation: Advances in Research**. (Vol.1), New York: Plenum Press.

⇒ & Sides, J.K. (1979). *Critical precedural variables related to the physiological effects of progressive relaxation: A review. Behavior Research and Therapy, 17*, 119-126.

⇒ Weerts, T.C., & Bernstein, D.A. (1977). *Behavioral assessment of anxiety*. In Ciminero, A.R., Calhourn, K.S. & Adams, H.E. (Eds.). **Handbook of Behavioral Assessment**. New York: Wiley.

Borkowski, J.G., Weyhing, R. & Carr, M. (1988). *Effects of attribution retraining on strategy-based reading comprehension in learning disability. Journal of Educational Psychology, 80*, 46-53.

Boutcher, S.H. & Landers, D.M. (1988). *The effects of vigorous exercise on anxiety, heart rate, and alpha activity of runners and nonrunners. Psychophysiology, 25*, 696-702.

Boutilier, M.A. & SanGiovanni, L. (1983). **The sporting woman**. Champaign, IL: Human Kinetics.

530

Bowers, K. (1968). *Pain, anxiety, and perceived control. Journal of Consulting and Clinical Psychology.32,* 596-602.

Boyd, M. & Callaghan, J., (1994). *Task and Ego Goal Perspectives in Organized Youth Sport.* Department of Physical Education, University of Southern California. *International Journal Sport Psychology, 22,* 411-424.

Bradley, P.B. (1958). *The central action of certain drugs in relation to the reticular formation of the brain.* In Jasper, H.H., Proctor, L.D., Knighton, R.S., Noshay, W.C. & Costello, R.T. (Eds.), *Reticular Formation of the Brain.* Boston: Little, Brown and Co.

Brady, J.V. & Hunt, H.F. (1955). *An experimental approach to the analysis of emotional behavior. Journal of Psychology, 40,* 313-324.

⇒ (1956). *Assessment of drug effects on emotional behavior. Science,* 123, 1033. Reprinted in Thompson, Pickens and Meisch (1970), 63-65.

Braskamp, L., Brandenburg, D. & Ory, J. (1984). *Evaluating teaching effectiveness: A practical guide.* Newburgy Park, CA: Sage.

Braun, D.L. & the Remington Pros (1969). *Trapshooting.* New York, N.Y.: The Benjamin Company, Inc.

⇒ (1967). *Skeet Shooting with D.Lee Braun.* New York: The Benjamin Company, Inc.

Brawley, .L.R., Carron, A.V. & Widmeyer, W.N. (1987*). Assessing the cohesion of sport teams: Validity of the Group Environment Questionnaire. Journal of Sport Psychology 9,* 89-108, 275-294.

⇒ & Carron, A.V. & Widmeyer, W.N. (1988) . *Exploring the relationship between cohesion and group resistance to disruption. Journal of Sport Psychology, 10,* 199-213.

Brewin, C. (1982). *Adaptive aspects of self-blame in coping with accidental injury.* In Antaki, C. & Brewin, C. (Eds.), *Attributions and psychological change: Applications of attributional theories to clinical and educational pratice,* 119-134. New York: Academic Press.

Briggs, F. (1963). *You Can be an Expert Rifleman.* New York, N.Y.: Grosset & Dunlap Publishers.

Broadbent, D.E. (1980). *The minimisation of models.* In Chapman, A.J. & Jones, D.M. (Eds.), *Models of Man,* 33-47. Leicester: British Psychological Society.

Brody, E.B., Hatfield, B.D. & Spalding, T.W. (1988*). Generalization of self-efficacy to a continuum of stressors upon mastery of a high-risk sport skill. Journal of Sport & Exercise Psychology, 10,* 32-44.

Brooks, L.W., Simutis, Z.M. & O'Neil, H.F. (1985). *The role of individual differences in learning strategies research.* In Dillon, R.F. & Schmeck, R.R. (Eds.), *Individual differences in cognition: Vol. 2.* New York: Academic Press.

Brooks-Gunn, J. & Reiter, E.O. (1990) *The role of pubertal processes in the early adolescent transition,* in Feldman, S. & Elliot,G. (Eds) *At the Threshold: the developing adolescent.* Cambridge, MA.: Harvard University Press.

Brophy, J. (1980) *Successful teaching strategies for the inner-city child. Phi Delta Kappan, 63,* 527-530.

Brown, A.L. & Barclay, C.R. (1976). *The effects of training specific memories on the metamnemonic efficiencv of retarded children. Child Psychology, 47,* 71-80.

⇒ & Campione, J.C., & Barclay, C.R. (1979*). Training self-checking routines for estimating test readiness: Generalization from list learning to prose recall. Child Psychology, 50,* 501-512.

⇒ (1978). *Knowing when, where, and how to remember: A problem of metacognition.* In R. Glaser (Ed.). ***Advances in instructional psychology****: Vol. 1,* 77-165. Hillsdale, NJ: Erlbaum.

⇒ & Campione, J.C. (1986). *Training for transfer: Guidelines for promoting flexible use of trained skills,* In Wade, M.G. (Ed.), ***Motor skill acquisition of the mentally handicapped****,* 257-271. Amsterdam: North-Holland.

⇒ Bransford, J.D, Ferrara, R.A. & Campione, J.C. (1983). *Learning, remembering, and understanding.* In Flavel, J.H. & Markman, E.M. (Eds.), ***Handbook of child psychology****: Vol. 3.* Cognitive *development* 177-226. New York: John Wiley & Sons.

Brown, H.J., Singer, R.N., Cauraugh, J.H. & Lucariello, G. (1985*). Cognitive style and learner strategy interaction in the performance of primary and related maze tasks. Research Quarterly for Exercise and Sport, 56,* 10-14.

Brown, I. & Inonye, K. (1978). *Learned helplessness through modelling: The role of perceived similarity in competence. Journal of Personality and Social Psychology, 36* (8), 900-903.

Brown, J. (1966). *Information theory.* In Foss, B.M. (Ed.) ***New Horizons in Psychology****,* 118-134. Harmondsworth: Penguin Books.

Brown, J.C. & Palincsar, A. (1982). *Inducing strategic learning from texts by means of informed self-control training. Topics in learning and learning disabilities 2,* 1-17.

Brown, M.R. (9/20/96). ***Flat Earth Society Flyer****. Microsoft Internet Explorer.*

Bruner, A. & Revusky, S.H. (1961). *Collateral behavior in humans. Journal of the Experimental Analysis of Behavior, 4,* 349-350.

Bryan, W.L. & Harter, N. (1899). *Studies on the telegraphic language: The acquisition of a hierarchy of habits. Psychological Review, 6,* 345-375.

Buchsbaum, M.S. (1979). *Tuning in on hemispheric dialogue. Psychology Today.* January, 100.

Buckert, U., Meyer, W. & Schmalt, H. (1979). *Effects of difficulty and diagnosticity on choice among tasks in relation to achievement motivation and perceived ability. Journal of Personality and Social Psychology, 37* (7), 1172-1178.

Bugelski, B.R. (1938). *Extinction with and without sub-goal reinforcement. Journal of Comparative Psychology, 51,* 109-117.

Bull, B. & Wittrock, M. (1973). *Imagery in the learning of verbal definitions,* British Journal of Educational Psychology, 43, 289-293.

Burton, D. & Martens, R. (1986). *Pinned by their own goals: An explanatory investigation into why kids drop out of wrestling. Journal of Sport Psychology, 8,* 183-197.

⇒ (1988). *Do anxious swimmers swim slower? Reexamining the elusive anxiety performance relationship. Journal of Sport and Exercise Psychology, 10,* 45-61.

⇒ (1989). *The impact of goal specificity and task complexity on basketball skill development. The Sport Psychologist, 3,* 34-47.

Buss, A.H. (1962). Two anxiety factors in psychiatric patients. *Journal of Abnormal and Social Psychology, 65,* 426-427.

Butt, D.S. (1987). ***Psychology of Sport: The behavior, motivation, personality, and performance of athletes***. New York: van Nostrand Reinhold Company.

Byrne, D. & Nelson, D. (1971). ***The attraction paradigm***. New York: Academic Press.

Calderaro, G., Dr. & Giampietro, P.G., *UIT Journal* (1/91). *Mental Health of Athletes and Mental Hygiene in Sport Medicine,* 48-51.

Campbell, B.A. & Church, R.M. ***Punishment and Aversive Behavior***. New York: Appleton-Century-Crofts.

Campbell, D.T. & Fiske, D.W. (1959). *Convergent and discriminant validation by the multitrait-multimethod matrix. Psychological Bulletin, 56,* 81-105.

Cannon, W.B. & Britton, S.W. (1927). *Studies on the conditions of activity in endocrine glands, XX. The influence of motion and emotion on medulliadrenal secretion. American Journal of Physiology, 79,* 433-465.

⇒ (1922). *New evidence for sympathetic control of some internal secretions. American Journal of Psychiatry, 2,* 15-30.

⇒ (1928). *The mechanism of emotional disturbance of bodily functions. The New England Journal of Medicine, 198,* 877-884.

⇒ (1932). ***The Wisdom of the Body***. New York: W.W. Norton.

Caprara, G.V., Renzi, P., D'Angello, D., D'Imperio, G., Rielli, I. & Travaglia, G. (1986). *Instigation to aggress and aggression: The role of irritability and emotional susceptibility. Aggressive Behavior, 12,* 78-83.

Carron, A.V. & Ball, J.R. (1977). *An analysis of the cause-effect characteristics of cohesiveness in intercollegiate hockey. International Journal of Sport Sociology, 12,* 49-60.

⇒ & Chelladurai, P. (1981) *The dynamics of group cohesion in sport. Journal of Sport Psychology, 3,* 123-139.

⇒ (1984). *Cohesion in sport teams.* In J.M. Silva and R.S. Weinberg (Eds.), ***Psychological foundations of sport***. Champaign, IL: Human Kinetics.

⇒ (1988). ***Group dynamics in sport***. London, Ontario: Spodym Publishers.

⇒ Widmeyer, W.N. & Brawley, L.R. (1985*). The development of an instrument to assess cohesion in sports teams: The Group Environment Questionnaire. Journal of Sport Psychology, 7,* 244-266.

Carver, C.S. & Scheier, M.F. (1981). ***Attention and self-regulation: A control theory approach to human behavior***. New York: Springer Verlag.

⇒ & Scheier, M.F. (1986). *Functional and dysfunctional responses to anxiety: The interaction between expectancies and self-focused at-*

tention. In Schwarzer, R. (Ed.), *Self-related cognitions in anxiety and motivation* 111-141. Hillsdale, NJ: Erlbaum.

⇒ & Scheier, M.F. (1988). *A control-process perspective on anxiety*. Anxiety Research, *1,* 17-22.

Case, R.W. (1984) *Leadership in sport: The situational-leadership theory. Journal of Physical Education. Recreation and Dance, 55 (1),* 15-16.

Casliello, U. & Umilta, C. (1988). *Temporal dimensions of mental effort in different sports. International Journal of Sport Psychology, 19,* 199-210.

Catania, A.C. (1966). *Concurrent Operants*. In Honig, W K (Ed.) *Operant Behavior: Areas of Research and Application,* 213-270. New York: Appleton-Century-Crofts.

Catania, A.C. (1968). (Ed.). *Contemporary Research in Operant Behavior.* This is a collection of experimental reports, which gives an excellent insight into operant conditioning. Glenview, Illinois: Scott, Foresman and Co.

Cavanaugh, J.C. & Borkowski, J.G. (1980). *Searching for metamemory-memory connections: A developmental study. Child Psychology, 16,* 441-453.

Champbeill, D.J. & Stanley, J.C. (1963). *Experimental and quasi-experimental designs for research.* Chicago, IL: Rand McNally.

Chatty, B.J. (1989). *Psychology in contemporary sport* (3rd Ed.). Englewood Cliffs, NJ: Prentice-Hall.

Chaumeton, N. & Duda, J.L. (1988). *It is how you play the game or whether you win or lose?: The effect of competitive level and situation on coaching behaviors. Journal of Sport Behavior, 11,* 157-174.

Chechoulin, S.I. (1923*). New observations upon extinction of the investigatory reflex. Archive Biol.. Sciences, xxiii.* 3-5, 1923.

Cheetham, D., & Landers, D. (1982) *A cinematographical analysis of rapid fire pistol shooting and running game target shooting.* Unpublished manuscript, Arizona State University, Tempe, AZ In Landers, D.M & Hunt, K.J., *Shooting Sports Research,* (1988) Washington, DC, National Rifle Association. pp104-107.

Chelladurai, P. & Arnott, M. (1985*) Decision styles in coaching: preferences of basketball players. Research Quarterly for Exereise & Sport, 56 (1),* 15-24.

Chelladurai, P. & Carron, A.V. (1981). *Applicability to youth sports of the leadership scale for sports. Perceptual and Motor Skills, 53,* 361-362.

⇒ & Saleh, S.D. (1980). *Dimensions of leader behavior in sports: development of a leadership scale. Journal of Sport Psychology, 2,* 34-45.

⇒ (1984a). *Leadership in sports.* In Silva, J.M., & Weinberg, R.S. (Eds.), *Psychological foundations of sport,* 329-339. Champaign, IL: Human Kinetics Publishers.

⇒ (1984b). *Discrepancy between preferences and perceptions of leadership behavior and satisfaction of athletes in varying sports. Journal of Sport Psychology, 6,* 27-41.

⇒ (1990). *Leadership in sports: A review. International Journal of Sport Psychology, 21,* 328-354.

⇒ & Malloy, D., Imamura, H. & Yamaguchi, Y. (1987). *A cross-cultural study of preferred leadership in sports. Canadian Journal of Sport Science, 12,* 106-110.

⇒ (1980). *Leadership in sports organizations. Canadian Journal of Applied Sport Sciences, 5,* 226-231.

Chen, D. & Singer, R.N., (1992). *Self-Regulation and Cognitive Strategies in Sport Participation.* People's Republic, China, Department of Exercise and Sport Sciences, University of Florida. *International Journal Sport Psychology, 23,* 277-300.

Cherry, N. (1978). *Stress, anxiety and work: A longitudinal study. Journal of Occupational Psychology, 51,* 259-270.

Chi, M. (1976). *Short-term memory limitations in children: Capacity of processing deficits? Memory and Cognition, 4,* 559-572.

⇒ Glaser, R. & Farr, M.J. (Eds.). (1988). **The nature of expertise.** Hillsdale, NJ: Erlbaum.

Chick, G.E., Loy, J.W. & Walsh, M. (1986) *Need for stimulation and sport involvement among adolescent males.* In Humphrey, J.H. & Veldon, L.V. (Ed.), **Psychology and sociology of sport.** Princeton, NJ: Princeton Book Company.

Church, R.M. (1963). *The varied effects of punishment on behavior. Psychological Review, 70,* 369-402.

Clark, E. & Coleman, J.C. (1992) **Growing Up Fast.** London: St Michael's Fellowship.

Clark, F.C. (1958). *The effect of deprivation and frequency of reinforcement on variable interval responding. Journal of the Experimental Analysis of Behavior, 1,* 221-228.

Clarke, J.C. & Jackson J.A. (1983). **Hypnosis and behavior therapy. The treatment of anxiety and phobias.** New York: Springer Publishing Company.

Classé, J.G., O.D., et.el., (2/96). *Association Between Eye and Hand Dominance and hitting, fielding and pitching skill among players of the Southern Baseball League. Journal of the American Optometric Association, Vol. 87,* 81-85.

Claxton, D.B. (1988). *A systematic observation of more or less successful high school tennis coaches. Journal of Teaching in Physical Education, 7* (4), 302-310.

Claxton, G. (1990). **Teaching to learn.** London: Cassell.

Cockerill, I.M. (1981). *Peripheral vision and hockey.* In I.M. Cockerill & W.W. MacGillivary (Eds.), **Vision and sport,** 54-63. Cheltenham, England: Stanley Thornes.

Cohen, C.J. (1980). *Human circadian rhythms in heart rate response to a maximal exercise stress. Ergonomics, 23,* 591-595.

Cohen, D.H. & Obrist, P.A. (1975). *Interactions between behavior and the cardiovascular system. Circulation Research, 37,* 693-706.

Cohen, P. (1990). *Bringing research into practice.* In Theall, M. & Franklin, J. (Eds.), **Student ratings of instruction; Issues for improving practice,** 123-132. San Francisco, CA: Jossey-Bass Inc.

Cohen, S. (1987). *Instructional alignment: Searching for a magic bullet. Educational Researcher, 16,* 175-20.

⇒ Kamarck, T. & Mermelstein, R. (1983). *A global measure of perceived stress. Journal of Health and Social Behavior, 24,* 385-396.

Cohn, P.J. (1990). *An exploratory study on sources of stress and athlete burnout in youth golf. The Sport Psychologist, 4,* 95-106.

Coleman, J.A. (circa 1975). *Personality and stress in the shooting sports.* A copy of her original research paper sent to Bob Hickey by Mrs. J.A. Coleman.

⇒ (1977). *Normal stress reactions in shooting. The Rifleman, 12,* 19-20.

⇒ (1978). *Psychology and shooting. UIT Journal,* 2.

⇒ (1980). *Personality and stress in the shooting sports. Journal of Psychosomatic Research, 24,* 287-296.

Coles, M.G.H. (1989). *Modern mind-brain reading: Psychophysiology, physiology, and cognition. Psychophysiology, 26,* 251-269.

Colley, A. (1987). *Sex roles in leisure and sport.* In Hargreaves, D.J. & Colley, A.M. (Eds.), ***The psychology of sex roles***. New York: Hemisphere.

⇒ Eglinton, E. & Elliott, E. (1987) *Sport Participation in Middle Childhood: Association with Styles of Play and Parental Participation,* Department of Psychology, University of Leicester, U.K. *International Journal Sport Psychology, 23,* 193-206.

⇒ Nash, J., O'Donnell, L. & Restorick, L. (1987). *Attitudes to the female sex role and sex-typing of physical activities. International Journal of Sport Psychology, 18,* 19-29.

⇒ Roberts, N. & Chipps, A. (1985). *Sex role identity, personality and participation in team and individual sports by males and females. International Journal of Sport Psychology, 16,* 103-112.

Colley, E.J. (1987). *Situational and trait determinants of competitive state anxiety. Perceptual and Motor Skills, 64,* 767-773.

Conrad, D.G., Sidman, M. & Herrnstein, R.J. (1958). *The effects of deprivation upon temporally spaced responding. Journal of the Experimental Analysis of Behavior, 1,* 59-65.

Contrada, R.J. (1989). *Type A behavior, personality hardiness, and cardiovascular responses to stress. Journal of Personality and Social Psychology, 57,* 895-903.

Conway, A. (1991). ***Instant People-Reading Through Handwriting***. North Hollywood, CA.: Newcastle Publishing, Co.

Cook, T.D. & Campbell, D.T. (1979). ***Quasi-experimentation: Design and Analysis Issues in Field Settings***. Chicago: Rand-McNally.

Coop, R.H., Dr. (8/1990). *Tempo. Mechanics. Alignment. None of them matters without...CONCENTRATION. Golf Illustrated,* 28-40.

Corbin, C.B., Jr. (1972). *Mental practice.* In W.P. Morgan (Ed.), ***Ergotenic aids and muscular performance***, 93-118. New York: Academic Press.

Costa, P.T. & McCrae, R.R. (1980). *Influence of extraversion and neuroticism on subjective well-being: Happy and unhappy people. Journal of Personality and Social Psychology, 38,* 668-678.

Costill, D.L., Flynn, M.G., Kirwan, J.P., Houmard, J.A., Mitchell, J.B., Thomas, R. & Park, S.H. (1988). *Effects of repeated days of intensified training on muscle glycogen and swimming performance.* Medicine and Science in Sports and Exercise, 20, 249-254.

Cowen, E.L., Gardner, E.A. & Zax, M. (1967). (Eds,): *Emergent approaches to mental health problems.* New York: Appleton-Century-Crofts.

Cox, R.H. (1990). *Sport psychology: Concepts and applications.* Dubuque, IA: Wm. C. Brown Publishers.

Cox, T. (1975). *The nature and measurement of stress.* Ergonomics, 28 (8), 1155-1163.

⇒ (1986). *Stress.* London: Macmillan Education Ltd.

⇒ Thirlaway, M., Gotts, G., & Cox, S. (1983). *The nature and assessment of general well-being.* Journal of Psychosomatic Research, 5 (27), 353-359.

Craske, M. & Craig, K. (1984). *Musical performance anxiety: The three-systems model and self-efficacy theory.* Behavior Research and Therapy, 22, 267-280.

Cratty, B.J. (1989). *Psychology in contemporary sport.* Englewood Cliffs, NJ: Prentice Hall.

Cronbach, L.J. & Snow, R.E. (1977). *Aptitudes and instructional methods: A handbook for research on interactions.* New York: Wiley & Sons.

Cronbach, L.J. (1951). *Coefficient alpha and tests of the internal consistency of tests.* Psychometrika, 16, 297-334.

Cross, D.R. & Paris, S.G. (1988). *Developmental and instructional analyses of children's metacognition and reading comprehension.* Journal of Educational Psychology, 80 131-142.

Crowne, D.P. & Marlowe, D. (1964). *The approval motive: Studies in evaluative dependence.* New York: Wiley.

Cumming, W.W. & Schoenfeld, W.N. (1960). *Behavior stability under extended exposure to a time-correlated reinforcement contingency.* Journal of the Experimental Analysis of Behavior, 3, 71-82.

⇒ (1966). *A bird's eye glimpse of men and machines.* In Ulrich, R., Stachnik, T. & Mabry, J. (Eds.). *Control of Human Behavior.* Glenview, 246-256. Illinois: Scott, Foresman and Company.

Cushman, J. (5/6/96). *EQ, not IQ, can determine success.* Tucson, AZ. Tucson Citizen.

Curtis, J.D. & Detert, R.A. (1981) *How to Relax: A Holistic Approach to Stress Management.*, Palo Alto: Mayfield Publishing Company.

Dahl, H. & Spence, D.P. (1971). *Mean heart rate predicted by task demand characteristics.* Psychophysiology, 7, 369-376.

Daniels, F.S. & Landers, D.M. (1981). *Biofeedback and shooting performance: A test of disregulation and systems theory* Journal of Sport Psychology, 3, 271-282.

⇒ & Landers, D.M., Hatfield, B.D. & Wilkinson, M.O. *Heart rate and respiration effects upon performance in elite rifle shooters.* American Marksman.

⇒ Landers, D.M. *UIT Journal* (1/86). *A test of disregulation and systems theory,* 22.

Daniels, J.T. & J.J. (1972). *Epinephrine and norepinephrine excretion during running training at sea level and altitude. Medicine and Science in Sport, 4,* 219-224.

Daniels, S. & Landers, Daniel M., *UIT Journal* (6/85). *Biofeedback and Shooting Performance, A Test of Disregulation and Systems Theory,* 16-21.

Danik, R.J., 27, Ellerslie Road, London, W12 7BN, tel+fax: +44 81 743 8685. Provided some translations of the slavic language books listed in this section, including (1) **Kopkh,** ed., **Shooting Sport And Teaching Methodology,** Moscow, 1986. (2) **Kinl',** V.A, **Shooting With Rifled Weapons,** Moscow, 1989. (3) **Weinstein (Vaynshteyn),** *Learn to Shoot Accurately,* Moscow, 1973. (4) **Weinstein (Vaynshteyn,** *Shooter And Trainer,* Moscow, 1977 (First published 1969). (5) **Yur'yev, A.A.,** **Competitive Shooting,** Moscow, 1973.

Dansereau, D. (1985). *Learning strategy research.* In Segal, J., Chipman, S. & Glaser,R. (Eds.), **Thinking and learning skills: Relating instruction to basic research:** *Vol. I,* 209-240. Hillsdale, NJ: Erlbaum.

Darrow, C.W. & Graf, C.G. (1945). *Relation of electroencephalogram to photometrically observed vasomotor changes in the brain. Journal of Neurophysiology, 8,* 449-462.

⇒ & Pathman, J.H. (1944). *Relation of heart rate to slow waves in the electroencephalogram during overventilation. The American Journal of Physiology,* 140.

⇒ & Stoup, M., Kris, C., Arnott, P., Brudo, C. & Ginsbury, N. (1973). *Cyclic respiratory and cardiac changes in EEG.* In Gullickson, G.R. (Ed.), **The Psychophysiology of Darrow.** New York: Academic Press.

Darwin, C.R. (1873). **On the Expression of the Emotions in Man and Animals.** London: Murray.

Davidson, R.J. & Schwartz, G.E. (1976). *The psychobiology of relaxation and related states: A multiprocess theory.* In Mostofsky, D.I. (Eds.), **Behavior Control and Modification of Physiological Activity.** Englewood Cliffs, N.J.: Prentice-Hall.

⇒ (1978). *Specificity and patterning in biobehavioral systems: Implications for behavior change. American Psychologist, 33,* 430-436.

⇒ & Schwartz, G.E. & Rothman, L.P. (1976). *Attentional style and the self-regulation of mode-specific attention: An electroencephalographic study. Journal of Abnormal Psychology, 85,* 611-621.

Davies, D.R. & Krkovic, A. (1965). *Skin-conductance, alpha-activity, and vigilance. American Journal of Psychology, 78,* 304-306.

Davis C. & Cowles, M.P. (1989). *A comparison of weight and diet concerns and personality factors among female athletes and non-athletes. Journal of Psychosomatic Research, 34,* 563-574.

⇒ & Mogk, J.P. (1994). *Some Personality Correlates of Interest and Excellence in Sport.* Graduate Programme in Exercise and Health

Sciences, York University, Canada: *International Journal Sport Psychology, 25*, 131-143.

⇒ (1992) *Body image, dieting behaviours, and personality factors among high performance female athletes. International Journal of Sport Psychology, 23*, 179-192.

Davis, C., Fox, J., Cowles, M.P., Hastings, P. & Schwass, K. (1990). *The functional role of exercise in the development of weight and diet concerns in women. Journal of Psychosomatic Research, 34*, 563-574.

Davis, M., Ph.D., Eshelman, E.R., M.S.W. & McKay, M., Ph.D. (1985). ***The Relaxation & Stress Reduction Workbook***. Oakland, CA., New Harbinger Publications.

Day, L.J. (1980). *Anticipation in junior tennis players.* In Groppel, J. & Sears, R. (Eds.), ***Proceedings of the International Symposium on the Effective Teaching of Racquet Sport***, 107-116. Champaign, IL.: University of Illinois.

De Groot, A.D. (1965). ***Thought and choice in chess***. Paris: Mouton & Company.

Demeter, Andrei, Dr. & Barani, Gavrila,. (5/78). *Contributions to a Cybernetic Interpretation of Performance Shooting, UIT Journal* 229+.

Denis, M. (1985). *Visual imagery and the use of mental practice in the development of motor skills. Canadian Journal of Applied Sport Science 10, 4s-16s.*

Derry, S.J. & Murphy, D.A. (1986). *Designing systems that train learning ability: From theory to practice Review of Educational Research, 56*, 1-39.

Descartes, R. (1637). ***Discourse on Method***. (1960). Translated by Wollaston A. Harmondsworth: Penguin Books, Ltd.

Dewey, D., Brawley, L.R. & Allard, F. (1989). *Do the TAIS attentional-style scales predict how visual information is processed? Journal of Sport & Exercise Psychology, 11*, 171-186

Dewey, J. (1896). *The Reflex Arc Concept in Psychology, Psychological Review 3*, 357-370.

Dews, P.B. (1970). *The theory of fixed-interval responding.* In Schoenfeld, W.N. (Ed.), ***The Theory of Reinforcement Schedules***, 43-61. New York: Appleron-Century-Crofts.

Di Lollo, J. (1980). *Temporal integration in visual memory. Journal of Experimental Psychology: General, 109*, 75-97.

Dickenson, J. (1977). ***A behavioral analysis of sport***. Princeton, NJ: Princeton Book. Co.

Diener, C.I. & Dweck, C.S. (1986). *An analysis of learned helplessness: The process of success. Journal of Personality and Social Psychology, 39*, 940-952.

Diethelm, O., Doty, E.J. & Milhorat, A.T. (1945). *Emotions and adrenergic and cholinergic changes in blood. Archives of Neurology and Psychiatry, 54*, 110-115.

Dilworth, C.B., Jr. (1975). *Visualization and the experience of poetry: A study of selected variables in reader response. Dissertation Abstracts International, 8*, 4978-A.

Dimond, S.J. & Farrington, L. (1977). *Emotional response to films shown to the right or left hemisphere of the brain measured by heart rate. Acta Psychologica, 41,* 255-260.

Dinsmoor, J.A. & Winograd, E. (1958). *Shock intensity in variable interval escape schedules. Journal of the Experimental Analysis of Behavior, 1,* 145-148.

DN News, (3/79). *Air Rifle Bullets, UIT Journal ,*119-121.

Dolphin, C., O'Briennnn, M., Cahill, N. & Cullen, J. (1980). :*Personality factors and some physiological correlates in athletes. Journal of Psychosomatic Research, 24,* 281-285.

Domey, R.L., Ph.D., (1/88). *Planning the Champion Shooter's Travel Across the Twilight Zones, UIT Journal,* 50-51.

⇒ (4/87). *Taking the First Sssteps Toward Being a Champion: Goal Setting - part II, UIT Journal,* 42-43.

Donaldson, M. (1992). *Human Minds, An Exploration.* New York, N.Y.: Penguin Press.

Donner, L. & Guerney, Jr, B.: (1969). *Automated group desensitization for test anxiety. Behav. Res. Theory. 7:* 1-13.

Donovan, C. (1990) *Adolescent sexuality, British Medical Journal, 63,* 935-941.

Downs, A.C. & Langlois, J.H. (1988). *Sex typing: Construct and measurement issues. Sex Roles, 18,* 87-100.

Doyle, J.C., Ornstein, R., & Galin, D. (1974). *Lateral specialization of cognitive mode: II. EEG frequency analysis. Psychophysiology, 11,* 567-577.

Dreyfus, H. & Dreyfus, S. (1986). *Mind over machine.* New York: Free Press.

Duda, J.L. & Nicholls, J.G. (1992). *Dimensions of achievement motivation in schoolwork and sport. Journal of Educational Psychology, 84,* 290-299.

⇒ & White, S.A. (1992). *The relationship of goal orientations to beliefs about success among elite skiers. The Sport Psychologist, 6,* 334-343.

⇒ (1988). *The relationship between goal perspectives, persistence, and behavioral intensity among male and female recreational participants. Leisure Sciences, 10,* 95-106.

⇒ (1989). *The relationship between task and ego orientation and the perceived purpose of sport among male and female high school athletes Journal of Sport and Exercise Psychology, 11,* 318-335.

⇒ (1992). *Motivation in sport settings: A goal perspective analysis.* In Roberts, G.C. (Ed.), *Motivation in sport and exercise,* 57-92. Champaign, IL: Human Kinetics.

⇒ (1993). *Goals A social cognitive approach to the study of achievement motivation in sport.* In Singer, R. Murphy, M. & Tennant, L.K. (Eds.), *Handbook on research in sport psychology,* 421-436. New York: Macmillan Publishing Co..

⇒ & Olson, L.K. & Templin, T.J. (1991). *The relationship of task and ego orientation to sportmanship attitudes and the perceived legitamacy of injurious acts. Research Quarterly for Exercise and Sport, 62,* 79-87.

Duffy, E. (1957). *The psychological significance of the concept of arousal or activation. The Psychological Review, 64,* 265-275
⇒ (1962). *Activation and Behavior.* New York: Wiley.
⇒ (1972). *Activation,* In Greenfield, N.S. & Sternbach, R.A. (Eds.), *Handbook of Psychophysiology.* New York.: Holt, Rinehart, and Winston.
Duncan, O.D. (1975). *Introduction to Structural Equation Models.* New York: Academic Press.
Dustman, R.E., Schenkenberg, T., & Beck,E.C. (1976). *The development of the evoked response as a diagnostic and evaluative procedure.* In Karru, R. (Ed.), *Developmental Psychophysiology of Mental Retardation.* Springfield, Illinois: Charles C. Thomas.
Dweck, C.S. & Leggett, E.L. (1988). A social-cognitive approach to motivation and personality. *Psychological Review, 95,* 256-273.
⇒ (1986). Motivational processes affecting learning. *American Psychologist, 41,* 1040-1048.
Dwyer, J. & Fischer, D. (1988) Psychometric properties of the coach's version of the leadership scale for sports. *Perceptual and Motor Skills, 67* (3), 795-798.
⇒ & Fischer, D. (1990) Wrestlers' perceptions of coaches' leadership as predictors of satisfaction with leadership. *Perceptual and Motor Skills, 71,* (2), 511-517.
Dynamit Nobel AG, *UIT Journal* (6/92). *Better Performance through Optimal Training (Part 2) A Sustematic Training Plan,* 26-27
⇒ *UIT Journal* (2/86). *In Firth opened a New Shooting Range for Sports Shooters,* 20.
Eagly, A.H. & Crowley, M. (1986). *Gender and helping behavior. Psychological Bulletin, 700* (3), 283-308.
Earl, L. & Stennett, R. (1987) *Student attitudes toward physical and health education in secondary schools* in Ontario. *CAHPER/ACSEPL Journal, 53* (4), 4-11.
Easterbrook, J.A. (1959). *The effect of emotion on cue utilization and the organization of behavior. Psychological Review, 66,* 183-201.
Ebbeck, K. & Weiss, M.R. (1988). *The arousal-performance relationship: Task characteristics and performance measures in track and field athletics. The Sports Psychologist, 2,* 13-27.
Edrington, D. (9/96). *A Palliative for Wandering Attention. Microsoft Internet Explorer.*
Egger, M.D. & Miller, N.E. (1962). *Secondary reinforcement in rats as a function of information value and reliability of the stimulus. Journal of Experimental Psychology, 64,* 97-104.
⇒ & Miller, N.E. (1963). *When is reward reinforcing?: an experimental study of the information hypothesis. Journal of Comparative and Physiological Psychology, 56,* 132-137.
Eichas, T. & Keane, V. (1993). *Relationships among perceived leadership styles, member satisfaction, and team cohesion in high school basketball play-*

ers. *Research Quarterly for Exercise and Sport Abstracts, 64* (Supplement), A101-102.

Eisdorfer, C., Doerr, H.O. & Follette, W. (1980). *Electrodermal reactivity: An analysis by age and sex. Journal of Human Stress, 6(4),* 39-42.

Eliason, M.M. (1907). *Restoration of extinguished reflexes by the use of unconditioned stimuli. Proc. Russian Med. Soc. in Petrograd,* vol. 74.

Elliot-Faust, D.J. & Pressley, M. (1986). *How to teach comparison processing to increase children's short-and long-term comprehension monitoring. Journal of Educational Psychology, 78,* 27-33.

Elliott, E.S. & Dweck, C.S. (1988*). Goals: An approach to motivation and achievement. Journal of Personality and Social Psychology, 54 (1),* 5-12.

Elmadjian, F., Hope, J.M. & Lamson, E.T. (1958). *Excretion rates of spinephrine and norepinephrine.* In Pincus, G. (Eds.), *Recent progress in hormone research* (Vol.14). New York: Academic Press.

Emmons, R.A. & Diener, E. (1986). *An interaction approach to the study of personality and emotion. Journal of Personality, 54,* 371-384.

Engel, B.T. (1960). Stimulus-response and individual-response specificity. *Archives of General Psychiatry, 2,* 305-313.

Englehardt, L. (1976-1978). *The application of biofeedback techniques with a public school setting. Preceedings of the Biofeedback Society of America.*

Engstrom, L.M. (1986). *The process of socialization into keep-fit activities. Scandinavian Journal of Sports Sciences, 8* (3), 89-97.

Enos, B. (9/1996). *Aiming with the Trigger: Developing Trigger Control.* Shooting Sports USA, Vol. 9 No.9. Fairfax, VA.: National Rifle Association of America.

Epstein, L.H. (1976). *Psychophysiological measurement in assessment.* In Hersen, M. & Bellack, A.S. (Eds.), *Behavioral assessment: A Practical Handbook.* Oxford: Pergamon Press.

Epstein, M.L. (1980). *The relationship of mental imagery and mental rehearsal to performance of a motor task. Journal of Sport Psychology, 2,* 211-220.

Epstein, S. & Fenz, W.D. (1967). *The detection of areas of emotional stress through variations in perceptual threshold and physilolgical arousal. Journal of Experimental Research in Personality, 2,* 191-199.

Ericsson, A. & Simon, H.A. (1983). **Protocol analysis: Analysing verbal reports as data.** Cambridge, MA: MIT Press.

Erlichman, H. & Wiener, M.S. (1980). *EEG asymmetry during covert mental activity. Psychophysiology, 17(3),* 228-235.

Erofeeva, M.N. (1913). *Contribution to the physiology of conditioned reflexes to injurious stimuli. Proc. Russian Med. Soc. in Petrograd,* vol. 80.

Essie Systems (1991). *Stress Map. Personal Diary Edition.* New York, N.Y.: Newmarket Press.

Estes, W.K. & Skinner, B.F. (1941). *Some quantitative properties of anxiety. Journal of Experimental Psychology, 29,* 390-400. Reprinted in Skinner (1972b), 512-523.

⇒ (1944). *An experimental study of punishment. Psychological Monographs,* 57 (Whole No. 263). Reprinted in Boe and Church (1968), 108-165.

542

⇒   (1969). *Outline of a theory of punishment*. In Campbell, B.A. & Church, R.M. (Eds.). *Punishment and Aversive Behavior, 57-82.* New York: Appleton-Century-Crofts.

⇒   (1975). *The state of the field: General problems and issues of theory and meta-theory*. In Estes, W.K. (Ed.), *Handbook of Learning and Cognitive processes: Vol.* 1, 1-21, Hillsdale, NJ: Erlbaum.

⇒   (1976). *Structural aspects of associate models for memory*. In Cofer, C.N. (Ed.), *The structure of human memory*, 31-53. San Francisco: Freeman.

Etzel, E. Dr. & Riesterer, U., *UIT Journal* (1/94). *Addressing Team Problems and Resolving Team Conflicts, 24.*

⇒   & Riesterer, U., *UIT Journal* (1/93). *Self Confidence: Part 3, Staleness, Slumps, and Burnout: Prevention and Treatment, 16-17.*

⇒   & Riesterer, U., *UIT Journal* (2/93). *Self-Confidence, Part 4, Flow: The Experience of Peak Shooting Performance, 20.*

⇒   & Riesterer, U., *UIT Journal* (6/92). *Self-Confidence: Part2,.* 60.

Evans, K.L., Thompson, T.J. & Smith, S., (1980). *FORSCOM/US ARMY MARKSMANSHIP UNIT M16A1 RIFLE AND .45 CAL PISTOL MARKSMANSHIP TRAINING EVALUATION: Research Report 1263.* Alexandria, Virginia: US Army Research Institute for the Behavioral and Social Sciences.

Evans, N.J. & Jarvis, P.A. (1980). *Group cohesion: A review and reevaluation. Small Group Behaviour, 2,* 4, 359-370.

Everett, J.J., Smith, R.E. & Williams, K.D., (1992). *Effects of Team Cohesion and Identifiability on Social Loafing in Relay Swimming Performance.* Department of Psychology, University of Washington, University of Toledo. *International Journal of Sport Psychology*, *23*, 311-324.

Eysenck H.J. & Eysenck, S.B.G. (1968 & 1975). *Manual for the Eysenck Personality Inventory.* San Diego: Educational and Industrial Testing Service.

⇒   (1981). *A Model for Personality*. Heidelberg: Springer-Verlag.

⇒   & Eysenck, S.B.G. (1975). *The Eysenck Personality Questionnaire (Adult Version).* London: Chigwell.

⇒   (1967). *The biological basis of personality*. Springfield, IL: Charles C. Thomas.

⇒   (1978). *Superfactors, P, E, and N in a comprehensive factor space. Multivariate Behavior Research, 13,* 475-482.

⇒   (1979). *Personality in sport. Medissport, 1,* 23-26.

⇒   & Nias, D.K.B. & Cox, D.N. (1982). *Sport and personality. Advances in Behavior Research and Therapy, 4,* 1-56.

Fantino, E. (1969). *Conditioned reinforcement, choice, and the psychological distance to reward*. In Hendry, D.P. (ED.). *Conditioned Reinforcement,* 163-191. Homewood, Illinois: The Dorsey Press.

Farkas, G. (1989). *Exposure and response prevention in the treatment of an okeanophobic triathlete. The Sport Psychologist, 3,* 189-195.

Faucette, N. (1987). *Teachers' concerns and participation styles during in-service education. Journal of Teaching in Physical Education, 6* (4), 425-440.

543

Feldman, K. (1976*). The superior college teacher from the student's view. Research in Higher Education, 5,* 243-288.

⇒ (1989) *Instructional effectiveness of college teachers as judged by teachers themselves, current and former students, colleagues, administrators, and external (neutral) observers. Research in Higher Education, 30,* 137-194.

Felton, M. & Lyon, D.O. (1966). *The post-reinforcement pause. Journal of the Experimental Analysis of Behavior, 9,* 131-134. Reprinted in Catania (1968), 72-74.

Feltz, D. & Mugno, D. (1983). *A replication of the path analysis of the casual elements in Bandura's theory of self-efficacy and the influence of autonomic perception. Journal of Sport Psychology, 5* (3), 263-277.

⇒ Landers, D. & Raeder, U. (1979). *Enhancing self-efficacy in high-avoidance motor tasks: A comparison of modelling techniques. Journal of Sport Psychology, I (2),* 112-122.

⇒ & Landers, D. (1983). *The effect of mental practice on motor skill learning and performance: A meta-analysis. Journal of Sport Psychology 5,* 25-57.

⇒ & Petlichkoff, L. (1983). *Perceived competence among interscholastic sport participants and dropouts. Canadian Journal of Applied Sport Sciences, 8,* 231-235.

Fenz, W.D. & Epstein, S. (1967). *Gradients of physiological arousal of experienced and novice parachutists as a function of an approaching jump. Psychosomatic Medicine, 29,* 33-51.

⇒ & Jones, G.B. (1972). *Individual differences in physiological arousal and performance in sport parachutists. Psychosomatic Medicine, 34,* 1-8.

⇒ (1975). *Coping mechanisms and performance under stress. In Landers, D.M. (Ed.), Psychology of Sport and Motor Behavior.* University Park, PA., College of Health, Physical Education, and Recreation, *The Pennsylvania State University HYPER Series Press.*

Ferrari, M., Pinard, A., Reid, L. & Bouffard-Bouchard, T. (1991). *The relationship between expertise and self-regulation in movement performance: Some theoretical issues. Perceptual and Motor Skills, 72,* 139-150.

Ferster, C.B. & Perrott, M.C. (1968). *Behavior Principles.* New York: Appleton-Century-Crofts.

⇒ and Skinner, B.F. (1957). *Schedules of Reinforcement.* New York: Appleton-Century-Crofts.

Feshbach, S., Weiner, B. & Bohart, A. (1996). *Personality,* (fourth edition). Lexington, MA.: D.C. Heath and Company.

Festinger, L., Schachter, S. & Back, K. (1950). *Social pressures in informal groups A study of human factors in housing. Stanford, CA:* Stanford University Press.

Fineman, L.T., *UIT Journal* (1/82). *Interview with Rainer K. Altenburger,* Sales Manager and Public Relations Director, Feinwerkbau, 31-32.

Finn, R. (1989, June). *Sports psychology: Part of winning edge. The Montreal Gazette,* D-7.

Fishwick, L. & Greendorfer, S. (1987). *Socialization revisited: A critique of the sport related research. Quest, 39,* 1-8.

Fiske, D.W. & Maddi, S.R. (1961). *Functions of varied experience.* Homewood, Illinois: Dorsey Press.

Fitts, P.M. (1962). *Factors in complex skill training.* In Claser, R. (Ed.), *Training research and education,* 111-139. New York: Wiley.

Flavell, J.H. (1978). *Metacognitive development.* In Scandura, J.M. & Brainerd, C.J. (Eds.), *Structural/process models of complex human behavior,* 213-245. Alphen a.d. Rijn: Sijthoff & Noordhoff.

⇒ (1979). *Metacognition and cognitive monitoring: A new area of cognitive developmental inquiry. American Psychologist 34,* 906-911.

⇒ (1981). *Cognitive monitoring.* In P. Dickson (Ed.), *Children's oral communication skills.* New York: Academic Press.

Fleury, M., Bard, C. & Carriere, L. (1982). *Effects of reduction of processing time and level of expertise in a multiple-choice decision task. Perceptual and Motor Skills, 55,* 1279-1288.

Fogarty, G.J. (1995). *Some Comments on the Use of Psychological Tests in Sport Settings.* Department of Applied Psychology, Unviersity of Southern Queensland, Australia: *International Journal of Sport Psychology, 26,* 161-170.

Fogle, D. (1982). *Toward effective treatment for music performance anxiety. Psychotherapy Theory, Research and Practice, 19,* 368-375.

Folkins, C.H. & Sime, W.E. (1981) *Physical fitness training and mental health. American Psychologist, 36,* 373-389.

Ford, N. (1991) *The Socio-sexual Lifestyles of Young People in South-west England* (Bristol, South-Western Regional Health Authority).

Forsyth, D.R. & McMillan, J.H. (1981). *Attributions, affect, and expectations: A test of Weiner's three dimensional model. Journal of Educational Psychology, 23,* 393-403.

Forzano, L.B. & Logue, A.W. (1995). *Self-control and impulsiveness in children and adults: Effects of food preferences. Journal of the Experimental Analysis of Behavior, 64,* 33-46.

Fox, L. (1962). *Effecting the use of efficient study habits. Journal of Mathetics, 1,* 75-86. Reprinted in Ulrich, Stachnik and Mabry (1966), 85-90.

Frane, J. (1988). *Description and estimation of missing data.* In Dixon, W.J. (Ed.), *BMDP statistical software manual Vol 2.* Berkeley: University of California Press.

Frankenhaeuser, M. & Johansson, G. (1976). *Task demand as reflected in catecholamine excretion and heart rate. Journal of Human Stress, 2,* 15-23.

⇒ (1971). *Behavior and circulating catecholamines. Brain Research, 31,* 241-262.

Franks, B.D. (1984). *Physical activity and stress: Part 1. Acute effects. International Journal of Physical Education, (4),* 9-16.

Frazier, S.E. (1987). *Introversion-Extraversion measures in elite and nonelite distance Gerorunners. Perceptual and Motor Skills, 64,* 867-872.

Freeman, G.L. (1948). *The energetics of human behavior*. Ithaca: Cornell University Press.

French, K.E. & Thomas, J.R. (1987). *The relation of knowledge development of children's basketball performance. Journal of Sport Psychology, 19*, 15-32.

French, S. & Van Houoten, P., Ph.D. (1987). *Never Say Lie.* Boulder, CO.: CEP, Inc.

Frenker, R. & Lambiotte, J. (1987). *A performance enhancement program for a college football team: One incredible season. The Sport Psychologist, I,* 224-236.

Friedman, N. (1953). *Imagery: From sensation to symbol. Journal of Aesthetics and Art Criticism, 12,* 25-37

Froehlich, W.D. (1978). *Stress, anxiety and the control of attention: A psychophysiological approach.* In Spielberger, C.D. & Sarason, I.G. (Eds.), *Stress and anxiety: Vol. 5.* New York: J Wiley and Sons.

Frost, R.O., Burish, T.G. & Holmes, D.S. (1978). *Stress and EEG-Alpha. Psychophysiology, 15,* 394-397.

Funk, S.C. & Houston, B.K. (1987).*Critical analysis of the Hardiness Scale's validity and utility. Journal of Personality and Social Psychology, 53, 572-578.*

Gagne, R. (1974). *Educational technology and the learning process. Educational Researcher, 3,* 3 -8.

Galin, D. & Ornstein, R. (1972). *Lateral specialization of cognitive mode: EEG study. Psychophysiology, 9,* 412-418.

Gallahue, D. (1985). *Toward positive discipline in the gymnasium. Psysical Educator, 42 (1),* 14-17.

Gallwey, T.W. (1974). *The Inner Game of Tennis.* New York: Random House.

Games, P.A. (1976). *Programs for robust analyses of ANOVA's with repeated measures. Psychophysiology, 13,* 603.

Ganellen, R.J. & Blaney, P.H. (1984). *Hardiness and social support as moderators of the effects of life stress. Journal of Personality and Social Psychology, 47,* 156-163.

Garfinkel, P.E. & Garner, D.M. (1982). *Anorexia nervosa: A multidimensional perspective.* New York: Brunner Mazel.

⇒ & Goldbloom, D.S. (1988). *Anorexia nervosa and bulimia nervosa.* In Garfinkel, P.E. (Ed.). *Anorexia nervosa and bulimia nervosa: Current update,* 3-9. Toronto: Department of Psychiatry, Toronto General Hospital, Eating Disorders Group.

Garner, D.M. & Olmsted, M.P. (1984). *Manual for Eating Disorder Inventory.* Odessa, FL: Psychological Assessment Resources, Inc.

⇒ & Olmsted, M.P. & Garfinkel, P.E. (1983). *Does anorexia nervosa occur on a continuum? International Journal of Eating Disorders, 2,* 11-20.

⇒ & Olmsted, M.P. & Poliuy, J. (1983). *The development and validation of a multidimensional eating disorder inventory for anorexia nervosa and bulimia. International Journal of Eating Disorders, 2,* 15-34.

⇒   & Olmsted, M.P., Polivy J., & Garfinkel, P.E. (1984). *Comparison between weight-preoccupied women and anorexia nervosa. Psychosomatic Medicine, 46,* 255-266.

⇒   & Rockert, W., Olmsted, M.P., Johnson, C., & Coscina, D.V. (1985). *Psychological principles in the treatment of bulimia and anorexia nervosa.* In Garner, D.M. & Garfinkel, P.E. (Eds.), **Handbook for psychotherapy for anorexia nervosa and bulimia,** 513-572. New York: The Guildford Press.

Gasser, T., Bacher, P. & Steinberg, H. (1985). *Test-retest reliability of spectral parameters of the EEG. Electroencephalographic and Clinical Neurophysiology, 60,* 312-319.

Gastaut, H., Roger, A., Corriol, J. & Haquet, R. (1951). *Etude electrographique du cycle d'excitabite cortical. EEG and Clinical Neurophysiology, 3,* 401-428.

Geissmann, G., *UIT Journal* (5/79). *Heinz Weissenberger, Maximum of 600 Points With the Rapid Fire Pistol,* 218.

Gellhorn, E. (1978). *The neurophysiological basis of anxiety: A hypothesis. Perspectives in Biology and Medicine,* 488-513.

Geron, E., Furst, D. & Rotstein, P. (1986). *Personality of athletes participating in various sports. International Journal of Sport Psychology, 17,* 120-135.

Gevins A.S., Zeithlen, G.M., Doyle, J.C., Schaffer, R.E., Yingling, C.D., Callawey, E. & Yeager, C.L. (1979). *EEG correlates of higher cortical functions. Science, 203,* 665-668.

Gibson, J.J. (1979). **The ecological approach to visual perception.** Boston, MA: Houghton-Mifflin.

Giebink, J., Stover, D. & Fahl, M. (1968). *Teaching adaptive responses to frustration to emotionally disturbed boys. J. cons. Psychol. 32:* 366-368.

Gill, D.L., Gross, J., & Huddleston, S. (1983). *Participation motivation in youth sports. International Journal of Sport Psychology, 14,* 1-14.

⇒   & Deeter, T.E. (1988). *Development of the sport orientation questionnaire. Research Quarterly for Exercise and Sport, 59,* 191-202.

⇒   Ruder, M.K. & Gross, J.B. (1982). *Open-ended attributions in team competition. Journal of Sport Psychology, 4,* 159-169.

Gill, J. (1981). *Different perspectives of the purpose for student evaluation of teacher performance at the community college level.* University Of Oregon, Eugene, OR.: Microform Publications.

Glaser, R. (Ed.) (1965). **Teaching Machines and Programmed Learning. 11. Data and Directions.** Washington, D. C.: National Education Association.

Glencross, D.J. (1973). *Temporal organization in a repetitive speed skill. Ergonomics, 16,* 765-776.

⇒   (1975). *The effects of changes in task conditions on the temporal organization of a repetitive speed skill. Ergonomics, 18,* 17-28.

⇒   (1977). *Control of skilled movements. Psychological Bulletin, 84,* 14-29

⇒   (1978). **Psychology and sport.** Sydney: McGraw-Hill.

547

Glencross, D.J., Whiting, H.T.A. & Abernethy, B., (1994). *Motor Control, Motor Learning and the Acquisition of Skill: Historial Trends and Future Directions*. School of Psychology, Curtin University of Technology, Australia, University of York, United Kingdom & Department of Human Movement Studies, University of Queensland, Australia. *International Journal Sport Psychology, 25,* 32-52.

Goetze, H. & Teubner, J. (1982). *Capacity for educational leadership according to the selfimage of student teachers. Theorie und Praxis der Koerperkultur, 31 (9),* 692-696.

Goldberg, E. & Costa, L.D. (1981). *Hemisphere differences in the acquisition and use of descriptive systems. Brain and Language, 14,* 144-173.

Goldstein, M.J., Jones, R.B., Clemens, T.L., Flagg, G.W. & Alexander, R.G. (1965). *Coping style as a factor in psychophysiological response to tension-arousing film. Journal of Personality and Social Psychology, 1,* 290-302.

Goleman, D. (1991). **Psychology Updates: Articles on Psychology** from The New York Times. New York, N.Y.: Harper Collins Publishers, Inc.

⇒   (9/8/1995). *EQ: Why your emotional intelligence quotient can matter more than IQ.* Gannett Newspaper: USA Weekend, Tucson Citizen

Goodman, L.S. & Gilman, A. (1955). **The pharmacologic Basis of Therapeutics.** New York: The MacMillan Company.

Goodwin, D. (1983). **Phobia: The facts.** Oxford: Oxford University Press.

Gopher, D. & Navon, D. (1980). *How is performance limited: Testing the notion of central capacity. Acta Psychologica, 46,* 161-180.

⇒   & North, R.W. (1977). *Manipulating the conditions of training in time sharing performance. Human Factors, 19,* 583-593.

⇒   (1984). *On the psychophysics of workload: why bother with subjective measures? Human Factors, 26* (5), 519-532.

⇒   & Brickner, M. & Navon, D. (1982). *Different difficulty manipulations interact differently with task emphasis:* Evidence for multiple resources. *Journal of Experimental Psychology: Human Perception and Performance, 8,* 146-157.

Gordon, T. (1970). **Parent effectiveness training.** New York: Wyden.

Gould, D. & Horn, T. (1984). *Participation motivation in young athletes.* In Silva III, J.M. & Weinberg S. (Eds**.), Psychological foundations of sport,** 359-370. Champaign, IL: Human Kinetics.

⇒   & Petlichkoff, L. (1988*). Participation motivation and attrition in young athletes.* In Smoll, F.L., Magill, R.A. & Ash, M.J. (Eds.), **Children in sport** (3rd ed.), 161-178. Champaign, IL: Human Kinetics.

⇒   & Weiss, M.R. (1981). *The effects of model similarity and model talk on self efficacy and muscular endurance. Journal of Sport Psychology, 2,* 69-81.

⇒   (1982). *Sport psychology in the 1980s: Status, direction, and challenge in youth sports research. Journal of Sport Psychology, 4,* 203-218.

⇒ & Feltz, D. & Weiss, M. (1985). *Motives for participating in competitive youth swimming. International Journal of Sport Psychology, 16,* 126-140.

⇒ & Feltz, D., Weiss, M. & Petlichkoff, L. (1982*). Participation motives in competitive youth swimmers.* In Orlick, T., Partington, J. & Salmela, J. (Eds.), ***Mental training for coaches and athletes,*** 57-59. Ottawa: Coaching Association of Canada.

⇒ & Horn, T. & Spreemann, J. (1983). *Competitive anxiety in junior elite wrestlers. Journal of Sport Psychology, 5,* 58-71.

⇒ & Horn, T.S. & Spreeman, J. (1983). *Source of stress in junior elite wrestlers. Journal of Sport Psychology, 5,* 58-71.

⇒ & Petlichkoff, L. & Weinberg, R.S. (1984). *Antecedents of, temporal changes in, and relationships between Competitive State Anxiety Inventory-2 subcomponents. Journal of Sport Psychology, 6,* 289-304.

⇒ & Weiss, M. & Weinberg, R. (1981). *Psychological characteristics of successful and nonsuccessful Big Ten wrestlers. Journal of Sport Psychology, 3,* 69-81.

Goulet, C., Bard, C. & Fleury, M. (1989). *Expertise differences in preparing to return a tennis serve: A visual information processing approach. Journal of Sport and Exercise Psychology, 11,* 382-398.

⇒ & Bard, C. & Fleury, M. (in revision). *Peripheral visual information processing in preparing to return a tennis serve. Human Movement Science.*

Graham, G. & Heimerer, E. (1981*). Research on teacher effectiveness: A summary with implications for teaching. Quest, 33,* 14-25.

Greendorfer, S.L. & Lewko, J.H. (1978). *Role of family members in sport socialization of children. Research Quarterly for Exercise and Sport, 49* (2), 146-152.

⇒ (1978). *Socialization into sport.* In C.A. Oglesby (Ed.), ***Women and sport: From myth to reality.*** Philadelphia: Lea & Febiger.

⇒ (1979). *Childhood sport socialization influences of male and female track athletes. Arena Review, 3,* 39-53.

⇒ (1983*). Shaping the female athlete: The impact of the family.* In Boutilier, M.A. & San Giovanni, L. (Eds.), ***The sporting woman.*** Champaign, IL: Human Kinetics.

Greenspan, M.J. & Feltz, D.L. (1989). *Psychological interventions with athletes in competitive situations: A review. The Sport Psychologist, 3,* 219-236.

Greenwald, A.G. (1970). *Sensory feedback mechanisms in performance control. Psychological Review, 77,* 73-99.

Gregson, J.F. & Colley, A. (1986). *Concomitants of sport participation in male and female adolescents. International Journal of Sport Psychology, 17,* 10-22.

Griffiths, T.J., Steel, D.H., Vaccaro, P., Allen, R. & Karpman, M. (1985). *International Journal of Sport Psychology, 16,* 113-119.

Grillner, S. (1975). *Locomotion in vertebrates: Central mechanisms and reflex interaction. Physiological Reviews, 55,* 247-304.

Grings, W.E., (1978). Dawson, M.E. *Emotions and Bodily Responses: A Psychophysiological Approach*. New York: Academic Press.

Grinker, R.R., Kordhin, S.J., Basowitz, H., Hamburg, D.A., Sabahin, M., Persky, H., Chevalier, J.A. & Board, F.A. (1957). *A Theoretical and experimental approach to problems of anxiety. Archives of Neurology and Psychiatry, 76*, 420-431.

Grouios, G. (1992). *The Effect of Mental Practice on Diving Performance*. Department of Neurology, Aristotelium University of Thessalonolo. Greece. *International Journal Sport Psychology, 23*, 60-69.

Grove, J.R. & Prapavessis, H. (1992). *Preliminary evidence for the reliability and validity of an abbreviated Profile of Mood States. International Journal of Sport Psychology, 23*, 93- 109.

Grusec, T. (1968). *The peak shift in stimulus generalization: equivalent effects of errors and non-contingent shocks. Journal of tbe Experimental Analysis of Behavior, 11*, 239-249.

Guertin, W.H. & Bailey, J.P. (1970). *Introduction to modern factor analysis*. Ann Arbor: Edwards Brothers, Inc.

Gullickson, G.R. (1973). *The Psychophysiology of Darrow*. New York: Academic Press.

Gundersheim, J. (1987). *Sensation seeking in male and female athletes and nonathletes. International Journal of Sport Psychology, 18*, 87-99.

Gunn, C.G., Wolf, S., Block, R.T. & Person, R.J. (1972). *Psychophysiology of the cardiovascular system*. In Greengield, N.S. & Sternbach, R.A. (Eds.), *Handbook of Psychophysiology*. New York: Holt, Rinehart, and Winston.

Gunn, H.E. & Gunn, V.C. (1980). *The Test Yourself Book*. Chicago, IL: Chicago Review Press.

Guttmann, M.C., Pollock, M.L., Foster, F. & Schmidt, D (1984). *Training stress in olympic speed skaters: A psychological perspective. The Physician and Sportsmedicine, 12*, 45-57.

Guyton, A.C. (1977). *Basic Human Physiology: Normal Function and Mechanisms of Disease*. Philadelphia, Saunders.

Haggins, S. (1985). *Movement as an emergent form: Its structural limits. Human Movement Science 4*, 119-148.

Hahn, W.W. (1973). *The hypothesis of Lacey: A critical appraisal. Psychological Bulletin, 79*, 59-70.

Haley, J. (1963). *Strategies of psychotherapy*. New York: Grune & Stratton.

Hall, C.R., Pongrac, J. &: Buckolz, E. (1985). *The measurement of imagery ability. Human Movement Science, 4*, 107-118.

⇒ & Pongrac, J. (1983). *Movement Imagery Questionnaire*. London, Ont: *The University of Western Ontario*.

⇒ & Rodgers, W.M. (1989). *Enhancing coaching effectiveness in figure skating through a mental skills training program. The Sport Psychologist, 3*, 142-154.

⇒ Rodgers, W.M. & Barr, K.A. (1990). *The use of imagery by athletes in selected sports. The Sport Psychologist, 4*, 1-10.

550

Hall, E.G. & Erffmeyer, E.S. (1983). *The effect of visuo-motor behavior rehearsal with videotaped modeling on free throw accuracy of intercollegiate female basketball players. Journal of Sport Psychology, 5,* 343-346.

⇒ & Erffmeyer, S.E. (1983). *The effect of visuo-motor behavior rehearsal with videotape modelling on free throw accuracy of intercollegiate female basketball players. Journal of Sport Psychology, 5,* 343-346.

Hall, H.K., Weinberg, R.S. & Jackson, A. (1987). *Effects of goal specificity, goal difficulty, and information feedback on endurance performance. Journal of Sport Psychology, 9,* 43-54.

Hall, S.J., Ph.D. (1995). **Basic Biomechanics,** second edition, 179-181. St. Louis, MO: Mosby-Year Book, Inc.

Halliwell, W. (1989). *Applied sport psychology in Canada. Journal of Applied Sport Psychology, 1,* 35-44.

Hamilton, M. (1959). *The assessment of anxiety states by rating. British Journal of Medicine and Psychology, 32,* 50-55.

Hamilton, S. & Fremouw, W. (1985). *Cognitive behavioral training for college free throw performance. Cognitive Therapy and Research, 9,* 479-483.

Harbin, G.M., Durst, L. & Harbin, D. (1989). *Evaluation of oculomotor response in relationship to sports performance. Medicine and Science in Sports and Exercise, 21,* 258-262.

Hardy, L. & Nelson, D. (1988). *Self-regulation training in sport and work. Ergonomics, 31,* 1573-1583.

Hargreaves, D., Stoll, L., Farnworth, S. & Morgan, S. (1981). *Psychological androgyny and ideational fluency. British Journal of Social Psychology, 20,* 53-55.

Harig, P.T., PhD. (1996). *Stress Management: A guide for senior leaders. Microsoft Internet Explorer.*

Harman, D.W. & Ray, W.J. (1977). *Hemispheric activity during affective verbal stimuli: An EEG study. Neuropsychologia, 15,* 457-460.

Harper, M. & Roth, M. (1962). *Temporal lobe epilepsy and the phobia-anxiety depersonalization syndrome. Comprehensive Psychiatry, 3,* 129-151.

Harre, D. (1982). *Principles of sports training.* Berlin, Germany: Sportverlag.

Harris, D. (1986). *Relaxation and energizing techniques for regulation of arousal* In Williams, J.M. (Ed.), *Applied sport pscyhology: Personal growth to peak performance,* 185-207. Palo Alto, CA: Mayfield.

Harris, D.V. & Harris, B.L. (1984) *The athlete's guide to sports psychology: Mental skills for physical people.* New York: Leisure Press.

⇒ (1986). *The psychology of the female runner.* In Drinkwater, B.L. (Ed.), *Female endurance athletes,* 59-74. Champaign, IL: Human Kinetics.

Harrison, J. (1987). *A review of the research on teacher effectiveness and its implications for current practice. Quest, 39 (1),* 36-55.

Harrison, R.P. & Feltz, D.L. (1981). *Stress inoculation for athletes: Description and case example. Motor Skills: Theory into Practice, 5 (1),* 53-61.

Hartford, H. (1973). *You Are What You Write.*New York, N.Y.: Macmillan Publishing Co.

Harzem, P. (1969). *Temporal discrimination*. In Gilbert, R.M. and Sutherland, N.S. (Eds.), *Animal Discrimination Learning*, 299-334. London: Academic Press.

Hassett, J.A. (1978). *A Primer of Psychophysiology*. San francisco: W.H. Freeman and Company.

Hatcher, J.S., Maj. (1995). *Textbook of Pistols and Revolvers*. Fairfax, VA.: The Firearms Classics Library of the National Rifle Association and It's National Firearms Museum.

Hatfield, B.D, (in press). *Exercise and mental health: A mechanistic discussion*. In Diaant L. (Ed.), *Issues in Mental Health*. Washington, DC: Hemisphere.

⇒ Landers, D.L. & Ray, W.J. (1984). *Cognitive processes during self-paced motor performance: An electroencephalographic profile of skilled marksmen*. Journal of Sport Psychology, 6, 42-59.

⇒ Landers, D.L. & Ray, W.J. (1987). *Cardiovascular-CNS interactions during a self-paced, intentional state: Elite marksmanship performance. Psychophysiology, 24, 542-549.*

Haughton, E. and Ayllon, T. (1965). *Production and elimination of symptomatic behavior*. In Ullmann, L.P. and Krasner, L. (Eds.). *Case Studies in Behavior Modification* 94-98. New York: Holt, Rinehart and Winston, Inc.

Haury, D.L. & Rillero, P. (1994). *Perspectives of Hands-On Science Teaching*. Columbus, OH.: The ERIC Clearinghouse for Science, Matyhematics, and Environmental Education.

Hayes, R.W. & Venables, P.H. (1970). *EEG measures of arousal during RFT performance in Noise. Perceptual and Motor Skills, 31,* 594.

Hearst, E., Koresko, M.B. and Poppen, R. (1964). *Stimulus generalization and the response-reinforcement contingency. Journal of tbe Experimental Analysis of Behavior, 7,* 369-380.

Hebard, G. (1961). Editor, *Catalogue*. Knoxville, IL.: Gil Hebard Guns.

⇒ (1973). *The Pistol Shooter's Treasury*, (second edition), Knoxville, IL.: Gil Hebard.

Heishman, M.F. & Bunker, L. (1989). *Use of mental preparation strategies by international elite female lacrosse players from five countries. The Sport Psychologist, 3,* 14-22.

Hendry, D.P. (1969). Reinforcing value of information: Fixed-ratio schedules. In Hendry, D.P. (Ed.) *Conditioned Reinforcement*, 300-341. Homewood, Illinois: The Dorsey Press.

Henry, C.E. & Darrow, C.W. (1973). Automatic factors in the relation of EEG to heart rate. In Gullickson, G.R. (Ed.), *The Psychophysiology of Darrow*. New York: Academic Press.

Herrnstein, R.J. & Hineline, P.N. (1966). *Negative reinforcement as shock-frequency reduction. Journal of the Experimental Analysis of Behavior, 9,* 421-430. Reprinted in Catania (1968), 211-220.

⇒ (1964). *Secondary reinforcement and the rate of primary reinforcement. Journal of the Experimental Analysis of Behavior, 7,* 27-36.

⇒ (1966). *Superstition*. In Honig, W.K. (Ed.). *Operant Behavior Areas of Research and Application*, 33-51. New York: Appleton-Century-Croft.

⇒ (1969). *Method and theory in the study of avoidance. Psychological Review, 76,* 49-69.

Heuer, H. (1988). *The laboratory and the outside world.* In Meijer, O.G. & Roth, K. (Eds.), *Complex movement behavior: The motor-action controversy,* 77-82. Amsterdam: North-Holland.

Heyman, S.R. (1987). *Research and interventions in sport psychology: Issues encountered in working with an amateur boxer. The Sport Psychologist, 1,* 208-223.

Heymans, C. & Neil, E. (1958). *Reflexogenic Areas of the Cardiovascular System.* Boston: Little Brown.

Hickey, B. (1985). *Mental Training.* Eagle River, AK.: ASCII.

Higginson, F. (9/1985). *Keep Pistol Shooting Simple.* InSights. Washington, D.C.: National Rifle Association.

Hilden, E.W. (5/1983). *Learning how to shoot a pistol.* InSights. Washington, D.C.: National Rifle Association.

Hilgard, E.R. & Marquis, (1940, 1961, 1968), (second edition), revised by Kimble, G.A. of Duke University, New York: Appleton-Century-Crofts.
⇒ (1986**). Divided consciousness.** *Multiple controls in human thought and action.* New York: Wiley.

Hill, J.P. & Lynch, M.E. (1982). *The intensification of gender-related role expectations during early adolescence.* In Brooks-Gunn, J. & Petersen, A.C. (Eds.), *Girls at puberty: Biological and psychological perspectives.* London & New York: Plenum.

Hillyard, S.A., Hink, R.F., Schwent, V.L. & Picton, T.W. (1973). *Electrical signs of selective attention in the human brain. Science.*

Hilts, P.J. (1974). *Behavior Mod.* New York, N.Y.: Bantam Books, Inc.

Himmelwright, A.L.A. (1928). *Pistol and Revolver Shooting.* New York, N.Y.: The MacMillan Company.

Hingtgen, J.N., Sanders, B.J. & De Myer, M.K. (1965). *Shaping co-operative responses in early childhood schizophrenics.* In Ullmann, L.P. and Krasner, L. (Eds.). *Case Studies in Behavior Modification.* New York: Holt, Rinehart and Winston, Inc.

Historical Developments of Marksmanship. (4/1960). Yer'yev, A.A., *Sportifnaya Strel'ba Iz Vintovki (Competitive Marksmanship With Rifle and Carbine).* US Army Intellegence translation No. *H-3205B.* Published for Instructional Purposes, Fort Benning, GA: U.S. Army Marksmanship Unit.

Hodges, L. & Carron, A.V. (1992). *Collective Efficacy and Group Performance.* Faculty of Kinesiology, University of West Ontario, Canada: *International Journal Sport Psychology, 23,* 48-59.

Hodges, W.P. (1968). *Effects of ego threat and threat of pain on state anxiety. Journal of Personality and Social Psychology, 8,* 264-273.

Hodgson, R. & Rachman, R.,II. (1974). *Desynchrony in measures of fear. Behavior Research and Theory, 12,* 319-326.

Hogan, P. & Santomier, J. (1984). *Effect of mastering swim skills on older adults' self efficacy. Research Quarterly, 55 (3),* 294-296.

Holland, J.G. (1957). *Technique for behavioral analysis of human observing.* Science, *125*, 348-350.

⇒ (1960). *Teaching machines: an application of principles from the laboratory. Journal of the Experimental Analysis of Behavior, 3,* 275-287. Reprinted in Ulrich, Stachnik and Mabry (1966), 75-84.

Hollin, C.R., Houston, J.C. & Kent, M.F. (1985). *Neuroticism, life stress concern about eating, body weight and appearance in a non-clinical population. Personality and Individual Differences 6,* 485-492.

Holt, J. (1982). *How children fail.* New York: De Lacorte Press.

Holz, W.C. & Azrin, N.H. (1961). *Discriminative properties of punishment. Journal of the Experimental Analysis of Behavior, 4,* 225-232. Reprinted in Catania (1968), 236-241.

⇒ & Azrin, N.H. (1962). *Interactions between the discriminative and aversive properties of punishment. Journal of the Experimental Analysis of Behavior, 5,* 229-234.

⇒ & Azrin, N.H. (1963). *A comparison of several procedures for eliminating behavior. Journal of the Experimental Analysis of Behavior, 6,* 399-406. Reprinted in Catania (1968), 221-227.

Honig, W.K. (Ed) (1966). *When first published, this was the authoritative review of this area of research.* **Operant Behavior Areas of Research and Application**. New York: Appleton-Century-Crofts.

Horgan, D.D., Millis, K. & Neimeycr, R.A. (1989). *Cognitive reorganization and the development of chess expertise. International Journal of Personal Construct Psychology, 2,* 15-36.

Horne, T. & Carron, A.V. (1985). *Compatibility in coach-athlete relationships. Journal of Sport Psychology, 7,* 137-149.

Houtmans, M.J.M. & Sanders, A.F. (1983). *Is information acquisition during large saccades possible? Bulletin of the Psychonomic Society, 21,* 127-130.

Howard, M., *UIT Journal* (5/82). *Prone Shooting and the Pregnant Woman,* 17.

Huband, E.D. & KcKelvie, J.S. (1986). *Pre and post game state anxiety in team athletes high and low in competitive trait anxiety. International Journal of Sport Psychology, 17,* 191-198.

Huberty, C.J. & Morris, J.D. (1989). *Multivariate analysis versus multiple univariate analyses. Psychological Bulletin, 105,* 3-2-308.

Hull, C.L. (1943). *Principles of Behavior.* New York: Appleton-Century-Crofts.

Hull, J.G., Van Treuren, R.R. & Virnelli, S. (1987). *Hardiness and Health: A critique and alternative approach. Journal of Personality and Social Psychology, 53,* 518-530.

Human Development Institute, Inc. (1967). *Improving communication in marriage.* Atlanta: *Hum. Develop. Institute.*

Humphreys, D.R. (1967). *Neuronal activity in the medulla oblongata of cat evoked by stimulation of the carotid sinus nerve.* In Kezdi, P. (Ed.), **Baroreceptors and Hypertension**. New York: Pergamon Press.

Hunt, H.F. & Brady, J.V. (1955). *Some effects of punishment and intercurrent anxiety on a simple operant. Journal of Comparative and Physiological Psychology, 48,* 305-310. Reprinted in Boe and Church (1968), 188-198.

554

Hurwitz, H.M.B. (1957). *Periodicity of responses in operant extinction. Quarterly Journal of Experimental Psychology, 9,* 177-184.

Husman, B.F. & Silva, J.M. (1984). *Aggression in sport: Definitional and theoretical considerations.* In Silva, J.M. & Weinberg, R.S. (Eds.), ***Psychological foundations of sport,*** 246-260. Champaign, IL: Human Kinetics.

Ilieva, G. (1987). *Some possibilities for purposeful development of a behaviour of a leader. Psikologia-Bulgaria, 15* (3), 24-28.

Ingvar, D.H. (1971). *Cerebral blood flow and metabolism related to EEG and cerebral functions. Acta Anaesthesiologica Scandinavica, 39,* 110-114.
⇒ (1972). *Patterns of thought recorded in the brain. Totus Homo, 4,* 98-103.

Instructor's Guide, Basic Pistol Marksmanship (1959). Washington, D.C.: National Rifle Association.

International Moving Target Guide (1970). Ft. Benning, GA.: The United States Army Marksmanship Training Unit.

International Moving Target Manual (1968 Edition). Ft. Benning, GA.: The United States Army Marksmanship Training Unit.

International Rifle Marksmanship Guide (1973 Edition). Ft. Benning, GA.: The United States Army Marksmanship Training Unit.

International Rifle Marksmanship Guide (1980 Edition). The United States Army Marksmanship Unit, Washington, D. C.: U.S. Government Printing Office.

International Rifle Marksmanship Manual (1968 Edition). Ft. Benning, GA.: The United States Army Marksmanship Training Unit.

Isaacs, I.D. & Finch, A.E. (1983). *Anticipatory timing of beginning and intermediate tennis players. Perceptual of Motor Skills, 57,* 451-454.

Isaacs, W., Thomas, J. & Goldiamond, I, (1960). *Application of operant conditioning to reinstate verbal behavior in psychotics. Journal of Speech and Hearing Disorders, 25,* 8-12. Reprinted in Ullmann and Krasner (1965), 69-73.

Jackson, C. (6/1992). *US Pistol Shooting.* Poway, CA.: Black Mountain Foundation.

Jackson, D.N., Hourany, L. & Vidmar, N.J. (1972). *A four-dimensional interpretation of risk-taking. Journal of Personality, 40,* 483-501.

Jackson, J. *Success in Prone Target Shooting Skills & Coaching Aids.* Imported by OK Weber Company, Eugene, Oregon.

Jagacinski, C.M. & Nicholls, J.G. (1987). *Competence and affect in task and ego involvement: The impact of social comparison information. Journal of Educational Psychology, 79,* 107-114.

Jahoda, G. (1970). *The Psychology of Superstition.* Harmondsworth: Penguin Books.

Janoff-Bulman, R. (1979). *Characterological vs. behavioral self-blame; Inquires into depression and rape. Journal of Personality and Social Psychology, 37,* 1798-1809.

Jasper, H.H. (1958). *Report of committee on methods of clinical examination in EEG*: Appendix: The ten-twenty electrode system of the International

Federation. *Electroencephalography and Clinical Neurophysiology, 10,* 371-375.

Jeka, L. & Kelso, J A.S. (1989). In Wallace, S.A. (Ed.), *Perspectives on the coordination of movement,* 151 170. Amsterdam: North-Holland.

Jenkins, H.M. & Harrison, R.H. (1960). *Effects of discrimination training on auditory generalization. Journal of Experimental Psychology, 59,* 246-253. Reprinted in Catania (1968), 140-145.

Jennings, J.R. & Hall, S.W. Jr. (1980). *Recall, recognition and rate: Memory and the heart. Psychophysiology, 17,* 37-46.

Johnson, H.J. & Campos, J.J. (1967). *The effect of cognitive tasks and verbalization instructions on heart rate and skin conductance. Psychophysiology, 4,* 143-150.

Johnston, J.M. & Pennypacker, H.S. (1971). *A behavioral approach to college teaching. American Psychologist, 26,* 219-244

Jones, B. (1980). *Decision making and hemispheric specialization. Acta Psychologica, 44,* 235-243.

Jones, C.M. & Miles, T.R. (1978). *Use of advance cues in predicting the flight of a lawn tennis ball. Journal of Human Movement Studies, 4,* 231-235.

Jones, J.G. Swain, A. & Cale, A. (1990). *Antecedents of multidimensional competitive state anxiety and self-confidence in elite intercollegiate middle-distance runners. The Sport Psychologist, 4,* 107-118.

⇒ Swain, A. & Cale, A. (1991). *Gender differences in precompetition temporal patterning and antecedents of anxiety and self-confidence. Journal of Sport and Exercise Psychology, 13,* 1-15.

Jones, L.F.,III,O.D., Classé, J.G., O.D., J.D., Hester, M., O.D. & Harris, K., O.D., (2/96). *Association Between Eye Dominance and Training for Rifle Marksmanship: A Pilot Study. Journal of the American Optometric Association, Vol. 67,* 73-76

Jordaan, W. & Jordaan, J. (1989). *Man in Context.* Johannesburg: Lexicon Publishers.

Kahneman, D. (1973). *Attention and effort.* Englewood Cliffs, N.J.: Prentice-Hall.

⇒ Slovic, P. & Tversky, A. (1982) (Eds.). *Judgement under uncertainty: Heuristics and biases.* New York: Cambridge.

Kalmikov, M.P. (1926). *The positive phase of mutual induction as observed in one and the same group of nervous elements of the cortex. Collected Papers, Physiol.. Labs. I.P. Pavlov, vol. i.* 2-3.

Kamal, A.F., Blais, C., Kelly, P. & Ekstrand, K., (1995). *Self-Esteem Attributional Components of Athletes Versus Nonathletes.* Department of Physical Education, University of United Arab Emirates, Child Studies Program, Brock University, St. Catherine, Canada & School of Psychology, University of Ottawa, Canada. *International Journal of Sport Psychology, 26,* 189-195.

Kamin, L.J. (1965). *Temporal and intensity characteristics of the conditioned stimulus.* In Prokasy, W.F. (Ed.). *Classical Conditioning: A Symposium,* 118-147. New York: Appleton-Century-Crofts.

Kampwirth T. & Bates, M. (1980). *Modality preference and teaching methods: A review of the research. Academic Therapy, 15,* 597-605.

Kandel, D. (1986). *Processes of peer influences in adolescence.* In Silbereisen, R.K., Eyferth, K. & Rudinger, G. (Eds.), **Development as action in context,** 203-227. Berlin: Springer-Verlag.

Kanfer, F.H. & Karoly, P. (1972). *Self-control: A behavioristic excursion into the lion's den. Behavior Therapy, 3,* 398-416.

Kasamatsu, A., Okima, T. & Takenaka, S. (1957). *The EEG of Zen and Yoga practitioners. Electroencephalography and Clinical Neurophysiology, 9,* 51-52.

Katz, J.I. (1986) *Long-distance running, anorexia nervosa, and bulimia: A report of two cases. Comparative Psychiatry, 27,* 74-78.

Kaufman, J.S. (1996). *Education and Research on Emotion & Cognition: Seeking Connections. Microsoft Internet Explorer.*

Kay, H. Dodd, D. and Sime, M. (1968). **Teaching Machines and Programmed Instruction.** Harmondsworth: Penguin Books, Ltd.

Kazdin A.E. & Bootzin, R.R. (1972). *The token ecomony: an evaluative review. Journal of Applied Behavior Analysis, 5,* 343-372.

Keele, S.W. (1968). *Movement control in skilled motor performance. Psychological Bulletin, 70,* 387-403.

Keele, S.W. (1982). *Learning and control of coordinated motor patterns: The programming perspective.* In Kelso, J.A.S. (Ed.), **Human motor hehavior: An introduction,** 161-186. Hillsdale, NJ: Lawrence Erlbaum Associates.

Kelleher, R.T. & Fry, W.T. (1962). *Stimulus functions in chained fixed-interval schedules. Journal of the Experimental Analysis of Behavior, 5,* 167-173. Reprinted in Catania (1968), 178-185.

⇒ & Morse, W.H. (1964). *Escape behavior and punished behavior. Federation Proceedings, 23,* 808-817. Reprinted in Thompson, Pickens and Meisch (1970), 613-631.

⇒ & Morse, W.H. (1968). *Determinants of the specificity of behavioral effects of drugs. Ergebnisse der Physiologie, 60,* 1-5.

⇒ (1966). *Chaining and conditioned reinforcement.* In Honig, W.K. (Ed.). **Operant Behavior: Areas of research and application,** 160-212. New York: Appleton-Century-Crofts.

⇒ Fry, W. & Cook, L. (1959). *Interresponse time distribution as a function of differential reinforcement of temporally spaced responses. Journal of the Experimental Analysis of Behavior, 2,* 91-106.

Keller, F.S. & Schoenfeld, W.N. (1950). **Principles of Psychology.** New York: Appleton-Century-Crofts.

Keller, F.S. (1968). *'Good-bye teacher'. Journal of Applied Behavior Analysis, 1,* 79-89.

Kelso, J.A.S. & Scholz, J.P. (1985). *Cooperative phenomena in biological motion.* In Haken, H. (Ed.), **Complex systems. Operational approaches in neurobiology, physical systems and computers,** 75-92. Berlin: Springer.

Kelso, J.A.S. & Tuller, B. (1985). *Intrinsic time in speech production. Journal of the Acoustical Society of America, Suppl. 1,* 77, 553.

⇒ & Wallace, S.A. (1978). *Conscious mechanisms in movement.* In G.E. Stelmach (Ed.), **Information processing in motor control and learning,** 79-116. New York: Academic Press.

⇒ (1981). *Contrasting perspectives on order and regulation in movement.* In Long, J. & Baddeley, A. (Eds.), **Attention and performance: IX,** 437-458. Hillsdale, NJ: Erlbaum.

Kendall, G., Hrycaiko, D., Martin, G.L. & Kendall, T. (1990). *The effects of an imagery rehearsal, relaxation and self-talk package on basketball game performance. Journal of Sport and Exercise Psychology, 12,* 157-166.

Kendall, S.B. (1969). *Discriminative and reinforcing properties of differential trace stimuli.* In Hendry, D.P. (Ed.). **Conditioned Reinforcement,** 261-280. Homewood, Illinois: The Dorsey Press.

Kennard, M.A. & Willner, M.D. (1943). *Correlation between electroencephalograms and deep reflexes in normal adults. Discussions of the Nervous System, 6,* 337-347.

Kenny, D.A (1975). *Cross-lagged panel correlations: A test for spuriousness. Psychological Bulletin, 82,* 887-903.

Keppel, G. (1982). *Design and analysis a researcher's handbook.* Englewood Cliffs, New Jersey: Prentice-Hall, Inc.

Ketterl, L., *UIT Journal* (2/86). *The Respiration during Precision Shooting with Sport Pistols, 6,* 60-61.

Kimiecik, J.C., Allison, M. & Duda, J. (1986). *Performance satisfaction, perceived competence, and game outcome: The competitive experience of Boys' Club Youth. International Journal of Sport Psychology, 3,* 255-268.

Kindler, U. & Riesterer, U., *UIT Journal* (1/88). *Exercise Program,* 60-61.

Kinl', V.A. Shooting With Rifled Weapons, Moscow, (1989). This is a very interesting book. It is a bright green, hard-back textbook for pedagogical institutes. Tthe title in Russian is much more economical. It is of interest for pistol shooters only from: **Chapter 8 (p. 112)** when he describes shooting in schools beginning with 9-10 year olds. Until Hickey read Danik's translation of this book he had not realized that the younger the child the higher the pulse rate: **(p. 131)** 6-8 year olds average 82-95, 9-10 year olds 72-88, 11 year olds 70-80. **Kinl'** gives a very interesting description of the anatomy, physiology and psychology of school-age children. **Chapter 9** deals with shooting in institutes of higher education. Finally, in **Chapter 10** he begins the discussion of the fundamentals of teaching and training methodology: establishment of shooting technique, methodology of teaching the elements of technique, the principles of teaching and training, planning a year's training, training during the preparatory period, training during the competition season, training during the transition period (post-competitive, staleness, loss of form, fatigue), contents of training periods (ideological preparation, physical, technical, tactical, psychological, theoretical}. **Chapter 11** discusses watching over the state of a sportsman's organism: auto-observation, medical, pedagogical and determination of a shooter's preparedness for competition. **Chapter 12** deals with the assessment/evaluation of the teaching-training process.

Kinnard, W.J., Aceto, M.D.G. & Buckley, J.P. (1962). *The effects of certain psychotropic agents on the conditioned emotional response behavior pattern of the rat. Psychopharmacologia, 3,* 227-230.

Kirsch, I. (1982). *Efficacy expectations or response predictions: The meaning of efficacy ratings as a function of task characteristics. Journal of personality and Social Psychology, 42* (1), 132-136

Kirschenbaum, D.S. & Bale, R.M. (1980). *Cognitive-behavioral skills in golf: Brain power golf.* In Suinn, R.M. (Ed.), **Psychology in sports: Methods and application,** 334-343. Minneapolis, MN: Burgess.

⇒ & Tomarken, A.J. (1982). *On facing the generalization problem: The study of self-regulating failure.* In P.C. Kendall (Ed.), **Advances in cognitive-behavioral research and therapy: Vol. 1,** 121-120. New York: Academic Press.

⇒ & Wittrock, D.A. (1984). *Cognitive-behavioral interventions in sport: A self-regulatory perspective.* In Silva, J.M. & Weinberg, R.S. (Eds.), **Psychological foundations of sport,** 81-88. Champaign, IL: Human Kinetics.

⇒ Ordman, A.A. M., Tomarken, A.J. & Holtzbauer, R. (1982). *Effects of differential self-monitoring and level of mastery on sports performance: Brain power bowling. Cognitive Therapy and Research, 6,* 335-342.

Kirsta, A. (1986). *The Book of Stress Survival.* New York, N.Y.: Simon & Schuster, Inc.

Kirwan, J.P., Costill, D.L., Flynn, M.G., Mitchell, J.B., Fink, W J., Neufer, D. & Houmard, J.A. (1988). *Physiological responses to successive days of intensive training in competitive swimmers Medicine and Science in Sports and Exercise, 20,* 255-259.

Klein, D.C., Fencil-Morse, E. & Seligman, M.E.P. (1976). *Depression, learned helplessness, and the attribution of failure. Journal of Personality and Social Psychology, 33,* 508-516.

Kleinknecht, R.A. (1986). *The anxious self: Diagnosis and treatment of fears and phobias.* New York: Human Sciences Press, Inc.

Klint, K.A. & Weiss, M.R. (1987). *Perceived competence and motives for participating in youth sports: A test of Harter's competence motivation theory. Journal of Sport Psychology, 9, 55-65.*

Klorman, R. & Ryan, R.M. (1980). *Heart rate, negative variationn, and evoked potentials during anticipation of affective stimulation. Psychophysiology, 17,* 513-523.

Knox, N. (1976). *Defense of Your Home is Your Choice, Guns & Ammo Home Defense Guns,* 3-6, Los Angeles, CA.: Peterson Publishing Co.

Kobasa, S.C. (1979). *Stressful life events, personality, and health: An inquiry into hardiness. Journal of Personality and Social Psychology, 37,* 1-11.

⇒ Maddi, S.R. & Coulington, S. (1981). *Personality and constitution as mediators in the stress illness relationship. Journal of Health and Social Behavior, 22,* 368-378.

⇒ Maddi, S.R. & Kahn, S. (1982). *Hardiness and health: A prospective study. Journal of Personality and Social Psychology, 42,* 168-177.

⇒ Maddi, S.R., Pucetti, M.C. & Zola, M.A. (1985). *Effectivenss of hardiness, exercise, and social support as resources against illness. Journal of Psychosomatic* Research, *29,* 525-533.

Koller, L. (1963). ***Complete Guide to Handguns****.* New York, N.Y.: Arco Publishing Co.

Kopkh, editor, (1986). ***Shooting Sport And Teaching Methodology,*** Moscow. A textbook (greenish-blue-cover), intended for physical education institutes.

Koupalov, P.S. (1915). *Initial generalization and subsequent specialization of conditioned reflexes. Archive of Biological Sciences, vol. xix.* No. 1.

⇒ (1926). *Periodical fluctuations in the rate of conditioned salivary secretion. Archive Biol. Sciences, vol. xxv.* No. 45.

Kraft, P. (1993) *Sexual knowledge among Norwegian adolescents, Journal of Adolescence, 16,* 3-21.

Krahenbuhl, G.S. (1971). *Stress reactivity in tennis players. Research Quarterly. 42,* 42-46.

⇒ (1975). *Adrenaline, arousal and sport. Journal of Sports Medicine, 3,* 117-121.

Kras, D. (1977). *The transcendental meditation technique and EEG alpha activity.* In Orne-Johnson, D.W. & Farrow, J.T. (Eds.), ***Scientific Research on the Transcendental Meditation Program****.* Collected papers (Vol. 1). Livingston Manor, NY.: Maharishi European Research University Press.

Krasner, L. & Ullmann, L.P. (1965). ***Research in Behavior Modification****.* New York: Holt, Rinehart and Winston.

⇒ (1964). *Behavior control and social responsibility. American Psychologist 17,* 199-204. Reprinted in Ulrich, Stachnik and Mabry (1966), 317-321.

Kreps, E.M. (1925). *Positive induction and irradiation of inhibition in the cortex. Pavlov Jubilee Vol.*

⇒ (1926). *The effect of prolongation of delay upon the excitability of the cortex. Archive of Biol. Sciences, vol. xxv.* Nos. 4.5.

Krilov, V.A. (1925). *Development of conditioned reflexes to stimuli acting through the blood (automatic stimuli). Pavlov Jubilee Vol.*

Krippner, S. & George, L. (1986). *Psi phenomena as related to altered states of consciousness.* In Wolman, B.B. & Ullman, M. (Eds.), ***Handbook of states of consciousness,*** 332-364. New York: Van Nostrand Reinhold.

Kruss, G. (1992) ***Young People and Health****.* Belfast: Whiterock.

Kugler, P.N. & Turvey, M.T. (1986). ***Information, natural law and the self-assembly of rhythmic movement****.* Hillsdale, NJ: Erlbaum.

Kuipers, H. & Keizer, H.A. (1988). *Overtraining in elite athletes: review and directions for the future. Sports medicine, 6,* 79-92.

560

Kurtz, B.E. & Borkowski, J.G. (1984). *Children's metacognition: Exploring relations among knowledge, process, and motivational variables. Journal of Experimental Child Psychology, 37.* 335-354.

Lacey, B.C. & Lacey, J.I. (1974). *Studies of heart rate and other bodily processes in sensorimotor behavior.* In Obrist, P.A., Black, A.H., Brener, J. & DiCara, L.V. (Eds.), *Cardiovascular Psychophysiology.* Chicago: Aldine.

⇒ & Lacey, J.I. (1978). *Two-way communication between the heart and the brain: Significance of time within the cardiac cycle. American Psychologist, 41,* 99-113.

Lacey, J. I. & Lacey, B.C. (1974). *On heart rate responses and behavior: A reply to Elliott. Journal of Personality and Social Psychology, 30,* 1-18.

⇒ (1950). *Individual differences in somatic response patterns. Journal of Comparative and Physiol Psychology,* (1950), *43,* 338-350.

⇒ & Lacey, B.C. (1958). *Verification and extension of the principle of autonomic response-stereotype. American Journal of Psychology, 71,* 50-73.

⇒ (1959). *Psychophysiological approaches to the evaluation of psychotherapeutic process and outcome.* In Rubinstein, E.A. & Paraloff, M.G. (Eds.), *Reasearch in Psychotherapy, Volumne I.* Washington, D.C.: American Psychological Association.

⇒ (1967). *Somatic response patterning and stress: Some revision of activation theory.* In Appley, M.H. & Trumbull, R. (Eds.), *Psychological stress: Issues in research,* 170-197. New York: Appleton-Century-Crofts.

⇒ (1969). *Autonomic indices of attention, readiness, and rejection of the external environment.* In Kimble, D.P. (Ed.), *Readiness to Remember.* New York: Gordon & Breach.

⇒ Bateman, D.E. & Van Lehn, R. (1953). *Autonomic response specificity.* An experimental study. *Psychosomatic Medicine, 15,* 8-21.

⇒ Kagan, J., Lacey, B.C. & Moss, H.A. (1963). The visceral level: Situational determinants and behavioral correlates of autonomic response patterns. In Knapp, P.G. (Ed.), *Expression of the Emotions in Man.* New York: International Universities Press.

⇒ & Lacey, B.C. (1970). *Some autonomic-central nervous system interrelationships.* In Black, P. (Ed.), *Physiological Correlates of Emotion.* New York: Academic Press.

Lack, D. (1943). *The Life of the Robin.* Harmondsworth: Penguin Books Ltd.

Lalli, J.S. & Mauro, B.C. (1995). *The paradox of preference for unreliable reinforcement: The role of context and conditioned reinforcement. Journal of Applied Behavior Analysis, 28,* 389-394.

Landers, D.M. (1978). Motivation and performance: The role of arousal and attentional factors. In W.F. Straub (Ed.), *Sport Psychology: An Analysis of Athlete Behavior.* Ithaca, New York: Mouvement Publications.

⇒ (1980), *The arousal-performance relationship revisited. Research Quarterly for Exercise and Sport, 51,* 77-90.

⇒ (1980). *Moving competitive shooting into the scientists' lab. American Rifleman, 5,* 36-37, 76-77.

561

⇒ & Wang, & Courtet, (1985) *Peripheral narrowing amoung experienced and inexperienced rifle shooters under low and high stress conditions. Research Quarterly for Exercise and Sport,* 56(2), 122-130, In Landers, D.M & Hunt, K.J., ***Shooting Sports Research***,(1988) Washington, DC, National Rifle Association. pp 36-37.

⇒ (1982). *Arousal, attention and skilled performance: Further considerations. Quest, 33* (2), 271-283.

⇒ (1989). *Controlling arousal to enhance sport performance.* In Tenenbaum, G. & Eiger, D. (Eds.), ***Proceedings of the Maccabiah-Wingate International Congress*** (Sport Psychology, 7-27). Netanya: Wingate Institute.

⇒ Daniels, F.S., Hatfield, B.D. & Ray, W.J., *UIT Journal* (4/83). *An Electroencephalographic (EEG) Study of Elite Rifle Shooters, Part 1,* 21-27.

⇒ Daniels, F.S., Hatfield, B.D. & Ray, W.J., *UIT Journal* (5/83). *An Electroencephalographic (EEG) Study of Elite Rifle Shooters, Part 2,* 29+.

⇒ Daniels, F.S., Hatfield, B.D. & Wilkinson, M.O., *UIT Journal* (5/82). *Heart Rate and Its Affects on Performance,* 22-28.

⇒ Petruzzello, S.J., Salazar, W., Crews, D.J., Kubitz, K. A., Han, M. & Gannon, T.L. (1994).(in press). *The influence of electrocortical biofeedback on performance in pre-elite archers. Medicine and Science in Sports and Exercise.* Exercise and Sport Research Institute, Arizona State University: *International Journal Sport Psycholo.,* 25, 313-330.

⇒ Wang, M.Q. & Courtet, P. (1985). *Peripheral narrowing among experienced and inexperienced rifle shooters under low- and high-time stress conditions. Research Quarterly for Exercise and Sport, 56,* 122-130.

⇒

Lang, P.J. (1968). *Fear reduction and fear behavior: Problems in treating a construct.* In Schlien, J.M. (Ed.), ***Research in Psychotherapy***. Washington, DC: American Psychological Association.

⇒ (1969). *The mechanics of desensitization and the laboratory study of fear.* In Franks, C.M. (Ed.), ***Behavior Therapy: Appraisal and Status***. New York: McGraw-Hill.

⇒ (1977). *The psychophysiology of anxiety.* In Akiskal, H. (Ed.), ***Psychiatric Diagnosis: Exploration of Biological Criteria***. New York: Spectrum.

Lanning, W. & Hisanaga, B. (1983). *A study of the relation between the reduction of competition anxiety and an increase in athletic performance. International Journal of Sport Psychology, 14,* 219-227..

Latane, B. (1986). *Responsibility and effort in organizations.* In Goodman, P. (Ed.), ***Groups and organizations***, 277-303. San Francisco: Jossey-Bass.

⇒ Williams, K.D. & Harkins, S.G. (1979*). Many hands make light the work. Journal of Personality and Social Psychology, 37,* 823-832.

562

Laties, V.G., Weiss, B., Clark, R.L. and Reynolds, M.D. (1965). *Overt 'mediating' behaviour during temporally spaced responding. Journal of the Experimental Analysis of Behavior 8*, 107-115. Reprinted in Catania (1968) 82-89.

Laughlin, N. & Laughlin, S. (1994). *The Relationship Between the Similarity in Perceptions of Teacher/Coach Leader Behavior and Evaluations of Their Effectiveness.* Human Performance Laboratory, University of San Francisco and San Francisco Community College. *International Journal Sport Psychology, 22*, 396-410.

⇒ & McGlynn, G. (1983). *The relationship between teacher and student (a) preferences for task-or relationship-motivated instruction and (b) degree of authoritarianism and student evaluations of teacher effectiveness. International Journal of Sport Psychology, 14 (1),* 27-40.

⇒ (1975). *The use of positive motivation in coaching. Scholastic Coach, 44 (9),* 66, 124-125.

Layden, M., M.D. (1977). *Escaping The Hostility Trap.* Englewood Cliffs, N.J.: Prentice-Hall.

Lazarevic, L., & Havelka, N. (1986). *Achievement motivation and sports activity.* In Unestahl, L.E. (Ed.), *Contemporary sport psychology,* 282-288. Orebro: Veje.

Lazarus, A.A. (1973). *Multimodal behavior therapy: Treating the basic id. Journal of Nervous and Mental Disease, 156,* 404-411.

Lazarus, R.S., Deese, J. & Osler, S.P. (1952). *The effects of psychological stress on performance. Psychological Bulletin, 49,* 295-317.

Lee, A.B. & Hewitt, J. (1987). *Using visual imagery in a flotation tank to improve gymnastic performance and reduce physical symptoms. International Journal of Sport Psychology, 18,* 223-230.

Lefebvre-Pinard, M. & Pinard, A.. (1985). *Taking charge of one's own cognitive activity: A moderator of competence.* In Neimark, E.D., De Lisi, R.& Newman, L. (Eds.), *Moderators of competence,* 191-211. Hillsdale, NJ: Erlbaum.

Lehrer, P.M. (1978). *Psychophysiological effects of progressive relaxation and alpha feedback in nonpatients. Journal of Consulting and Clinical Psychology, 46,* 389-404.

⇒ Schoicket, S., Carrington, P. & Woolfolk, R.L. (1980). *Psychophysiological and cognitive responses to stressful stimuli in subjects practicing progressive relaxation and clinically standardized meditation. Behavior Research and Therapy, 18,* 293-303.

Lemmon, V., PhD. (1996). *How to talk to children in schools.* Cleveland, OH.: Case Western Reserve University.

Lemonick, Michael D. (July 17, 1995). *Glimpses of the Mind,* 44-52. New York, N.Y.: Time Inc.

Lenney, E. (1977). *Women's self-confidence in achievement situations. Psychological Bulletin, 84,* 1-13.

Lent, R., Brown, S. & Larkin, K. (1984). *Relation of self-efficacy expectations to academic achievement and persistence. Journal of Counselling Psychology, 31* (3), 356-362.

Leon, G.R. (1984). *Anorexia nervosa and sports activities. Behavior Therapist, 7,* 9-10.

LePoncin, M., Levine, M. & translated by Blair, L. (1990). **Brain Fitness.** *A proven program to improve your memory, logic, attention span, organizational ability, and more.* New York, N.Y.: Random House, Inc.

Lewko, J.H. & Ewing, M.E. (1980). *Sex differences and parental influence in sport involvement of children. Journal of Sport Psychology, 2,* 62-68.

Lewthwaite, R. & Scanlan, T.K. (1989). *Predictors of competitive trait anxiety in male youth sport participants. Medicine and Science in Sports and Exercise, 21,* 221-229.

⇒ (1990). *Threat perception in competitive trait anxiety: The endangerment of important goals. Journal of Sport & Exercise Psychology, 12,* 280-300.

Licht, B.G. & Dweck, C.S. (1984). *Determinants of academic achievement: The interaction of children's achievement orientations with skill area. Developmental Psychology, 20,* 628-636.

Linden, J.J. & Stollak, C.E. (1969). *The training of undergraduates in play techniques. Journal clinical Psychology. 25,* 213-218.

Lindsley, D.B. (1951). *Emotion.* In Stevens, S.S. (Ed.), **Handbook of Experimental Psychology.** New York: Wiley.

⇒ (1952). *Psychological phenomena and the electroencephalogram. EEG and Clinical Neurophysiology, 4,* 443-456.

Littman, R.A. (1994). *Bekhterev and Watson Rang Pavlov's Bell: A Reply to Catania's Query.* A Psycoloquy sponsored by the American Psychological Association. Eugene, OR., *Department of Psychology, University of Oregon.*

Lloyd, J.W., Eberhardt, M.J. & Drake, G.P., Jr. (1996). *Group versus individual reinforcement contingencies within the context of group study conditions. Journal of Applied Behavior Analysis, 29,* 189-200.

Locke, E.A. & Latham, G.P. (1985). *The application of goal setting to sports. Journal of Sport Psychology, 7,* 205-222.

Lorens, S.A. & Darrow, C.W. (1962). *Eye movements, EEG< GSA, and EKG during mental multiplication. Electroencephalography and Clinical Neurophysiology, 14,* 739-746.

Lösel, Heinz, Dr., *UIT Journal* (1/79). *Alcohol - No Means to Improve Your Performance,* 25-27.

⇒ (1/81). *Missed Shots in Clay Pigeon Shooting as a Result of Visual Hallucinations,* 16+.

⇒ (1/86). *Sense of Position, Sense of Movement, and Sense of Strength,* 18-21.

⇒ (1/87). *Nutrition and Athletic Performance,* 12-18.

⇒ (1/88). *Criteria for the Determination of Talent in the Competitive Sport of Shooting, Part 3,* 14, 15, 18, 19, 20.

⇒ (1/91). *Sauna - What the Sport Doctor Has to Say About This, Part 3*, 14.

⇒ (1/92). *Count Down Has Already Started - 1992 Olympic Games in Barcelona - part 3*, 12.

⇒ (1/95). *Color Filter - Necessity or Psychological Effect?*, 8.

⇒ (1/96). *Conditioned Reflex and the Psychology of Learning*, 8+.

⇒ (12/93). *Alcohol Controls in Highly Competitive Sports*, 8.

⇒ (1994). *Electronic Scoring for Rapid Fire Pistol and Sport Pistol Events.*

⇒ (2/78). *A New Filter for Shooting Spectacles*, 61-62.

⇒ (2/79). *The Importance of Rifle Shooters Avoiding Backstrain*, 71+.

⇒ (2/82). *Acclimatization to Regional Influences*, 11+.

⇒ (2/83). *Additional Medical Examinations for Master Shooters*, 26.

⇒ (2/84). *Important Medical Aspects on Sport Referring to the Olympic Games in Summer 1984, Part 4*, 18-20.

⇒ (2/86). *Colour Filtres and Sport Shooting*, 12-19.

⇒ (2/87). *Protein*, 8-14.

⇒ (2/91). *The Use of an Electro-encephalogram to Evalulte Concentrative Meditation during the Aiming and Firing Processes in Sport Shooting*, 8, 9, 11.

⇒ (2/92). *Conduct on the Rifle Range*, 8+.

⇒ (2/93). *Chiropractic and Osteopathy*, 38+.

⇒ (2/93). *Pregnancy and Sport Shooting*, 8.

⇒ (2/94). *Rifle Shooting: Kneeling Position, Part 2*, 8.

⇒ (3/81). *The State of Development of the Swiss Firearms Laws*, 13-17.

⇒ (3/84). *Important Medical Aspects on Sport Referring to the Olympic Games in Summer 1984*, 13-19.

⇒ (3/86). *Holding Power and Blood Circulation in the Process of Duell Shooting*, 20-23.

⇒ (3/91). *Insufficient Sleep Restricts Performance Ability*, 16, 17, 20.

⇒ (3/92). *Does Lead Pose a Special Danger to Sport Shooters?*, 8.

⇒ (3/94). *Light and Dark Vision*, 8.

⇒ (4/79). *Autogenous Training*, 159-162.

⇒ (4/85). *Even an Orthopedic Grip Does Not Fit for Ever*, 22-24.

⇒ (4/86). *Televised Shooting Sport - A New Religion?*, 44-45.

⇒ (4/87). *Criteria for the Determination of Talent in the Competitive Sport of Shooting*, 6-7.

⇒ (4/91). *Prophylactic Measures against Infectious Diseases*, 8-9.

⇒ (4/92). *Does Lead Pose a Special Danger to Sport Shooters?*, 8.

⇒ (4/92). *The Wellness Program - A Key to Optimal Training*, 24.

⇒ (4/93). *Alcohol Controls in Highly Competitive Sports, Part 2*, 8.

⇒ (4/96). *Electrolyte Substitution even during a Competition*, 10-13.

⇒ (5/78). *Pre-Breakfast Fitness Flip*, 233.

⇒ (5/79). *Sense of Hearing, Auditory Defects and Individual Protection of Hearing*, 215-217.

⇒ (5/82). *Grand Prix Moskau*, 26.

⇒ (5/83). *Important Medical Aspects on Sport Referring to the Olympic Games in Summer 1984*, 32-35.

⇒ (5/86). *The Larval Potassium Deficiency and Possibilities of its Determination*, 8-12.

⇒ (5/89). *Cigarette Smoking - A Factor which Impairs the Ability to Perform in Sport Shooting*, 12-13.

⇒ (5/90). *Sauna - What the Sport Doctor Has to Say About This*, 8.

⇒ (5/91). *The Count Down Has Already Started 1992 - Olympic Games in Barcelona*, 8-10.

⇒ (5/92). *Does Lead Pose a Special Danger to Sport Shooters?*, Part 3, 6-8.

⇒ (5/95). *Posture*, 8-15.

⇒ (6/85). *How Does The Sense of Touch and Contact Develop?*, 28-31.

⇒ (6/86). *CISM World Championships in Ota, Portugal from August 2th - 11th, 1986*, 44-45.

⇒ (6/86). *Nutrition and Athletic Performance*, 10+.

⇒ (6/89). *Stress Related Vibrations pose Absolutely no Threat to the Sport Shooter!*, 8-12.

⇒ (6/90). *Sauna - What the Sport Doctor Has to Say About This*, 10-13.

⇒ (6/91). *Fair Play*, 58.

⇒ (6/91). *The Count Down Has Already Started - 1992 Olympic Games in Barcelona - part 2*, 8-11.

⇒ (6/92). *A Posibillity for the Stabilization of Posture during Prone Rifle Shooting*, 12+.

⇒ (6/92). *First Aid for Sport Shooters during a Competition*, 42+.

⇒ (6/94). *All About The Perception of Colors, Part 3*, 10.

⇒ *What a Sport Shooter Should Know About Doping*, 6-7.

⇒ (1/94). *Rifle Shooting: Kneeling Position, Part 1*, 12.

Lowengard, M. (1975). *How to Analyze Your Handwriting*. London: Marshall Cavendish Publications Limited.

Lugs, J. (1968). *A History of Shooting*. Czechoslovokia: Spring Books.

Lumsdaine, A.A. & Glaser, R. (Eds.) (1960). *Teaching Machines and Programmed Learning: A Source Book*. Washington, D. C.: National Education Association.

Mackay, C., Cox, T., Burrows, G. & Lazzerini, T. (1978). *An inventory for the measurement of self-reported stress and arousal. British Journal of Socioclinical Psychology, 17*, 283-284.

Mackay, D.G. (1982). *The problem of flexibility, fluency and speed-accuracy trade-off in skilled behavior. Psychological Review 89, 5*, 483-506.

MacNeilage, P.F. (1966). *Changes in electroencephalogram and other physiological measures during serial mental performance. Psychophysiology, 2*, 344-353.

Maddi, S.R. & Kobasa, S.C. (1984). *The hardy executive: Health under stress*. Chicago: Dorsey.

Maddi, S.R. (1987). *Hardiness training at Illinois Bell Telephone*, In Opatz, J.P. (Ed.), *Health promotion evaluation*. Stevens Point, WI: National Welfare Institute.

Madsden, C.H. (1965). *Positive reinforcement in the toilet training of a normal child: a case report*. In Ullmann, L.P. and Krasner, L. (Eds.). *Case Studies in Behavior Modification*, 305-307. New York: Holt, Rinehart and Winston, Inc.

Maehr, M. & Nicholls, J.G. (1980). *Culture and achievement motivation: A second look*, In N. Warren (Ed.), *Studies in cross-cultural psychology: Vol 2*, 221-267. London: Academic.

Magill, R.A. (1989). *Motor learning: Concepts and applications*, (3rd edition). Dubuque, IA: William C. Brown.

Mahoney, J. (1979). *Cognitive skills and athletic performance*. In P. Kendall & S. Hollan (Ed.), *Cognitive-Behavioral interventions theory, research, and procedures*, 423-443. New York: Academic.

Mahoney, M.J. & Avener, M. (1977). Psychology of the elite athlete: An exploratory study. *Cognitive Therapy and Research, 1,* 135-151.

⇒ (1989). Psychological predictors of elite and nonelite performance in olympic weightlifting. *International Journal of Sport Psychology, 20,* 1-12.

⇒ Gabriel, T.J. & Perkins, T.S. (1987). *Psychological skills and exceptional athletic performance. The Sport Psychologist, 1,* 181-199.

Malmo, R.B. (1957). *Anxiety and behavioral arousal. Psychological Review, 64,* 276-287.

⇒ (1959). *Activation: A neuropsychological dimension. Psychological Review, 66,* 367-386.

⇒ (1972). *Overview.* In Greenfield, N.S. & Sternbach, R.A. (Eds.), *Handbook of Psychophysiology*. New York: Holt, Rinehart, and Winston.

⇒ (1975). *On Emotions, Needs, and our Archaic Brain*. New York: Holt, Rinehart, and Winston.

Mandler, G. & Kremen, I. (1958). *Automatic feedback: A correlational study. Journal of Personality, 26,* 388-399.

⇒ Mandler, J.M. & Uviller, E.T. (1958). *Autonomic feedback: The perception of autonomic activity. Journal of Abnormal and Social Psychology, 56,* 367-373.

Manning, S.K. & Melchiori, M.P. (1974). *Words that upset urban college students: Measured with GSRX and rating scales. Journal of Social Psychology, 94,* 305-306.

Marks, D.F. (1973). *Visual imagery differences in the recall of pictures. British Journal of Psychology 64,* 17-24.

Marks, I. (1969). *Fears and phobias.* New York: Academic Press.

Marksmanship Instructors' and Coaches Guide (1968). Ft. Benning, GA.: The United States Army Marksmanship Training Unit.

Marksmanship Instructors' and Coaches Guide (1972). Ft. Benning, GA.: The United States Army Marksmanship Training Unit.

Marksmanship Instructors' and Coaches Guide (1987). Ft. Benning, GA.: The United States Army Marksmanship Training Unit.

Marlowe, D. & Crowne, D.P. (1964). Marlowe-Crowne social-desirability scale norms. In Crowne, D.P. & Marlowe, D. (Eds.), *The approval motive,* 209-212. New York: Wiley.

Marsh, H. (1987). *Students' evaluations of university teaching: research findings, methodological issues, and directions for future research. International Journal of Educational Research, 11,* 253-388.

Martel, D., Brunelle, J. & Spallanzani, C. (1991). *Leadership style and implications for athletes. Canadian Association of Health. Physical Education and Recreation Journal, 57.*

Marteniuk, R.G. (1976). *Information processing in motor skills.* New York: Holt, Rinehart & Winston.

Martens, R. & Gill, D.L. (1976). *State anxiety among successful and unsuccessful competitors who differ in competitive trait anxiety, Research Quarterly, 47,* 698-708.

⇒   & Peterson, J.A. (1971). *Group cohesiveness as a determinant of success and member satisfaction in team performance. International Review of Sport Sociology, 6,* 44-61.

⇒   & Simon, J.A. (1976). *Comparison of three predictors of state anxiety in competitive situations. Research Quarterly, 47,* 381-387.

⇒   (1971). *Anxiety and motor behavior. Journal of Motor Behavior, 3,* 151-179.

⇒   (1974). *Arousal and motor performance.* In Wilmore, J.H. (Ed.), *Exercise and Sport Science Reviews,* Vol. 2. New York: Academic Press.

⇒   (1975) *Social psychology and physical activity.* New York: Harper & Row.

⇒   (1977). *The sport competition anxiety test.* Champaign, IL: Human Kinetics.

⇒   Burton, D, Vealey, R.S., Bump, L.A. & Smith, D.E. (1990). *The competitive state anxiety inventory-2* (CSAI-2). In Martens, R., Vealey, R.S. & Burton,D. (Eds.), *Competitive anxiety in sport,* 117-190. Champaign, IL: Human Kinetics.

⇒   Burton, D., Rivkin, F. & Simon, J. (1980). *Reliability and validity of the Competition State Anxiety Inventory* (CSAI). In Nadeau, C.H., Halliwell, W.C., Newell, K.M. & Roberts, G.C. (Eds.), *Psychology of motor behavior and sport-1979,* 91-99. Champaign, IL: Human Kinetics.

⇒   Christina, R.W., Ph.D., Harvey, J.S., Jr., M.D. & Sharkey, B.J., Ph.D. (1983). *Coaching Young Athletes.* Champaign, IL.: Human Kinetics Publishers, Inc.

Martin, B. (1961). *The assessment of anxiety by physiological-behavioral measures. Psychological Bulletin, 58,* 234-255.

Maslow, A.H. (1976). *The farther reaches of human nature. New* York: Penguin Books.

Mason, E.J. & Bramble, W.J. (1978). *Understanding and Conducting Research / Applications in Education and the Behavioral Sciences.* U.S.A., McGraw-Hill, Inc.

Mason, J.O. & Powell, K.E. (1985). *Physical activity, behavioral epidemiology, and public health. Public Health Reports, 100* (2), 113-115.

Matsuda, I., Inomata, K., Ochiai, Y., Kaga, H., Shiroyama, G., Sugihara, T., Fujita, A. & Ito, S. (1981). *Research on athletes' psychological aptitudes for sports (No.3). 1981's Reports of Sports Science Research of the Japanese Committee for Sports Science (Report No.3).* Tokyo: the *Japanese Committee for Sports Science.* (In Japanese).

Matteo, S. (1986). *The effect of sex and gender-schematic processing on sport participation. Sex Roles, 15,* 417-432.

Mauro, B.C. & Mace, F.C. (1966). *Differences in the effect of pavlovian contingencies upon behavioral momentum using auditory versus visual stimuli. Journal of the Experimental Analysis of Behavior, 65,* 389-399.

Maynard, I.W. & Howe, B.L. (1987). *Interrelations of trait and state anxiety with game performance of rugby players. Perceptual and Motor Skills, G4,* 599-602.

McArdle, W.D., Katch, F.I. & Katch. V.L. (1981). *Exercise physiology energy, nutrition, and human performance.* Philadelphia: Lea & Febiger.

McAuley, E. & Duncan, T.E. (1989). *Causal attributions and affective reactions to disconfirming outcomes in motor performance. Journal of Sport and Exercise Psychology, 11,* 187-200.

⇒ & Gill, D. (1983). *Reliability and validity of the physical self-efficacy scale in a competitive sport setting. Journal of Sport Psychology, 5,* 410-418.

⇒ (1985). *Modeling and self-efficacy: A test of Bandura's model. Journal of Sport Psychology, 7,* 283-295.

⇒ Russell, D. & Gross, J.B. (1983). *Affective consequences of winning and losing: An attributional analysis. Journal of Sport Psychology, 5,* 278-287.

McClelland, D.C. (1961). *The achieving society.* Princeton: Van Nostrand.

McClintic, J.R. (1978). *Physiology of the Human Body.* New York: Wiley & Sons, Inc.

McCombs, M.L. (1988). *Motivational skills training: Combining metacognitive, cognitive, and affective learning strategies.* In Weinstein, C.E., Goetz, E.T. & Alexander, P.A. (Eds.), *Learning and study strategies: Issues in assessment and evaluation,* 141-169. New York: Academic Press.

⇒ (1989). *Self-regulated learning and academic achievement: A phenomenological view.* In Zimmerman, B.J. & Schunk, D.H. (Eds.), *Self-regulated learning and academic achievement theory, research, and practice: Progress in cognitive development research,* 51-82. New York: Springer-Verlag.

McConnell, J.V. (1977). **Understanding Human Behavior**, second edition. New York, N.Y.: Holt, Rinehart and Winston.

McDonald, S.A. & Hardy, C.J. (1990). *Affective response pattern of the injured athlete: An exploratory analysis. The Sport Psychologist, 4,* 261-274.

McGivern, E. (1938). *Ed McGivern's Book on Fast and Fancy Revolver Shooting and Police Training.* Springfield, Mass.: The King Richardson Company. (1984). New Win Publishing.

McGuigan, F.J. (1978). *Covert functioning of the motor system.* In G.E. Schwartz & D. Shapiro (Eds.), *Consciousness and self-regulation: Advances in research and theory: Vol. 2,* 256-293. New York: Plenum Press.

McGuinness, D. & Pribram, K. (1980). *The neuropsychology of attention*: Emotional and motivational controls. In Wittrock, M.C. (Ed.), *The Brain and Psychology.* New York: Academic Press.

McKearney, J.W. (1969). *Fixed-interval schedules of electric shock presentation: extinction and recovery of performance under different shock intensities and fixed-interval durations. Journal of the Experimental Analysis of Behavior 12,* 301-313.

⇒ (1972). *Maintenance of responding under schedules of response-produced electric shock.* In Gilbert, R.M. and Keehn, J.D. (Eds). *Schedule Effects: Drugs, Drinking and Aggression,* 3-25. Toronto: University of Toronto Press.

McKenzie, T.L. & Rushall, B.S. (1974). *Effects of self-recording on attendance and performance in a competitive swimming training environment. Journal of Applied Behavior Analysis, 7,* 199-206.

McLeod, P. (1980). *What can probe RT tell us about the attentional demands of movement?* In Stelmach, G.E. & Requin, J. (Eds.), *Tutorials in Motor Behavior,* 579-589. Amsterdam: North-Holland Publishing Company.

⇒ (1987). *Visual reaction time and high-speed ball games. Perception, 16,* 49-59.

McNair, D.M., Lorr, M. & Dropplemann, L.F. (1992). *Profile of Mood States Manual..* San Diego: Educational and Testing Service.

Medicine. UIT *Journal* (4/96). *The triggering process seen from the viewpoint of sports medicine - part 1, 6-9.*

Mehrabian, A. & Bank, L. (1978). *A questionnaire measure of individual differences in achieving tendency. Educational and Psychological Measurement, 38,* 475-478.

Merton, R.K. (1969). *Social structure and anomie.* In W.L. Wallace (Ed.), *Sociological theory,* 162-183. London: Heinemann.

Meyer, G.J. & Shack, J.R. (1989). *Structural convergence of mood and personality: Evidence for old and new directions. Journal of Personality and Social Psychology, 57,* 691 -706.

Meyer, M.C., Sterling, J.C., & LeUnes, A. (1988). *Personality characteristics of the collegiate rodeo athlete. Journal of Sport Behavior, 11,* 59-65.

Meyers, A.W., Cooke, C. J., Cullen, J. & Liles, L. (1979). *Psychological aspects of athletic competitors: A replication across sport. Cognitive Therapy Research, 3,* 316-366.

Michael, J.L. (1970). *Rehabilitarion.* In Neuringer, C. and Michael, J.L. (Eds.). *Behavior Modification in Clinical Psychology,* 52-85. New York: Appleton-Century-Crofts.

Millenson, J.R. & De Villiers, P. (1972). *Motivational properties of conditioned anxiety.* In Gilbert, R.M. and Millenson, J.R. (Eds.). *Reinforcement Behavioral Analysis,* 97-127. New York: Academic Press.

⇒ (1967) *Principles of Behavioral Analysis. An introductory text in psychology, written from the point of view of an operant conditioner.* New York: Macmillan.

Miller, A. (1986). *Brief reconstructive hypnotherapy for anxiety reactions: Three case reports. American Journal of Clinical Hypnosis, 28,* 138-146.

Miller, B.P. & Miller, A.J. (1985). *Psychological correlates of success in elite sportswomen. International Journal of Sport Psychology, 16,* 289-295.

Miller, G.A. (1969). *Psychology as a means of promoting human welfare. American J. Psychology.* 24: 1063-1075.

Miller, M. (1993). *Efficacy Strength and Performance in Competitive Swimmers of Different Skill Levels. Faculty of Physical Education,* University of Calgary, Canada: *International Journal Sport Psychology, 24,* 284-296.

Miller, N.E. & Carmona, A. (1967). *Modification of a visceral response, salivation in thirsty dogs, by instrumental training with water reward. Journal of Comparative and Physiological Psychology, 63,* 1-6.

⇒ (1969). *Learning of visceral and glandular responses. Science 163,* 434-445.

Miller, R.B. (1974). A *method for determining task strategies.* American Institutes for Research. Technical Report AFHRL-TR- 74-26. Springfield, VA: *National Technical Information Service.*

Minas, S.C. (1978). *Mental practice of a complex motor skill. Journal of Human Movement Studies, 4,* 102-107.

Minsky, M. (1986). *The Society of Mind.* New York, N.Y.: Simon and Schuster.

Mischel, W. (1968). *Personality and Assessment.* New York: Wiley.

Mizusawa, K., Sweeting, R.L. & Knouse, S. (1983). *Comparative studies of color fields, visual acuity fields, and movement perception limits among varsity athletes and nonvarsity groups. Perceptual and Motor Skills, 56,* 887-892.

Molander, B. & Backman, L. (1989). *Age differences in heart rate patterns during concentration in a precision sport: Implications for attentional functioning. Journal of Gerontology: Psychological Sciences, 44,* 80-87.

Monez, K. *The Smallest World Champion, UIT Journal* (3/81), 10-12.

Morgan, C.L. (1894). *An Introduction to Comparative Psychology.* London: Scott.

Morgan, M.J. (1968). *Negative reinforcement.* In Weiskrantz, L (Ed.). *Analysis of Bebavioral Change,* 19-49. New York: Harper and Row.

Morgan, P., Horstman, D.H., Cymerman, A. & Stokes, J. (1983). *Facilitation of physical performance by means of a cognitive strategy. Cognitive Therapy and Research, 7,* 251-264.

Morgan, W.P. & Johnson, R.W. (1978). *Personality characteristics of successful and unsuccessful oarsmen. International Journal of Sport Psychology, 9,* 55-56.

571

⇒ & Pollock, M.L. (1977). *Psychological characterization of the elite distance runner.* In Milvy, P. (Ed.), **Annals of the New York Academy of Sciences, 301.** New York: New York Academy of Sciences.

⇒ (1979, March). *Anxiety reduction following acute physical activity. Psychiatric Annals. 9*, 141-147.

⇒ (1980). *Test of champions: The iceberg profile. Psychology Today, 14.*

⇒ (1985). *Affective beneficence of vigorous physical activity. Medicine and Science in Sports and Exercise, 17*, 94-100.

⇒ (1985). *Selected psychological factors limiting performance: A mental health model.* In Clarke, D.H. & Eckert, H.M. (Eds.). **Limits of human performance**, 70-80. Champaign, IL: Human Kinetics.

⇒ (1987). *Reduction of state anxiety following acute physical activity.* In Morgan, W. P. & Goldston, S.E. (Eds.), **Exercise and mental health**, 105-109, 155-159. Washington DC: Hemisphere.

⇒ Brown, D. R., Raglin, J.S., O'Connor, P.J. & Ellickson, K.A. (1987). *Psychological monitoring of overtraining and staleness. British Journal of Sports Medicine, 21*, 107-114.

⇒ Costill, D.1L., Flynn, M.G., Raglin, J.S. & O'Connor, P.J. (1988). *Mood disturbance following increased training in swimmers. Medicine and Science in Sports and Exercise, 20*, 408-414.

⇒ Costill, D.L. (1972). *Psychological characteristics of the marathon runner. Journal of Sports Medicine and Physical Fitness, 12*, 42-46.

⇒ Costill, D.L., Flynn, M.G., Raglin, J.S., & O'Connor, P.J. (1988) *Mood disturbance following increased training in swimmers. Medicine and Science in Sports and Exercise, 20*, 408-414

Morris, D. (1967). **The Naked Ape.** London: Jonathan Cape.

Morris, W.N. (1989). **Mood: The frame of mind.** New York: Springer-Verlag.

Morse, W.H. & Kelleher, R.T. (1970). *Schedules as fundamental determinants of behavior.* In Schoenfeld, W.N. (Ed.). **The Theory of Reinforcement Schedules**, 139-185. New York: Appleton-Century-Crofts.

Mowrer, O.H. (1947). *On the dual nature of learning as a reinterpretation of 'conditioning' and 'problem-solving'. Harvard Educational Review, 17*, 102-148.

Muenzinger, K.F. (1934). *Motivation in learning: 1. Electric shock for correct response in the visual discrimination habit. Journal of Comparative and Physiological Psychology, 17*, 267-277. Reprinted in Boe and Church (1968), 14-26.

Mumford, B. & Hall, C. (1985). *The effects of internal and external imagery on performing figures in figure skating. Canadian Journal of Applied Sport Sciences, 10*, 171-177.

Mundy-Castle, A.C. (1953*). Electrical responses of the brain in relation to behavior. British Journal of Psychology, 44*, 318-329.

Murdock, M. (1974). *41ˢᵗ World Shooting Championships - Thun, Switzerland.* Mesa, AZ.: United States Women's International Rifle Organization.

Murphy, S.M. & Woolfolk, R.L. (1987). *The effects of cognitive interventions on competitive anxiety and performance on a fine motor skill accuracy task. International Journal of Sport Psychology, 18,* 152-166.

Musselwhite, R. (1970). *Why Navy Scores Shoot Upward.* Washington, D.C.: The American Rifleman.

Myers, A.M. & Lips, H. (1978). *Participation in competitive amateur sports as a function of psychological androgyny. Sex Roles, 4,* 571-578.

Myerson, J. & Green, L. (1995). *Discounting of delayed rewards: Models of individual choice. Journal of the Experimental Analysis of Behavior, 64,* 263-276.

Namënyl, J. *UIT Journal* (5/81). *The Miracle of Miracles,* 31.

Nation, J.R. & LeUnes, A. (1983). *Personality characteristics of intercollegiate players as determined by position, classification, and redshirt status. Journal of Sport Behavior, 6,* 92-101.

National Smallbore Rifle Association of Great Britain (Video 1992). *Sportliches Pistolenschielen, Teil I.*

National Smallbore Rifle Association of Great Britain (Video 1992). *Sportliches Pistolenchielen, Teil II.*

Neiss, R.. (1988). *Reconceptualizing arousal: Psychological states in motor performance. Psychological Bulletin, 103,* 345-366.

Neisser, V. (1976). *Cognition and reality: Principles and implications of cognitive psychology.* San Fransico: Freeman.

Neitz, E.A. (1907). *Mutual interaction of conditioned reflexes. Bulletin of Military Med. Acad.,* 1908; Preliminary Commun. *Proc. Russian Med. Soc. in Petrograd, vol. 74.*

Nemethy, I. *UIT Journal* (1/93). *The Individual psychological preparation of a female sport shooter,* 46-47.

Nemiah, J.C. (1963). *Emotions and gastrointestinal disease.* In Lief, H., Lief, V.F. & Lief, N.R. (Eds.). *The Psychological Basis of Medical Practice,* 233-244. New York: Hoeber.

Nettleton, B. (1979). *Attention demands of ball-tracking skill. Perceptual and Motor Skills, 49,* 531-534.

Neuringer, A.J. (1970). *Superstitious key-pecking after three peck produced reinforcements. Journal of the Experimental Analysis of Behavior, 13,* 127-134.

⇒ & Chung, S. (1967). *Quasi-reinforcement: Control of responding by a percentage reinforcement schedule. Journal of the Experimental Analysis of Behavior, 10,* 417-424.

Newell, A. & Rosenbloom, P.S. (1981). *Mechanisms of skill acquisition and the law of practice.* In Anderson, J.R. (Ed.), *Cognitive skills and their acquisition,* 1-51. Hillsdale, NJ: Lawrence Erlbaum Associates.

Newell, K.M. (1985). *Coordination, control and skill.* In Goodman, D., Wilberg, R.B. & Franks, I.M. (Eds), *Differing perspectives in motor learning, memory and control,* 295-317. Amsterdam: North-Holland.

Nicholls, J.G. (1978). *The development of the concepts of effort and ability, perception of own attainment, and the understanding that difficult tasks require more ability. Child Development, 49,* 800-814.

573

⇒   (1980). *The development of the concept of difficulty. Merrill-Palmer Quarterly, 26*, 271-281.

⇒   & Miller, A.. (1984). *Development and its discontents: The differentiation of the concept of ability.* In J. Nicholls (Ed.), **Advances in motivation and achievement: The development of achievement motivation**. Greenwich, CT: JAI Press.

⇒   (1984). *Achievement motivation: Conceptions of ability, subjective experience, task choice, and performance. Psychological Review, 91*, 328-346.

⇒   (1989). **The competitive ethos and democratic education**. Cambridge, MA: Harvard University Press.

⇒   (1992). *The general and the specific in the development and expression of achievement motivation.* In G.C. Roberts (Ed.), **Motivation in sport and exercise**, 31-56. Champaign, IL: Human Kinetics.

Nideffer, R.M. (1981). **The Ethics and Practice of Applied Sport Psychology**. Ann Arbor, MI.: Mouvement Publications.

⇒   (1985). **Athlete's guide to mental training**. Champaign, IL: Human Kinetics Publishers.

⇒   (1986). *Concentration and attention control training.* In Williams, J.M. (Ed.), **Applied sport psychology: Personal growth to peak performance**, 257-284. Palo Alto, CA: Mayfield.

⇒   Dufresne, P., Neswig, D. & Selder, D. (1980). *The future of applied sport psychology. Journal of Sport Psychology, 2*, 170-174.

Nightline, (1988, February). *Sport Psychology. Journal Graphics.* New York: ABC.

Nikolaev, P.N. (1911). *Analysis of complex conditioned reflexes. Archive Biol. Sciences, vol. xvi.* No. 5.

Nisbett, R.E. & Wilson, T.D. (1977). *Telling more than we can know: Verbal reports on mental processes Psychological Review, 84*, 231-259.

Nonte, G.C., Jr. (1975). **Pistol & Revolver Guide**. South Hackensack, N.J.: Stoeger Publishing Company.

Nordin, M., R.P.T., Dr. Sci. & Frankel, V.H., M.D., Ph.D. (1989). **Basic Biomechanics of the Musculoskeletal System**. Philadelphia, PA.: Lea & Febiger.

Noruzze, G. & Magoun, H.W. (1949). *Brain stem reticular formation and activation of the EEG. Electroencephalography and Clinical Neurophysiology, 1*, 455-473.

NRA Basic Pistol Instruction (1987). Washington, D.C.: National Rifle Association of America.

NRA Junior Rifle Shooting (1993). Washington, D.C.: National Rifle Association of America.

NRA...Illustrated Shooting Handbook (1962). Washington, D.C.: National Rifle Association of America.

NRA Police Firearms Instructor Manual (1968). Washington, D.C.: National Rifle Association of America.

NRA Pre-Coach School Study Guide (1979). Washington, D.C.: National Rifle Association of America.

NRA Shooting Sports Camp Planning Guide (1996). Safety and Education Division, Fairfax, VA.: National Rifle Association of America.

Nutbeam, D., Aaro, L.E. & Catford, J. (1989). *Understanding children's health behaviour: the implications for health promotion for young people. Social Sciences and Medicine, 29* (3), 317-325.

O'Connell, A. & O'Connell, V. (1974). *Choice and Change, The Psychology of Holistic Growth, Adjustment, and Creativity*, fourth edition. Englewood Cliffs, N.J.: Prentice-Hall, Inc.

O'Connell, L. (11/5/1995). *Keeping your cool: Happier living is linked to emotional intellegence.* Tucson, AZ.: The Arizona Daily Star.

O'Halloran, A. & Gauvin, L., (1994). *The Role of Preferred Cognitive Style in the Effectiveness of Imagery Training.* School of Graduate Studies and Department of Exercise Science, Concordia University, Canada. *International Journal Sport Psychology, 25,* 19-31.

O'Connor, K.A. & Webb, J.L. (1976). *Investigation of personality traits of college female athletes and nonathletes. Research Quarterly, 47,* 203-210.

Oldham, J.M., M.D. & Morris, L.B. (1990). *The Personality Self-Portrait: Why You Think, Work, Love, and Act the Way You Do.* New York: Bantam Books.

Olds, J. (1956) *Pleasure centers in the brain. Scientific American, 195,* 105-116.

Ollendick, T.H. & Murphy, M.J. (1977). *Differential effectiveness of muscular and cognitive relaxation as a function of locus of control. Journal of Behavior Therapy and Experimental Psychiatry, 8,* 223-228.

Olson, J. (compiled by).*Famous Automatic Pistols and Revolvers*, Volume 2. Jolex Inc.

O'Malley, M.N. & Gillette, C.S. (1984). *Exploring the relationship between traits and emotions. Journal of Personality, 52,* 274-284.

Orbist, P.A. (1968). *Heart rate and somatic-motor coupling during classical aversive conditioning in humans. Journal of Experimental Psychology, 77,* 180-193.

⇒ (1976). *The cardiovascular-behavior interaction as it appears today. Psychophysiology, 13,* 95-107.

⇒ Howard, J.L., Lawler, J.E., Galosy, R.A., Meyers, K.A. & Gabelein, C.J. (1974). *The cardiac-somatic interaction.* In Obrist, P.A., Black, A.H., Brener, J. & Dicara, L.A. (Eds.), *Cardiovascular psychophysiology*. Chicago: Aldine.

⇒ Webb, R.A., & Sutterer, J.R. (1969). *Heart rate and somatic changes during aversive conditioning and a simple reaction time task. Psychophysiology, 5,* 696-723.

Orlick, T. & Partington, J. (1986). *Psyched.* Ottawa: Coaching Association of Canada.

⇒ & Partington, J.T. (1987). *The sport psychology consultant: Analysis of critical component as viewed by Canadian Olympic athletes. The Sport Psychologist, 1,* 4-17.

⇒ & Partington, J.T. (1988). *Mental links to excellence. The Sport Psychologist, 2,* 105-130.

⇒ (1986). *Psyching for sport: Mental training for athletes.* Champaign, IL: Leisure Press.

⇒ (1990). *In pursuit of excellence: How to win in sport and life through mental training,* second edition. Champaign, IL: Human Kinetics.

Orne, M.T. & Paskewitz, D.A. (1974*). Aversive situational effects on alpha feedback training. Science, 186,* 458-460.

Ornstein, P.A. & Naus, M.J. (1978). *Rehearsal processes in children's memory.* In Ornstein, P.A. (Ed.), *Memory development in children,* 155-194. Hillsdale, NJ: Lawrence Erlbaum Associates.

Ott, L. (1977). *An Introduction to Statistical Methods and Data Analysis.* North Scituate, Massachusetts: Duxberg Press.

Oxendine J.B. (1970). *Emotional arousal and motor performance. Quest, 13,* 23-32.

Paillard, J. & Amblard, B. (1985). *Static versus kinetic visual cues for the processing of spatial relationships.* In Ingle, D.J., Jeannerod, M., & Lee, D.N. (Eds.), *Brain mechanism of spatial vision.* The Hague: Martinos Nihjoff.

⇒ (1985). *Development and acquisition of motor skills: A challenge prospect for Neuroscience.* In Wade, M.G. & Whiting, H.T.A. (Eds.), *Motor development in children: Aspects of coordination and control,* 12-32. Dordrecht: Martinus Nijhoff.

Paivio, A. (1971). *Imagery and verbal processes.* New York: Holt, Rinehart and Winston.

⇒ (1985). *Cognitive and motivational functions of imagery in human performance. Canadian Journal of Applied Sport Science, 10,* 22s-28s.

⇒ (1986). *Mental representations: A dual coding approach.* New York: Oxford University.

Palacio, J. & Salmela, J.H. (1986). *Identified roles, programmes and models of sport psychology in North America. International Journal of Sport Psychology, 17,* 311-326.

Palincsar, A.S. & Brown, A.L. (1984). *Reciprocal teaching of comprehension-monitoring activities. Cognition and Instruction, 1,* 117-175.

Palladin, A.V. (1906). *Development of artificial conditioned reflex to a sum of two stimuli. Proc. Russian Med. Soc. in Petrograd, vol. 73.*

Palmer, D.J. & Goetz, E.T. (1988). *Selection and use of study strategies: The role of the studier's beliefs about self and strategies.* In Weinstein, C.E., Goetz, E.T. & Alexander, P.A. (Eds.), *Learning and study strategies: Issues in assessment and evaluation,* 41-61. New York: Academic Press.

Paris, D.G., Cross, C.R., & Lipson, M.Y. (1984). *Informed strategies for learning: A program to improve children's reading awareness and comprehension. Journal of Educational Psychology, 76,* 1239-1252.

Paris, S.G. (1978). *The development of inference and transformation as memory operations.* In P.A. Ornstein (Ed.), *Memory development in children,* 101-128. Hillsdale, NJ: Erlbaum.

Parker, H.E. (1981). *Visual detection and perception in netball.* In Cockerill, I.M. & Mac Gillivary, W.W. (Eds.), *Vision and sport,* 42-53. Cheltenham: Stanley Thomas.

Parrot, J. (1973). *The measurement of stress and strain.* In Singleton, N.T., Fox, J.G. & Whitfield, D. (Eds.), *Measurement of man at work.* London: Taylor and Francis.

Partington, J.T. & Orlick, T. (1987). *The sport psychology consultant: Olympic coaches' views. The Sport Psychologist, 1,* 95-102.

⇒ & Shangi, G.M. (1992). *Developing and Understanding of Team Psychology.* Department of Psychology, Carleton University, Canada. *International Journal Sport Psychology, 23,* 28-47.

Passer, M.W. & Scanlan, T.K. (1980). *The impact of game outcome on the post-competition affect and performance evaluations of young athletes.* In Nadeau, C.H., Halliwell, W.R., Newell, K.M. & Roberts, G.C. (Eds.), *Psychology of motor behavior and sport - 1979* 100-111. Champaign, IL: Human Kinetics.

⇒ (1982). *Children in sports: Participation motives and psychological stress. Quest, 33,* (2), 231-244.

Patriksson, G. (1981). *Socialization to sports involvement. Influences of parents and peers. Scandinavian Journal of Sports Sciences, 3 (l),* 27-32.

Patterson, C.R. (1965). *An application of conditioning techniques to the control of a hyperactive child.* In Ullmann, L.P. & Krasner, L. (Eds.). *Case Studies in Behavior Modification,* 370-375. New York: Holt Rinehart and Winston, Inc.

Paul, G.L. & Bernstein, D.A. (1973). *Anxiety and Clinical Problems: Systematic Desensitization and Related Techniques.* New York: General Learning Press.

⇒ (1969). *Outcome of systematic desensitization I: Background procedures and uncontrolled reports of individual treatment.* In Franks, C.M. (Ed.), *Behavior Therapy: Appraisal and Status.* New York; McGraw-Hill.

⇒ (1969). *Physiological effects of relaxation training and hypnotic suggestion. Journal of Abnormal Psychology, 74,* 425-437.

Pavlov, I.P. (1927). *Conditioned Reflexes, Lectures I-XXIII.* G.V. Anrep, Trans. London: *Oxford University Press,* (Reprinted, New York: Dover Publications 1960).

⇒ *Twenty years of objective study of the higher nervous activity of animals. Articles, 1-36.*

Peters, T.J. & Waterman, R.H. (1982). *In search of excellence.* New York: Harper & Row.

Petrova, M.K. (1925). *Pathological deviations of the inhibitory and excitatory process in a case of their clashing. Collected Papers, Physiol. Labs. I.P. Pavlov,* vol. i. Nos. 2-3.

⇒ (1925). *The combatting of sleep: the mutual counterbalancing of the excitatory and inhibitory processes. Pavlov Jubilee Vol.*

Peverly, S.T. (1991). *Problems with the knowledge-based explanation of memory and development. Review of Educational Research, 61,* 71-93.

Pew, R.W. (1966). *Acquisition of hierarchical control over the temporal organization of a skill. Journal of Experimental Psychology, 71,* 764-771.

Piaget, J. & Inhelder, B. (1971). **Mental imagery in the child** New York: Basic Books.

Pickering, T. (1775). **An Easy Plan of Discipline for a Militia**. Salem, New-England.

Pinel, J.P. & Schultz, T.D. (1978). *Effect of antecedent muscle tension levels on motor behavior. Medicine and Science in Sport, 10,* 177-182.

Ping, Ye., (1993). *Competitive Motives as Predictors of Cognitive Trait Anxiety in University Athletes.* Chukyo University, Japan. *International Journal Sport Psychology, 24,* 259-269.

Pinneo, L.R. (1961). *The effects of induced muscle tension during tracking on level of activation and performance. Journal of Experimental Psychology, 62,* 523-531.

Pistol Marksmanship Guide (1972). Ft. Benning, GA.: The United States Army Marksmanship Training Unit.

Pistol Marksmanship Guide (1981). The United States Army Marksmanship Unit, Washington, D.C.: The U.S. Government Printing Office.

Pistol Marksmanship Manual (1969). Ft. Benning, GA.: The United States Army Marksmanship Training Unit.

Pistols and Revolvers (1953). FM 23-35. Washington, D.C.: United States Printing Office.

Pistols and Revolvers (1960). FM 23-35, AFM 50-17. Washington, D.C.: Departments of the Army and the Air Force.

Podkopaev, N.A. & Grigorovich, L.S. (1924). *The development of symmetrical positive and negative reflexes. Vrashebnoe Delo,* Nos. 1-2, 3-4.

⇒ (1924). *Determination of the exact moment at which irradiation of inhibition begins. I.P. Pavlov Jubilee Volume,* (abstract in *Physiol. Abstracts, vol. viii.* 1924).

⇒ (1924). *The mobility of the inhibitory process.* **Collected Papers of Physiol. Lab. of I.P. Pavlov,** vol. vii. No.1, (abstract in *Physiol. Abstracts, vol. viii.* 1924).

⇒ (1925). *Development of a conditioned reflex to an automatic (direct) stimulus.* **Collected Papers of Physiol. Labs. I.P. Pavlov,** *vol. i.* 2-3, 1926 (abstract, *Zentralblatt fur die gesammte Neurologie und Psychiatrie,* Bd. xxxix.).

Porter, K. & Foster, J. (1986). *The mental athlete.* Dubuque, IA.: Wm. C. Brown Publishers.

Posner, M.I. (1978). *Chronometric explanation of mind.* Hillsdale, NJ: Erlbaum.

⇒ (Ed.). (1989). *Foundations of cognitive science.* Bradford Brook, Cambridge, MA.: MIT Press.

Potehin, S.I. (1911). *Contributions to the physiology of internal inhibition of conditioned reflexes. Thesis, Petrograd,* 1911; Preliminary communication, *Proc. Russian Med. Soc. in Petrograd, vol. 78.*

⇒ (1911). *The pharmacology of conditioned reflexes. Proc. Russian Med. Soc. in Petrograd, vol. 78.*

Poulton, E.C. (1957). *On prediction of skilled movements. Psychological Bulletin, 54,* 467-478.

Powis, R.L. (1985). *The Human Body and Why It Works.* Englewood Cliffs, N.J.: Prentice-Hall.

Prapavessis, H. & Carron, A.V. (1988). *Learned helplessness in sport. The Sport Psychologist, 2,* 189-201.

⇒ & Grove, J.R., (1994). *Personality Variables as Antecedents of Precompetitive Mood States.* Department of Human Movement Studies, University of Western Australia. *International Journal Sport Psychology,* 25, 81-99.

Pratt, R.W. & Nideffer, R.M. (1981). *Taking Care of Business.* A manual to guide the refinement of Attention Control Training developed by Dr. Nideffer. San Diego, CA.: Enhanced Performance Associates.

Pressley, M. & Ghatala, E.S. (1989). *Metacognitive benefits of taking a test for children and young adolescentes. Journal of Experimental Child Psychology, 47,* 430-450.

⇒ (1979). *Increasing children's self-control through cognitive interventions. Review of Educational Research, 49,* 319-370.

⇒ Borkowski, J.G. & O'Sullivan, J. (1988). *Children's metamemory and the teaching of memory strategies.* In Forrest-Pressley, D.L., Mackinnon, G.E. & Waller, T.G. (Eds.), *Metacognition, cognition, and human performance: Vol. 1* 111-153. New York: Academic Press.

⇒ Borkowski, J.G. & Schneider, W. (1987). *Cognitive strategies: Good strategy users coordinate metacognition and knowledge.* In Vasta, R. & Whitehurst, G. (Eds.), *Annals of child development: Vol. 4.* Greenwich, CT: JAI Press.

⇒ Heisel, B.E., McCormick, C.G. & Nakamura, G.V. (1982). *Memory strategy instruction with children.* In Brainerd, C.J. & Pressley, M. (Eds), *Progress in cognitive development research: Vol. 2. Verbal processes in children* 125-159. New York: Springer-Verlag.

Pullum, B. & Hanenkrat, F.T.(1973, 1975). *Position Rifle Shooting.* South Hackensack, N.J.: Stoeger Publishing Company.

⇒ (1977). *Psychology of Shooting. Schiessportschule Dialogues, 1,* 1-17.

Quarti, Q. & Renaud, J. (1964). *A new treatment of constipation by conditioning:* a preliminary report. In Franks, C.M. (Ed.). *Conditionmg Techniques in Clinical Practice and Research.* New York: Springer. Reprinted in Ulrich, Stachnik & Mabry (1966), 138-143.

Rabkin, J.G., & Streuning, E.L. (1976). *Life events, stress and illness. Science, 194,* 1013-1020.

Rachlin, H. (1970). *Introduction to Modern Behaviorism.* A very clear *and well-written introduction to operant conditioning.* San Francisco: W. H. Freeman and Co.

Raglin, J.S., Eksten, F. & Garl, T. (1995). *Mood State Responses to a Pre-Season Conditioning Program in Male Collegiate Basketball Players.* Department of Kinesiology and Athletics, Indiana University. *International Journal Sport Psychology, 26,* 214-225.

Railo, W. (1986). *Willing to win.* Naarden, Holland: Amax Export Bv.

Rasenkov, I.P. (1924). *Modifications of the excitatory process in the cortex under some complex conditions.* **Collected Papers, Physiol. Labs. I.P. Pavlov,** vol. i. No. 1.

Raugh, D. & Wall, A. (1987). *Measuring sports participation motivation. International Journal of Sport Psychology, 18,* 112-119.

Ray, O.S. (1964). *Tranquilizer effects as a function of experimental anxiety procedures. Archives Internationales de Pharmacodynamie et de Therapie, 153,* 49-68

Ray, W.J. & Cole, H.W. (1985*). EEG alpha activity reflects attentional demands, and beta activity reflects emotional and cognitive processes. Science, 228,* 750-752.

⇒   Frediani, A.W. & Harman, D. (1977*). Self-regulation of hemispheric activity. Biofeedback and Self-Regulation, 2(2),* 195-199.

Reddy, M.J. (1979). *The conduit metaphor - a case of frame conflict in out language.* In Ortony, A. (Ed.), *Metaphor and thought,* 284-324. London: Cambridge University Press.

Reese, E.P. (1966). *The Analysis of Human Operant Behavior.* Dubuque, Iowa: Wm. C. Brown Co.

Reichenbach, W. (1937) *Automatic Pistol Marksmanship,* Plantersville, South Carolina: Small-Arms Technical Publishing Company.

Reinkemeier, Heinz, (1992), *On the Training of Shooters,* vol. 1, Translated and published by the National Smallbore Rifle Association of Great Britain (translated by Stan Greer with assistance from Bill Murray)

⇒   (1993), *On the Training of Shooters,* vol. 2, Translated and published by the National Smallbore Rifle Association of Great Britain (translated by Stan Greer with assistance from Bill Murray).

Reschjotilow, W., *UIT Journal* (5/79). *Who'll Storm Olympia's Peak?,* 232.

Reynolds, G.S. (1961a). *Behavioral contrast. Journal of the Experimental Analysis of Behavior, 4,* 57-71.

⇒   (1961b). *Relativity of response rate and reinforcement frequency in a multiple schedule. Journal of the Experimental Analysis of Behavior, 4,* 179-184.

⇒   (1968), *A Primer of Operant Conditioning.* Glenview, Illinois: Scott, Foresman and Co.

Reynolds, W.M. (1982). *Development of a reliable and valid short form of the Marlowe-Crowne Social Desirability Scale. Journal of Clinical Psychology, 38,* 119-125.

Rhodewalt, F. & Aguostsdottir, S. (1984). *On the relationship to the Type A behavior pattern: Perception of life events versus coping with life events. Journal of Research in Personality. 18,* 212-223.

⇒   (1989). *Self-handicappers: Individual differences in the preference for anticipatory self-protective acts.* In Higgings, R.L. & Snyder, C.R. (Eds.), *Self-handicapping: The paradox that isn't.* 69-173. New York: Plenum.

580

⇒ Saltzman, A.T. & Wittmer, J. (1984). *Self-handicapping among competitive athletes: The role of practice in self-esteem protection.* Basic and Applied Social Psychology, 5, 197-209.

Rice, J. (9/15/95). *Fear is good.* Gannett Newspaper, USA Weekend. Tucson AZ.: Tucson Citizen

Richardson, A. (1967a). *Mental practice: A review and discussion, Part I.* Research Quarterly for Exercise and Sport, 38, 95-107.

⇒ (1967b). *Mental practice: A review and discussion, Part II.* Research Quarterly for Exercise and Sport, 38, 263-273.

⇒ (1969). *Mental imagery.* New York: Springer.

⇒ (1977). *Verbalizer-visualizer: A cognitive style dimension. Journal of Mental Imagery, 1,* 109-126.

Richardson, P.A., Adler, W. & Hankes, D. (1988). *Game, set, match: Psychological momentum in tennis. The Sport Psychologist, 2,* 69-76.

Rickard, H.C. & Mundy, M.B. (1965). *Direct manipulation of stuttering behavior: an experimental-clinical approach.* In Ullmann, L.P. and Krasner, L. (Eds.). *Case Studies in Behavior Modification,* 268-274. New York: Holt, Rinehart and Winston, Inc.

Rickles, W.H. (1972). *Central nervous system substrates of some psychophysiological variables.* In Greenfield, N.S. & Sternbach, R.A. (Eds.), *Handbook of Psychophysiology,* New York: Holt, Rinehart, and Winston.

Riddick, C.C. (1984). *Comparative psychological profiles of three groups of female collegians: Competitive swimmers, recreational swimmers, and inactive swimmers. Journal of Sport Behavior, 7,* 160-174

Riesterer, Uwe, & Etzel, Ewald Dr., *UIT Journal* (2/92). *Coaching - Part 5, Team Communication,* 16-17.

⇒ & Etzel, Ewald, Dr., *UIT Journal* (1/91). *Coaching: Part 2, Selecting a Coaching Style,* 58-59.

⇒ & Etzel, Ewald, Dr., *UIT Journal* (1/92). *Communication and Shooting Coach Effectiveness, Part 4.* 30.

⇒ & Etzel, Ewald, Dr., *UIT Journal* (4/92). *Retirement from Shooting: An Inevitable Transition, Part 6,* 18-19.

⇒ & Etzel, Ewald, Dr., *UIT Journal* (6/90). *The Role of the Shooting Coach,* 60-61.

⇒ *UIT Journal* (1/81). *The Methodical Teaching Programme of Rifle Shooting,* 8-12.

⇒ *UIT Journal* (2/81). *The Methodical Teaching Programme of Rifle Shooting,* 13-17.

⇒ *UIT Journal* (3/86). *Learning and Teaching,* 24-27.

⇒ *UIT Journal* (4/81). *The General Build-up Phase,* 16-19.

⇒ *UIT Journal* (5/86). *Teaching Methods,* 36-37.

⇒ *UIT Journal* (1/92). *Coaching - Part 4, Psychological Factors of Shooting Sports Producing Behaviour Permanence.*

⇒ *UIT Journal* (6/85). *Trainer - Shooter - Interaction,* 56-58.

Rifle Instructors and Coaches Guide (1964 Edition). Ft. Benning, GA.: United States Army Marksmanship Training Unit.

Rifle Instructors and Coaches Guide (1965 Edition). Ft. Benning, GA.: United States Army Marksmanship Training Unit.

Rigby, W.R. (1976). *A Review of Sports Psychology Literature in Rifle Marksmanship*. National Technical Information Service Report #3206. Springfield, VA.: U.S. Department of Commerce.

⇒ (1980) *Personality characteristics of United States international rifle shooters.* Unpublished doctoral dissertation, University of Maryland, College Park, Maryland. In Landers, D.M & Hunt, K.J., *Shooting Sports Research*, (1988) Washington, DC, National Rifle Association. pp 38-40.

Ripoll, H. (1991). *The understanding-acting process in sport: The relationship between the semantic and the sensorimotor visual function. International Journal of Sport Psychology, 22,* 221-243.

Roberts, C.C. (1984). *Toward a new theory of motivation in sport: The role of perceived ability.* In Silva, J.M. & Weinberg, R.S. (Eds.), *Psychological foundations of sport,* 214-228. Champaign, IL.: Human Kinetics

Roberts, D. & Bristow, A.P.(1969) *An Introduction to Modern Police Firearms.* Encino, CA.:Glencoe Publishing Co., Inc.

Roberts, G.C. (1984). *Achievement motivation in children's sport.* In Nicholls, J.G. (Ed.), *Advances in motivation and achievement: Vol. 3. The development of achievement and motivation,* 251-281. Greenwich, CT: JAI Press.

⇒ Kleiber, D.A. & Duda, J.L. (1981). *An analysis of motivation in children's sport: The role of perceived competence in participation. Journal of Sport Psychology, 3,* 206-216.

⇒ Spink, K.S. & Renberton, C.I. (1985). *Learning experiences in sport psychology.* Champaign, IL.: Human Kinetics.

Robertson, I. (1982). *Sport in the lives of Australian children.* In Orlick, T., Partington, J., & Salmela, J. (Eds.), *Mental training for coaches and athletes,* 56-57. Ottawa: Coaching Association of Canada.

Robinson, D.W. & Howe, B.L. (1987). *Causal attribution and mood state relationships of soccer players in a sport achievement setting. Journal of Sport Behavior, 10,* 137-146.

⇒ (1985). *Stress seeking: Selected behavioral characteristics of elite rock climbers. Journal of Sports Psychology, 7,* 400-404.

Rodgers, W., Hall, C. & Buckolz, E., (in press). *The effect of an imagery training program on imagery ability, imagery use, and figure skating performance. Journal of Applied Sport Psychology.*

Rogers, C.R. & Skinner, B.F. (1965). *Some issues concerning the control of human behavior. Science, 124,* 1057-1066. (Reprinted in Ulrich, Stachnik & Mabry (1966), 301-316.

Rogosa, D.A. (1980). *Critique of cross-lagged correlation. Psychological Bulletin, 88,* 245-258.

Rohwer, W.D., Jr. (1970). *Images and pictures in children's learning: Research results and educational implications. Psychological Bulletin, 73,* 393-403

Rose, D.J. & Christina, R.W. (1990). *Attention demands of precision pistol-shooting as a function of skill level. Research Quarterly for Exercise and Sport. 61 ,*111-113.

Rosenberg, B.G. & Sutton-Smith, B. (1964). *The measurement of masculinity and femininity in children: An extension and revalidation. Journal of Genetic Psychology, 104,* 259-264.

Rosenberg, M. (1965). *Society and the adolescent self-image.* Princeton, NJ: Princeton University Press.

Rosenthal, I.C. (1926). *The mutual interactions of the excitatory and inhibitory processes (a new type of differectiation of tactile conditioned stimuli).* **Collected Papers of the Physiol. Lab. of I.P. Pavlov,** *vol. i.* Nos. 2-3.

Rosenthal, I.S. (1923). *A static state of irradiation of excitation. Archive of Biol. Sciences, vol xxiii.* Nos. 1-3.

⇒ (1924). *Upon the specialization of conditioned reflexes. Archive of Biol. Sciences, vol. xxiii.* Nos. 4-5.

Ross, J.G., Pate, R.R., Caspersen, C.J., Damberg, C.L. & Svilar, M. (1987). *Home and community in children's exercise habits. JOPERD* (Public Health Service, Office of Disease Prevention and Health Promotion, U.S. Department of Health and Human Services), Nov-Dec, 85-95.

Rotella, R.J., Gansneder, B., Ojala, D. & Biling, J. (1980). *Cognitions and coping strategies of elite skiers: An exploratory study of young developing athletes. Journal of Sport Psychology, 2,* 350-354.

Rothstein, A.L. (1977). *Prediction in sport: visual factors.* In Stadulis, R.E. (Ed.), **Research and practice in physical edcuation.** Champaign, IL.: Human Kinetics Publishers.

Rotter, J. (1966). *Generalized expectancies for internal versus external control of reinforcement. Psychological Monographs, 80,* 609.

⇒ Seeman, M. & Livera, S. (1962). *Internal vs. external focus of control of reinforcement.* In Washburne, N.F. (Ed.), **Decisions, values and groups**: *Vol. 2,* 473-516. London: Pergamon.

Rouse, M.W., DeLand, P., Christin, R. & Haweley, J. (1988). *A comparison study of dynamic visual acuity between athletes and nonathletes. Journal of the American Optometric Association, 59,* 946-950.

Rowland, G.L., Franken, R.E. & Harrison, K. (1986). *Sensation seeking and participation in sporting activities. Journal of Sport Psychology, 8,* 212-220.

Roy, E.A. (1983). *Neuropsychological perspectives on apraxia and related disorders.* In R.A. Magill (Ed.). **Memory and control of action,** 293-320. Amsterdam: North-Holland.

Rubin-Rabson, G.A. (1941). *A comparison of two forms of mental rehearsal and keyboard overlearning, Journal of Educational Psychology, 32,* 593-602.

Rumelhart, G.E. (1989). *The architecture of mind: A connectionist approach.* In Posner, M.I. (Ed.), **Foundations of cognitive science,** 133-160. Bradford Brook, Cambridge, MA: MIT Press.

Russell, D. (1982). *The Causal Dimension Scale: A measure of how individuals perceive causes. Journal of Personality and Social Psychology, 42,* 1137-1145.

583

Ryan, D.E., Blakeslee, T. & Furst, M. (1986*). Mental practice and motor skill learning: An indirect test of the neuromuscular feedback hypothesis. International Journal of Sport Psychology, 7,* 60-70.

Ryckman, R.M. & Hamel J.,(1993). *Perceived Physical Ability Differences in the Sport Participation Motives of Young Athletes.* Department of Psychology, University of Maine: *International Journal Sport Psychology, 24,* 270-283.

⇒ Robbins, M.A., Thornton, B. & Cantrell, P. (1982). *Development and validation of a physical self-efficacy scale. Journal of Personality and Social Psychology, 42,* 891-900.

Ryle, G. (1949). *The Concept of Mind.* London: Hutchinson.

Sachs, M.L. & Buffone, G.W. (Eds.). (1984). *Running as therapy: An integrated approach.* Lincoln: University of Nebraska Press.

Sackeim, H.A. & Gur, R.C. (1978). *Lateral asymmetry in intensity of emotional expression. Neuropsychologia, 16,* 473-481.

Salminen, S. & Liukkonen, J., (1994). *The Convergent and Discriminant Validity of the Coach's Version of the Leadership Scale for Sports. International Journal Sport Psychology, 25,* 119-127.

⇒ (1985). *Cohesion and success of ice-hockey teams: A cross-lagged panel correlation summary. Proceedings of the VI World Congress of Sport Psychology, 6,* 1-8.

Saltzman, E. & Kelso, J.H.S. (1987). *Skilled actions: A task-dynamic approach. Psychological Review, 94,* 84-106.

Sanak, V., *UIT Journal,* (6/93). *Dry Training,* 50.

Sandman, C.A. & Walker, B.B. (1985). *Cardiovascular relationship to attention and thinking.* In Rental, V.M., Corson, S.A. & Dunn, B.R. (Eds.), **Psychophysiological aspects·of reading and learning**, 95-122. New York: Gordon & Breach.

Sanford, F.N. (1955). *Creative health and the principle of habeas mentem. American Journal. Psychology. 10*: 829-835.

Sarason, S.B., Mandler, G. & Craighill, P.G. (1952). *The effects of differential instructions on anxiety and learning. Journal of Abnormal and Social Psychology, 47,* 561-565.

SAS Institute Inc. (1985). *SAS user's guide: Statistics version 5th edition.* Cary, NC: SAS Institute Inc.

Savelsbergh, G.J.P. & Bootsma, R.J., (1994). *Perception-Action Coupling in Hitting and Catching.* Faculty of Human Movement Sciences, Free University, The Netherlands: *International Journal of Sport Psychology, 23,* 331-343.

Savich, A.A. (1913). *Further contributions to the study of the influence of conditioned reflexes one upon another. Thesis, Petrograd.*

Scanlan, T.K. & Lewthawaite, R. (1984). *Social psychological aspects of competition for male youth sport participants: I. Predictors of competitive stress. Journal of Sport Psychology,* 208-226.

⇒ & Lewthwaite, R. (1989). *From stress to enjoyment: parental and coach influences on young participants.* In Brown, E.W. & Branta,

C.F. (Eds.), *Competitive sports for children and youth*, 41-48 Champaign, IL: Human Kinetics.

⇒ & Lewthwaite, T. (1986). *Social psychological aspects of competition for male youth sports participants: IV. Predictors of enjoyment. Journal of Sport Psychology, 8*, 25-35.

⇒ & Passer, M.W. (1978). *Factors related to competitive stress among male youth sport participants. Medicine and Science in Sport, 10*, 103-108.

⇒ & Passer, M.W. (1980). *Self-serving biases in the competitive sport setting: An attributional dilemma. Journal of Sport Psychology, 2*, 124-136.

⇒ & Ragan, J.T. (1978). *Achievement motivation and competition: Perceptions and responses. Medicine and Science in Sports, 10*, 276-281.

⇒ (1978). *Perceptions and responses of high and low competitive trait-anxious males to competition. Research Quarterly, 49*, 520-527.

⇒ Ravizza, K. & Stein, G.L. (1989). *An in-depth study of former elite figure skater. Journal of Sport & Exercise Psychology, 11*, 54-83.

Scheehan, P.W. (1967). *A shortened form of Betts' Questionnaire Upon Mental Imagery. Journal of Clinical Psychology, 23*, (2), 368-389.

Scheier, M.F. & Carver, C.S. (1985). *Optimism, coping, and health: Assessment and implications of generalized outcome expectancies. Health Psychology, 4*, 219-247.

⇒ & Carver, C.S. (1987). *Dispositional optimism and physical well-being: The influence of generalized outcome expectancies on health. Journal of Personality, 55*, 169-210.

Schliesman, E.S. (1987). *Relationship between the congruence of preferred and actual leader behavior and subordinate satisfaction with leadership. Journal of Sport Behavior, 10*, 157-166.

Schmeck, R.R. (1983). *Learning styles of college students.* In Dillon, R.F. & Schmeck, R.R. (Eds.), *Individual differences in cognition: Vol.* 233-279. New York: Academic Press.

⇒ (1988). *An introduction to strategies and styles of learning.* In Schmeck, R.R. (Ed.), *Learning strategies and learning styles,* 1-19. New York: Plenum.

Schmid, A. & Peper, E. (1986). *Techniques for training concentration.* In Williams, J.M. (Ed.), *Applied sport psychology: Personal growth to peak performance,* 274-284. Palo Alto, CA: Mayfield.

Schmid, W.D. (1989). *Heart rate patterns of archers while shooting. Fiziologia Cheloveka, 15*, (1), 64-68.

Schmidt, R.A. & Stull, G.A. (1970). *Premotor and motor reaction time as a function of preliminary muscular tension. Journal of Motor Behavior, 2*, 96-110.

⇒ (1975). *A schema theory of discrete motor skill learning, Psychological Review, 82*, 225-260.

⇒ (1976). *The schema as a solution to some persistent problems in motor learning theory*. In Stelmach, G.E. (Ed.), ***Motor control: Issues and trends***, 41-65. London: Academic Press.

⇒ (1980). *Past and future issues in motor programming. The Research Quarterly for Exercise and Sport, 51*, 122-140.

⇒ (1988). ***Motor control and learning: A behavioural approach***, 2nd. Ed. Champaign, IL: Human Kinetics.

⇒ (1991). **Motor Learning & Performance**. Champaign, IL.: Human Kinetics Books.

⇒ & McCabe, J.F. (1976). *Motor program utilization over extended practice. Journal of Human Movement Studies, 2*, 239-242.

Schneider, W., Dumais, S.T. & Shiffrin, R.M. (1984). *Automatic and control processing of attention*. In Parasuraman, R. & Davies, D.R. (Eds.), *Varieties of attention*, 1-27. New York: Academic Press.

Schoenfeld, W.N. (1950). *An experimental approach to anxiety, escape and avoidance behavior*. In Hoch, P.H. & Zubin, J. (Eds.). *Anxiety*, 70-90. New York: Grune and Stratton.

⇒ (1957). *Discussion of four research papers*. In Hoch, P.H. & Zubin, J. (Eds.). ***Experimental Psychopathology***, 55-65. New York: Grune and Stratton.

⇒ (1970) (Ed.). ***The Theory of Reinforcement Schedules***. New York: Appleton-Century-Crofts.

⇒ Cumming, W.W. & Hearst, E. (1956). *On the classification of reinforcement schedules. Proceedings of the National Academy of Science, 42*, 563-570.

Scholz, J.P. & Kelson, J.A.S. (1989). *A quantitative approach to understanding the formation and change of coordinated movement patterns. Journal of Motor Behavior, 21* (2), 122-144.

Schülein, H., *UIT Journal*, (6/83). *Importance of Shooting in Other Sports*, 33-34.

Schuri, U. & von Cramon, D. (1981). *Heart rate and blink rate responses during mental arithmetic with and without continuous verbalization of results. Psychophysiology. 18*, 650-653.

Schuster, C.R., Dockens, W.S. & Woods, J.H. (1966). *Behavioral variables affecting the development of amphetamine tolerance. Psychopharmacologia, 9*, 170-182. Reprinted in Thompson, Pickens and Meiseh (1970), 539-551.

Schuster, R.H. (1969). *A functional analysis of conditioned reinforcement*. In Hendry, D.P. (Ed.). ***Conditioned Reinforcement***, 192-234. Homewood, Illinois: The Dorsey Press.

Schwartz, G. E., Davidson, R.J. & Coleman, D.J. (1978). *Patterning of cognitive and somatic processes in the self-regulation of anxiety: Effects of meditation vs. Exercise. Psychosomatic Medicine, 40*, 321-328.

⇒ (1977). *Biofeedback and patterning of autonomic and central processes: CNS—cardiovascular interactions*. In Schwartz, G.E. & Beatty, J. (Eds.), ***Biofeedback: Theory and Research***. New York: Academic Press.

⇒ (1977). *Psychosomatic disorders and biofeedback: A psychobiological model of disregulation.* In Maser, J.D. & Seligman, M. (Eds.), ***Psychopathology: Experimental models.*** San Francisco: Freeman.

⇒ (1978). *Psychobiological foundations of psychotherapy and behavior change.* In Garfield, S.L. & Bergin, A.E. (Eds.), ***Handbook of Psychotherapy and Behavior Change: An Empirical Analysis*** (second ed.). New York: Wiley.

⇒ Davidson, R.J. & Goleman, D. (1978). *Patterning of cognitive and somatic processes in the self-regulation of anxiety: Effects of meditation versus exercise. Psychosomatic Medicine, 40,* 321-328.

⇒ Davidson, R.J. & Maer, F. (1975). *Right hemispheric lateralization for emotion in the human brain: Interaction with cognition. Science, 190,* 286-288.

Seabourne, T.G., Weinberg, R. & Jackson, A. (1984). *The effect of individualized practice and training of visuo-motor behavior rehearsal in enhancing karate performance. Journal of Sport Behavior, 7,* 58-67.

⇒ Weinberg, R.S., Jackson, A. & Suinn, R.M. (1985). *Effect of individualized, non-individualized and package intervention strategies on karate performance. Journal of Sport Psychology, 7,* 40 50

Seefeldt, V.D., Gilliam, T., Blievernicht, D. & Bruce, R. (1978). *Scope of youth sports programs in the state of Michigan.* In Smoll F.L. & Smith R.E. (Eds.), ***Psychological perspectives in youth sports,*** 17-67. Washington, D.C: Hemisphere.

Selye, H. (1977). ***Stress without distress. Teach yourself books.*** Great Britain: Hodder and Staughton.

Serpa, S., Pataco, V. & Santos, F. (1991). *Leadership patterns in handball international competition. International Journal of Sport Psychology, 22,* 78-89.

Sersen, E.A., Clausen, J. & Lidsky, A. (1978). *Autonomic specificity and stereotype revisited. Psychophysiology, 15,* 60-67.

Service Rifle Coach's Performance Check List and Examination (SAFS/SR-AA/RMCC), (1972). Ft. Benning, GA.: United States Army Marksmanship Training Unit.

Service Rifle Marksmanship Manual, (1968 Edition). Ft. Benning, GA.: United States Army Marksmanship Training Unit.

Shagass, C. (1972). *Electrical activity of the brain.* In Greenfield, H.S. & Sternbach, R.A. (Eds.), ***Handbook of Psychophysiology.*** New York: Holt, Rinehart, & Winston.

Shangi, G.M. & Carron, A.V. (1987). *Group cohesion and its relationship with performance and satisfaction among high school basketball players. Canadian Journal of Sport Sciences, 12,* 20.

Shapiro, D. & Lehrer, P.M. (1980). *Psychophysiological effects of autogenic training and progressive relaxation. Biofeedback and Self-regulation, 5,* 249-255.

⇒ & Schmidt, R.A. (1982). *The schema theory: Recent evidence and developmental implications,* In Kelso, J.A.S. & Clark, J.E. (Eds.),

587

The developmental of movements control and coordinations, 82-99. New York: Wiley.

Sharit, J., Salvendy, G. & Deinseroth, M.P. (1982). *External and internal attentional environments. I. The utilization of cardiac deceleratory and acceleratory response data for evaluating differences in mental workload between machine-paced and self-paced work. Ergonomics, 25,* 107- 120.

Sharpe, T., Brown, M. & Crider, K. (1995). *The effects of a sportsmanship curriculum intervention on generalized positive social behavior of urban elementary school students. Journal of Applied Behavior Analysis, 28,* 401-416.

Shaw, W.A. (1939). *Imaginary exercise, Newsweek, 14,* 30-31.

Sheikn, A.A. & Panagiotou, N.C. (1975). *Use of mental imagery in psychotherapy: A critical review. Perceptual and Motor Skills, 41,* 555-585.

Sherif, M. & Sherif, C. (1979). *Research on intergroup relations.* In Austin, W.G. & Worchel S. (Eds.), **The social psychology of intergroup relations,** 7-18. Belmount, CA: Wadsworth.

Shik, M.L. & Orlovskii, G.N. (1976). *Neurophysiology of a locomotor automatism. Physiological Reviews, 56,* 485-501.

Shishlo, A.A. (1910). *Thermal centres in the cortex of the hemispheres; sleep as a reflex. Thesis,* Petrograd, 1910; Prelim. Commun. *Russian Med. Soc. in Petrograd, vol. 77.*

Shooting FUNdamentals (Video 1988). *4-H Development.* Minnesota Extension Service and Daisy Manufacturing Co.

Shuell, T.J. (1986*). Cognitive conceptions of learning. Review of Educational Research, 56,* 411-436.

Sidman, M. (1955*). Technique for assessing the effects of drugs on timing behavior. Science, 122,* 925. Reprinted in Thompson, Pickens and Meisch (1970), 511-513.

⇒ (1960). *Tactics of Scientific Research.* New York: Basic Books.

⇒ (1964). Anxiety. *Proceedings of the American Philosophical Society, 108,* 478-481.

Sievers, A. & Briggs, F. (1979*). Success in the Shooting Sports, Tools for Instant Achievement.*

Silva, J.M. (1983). *Covert rehearsal strategies.* In M.H. Williams (Ed.), **Ergogenic aids in sport,** 253-274. Champaign, IL: Human Kinetics.

⇒ (1984). *Factors related to the acquisition and exhibition of aggressive sport behavior.* In Silva, J.M. & Weinberg, R.S. (Eds.), **Psychological foundations of sport,** 261-273. Champaign, IL: Human Kinetics.

⇒ Hardy, C.J. & Crace, R.K. (1988). *Analysis of psychological momentum in intercollegiate tennis. Journal of Sport and Exercise Psychology, 10,* 346-354.

⇒ Shultz, B.B., Haslam, R.W., Martin, T.P. & Murray, D.F. (1985). *Discriminating characteristics of contestants at the United States Olympic wrestling trials. International Journal of Sport Psychology, 16,* 79-102.

Simon, H.A. & Chase, W.G. (1973). *Skill in chess. American Scientist, 61,* 394-403.

⇒ & Gilmartin, K. (1973). *A simulation of memory for chess positions. Cognitive Psychology, 5,* 29-46.

⇒ (1979). *Information processing models of cognition. Annual Review of Psychology, 30,* 363-396.

Simon, H.H. & Kaplan C.A. (1989). *Foundations of cognitive science.* In M.I. Posner (Ed.), **Foundations of cognitive science,** 1-48. Cambridge, MA: MIT Press.

Simons, B. & Taylor, J., (1992). *A Phychosocial Model of Fan Violence in Sports.* School of Psychology, Nova University. *International Journal of Sport Psychology, 23,* 207-232.

Singer, R.N. (1986). **Peak performance... and more,** Ithaca, NY: Mouvement.

⇒ & Suwanthada, S. (1986). *The generalizability effectiveness of a learning strategy on achievement in related closed motor skills. Research Quarterly for Exercise and Sport. 57,* 205-214.

⇒ (1978). *Motor skills and learner strategies.* In O'Neil, H.F. (Ed.), **Learning strategies,** 79-106. New York: Academic Press.

⇒ (1986). *Children in physical activity: Motor learning considerations.* In Stull, A. & Eckert, H.M. (Eds.), **The Academy Papers: The effects of physical activity on children,** 64-74. Champaign, IL: Human Kinetics.

⇒ (1988). *Strategies and metastrategies in learning and performing self-paced athletic skills. The Sport Psychologist, 2,* 49-68.

⇒ DeFrancesco, C. & Randall, L.E. (1989). *Effectiveness of a global learning strategy practiced in different contexts on primary and transfer self-paced motor tasks. Journal of Sport and Exercise Psychology, 11,* 290-303.

Siriatsky, V.V. (1925). *Pathological deviations in the activity of the central nervous system in the case of clashing of excitation and inhibition. Russian Jour. Physiol., vol. viii.* Nos. 3-4.

Skinner, .B.F. (1948). **Walden Two.** *Skinner's novel about life in a commumty based on behavioural principles.* New York: Macmillan.

⇒ (1938). **The Behavior of Organisms.** *The original theoretical exposition and experimental report on which current operant conditioning is largely based.* New York: Appleton-Century-Crofts.

⇒ (1953). **Science and Human Behavior.** *A nontechnical account of the experimental analysis of behaviour as it is applied to a wide range of human activities.* New York: Macmillan.

⇒ (1957). **Verbal Behavior.** *An extension of Skinner's approach to verbal behaviour in general.* New York: Appleton-Century-Crofts.

⇒ (1968). **The Technology of Teaching.** *Some of Skinner's more influential papers on psychology and education.* New York: Appleton-Century-Crofts.

⇒ (1969). **Contingencies of Reinforcement: a Theoretical Analysis.** *A general and spirited advocacy of radical behaviourism in psychology.* New York: Appleton-Century-Crofts.

589

⇒ (1972a). ***Beyond Freedom and Dignity***. *A general statement of Skinner's approach to psychology and to man*. London: Jonathan Cape Ltd.

⇒ 1972b). ***Cumulative Record***. (3rd Edition). *A collection of Skinner's papers on a wide range of topics: experimental psychology, educational technology, abnormal behaviour, science and human behaviour, etc*. New York: Appleton-Century-Croft.

Slovic, P. & Lichtenstein, S. (1971). *Comparison of Bayesian and Regression approaches to the study of information processing in judgment. Organizational Behavior and Human Performance 6*, 649-744.

Slusher, H.S. (1964). *Personality and intelligence characteristics of selected high school athletes and nonathletes. The Research Quarterly, 35*(4), 539-545.

Small Arms Firing School Camp Perry, Ohio Rifle Coaches Guide, (1961). Ft. Benning, GA.: U.S. Army Advanced Marksmanship Unit.

Small Arms Marksmanship Manual (1971). Bureau of Naval Personnel, NAVPERS 93863.

Smith, N.J. (1980). *Excessive weight loss and food aversion simulating anorexia nervosa. Pediatrics, 66*, 139-142.

Smyth, M. (1995). *An Introduction to Blink Relfex Research*. Psychology Dept., University of Western Australia. *Microsoft Internet Explorer*.

⇒ (1995). *How do we Measure a Blink?* Psychology Dept., University of Western Australia. *Microsoft Internet Explorer*.

⇒ (1995*). Using the Modified Blink Reflex to Index Speed of Processing*. Psychology Dept., University of Western Australia. *Microsoft Internet Explorer*.

Snoody, G.S. (1926). *Learning and stability. Journal of Applied Psychology, 10*, 1-36.

Solomon, S. (1978). ***Knowing Your Child Through His Handwriting and Drawings***. New York: Crown Publishing, Inc.

Solomonov, O.S. & Shishio, A.A. (1910). *Conditioned reflexes and sleep. Proc. Russian Med. Soc. in Petrograd, vol. 77*.

Solyom, L., Freeman, R.J. & Miles, J.E. (1982). *A comparative psychometric study of anorexia nervosa and obsessive neurosis. Canadian Journal of Psychiatry, 27*, 282-286.

Sonstroem, R.J. & Bernardo, P. (1982). *Intraindividual pregame state anxiety and basketball performance: A re-cxamination of the inverted-U curve. Journal of Sport Psychology, 4*, 235-245.

Souck, G. & Carlson, A.D. (1976). ***Computers in Meurobiology and Behavior***. New York: Wiley.

Spence, J.T., & Spence, K.W. (1966). *The motivational components of manifest anxiety: Drive and drive stimuli*. In C.D. Speilberger, C.D. (Ed.), ***Anxiety and Behavior***, 291-326. New York: Academic Press.

⇒ Helmreich, R.L. & Stapp, J. (1974). *The Personal Attributes Questionnaire*.

⇒ & Chase, P.N. (1996). *Speed analyses of stimulus equivalence. Journal of the Experimental Analysis of Behavior, 65*, 643-659.

590

Sperry, R.W. (1974). *Lateral specialization of cerebral function in the surgically separated hemispheres*. In McGuigan, F.J. & Schoonover, R.A. (Eds.), *The Psychophysiology of Thinking*. New York: Academic Press.

Spielberger, C.D. (1966). *Theory and research on anxiety*. In Spielberger, C.D. (Ed.), *Anxiety and Behavior*. New York: Academic Press.

⇒ (1972). *Anxiety as an emotional state*. In Spielberger, C.D. (Ed.), *Anxiety: Current trends in theory and research: vol. I*, New York: Academic.

⇒ Gorsuch, R.L. & Luschene, R.E. (1970). *Manual for the State-Trait Anxiety Inventory*. Palo Alto, CA,: Consulting Psychologists Press.

Spigolon, L. & Annalisa, D. (1985). *Autogenic training in frogmen*. International Journal of Sport Psychology, 16, 312-320.

Spong, P., Haider, M. & Lindsley, D.B. (1965). *Selective attentiveness and cortical evoked responses to visual and auditory stimuli*. Science, 148, 395-397.

SPSS Inc. (1986). *SPSS-X User's Guide*, second ed. New York: Mc Graw Hill.

Starkes, J.L. & Deakin, J. (1984). *Perception in sport: A cognitive approach to skilled performance*. In Straub, W.F. & Williams, J.M. (Eds.), *Cognitive sport psychology*, 115-128. Lansing, NY: Science Assocs. Sport.

⇒ (1987). *Skill in field hockey: The nature of the cognitive advantage*. Journal of Sport Psychology, 9, 146-160.

⇒ (1990). *Eye-hand coordination in experts: from athletes to micro-surgeons*. In Bard, C., Fleury, M. & Hay, L. (Eds.), *Development of eye-hand coordination across the lifespan*, 309-326. Columbia, South Carolina:University Press.

Statistical Analysis System. (1985). *SAS user's guide: Statistics*. Cary, NC: SAS Institute Inc.

Steele, W.G. & Koons, P.B. (1968) *Cardiac response to mental arithmetic under quiet and white noise distraction*. Psychonomic Science, 176, 1344-1346

Stelmach, G.E. & Diggles, V.A. (1982). *Control theories in motor behavior*. Acta Psychologica, 50, 83-105.

Stennett, R.G. (1957). *The relationship of alpha amplitude to the level of palmer conductance*. Electroencephalography and Clinical Neurophysiology, 9, 131-138.

Steptoe, A. & Cox, S. (1988). *The short-term influence of high and low intensity physical exercise on mood*. Psychology and Health, 2, 91-106.

⇒ & Fidler, H. (1987). *Stage fright in orchestral musicians: A study of cognitive and behavioral strategies in performance anxiety*. British Journal of Psychology, 78, 241 -249.

Stern, R.M. (1976). *Reaction time and heart rate between the GET SET and GO of simulated races*. Psychophysiology, 13, 149-154.

⇒ Ray, W.J. & Davis, C.M. (1980). *Psychophysiological Recording*. New York: Oxford University Press.

Sternbach, R.A. (1966). *Principles of Psychophysiology*. New York: Academic Press.

Stillings, N.A. (Ed.). (1987). *Cognitive science: An introduction*. Cambridge, MA: MIT Press.

591

Stock, J. & Cervone, D. (1990). *Proximal goal-setting and self-regulatory processes. Cognitive Therapy and Research, 14,* 483-498.

Stokes, T.F. & Baer, D.M. (1977). *An implicit technology of generalization. Journal of Applied Behavior Analysis, 10,* 349-368.

Stonehill, E. & Crisp, A.H. (1977). *Psychoneurotic characteristics of patients with anorexia nervosa before and after treatment and at follow-up 4-7 years later. Journal of Psychosomatic Research, 21,* 187-193.

Stoubova, M.M. (1914). *Further contributions to the study of the significance of time as a conditioned stimulus. Thesis, Petrograd.*

Straub, W.F. & Williams, J.M. (Eds), **Cognitive sport psychology,** 191-198. Lansing, NY: Sport Sciences Associates.

⇒   (1989). *The effect of three different methods of mental training on dart throwing performance. The Sport Psychologist, 3,* 219-236.

Stretch, R. (1972). *Development and maintenance of responding under schedules of electric-shock presentation.* In Gilbert, R.M. and Millenson, J.R. (Eds.). **Reinforcement: Behavioral Analysis,** 67-95. New York: Academic Press.

Stromme, S.B., Harlem, O.K., et al. (1982). *Physical activity and health. Summary and main conclusions. Scandinavian Journal of Social Medicine, Supplementum, 19,* 9-26.

Stroyanov, V.V. (1925). *Development of a conditioned reflex to, and differentiation of, compound stimuli. Pavlov Jubilee Vol.*

Stubbs, D.A. (1971). *Second-order schedules and the problem of conditioned reinforcement. Journal of the Experimental Analysis of Behavior, 16,* 289-314.

Stunkard, A.J. & Albaum, J.M. (1981). *The accuracy of self-reported weights. The American Journal of Clinical Nutrition, 34,* 1593-1599.

Suberi, M. & McKeever, W.F. (1977). *Differential right hemispheric memory storage of emotional and non-emotional faces. Neuropsychologia, 15,* 757-768.

Suinn, R. (1984). *Visual motor behavior rehearsal: The basic technique. Scandinavian Journal of Behavior Therapy, 13,* 131-142.

⇒   (1987). *Behavioral approaches to stress management in sports.* In J. May & M. Asken (Eds.), **The psychological health of the athlete** 59-75. Elmsford, NY: Pergamon.

⇒   (1972). *Removing emotional obstacles to learning and performance by visuo-motor behavior rehearsal. Behavioral Therapy, 31,* 308-310.

⇒   (1983). *Imagery and sports,* In Sheikh, A.A. (Ed), **Imagery: Current theory, research, and application,** 507-534. New York: John Wiley.

Summers, J.J. (1989). *Motor programs,* In Holding, D.H. (Ed.), **Human skills,** 46-69, second ed. Chichester: John Wiley.

Swain, A. & Jones, G. (1992). *Relationship between sport achievement orientation and competitive state anxiety. The Sport Psychologist, 6,* 42-53.

592

Sweeney, G. & Horan, J. (1982). *Separate and combined effects of cue controlled relaxation and cognitive restructuring in the treatment of musical performance anxiety. Journal of Counseling Psychology, 29,* 486-497.

Sweet, J. (1973). *Competitive Rifle Shooting.* Maroubra, N.S.W., Australia:. Shooting Book Publisher

Syer, J. & Connolly, C. (1987). *Sporting body, sporting mind.* London: Simon & Schuster Ltd.

Szasz, T. (1961). *The Myth of Mental Illness: foundations of a theory of personal conduct.* New York: Hoeber-Harper.

Tabachnick, B.G. & Fidell, L.S. (1983) *Using multivariate statistics.* New York: Harper & Rowe.

Tajfel, H. & Turner, J. (1979). *An integrative theory of intergroup conflict.* In Austin W.G. & Worchel S. (Eds.), *The social psychology of intergroup relations,* 33-48. Belmount, CA: Wadsworth.

Taylor, H.L. Jacobs, D.R., Schucker, B., Knudsen, J., Leon, A.S., & Debacker, G. (1978). *A questionnaire for the assessment of leisure time physical activities. Journal of Chronical Disorders, 31,* 741-755.

Teitge, D.W. (1983). *Minding the team: A median approach to competitive coaching. Journal of Sport Sociology, 18,* 83-98

Tellegen, A. & Atkinson, G. (1974). *Openness to absorbing and self-altering experiences (<<Absorption>>), a trait related to hypnotic susceptibility. Journal of Abnormal Psychology, 83,* 268-277.
 ⇒ (1985). *Structures of mood and personality and their relevance to assessing anxiety, with an emphasis on self-report.* In Tuma, A.H. & Maser, J.D. (Eds.), *Anxiety and the anxiety disorders.* 681-706. Hillsdale, NJ: Erlbaum.

Ten-Cate, J.J. (1921). *Contributions to the study of irradiation and concentration of extinctive inhibition. Bulletin of the Institute of Lesgaft, vol. 3.*

Terrace, H.S. (1963a). *Discrimination learning with and without 'errors'. Journal of the Experimental Analysis of Behavior, 6,* 1-27.
 ⇒ (1963b). *Errorless transfer of a discrimination across two continua. Journal of the Experimental Analysis of Behavior, 6,* 223-232. Reprinted in Catania (1968), 155-161.
 ⇒ (1964). *Wavelength generalization after discrimination learning with and without errors. Science, 144,* 78-80
 ⇒ (1966). *Stimulus control.* In Honig, W.K. (Ed.). *Operant Behavior: Areas of Research and Application.* New York: Appleton-Century-Crofts.

Thakur, G.P. & Thakur, M., (1980). *Personality differences between the athlete and the non-athlete college males. International Journal of Sport Psychology, 11,* 180-188.

Thayer, R.E. (1978). *Toward a psychological theory of multidimensional activation* (arousal). *Motivation and Emotion, 2,* 1-34.

The Advanced Pistol Marksmanship Manual (1964 Edition). Ft. Benning, GA.: United States Army Marksmanship Training Unit.

The Basics of Pistol Shooting (1991). *Significant contributions of knowledge and skills were given by the following:* Arenson, N.R., Dr., McElroy, B.R.,

Pinaud, L.H., Reeves, H., Walsh, W.R., Col. & White, J.C. Washington, D.C.: The National Rifle Association of America.

The Basics of Rifle Shooting (1991). Washington, D.C.: National Rifle Association of America.

The Effective Shooting Coach (1987). *A collection of articles, vol.1.* Washington, D.C.: National Rifle Association of America.

The Handbook of Free Rifle Shooting (1965 Edition). Ft. Benning, GA.: United States Army Marksmanship Training Unit.

The Marksmanship Instructors' Service Rifle Marksmanship Guide (1971). Ft. Benning, GA.:The United States Army Marksmanship Training Unit.

The Service Rifle Marksmanship Guide (1973). Ft. Benning, Ga.: The United States Army Marksmanship Unit.

Thomas, C.E. (1983). *Sport in a philosophic context.* Philadelphia: Lea & Febiger.

Thomas, J.R., French, K.E. & Humphries, C.A. (1986). *Knowledge development and sport skill performance: Directions for motor behavior research. Journal of Sport Psychology, 8,* 259-272.

Thompson, R.F., Lindsey, B. & Mason, G. (1966). *Physiological psychology.* In J.B. Sidowaki (Ed.), *Experimental Methods and Instrumentation in Psychology.* New York: McGraw-Hill.

Thompson, T. & Schuster, C.R. (1968). *Behavioral Pharmacology.* Englewood Cliffs, New Jersey: Prentice-Hall, Inc.
⇒ Pickens, R. and Meisch, R.A. (Eds.) (1970). *Readings in Behavioral Pharmacology.* New York: Appleton-Century-Crofts.

Thorndike, E.L. (1913). *Educational Psychology, Vol. 2. The Psychology of Learning.* New York: Teacher's College, Columbia University.
⇒ (1932). *The Fundamentals of Learning.* New York: Teacher s College, Columbia University.

Thornton, B., Ryckman, R.M., Robbins, M.A., Donolli, J. & Biser, G. (1987). *Relationship between perceived physical ability and indices of acutal physical fitness. Journal of Sport Psychology, 9,* 295-300.

Tihomirov, N.P. (1910). *The intensity of stimulus as an independent conditioned stimulus. Proc. Russian Med. Soc. in Petrograd, vol. 77.*

Trefethen, J.B., & Serven, J.E. (1967). *Americans and Their Guns.* Harrisburg, PA.: Stackpole Company.

Tretilova, T.A. & Rodimki, E.M. (1979). *Investigation of the emotional state of rifle shooters. International Sport Sciences, 1,* 745.

Tucker, D.M., Roth, R.S., Arneson, B.A. & Buckingham, V. (1977). *Right hemisphere activation during stress. Neuropsychologia, 15,* 697.

Turvey, M.T., Fitch, H.L., & Tuller, B. (1982). *The Bernstein perspective: I. The problems of degrees of freedom and context conditioned variability.* In J.A.S. Kelso (Ed.), *Human motor behavior: An introduction,* 239-252. Hillsdale, NJ: Erlbaum.
⇒ Shaw, R.E. & Mace, W. (1978). *Issues in the theory of action: Degrees of freedom, coordinative structures and coalitions.* In J. Requin (Ed.), *Attention and Performance VII,* 187-201. Hillsdale, NJ: Erlbaum.

594

Sources of Successful Pistol Shooting

Tutko, T.A. & Richards,].M. (1971). *Psychology of coaching.* Boston: Allyn and Bacon.

Tversky, A. & Kahneman, D. (1973). *Availability: A heuristic for judging frequency and probability.* Cognitive Psychology, 5, 207-232.

UIT Journal (6/92). Olympic Games.

Ullman, L.P. & Krasner, L. (Eds) (1965). *Case Studies in Behavior Modification.* New York: Holt, Rinehart and Winston.

⇒ & Krasner, L. (1969). *A Psychological Approach to Abnormal Behavior.* Englewood Cliffs, N.J.: Prentice-Hall, Inc.

Ulrich, R., Stachnik, T, & Mabry, J. (Eds.) (1966). *Control of Human Behavior.* Glenview, Illinois: Scott, Foresman & Co.

⇒ Stachnik, T. & Mabry, J. (Eds) (1970). *Control of Human Behavior 11: From Cure to Prevention.* Glenview, Illinois: Scott, Foresman and Co.

Ulrich, R.E., Hutchinson, R.R. & Azrin, N.H. (1965). *Pain-elicited aggression.* The Psychological Record, 15, 111-126.

US Army Pistol Marksmanship Guide (1981). U.S. Government Printing Office:

Vallerand, R.J. (1983). *Attention and decision making a test of the predictive validity of the test of attentional and interpersonal style (TAIS) in a Sport setting.* Journal of Sport Psychology, 5, 449-459.

⇒ (1987). *Antecedents of self-related affect in sport: Preliminary evidence on the intuitive-reflective appraisal model.* Journal of Sport Psychology, 9, 161-182.

⇒ Colavecchio, P.G. & Pelletier, L.G. (1988*). Psychological momentum and performance inferences: A preliminary test of the antecedents - consequences psychological momentum model.* Journal of Sport and Exercise Psychology, 10, 92-108

Van Rossum, J.H.A. (1988). *Motor development and practice: The variability of practice hypothesis in perspective.* Amsterdam: Free University Press.

Van Wieringen, P.C.W. (1988). *Kinds and levels of explanation: Implications for the motor systems versus action systems controversy.* In Meijer, D.G. & Roth, K. (Eds.), *Complex movement behaviour: The motor-action controversy,* 87-120. Amsterdam: North-Holland.

Vanek, M. & Cratty, B. (1970). *Psychology of the superior athlete.* New York: MacMillan.

Vealey, R.S. (1986). *Conceptualization of sport confidence and competitive orientation: Preliminary investigation and instrument development.* Journal of Sport Psychology, 8, 221-246.

Verhave, T. (Ed) (1966). *The Experimental Analysis of Behavior.* New York: Appleton-Century-Crofts.

vos Savant, M. & Fleischer, L. (1990). *Brain Building.* New York: Bantam Books.

Vygotsky, L.S. (1962). *Thought and Language.* Cambridge, MA: MIT Press.

Walker, B.B. & Sandman, C.A. (1979). *Human visual evoked responses are related to heart rate.* Journal of Comparative and Physiological Psychology, 93, 717-729.

Wall, A.E. (1986). *A knowledge-based approach to motor skill acquisition.* In Wade, M.G. & Whiting, H.T.A. (Eds.), *Motor-development in children: Aspects of coordination and control,* 33-49. Dordrecht: Martinus Nijhoff.

Wall, A.E., McClements, J., Bouffard, M., Findlay, H. & Taylor, M.J. (1986). *A knowledge-based approach to motor development: Implications for the physically awkward. Adapted Physical Activity Quarterly, 2,* 21-42.

Wallace, R.K. (1970). *Physiological effects of transcendental meditation. Science, 213,* 1143-1152.

⇒ Benson, H, & Wilson, A.F. (1971). *A wakeful hypometabolic physiologic state. American Journal of Physiology, 221,* 795-799.

Wang, C.C., Marple, H.D. & Carlson, H. (1975). *EEG desynchronization during pitch discrimination. Journal of Auditory Research, 15,* 140-145.

Wankel, L.M. & Kreisel, P.S.J. (1985a). *Factors underlying enjoyment in youth sports: Sport and age group comparisons. Journal of Sport Psychology, 7,* 51-64.

⇒ & Kreisel, P.S.J. (1985b). *Methodological considerations in youth sport motivation research: A comparison of open-ended and paired comparison approaches. Journal of Sport Psychology, 7,* 65-74.

Wann, D.L. & Hamlet, M.A. (1995). *Author and Subject Gender in Sports Research.* Department of Psychology, Murray State University. *International Journal of Sport Psychology, 26,* 225-232.

War Department, Office of the Chief of Staff, (1909). *Provisional Small Arms Firing Manual: For the United States Army and For the Organized Militia of the United States.* Washington, D.C.: Government Printing Office.

Warm, J.S., Richter, D.O., Sprague, R.L., Proter, P.K. & Schumsky, D.A. (1980). *Listening with a dual brain: Hemispheric asymmetry in sustained attention. Bulletin of the Psychonomic Society, 15,* 229-232.

Warren, W.H., Jr. & Shaw, R.E. (1985). *Events and encounters as units of analyis of ecological psychology.* In Warren, W.M., Jr. & Shaw, R.E. (Eds.), *Persistence and change,* 2-27. Hillsdale, NJ: Erlbaum.

Watkins, D. (1984). *Students' perceptions of factors influencing tertiary learning. Higher Education Research and Development, 3,* 33-50.

Watson, G.G. (1986). *Approach-avoidance behavior in team sports: An application to leading Australian national hockey* players. *International Journal of Sport Psychology, 17,* 130-155.

Watson, J.B. (1924). *Behaviorism.* Chicago: University of Chicago Press.

Weber, A., Fussler, C., O'Hanlon, J.F., Gierer, R. & Grandjean, E. (1980). *Psychophysiological effects of repetitive tasks. Ergonomics, 23(11),* 1033-1046.

Webster, J.G. (1978). (Ed.), *Medical Instrumentation: Application and Design.* Boston: Houghton Mifflin Company.

Weibe, D.J. (1991). *Hardiness and stress moderation: A test of proposed mechanisms. Journal of Personality and Social Psychology, 60,* 89-99.

Weinberg, R.S. (1985). *Relationship between self-efficacy and cognitive strategies in enhancing endurance performance. International Journal of Sport Psychology, 17,* 280-292.

⇒ Gould, D. & Jackson, A. (1979) *Expectations and performance: An empirical test of Bandura's self-efficacy theory. Journal of Sport Psychology, 1,* 320-331.

⇒ Gould, D., Yukelson, D. & Jackson, A. (1981). *The effect of preexisting and manipulated self-efficacy on a competitive muscular endurance task. Journal of Sport Psychology, 3 (4),* 345-354.

⇒ Seaborne, T. & Jackson, A. (1981). *Effects of visuo-motor behavior rehearsal, relaxation and imagery on karate performance. Journal of Sport Psychology, 3,* 228-238.

⇒ Seaborne, T. & Jackson, A. (1987). *Arousal and relaxation instructions prior to the use of imagery. International Journal of Sport Psychology, 18,* 205-214.

⇒ & Hunt, V.V. (1976*). The interrelationships between anxiety, motor performance and electromyography. Journal of Motor Behavior, 9,* 219-224.

⇒ & Jackson, A. (1989). *The effects of psychological momentum on male and female tennis players revisited. Journal of Sport Behavior, 12,* 167-179.

⇒ (1982). *The relationship between mental preparation strategies and motor performance. A review and critique, Quest, 33,* 195-213.

⇒ Bruya, L., Longino, J. & Jackson, A. (1988). *Effect of goal promixity and specificity on endurance performance of primary-grade children. Journal of Sport and Exercise Psychology, 10,* 81-91.

⇒ Yukelson, D. & Jackson, A. (1980). *Effect of public and private efficacy expectations on competitive performance. Journal of Sport Psychology, 2,* 340-349.

Weiner, B. (1985). *An attributional theory of achievement motivation and emotion. Psychological Review, 92,* 548-573.

⇒ Russell, D. & Lerman, D. (1978). *Affective consequences of causal ascriptions.* In Harvey, J.H., Ickes,W.J. & Kidd, R.F. (Eds.), *New directions in attribution research: Vol. 2,* 59-88. Hillsdale, NJ: Erlbaum.

⇒ Russell, D. & Lerman, D. (1979). *The cognition-emotion process in achievement-related contexts. Journal of Personality and Social Psychology, 37,* 1211-1220.

Weinstein (Vaynshteyn), ***Learn to Shoot Accurately*** (1973), Moscow, This is intended for beginners.

Weinstein (Vaynshteyn), *Shooter And Trainer* (1977), Moscow, (First published 1969). This book is **Weinstein's** most famous book. The the first 108 pages deal with rifle shooting techniques. page 109 forward, deal exclusively with pistol shooting techniques. One thing you will quickly notice is that there are relatively few illustrations, which only serves to emphasize the differences between European and American cultures. He notes,

597

before WWII, the Estonians fought too much adrenaline by keeping their shooters up all night before an important championship.

Weiss, B. & Laties, V.G. (1961), *Changes in pain tolerance and other behavior produced by salicylates. Journal of Pharmacology and Experimental Therapeutics, 131,* 120-129. (Reprinted in Thompson, Pickens and Meisch (1970), 368-382.

⇒ (1970). *The fine structure of operant behavior during transition states.* In Schoenfeld, W.N. (Ed.). **The Theory of Reinforcement Schedules,** 277-311. New York: Appleton-Century-Crofts.

Weiss, M.R. & Bredemeier, BJ. (1983). *Developmental sport psychology: A theoretical perspective for studying children in sport. Journal of Sport Psychology, 5,* 216-230.

⇒ & Friedrichs, W.D. (1986). *The influence of leader behaviors, coach attributes, and institutional variables on performance and satisfaction of collegiate basketball teams. Journal of Sport Psychology, 8,* 332-346.

Welch, G., Hall, A. & Walkey, F. (1988). *The factor structure of the Eating.* Disorder Inventory. *Journal of Clinical Psychology,* 44, 51-56.

Welford, A.T. (1960). *The measurement of sensory-motor performance: survery and reappraisal of twelve years' progress. Ergonomics, 3,* 189-230.

⇒ (1974). *Stress and Performance.* In Welford, A.T. (Ed.), **Man under stress.** London: Taylor and Francis.

Wells, W.R.,II, (1993). **Shots That Hit.** *A Study of U.S. Coast Guard Marksmanship: 1790-1985.* United States Coast Guard Historian's Office.

Wenger, M.A., Clemens, T.L., Coleman, D.R., Cullen, T.D. & Engel, B.T. (1961). *Autonomic response specificity. Psychosomatic Medicine, 23,* 185-193.

Westman, M. (1990). *The relationship between stress and performance: The moderating effect of hardiness. Human Performance,* 3, 141-155.

Weston, P.B., (1970). **The Handbook of Handgunning.** New York, N.Y.: Crown Publishers.

Wexler, B.E. (1980). *Cerebral laterality and psychiatry: A review of the literature. American Journal of Psychiatry, 137,* 279-291.

Whaley, D.L. & Malott, R. W. (1971). **Elementary Principles of Behavior.** New York: Appleton-Century-Crofts.

White, S.A. & Duda, J.L., (1994). *The Relationship of Gender, Level of Sport Involvement, and Participation Motivation to Task and Ego Orientation.* Illinois State University, USA, Purdue University, USA. *International Journal Sport Psychology, 25,* 4-18.

Whiting, H.T.A. (1969). **Acquiring ball skills.** London: Bell.

⇒ (1978). *Input and perceptual processes in sports skills.* In Glencross, D.J. (Ed.), **Psychology in sport,** 22-47. Sydney: McGraw-Hill.

⇒ (1982). *Skill in sport - a description and prescriptive appraisal.* In Salmela, J.H., Partington, J.T. & Orlick, T. (Eds.), **New paths of sport learning and excellence** 7-13. Ottawa: Sport in Perspective Inc.

⇒ (Ed.) (1984). *Human motor action: Bernstein reassessed.* Amsterdam: North-Holland.

⇒ (1984) *Aggression-performance relationship in sport.* In Silva, J.M. & Weinberg, R.S. (Eds.), *Psychological foundations of sport,* 274-286. Champaign, IL: Human Kinetics.

⇒ Brawley, L.R. & Carron, A.V. (1985). *The measurement of cohesion in sport teams: The group enrironment questionnaire.* London, Ontario: Sports Dynamics.

Wike, W.L. (1966). *Secondary Reinforcement Selected Experiments.* New York: Harper and Row.

Wilkinson, M.O., Landers, D.M. & Daniels, F.S.(1981). *Respiration patterning as related to performance in elite and subelite rifle shooters. The American Marksman, 6,* 8-9.

Williams, C. (1994). *Arnie Vitarbo: National Pistol Coach.* InSights.

Williams, C.D. (1959). *The elimination of tantrum behaviour by extinction procedures. Journal of Abnormal and Social Psychology,* 59, 269. Reprinted in Ullmann and Krasner (1965). 295-296.

Williams, J.M. (1980). *Personality characteristics of the successful female athlete.* In W.F. Straub (Ed.), *Sport psychology: An analysis of athlete behavior.* Ann Arbor: McNaughton Gunn.

Williamson, D.A., Kelley, M.L., Davis, C.J., Ruggiero, L. & Blouin, D.C. (1985). *Psychopathology of eating disorders: A controlled comparison of bulimic, obese, and normal subjects. Journal of Consulting and Clinical Psychology, 53,* 161-166.

Willis, J.D. & Layne, B.H. (1988*). A validation study of the sport-related motives scales. Journal of Applied Research in Coaching and Athletics, 3,* 299-307.

⇒ (1982). *Three scales to measure competition-related motives in sport. Journal of Sport Psychology, 4,* 338-353.

Willis, M.P. (1967). *Stress effects on skill. Journal of Experimental Psychology,* 74, 460-465.

Wilson, V.E., Berger, B.G. & Bird, E.I. (1981). *Effects of running and of an exercise class on anxiety. Perceptual and Motor Skills, 53,* 472-474.

⇒ Morley, N.C. & Bird, E.I. (1980). *Mood profiles of marathon runners, joggers, and non-exercisers. Perceptual and Motor Skills, 50,* 117-118.

Windholz, George;(1990). & Kuppers, James R. *Pavlov and the Nobel Prize award,* U North Carolina, Charlotte, US. *Pavlovian Journal of Biological Science.* Vol 25(4) 155-162, Oct-Dec.

Wine, J.D. (1980). *Cognitive-attentional theory of test anxiety.* In Sarason, I.G. (Ed.), *Test anxiety Theory, research and applications,* 349-385. Hillsdale, NJ: Erlbaum.

⇒ (1982). *Evaluation anxiety: A cognitive-attentional construct.* In Krohne, H.W. & Laux, L. (Eds.), *Achievement, stress, and anxiety,* 207-219. Washington, DC: Hemisphere.

Wold, B. & Anderson, N., (1992). *Health Promotion Aspects of Family and Peer Influences on Sport Participation.* Research Center for Health Promotion, University of Bergen, Norway. *International Journal of Sport Psychology*, 23, 343-359.

Wolf, M.M., Risley, T. & Mees, H. (1964). *Application of operant conditioning procedures to the behavior problems of an autistic child. Behaviour Research and Therapy, 1,* 305-312. Reprinted in Ulrich, Stachnik and Mabry (1966), 187-198.

Wolman, B.B. (1973). *Dictionary of Behavioral Science*. New York, N.Y.: Van Nostrand Reinhold Company.

Woods, J.B. (1976). *Kids and Guns do Mix, Guns & Ammo Home Defense Guns*, 35, 39-41, 95. Los Angeles, CA.: Peterson Publishing Co.

Woolfolk, R.L., Parrish, M.W. & Murphy, S.M.. (1985). *The effects of positive and negative imagery on motor skill performance. Cognitive Therapy and Research*, 9, 335-342.

World Health Organization. (1985). *Health behaviour in schoolchildren. A cross-national survey. PROTOCOL*, WHO, Regional Office for Europe-HED.

Wortman, C.B., Panciera, L., Shusterman, L. & Hibscher, J. (1976). *Attributions of causality and reactions to uncontrollable outcomes. Journal of Experimental Social Psycholo*gy, *12,* 301-316.

Yan Lan, L. & Gill. D.L. (1984). *The relationship among self-efficacy, stress responses, and a cognitive feedback manipulation. Journal of Sport Psychology, 6,* 227-238.

Yanovski, A. & Fogel, M.L. (1978). *Some diagnostic and therapeutic implications of visual imagery reactivity. Journal of Mental Imagery, 2,* 301-302.

Yerkes, R.M. & Dodson, J.D. (1908). *The relation of strength of stimulus to rapidity of habit-formation. Journal of Comparative Neurology and Psychology, 18,* 459-482.

Youmans, W.B. (1967). *The visceral nervous system and skeletal muscle activity. American Journal of Physiology and Medicine, 46,* 173-183.

Yukelson, D., Weinberg, R. & Jackson, A. (1984). *A multidimensional group cohesion instrument for intercollegiate basketball teams. Journal of Sport Psychology, 6,* 103-117.

Yur'yev, A.A. (1973). *Competitive Shooting, Techniques & Training for Rifle, Pistol and Running Game Target Shooting*. English translation edited by Gary L. Anderson. Original copyright by Fizkul'tura i Sport, Moscow. Copyright 1985 by V.H. Winston & Sons and the National Rifle Association of America, Inc.

Zaichkowsky, L. & Fuchs, C.Z. (1988). *Biofeedback applications in exercise and athletic performance. Exercise and Sport Science Reviews, 16,* 381-419.

Zander, A. (1971). *Motives and goals in groups*. New York: Academic Press.

Zeliony, G.P. (1909). *A special type of conditioned reflexes. Archive Biol. Sciences, vol. xiv.* No. 5.

Zillman, D. (1971). *Excitation transfer in communication-mediated aggressive behavior. Journal of Experimental Social Psychology, 7,* 419-434.

Zimbardo, P.G., Ebbesen, E.B. & Maslach, C. (1977). *Influencing attitudes and changing behaviour,* 2nd edition. Reading, MA: Addison Wesley.

600

Zimmerman, B.J. (1986). *Becoming a self-regulated learner: Which are the key subprocesses? Contemporary Educational Psychology, 11,* 307-313.

⇒ (1989). *Models of self-regulated learning and academic achievement.* In Zimmerman, B.J. & Schunk, D.H. (Eds.), **Self-regulated learning and academic achievement theory, research, and practice: Progress in cognitive development reasearch,** 1-26. New York: Springer-Verlag.

Zimmerman, E.H. & Zimmerman, J. (1972). *The alteration of behavior in a special classroom situation. Journal of the Experimental Analysis of Behavior, 5,* 59-60 Reprinted in Ulrich, Stachnik and Mabry (1966), 94-96

Zucker, P., Avener, J., Bayder, S., Brotman, A., Moore, K. & Zimmerman, J. (1985). *Eating disorders in young athletes. The Physician and Sportsmedicine, 13,* 88-106.

Zuckerman, D.M., Colby, A., Ware, N.C. & Lazerson, J.S. (1986). *The prevalence of bulimia among college students. American Journal of Public Health, 76,* 1135-1137.

Zuckerman, M. (1971). *Dimensions of sensation seeking. Journal of Consulting and Clinical Psychology, 36,* 45-52.

⇒ (1979). **Sensation seeking,** Hillsdale, NJ: Lawrence Erlbaum Associates.

⇒ (1983). *Sensation seeking and sports. Personality and Individual Differences, 4,* (3), 285-292.

⇒ Kuhlman, D.M. & Camac, C (1988). *What lies beyond E an N Factor analyses of scales believed to measure basic dimensions of personality. Journal of Venality and Social Psychology, 54,* 96-107.

Zurich, Riwosa, A.G., *UIT Journal* (3/86). *Why do Shooters Wear Hearing Protectors?,* 62-63.

Appendix A

Art Sievers

Lieutenant Commander Arthur W. Sievers, USN
on the right, being congratulated by LCDR Lannie Conn
upon his retirement from the Navy in October, 1970.

Lieutenant Commander Arthur W. Sievers, USN

PISTOL CHAMPS . . . Four of Lieutenant Commander Arthur W. Sievers' All American Pistol Team members were on hand to wish him well following his retirement from the Navy. Flanking the long-time Naval Academy Small Arms Instructor are Midshipman Gerry D. Appenfelder (left); Ronald M. DeLoof (second left); Sievers; Midshipmen Robert C. Mayes (second right) and Stephen C. Kanopa (right). Of the 5000 midshipmen coached by Sievers, 25 have been named to the All American Pistol Team.

Sievers initial contact with the military was on May 5, 1935, when he moved from the rank of Eagle Scout in the Boy Scouts to enlisting as a private in the 151st Field Artillery of the Minnesota National Guard. When Sievers signed this initial contract, he unknowingly committed himself to what turned out to be 35 and a half years of service to the military of his country. This route would carry him through 22 enlisted grades and four officer ranks in three U.S. military services, culminating in his retirement in 1970 as Lieutenant Commander, after completing his last thirty years in active naval service. Sievers felt extremely fortunate to complete his last six years as the Smallarms Marksmanship Instructor, Naval Station, Annapolis, and coach of the Midshipman Pistol Team.

Sievers carried a 40 man pistol squad at the Naval Academy, 20 Varsity and 20 Freshmen. Few coaches in this country have ever seen a squad this size, let alone have an opportunity to work with them.

604

NATIONAL RIFLE ASSOCIATION OF AMERICA
INCORPORATED 1871

1600 RHODE ISLAND AVENUE
WASHINGTON, D.C. 20036

OFFICE OF THE
SECRETARY

June 17, 1970

Rear Admiral James Calvert, U. S. N.
Superintendent
United States Naval Academy
Annapolis, Maryland   21402

Dear Admiral Calvert:

      The Board of Directors of the National Rifle Association
of America, in Annual Meeting, on April 8, 1970, in New Orleans,
Louisiana, unanimously adopted a resolution of commendation to
Lieutenant Commander Arthur Sievers, U. S. N.

      Commander Sievers served as coach of the United States
Palma Team which won the Palma Trophy Match at the Connaught Ranges
in Ottawa, Canada, in 1969. In his service to the team and to the
shooters of the United States, Commander Sievers contributed gener-
ously of his time and expertise as a rifle coach, much to the credit
of the United States and to the United States Navy.

      I enclose an engrossed copy of the resolution adopted by
the NRA Board of Directors with the request that at an opportune
time you present this document to Commander Sievers with the thanks
and appreciation of the National Rifle Association of America and
the shooters of the United States.

Sincerely,

Frank C. Daniel
Secretary

FCD/jan
enclosure

cc: Admiral Thomas H. Moorer
     Chief of Naval Operations

3 0 JUN **1970**

FIRST ENDORSEMENT on Frank C. Daniel, National Rifle
Association of America ltr of 17 Jun 1970

From: Superintendent, U. S. Naval Academy
To: Lieutenant Commander Arthur Sievers, USN

1.   The National Rifle Association of America resolution
honoring Lieutenant Commander Arthur Sievers, USN, is
forwarded with sincere congratulations and appreciation
for your services to the Naval Academy as the Small Arms
Marksmanship Instructor and Pistol Coach during the past
five and one half years.

JAMES CALVERT

Sievers is the only person, coach or shooter to be awarded an NRA Board of Directors Resolution acknowledging his exemplary services to the United States Palma Team enabling the team to win the international match. This was a historic first and has never been repeated for any shooter or coach in the history of the National Rifle Association.

1964, Art Sievers

In 1964, Sievers, at the time of this picture, had coached seven National Navy rifle squads as can enlisted man. 1964 is significant in Sievers career in that he coached his 8th National Navy Rifle Squad as an officer. LTJG Sievers, in that year, was the oldest LTJG in the United States Navy at age 47.

At the culmination of his career in 1970 he had coached ten Navy Squads, nine rifle and 1 pistol. In 1969, he coached the successful United States Palma Team to victory in Canada.

As a shooter, in 1958, Sievers was a member of a Navy 4-man smallbore rifle team and they shot a National Record in the 100 any sight match.

606

NATIONAL RIFLE ASSOCIATION
OF AMERICA

Resolution

WHEREAS, American riflemen are now participating in long-range rifle matches with other English speaking countries of the world, such competition being a revival of the Palma Trophy Matches, the memory of which for nearly a hundred years has been marked by prestige, traditions, and color, supported by the Royal House of Great Britain and by the Presidency of the United States; and

WHEREAS, The team representing the United States of America by a long series of qualifying competition consists of the best long-range marksmen in this country, and the superlative performance expected of the American teams depends overwhelmingly upon the quality of leadership and proficiency of the coaching available, and

WHEREAS, Lieutenant Commander Arthur Sievers, U.S. Navy, served the American team as coach at Connaught Ranges, Ottawa, Canada, in 1969, in an outstanding and exemplary manner, thus contributing to the splendid victory of our team there under most difficult conditions, bringing thereby great credit to himself, our team, and the U.S. Navy which he represented in successful support of the National Rifle Association shooting program; now, therefore, be it

RESOLVED, That the Board of Directors of the National Rifle Association in meeting assembled here in New Orleans, Louisiana, April 8, 1970, expresses its gratitude to Lieutenant Commander Arthur Sievers, United States Navy, and that this resolution suitably prepared, be presented to him.

Attest:

_____
Secretary

Appendix B

Bob Hickey

Bob Hickey has been training shooters since 1952. He is an NRA Training Counselor, having been appointed in 1958. His individual rifle shooting activities have won him state rifle championships in Illinois, Wisconsin, New Mexico and Alaska. In 1959, his score of 299 out of 300 won the Intercollegiate Rifle Championship. He is also a two time All-American Rifle Team selection. At Camp Perry, in the Nationals of 1971, he won one of the 50 yard, any sights matches, with a perfect score of 400 out of 400, with 40 X's. He was honored by the State of Alaska as one of the 50 *Champions of Sport*, during the celebration of the 50 years of the Purchase of Alaska from Russia.

However, Hickey's principal field of expertise has been in coaching others in shooting. He has coached junior rifle clubs, junior pistol clubs, summer recreational camps, public junior high school rifle teams, university rifle teams, state junior rifle teams, the Armed Forces Special Weapons Project High Power Rifle Teams and has organized and conducted junior rifle team shooting tours of England and Scotland.

He is a teacher and psychological social worker by profession. He spent 30 years in Alaska. His retirement to Arizona allowed him to implement his decision to establish a more efficient pistol coaching system. This led to his involvement with Art Sievers, as a result of the recommendation of David Lyman, of the Blue Trail Range in Wallingford, Connecticut, the best range on the East Coast.

Hickey is probably the only coach in the United States to have coached both junior rifle and junior pistol teams to individual and team multiple National Records.

He is the author of the best selling shooting book titled, *Mental Training*. He is also the author of articles in computer magazines and *The American Rifleman*. He is the first to have placed a series of shooting poems in the public domain with his book titled, *Laundry Room Poems*.

608

Appendix C

Personality Inventories For Shooters

Shooter's Personality Inventory

Name:_____ Date: _____ Age: _____

1. **Try to imagine that you overhear two people whom you know very well talking about someone. After a while they say something which makes you realize that they are talking about you as what they say fits pretty closely with how you think other people see you. Which of the following statements is closest to the one that you "overheard"?**

a. "X" seems to be a pretty much on an even keel kind of person. Nothing much troubles him/her.

b. I like "X", but I wish he/she wasn't so fussy and finicky.

c. Poor "X" always seems to have something the matter with him/her.

d. "X" is very moody, don't you think? I wish he/she was a bit easier to get on with.

e. I simply don't understand "X.". I wish I knew what made him/her tick.

Closest To The One I "overheard."

▢

2. **Here's a question about your relationships with the opposite sex. Which of the following most commonly corresponds to your own case? Exclude siblings from your answers.**

a. I find it extremely easy to get along with members of the opposite sex.

b. I am unable to form a happy relationship with anyone of the opposite sex and I find this very worrying.

c. On the whole I get along well with members of the opposite sex, but I have difficulties or upsets from time to time..

d. Occasionally I get along well with men/women, boys/girls, but most times it's not too easy.

e. I haven't started an active love life yet and I find it a very troubled and uncertain idea when I do think about it.

f. I cannot find any statement above that is anywhere near my own case.

Most Commonly Corresponds To My Own Case:

☐

3. **Here are six statements. Show whether you strongly agree, agree, disagree, or strongly disagree with each.**

a. Politicians tend to be concerned with advancing themselves rather than helping ordinary people.

Strongly Agree	Agree	Strongly Disagree	Disagree
☐	☐	☐	☐

b. Spare the rod and spoil the child may be an old-fashioned saying, but there is certainly a good deal of truth in it.

Strongly Agree	Agree	Strongly Disagree	Disagree
☐	☐	☐	☐

c. Most people who suffer from emotional disturbances could benefit from more firmness and less sympathy.

Strongly Agree	Agree	Strongly Disagree	Disagree
☐	☐	☐	☐

610

d. Homosexuality is basically wrong and is a matter for punishment rather than acceptance.

Strongly Agree ☐ **Agree** ☐ **Strongly Disagree** ☐ **Disagree** ☐

e. People who become alcoholics have only themselves to blame.

Strongly Agree ☐ **Agree** ☐ **Strongly Disagree** ☐ **Disagree** ☐

f. An untidy house denotes an untidy mind.

Strongly Agree ☐ **Agree** ☐ **Strongly Disagree** ☐ **Disagree** ☐

4.   Indicate which of the statements below most closely agrees with your overall picture of your attitude to life.

a. I feel full of confidence about the future for most of the time.

b. I'm pretty optimistic about things on the whole.

c. Sometimes I feel optimistic, sometimes pessimistic about the way things are going to turn out.

d. Occasionally I feel optimistic, but mostly I'm not too hopeful or happy about my future.

e. The future looks pretty black to me most of the time..

Most Closely Agrees With My Attitude To Life.

☐

611

5.   **Indicate the questions to which you answer yes.**

a. Are you having difficulty getting off to sleep at night?

Yes   No
☐   ☐

b. Do you tend to be troubled by "dizzy spells" or "shortness of breath"?

Yes   No
☐   ☐

c. Do you dislike the idea of foreign travel?

Yes   No
☐   ☐

d. Do you have what you feel to be an unreasonable fear of high places or open spaces?

Yes   No
☐   ☐

e. Do you often find yourself needing to cry?

Yes   No
☐   ☐

f. Do you dislike shyness in others?

Yes   No
☐   ☐

g. Do you have to check things that you do over and over again?

Yes   No
☐   ☐

Appendix C

h. Have you ever had the feeling that you are just about to "go to pieces" in your mind?

Yes ☐   No ☐

i. Does the thought of being in a closed space like an elevator or a tunnel upset you??

Yes ☐   No ☐

j. Do you tend to wake up unusually early in the mornings?

Yes ☐   No ☐

k. Do you suffer from indigestion and upset stomach rather a lot?

Yes ☐   No ☐

l. Do crowds of people make you feel a bit panicky?

Yes ☐   No ☐

m. Are you interested in current affairs and politics?

Yes ☐   No ☐

n. Does life seem to you to be "too much effort"?

Yes ☐   No ☐

o. Do you often worry about mistakes you have made in the past?

Yes ☐   No ☐

p. Are you at your happiest when you are being kept really busy?

Yes ☐ No ☐

q. Have you been suffering from poor appetite recently?

Yes ☐ No ☐

r. Do you enjoy watching thrillers on TV?

Yes ☐ No ☐

s. Do you find it difficult to look at pictures of any creepy-crawly animal, spider or worm?

Yes ☐ No ☐

t. Do you get strange tingling or burning sensations in different parts of your body?

Yes ☐ No ☐

u. Does it worry you quite a lot if you see an untidy room or house?

Yes ☐ No ☐

v. Do you often have the feeling that you are going to faint?

Yes ☐ No ☐

w. Are you interested in cross word puzzles?

Yes ☐ No ☐

x. Are you really scared of heights?

Yes	No
☐	☐

y. Do you get unusually tired rather easily?

Yes	No
☐	☐

z. Are you good at quickly analyzing a complex situation such as which of four or five kids started a fight?

Yes	No
☐	☐

aa. Does the prospect of a journey or voyage of any kind unsettle you?

Yes	No
☐	☐

bb. Would you describe yourself as a person who worries a lot?

Yes	No
☐	☐

cc. Do you find that you get unusually annoyed if someone prevents you from doing something that you want to do?

Yes	No
☐	☐

dd. Are you interested in athletics?

Yes	No
☐	☐

6.   **Here are some drugs that people take to help them when under stress of one kind or another. Say honestly whether you use them never, occasionally or regularly.**

a. Aspirin or tranquilizers

Never	Occasionally	Regularly
☐	☐	☐

b. Sleeping pills of any kind.

Never	Occasionally	Regularly
☐	☐	☐

c. Herbal tonics or medicine

Never	Occasionally	Regularly
☐	☐	☐

d. Alcohol

Never	Occasionally	Regularly
☐	☐	☐

Personality Test Answers

Add up the A, B, C and D scores separately. Then add them together for the total score.

1a = 0	1b = 4C	1c= 4D	1d=4A	1e= 0	

2a= 0	2b= 3C	2c= 0	2d= 3A	2e= 0	2f= 3A

	Strongly Agree	Agree	Disagree	Strongly Disagree
3a	**4D**	**2D**	**0**	**0**
3b	**4C**	**2C**	**0**	**2A**
3c	**4C**	**2C**	**0**	**2A**
3d	**4D**	**2D**	**0**	**0**
3e	**4C**	**2C**	**0**	**0**
3f	**4C**	**2C**	**0**	**2A**

4a= 0	4b= 0	4c= 2A	4d =4A	4e= 6A

Scores For 5 are for YES answers ONLY

5a= 2C	5b= 2D	5c= 0	5d= 4B	5e= 2A
5f= 0	5g= 2C	5h= 2D	5I= 4B	5j= 2A
5k= 2D	5l= 4B	5m= 0	5n= 2A	5o= 2C
5p= 2C	5q= 2A	5r= 0	5s= 4B	5t= 2D
5u= 2C	5v= 2D	5w= 0	5x= 4B	5y= 2A
5z= 2A	5aa= 4B	5bb= 2A	5cc= 2C	5dd= 0

	Never	Occasionally	Regularly
6a	**0**	**1D**	**2D & 2A**
6b	**0**	**1C**	**2C & 2A**
6c	**0**	**1C**	**2C & 2A**
6d	**0**	**1C**	**2C & 2A**

Shooter Personality Test Analysis

Table A

1-10 This is a suspiciously low score. There could be two reasons for this, either the shooter misread the instructions, or the coach has made an error in the scoring in some way, or another possibility, the shooter has not been honest when filling out the questionnaire. In theory it would be possible for someone to be so well adjusted that he could produce the score the shooter has recorded, but he would certainly be leading a very dull and unchallenging life. Have the shooter take a look at the questions again and suggest he try to be a bit franker this time.

11-25 This is the "normal" range of response. No human being is completely well-adjusted, but the answers the shooter has given reveal that he or she is striking a reasonably satisfactory balance between his or her personality and the stresses of the world around him or her. Some degree of irrational or "neurotic" behavior exists in everyone and in many ways helps to make their personality somewhat more interesting. As a coach, you should look, however, at the distribution of the shooter's scores in the four personality strains, A, B, C and D. If the shooter's score is fairly evenly drawn from each of the four personality strains then the shooter is indeed *"well-balanced."* If the preponderance is within two strains, this will give the pistol coach a clue as to those areas of the shooter's personality where the adjustment will be somewhat less easy. When a major contribution to the shooter's score comes from only one of the strains, it implies a more marked imbalance. To interpret this tendency see Table B.

26-45 No human being is totally free of emotional stress and most people compensate for this stress by a degree of inconsistent behavior. The pistol shooter's score indicates that there may be a measurable component of the shooter's psychological make-up. This in itself should not be a matter for worry, but it does suggest to the coach that the pistol shooter does seem to be having hard time with his life and some of its problems. This is largely a matter of personal adjustment. But mentally such stresses as are reflected in the shooter's score are due to unresolved conflicts, for example, an unresolved pistol shooting problem or an unsatisfactory performance in a class at school or perhaps some ambiguity about just what the shooter's relationship with the opposite sex is supposed to be. At this stage of the junior pistol shooter's life this is quite normal. Congratulate the pistol shooter on being normal.(see Table B)

46-60 There is little doubt from the junior pistol shooter's score that the shooter leads an erratic and troubled emotional life. If the pistol shooter is young, say under 15, this could well be a passing phase brought on by the enormous stresses of the transition through puberty and into adult life. If the shooter is older, it suggests that he or she is being faced with crises and conflicts which the shooter is finding very hard to resolve. As long as these conflicts remain, the strong neurotic aspect of the shooter's character will also remain. It is important to realize however, that neurotic responses do represent the fact that the individual is struggling to solve his problems. In that sense, therefore, the shooter's high score is nothing to be ashamed of. However, there's no doubt that life is giving the pistol shooter a bit of a hard time at the moment and there would be an obvious advantage to trying to resolve some of those conflicts. Perhaps it's not easy for the shooter to even identify what they are. Check to see if the shooter has friend, teacher, or member of the family in whom the shooter can confide. This often helps to highlight the route out of the problem. The coach should also look at the distribution of the shooter's scores among the four personality strains. (see Table B)

Over 60   This is an exceedingly high score by any standard and either the shooter is passing through a highly critical time of the shooter's life, in which case the scores are probably inflated and will later decline, or the coach has mis-scored or misinterpreted the questionnaire. If after rechecking the shooter's scores they still retain the same high score, then the coach should seriously set about trying to obtain the shooter's permission to discuss this score with the shooter's parents or guardian, so as to solve the problems which are obviously troubling the shooter. If the shooter chooses not to have the coach involve the parent, suggest a long chat with a close and trusted friend may help the shooter to find out exactly what these problems are.

Table B

The four scores A, B, C and D represent four major personality traits. Each of these represents a method by which the individual attempts to deal with problems and difficulties in his life, which could be solved by *"normal"* means. The difficulty is that often the conflicts which bring about neurotic disturbance are unclear to the coach, and thus he is simply unable to suggest to the shooter the correct steps to change them.

Clinical psychologists recognize a large number of different *"Neurotic states,"* but for simplicity's sake we have grouped them in this questionnaire into four categories: **(A) Anxiety, (B) Phobic, (C) Obsessive and (D) Hysterical**. **Anxiety** states tend to be dominated by feelings of depression and general uneasiness. **Phobic** states are dominated by irrational and unrealistic fears. **Obsessive** states are dominated by a tendency towards a rigid personality and pre-occupation with trivial detail. **Hysterical** states are dominated by physical and psychological symptoms of one kind or another.

620

As a general guide to interpretation the coach can say that if the shooter's overall score is less than 25 and no individual trait score exceeds 10, the shooter's personality pattern in these areas can be described as normal. An individual score of over 10 does not, at this level, mean very much, but it does give the coach a clear indication that any psychological stresses, the shooter experiences, will tend to be reflected in distortions in this particular area.

When overall scores lie between 25 and 40, there is again little to be said if the distribution is evenly balanced. Individual trait scores of over 10 are indicative of a particular strain and tension in that area, whereas individual scores of over 10, in the case of **Phobic**, over 15 in the case of **Anxiety** and **Hysteric** and over 10 in the case of **Obsessive,** suggest a marked imbalance in the way the shooter copes with stress.

For those with lower total scores and any individual score not more than half of the total the following simple rule applies:

If it is a moderate **Obsessive** score: suggest the shooter try to be a little less fussy and more tolerant of others. The shooter's intolerance is really intolerance of himself or herself. If this characteristic is allowed to remain a dominate trait of the shooter's personality, it could cause the shooter some problems in the future, if it is allowed unchecked expansion. For example, there is a woman whose **Obsessive** trait was allowed to develop all through junior high and high school. When she got to college, the **Obsessive** trait had become so all embracing that she never turned in an assignment paper. Thus she did not graduate. She was a highly intelligent person, but she was never able to be satisfied with any paper she wrote, so she just did not turn any in for credit in any class.

For shooters, this has implications in whether and when the shooter decides to move the trigger finger. The shooter with this **Obsessive** trait is continually interrupting the conditional reflex between the eye-brain-finger. Shooters with this moderate **Obsessive** trait tend to spend an over amount of time looking at the sights, and trying to establish perfect alignment on a particular point, when they are not physically capable of holding the sights perfectly aligned on a point. This act of trying to hold the sights perfectly aligned on a specific point is really a physical impossibility. It is contrary to Newton's finding about gravity and the laws of motion.

Solution To Try: Since holding the pistol up for extended periods tires out the muscles of the body concerned with this effort, the shooter must make a conscious effort to move the finger as the sights become aligned with his or her desired area, not trying to wait to achieve PERFECT sight alignment on a particular point. This will assist in developing the eye-brain-finger conditional reflex in a way which will at the same time promote the development of less of an obsessive personality. The shooter needs:

1) to have one of the Conditional Reflex Forms run each practice session.
2) to work up to completely filling out the dry firing chart and noting the time it takes to fire 100 shots, excluding the time taken to rest between series of shots.

Appendix D

Attitude Inventory For Shooters

Add the shooter's

☞extroversion (**E**) and then

Add the shooter's:

☞introversion (**i**) scores independently.

☞Subtract the smaller of the two from the other, whichever it may be.

For example, if you have an **E** score of 30 and an **i** score of 17, you should take 17 from 30, which leaves you with an **E** score of 15.

$$\mathbf{E} = 30$$
$$\underline{\mathbf{-i} = 17}$$
$$\mathbf{13}$$

Add on the shooter's special time score based on the amount of time taken to complete the test. For example, if the shooter has an **E** score of 30 and an **i** score of 17, subtract 17 from 30, which leaves you with an **E** score of 13. Then if the shooter finished the inventory in less than 5 minutes, add 25E to the shooter's score of 13 which gives a total result of 38.

$$\mathbf{E} = 30$$
$$\underline{\mathbf{-i} = 17}$$
$$13$$
$$\underline{\textbf{Time} = 25}$$
$$38$$

Time Bonus

5 minutes or less	**25E**	**16 minutes**	**5i**
6 minutes	**20E**	**17 minutes**	**10i**
7 minutes	**15E**	**18 minutes**	**15i**
8 minutes	**10E**	**19 minutes**	**20i**
9 minutes	**5E**	**20 minutes**	**25i**
10-15 minutes	**0**	**21 minutes or over**	**30i**

Attitude Inventory For Shooters

Name:_____ Date:_____ Age:_____

Beginning Time:_____ Ending Time:_____

Total Minutes:_____

---

1. Here are five statements reflecting attitudes to conversation. Read them carefully and choose the statement which most closely matches your own feelings.

a. I tend to be a talkative and forward conversationalist, perhaps too talkative and forward for a lot of people's tastes.

b. I tend to be talkative and often take the lead in group conversations.

c. I'm afraid I'm simply a bad conversationalist.

d. I enjoy conversation but would as soon listen as talk.

e. I find myself generally ill at ease in a situation where I am likely to be drawn into conversation.

Most Closely Matches My Feelings:

2. Here are five statements reflecting attitudes to using the telephone. Read them carefully and choose the statement which most closely matches your feelings.

624

a. I can carry on a good conversation on the telephone, but much prefer to see people face to face, if I am to really get across to them.

b. The telephone fails for me principally because I cannot see the face of the person I am talking to.

c. I can use the telephone when I have to but find it a limited instrument for communication.

d. I find that when I use the telephone I can communicate very easily with people and get through to them in surprising depth.

e. I feel positively ill at ease on the telephone.

Most Closely Matches My Feelings:

3. You have won a choice of the following holidays in a competition, with all expenses paid. Look at them carefully and choose the one which you would <u>most enjoy</u>, and the one you would <u>least enjoy</u>.

a. A month in a luxury holiday camp with sun, surf, music, everyone eating at a central table and good company.

b. A small but really neat and comfortable hotel in a quiet, remote part of the country where walking, fishing or other gentle amusements are possible

c. A house party at the home of a wealthy author friend whose other guests are mainly writers, artists and people with creative interests.

d. The opportunity to devote yourself entirely to doing something that you have always wanted to do -- learning to fly, reading Gibbon's *Decline and Fall*, writing a book, visiting every movie theater you can.

e. A quiet holiday with family or friends in a quiet motel or hotel.

f. A month's tour in a luxurious bus of historical and cultural centers in every country of Europe.

Most Enjoy: Least Enjoy

☐   ☐

4. In an evening's television viewing, which of the following do you prefer to watch <u>most</u> and which <u>least</u>?

a. An old feature film.

b. A panel discussion on a serious subject in the news.

c. A lightweight talk show, such as *The Tonight Show.*.

d. An uninhibited comedy show which includes dirty jokes and disgusting language.

e. A modern play with psychological undertones.

f. A live boxing match.

Most Enjoy: Least Enjoy

☐   ☐

5. Here are various ways you might spend a spare evening. Indicate the evening which you would <u>most</u> and <u>least</u> enjoy.

a. You and half a dozen friends in the basement of a cheery, lively home where darts and perhaps some music are on hand.

b. An evening with a close friend at the movie theater.

c. A really swinging party with lots of good food, drink and company.

d. An evening at home listening to music or reading.

e. A small dinner party at a friend's home with plenty of enjoyable conversation.

f. An evening at home watching good TV.

626

Most Enjoy:

Least Enjoy

6. Which most closely matches your own attitudes to taking decisions?

a. I am scared sometimes about the consequences of decisions and often put off making them.

b. I like to have time to think, but when I make my mind up I'm firm about it.

c. I come to quick decisions, but they are generally well-balanced, and not overly-hasty.

d. If I make rapid decisions they tend to be wrong; if I consider them carefully they tend to be right.

e. I can make decisions with great speed, but sometimes wish that I was not so impulsive.

f. I tend to find it difficult to make decisions.

Most Closely Matches My Attitudes:

7. Choose the statement which most closely matches your own feelings or experience.

a. I would never hurt anyone physically unless I had to in self-defense, but then I would fight hard.

b. I find the idea of human beings fighting each other repulsive.

c. I do not deliberately seek out trouble, but have had to resort to physical violence on more than one occasion.

d. I have frequently been involved in arguments which could easily lead or have led to violence.

e. I would never under any circumstances fight physically with another person.

Most Closely Matches My Feelings:

8. Choose the statement which most closely reflects your own level of work or productivity.

a. I think I am pretty average in the amount of work I get through.

b. I am capable of a high level of steady, productive work which doesn't vary too much from one week to the next.

c. I am not very productive and most work for me is hard work.

d. Sometimes I am highly productive, other times unproductive, but most times I'm fairly average.

e. I find I can get through a tremendous amount of work If I want to, but it seems to come in bursts.

Most Closely Reflects My Own Level of Work:

9. In this question you must try to rate yourself not according to how you feel about yourself, but how you believe <u>others</u> feel about you. On the whole other people probably view me as:

a. Good company sometimes, but very poor company other times.

b. Exceedingly active and outgoing, possibly even somewhat overactive and pushy.

c. Pretty much of a bore for one reason or another.

d. Active, friendly and pleasant, lively company.

e. More or less average in terms of activity and friendliness.

f. A rather hesitant type of personality.

Other People Probably View Me As:

☐

10. If I could see myself as others see me, I'd be:

a. Disappointed at their poor image of me.

b. Somewhat more pleased than I thought I'd be.

c. Very pleased and flattered.

d. Horrified.

e. Surprised at some aspects of my personality which I had been unaware of.

f. Not surprised to find my own faults clearly spotlighted.

I'd Be:

☐

11. Which of the following most closely matches your attitude to shopping or buying things?

a. I usually spend whatever I want to, but what else is money for?

b. I am often rather foolish when it comes to shopping and frequently end up buying things that I don't really want.

c. I am a fairly responsible shopper and on the whole buy within my means.

d. I don't enjoy shopping for major items as I feel that the risk of making a mistake is too great.

e. I hate shopping of any kind.

Most Closely Matches My Attitude:

☐

12. For each of the following statements say whether you agree or disagree or whether you are not sure.

a. The world would be a better place if people had to explain their decisions to someone else before they were able to carry them out.

Agree	Disagree	Not Sure
☐	☐	☐

b. Man is an aggressive creature who must adjust, however, to the requirements of society.

Agree	Disagree	Not Sure
☐	☐	☐

c. Credit cards are a menace since they make people spend more than they can afford.

Agree	Disagree	Not Sure
☐	☐	☐

d. There is no surer way of getting a boring decision than by putting it to a committee.

Agree	Disagree	Not Sure
☐	☐	☐

e. Unstable people tend to be a bit concerned with their own problems.

Agree	Disagree	Not Sure
☐	☐	☐

f. Variety is the spice of life.

Agree	Disagree	Not Sure
☐	☐	☐

13. Which of the following <u>(assuming you had to do one)</u> would you enjoy doing <u>most</u> and which <u>least</u>?

a. Tackle a big cataloging task for the school library.

b. Act as treasurer of a sports or social club.

c. Take the lead in a school play.

d. Start a youth chapter of a local political party at my school.

e. Do an absolutely huge jigsaw puzzle.

f. Get thoroughly acquainted with the latest development in psychological theory.

Most Enjoy: Least Enjoy

☐   ☐

QUESTIONS 14-16 FOR MALES ONLY

14. Forgetting purchase price, resale value, garaging and running costs, etc., and assuming you are old enough to drive, which of the following cars appeals to you the most and which the least?

a. Rolls-Royce Corniche
b. Ferrari   **g.** Ford Granada
c. Rover 3500   **h.** Mercedes
d. Volkswagen   **i.** Jaguar E-type
e. Ford Mustang   **j.** Mercury Cougar
f. Ford Thunderbird   **k.** Not sure.

Appeals Most   Appeals Least

☐   ☐

15. Your closest friend has to choose a car from the above list which he or she feels suits your personality best, not necessarily your price range. Which would he or she pick?

631

He or she would pick:

☐

16. Does your choice match your friend's choice?

Yes   No

☐   ☐

QUESTIONS 17-19 FOR FEMALES ONLY

17. Forgetting your present age, job, training, background, which of the following jobs would appeal to you most if you had freedom of choice and you had to pick one, and which the least?

a. Head of a big university library.
b. Secretary to a famous film producer.
c. World-class athlete.
d. A successful fashion model.
e. Brilliant psychologist.
f. Principal of a modern progressive school.
g. Housewife with a happy home and family.
h. Successful authoress.
i. Film, stage or music star.
j. Wife of a successful but rather reclusive author.
k. Not sure.

Appeals Most   Appeals Least

☐   ☐

18. Your closest friend has to decide which of the above jobs would be most suited to your character and personality, not necessarily to your age, ability or prospects. Which do you think he or she would select?

He or she would pick:

☐

19. Does your choice match your friend's choice"

Yes   No

Attitude Test Answers

1a= 3E	1b= 5E	1c= 3i	1d= 0	1e= 5i

2a= 3E	2b= 3i	2c= 0	2d= 5E	2e= 5i

Most Enjoy:	3a= 5E	3b= 3i	3c= 2E
	3d= 5i	3e=2i	3f= 3E

Least Enjoy:	3a= 5i	3b= 3E	3c= 2i
	3d= 5E	3e= 2E	3f= 3i

Most Enjoy:	4a = 0	4b= 4i	4c= 0
	4d= 2E	4e= 2i	4f= 4E

Least Enjoy:	4a= 0	4b= 4E	4c= 0
	4d= 2i	4e= 2E	4f= 4i

Most Enjoy:	5a= 3E	5b= 1i	5c= 5E
	5d= 5i	5e= 1E	5f= 3i

Least Enjoy:	5a= 3i	5b= 1E	5c= 5i
	5d= 5E	5e= 1i	5f= 3E

6a= 5i	6b= 1E	6c= 5E	6d= 3i	6e= 3E	6f= 1i

7a= 0	7b= 5i	7c= 3E	7d= 5E	7e= 3i

8a= 3i	8b= 5E	8c= 5i	8d= 0	8e= 3E

9a= 0	9b= 3E	9c= 5i	9d= 5E	9e=0	9f= 3i

10a= 3E	10b= 2i	10c= 5E	10d= 5i	10e= 0	10f=0

11a= 5E   11b= 3E   11c= 0   11d= 3i   11e= 5i

Agree: 12a= 5i   12b= 0   12c= 3i   12d= 2E
              12e= 3E   12f= 3E

Disagree: 12a= 3E   12b= 0   12c= 3E   12d= 5i
              12e= 5i   12f= 3i

Not Sure: 12a= 2i   12b= 2i   12c= 2i   12d= 2i
              12e= 2i   12f= 2i

Most Enjoy: 13a= 2i   13b= 2E   13c= 5E   13d= 5E
              13e= 5i   13f= 5i

Least Enjoy: 13a= 2E   13b=2i   13c= 5i   13d= 5i
              13e= 5E   13f= 5E

Appeals Most: 14a= 4E   14b= 5E   14c= 5i   14d= 1i
              14e= 1E   14f= 1E   14g= 5i   14h= 1i
              14i= 4E   14j= 5i   14k= 5i

Appeals Least: 14a= 4i   14b= 5i   14c= 5E   14d= 1E
              14e= 1i   14f= 1i   14g= 5E   14h= 1E
              14i= 4i   14j= 5E   14k= 5i

15a= 4E   15b= 5E   15c= 5i   15d= 1i   15e= 1E
          15f= 1E   15g= 5i   15h= 1i   15i= 4E
          15j= 5i   15k= 5i

16   Yes= 5E   No= 0

Appeals Most: 17a= 2E   17b= 5E   17c= 2i   17d= 5E
              17e= 2E   17f= 2E   17g= 5i   17h= 2i
              17i= 5E   17j= 5i   17k= 5i

Appeals Least: 17a= 2i   17b= 5i   17c= 2E   17d= 5i
              17e= 5E   17f= 2i   17g= 2E   17h= 2E
              17i= 5i   17j= 5E   17k= 5i

18a= 2E	18b= 5E	18c= 2i	18d= 5E	18e= 2E	18f= 2E
18g= 5i	18h= 2i	18i= 5E	18j=5i	18k= 5i	

19	Yes= 5E	No= 0

Analysis

Over 100 E   An E score of more than 100, if the questionnaire has been frankly and honestly filled out, represents a quite abnormal degree of extroversion, so much in fact that it would suggest a distinctly unbalanced personality. All tests become very inaccurate at their extremes, but any score of a hundred or over would be quite remarkable. The most probable explanation of this is the pistol shooter has either misunderstood some of the questions or the coach has misinterpreted the scoring.

76 E to 100 E   This is an unusually high score and if the pistol shooter has filled out the questionnaire and the coach has scored it correctly, then this suggests that the shooter is exceptionally extroverted in comparison with most people and may be considered rather overbearing by some. The question now arises as to what the coach can or should do about it. If the coach is already aware that this side of the shooter's personality is hindering the shooter, in the shooting training process to one degree or another, then the coach will have to strive to curb it a little. The best and simplest strategy is to help the shooter to try to form a more accurate image of himself or herself.

51 E to 75 E   This high score indicates that the shooter's personality is marked by an unquestionable extroversion. The chances are that the shooter has adjusted his or her school or life style to his or her personality. If not, then the coach should take steps to make this adjustment as it pertains to shooting. Strong extroversion is often

635

accompanied by a high drive to succeed and provided that the shooter can avoid being pushy, it can be a useful trait.

31 E to 50 E   With a score such as this, the shooter is clearly extroverted and most people will probably judge the shooter to be so when they know him or her well. Those scoring in the 30s however may not be immediately recognizable as extroverts to others. No adjustment is required for this normal, healthy trait, but all extroverts should be encouraged by the coach to make the most of their special potential for good social relationships. The coach should bear in mind that many of the shooting champions never feel comfortable in social situations. With this in mind, the coach should refrain from pushing shooters into strained social circumstances.

11 E to 30 E   In balance this shooter's personality is extroverted. The bias is fairly mild and the shooter may not even be aware that it exists in himself or herself. If the shooter has been considering himself or herself to be *introverted,* it may be that a few minor changes in the shooter's life style are called for! For example, the shooter may find some forms of social interaction, while not unenjoyable, to be somehow stressful, without knowing quite why. This stress can be alleviated by doing more what the shooter wants to do rather than what he or she thinks everyone expects them to do.

10 E to 10 i This shooter's personality is neither introverted nor extroverted and along this dimension of personality, the shooter can be described as being "balanced." This is neither good nor bad, but on the whole the shooter gains because he or she is acceptable to both introverts and extroverts and they should find it easy to form relaxed social relationships.

10 i to 30 i On the whole this shooter's personality is introverted. It is a fairly mild bias however. For example, the shooter may find some forms of social intercommunication, while not unpleasant, to be somehow fast-paced, without knowing quite why. This pressure can be alleviated by the shooter doing more of what he or she desires to do rather than what he or she considers they should do.

31 i to 50 i This is a very clear introvert score and most people who know this shooter will classify him or her as introverted or shy. If the shooter's score is in the 30s however, the shooter may have been able to conceal this aspect of their personality, consciously or unconsciously. This is fine as long as it does not cause the shooter stress by exposing the shooter to complicated social situations which the shooter does not really enjoy.

51 i to 75 i The dominating feature of this shooter's personality is a marked introversion. The chances are that the shooter's school and life style have long ago been adjusted to accept the situation. The shooter will not really enjoy large gatherings of people and social situations. Most introverts tend to turn their energies towards intellectual pursuits which do not require interaction with other people, reading, shooting, appreciating music and creative hobbies.

76 i to 100 i This very high score denotes a quite unusual imbalance towards introversion. Many people the shooter knows will probably consider the shooter shy to an unusual extent. There is not a great deal that the shooter can do about this except to come to terms with it. As a coach, do not be tempted to force the shooter into social interaction which the shooter does not really enjoy and is never likely to enjoy.

Over 100 i Assuming that this questionnaire has been honestly filled out, the shooter's **i** score of over 100 represents a quite abnormal bias towards introversion. The shooter is certainly exceedingly shy and must lead a highly restricted social life. The most likely explanation though, is that the shooter has not filled out the questionnaire accurately.

Appendix E

Lesson Plans For A Junior Pistol Team

Purpose Of These Exercises

Shooter to teach himself or herself to move the trigger finger instantaneously when the front sight arrives at the preselected area of the target.

Lesson Plan A

1	2
Visually Align the barrel with the eye, using the top of the front sight as a reference, point the aligned system at the area where you want the indicator (bullet hole) to appear..	Instantaneous Smooth Trigger Finger Movement

I. Training The Conditional Reflex:

    A. Live firing with dry firing exercise
    B. Shooters to load two rounds in the magazine
    C. Fire a shot
    D. Recover the sight alignment
    E. Keep the arm up and
    F. Fire the second shot
    G. Recover the sight alignment
    H. Keep the arm up and
    I. Then dry fire one shot
    J. Record the sight alignment observed at the moment of trigger let-off

K. Repeat this 20 times for a total of 80 shots and 20 dry fires

Lesson Plan B

1	2
Visually Align the barrel with the eye, using the top of the front sight as a reference, point the aligned system at the area where you want the indicator (bullet hole) to appear..	Instantaneous Smooth Trigger Finger Movement

I. <u>Shot Group Match</u> of 20 shots w/.22 on blank target.
Setup targets at 10 meters.

II. <u>Training The Conditional Reflex</u>.
    A. 40 shots at 25 meters slow fire using the single shot loading technique without the magazine.
    B. Recover the sight alignment after the shot recoil.
    C. Then Dry Fire another shot.
    D. Allow 15 minutes for this exercise.

III. <u>Video Analysis Training</u>
    A. During Phases I & II of today's training, Mr. Hickey will be using the camcorder to record individual training.
    B. Shooters **must** have about **5 feet** between frames and the shooters on either side of their firing points.
    C. After the range is cleaned, we will retire to the trailer for analysis of shooter training.
    D. The pistols will be cleaned after the video analysis.

Targets to be scored at end of the practice session.

Lesson Plan C

1	2
Visually Align the barrel with the eye, using the top of the front sight as a reference, point the aligned system at the area where you want the indicator (bullet hole) to appear..	Instantaneous Smooth Trigger Finger Movement

Pro-Marksman Shooters

1. On the range with the air pistol.
2. Put 1 blank target on each frame.
3. Fire 20 shots at the middle of it.
4. Score the blank target's group.
5. Cut it out, tape it and record it in your handbook.
6. Then put up 4 bullseye targets.
7. Fire 10 shots at each bullseye target.
8. Score each target and record it in your handbook if it scores 30 points or better.
9. Upon earning your Marksman I Proficiency Award, put up another blank target.
10. Fire 20 shots at the target.
11. When the range is safe, take a target down range.
12. Then move the frame to 25 yards and join the other shooters in the rest of the training.

Intermediate Shooters

I. **Shot Group Match** of 20 shots w/.22 on blank target.
   Setup targets at 10 meters.

Score targets and place in front of record box.

II. **Training the Conditional Reflex.**
   A. 40 shots Rapid Fire at 10 meters.
   B. This means 8 strings of 5 shots each, in 10 seconds.
   C. Wait and score after all 40 shots are fired.

640

Appendix E

III. Training the Conditional Reflex.

100 shots Rapid Fire, in 5 shot strings of 10 seconds
This means 20 strings of 5 shots each
Wait and score after all 100 shots are fired

Everyone, **Clean** the gun you used.

Lesson Plan D

1	2
Visually Align the barrel with the eye, using the top of the front sight as a reference, point the aligned system at the area where you want the indicator (bullet hole) to appear..	**Instantaneous Smooth Trigger Finger Movement**

*Shooter to teach himself or herself the shooting platform which is most **efficient** for himself or herself.*

I. Establishing the Shooting Platform

    A. Have the students pair up and open their books to the page in their hand books showing how to do this. (This is available in Chapter 5 of this book.)

    B. Working in pairs, follow the directions, use coach/pupil method.

    C. Coach of coach/pupil pair to read the **Rationale** and then the **Directions**

    D. Pairs then switch and repeat the **whole process**

Lesson Plan E

1	2
Visually Align the barrel with the eye, using the top of the front sight as a reference, point the aligned system at the area where you want the indicator (bullet hole) to appear..	**Instantaneous Smooth Trigger Finger Movement**

Objectives

1. To introduce the concept of *strategy* in dealing with the upcoming Preliminary Try Out (PTO) shooting match in Phoenix at the Phoenix Rod & Gun Club South Mountain Range on July 22, 1995.
2. To prepare shooters for match conduct & the use of the *International Pistol Rule* book.
3. To reinforce the attitude of range courtesy and safety

Methods

To introduce the concept of *strategy* in dealing with the upcoming Preliminary Try Out (PTO) shooting match in Phoenix at the Phoenix Rod & Gun Club South Mountain Range on the 3rd weekend of the month.

We will shoot the Air Pistol Match, 60 shots for the boys and 40 shots for the girls. We will also shoot the Sport Pistol Match.

Considerations:

1. The Air Pistol range only has five firing points. Since there will be other people shooting, we may get to have only three or so people shoot the air pistol at a time. So, among ourselves, we need to set up our own internal club relays.

2. Everyone will shoot the 11:00 AM Sport Pistol relay.

To prepare shooters for match conduct & the use of the
International Pistol Rule **book.**
Go Over Rules:

- [ ] 9.1
- [ ] 9.2
- [ ] 9.3
- [ ] 9.4
- [ ] 9.5
- [ ] 9.11
- [ ] 9.17
- [ ] 9.19
- [ ] 9.20
- [ ] 9.26
- [ ] 9.32
- [ ] 9.36
- [ ] 14.1
- [ ] 14.3
- [ ] 14.3.1
- [ ] 14.10 (b)
- [ ] 15.3

To teach range courtesy and safety.
Stress safety and courtesy through quiet attention.

Discuss kinds of range conditions the shooters may encounter during a match and what to do about unsafe conditions. Stress team self-monitoring.

If you see or hear someone becoming loud or just plain fooling around, go up to them and quietly remind them that our team is on display and to cool it down. Do it as you have seen the coach do it, quietly and without drawing much attention to the person.

Lesson Plan F

1	2
Visually Align the barrel with the eye, using the top of the front sight as a reference, point the aligned system at the area where you want the indicator (bullet hole) to appear..	Instantaneous Smooth Trigger Finger Movement

1. Discuss 1995 Grand Canyon Games Results
2. 22 caliber training
3. Live firing with dry firing exercise
4. Use the Dry Firing Chart
5. Shooters to fire one live fire shot, then one dry fire,
6. Then another live fire shot as a single exercise.
7. Repeat this 40 times for a total of 40 shots and 40 dry fires.

Appendix F

Forms For Measuring The Conditioned Reflex In Pistol Shooters

These forms are discussed in Chapter 9. These forms are maintained in a computer. Hickey has a small notebook computer which is used to record the observations. The charts are then generated by the computer program. At the time of the writing of this book, the forms are in the Microsoft Excel For Windows program. Thus, they are in the "*.xls" format. However, the forms lend themselves to paper scoring also.

The important point about maintaining forms is that you then have a history of the shooter's progress. When using a computer, it is quite easy to generate a form to place in your coach's notebook and to also provide one for the shooter to place in his or her notebook.

This allows both the coach and the shooter to have a common reference point when the shooter's performance is discussed. Most commonly, the purpose is to maintain a record of the shooters conditional reflex acquisition. But, another important purpose of maintaining such forms is to allow the coach to evaluate the efficiency and effectiveness of the shooter's training. This permits the coach to help the shooter to define the objects and functional principles of the system under which he or she is training. This way the coach can make suggestions about actions to develop the shooter's conditional reflex more efficiently.

Daily Shooting Report
Date: 5/3/96 Friday

Name: Danielle Dancho

	Shot 1	Shot 2	Shot 3	Shot 4	Shot 5	Shot Time Average	Total	
Series 1	1	4	6	6	6		23	
Time 1	3	2	3	3.2	3.5	2.94		
Series 2	8	6	6	7	6		33	56
Time 2	3.1	3.5	4	3.1	5	3.74		
Series 3	5	9	9	8	4		35	
Time 3	3.5	4.6	3	3	3	3.42		
Series 4	6	10	7	8	5		36	71
Time 4	2.5	2.5	2.1	3	3	2.62		
Series 5	6	8	6	4	6		30	
Time 5	2.7	3.5	2	2	2	2.44		
Series 6	6	5	9	10	7		37	67
Time 6	3	4	4	4	2	3.4		
Series 7	7	5	8	6	8		34	79
Time 7	3.5	3	3	3.5	3	3.2		273
Series 8	8	10	8	9	10		45	
Time 8	3	2.8	2.5	2.6	4.6	3.1		
Series 9	10	10	5	9	7		41	
Time 9	3	3.2	2.6	3.1	3.4	3.06		
Series 10	8	7	7	10	4		36	77
Time 10	2	3.3	3	3.5	2.3	2.82		
Series 11	6	6	8	6	6		32	
Time 11	4	3.1	3.2	4	2.2	3.3		
Series 12	6	9	10	8	8		41	73
Time 12	5	2.2	3.1	4	2.6	3.38		

Average Time Per Shot: 2.8 seconds

Total Score For 60 Shots: 423
Shot Average: 7.05

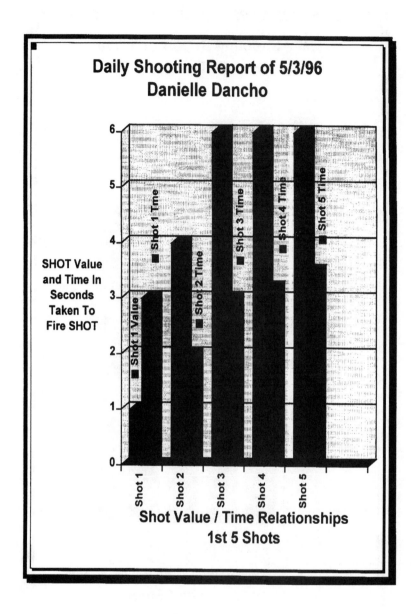

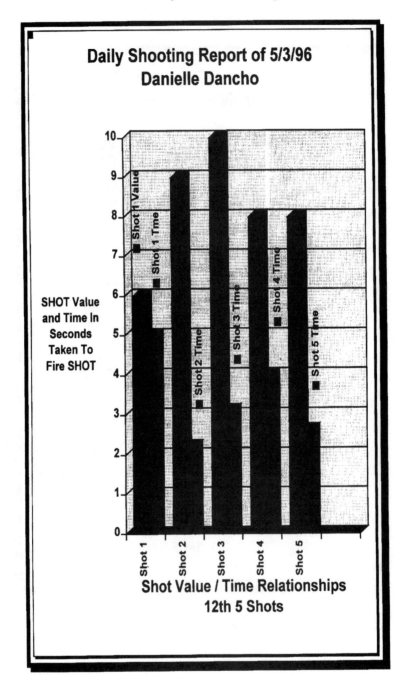

Appendix G

Form For The Coach's Observations of Personality Traits of Pistol Shooters

Coach's Notes	
1. Age: 10	
2. Birthdate: 7/31/85	
3. School Attitude: School's okay	
4. How do you respond when your parent asks you "How'd it go today?" give out with your usual, "Nothing"	
5. Best Liked School Subject: Math	
6. Most Average School Subject: Spelling	
7. Subject With Grade Problems: Science	
8. Amount of Daily Time Watching TV: 1	
9. Amount of Daily Homework Time: 2	
10. Wake-Up Time: 7:00:00 AM	
11. Bed Time: 10:00:00 PM	
12. My Teachers Mostly: like me	
13. Day Dreaming: Never	
14. When I Get Home From School: usually do not have anything to do	
15. I Joined The Pistol Team Because: I want to learn how to hunt with a pistle.	

What we have done is to put this information, from our *Test #1*, into a database. We then merge the information with the form in our word processor. We use Microsoft Access For Windows 95.

Index

Index

Anderson, Gary, 88, 110, 149
androgynous, 362
angular misalignment, 85, 101, 118,
    147, 149, 161, 275, 276, 279
anxiety, 403, 410, 411, 412
arc of movement, 59, 60, 94, 95,
    250, 340-341, 446, 453, 458,
    469, 470, 477, 480, 490, 495
arcades, 263+
archery, 423
area aiming technique, 283
Aristotle, 104
arm swing, 450
arousal, 256, 257, 367, 369, 412,
    418, 489
Ash, David, 377
Askins, Col. Charles, 91, 132-138,
    140
attention, 70, 80, 90, 91, 95, 98,
    111, 112, 117-119, 123, 127,
    133, 138, 143, 148, 152, 158,
    161, 162, 315, 323, 438, 446,
    453, 455, 457, 465, 476, 477,
    481, 484, 496, 498, 499, 501,
    502, 505, 510, 513
    reflex, 498
    voluntary, 498, 499
attitude, 253, 308, 323, 328, 334,
    341, 353, 367, 381, 383, 397,
    398, 400, 401, 421, 422, 423,
    432,
attorney, 219
Australian Junior National Team,
    178
autogenic training, 425, 426
automatic, 173, 176, 184, 309, 311,
    315, 316, 317, 328, 438, 444,
    451, 458, 463, 466, 478, 479,
    506-509, 512, 513, 515
automatic process, 365, 366, 380
autonomic nervous system, 438,
    439, 458, 459
average beginner, 135
avoiding a bad performance, 380
awareness, 217, 218, 227, 237, 249,
    265, 367, 382, 393, 395, 403
axis of the bore, 127

B

ballpark size, 91, 293
Barani, Gavrila, 453-456, 462, 463,
    466, 477-479
Barlow, Brigadier J. A. C.B.E.,
    p.t.s.c, 126
barrel, 275-281, 286
Barstow, Brent "Bugsy", 48, 170,
    197, 330, 369, 432
Barstow, Geoffrey, 330, 432
Basic Head Position, 156, 243
Basic Rifle Shooting, A Better Way,
    224
Bassham, Lanny, 444
behavior, 256, 257
    Operant, 438
behavioral components, 374
benchrest, 182, 184, 187, 211, 311,
    316, 319, 320
Benito Juarez Championships, 491
Benner, Huelet, 91
Bisley, 48, 335
Black Mountain Shooting Club, 178
Blair, Vince, 324, 330
blank target, 52, 188, 189, 239, 247,
    248, 270, 272
Blankenship, Bill, 95, 116, 123,
    175, 179, 315, 366, 425, 438,
    444, 445, 448, 449, 462, 463,
    465, 466, 474, 475, 476-481,
    506-509, 511, 513
blink, 279
bottle lifting, 256, 358
Boy Scouts Explorer Program, 179
breathing, 54, 55, 112,115, 116,
    186, 192, 197, 202, 207, 283,
    309, 359, 365, 366, 367, 383
Briggs, Frank, 46
British, 48, 49, 52, 335
Browning Buckmarks, 182
Brugh, Major Larry U.S.A., 298
Bulgarians, 353
bully, 265

651

Index

G

H

Index

hypocrisy, 264

I

illuminated gun sights, 292
image rehearsal, 262
imagery training, 262, 263
immune defense system, 367
immutable laws of nature, 314
Inconsiderate, 264
Indicate as desired, 85
Indicating System, 84, 85, 93, 102
Individual Shot Goal, 354, 361, 384, 386
ineffective communicators, 349
inferiority complex, 264
initiative, 332
innovative techniques, 297
Insights, 186
instantaneous smooth, 60, 311, 355, 444, 474, 481
instructional materials, 226
Instructor/coach shooter relations, 431
intellectual balance, 264
intellectual imagination, 264
intellectual needs, 401
intercollegiate, 257, 259
Intercollegiate Pistol Championships, 273
internal alignment, 127, 355
Internal Alignment System, 82, 87, 102
internal self honesty, 374, 375, 385
internal self-worth, 370
internally aligned system, 303
interrupted trigger pressure, 469
interscholastic, 257, 259
introversion, 392, 402

J

Jackson, Art, 149
Jackson, Charlie, 177, 182
Jackson, John, 329
jealousy, 264

jerk, 279, 282, 446, 462, 476, 478, 480, 481, 507
joys of sex, 346
Junior Olympic Development Team, 191
junior pistol program, 180, 182, 184, 185
Junior Team record, 472
Juniors under the age of 12, 182

K

Kearney, Jay T., 466
kicking feet, 226
kids and handguns, 219
killer instinct, 340, 341
kinesthetic reaction, 159
Kinl', V.A, 165
kitchen, 216, 225
knowing the difference, 347

L

Landers, D.M., 116, 423, 491
Lara, Kelly, 330
Lara, Mike, 330
Lara, Ryan, 330
laws of gravity, 314
laws of motion, 307, 311, 314, 477
lead exposure, 220
lectures, 182, 197, 307
liability Insurance, 185
liability items, 219
Libet, Benjamin, 176
ligament control, 362
locomotion, 450, 451, 455
longitudinal study, 405
Lösel, Dr. Heinz, 87, 88, 472
lousy lover, 345
low efficacy, 428
low expectations, 429
low self-efficacy, 256, 257
Loyer, Surfman Stanley L., 167, 294

Index

P

O

Q

R

Index

V

W

Y

NRA Field Representative for Arizona and New Mexico, H. Dean Hall, presents $4,000.00 grant from the Friends of NRA State Committee to the Saguaro Shooting Sports Club. Accepting are, on the left, club treasurer, Cade Wilson and in the middle, club president, Candace Abrams.

SUCCESSFUL PISTOL SHOOTING

By
Bob Hickey
and
Art Sievers

STP Books

Limited Edition	Book Number
First Printing	